Greatest Musicals

ABE LAUFE

DAVID & CHARLES
Newton Abbot   London

782·81/223240

To the memory of my mother and father

ISBN 0 7153 7712 4

Library of Congress Catalog Card Number 77-7922

© Abe Laufe 1969, 1970, 1973, 1977

PICTURE CREDITS: Mary Bryant, 17; Fred Fehl, 4, 5, 6, 7, 8, 10; Sy Friedman, 16; Martha Swope, 15, 18, 19, 20; Museum of the City of New York, 2, 3; The New York Public Library, John H. James Collection, 1; Zodiac, 9, 11, 12, 13, 14.

First published in the USA by Funk & Wagnalls, New York
First published in the United Kingdom by David & Charles, 1978

Printed in Great Britain
by Redwood Burn Limited Trowbridge & Esher
for David & Charles (Publishers) Limited
Brunel House Newton Abbot Devon

Acknowledgments

I want to thank the following people for their cooperation and assistance in preparing this book:

Dr. Ford and Mrs. Harriet Curtis, who made available all resources of the Ford and Harriet Curtis Theatre Collection of the University of Pittsburgh;

Dr. Ford Curtis, for his sage advice in handling conflicting evidence and for his assistance in locating theatrical data;

Dr. Edmund G. Wilson, for making available his collection of musical comedy files, original cast albums, and theatrical books, and also for his expert advice on musicology;

Mr. Julian S. Bach, Jr., and Miss Natalie Bowen, for their encouragement and direction;

Mr. Hobe Morrison of *Variety*, for his graciousness in answering queries;

Miss Mary Bryant, for making it possible to complete the research for *Cabaret*;

Mr. Richard Gilston and Mr. George Caldwell, for their many suggestions in shaping the final manuscript;

Miss Minda Tessler and Miss Irene Thomas, for their technical assistance;

Dr. Benjamin Perlow and Mrs. Anna Perlow, for their patience and understanding during the arduous months of preparation;

Dr. Edward Pfau of Wisconsin State University, for his helpful suggestions and corrections;

Miss Dyanne Hochman, for making it possible to complete the research for *Hair*;

Miss Evelyn O'Connor, for her excellent assistance with illustrations for the second edition.

A very special thanks to Miss Hannah E. Bechtel for her invaluable assistance in research and writing.

Special thanks also to Mr. John Madden of *Variety*, without whose help I would not have been able to complete the statistical records for this edition.

Mr. Alan Hewitt for his suggestions and corrections on the text.

Contents

Illustrations follow pages 120, 258, and 370

Introduction:
What Makes Musicals Run?

FROM ITS early beginnings in the burlesque-extravaganza
and the operetta patterned on European models, the American
musical comedy theater has developed into a uniquely American
art form which more than one historian of the theater has called
America's greatest contribution to worldwide theatrical entertainment. Five musicals—*Of Thee I Sing, South Pacific, Fiorello!, How
to Succeed in Business Without Really Trying,* and *A Chorus Line*
—have won Pulitzer Prizes, not as musicals but as the best dramas
of the year in which they were produced. *Carousel* and *Wonderful
Town* were selected to represent the musical theater at the 1957
World's Fair in Brussels. More recently the phenomenal success
abroad of *My Fair Lady, Fiddler on the Roof,* and *A Chorus Line*
has brought even further distinction to this American dramatic
form.

Musical comedy has also become big business. Skyrocketing
production costs, higher admission prices, increased gross receipts,
as well as higher salaries for performers, musicians, electricians,
and stagehands have raised statistical reports for individual shows
from the hundreds of thousands into the millions. An investment
of $200,000, considered high in the 1940s, would not cover even
half the cost of producing a low-budgeted musical in the 1970s.
Yet increased costs have not cut down on the number of new productions. The phenomenal financial success of *Hello, Dolly!,*

Fiddler on the Roof, My Fair Lady, and *A Chorus Line* has inspired Broadway angels to take the big gamble on other productions.

Higher admission prices have almost doubled gross receipts. A weekly gross of $40,000 for a musical, a phenomenal figure in the 1920s, would mean failure in the 1970s. Some theatrical observers believe that the high admission prices of $15, $17.50, and even $20 a ticket are curtailing the runs of shows because fewer patrons will pay such prices for live musical entertainment when television spectaculars are free. And yet since the publication of the third edition of this book, seventeen musicals have run 500 or more consecutive performances. Even the reputed prices of $25 and $50 a ticket bought from under-the-counter speculators have not affected the hit musicals. Nor are these high prices a recent development. In the 1920s, exorbitant prices were being charged at the box office in at least two cases, to attract theatergoers who wanted to boast that they had attended a certain special performance. In 1926, tickets for the opening performance given by Raquel Meller, famous Spanish singer and entertainer, were $27.50; and, that same season, probably as a publicity stunt, George White doubled the price for the first ten rows of *Scandals* on opening night. One story told on Broadway concerns a famous musical star who attended that premiere, got tired when the show was still running at 1:30 A.M., pulled a screwdriver out of his pocket, and began taking the seat apart. "I paid fifty-five dollars for this seat," he said, "and at that price I'm taking it home with me."

For the average musical, a run of 500 consecutive performances on Broadway should indicate a hit, but the chapter "These Also Ran" deals with recent long-running musicals that have been financial failures. *What Makes Sammy Run?* closed after 540 performances with a loss of $285,000. *Golden Boy* closed after 569 performances and lost approximately $120,000. In any discussion of musical hits, therefore, the actual length of the run is not always an indication of the financial success of the show. The arbitrary figure of 500 consecutive performances in New York, nevertheless, is used here as the standard for placing a production in the hit category. The 500-performance mark not only helps establish the tremendous success of earlier long-runs but also explains the economic necessity of long runs for current shows. Although the productions included in "These Also Ran" are financial failures, they cannot be excluded from the list of hit shows because their long runs indicate at least popular success.

Theatrical statisticians may disagree about the numbers of performances credited to various musicals, for sources which supply this information are not always in agreement. Should the run of *Flower Drum Song*, for example, be listed as 600 performances, as it is in the *Best Plays* series, or should it be 602 performances, the figure given by *The New York Times?* Did *Oklahoma!* run for 2,208 performances or do the 40 extra matinees performed for servicemen only belong in the final tabulation of 2,248 performances? *Milk and Honey* is credited with 570 performances by some sources, 543 by others.

In cases where the number of performances has not been reported consistently, the figures used in this book are those found in the majority of sources checked. The number of weeks a show has run and the estimates of gross receipts have, for the most part, been based on figures given in *Variety*.

Theatergoers are undoubtedly familiar with many of the following terms, but the explanations are included to avoid any possible misunderstanding. *Book musical* refers to a production which develops a plot and which uses songs and dances either to augment or to develop the action. *Operetta* refers to an opera whose music and plot are less serious than those found in grand opera. The score usually demands trained singers who can handle more difficult numbers than those usually included in musical comedies. A *sleeper* is an unexpected hit, a show which becomes a greater success than the management anticipated. *Burlesque,* particularly as used in the opening chapters, refers to a type of family entertainment popular at the turn of the century. Burlesque productions of that time usually satirized dramatic hits. For example, the burlesque of *Cyrano de Bergerac* was called *Cyranose de Bric Brac. Burlesque extravaganza* refers to a lavish burlesque production.

Broadway's Greatest Musicals

The Early Hits:
1884 to 1927

THE FIRST three stage productions to run for more than 500 performances on Broadway were all musicals: *Adonis*, produced in 1884; *A Trip to Chinatown*, produced in 1891; and *Florodora*, produced in 1903. By 1919 the number of long-running productions totaled ten, of which only four were musicals.

No book musical or operetta produced in the 1930s played for 500 consecutive performances, and only three musical revues produced in this decade exceeded the 500-performance record. Furthermore, none of the well-known, opulent revues of the 1920s and 1930s, such as Florenz Ziegfeld's *Follies*, George White's *Scandals*, or Earl Carroll's *Vanities*, ever reached the 500 mark. Successful road tours for these revues made extended runs in New York financially unnecessary and also enabled the producers to present new, annual editions on Broadway.

The musical comedy which tells a story, regardless of how thin or tenuous the plot may be, has always been popular in the American theater. The very early hit musicals, however, were, for the most part, quite different from today's musicals of distinction.

Several theatrical histories call *Adonis*, the first musical to establish a long run, a burlesque; others refer to it as a burlesque-extravaganza. Burlesque of the 1880s, unlike the burlesque of later years, was family entertainment that satirized current stage attractions, popular fiction, or well-known public figures. *Adonis* burlesqued the story of Pygmalion and Galatea; its principal attraction was not its story, however, but rather its star, Henry E. Dixey, a matinee idol who sang, danced, and wore his silk tights with such aplomb that women flocked to the theater just to see him. Photographs showing Dixey in costume for *Adonis* seem to confirm the historical accounts of his charm. Dixey's personal attractiveness, his singing, his dancing, and his remarkable ability as a comedian kept *Adonis* running in New York for two seasons. A great number of theatergoers came to see the show over and over again because Dixey and William F. Gill, who co-authored the script and lyrics, constantly changed the dialogue and added new songs dealing with items of current interest. The basic plot, however, tells a highly satirical story of a statue that comes to life and becomes involved in a series of improbable adventures. Unfortunately, no actual playscripts have survived.

Before bringing the production into New York, Dixey played *Adonis* in Chicago. After a two-year run in Manhattan, he toured with the show throughout the United States and also took it to London. Throughout his career, his name was identified with *Adonis,* but it was Dixey rather than the play that audiences came to see.

The record of 603 performances in New York established by *Adonis* remained unbroken for almost a decade. But *A Trip to Chinatown,* by Charles Hoyt, with music by Percy Gaunt, surpassed it. Following the example set by *Adonis,* this offering also played a road tour before opening in New York in 1891. The touring production and the one that played in New York must have differed, however, for the text—published by the Princeton University Press in 1941 and edited by Douglas L. Hunt—contains two third acts, one from a prompter's copy of the play, the second from the copy in the New York Public Library. Discussions of the play in theatrical histories reveal further dissimilarities. References to songs, dance numbers, and even cast members are never quite the same; some sources list J. Aldrich Libby and Miss Loie Fuller as the principal actors, while Hunt's edition lists a completely different cast for the opening performance in New York on November 9, 1891, the date generally given for the première. One source cites the New York opening as August, 1893, but this could well refer to a revival. Even the actual number of consecutive performances credited to the show varies from 300 to 630 to 657.

At least two songs still sung today, "Reuben, Reuben" (sometimes called "Reuben and Cynthia") and "The Bowery," were definitely used in the New York production. There are conflicting reports about a third popular song, "After the Ball," by Charles K. Harris. Undoubtedly this number was interpolated into the show when one of the road companies played in Milwaukee, and it may also have been used in New York. Some historians doubt that Hoyt would have used the song since he was known to prefer his own material. Still others report that the song was the hit of the show. Thirty-some years later, "After the Ball" again proved to be a show-stopper when Magnolia sang it in *Showboat*.

A Trip to Chinatown probably included Loie Fuller's famous butterfly dance, in which she used her skirt to represent the butterfly's wings; but again no specific reference to the dance appears in the text, and the number may have been interpolated after the New York opening.

Records show that many companies presented *A Trip to Chinatown* on the road while the New York production was running. For a short time, a road company actually played in New York at a second theater while the first New York company was still drawing large audiences. Since all evidence points to more than one script being used by different companies, it is understandable that one program would call the character named Flirt a friend of Tony Gay and another Mrs. Guyer's maid. When one historian, therefore, mentions timely jokes about temperance and woman suffrage in the play, and another, referring to a different text, describes jokes about doctors and widows, both are undoubtedly accurate. There is general agreement that Hoyt did not approve of interpolated material, and that the basic plot dealt with a wealthy bachelor, Mr. Ben Gay, who refuses to allow his niece and nephew and their friends to go to San Francisco's Chinatown. The young people, however, are using the trip to Chinatown as a pretext, their real purpose being to attend a masked ball at the Riche Restaurant. The Widow Guyer sends a note to Mr. Rashleigh Gay, the nephew, explaining that she will meet him at the restaurant; but the letter is delivered by mistake to Uncle Ben Gay who is delighted to think that the widow wishes to arrange a rendezvous. To divert suspicion, Ben tells the young people he has changed his mind and will permit them to go to Chinatown after all. The second act finds all the principals at the Riche Restaurant. The stage reveals two separate dining rooms. Ben Gay is alone in the first; the rest of the cast, in the second. The humor, such as it was, stemmed from a series of mix-ups—orders being sent to the wrong room, people trying to avoid being discovered, and Uncle Ben finally getting the check for both rooms and discovering that he does not have his wallet with him. Luckily he sees his friend, Mr. Strong, who has been in still a third room, and borrows one hundred dollars from him. The two different versions of the last act printed in the Princeton text ultimately arrive at the same point: the characters all explain their actions, after which Uncle Ben takes them all to dinner.

A Trip to Chinatown is a farce with music rather than a musical comedy. The songs and dances are all performed by the principal characters—Rashleigh Gay, Welland Strong, Wilder Daly, and Flirt—whose humorous names are typical of those that had popular appeal not only in the 1890s but also as late as the 1920s in novels, comic strips, and two-reel motion pictures.

A great deal of the play's drawing power at the box office must be credited to Charles Hoyt, one of the most popular playwrights of his time. Audiences enjoyed the fast pace of *A Trip to Chinatown,* the ridiculous characters, the familiar jokes, and, above all, the music. Some of the songs used, such as "Pushing the Clouds Away," "Out for a Racket," and "The Chaperone," are totally unfamiliar to modern audiences; but the popularity even today of "Reuben, Reuben" and "The Bowery" helps explain why *A Trip to Chinatown* established a record of 657 performances. The sheet music sales for these two songs were extremely high. The sales for the third hit song associated with the show, "After the Ball," were reported to have been in the millions.

The "Florodora Sextette" ("Tell Me Pretty Maiden") illustrates even more clearly how one song helped a show become a popular success. It was the girls who appeared in the number, however, rather than the song itself, that made the show famous. *Florodora* ran for more than 400 performances in London before its opening in New York in November 1900, to satisfactory, but not enthusiastic, reviews. Box office receipts for the first week or two gave no evidence that *Florodora* would develop into a hit. Stories about the beauty and charm of the *Florodora* girls, however, soon attracted theatergoers. Critics called the girls "goddesses," or "the most beautiful women on the stage." Their performances, particularly in the "Florodora Sextette," enchanted the men, for, at the end of each number, according to people who saw the show, the girls would smile and wink, usually at some man in the audience, as they exited. This personal touch, an innovation in the musical theater, entranced the young beaux who crowded the theater night after night to see the girls and to lavish expensive gifts upon them. Many men bought seats down front for almost every performance, came into the theater just in time to see the sextette in the second act, and left after the last encore.

So many stories have circulated about the *Florodora* sextette that it is almost impossible to separate fact from fancy. Many of the girls received gifts of jewelry, furs, champagne, and flowers. One beauty, who received tips on the stock market from an admirer, built up a sizeable fortune. The members of the original sextette were Margaret Walker, Daisy Greene, Marjorie Relyea, Vaughn Texsmith, Marie Wilson, and Agnes Wayburn; but according to some critics, replacements were constantly entering the cast, for the girls married wealthy men or found wealthy admirers and dropped out of the show with such frequency that more than 70 girls were reputed to have appeared in the sextette as replacements during the New York run.

Because *Florodora* was an English import, anthologies of the American theater often omit references to the show. Many theatergoers too young to have seen the operetta, therefore, know little about the production except for its title and the stories of its fabulous girls. Even the title has been misspelled as "Floradora" so often that many people question the correct spelling.

The text reveals that the title does not refer to the heroine, whose name is Dolores, but to an island in the Philippines and to a perfume named for the island. Dolores' father had owned the company which made the famous perfume, but, when he died, Cyrus W. Gilfain, an American, had stolen his business. The first act is set on the island of Florodora, where Dolores is now working for Gilfain. Frank Abercoed, who is really Lord Abercoed, arrives on the island to act as Gilfain's manager. Tweedlepunch, the comic in the show, is a detective searching for the girl who rightfully owns the perfume business. He comes to the island disguised as a traveling showman. When Gilfain discovers that Frank and Dolores have fallen in love, he pays Tweedlepunch to get Dolores out of the way by marrying her off. Lady Holyrood, who wants to marry Frank and who has come to the island with Gilfain's daughter Angela, joins in the plot. Frank, however, refuses to marry Lady Holyrood, and Gilfain discharges him. As the first act ends, Frank is leaving for England, and Dolores is planning to follow him.

The second act is set at Abercoed Castle, Frank's ancestral home in Wales. Gilfain, who has become the new owner of the castle, refuses to allow Frank to enter his former home, but Frank defies orders and maneuvers his way inside, taking Dolores and Tweedlepunch with him. Once inside, Tweedlepunch confronts Gilfain and then spins a weird ghost story that terrifies Gilfain into admitting that he has stolen the perfume business. Even more important, Gilfain returns the properties he has taken from Dolores and Frank. The final curtain comes down on a triple happy ending. Frank marries Dolores; Gilfain marries Lady Holyrood; and Gilfain's daughter, Angela, marries Captain Donegal, a member of the Life Guards.

The original New York cast included Edna Wallace Hopper as Lady Holyrood; Fannie Johnston as Dolores; R. E. Graham as Gilfain; Cyril Scott as Donegal; and Willie Eduoin, who had appeared in the London production, as Tweedlepunch. The real stars of the show, however, were the six friends of Angela who sang the *Florodora* sextette in the second act. Evelyn Nesbit, a stage beauty who later became a front-page headline, was not in the original cast but joined the show during its run.

The number of performances credited to *Florodora* varies from 505 to 553, but there is a valid explanation for this wide range; the original production closed on January 25, 1902, after a total of 505 performances and reopened two days later with a different company for an additional 48 performances. A revival of *Florodora* in April, 1920, ran for only a short time, although critics still praised the beautiful sextette. The producers had modernized the costumes for the entire cast, and introduced a novel idea by presenting two sextettes. The girls in the first group wore modern costumes; the girls in the second group were dressed just like the *Florodora* girls in the original production.

Two long-running musicals, *Irene* and *Sally,* which had excellent chorus routines, familiar stories, lilting musical scores, and appealing heroines, reflected the new type of musical production that made the 1920 version of *Florodora* seem outdated.

Irene, produced in 1919, was a variation of the Cinderella story. Irene O'Dare, a poor but honest working girl, delivers a package to the home of Prince Charming, the wealthy Donald Marshall. Impressed by her charm, Marshall sends Irene to the famous dress establishment run by Mme Lucy, who hires Irene to model beautiful gowns. To complicate the plot, Irene, who has been invited to a party, takes an elegant blue gown out of the shop without permission, expecting to return it unnoticed the next morning. Irene is caught, of course, but all works out for the best, and she marries the wealthy Donald Marshall, who turns out to be the real owner of Mme Lucy's establishment.

Irene's version of *Cinderella* has two variations. In the first, it is Irene's mother, and not the wealthy Marshalls, who opposes the marriage, though Donald finally convinces Mrs. O'Dare that he is the right husband for her daughter. In the second, the owner of the dress establishment conceals his true identity by using the name Mme Lucy, a plot variation that appeared again in a later musical, *Roberta,* the story of a football hero who inherits a dress shop.

Irene appealed to everyone who liked rags-to-riches success stories. Its charm, however, came not so much from its familiar plot as from a really delightful score. One song, "Alice Blue Gown," has become a standard; the score also included "Irene," still played occasionally, and "Castle of My Dreams," based on Chopin's "Minute Waltz."

The New York cast featured Edith Day, as Irene. The show toured the United States successfully while the original company established a record run of 670 performances in New York. As a matter of fact, *Irene* had the largest number of touring companies of any musical production up to that time. *Irene* proved to be equally successful in at least two motion picture versions. The first starred Colleen Moore; and the second, Anna Neagle and Ray Milland. In the latter film, the director set off "Alice Blue Gown" by filming the song sequence in Technicolor and keeping the rest of the film in black and white.

Irene's record of 670 performances, the longest run for a musical comedy with a story-line, remained unsurpassed for over twenty-five years to be exceeded finally by *Oklahoma!* in the 1940s.

Sally, produced in 1920, followed the same Cinderella pattern as *Irene*. Sally works in a Greenwich Village restaurant where "Connie"—in reality the former Grand Duke Constantine, forced out of a Balkan country by a revolution—is a waiter. Connie takes Sally to a party given by one of his wealthy Long Island friends, at which a famous Russian ballerina is scheduled to entertain his guests. She fails to arrive, and Connie introduces Sally as the dancer. Sally, of course, enchants her audience and gets an offer to appear in the *Ziegfeld Follies*. She becomes a star and marries wealthy Blair Farquar, whom she had met at the party. Connie also finds romance and marries a beautiful society woman. The plot has few surprises. The audiences know almost from the start how the stereotyped characters will react and how the story will end.

Ziegfeld originally had planned to feature Marilyn Miller, Leon Errol, and Walter Catlett in three separate productions, but decided to use all three players in the same vehicle when he found that the script for *Sally* could easily be tailored to fit not only the scintillating Miss Miller, but also the comic talents of Errol and Catlett. Although Marilyn Miller had previously appeared in Broadway reviews, she made her first musical comedy appearance in *Sally* and delighted the critics and the audiences with her acting as well as her singing and dancing. Leon Errol, as Connie, had ample opportunity to demonstrate his famous rubber-leg dancing and his ability to keep pace with Miss Miller in their duets. Walter Catlett, as Otis Hooper, a press agent who helps Sally become a star, had his moments of raucous comedy. Ziegfeld also cast one of his glamorous showgirls, Dolores, a six-foot beauty, to play the society woman who marries Connie.

Marilyn Miller and Leon Errol dominated the show, but

Ziegfeld made certain the production had other elements that would please theatergoers. Joseph Urban, who designed Ziegfeld's spectacular sets and costumes for the *Follies,* designed equally lavish sets for *Sally.* Ziegfeld selected both the showgirls and the chorus girls for their beauty as well as for their dancing ability. Jerome Kern's score was delightful. "Look for the Silver Lining," the hit song of the show, became synonymous with Marilyn Miller. Her later film biography, starring June Haver, was released under that title. Judy Garland also sang the number when she played Marilyn Miller in the film biography of Jerome Kern, *Till the Clouds Roll By.*

Other popular songs in *Sally* included "The Little Church Around the Corner," "Sally," and two numbers, "Wild Rose" and "Whip-poor-will," which are still heard occasionally on television and radio programs. The happy combination of Kern's music, Ziegfeld's lavish production, and Marilyn Miller's charm kept *Sally* running for 570 performances.

In 1948, Bambi Linn and Willie Howard appeared in a revival of *Sally.* Miss Linn danced beautifully and Willie Howard's antics amused the critics, but audiences in the late 1940s, accustomed to more sophisticated musical comedies, found the story stilted. Although the revival included well-known hit songs from other Jerome Kern musicals, the opulence of Ziegfeld's original production, the enchanting Miss Miller, and the very funny Mr. Errol were missing. The revival closed after 36 performances.

A revival of the all-Negro musical *Shuffle Along,* in 1952, proved to be even less successful than the revival of *Sally.* Critics had referred to the original *Shuffle Along,* produced in 1921, as a revue, for the story element was negligible. The plot, dealing with a mayoralty race, served primarily as a framework for extensive musical numbers. The principal attractions of the production were its excellent singers, frenzied dancers, and the songs of Noble Sissle and Eubie Blake. Audiences enjoyed the numbers "Bandanna Days" and "Love Will Find a Way." "I'm Just Wild About Harry" not only became the hit of the show but had sufficient appeal to remain a popular favorite still sung today. Florence Mills, along with Sissle and Blake, appeared in the original production which started in Harlem and then moved to Broadway where it opened on May 23, 1921, and ran for 504 performances. Sissle and Blake also appeared in the 1952 revival which lasted for only four performances—a failure that reflected a significant change in public taste.

Unlike *Sally* and *Shuffle Along*, *Blossom Time* reappeared on Broadway many times in successful revivals after its first long run in 1921. *Blossom Time*, for which Sigmund Romberg adapted Franz Schubert's melodies, started a vogue of popular operettas in the 1920s that resulted in two additional long-running musicals with scores by Romberg and two with scores by Rudolf Friml.

Blossom Time was supposedly based on Schubert's life, but the authors changed dates and events. The operetta, therefore, is a purely fictional story which begins with Schubert as a rather homely, shy young man. He meets Mitzi, Kitzi, and Fritzi, the daughters of Mr. Kranz, who becomes his patron. Schubert falls in love with Mitzi and writes a love song for her, but he asks his friend, the handsome Baron Schober, to sing it. Mitzi becomes enchanted with Schober, and the heartbroken Schubert begins writing a symphony based on the melody but changes his mind and does not finish the composition. Schubert becomes ill and then, as one of his last works, writes "Ave Maria."

The production was based on the European operetta, *Das Dreimädlerhaus* by A. M. Willner and H. Reichert, for which H. Berte had adapted the music from melodies by Schubert. Although Berte's adaptations are seldom heard today, George Feyer's piano record, "Memories of Viennese Operettas," includes selections from Berte's score for *Das Dreimädlerhaus*. Dorothy Donnelly re-adapted the operetta and Sigmund Romberg re-adapted the score and blended the sentimental plot with a great number of beautiful songs.

Critics have objected to the story of *Blossom Time* because it fictionalized Schubert's life. Several critics, in fact, have called the operetta simply a variation of *Cyrano de Bergerac*. On the other hand, critics have almost unanimously praised Romberg's skillful adaptation of Schubert's classical compositions to the requirements of the popular musical. Such songs as "Serenade," "Ave Maria," and "Song of Love"—which became the hit of the show—helped make *Blossom Time* one of Romberg's most successful operettas. The excellent singing and tuneful score overshadowed the conventional plot and gave *Blossom Time* a total run of 592 performances. The figure has sometimes been given as 572 but either total indicates the operetta's great popular appeal. The fact that *Blossom Time* closed for a month at the end of the first season may possibly explain the variance in totals. If all Broadway revivals were included in the final tabulation, the number of performances would be much greater.

The original cast included Bertram Peacock as Schubert, Olga Cook as Mitzi, and Howard Marsh as Schober; but cast changes and second companies did not seem to affect the show's box office appeal, for *Blossom Time* became a favorite all over the United States. Several road companies toured annually during the early 1920s, and, occasionally, one of these companies would play a two- or three-week revival in New York before re-embarking on tour. For quite a number of years at least one company of *Blossom Time* was appearing somewhere in the United States. *Blossom Time* also proved to be a forerunner of the long-running musicals produced in the 1940s which used adaptations of music written by Grieg (*Song of Norway*), Borodin (*Kismet*), and Bizet (*Carmen Jones*).

Howard Marsh, the original Baron Schober in *Blossom Time,* also appeared in Romberg's next long-running musical, *The Student Prince,* produced in 1924. Dorothy Donnelly adapted the operetta from the drama *Old Heidelberg* by Wilhelm Meyer-Forster, following rather closely the version played by Richard Mansfield.

The story concerns Prince Karl Franz, who comes to Heidelberg as a student and falls in love with Kathie, the waitress at the college inn. When his grandfather, the king, dies, Prince Karl is forced to return home to become the new monarch. Two years later, he comes back to say goodbye to Kathie before marrying Princess Margaret.

Just as *Blossom Time* was reminiscent of *Cyrano de Bergerac, The Student Prince* was reminiscent of many novels dealing with unrequited romance and the obligation of royal heirs to marry members of other royal families. Before *The Student Prince* opened, rumors on Broadway indicated that the producers wanted

the operetta to have a happy ending; nevertheless, Romberg insisted that Prince Karl Franz return to his kingdom. Most certainly in the 1920s this ending was not too far removed from the
unhappy endings of such popular novels as *The Prisoner of Zenda*
or *Rupert of Hentzau,* which also dealt with thwarted romances
and royal marriages.

In both *Blossom Time* and *The Student Prince* the plots were
secondary to Romberg's music. Moreover, *The Student Prince*
gave Romberg the opportunity to write what many critics have
called his finest score. The melodies were original rather than
adaptations; but the songs were not of the conventional type
usually sung in musical comedies, and the score required excellent
singers who could handle the counterharmonies and extensive
ranges in the duets, the demanding solos, and the lusty male
chorus numbers.

In the original company, Howard Marsh and Ilse Marvenga
played Prince Karl and Kathie. The hit songs included "Deep in
My Heart," "Serenade," "Just We Two," and the robust "Drinking Song" which featured a male chorus. The popular appeal of
Romberg's music is evidenced by the successful recordings of *The
Student Prince,* one featuring Nelson Eddy, Risë Stevens; another
with Jan Peerce as Prince Karl, Roberta Peters, and Georgio
Tozzi. The pleasure of hearing the delightful melodies sung by
excellent voices helps explain why the original production ran 608
performances, the longest run for any Romberg musical.

Historians of the drama do not always agree on the number of
touring companies that performed *The Student Prince,* but they
do agree that there were more road companies than for *Blossom
Time,* and possibly even more revivals. The Broadway revival in
1943 proved very successful, with a run of more than 150 performances during the hot summer months from June through September. In the summer of 1966, a successful revival of *The
Student Prince* on the West Coast again proved its popular appeal.

The Student Prince was filmed twice, but neither version was
comparable to the stage production. It would be difficult for
younger theatergoers accustomed to spoken dialogue and musical
sound tracks to understand how the silent motion picture starring
Norma Shearer and Ramon Novarro could have appealed to

audiences. Even an orchestral accompaniment in the larger motion-picture houses, or an organist or pianist in the smaller theaters, was not a substitute for the voices of Prince Karl and Kathie singing "Deep in My Heart." The talking-picture version had the benefit of Mario Lanza's voice, but the studio officials and Mr. Lanza became involved in a prolonged argument after the songs had been recorded, and the picture was finally released with Lanza's voice on the sound track but with Edmund Purdom playing the title role. Music lovers who objected to dubbed voices on the screen contented themselves with buying Lanza's recording of the songs rather than seeing the picture.

The New Moon, the third Romberg operetta in a decade to achieve a long run, was not an adaptation of an older drama. It followed the same sentimental pattern as *Blossom Time* and *The Student Prince,* however, and told a romantic story based on the life of a historical figure. The operetta opened out of town in December 1927, received poor notices, and closed. Oscar Hammerstein II, Frank Mandel, and Lawrence Schwab completely rewrote the book and lyrics; Romberg rewrote the music; and the producers brought in a new cast. In the fall of 1928 the revised version reopened on tour, received better notices, and started a long run on Broadway in September 1928.

The setting for Act I is New Orleans in 1788. The hero, Robert, a nobleman wanted by the French government, escapes from the French police by coming to New Orleans as a bond servant to the wealthy Monsieur Beaunoir. He and Marianne, Beaunoir's daughter, fall in love, but Robert does not reveal his true identity. When Captain Paul Duval arrives on a ship called *New Moon* to find Robert and take him back to France, Robert eludes him, goes to the tavern, and denounces a Mr. Ribaud as the spy who betrayed him. Robert returns to the Beaunoir mansion while a party is in progress, finds Marianne, and they sing the love duet, "Wanting You."

As the second act opens, Robert, who has been arrested by Ribaud and Duval, is aboard ship en route back to France. Marianne has also maneuvered to get aboard. Robert's friend Philippe helps organize a mutiny that results in Duval and Ribaud being put ashore on a Florida reef. The mutineers then land on a small island nearby and have several clashes with Duval, until another ship arrives with the news that France is now a republic. This report clears the way for Robert to marry Marianne and also to become leader of the island community that will be a part of the new French Republic.

The New Moon was a much more lavish production than *Blossom Time* or *The Student Prince*. The cast wore elaborate costumes in the first act, particularly in the scenes set in the Beaunoir mansion. The second act aboard ship and on the island emphasized stage settings rather than costumes, providing an effective contrast to the opulence of Act I.

The popular appeal of the operetta, which ran for 509 performances, must be credited to the music and lyrics rather than to the story. Even drama critics who derided the plot agreed that the melodies, particularly as sung by Robert Halliday, as Robert, and Evelyn Herbert, as Marianne, provided a delightful evening's entertainment.

Music critics who maintain that *The Student Prince* has Romberg's best score also say that *The New Moon* has Romberg's most popular score, for the operetta probably contains more familiar melodies than any other Romberg musical. "Lover, Come Back to Me," often called Romberg's best-known work, has an exceptionally lyrical bridge based on a phrase from Tschaikovsky's "June Barcarolle." Musicologists have also suggested that the opening phrase of "One Kiss" bears a strong resemblance to the opening bars of Vincent Youmans' "No, No, Nanette." The similarities among the melodies aid rather than detract from the enjoyment, for audiences familiar with both compositions find the Romberg score easy to remember. *The New Moon* also includes the well-known "Softly, As in a Morning Sunrise," "Wanting You," and the virile male chorus number, "Stouthearted Men," which is as robust as the "Drinking Song" in *The Student Prince*.

. In the early days of talking pictures, Metro-Goldwyn-Mayer filmed *The New Moon* with opera stars Lawrence Tibbett and Grace Moore. The producers, evidently dissatisfied with the plot, had the story rewritten and the locale changed. The hero, played by Tibbett, now became Lieutenant Michael Petroff; the heroine, played by Grace Moore, Princess Tanya Strogoff; and the locale, the Russian Steppes. M-G-M refilmed *The New Moon* in 1940 with Jeannette MacDonald and Nelson Eddy, again changing the characters but retaining the Romberg score and Hammerstein lyrics.

The stage versions of all three long-running Romberg operettas have never been changed in their revivals on Broadway, in summer stock, and in local productions throughout the United States. With the emphasis on actors rather than on singers in the musicals of the 1960s, the success of another Broadway revival would now depend upon the ability of the actors to handle Romberg's melodies. If the voices were musically inadequate, the audience would become conscious of the stilted dialogue and raise more objections to the implausible plot than did the critics of the 1920s.

Romberg's long-running musicals were equalled in popularity by *Rose Marie* and *The Vagabond King* produced in the mid-1920s with scores by Rudolf Friml. *The Vagabond King*, an adaptation of an earlier drama, followed the Romberg pattern; but *Rose Marie*, produced in 1924, had an original and relatively simple story written by Otto Harbach and Oscar Hammerstein II, which the critics liked much better than the stereotyped plots of a great many musicals presented during those years.

The story begins in Saskatchewan, in the Canadian Rockies. Rose Marie La Flamme and Jim Kenyon of the Northwest Mounted Police are in love, but Jim is unjustly accused of killing Black Eagle. To save Jim's life, Rose Marie agrees to marry the villain, Edward Hawley. Meanwhile the Canadian Mounties, led by Sergeant Malone, go into action. Before they trap the real killer and prove Jim's innocence, the scene has shifted to Quebec and the famous Chateau Frontenac and then back to a mountain pass in the Rockies, but by the final curtain, the real killer has been exposed and Rose Marie and Jim reunited.

The contrast in settings from the outdoor scenes in the Canadian Rockies to the indoor scenes in Quebec—including one episode in the dazzling ballroom of the Chateau Frontenac—intrigued audiences. The score also provided a series of contrasts that ranged from duets and solos to choral and dance numbers. The authors integrated the songs with the action, and, in the program for the original production, did not list individual musical numbers. Several of the songs, however, which became popular even out of context, included the popular "Indian Love Call" with its "yoo-hoo-hoo" lyrics; the title song; the male chorus numbers, often as hearty as Romberg's, particularly the opening song of the Canadian Mounties; and "Totem Tom-Tom," a production number in which the chorus girls, colorfully dressed as totem poles, stopped the show with their effective dancing. The program credits the music to both Rudolf Friml and Herbert Stothart, but the best-known melodies are those written by Friml.

The excellent voices of Dennis King and Mary Ellis, who played the lovers, also helped *Rose Marie* become a popular success. Miss Ellis, who had previously sung with the Metropolitan Opera Company, received glowing notices in her Broadway musical comedy debut. Most of the critics were enthusiastic about her singing; several were nearly ecstatic about her acting and her beauty.

The long run of 557 performances may be attributed to a great many causes: the beautiful Canadian settings; the exciting action; the colorful Canadian Northwest Mounted Police; the Indian totem-pole dance; the skillful blending of songs and plot; the excellent cast; and Rudolf Friml's appealing score. *Rose Marie* has also remained a popular attraction in revivals. Patrice Munsel, for example, has used *Rose Marie* as a vehicle for her guest appearances with summer operetta companies.

Metro-Goldwyn-Mayer made three motion-picture versions of *Rose Marie*. The producers thought the plot sufficiently absorbing to film *Rose Marie* the first time as a silent picture, with Joan Crawford in the leading role. The last remake starred Ann Blyth and Howard Keel, but the most popular version starred the famous team of Jeannette MacDonald and Nelson Eddy.

Miss MacDonald also co-starred in the film version of Rudolf Friml's second long-running musical, *The Vagabond King*, with Dennis King who had originated the role of Francois Villon in the stage production. *The Vagabond King*, adapted from the drama *If I Were King* by Justin Huntley McCarthy, opened in September 1925. The original play starring E. H. Sothern ran for 56 performances in 1901 and was revived in 1902, 1907, 1913, and 1916.

The Vagabond King followed McCarthy's drama but thinned out the plot, for dialogue had to be cut and scenes changed to allow time for Friml's excellent score. Brian Hooker and W. H. Post, the adapters, maneuvered the scenes, telescoped the action skillfully, and wrote excellent lyrics for Friml's melodies.

The story deals with Francois Villon, leader of a group of vagabonds, who offers to help King Louis XI fight against Burgundy. The King, deciding to humble the haughty Katherine De Vaucelles, makes Villon a king for a day on the condition that during that time, Villon must get the lady to fall in love with him; if he fails, he is to be hanged. Although Villon succeeds in making love to Katherine, he gets trapped in his fight against the Burgundians and is rescued by his true love, Huguette, who dies saving his life. Aided by his vagabonds, Villon prevents the Burgundians from taking Paris, and, by royal decree, marries a noblewoman at the court.

The vigorous action, Dennis King's excellent performance as Villon, and Friml's melodic score made *The Vagabond King* one of the season's greatest musical successes, with a total of 511 performances. *The Vagabond King* was also called one of Friml's best contributions to the American musical theater, for his melodies superbly enhanced both the romantic and the roguish aspects of the story. Katherine's "Only a Rose" and "Some Day," and Huguette's plaintive "Waltz" were typical of the romantic numbers audiences enjoyed. To many theatergoers, however, the high point of the operetta was "Song of the Vagabonds," a stirring number for male voices sung by Villon and his followers. Its tempo and infectious lyrics made the song not only the hit of the show but also a popular favorite still sung today by male choruses.

The emphasis upon romantic plots and operatic singing in the Friml-Romberg operettas did not influence two long-running musical comedies produced in the later 1920s that reverted back to the frothy stories of *Irene* and *Sally*. *Sunny*, produced in 1925, and *Good News,* produced in 1927, concentrated on comedy, beautiful girls, and lilting tunes.

Charles Dillingham, who produced *Sunny*, set out to equal Ziegfeld's successful *Sally* by using the same star, Marilyn Miller, and the same composer, Jerome Kern. Dillingham assembled a cast that included Jack Donahue, a dancing comedian who later became Miss Miller's dancing partner in other musicals; Clifton Webb and his dancing partner, Mary Hay; Cliff Edwards, better known as Ukulele Ike, who left the show before the end of the run and was replaced by Borrah Minevitch; Paul Frawley, who played the juvenile lead; and George Olsen's band, one of the favorite orchestras of the decade. Oscar Hammerstein II and Otto Harbach then created a musical comedy that gave each performer the chance to do his specialty and yet did not detract from Miss Miller's starring role, which capitalized on her singing, dancing, and ability to charm audiences.

Despite the handicap of having had to fit the story to the cast, Harbach and Hammerstein concocted a pleasant potpourri that became the season's musical sensation. The story deals with Sunny, a bareback rider in the circus, who meets Tom Warren, an American soldier, when she is entertaining the American troops in France during World War I. Later, in England, where she is performing with the circus, she meets Tom again. To avoid having to remarry the circus owner whom she had divorced, Sunny becomes a stowaway on the same ship that is taking Tom back to America. Complications ensue, but Sunny sings and dances her way to success, and, of course, marries Tom.

The plot was unimportant in establishing the show's long run, for the writers sacrificed story coherence to emphasize music and dancing. The principal attractions were Marilyn Miller, who enjoyed another personal triumph, and Jerome Kern's melodic score, particularly the lilting "Who?" which rivals and perhaps even excels "Look for the Silver Lining" in popularity today. Kern stressed the question *who?* by holding it for several beats while the orchestral accompaniment changed harmony. Two other songs, "D'ye Love Me?" and "Sunny," both popular during the Broadway run, are still played occasionally on radio and television.

Audiences enjoyed the circus atmosphere, the specialty numbers, the comedy of Joseph Cawthorn as the circus owner, and the dancing by Marilyn Miller and Jack Donahue. The production—which equalled Ziegfeld's *Sally* in lavishness—plus Kern's music and Marilyn Miller's box office magnetism, kept *Sunny* on Broadway for 517 performances.

George Olsen's orchestra, one of the specialty features in *Sunny*, also appeared in *Good News*, a lively musical with excellent songs, vigorous dance routines, and a typically thin plot that lampooned college life and football heroes. The setting is Tait College, a coeducational school in a small town. The hero, Tom Marlowe, captain of the football team, is failing astronomy and will be declared ineligible for the big game of the season if he does not pass his examination. Although Connie Lane, who loves Tom, thinks he is in love with the campus siren, she tutors him and helps him pass the course. In the big game, Tom makes a long run but fumbles. Bobby Randall recovers the ball and wins the game for Tait. Tom and Bobby are the heroes of the day, and Tom finally convinces Connie that she is the girl he really loves.

Good News opened during the football season in September 1927, but the slight story had enough appeal to create a demand for tickets that lasted throughout the entire year. The collegiate atmosphere served as the background for jokes about sororities, fraternities, athletes, and college life. The energetic cast kept the audience laughing even when the situations were based on old gags. One of the girls, for example, sneaks into the men's dormitory for a rendezvous with a football player. When the coach unexpectedly begins making a check on the rooms, the boy hides the girl under the bed. The audience thinks the coach is unaware of the girl, but, as he turns to leave, the coach says goodbye to the boy, hits the top of the bed, says goodbye to the girl, and walks off stage to one of the biggest laughs in the show.

The rah-rah story by Lawrence Schwab and B. G. deSylva, the lyrics by deSylva and Lew Brown, the music by Ray Henderson, and the energetic dancing and singing by the youthful cast, blended together to make *Good News* fast-paced entertainment. No less than five of the songs were soon being played by dance bands and orchestras all over the country, which helped to stimulate box office receipts. Two of these numbers, "Varsity Drag" and "Good News," sung by Zelma O'Neal, stopped the show—the Varsity Drag, in fact, developed into the dance fad of the year. "Lucky in Love," "The Best Things in Life Are Free," and "Just Imagine" rounded out the quintet of hit numbers that kept *Good News* running for 551 performances.

These thirteen long-running musicals from *Adonis* to *Good News*—frivolous operettas, raucous comedies, and lavish star-vehicles—set the pattern for popular musical productions in the American theater from 1884 to 1927.

Show Boat

IN DECEMBER 1927, three months after *Good News* had opened, *Show Boat* arrived at the Ziegfeld Theater and immediately established itself not only as the major musical show of the 1920s but also as one of the finest musicals ever produced in the United States. Many critics, in discussing the development of the American musical theater, cite *Show Boat* as the production that set new standards for producers, composers, and librettist. According to most drama historians, *Show Boat* was the first musical play to combine the extravagant scenery and costumes of the earlier shows with a serious dramatic plot, integrating dance, song, and drama into a spectacular production that subsequent shows may have equalled, but not surpassed.

Produced by Florenz Ziegfeld, Jr., with music by Jerome Kern and libretto and lyrics by Oscar Hammerstein II, *Show Boat* was based on Edna Ferber's successful novel. It was the second production on which Hammerstein and Kern had collaborated. Both men also worked on the staging and production, for Ziegfeld, convinced that they could by themselves mold the show into a superior musical, never hired a formal director.

The story concerns Cap'n Andy Hawks and his wife, Parthy Ann, who own the show boat "Cotton Blossom"; their daughter Magnolia; and Gaylord Ravenal, a handsome but irresponsible gambler. When Julie, the mulatto leading lady of the "Cotton Blossom," and her husband, Steve, the leading man, are forced to leave the show because their mixed marriage is considered unlawful, Gaylord and Magnolia take over the leads, fall in love, and marry. They go to Chicago, where they are happy until Gaylord's luck fails him. Realizing that he cannot give up gambling, Gaylord leaves Magnolia and their daughter Kim. Magnolia starts a new career as a singer at the Trocadero Café, where she is a great success. Years later, Kim becomes the star of the show on the "Cotton Blossom" and reunites her parents.

Show Boat did not follow the traditional pattern of musical comedy, for not only did the story deal with a romance that resulted in unhappiness, but the entire production ended on a bittersweet note. The marriage of Julie and Steve, probably the first time miscegenation had ever been depicted in the musical theater, also ended unhappily. The show even broke away from the traditional musical comedy opening in which the chorus girls sing a number for the "tired businessman." As the curtain rose, Negro dock hands carrying bales of cotton across the stage sang about their work, using a melody that later became part of the famous "Ol' Man River."

Most of the critics welcomed these innovations and wrote enthusiastic reviews. Several even predicted that *Show Boat* would start a new trend in musical entertainment. At least three of the long-running musicals in the 1940s fulfilled their prophecy. Most certainly the miscegenation in *South Pacific,* the all-Negro cast in *Carmen Jones,* and the unhappy marriage in *Carousel* reflected in varying degrees the influence of *Show Boat.* Significantly enough, Oscar Hammerstein II had written the lyrics for all four productions.

Audiences heartily agreed with the critics, and their enthusiastic word-of-mouth advertising created so great a demand for tickets that Ziegfeld made plans to organize a second New York company that would present *Show Boat* simultaneously with the first, a practice that would have paralleled the double showing of *A Trip to Chinatown* in the 1890s. Ziegfeld later abandoned the idea of a second company, but kept *Show Boat* on Broadway for 572 performances before sending it on tour. In 1932 he reopened the production on Broadway at a time when the Depression had affected theater gross receipts, attendance had dropped sharply for most plays, and several musicals had closed abruptly. Yet, despite the adverse times, the second run of *Show Boat* continued for 180 performances.

Its tremendous popular appeal cannot be credited to any one cause. The elaborate Ziegfeld production, the excellent cast, the Hammerstein lyrics and libretto, and the Kern music all combined to make *Show Boat* a memorable experience for theatergoers. The sets by Joseph Urban and the magnificent costumes by John Harkrider were dazzling. The elaborate settings, which changed with amazing rapidity, required skillful maneuvering of encores and reprises sung in front of the curtain to allow time for scene changes. Yet the production moved quickly from the levee to various rooms on the "Cotton Blossom," the auditorium on the boat, the Midway at the Chicago Fair of 1893, the Trocadero Music Hall, the convent school that Kim attended, and back to the "Cotton Blossom." Every scene revealed Ziegfeld's unerring taste and precise attention to details. The out-of-town opening was reported to be a typical overly-long Ziegfeld production, for he usually waited until the tryout period before cutting the numbers that seemed to impede the action. Historians differ on the deletions Ziegfeld made in *Show Boat,* but most sources estimate that he eliminated at least one hour of running time to whittle the show into the customary three-hour maximum length. As a result the final production in New York was tight and well-integrated.

Ziegfeld also used the same care in selecting his cast. Charles Winninger proved to be an ideal Cap'n Andy; Edna Mae Oliver was superb as the shrewish and yet strangely sympathetic Parthy Ann Hawks; Howard Marsh, familiar to Broadway audiences for his roles in Romberg operettas, played Gaylord Ravenal; Eva Puck and Sammy White played Ellie and Frank, the young comedians; and Jules Bledsoe, as Joe, sang "Ol' Man River" magnificently. Ziegfeld saw Norma Terris in a musical review, decided that she was the perfect choice for Magnolia, and signed her even though he had already assigned the role to another actress who later sued him for breach of contract. Ziegfeld discovered Helen Morgan in the revue *Americana* and signed her to play Julie, the role that made her a star.

Cast changes seemed to have little effect on the show's popularity. When Ziegfeld brought *Show Boat* back to Broadway in 1932, Irene Dunne, who had understudied Norma Terris, was the new Magnolia; Dennis King replaced Howard Marsh as Gaylord;

and Paul Robeson replaced Jules Bledsoe as Joe. The 1946 revival had a completely new cast featuring Carol Bruce as Julie, Charles Fredericks as Ravenal, Kenneth Spenser as Joe, Ralph Dumke as Cap'n Andy, and Buddy Ebsen and Collette Lyons as Frank and Ellie. Richard Rodgers and Oscar Hammerstein II, who produced the revival, even persuaded Jan Clayton to leave their own hit show, *Carousel,* and play Magnolia. The 1946 production brought nostalgic reviews from critics who had seen *Show Boat* in 1927 and who again rated it as one of the musical theater's finest musical plays.

Most musical comedy producers are delighted when audiences remember one or two songs; most audiences, on the other hand, know almost all the music from *Show Boat,* for each new revival seems to make the public aware of another beautiful melody. "Ol' Man River" and "Make Believe" became popular during the first run of the show, as did "Why Do I Love You?" and "Can't Help Lovin' Dat Man." Yet none of these songs reached the saturation point from being overplayed on radio or television programs. On the other hand, infrequent playing of the lovely waltz, "You Are Love," has made its occasional airings as welcome as if it were being heard for the first time.

Kern and Hammerstein had decided that every song should fit a specific situation, but they made two exceptions. Kern had originally written "Bill," with lyrics by P. G. Wodehouse, for *Oh, Lady, Lady!* but decided the song was not right for that show; he did, however, keep the melody as part of the background music in the first act. A year or so later, Kern thought of having Marilyn Miller sing it in *Sally* but decided it was not the right number for her. When Helen Morgan was signed for *Show Boat,* Kern knew she was the right girl to sing the song. Because Miss Morgan was sitting on top of the piano in the orchestra pit when Ziegfeld saw her in *Americana,* Kern and Ziegfeld had her sing "Bill" from atop a piano. At the end of the scene, Miss Morgan came out front while the sets were being changed, leaned against the proscenium arch, and sang another chorus. Kern's reluctance to use the song until he met Miss Morgan explains why "Bill" is sung less frequently than most of the other hit numbers, for "Bill" needs a very special singer to do justice to the words and music. In the program for the 1946 revival Oscar Hammerstein II, who had always insisted that P. G. Wodehouse receive proper credit for the lyrics, inserted a special note calling attention to the fact that Wodehouse, not Hammerstein, had written the number.

Kern and Hammerstein also interpolated another song which neither of them had written. When Magnolia's debut in the Trocadero threatens to be a failure, Cap'n Andy gets her to sing an old number and persuades everyone on stage to join in the chorus. Instead of writing a new song, Kern and Hammerstein wisely selected the old favorite "After the Ball," which gave the scene authenticity and still did not detract from Kern's superb score.

Symphony orchestra conductors have given Kern's score for *Show Boat* further distinction by performing it in concert halls and on recordings. Hammerstein later wrote a special concert version with narrative passages.

Show Boat's run of 572 performances may seem low in comparison with more recent musicals that have played more than 1,500 performances, but if all the Broadway revivals of *Show Boat* were tabulated, the number of performances would be well over 1,000. The 1927–1928 run of 572 performances indicates greater popular appeal than a similar run would in the 1960s because competition was much greater. The night before *Show Boat*'s première, for example, eleven new productions opened on Broadway. In the 1960s eleven new productions in one month would be extraordinary.

In 1927, *Show Boat* grossed $50,000 a week, a sum that would mean failure for the average musical today. Rising production costs and higher salaries would make the extensive cast and elaborate settings of the original *Show Boat* financially impracticable. Even the 1946 revival, which ran for 418 performances, is reputed to have lost money. Later revivals trimmed down the cast, cut down on the sets, and eliminated the lavishness with which Ziegfeld had endowed his production. Even with these economies, *Show Boat* remained a visual and musical delight. The 1966 revival at the New York State Theater in Lincoln Center, however, came much closer to the original Ziegfeld production than any of the earlier revivals. Most of the critics wrote rave reviews as if they were welcoming a new musical, and only one dissenter bemoaned the sentimental story and the musical emphasis on violin crescendos.

The superb cast, which had been selected with as much care as had gone into choosing the original players, made *Show Boat* an exciting evening in the theater. Barbara Cook as Magnolia, David Wayne as Cap'n Andy, Margaret Hamilton as Parthy Ann, Stephen Douglas as Ravenal, William Warfield as Joe, Allyn McLerie as Ellie, Eddie Phillips as Frank, and Rosetta LeNoire as Queenie were all excellent. The great surprise of the show, however, proved to be Constance Towers as Julie. A dark wig converted the blond Miss Towers into a breathtakingly beautiful brunette who looked much more realistic as the mulatto Julie than even Miss Morgan had. One critic said he once thought that no one could have equalled Miss Morgan, but that Miss Towers was as good as Miss Morgan and possibly even better. Miss Towers was indeed excellent, both visually and vocally, when she sang "Can't Help Lovin' Dat Man," and in the second act, she stopped the show with "Bill." Margaret Hamilton gave a most effective performance as Parthy Ann. The theatergoers who remembered her as the wicked witch in *The Wizard of Oz* were delighted to see her as the stern Parthy.

Some critics said that the 1966 revival had all the opulence of the original Ziegfeld production, but this statement is not quite accurate. The sets, although attractive, were not of the same type that Ziegfeld had used. The revival used a revolving showboat that turned to reveal sides of the boat and gangplank, or the kitchen, but Ziegfeld's production gave the audience the impression that it was seeing an entirely new stage set for each scene. Several changes were also made in the action. In Ziegfeld's production, Magnolia's debut in the Trocadero was a miserable failure until Cap'n Andy told her to sing "After the Ball" and then cajoled the audience into singing with her. In the revival, Magnolia began with "After the Ball" and was booed by the audience; Cap'n Andy then stood, said nothing, but motioned as though he were directing, and gradually, as the café patrons responded to his beguiling grin, Magnolia gained confidence and became a sensation. In the original production Norma Terris, who appeared as Magnolia, also played the grown-up daughter Kim. But in the revival Magnolia and Kim were played by two different actresses. An interesting addition was a sequence that took place in front of the curtain while the extensive sets were being changed; Cap'n Andy did a short dance with Parthy Ann, and the wholesome sentiment of the scene gave Parthy Ann a warmth that the original characterization did not have.

Though the 1966 production did not parallel Ziegfeld's, it did have a far more extensive cast and more elaborate sets and costumes than most of the musicals presented on Broadway in the 1960s. To older audiences, the revival of *Show Boat* brought nostalgic joy. Younger theatergoers who had heard of the charms of *Show Boat* but had never seen it were as impressed by the music, the excellent cast, and the opulent production as the original theatergoers had been in 1927.

Show Boat has retained its popularity as a stage production despite three motion-picture versions. The first, filmed in 1929 as a silent picture, featured Laura La Plante as Magnolia, Joseph Schildkraut as Gaylord, and Alma Reubens as Julie. Before the picture was released, the transition from silent films to sound had created chaos in Hollywood. Pictures were scrapped and remade with new casts; producers, in an effort to salvage completed films, added one or two reels with spoken dialogue; other producers added musical sound tracks. The producers of *Show Boat* followed this last practice by adding a sound track with background music, but, unfortunately, they did not use the Hammerstein-Kern score. In the last reel, Joe sang one song that in no way could compare with "Ol' Man River," and audiences familiar with the stage play were disappointed. Technicolor and other tinted film processes had not yet been perfected, and the dull combination of subtitles and black-and-white photography failed to capture the charm *Show Boat* had had as a musical play.

The second version, an excellent motion picture released in 1936, featured Irene Dunne, Allan Jones, Helen Morgan, Charles Winninger, and Paul Robeson. One newspaper critic, in fact, cited this version of *Show Boat* to explain why he believed that talking pictures would eventually destroy the living theater; the man who sat in the last row of the balcony could see and hear Helen Morgan singing "Bill" as clearly as the man who sat down front; it also cost far less to see a motion picture than it did to see a stage play. Judy Garland was scheduled to play Julie in the third film version, released in 1951, with Howard Keel as Gaylord Ravenal and Kathryn Grayson as Magnolia; but Miss Garland's quarrel with the studio resulted in Ava Gardner's playing the role with dubbed vocals on the sound track. None of the three film versions has seriously affected the popular appeal of the stage production, however, for almost every year *Show Boat* is presented somewhere in the United States, particularly during the summer musical season.

The 1950s and 1960s have brought longer-running musicals that offer excellent scores and dramatic plots, and incorporate many of the innovations begun by *Show Boat*. Few musicals, however, have equalled *Show Boat* in endurance. The combination of Edna Ferber's poignant story, Jerome Kern's music, Oscar Hammerstein II's lyrics, and the nostalgic charm of the entire production not only gave *Show Boat* popular appeal but also made it the first distinguished, dramatic, long-running musical comedy to be as heartily endorsed by audiences as by critics.

The Depression Years
(1929 to 1939)

MUSICAL COMEDIES suffered through lean years on Broadway from 1929 to 1939. The stock-market crash, followed by the Depression, cut box-office receipts so sharply that several hit musicals that had opened before the crash were forced to close abruptly. Motion pictures flooded the screen in the 1930s and their lower admission prices cut theater attendance to such an extent that in 1935 only four productions spanned the summer season.

Several dramas in the 1930s barely passed the 500-performance record. Only two musical revues—*Hellzapoppin* and *Pins and Needles,* both produced in the late 1930s—had long runs; but no musical comedy or operetta produced in the same decade reached the 500-performance mark. In fact only four musicals—*Of Thee I Sing, Anything Goes, DuBarry Was a Lady,* and *Louisiana Purchase*—passed the 400-performance record. The minimum of 500 performances should eliminate these musicals from a list of hit shows, but all four deserve further discussion because each made a strong contribution to the history of the musical theater, giving it distinction as a dramatic art form, establishing new musical stars, and enhancing the reputations of the composers and lyricists involved.

Of Thee I Sing, produced December 26, 1931, ran for 441 performances, a remarkable run for the Depression period. The Pulitzer Prize Committee named the show as the best play of the year, and drama commentators said that it represented the first significant musical comedy produced in the United States. Critics

31

hailed George Gershwin's melodies and Ira Gershwin's lyrics, the book by Morrie Ryskind and George S. Kaufman, and the excellent cast which included William Gaxton as Wintergreen, the Presidential candidate; Victor Moore as Throttlebottom, the Vice Presidential candidate; and Lois Moran as the girl who marries Wintergreen. The dancing star was George Murphy, now Senator Murphy of California.

The plot, a satire on American Presidential elections, concerned Wintergreen's campaign for President, Throttlebottom's selection as Vice President, the romance between Wintergreen and a French girl whom he was supposed to marry for political reasons, and his eventual marriage to Mary Turner, the all-American girl. Wintergreen's campaign has one major issue—"Love." To help the campaign, he stages a beauty contest in Atlantic City, with the prize-winning girl to marry Wintergreen and become the First Lady. The song hit "Love Is Sweeping the Country" depicts the success of the campaign, for Wintergreen does win the election. Instead of marrying Diana Deveraux, the beauty contest winner, however, he marries Mary Turner. Unfortunately, Diana proves to be the descendant of a whole chain of illegitimate relatives of Napoleon; an international crisis begins to develop, and Wintergreen is threatened with impeachment. Mary gives birth to twins, however; the politicians decide that under such circumstances Wintergreen cannot be impeached; and Throttlebottom willingly marries Miss Deveraux at the suggestion of diplomats who remind him that the Vice President must assume the duties the President cannot perform.

If the theory that ridicule is often the most effective form of criticism is true, then *Of Thee I Sing* proved to be a most effective criticism of the Washington situation. In the throes of the Depression, the play had more than timely appeal as it lampooned hush-hush scandals, nonsensical debates, party politics, under-the-counter deals, political campaigns, and ridiculous bids for votes. The hopeless position of the Vice President also came in for its share of satire, for poor Throttlebottom could not be identified by the guards, was refused admission to the White House, and was asked to provide two references before he would be permitted to use the library. The play's barbed criticism, which if handled seriously might have aroused an irate public, was glossed over with ludicrous comedy and appealing music.

The producers reasoned that since *Of Thee I Sing* had been so successful, surely a sequel written by the same librettists, lyricist, and composer, and with the same cast, would also be a box-office hit. *Let 'Em Eat Cake,* however, did not impress the critics and the show failed. A subsequent road tour which the producers hoped would recoup their losses also failed. At the end of the final matinee performance, William Gaxton is said to have stepped in front of the curtain and asked the audience if it had enjoyed the show. When the applause died down, Gaxton is reported to have declared that the critics did not like it and were putting ninety people out of work.

The apathy of both the critics and the public toward *Let 'Em Eat Cake* is understandable, for the story lacked the freshness of *Of Thee I Sing,* the music did not have the popular appeal of Gershwin's earlier score, and, most important of all, the timeliness of the humor was gone.

Of Thee I Sing's 1952 revival on Broadway gave further proof that its humor and criticism were of topical rather than universal appeal. The story and satire seemed dated, and even the excellent score and competent cast could not keep the show running for more than 72 performances. Despite this failure, however, historians of the theater still refer to *Of Thee I Sing* as a classic and emphasize the contributions it made to American theatrical history. First, it proved to be a forerunner of political and musical satires such as the Rodgers and Hart musical *I'd Rather Be Right,* in which George M. Cohan gave a superb performance as Franklin D. Roosevelt, and the long-running Pulitzer Prize musical *Fiorello!,* which dealt with New York's popular Mayor La Guardia. Secondly, *Of Thee I Sing* established the precedent that a musical comedy could have sufficient merit to receive a Pulitzer award for drama.

In November 1934, William Gaxton and Victor Moore again co-starred in another musical, *Anything Goes,* which played for 420 performances during the lean years of the 1930s. The excellent teamwork and hilarious individual performances of Gaxton and Moore helped make the show a success, but credit for the box-office sales must also be given to the composer Cole Porter, and, more specifically, to Ethel Merman. Ever since singing "I Got Rhythm" in Gershwin's *Girl Crazy*, Merman had become increasingly prominent as a musical comedy performer. Her subsequent appearances in George White's *Scandals*, in which she introduced "Life Is Just a Bowl of Cherries," and in *Take a Chance*, in which she sang "Eadie Was a Lady," proved that she could make any of her songs show-stoppers. *Anything Goes*, however, gave Merman more than just one good song, for she made famous such now-classic Porter songs as "You're the Top" in a duet with Gaxton, the tricky rhythmic number "I Get a Kick Out of You," the jubilant "Blow, Gabriel, Blow," and the intricate, syncopated title song "Anything Goes." A great many theatergoers felt that, despite the presence of Gaxton and Moore, the show was Merman's vehicle, for she had the best musical numbers in the score and handled them superbly.

Historians of the theater record that *Anything Goes*, as originally written by P. G. Wodehouse and Guy Bolton, dealt with an assortment of odd characters who were shipwrecked, but that just as the comedy was ready to go into production, the Morro Castle disaster occurred, forcing Howard Lindsay and Russel Crouse, who were asked to rewrite the book, to cut the entire story line dealing with a shipwreck, although they did keep the characters aboard a luxury liner. The new plot centered around a romance between Gaxton and Bettina Hall. Gaxton, a wealthy playboy, has come on board in pursuit of Miss Hall, but he has not taken the time to book passage. He asks Victor Moore, who is disguised as a minister but is really Public Enemy Number 13, to help him avoid being caught. In the course of the mad antics, Gaxton assumes a number of disguises and finally wins Miss Hall. Only Moore is left dissatisfied at the finale, for to his annoyance he learns that the FBI no longer is interested in hunting him down and has labeled him "harmless."

Merman's successful performance as Rose Sweeney, a night-club singer, in *Anything Goes* still did not put her into solo starring roles, but her popularity with critics and with audiences was a definite asset to *DuBarry Was a Lady*, produced in 1939, in which she co-starred with Bert Lahr. That score, too, had been written by

Cole Porter, but several critics felt that it was not up to the standard he had set in *Anything Goes*.

The zany plot was a ludicrous satire on French royalty. Lahr, a washroom attendant in a nightclub, is in love with Merman, the star of the floor show. Lahr wins a fortune in a sweepstakes, and buys the club, hoping to win Merman's affection. He mistakenly drinks a Mickey Finn that he had prepared for Merman's sweetheart, falls asleep and dreams that he is King Louis XIV and Merman is Mme DuBarry, most of the action from then on centering about his futile attempts to compromise Miss Merman. At the finale, Lahr awakes from his dream and resigns himself to Merman's marrying the man she really loves.

The cast also included Betty Grable, who had left Hollywood to try her luck on Broadway and who enhanced the stage with her beauty and her shapely legs. Her success in the musical led to starring roles in Hollywood. Benny Baker, who appeared in many of the scenes with Bert Lahr, proved to be an admirable foil for Lahr's drolleries. The show girls were statuesque beauties, but despite their loveliness, and in spite of the famous Grable legs, Ethel Merman overshadowed all the other women in the cast. Her brash performance, her extraordinary enunciation, and her ability to cope with Lahr in the most ludicrous situations proved that she had become an expert comedienne as well as a top-ranking singer.

Critics who liked Porter's songs referred specifically to "Katie Went to Haiti," but the only number from the show that is heard today is "Friendship," a duet sung by Merman and Lahr with each chorus becoming more nonsensical than the preceding one. Merman's lusty singing and Lahr's expert mugging made the number the comedy hit of the production.

The Merman-Lahr combination, the line of beautiful show girls, and the opulent settings and costumes comprised excellent entertainment in "the tired businessman" tradition and kept *DuBarry Was a Lady* running for 408 performances.

Louisiana Purchase, which opened on May 28, 1940, starred William Gaxton and Victor Moore in their third run of more than 400 performances in less than ten years. Morrie Ryskind, co-author of *Of Thee I Sing,* wrote the book, based on a story by B. G. deSylva. Songs and lyrics were by Irving Berlin, whose musical revue *As Thousands Cheer,* produced in 1932, reached a high record of 400 performances during the Depression era. The cast also included Irene Bordoni, a popular musical star in the 1920s, and Vera Zorina, the ballerina who had captivated audiences in the Rodgers and Hart musical *I Married an Angel.*

Gaxton played a lawyer involved in a questionable deal concerning something called "The Louisiana Purchase Company," and Moore played Senator Oliver P. Loganberry, who has come down to New Orleans to investigate the situation. In order to stop Moore from revealing what he has learned, Gaxton, aided by Irene Bordoni as Mme Bordelaise, Vera Zorina as a dancer, and Carol Bruce as a glamour girl, attempts to involve the Senator in a scandal, even to the point of hiding a woman in his bedroom. Though Moore manages to outwit the crooks, there is a happy ending for all.

The cast was responsible in no small measure for the show's success, for Gaxton and Moore again demonstrated their excellent teamwork. Irene Bordoni singing "It's a Lovely Day Tomorrow" brought back nostalgic memories to New York theatergoers who remembered her delightful romps in musical frolics. Vera Zorina intrigued audiences particularly in her ballet number, an unusual combination of dancing and dialogue in which she performed intricate dance steps while soliloquizing about the possibility of a marriage to Moore. Carol Bruce ably handled the title number.

The general tunefulness of the Berlin melodies pleased audiences and most critics. Several of the songs, including "It's a Lovely Day Tomorrow" and "Louisiana Purchase," are still played frequently. The competence and popularity of the cast, and the fast-paced humor, helped *Louisiana Purchase* run for 444 performances, the longest run for any musical comedy in the decade.

No other book musical in the ten-year period from 1930 to 1940 equalled the runs of *Of Thee I Sing, Anything Goes, Du-Barry Was a Lady,* or *Louisiana Purchase.* These productions were less popular than the longer-running musical shows of the 1940s and 1950s, but all four paved the way for the full acceptance of musical comedies as drama, and enhanced the reputations of Ethel Merman, Cole Porter, Irving Berlin, and George Gershwin.

The Booming
World War II Years

THE 1940s brought a new decade of prosperity to the musical theater. In the Ziegfeld tradition of the 1920s, producers were still catering to the tired businessman by presenting him with an array of beautiful show girls who did little more than wear elaborate costumes and parade gracefully across the stage. The chorus girls, however, were chosen for their ability to sing and dance; one critic said he thought the average star of the 1920s did not have half the talent of the average chorine of the 1940s. So much emphasis was placed upon talent, in fact, that one musical show ran into serious problems when the producers discovered that one of the frontline chorus girls was too beautiful and, by contrast, made the other chorus girls look far less attractive. To fire her would have been disastrous. Publicity experts for rival producers might have capitalized on the situation and written barbs implying that the one thing a tired businessman would not find in the show was a pretty girl. In the musical motion pictures of the 1940s, such a problem would have been solved very easily by making the girl a star, but on Broadway, the producers used another solution. They simply moved the girl to the back line of the chorus and made her beauty less conspicuous.

Lavish productions were still popular, and producers spent money freely on costumes and scenery. It is said that when the producers of an early 1940s musical became aware at the last moment that the costumes for one chorus routine clashed with the scenery, they promptly ordered a whole set of new costumes in order to retain the more expensive stage setting. One producer, in discussing the probable solution to such a problem in the 1960s, said that he would shift the scenery or perhaps have a new number written to suit the costumes because it was too expensive to scrap anything already made.

In the 1960s Lucille Ball wore dungarees throughout most of *Wildcat,* and Gwen Verdon wore the same basic black outfit pictured in the advertisements for *Sweet Charity* for most of the proceedings on stage. In the 1940s, however, the emphasis was still upon many changes of costume, particularly for the star; elaborate outfits for the show girls; and lavish sets. Typical of such productions was *Panama Hattie.*

The long barren period that had begun after *The New Moon* opened in September 1928, and during which no musical comedy ran for 500 performances, ended on October 20, 1940, with the production of *Panama Hattie.* This musical, with book by Buddy deSylva and Herbert Fields, and music and lyrics by Cole Porter, established three new firsts on Broadway: the first of Ethel Merman's starring roles, as well as her first long-running musical; the first Cole Porter show to run for more than 500 performances; and the first musical comedy in twelve years to become a long-running hit with 501 performances.

The leading character, Panama Hattie, was patterned after the typical hard-boiled, outspoken, brash young women Merman had played in earlier musicals. Hattie Maloney is a nightclub singer in the Panama Canal Zone. She falls in love with Nick Bullett, of the socially prominent Philadelphia Bulletts, who is serving in the Armed Forces. Nick is divorced and has custody of his eight-year-old daughter Geraldine. Hattie and Nick decide to marry, and Hattie insists that Geraldine come to Panama before the wedding, for she wants the girl to approve of the marriage. When young Geraldine arrives with the family butler, she laughs at Hattie's garish costumes and her vulgarity. Things look bad for the marriage until Hattie overhears a plot to blow up the canal. With the help of three sailors, she foils the plot, becomes a heroine, wins over young Geraldine, and clears the way for her marriage to Nick.

The plot, of course, was of secondary importance, for the show had obviously been tailored to fit Merman. Most of the critics praised the Cole Porter score, particularly the numbers sung by Miss Merman. The late W. C. Fields openly admitted that he hated doing scenes with children because they always stole the spotlight; but Merman had no such fears as she and young Joan Carroll, who played Geraldine, sang "Let's Be Buddies" and made it a smash hit and, oddly enough, the only song which seems to have survived the show.

The cast included several players who were new to Broadway audiences. *Panama Hattie* predated Michael Todd's *Star and Garter* in bringing burlesque actors to the Broadway stage. One of these performers, Rags Ragland, was making his first appearance on Broadway after years in burlesque; he impressed motion picture scouts and later became a popular featured player at Metro-Goldwyn-Mayer studios. Ragland was not the only member of the cast for whom *Panama Hattie* provided a direct route to a motion-picture contract. Betty Hutton, formerly a vocalist with Vincent Lopez's orchestra, performed two of her typical scatter-brained routines in *Panama Hattie*. She jumped and bounced all over the stage as she sang, just as she had done with the Lopez orchestra, and received a film contract by the end of the New York run. James Dunn, who played Nick Bullett, and Arthur Treacher, who played the butler, reversed the procedure by coming to Broadway after successful careers in motion pictures. *Panama Hattie* was appearing on Broadway during the great Shirley Temple craze; Dunn, who had played Shirley Temple's father in one film, proved to be an ideal choice for Nick, father of eight-year-old Geraldine. Arthur Treacher's reputation as filmdom's perfect butler made him the logical choice for Geraldine's butler.

Most of the critics found the production highly entertaining. Some made particular mention of the colorful settings and costumes by Raoul Pène du Bois; others singled out the burlesque comedians who gagged their way through familiar routines; still others enjoyed the exciting dancing of Carmen D'Antonio; and almost all complimented the beautiful girls. Even the dissenters hedged their negative comments with reservations. One critic, for example, said he was pleased that young Joan Carroll was not on stage when the sailors swapped bawdy jokes. Opinions were mixed, too, on Betty Hutton's frenzied performance. Reviewers were almost unanimously effusive in their praise of Merman, however. With her flashy costumes and her brassy songs, Merman won over the audience as completely as she did young Geraldine. Regardless of how farfetched the possibility of her marriage to socialite Nick Bullett might have seemed, Merman made the audiences want her to triumph by getting Nick, and when she did, everyone was happy. Moreover, Merman's perfect enunciation immeasurably helped the Porter lyrics. Merman was not and is not, as some critics have suggested, merely "a shouter." Volume is not her only attribute; her ability to be heard in the last row of the balcony is due to her extraordinary ability to project her voice and enunciate.

Proof that Merman well deserved the star billing she received in *Panama Hattie* is illustrated by the fact that without her the production did not prove to be popular. Critics of the road show, which featured another star in Merman's role, were dissatisfied with the production; and in a large Eastern city, a summer stock production with another well-known star proved equally disastrous, for the critics said the show without Merman was ridiculous. Merman was the perfect choice as Hattie, for Porter's music and lyrics and the plot were tailored to fit her talents. It was Merman's magnetic personality and sparkling performance that brought people to the theater for 501 performances to make *Panama Hattie* the first long-running musical hit in the 1940s.

Some historians of the theater have credited the popular success of *Panama Hattie* to the public's search for raucous entertainment in that year before the war. But this desire for escape entertainment is more directly responsible for the success of Cole Porter's next musical, *Let's Face It!* starring Danny Kaye, which opened October 21, 1941.

Let's Face It! with music and lyrics by Cole Porter and book by Herbert and Dorothy Fields, was based on a popular comedy, *Cradle Snatchers,* by Russell Medcraft and Norma Mitchell, produced in 1925. The original play dealt with three women who discover that their husbands are philanderers. To make their husbands jealous, the three matrons hire three young college boys to make love to them. They invite the boys to a champagne party and get the boys tipsy. The plot then develops into a series of variations on the theme of whether the ladies would seduce or be seduced by the young men. The husbands return at the height of the party and make accusations; the wives make counter-accusations; the play ends with the young men still uncompromised but with the wives having gained the upper hand. In the original cast the wives were played by Mary Boland, Edna Mae Oliver, and Margaret Dale, all popular actresses of the 1920s. Two of the college boys were played by young men who later achieved stardom in Hollywood: Humphrey Bogart and Raymond Guion, who later changed his name to Gene Raymond.

Herbert and Dorothy Fields updated the story by making the young men Army inductees at Camp Roosevelt, and added three young girl friends of the inductees to provide further complications. The Fieldses emphasized the story of one inductee, Jerry, played by Danny Kaye, whose sweetheart, Winnie Potter, misunderstands his behavior with Maggie Watson, one of the three matrons, played by Eve Arden. At the final curtain, the inductees and their girl friends are reunited, and the wives return to their husbands.

By October 1941, the draft had gained momentum, New York audiences were aware of the impending war in Europe, and the revised version dealing with the experiences of young inductees made *Let's Face It!* timely, topical, and the proper kind of entertainment for theatergoers wanting to see the funny side of Army life.

Before *Let's Face It!* Danny Kaye had appeared in only two Broadway productions. The first, *The Straw Hat Review,* brought him good notices but did not push him into stardom. In the second, Gertrude Lawrence's star-vehicle *Lady in the Dark,* he played the supporting role of an effeminate photographer. His big number in that show came in the dream sequence when he sang "Tchaikovsky," a tongue-twisting number which required him to rattle off the names of 60 Russian composers in 90 seconds. There are several stories about "Tchaikovsky," most of them indicating that on the opening night Kaye received a tremendous ovation after that number. Kaye knew that if it met with too much applause, Miss Lawrence might exercise her prerogative as star and demand that the song be taken out of the show. According to one report, Kaye is supposed to have pleaded with the audience not to applaud; but the more he pleaded, the more applause he received. One commentator said that Miss Lawrence was furious, but someone backstage told her that if she were really a star, she would go out front and top Kaye in her next number. Miss Lawrence apparently did just that. In the biography *Gertrude Lawrence as Mrs. A,* Richard Aldrich, Miss Lawrence's husband, repudiated the story that Miss Lawrence considered cutting the number. In his version, Miss Lawrence insisted that Kaye keep the song, but on opening night she sang "Jenny," the song that followed "Tchaikovsky," differently from the way she had rehearsed it. Imitating a tough singer in a low dive, she gyrated with bumps and grinds that resembled a routine performed in a Minsky burlesque show. As a result she received a tremendous ovation.

Lady in the Dark had catapulted Danny Kaye to stardom. After his opening performance in *Let's Face It!,* the rave reviews made him as big a drawing power at the box office as Cole Porter. According to reports, the show had not gone well in rehearsal, but on opening night, Kaye's agile handling of special material made *Let's Face It!* the hit of the season. Kaye's two most popular routines were specialty numbers written by his wife, Sylvia Fine, and Max Leibman. Both numbers were typical of the specialties Kaye had used in personal appearances. The first, "A Modern Fairy Tale," was delightful, but it was the second number, "Melody in Four F," that proved to be the high spot of the show. In some respects its tongue-twisting double-talk resembled "Tchaikovsky." The routine also became the high spot of Kaye's first Hollywood film, *Up in Arms.*

Porter's songs for Kaye capitalized on his ability to enunciate polysyllabic tongue-twisters at breakneck speed. In "Let's Not Talk About Love," for example, the song began in conventional rhythm, then switched to double time with Kaye singing in lightning, staccato tempo, then reverted to the original rhythm for the lyrics that included the song title. A second Porter song, "Farming," epitomized Porter's sophisticated, café-society lyrics by dropping the names of such prominent personalities as Mae West, Katharine Cornell, George Bernard Shaw, and Lady Mendel.

The cast of *Let's Face It!* also included such clever performers as Benny Baker; Vivian Vance, who later appeared with Lucille Ball in "I Love Lucy"; Eve Arden, who became a featured player in Hollywood, a television star, and more recently the star in the Chicago company of *Hello, Dolly!;* Helena Bliss, who played one of the principal roles in the long-running operetta *Song of Norway;* and Nanette Fabray, who became a star when she replaced Celeste Holm in *Bloomer Girl.* Despite the excellent supporting cast, it was Kaye's dynamic performance and bubbling personality that made *Let's Face It!* the popular comedy success of the season. José Ferrer, who replaced Danny Kaye in February 1943, also gave a creditable performance, but the songs and special material had been tailored too closely to Kaye. The show suffered without him, and one month later closed with a total of 547 performances.

The motion-picture version co-starred Bob Hope and Betty Hutton, but even Miss Hutton, who was given Kaye's double-time songs, was no match for the Porter lyrics, and the motion picture did not draw the same enthusiastic response as the stage production.

Ethel Merman and Danny Kaye demonstrated the power of stars to make musical comedies long-running hits, but the 1942–43 theatrical season introduced a new means of achieving popular success—an emphasis on melodies by famous composers. *Rosalinda,* based on Johann Strauss's *Die Fledermaus,* opened in October 1942, and became one of the biggest hits of the season. It inspired a series of revivals of the famous operettas of the 1920s, such as *The Student Prince* and *The Vagabond King,* and started a cycle of new operettas, several of which became long-running successes.

Searching for a show that would be a popular as well as an artistic success, the New York Opera Company wisely selected *Die Fledermaus,* for the operetta had been presented under various titles at least four times before *Rosalinda* opened. George C. Odell's *Annals of the New York Stage* lists the first production of *Die Fledermaus* as October 1879; the first revival took place in April 1885 with De Wolf Hopper. The next production, this time entitled *The Merry Countess,* was presented in 1912 with a cast that included the famous Dolly Sisters. A third version of the story, now called *A Wonderful Night* and rewritten by Fanny Todd Mitchell, was presented in 1929. And four years later, still a different version, this time called *Champagne Sec,* opened in October 1933, with Peggy Wood, Helen Ford, George Meader, and a very young and delightful Kitty Carlisle singing the role of Prince Orlofsky.

The 1942 production of *Rosalinda* was based on the Max Reinhardt version of Strauss's operetta, and was written by Gottfried Reinhardt and John Meehan, Jr., with lyrics by Paul Kerby. The adapters followed the original story but updated situations and dialogue. Erich Korngold, an authority on Strauss, interpolated familiar Strauss music, including a passage from the well-known "Tales of the Vienna Woods," to augment the original score.

The cast and staff for *Rosalinda* included several European artists who had come to this country as refugees. Among these were Dr. Korngold, who conducted the orchestra; and Oscar Karlweis, a popular comedian in Vienna and Berlin, who played Prince Orlofsky, a role usually sung by a woman. The feminine leads, both American singers, were Dorothy Sarnoff, who later played a leading role in *The King and I,* and Virginia McWatters, a Philadelphia socialite making her New York debut as Adele. José Limon and Mary Ellen were the principal dancers. During the first few weeks, the operetta did only modest business. The excellent staging and capable cast, however, pleased audiences and, as the season progressed and the theaters in New York began prospering because of the influx of military personnel and visitors, *Rosalinda* became a hit.

The reviews alone would not have accounted for the long run, for some of the critics used terms such as "streamlined Strauss" or "Biedermeier Jitterbugging" and were divided in their opinions of the performers. One critic, for example, rated Everett West, who played Alfredo, as the best singer in the show; another thought West's voice was among the weakest. Opinion was equally divided on the merits of Dorothy Sarnoff as Rosalinda and Virginia McWatters as Adele. One critic, playing it safe, admitted that although the voices may not have been the best, at least the singers did not look like singers.

To its credit *Rosalinda* boasted a lavish production, a fine ballet, and the excellent Strauss music. The story was slightly ridiculous, but no more so than the stories of many earlier long-running musicals. Moreover, New York was crowded with people looking for different types of theatrical entertainment. For those who wanted an old-fashioned operetta which emphasized music rather than plot and permitted audiences to sit back, relax, and listen to lilting melodies, *Rosalinda* was an ideal choice.

The plot concerns Baron Eisenstein, who is facing a jail sentence; his wife, Rosalinda, who is upset lest this prevent her from attending a masked ball; and her maid Adele. Eisenstein leaves the house, and Alfredo, Rosalinda's lover, arrives. When the jail warden comes to arrest the Baron, Alfredo is forced to pose as Rosalinda's husband; the warden, thinking he has arrested the real Baron, takes Alfredo to jail.

The second act is set in Prince Orlofsky's palace where the masked ball is in progress. Rosalinda arrives masked, as does Adele, disguised as a member of the nobility. Adele enchants many of the men, but Rosalinda is wooed by her own husband, who does not recognize her. Rosalinda plays up to the Baron and steals his prize possession, a pocket watch that chimes.

The third act takes place outside the jail where Alfredo is still behind bars. All the major characters appear on the scene for various reasons. Adele comes to the jail hoping for an audition and sings an aria to demonstrate her talent. The Baron arrives, learns that he has been wooing his own wife, and also discovers that Alfredo has been Rosalinda's lover. He is, however, unable to defend himself when Rosalinda shows him the watch she has stolen. By the final curtain, all complications are smoothed out in time for the obligatory happy ending.

Though the music was the show's greatest asset, with its lyrical solos and charming duets, the comedy numbers were cleverly placed; and the entire operetta had a pace, color, and spectacle that enabled it to last for 581 performances.

Rosalinda might still be popular in revival today if the Metropolitan Opera Company had not presented its own version of *Die Fledermaus* with new lyrics by Garson Kanin and found it to be one of the most popular productions in its repertoire, both in New York and on tour. Although the Baron, Rosalinda, and Alfredo remained the most important characters, the role of Adele became a favorite particularly of such coloratura sopranos as Lily Pons, Roberta Peters, and Patrice Munsel, all of whom made Adele's aria "Look Me Over Once" one of the highlights of the opera. Further proof that *Die Fledermaus* is still popular is the fact that the Metropolitan Opera Company signed Kitty Carlisle for six performances during the 1966–67 opera season to repeat the role of Prince Orlofsky which she had sung in *Champagne Sec*.

Rosalinda inspired revivals of older operettas, but it also must have whetted public interest for the several new musical productions that followed during the war years. One of these, *Carmen Jones,* which opened in 1943, astounded many theatergoers who did not believe that grand opera could ever be popular enough to sustain a continuous run of 500 performances.

In many respects the original story and music of *Carmen Jones* were more familiar than the plot and score of *Rosalinda. Carmen* had long been a popular opera. Audiences knew many of the melodies, particularly such arias as "Habañera" and the "Toreador Song." The dramatic situations, too, had popular appeal. Prosper Mérimée's original story had been widely read. Paramount Pictures had made a silent motion picture based on *Carmen* starring Geraldine Farrar, one of the better-known Carmens at the Metropolitan Opera. Several talking motion-picture versions were produced under various titles, using only the story or including Bizet's score merely as background music.

Carmen Jones was by no means the same type of adaptation as *Rosalinda,* which had retained the original plot of *Die Fledermaus,* as well as the original location and character names. Oscar Hammerstein II, who wrote the adaptation, used the Bizet score almost intact except for changing the order of one or two numbers. He also followed Mérimée's story as adapted by Meilhac and Halévy, but modernized it by changing the location and the names of the characters, and writing completely new lyrics. Certainly the lyrics in "Seguidilia" from *Carmen* bore no resemblance to "Dere's a Café on de Corner" in *Carmen Jones.* "Habañera" became "Dat's Love," and the rousing "Toreador Song" emerged as "Stan' Up and Fight."

Carmen tells the story of a worker in a cigarette factory who is arrested when she gets into a fight with one of the other girls. Placed in the custody of Don José, a soldier, she soon entices him into a torrid love affair, and they run off together. Carmen meets Escamilio, a toreador, and tries to get rid of Don José. In the final scene the jilted Don José stabs Carmen and kills himself.

Hammerstein kept the same basic plot but changed the Spanish cigarette factory to a parachute factory in the South. One source specifies that the location for Act I in *Carmen Jones* is in Harlem, but the program cites the factory location as being in a Southern town. Don José the soldier became Joe, a member of the Military Police assigned to guard the factory; Escamilio the toreador became Husky Miller, a prizefighter. The plot, however, still dealt with a factory girl who fights with a co-worker, is arrested, and placed in custody of an M.P., whom she seduces. She lures him into deserting his post to take her to Chicago where she meets Husky Miller. In the final scene, outside the sports arena where Husky is fighting, Joe stabs the fickle Carmen and kills himself.

Carmen Jones is not easy to classify, for although the program refers to the production as "a musical play" rather than an opera, it is really a combination of both. Some critics refer to it as a drama because Hammerstein changed the recitative passages to straight dialogue, but musicologists point out that in doing so, Hammerstein was following the original version of the opera in which Bizet had also made use of dialogue.

Many critics praised the showmanship of Billy Rose, the producer. Howard Barnes, reviewer for the New York *Herald-Tribune,* felt that in blending theater, spectacle, song, and dance, Rose had proved that opera could be as entertaining as any other theatrical form. Most certainly Rose's contribution to the great success of *Carmen Jones* cannot be minimized, for it was he who assigned Howard Bay to do the sets and Raoul Pène du Bois the costumes, and the result was a visual delight, particularly as the audience became aware of color harmonies in both the sets and the costumes. For example, the opening scene contrasted shades of red, yellow, brown, and orange. The night club scene in Act I used only shades of purple, but the colors ranged from very light lavender to dark heliotrope. The Chicago scene effectively contrasted blues that varied from very light aqua to dark navy. And the final scene outside the sports arena contrasted black and white with vivid touches of bright red. Since both costumes and sets were variations of the same colors, each change of scene and costume provided a decided contrast to the preceding one, and the entire production was an ever-changing spectacle of color.

Because of the strenuous demands the score made upon the leading singers, Rose cast two players in each of the principal roles—one for the matinees and one for the evenings—and, according to critics, all these singers were excellent, even though all were nonprofessionals making their first Broadway appearances. Muriel Smith, who sang Carmen in the evenings, had been a camera-store clerk in Philadelphia; Luther Saxon, who played Joe in the evenings, had been a checker in the Philadelphia Navy Yard; and Glenn Bryant, who played Husky Miller for all performances, was a New York City policeman.

Most of the critics characterized Hammerstein's adaptation as brilliant. He was praised for avoiding jazz rhythms, for "singing the music straight," and for allowing the dances to deviate from the type of ballet usually seen in operas without resorting to the shuffling dances typical of Broadway musicals.

There were several dissenting voices, however, from opera lovers who objected to certain of Hammerstein's additions to the original action. They were appalled, for example, by Cosey Cole's frenzied drum solo in the cabaret scene, although theater critics thought the drum beating appropriate to the action. They also were displeased with an episode in which the vocalists chugged along stage as they sang about taking a train to Chicago. One or two felt that the singers could not cope with Bizet's music, and one opera historian wondered what Bizet's reaction would be if he could return to earth and see *Carmen Jones*.

Yet even the dissenters agreed that Billy Rose's production was visually effective and that Hammerstein's completely new lyrics were far better than the usual English translations of foreign lyrics. This is not altogether a valid comparison, for Hammerstein had escaped the pitfalls of most translations because the very nature of his libretto permitted him to change not only the lyrics but also the original ideas of the arias. Hammerstein's achievement, in fact, is all the more remarkable when compared with operas which have been presented with English lyrics. To maintain the original melodies and orchestrations, translators have often written lyrics that force singers to slur and distort words to such an extent that the lyrics sound ridiculous.

Hammerstein, however, not only wrote lyrics that fit the melodies but also made them intelligible by meticulously selecting words that permitted the singers to enunciate each syllable clearly. This feat is all the more remarkable if reports about Hammerstein's writing habits are true. Richard Rodgers is reputed to have said that Hammerstein would send him a complete set of lyrics for which he would then set the musical pattern. Yet in *Carmen Jones,* Hammerstein completely reversed this process. He took an entire operatic score and adapted his lyrics to fit the musical phrasing.

The significance of Hammerstein's accomplishment is probably best illustrated by the fact that other producers and writers tried to convert standard operas into popular fare and failed. *Carmen Jones* remains unique in that it is the only adaptation of a classical opera to the popular stage that became a long-running hit, with a total of 503 performances.

In his review of *Carmen Jones,* one critic expressed his delight that Hammerstein had not presented new and distorted versions of Bizet's music, as Romberg had done with Schubert's melodies for *Blossom Time.* In *Song of Norway,* which opened in August 1944, George Forrest and Robert Wright used Edvard Grieg's melodies but followed the Romberg approach by converting the music into more conventional song and dance forms. *Song of Norway* also resembled *Blossom Time* in plot development, for both operettas were fictionalized biographies of famous composers. Critics who objected to the liberties taken with Grieg's life disparaged the story in much the same way that they had ridiculed the plot of *Blossom Time.* Several critics thought the action in *Song of Norway* was contrived, lacked dramatic appeal, and moved too slowly. One critic admitted that he did not know if the various incidents were true but said they sounded logical; another declared that Grieg's life could not have been as dull as the operetta. Most reviewers agreed, however, that it was the presence of Grieg's music that made the production palatable.

Milton Lazarus, who wrote the book, based the plot on a play by Homer Curran. Grieg's father, who is in the fish business, would like his son to work with him, but Edvard prefers to write music. His best friend, Rikard, is also his rival for the affections of Nina. Grieg meets Countess Louisa Giovanni, an opera singer, and becomes her accompanist on a concert tour. Rikard finally convinces Grieg that he can write the music of his native land only if he returns home, and in the final scene, Edvard and Nina are reunited.

Song of Norway first opened on the West Coast as a Los Angeles Civic Light Opera Company presentation and received good notices. When the production opened in New York, Californians referred to the operetta as the West Coast's gift to Broadway, for that production became one of the most successful musicals in a very prosperous theatrical season. Most critics were kind to the cast, particularly to Lawrence Brooks as Grieg, Helena Bliss as Nina, Robert Schafer as Rikard, and Sig Arno as Count Peppi. They were especially glowing in their praise of Irra Pettina whose characterization of the temperamental opera singer brought life to a dull plot.

The dancing by the famous Ballet Russe de Monte Carlo, with choreography by George Balanchine, proved to be one of the high spots in the show. When the production opened, all of the principal members of the company including Alexandra Danilova, Frederick Franklin, Maria Tallchief, Nathalie Krassovska, Leon Daniellan, and Ruthanna Boris, appeared in the dance sequences. The dancing in *Song of Norway,* however, was not all ballet; the choreography also included peasant dancing and stately waltzes.

In spite of the excellent dancers and engaging leading singers, *Song of Norway* might have been a dull failure had it not been for Grieg's music. On this point the critics concurred almost unanimously. One review even carried the headline "Grieg's tunes save his life." A musical historian who had objected to *Carmen Jones,* even though Hammerstein did not change Bizet's music, completely reversed his point of view in reference to *Song of Norway* by saying that the music in its present adaptation was still faithful to the Norwegian spirit and would give a great many people the chance to become better acquainted with Grieg's fine compositions. Several passages of Grieg's piano concerto were played without any changes; but most of Grieg's melodies were adapted into tuneful, delightful songs. Among the numbers used, in addition to the *Peer Gynt Suite,* were Grieg's well-known "Ich Liebe Dich" which became "I Love You"; "Strange Music," based in part on "Nocturne" and "Wedding in Troldhaugen," became the love duet as well as the hit of the show; other Grieg compositions incorporated into the score included "Norwegian Dance," which became a lively dance number, "Freddy and His Fiddle"; "Papillon"; and "Albumblatt." A great deal of the music, such as the piano concerto and "Anitra's Dance," sounded familiar, but none of it had been played on radio to the extent that audiences would have grown tired of hearing it. In fact, many people who thought they knew little or nothing about Grieg's music were agreeably surprised to find that they recognized quite a few melodies in the score.

Drama historians have ranked *Song of Norway* with such operetta classics as *Rose Marie, The Student Prince, Rosalinda,* and *Blossom Time,* but the success of these productions did not mean that all operettas patterned after the same formula would be assured of long runs. *Polonaise,* for example, produced in 1945 and based on Chopin's well-known compositions, ran for only 113 performances. *Rhapsody,* produced during the same season as *Song of Norway,* had opulent scenery, lyrics by John LaTouche, a cast that included such excellent dancers as Patricia Bowman and George Zoritch, and music by Fritz Kreisler. Yet this production, which represented an investment of $200,000—a fantastic sum for the 1940s—lasted for only 13 performances.

Song of Norway closed with the phenomenal record of 860 performances, making it not only the musical hit of the season but also the longest running operetta in the history of the New York theater. The length of the run is even more remarkable in view of the fact that most of the original ballet members left the cast during the first year's run.

The popularity of *Song of Norway,* however, was not limited to the war years. In 1958 Guy Lombardo and Leonard Ruskin presented it at the Jones Beach Marine Theater, and, according to their reports, 400,000 people saw the show during its ten-week run. The operetta was presented at Jones Beach the following season, and reports from audiences indicate that one important visual asset was a body of water between the stage and the audience, which permitted the producers to simulate a Norwegian wharf complete with a fishing fleet, a Viking ship, and even a floating iceb:rg. Revivals of *Song of Norway* in summer stock companies throughout the United States have also been very successful.

The revival of Victor Herbert's *The Red Mill* that opened on Broadway October 16, 1945, profited from the success of *Song of Norway,* but not because it resembled the Grieg biographical musical. *The Red Mill* came to Broadway at a time when critics and audiences were surfeited with operettas patterned after *Rosalinda* and *Song of Norway: Mr. Strauss Goes to Boston* (1945) lasted only 12 performances; *Polonaise* closed after 113; *Marinka* (1945), a musical version of the Mayerling tragedy, had a slightly better run of 165 performances, but still not enough of a run to make it a major success. Despite its creaky plot, *The Red Mill* seemed fresh in contrast to the labored imitations of *Song of Norway.* The familiar music gave it a nostalgic charm that helped the operetta become the first revival to run for more than 500 performances.

The 1906 production of *The Red Mill* with music by Victor Herbert and book and lyrics by Henry Blossom was tailored to fit the talents of the famous team of Montgomery and Stone, who had intrigued audiences a season or two earlier in *The Wizard of Oz.* Montgomery and Stone reportedly romped through the operetta as if it were a series of vaudeville routines rather than a musical with a definite story line, but their zany antics helped *The Red Mill* run 274 performances, the longest run for any Herbert operetta during his lifetime. In addition to the drawing power of the starring comedians, curious theatergoers were lured to the box office by an electric sign, reputed to be the first moving electric sign on Broadway, which advertised the show. The principal attraction, however, was neither the sign nor the cast so much as it was Herbert's delightful music, for the score contained one hit after another, including the enchanting "Moonbeams"; "When You're Pretty and the World Is Fair"; the love song "Because

You're You"; the charming "In Old New York"; and the show-stopper "Every Day Is Ladies Day with Me."

The number of hit songs in *The Red Mill* was not character-istic of the average musical show. Most composers were delighted if they had one or two numbers which the public accepted as hits, but *The Red Mill* had so many hit songs that many theatergoers knew almost the entire score. Very few of the early musicals with the exception of *Show Boat* could equal the Herbert operetta in the number of song hits.

Music critics often called Victor Herbert the leading composer of light opera in America and ranked him with Arthur Sullivan of England and Jacques Offenbach of France. His music was kept alive on radio, on records, in amateur productions, and in motion pictures even though the vogue for his operettas was over by the late 1920s. Most of his operettas required trained voices, and the average amateur group had difficulty finding singers who could handle his intricate melodies. Paradoxically, since *The Red Mill* had not only one of Herbert's most popular but also one of his most simple scores, it proved to be the greatest popular success of his career. The revival in 1945 profited from this, for, as one high school operetta coach said when she heard about the revival, "If everybody who ever directed, or acted, or sang in *The Red Mill* were to see the show, it could run for a year on Broadway."

People on the West Coast could have called *The Red Mill* their second gift to Broadway, for its revival began there as the Los Angeles Civic Light Opera Company's opening production for the spring season of 1945. The program indicated that the musical had been revised, for in addition to listing Herbert and Blossom as composer and librettist, the credits also included Milton Lazarus as author of the book and Forman Brown as author of additional lyrics. Comedian Billy Gilbert, known to motion picture fans as the sneezing comic, directed the production which featured Eddie Foy, Jr., Lee Dixon, Nancy Kenyon, Dorothy Stone, Charles Collins, and Morton Bowe. The successful West Coast run prompted the producers to bring the show to New York with Eddie Foy, Jr. and Michael O'Shea playing the Montgomery and Stone roles for a limited run of eight weeks. The excellent reviews and enthusiastic public response soon changed that plan and the show settled down for a long run. Foy and O'Shea stayed with the operetta longer than they had planned; when they finally left the cast, Jack Whiting and Jack Albertson came in as excellent replacements.

The revival offered a new type of popular entertainment for younger theater patrons who had heard about Victor Herbert, had enjoyed his music, but had never seen a professional production of any of his operettas. Many critics praised the producers for not updating the story, but their assumption that it had remained entirely unchanged is not correct. The revival did follow the original story line. Many of the comic routines were patterned after those of the original production, but the producers did make several changes. The role played by Dorothy Stone, daughter of the famous comedian and sister of Paula Stone, the show's co-producer, was enlarged to include several dance numbers for Dorothy and her husband, Charles Collins. Some of the old jokes, too, had been eliminated, but the plot remained basically the same.

Act I takes place in Holland outside an inn called "The Sign of the Red Mill." Two stranded, penniless Americans, "Con" Kidder and "Kid" Conner, try to avoid paying their bill by climbing out of a window, but the burgomaster catches them and takes them to jail. The innkeeper consents to their being released if they will work out their bill. "Con" Kidder becomes an interpreter; "Kid" Conner, a waiter. When "Con" and "Kid" learn that Gretchen, the innkeeper's daughter, cannot marry Captain Van Damm, the man she loves, because she is being forced to marry the Governor of Zeeland, they promise to help her elope with the dashing Captain. The innkeeper discovers the plot, however, and he and the burgomaster lock Gretchen in the mill. At the finale of the first act, Gretchen, aided by "Kid" and "Con," escapes by climbing out of the window and coming down safely on a wing of the revolving windmill.

Act II takes place at the burgomaster's house. Everything is set for the wedding of the Governor and Gretchen, but it is discovered that the bride is missing. The innkeeper offers a reward for the return of his daughter and even sends for the famous detective Sherlock Holmes. The ensuing search for Gretchen enables "Con" and "Kid" to assume a number of disguises, including, of course, those of Sherlock Holmes and Doctor Watson, as they go through a hilarious routine of questioning, searching, and probing for missing evidence. When the innkeeper finally learns that Captain Van Damm will inherit a large fortune, he withdraws his objections to the marriage. The Governor of Zeeland decides that he can be just as content married to another very personable young woman, and everybody is happy at the final curtain.

Old-timers who had seen the original production as well as the revival said that many of the jokes they remembered were no longer in the script, but that the old-fashioned fun, the humorous gags, and the comic routines made the revival every bit as enjoyable as the original production. The fact that Mr. and Mrs. Fred Stone attended the New York opening also drew attention, with several reviewers commenting that audiences must have been delighted to see the Stones enjoying with parental pride an operetta produced by one daughter and featuring another.

Most of the critics were enthusiastic about the performance of Eddie Foy, Jr. as "Kid" Conner. Burton Rascoe compared him with Bobby Clark, and added that Foy was not only an expert comedian and effortless dancer but also an expert pantomimist. The critics' enthusiasm for Foy was shared by the public. He regaled audiences with his antics, particularly when he would step out of character, walk to the footlights, and talk directly to those sitting out front. The critics also singled out for special praise the performances of Michael O'Shea as "Con" Kidder, and Edward Dew as the Governor. Dew stopped the show every time he sang "Every Day Is Ladies Day." Odette Myrtil as a vivacious French lady pleased most of the critics, although one or two thought she was overly exuberant. A few critics felt that Dorothy Stone overacted in the dramatic scenes, but all praised her dancing. Even those reviewers who had objections to the cast or to the dated story admitted that they had enjoyed the show as a whole. According to stories heard along Broadway, some of the critics are reported to have come back to the show after opening night just to hear the lilting Herbert melodies.

Probably in keeping with the precedent set by *Oklahoma!* the producers did insert a ballet, but most of the dancing reflected the more conventional routines of earlier musicals. One critic echoed the opinion of a great many theatergoers when she said that most of these dance routines were a decided relief from the overabundance of ballet in contemporary musicals.

In addition to its music, its dancing, its expert comedians, and its nostalgic charm, the revival of *The Red Mill* had still another attribute that helped account for its long run. In a period filled with Broadway revues featuring former burlesque stars, musical comedies that included rowdy songs with double-entendre lyrics, and dramas emphasizing illicit romance, *The Red Mill* was the exception—an operetta that could still be called family entertainment. *The Red Mill* was an evening of old-fashioned charm, and its run of 531 performances proved that a revival could be a resounding hit.

V

Oklahoma!

Oklahoma! opened on March 31, 1943 and helped to change the whole concept of musical theater in New York. It set more precedents than any other musical produced during the war years and had more imitators than either *Song of Norway* or *Rosalinda.* At least three long-running musical hits in the mid–1940s imitated *Oklahoma!* by using the same ballet techniques, the same production methods, and, in one instance, even some of the same performers. And there were as many, if not more, musical comedies which tried but failed to capture the qualities that made *Oklahoma!* the longest running musical comedy in the world for eighteen years.

Oklahoma! is credited with a great many firsts: the first musical to tell a serious story; the first musical to introduce ballet; and the first musical to receive recognition as a literary drama. All of these firsts are only half true. *Oklahoma!* was certainly not the first serious musical on Broadway. *Show Boat,* which dealt with the separation and bittersweet romance of Magnolia and Ravenal as well as the episode of miscegenation between Julie and Steve, had, after all, preceded it by 16 years. *Oklahoma!,* however, impressed the critics as a serious musical because it included a scene in which a man was killed on stage. Agnes de Mille's choreography for *Oklahoma!* was developed from her work on Aaron Copland's *Rodeo,* which had been performed by the Ballet Russe, but this was not the first use of ballet in musical comedy. Marilyn Miller had introduced several ballet numbers in her hit musicals; and Vera Zorina, who had been a prima ballerina, performed ballets in the musicals of the 1930s—the most notable being "Slaughter on Tenth Avenue," which she danced with Ray Bolger in the Rodgers and Hart musical *On Your Toes,* produced in 1936. Moreover, Rodgers wrote "Slaughter on Tenth Avenue" specifically as a ballet, but for the ballets in *Oklahoma!* he used fragments of songs heard throughout the show. It is true that several members of the Critics' Circle voted *Oklahoma!* the best drama of the year, and it is also true that the Pulitzer Committee did award a special citation to *Oklahoma!;* but neither the Pulitzer Committee nor the Critics' Circle awarded a prize for drama in the season of 1942–43. On the other hand, *Of Thee I Sing,* produced in 1931, did win the Pulitzer Prize, not for a musical but for a drama.

Lynn Riggs's comedy *Green Grow the Lilacs,* the source for *Oklahoma!,* had been presented by the Theatre Guild in the 1930–31 season with Franchot Tone and June Walker heading the cast. The Guild had decided that the comedy needed musical numbers and added Western songs, cowboy ballads, and chorus numbers, but *Green Grow the Lilacs* did not prove to be a popular box-office attraction. It ran only 64 performances, the subscription period for Guild members, and then was sent on tour to the Guild subscription cities.

The Guild had often discussed reviving the show but had made no definite plans. When Theresa Helburn suggested that *Green Grow the Lilacs* be made into a musical comedy, the Guild had only $30,000 left in its treasury. Miss Helburn arranged for Rodgers and Hammerstein to work as a team, but the reports on how this was accomplished differ. Lawrence Langner, the most authoritative source, says in *The Magic Curtain* that it was Rodgers who suggested that Hammerstein write the lyrics. All sources agree, however, that Rodgers and Hammerstein wanted to work together. Broadway show people were skeptical about the new writing team, for Rodgers had written with only one other lyricist, Lorenz Hart; and Hammerstein, who had written with several composers as well as other lyricists, had not been associated with a hit show since the 1930s. It should be noted that *Oklahoma!* preceded Hammerstein's later, highly successful *Carmen Jones* on Broadway.

Rouben Mamoulian, who had directed *Porgy and Bess* for The Theatre Guild, was signed as director. Lemuel Ayers was signed to do the sets; Miles White, the costumes; and Agnes de Mille, at the suggestion of Lawrence Langner, was hired to do the choreography. Even before the show went into rehearsal, however, the Guild was beset with problems, of which the most serious was finding financial backers. The directors of the Guild rented studios in Steinway Hall and held a series of auditions to raise the proper amount, which Langner quotes as $100,000. Since the motion picture rights had not been cleared, the Guild could not hope to sell the picture rights to help defray production costs.

Backers were reluctant to invest in the production for a number of reasons. *Green Grow the Lilacs* had not been a popular play; Hammerstein had not had a hit since the 1930s; Richard Rodgers, although a highly respected composer, was working for the first time without Lorenz Hart; the Guild was in financial trouble and this production could well have been another failure in a series of noncommercial shows; the cast contained no star names that might have drawing power at the box office; Agnes de Mille had never worked in musical comedy before; and although Mamoulian had staged *Porgy and Bess* admirably, that production had not been a financial success. Throughout all the troubles, Theresa Helburn maintained her faith in the show that some critics began dubbing "Helburn's Folly."

The musical opened with the title *Away We Go* in New Haven, where it did not impress theatergoers. Several New Yorkers who saw the production on its pre-Broadway tour in New Haven, and later in Boston, were skeptical. One producer told the Guild that the show had little chance to succeed on Broadway because it was too clean, had no bawdy jokes or striptease girls, and would not appeal to the people who were crowding theaters that featured more raucous entertainment. This statement, however, was not entirely true, for *Oklahoma!* did have earthy humor in several of the scenes, particularly those involving Ado Annie, the Persian peddler, and Gertie Cummings. Hammerstein's lyrics were also clever and adult in their earthiness, but they were definitely not of the juvenile, vulgar type that occurred in several productions then current on Broadway. Other critics thought the show would suffer because it defied tradition: a man was killed on stage, and the chorus girls did not appear until the first act had run almost 45 minutes, which was definitely contrary to the old joke in show business that the average businessman could tell whether he would or would not like a musical comedy before the curtain was halfway up.

During the tryout, the authors made significant revisions. Hammerstein wrote additional lyrics for "All er Nothing," the duet sung by Ado Annie and Will Parker. In Boston, the title was changed to *Oklahoma,* and the routine for the song "Oklahoma" was restaged to make it a rousing number for the entire ensemble. Before the New York opening, the producers decided to add the exclamation point to the title. Advance stories about the show were still pessimistic, and on the Broadway opening night, there were empty seats in the theater. By intermission, however, everyone connected with the show knew it would be a hit, although it is doubtful that anyone suspected *Oklahoma!* would break the world's record for consecutive performances for a musical production—a record set by *Chu-Chin-Chow* in London during World War I.

The critics wrote rave reviews calling the show "truly delightful," "beautifully different," "colorful," "jubilant," "refreshing," "charming," and "completely enchanting." Several critics wrote glowing reviews of the score. One called it the finest he had ever heard, and another said he liked the Rodgers and Hammerstein combination better than that of Rodgers and Hart. The old-fashioned melodramatic quality of the plot, with the villain pursuing the innocent heroine; the enthusiasm of the youthful cast; the spectacular dancing—particularly the can-can girls—and the excellent integration of music and plot all came in for their share of favorable comment.

After opening night, long lines appeared at the box office. Newspaper columnists increased the staggering demand to see *Oklahoma!* by printing stories about the difficulty of obtaining tickets. In recent years, this type of publicity has become a public relations ploy to stir people to go to the theater, but *Oklahoma!* was one of the first shows on Broadway to get such consistent newspaper coverage about the scarcity of tickets. To have seen *Oklahoma!* during the early part of its run became a status symbol among certain theatergoers.

The miraculous transformation of *Green Grow the Lilacs* into a record-breaking success was not the work of any one person. Rodgers and Hammerstein deserved much of the credit, for although they followed the original plot, they speeded up the action, added the humor which the play had lacked, and provided excellent music and lyrics. Agnes de Mille also deserved accolades for her choreography. She skillfully used dance routines, particularly ballet sequences, to help develop the plot; and Rouben Mamoulian earned equal credit for skillfully integrating the plot, the music, and the dancing. The integration, in fact, is so complete that an explanation or listing of the musical numbers definitely belongs in a synopsis of the plot.

The setting is the Indian territory that later became the state of Oklahoma; the time is about 1907, the year of Oklahoma's statehood. As the curtain rises on the opening scene in front of Laurey's house, Aunt Eller is churning butter. Curly, a handsome cowboy, comes looking for Laurey, singing "Oh, What a Beautiful Mornin'." When Laurey comes on stage and pretends that she is not interested in Curly, he asks her to go to the box social with him and sings "The Surrey with the Fringe on Top." This almost breaks down Laurey's resistance, until Curly admits that he has made up the whole thing. Very soon the cowhands arrive with Will Parker, who has just come back from Kansas City, and he sings "Kansas City" to tell about all the amazing things he has seen, including a burlesque house. Will then performs the first dance routine in the show. "Kansas City" is a doubly effective song, for its lyrics are clever, slightly earthy but not offensive, and its rhythmic melody provides the perfect accompaniment for a lively dance routine.

After the dance number, Will accuses Ado Annie of flirting with other men while he has been away, and Ado Annie sings her explanation, "I Cain't Say No." Here again Hammerstein's lyrics contain earthy humor, but the witty lines and Ado Annie's innocent bewilderment make the number delightful rather than offensive. One of the men with whom Ado Annie has flirted is Ali Hakim, the Persian peddler, who dodges shotgun weddings and sells questionable merchandise. He sells Laurey a bottle of "Egyptian Elixir," a potion that he assures her will conjure up dreams about her future.

The chorus girls finally appear on stage. They are on their way to the box social, and among them is Gertie Cummings who has a loud, annoying laugh. When Gertie makes a fuss over Curly, Laurey is displeased and agrees to go to the social with Jud Fry, the disreputable farmhand who works for her and Aunt Eller. To show her indifference, Laurey sings "Many a New Day." The girls then follow with their first dance routine. Here Agnes de Mille introduced a novel touch in which Joan McCracken, as "the girl who falls down," pretends to fall in the middle of the sprightly number, then quickly gets up again as if embarrassed, and continues dancing.

As the scene ends, Laurey regrets that she has promised to go to the social with Jud. She and Curly sing "People Will Say We're in Love," a different type of love song, in which they ask each other not to be attentive so that people will not suspect they really are in love.

The second scene takes place in Jud's living quarters in the smokehouse. The walls are covered with pictures resembling pages from the old *Police Gazette*. Curly comes to warn Jud to keep away from Laurey, and, pretending to be jesting, suggests that Jud ought to hang himself. He then sings the mournful "Pore Jud," which describes what people would say about Jud if he were lying in his coffin. Curly, sounding almost like a revivalist, even gets Jud to join in the song, and later tricks him into admitting that he had killed a man. When Curly tells Jud to stay away from Laurey, Jud begins to threaten him, but, fortunately, Ali Hakim arrives. After Curly has left, Jud asks Ali if he could sell him a new gadget that looks like a telescope but which contains a hidden knife. Ali, however, says he does not have the gadget.

In the third scene, Laurey uses the "Egyptian Elixir" to help make up her mind. She sings "Out of My Dreams," and the ballet that follows dramatizes the struggle between Jud and Curly and ends with the victorious Jud carrying Laurey off stage. The ballet music consists of fragments used earlier in the show, and the chorus girls, dressed in can-can outfits, remind the audience not only of the burlesque theater in the song "Kansas City" but also of the pictures in Jud's room. Laurey comes out of her dream and reluctantly leaves for the box social with Jud.

Act II introduces only three new songs, a decided break from the traditional musical comedy pattern. As the act opens, the box social is in full swing. The entire ensemble sings "The Farmer and the Cowman" and then does a spirited square dance. When the picnic boxes are put up for sale, the bidding is spirited, but the bidding for Laurey's develops into a contest between Jud and Curly, who finally puts up his harness, his gun, and everything else he owns that can be sold, until he outbids Jud. To show there are no hard feelings, Jud pulls out the telescope he had described earlier to Ali and almost persuades Curly to look into the lethal gadget, but Aunt Eller, warned by the peddler, interrupts and insists that Curly dance with her. This gives Jud a chance to take Laurey to the back porch. Laurey, frightened by Jud's menacing gestures, tells him he is fired, and Curly arrives just in time to send the threatening Jud away. Still frightened, Laurey rushes into Curly's arms and they reprise the duet "People Will Say We're in Love."

Before the next change of scene, Will and Ado Annie are in front of the curtain where they sing the very humorous "All 'er Nothing," in which Will tells Ado Annie very firmly how things will have to be when they are married. In the final chorus, Ado Annie pretends that she will be a very dutiful wife—until the last two lines, when she suggests that if Will is out carousing she might be doing the same.

The final scene takes place three weeks later, in front of Laurey's house. Curly and Laurey have just been married. After the cowmen, farmers, and girls arrive, Aunt Eller says that Oklahoma, which has just become a state, should be a fine place for the young people to live. This statement cues the entire ensemble into the rousing choral number "Oklahoma," with the final chorus starting almost in a whisper and then building to a dramatic climax. Fittingly, "Oklahoma" was adopted as that state's official song in 1953.

The men decide that this is the time to have a shivaree for the newly married couple. Just as the shivaree is getting underway and the men have dragged Curly on stage, Jud, who has been away for three weeks, suddenly turns up. He is drunk, has a long knife, and rushes for Curly; but in the tussle, Jud falls on his own knife and is killed. The sheriff wants to take Curly to jail, but Aunt Eller insists that he cannot do this on Curly's wedding night. Everyone agrees that the trial should be held immediately, and, of course, Curly is acquitted. The men then wheel onto the stage a surrey with a fringe on top, put the young couple into it, and the entire ensemble reprises the rousing "Oklahoma."

Oklahoma! proved to be a prosperous hit for everyone connected with it. It established Rodgers and Hammerstein as the top writing team on Broadway. It broke all previously existing box-office records and brought enormous profits both to the Guild and to the backers. According to the June 7, 1950, issue of *Variety,* the Guild's share of the profits up to that date amounted to more than $2,790,000. Additional revenue came from the sale of more than one million record albums, for *Oklahoma!* was one of the first musical comedies to be recorded with the original cast.

Both the critics and the public approved of the excellent original cast: Alfred Drake as Curly; Joan Roberts as Laurey; Betty Garde as Aunt Eller; Lee Dixon (probably better known to audiences than most of the performers because of his motion pictures) as Will; Celeste Holm as Ado Annie; Joseph Buloff as Ali; and Howard da Silva as Jud. *Oklahoma!* elevated these players to starring or featured roles in other productions just as it did Katharine Sergava and Marc Platt, the principal ballet dancers, and dance company members Joan McCracken and Bambi Linn. The show continued playing to capacity houses as the cast underwent change after change in the major roles. Among the many replacements who became stars or featured players were Howard Keel, Shelley Winters, John Raitt, Isabelle Bigley, Iva Withers, and Florence Henderson.

Because of the great demand for tickets the producers were unable to participate in the program of distributing unsold tickets free to servicemen through the USO offices, but they did more than their share in making *Oklahoma!* available to servicemen. When the producers organized a road company to play the major cities in the United States, they also organized a touring company to play at USO bases and thus bring the show directly to the men and women in the Armed Services. During the war years, the show is reputed to have played to more than 1,500,000 servicemen overseas. The management also instituted a series of Tuesday matinees in New York, with attendance limited to servicemen and tickets selling at one half the regular box-office price. At the School for Personnel Services in Lexington, Virginia, a base which trained officers and enlisted men to produce soldier shows, the management permitted the school to do a production using songs and dialogue from *Oklahoma!* during the first year of the New York run. The Armed Services Forces distributed free recordings of the score to most military bases, and reports from these bases indicated that the troops were delighted to hear the superb orchestral arrangements of the fine score.

Oklahoma! broke all existing musical comedy records by running five years and nine weeks for a total of 2,248 consecutive performances. Originally the figure was quoted as 2,208, but John Chapman correctly insisted that the record should include the forty extra matinees for servicemen since they were performances for which tickets had been sold. *Oklahoma!* became the third longest-running attraction in the history of the New York theater, a record exceeded at that time only by two non-musical plays, *Life with Father* with 3,224 performances and *Tobacco Road* with 3,182.

Oklahoma! touring companies played all over the United States during the next ten years and the show is also reported to have set a world's record in the number of foreign touring companies—Sweden, Denmark, Australia, France, Germany, England, Canada and South America all welcomed *Oklahoma!* In his discussion of the London production, Lawrence Langner explained that the Guild selected the type of cast it felt would best please English audiences. Howard Keel, who played Curly, was tall, handsome, and sang well; personable Betty Jane Watson played Laurey; the chorus men were over six feet tall and looked like virile cowmen; the chorus girls were selected for their attractiveness on stage as well as for their ability to sing and dance. This careful planning not only made the show a great critical success in London but also helped it establish a run of 1,151 performances, which broke all records in the 287-year history of the Drury Lane Theatre.

Drama historians have no difficulty in explaining why *Oklahoma!* proved to be the greatest success of the American musical comedy theater. It had one of the most unusual and delightful scores in the history of the theater. The lyrics were not only clever but had humor, freshness, and a definite connection with the plot. From the opening "Oh, What a Beautiful Mornin' " to the exciting finale "Oklahoma" almost every number was a hit song, and within months after the show had opened, audiences were familiar with most of the score. One of the few numbers that did not become an instant favorite, "The Farmer and the Cowman," developed into a popular hit after the motion-picture version was released. Secondly, all the elements of the show blended together. The music, the lyrics, and the ballet were all integral parts of the plot, which thus never had to slow down for a musical interlude or specialty number. The ballet also proved to be a refreshing change from the ordinary chorus routine. The dancing was definitely Western style, and, in some of the routines, such as the square dance that opened Act II, the choreography emphasized zest and humor. The plot, too, was appealing. Instead of the standard Cinderella romance or the farcical comedies of earlier musicals, *Oklahoma!* told a sprightly story of the West; and stories of the West have always found an enthusiastic audience in the United States.

The motion-picture version, however, surprised a great many theatergoers who had hoped that it would live up to their vivid impressions of the stage production. Motion-picture audiences were surprised to learn, for example, that the film was made not in Oklahoma but in Kansas, because the producers thought the scenery in that state would be better. Some of the lyrics were made a bit less adult, and this, too, displeased people who knew all the original words. Most of the critics wrote favorable reviews; several particularly liked Charlotte Greenwood as Aunt Eller and Gordon MacRae as Curly. Others found the sound and photography excellent; but many were disappointed. One critic, for example, thought that only the Rodgers and Hammerstein songs saved the picture from being a very ordinary one. Perhaps the film failed to capture the enthusiastic acclaim of the original play simply because the story and production no longer seemed fresh and different.

The reaction to revivals in New York also reflected changing attitudes. As late as 1951, a two-month revival on Broadway with the national touring company still received rave reviews, but only two years later, critics were less enthusiastic about a presentation that played for five weeks at the New York City Center. The critics knew that featured performers appeared in City Center productions for minimum Equity salaries; that rehearsal time was often not long enough to give even experienced actors time to perfect performances; and that City Center shows did not have the advantage of out-of-town tryouts. Nevertheless, several reviewers said they thought the production was a little rough and that they found the show less attractive than it had been in earlier years. In spite of an excellent cast, the 1965 revival at City Center played to appreciative but not wildly enthusiastic audiences. People who had seen *Oklahoma!* in the 1940s still enjoyed the production and realized that if much of it had become dated in the 1960s, it was not the fault of the show. Twenty years of musicals that had imitated the dancing, the story line, and even the staging of *Oklahoma!* had changed public reaction.

One aspect of *Oklahoma!*, however, is as delightful today as it was in 1943. People have not grown weary of the melodies or the lyrics, and such songs as "People Will Say We're in Love," "Surrey with the Fringe on Top," and "Oh, What a Beautiful Mornin'" still enchant listeners and explain why *Oklahoma!* established a record for musical comedy runs that has been surpassed only by *My Fair Lady*.

The Mid 1940s

THE SUCCESS of *Oklahoma!* influenced the production of the musicals that followed, particularly those produced during the 1943–44 season. Every producer wanted a show that could capture the same wide audience appeal. Ballets were considered so essential that they were injected into musical comedies whether they fit the plot or not. In fact, ballet became so common in the theater that within a few years the same critics who had praised the dance routines in *Oklahoma!* became almost ecstatic when leading players or a chorus line would break into an old, familiar tap routine. In the year that followed the premiere of *Oklahoma!* producers knew that any new musical would suffer by comparison if it failed to present an integrated plot, if it offered an inferior score, or if it had a cast less zestful than the young players in *Oklahoma!*

Perhaps this fear of comparison explains why the period from June 1943, to October 1943, saw only one new musical comedy open during a four-month span; three new musical revues failed to catch public interest; and although New York was crowded with people clamoring to see hit shows, the remaining musical productions were all revivals of well-known hits, of which only one, *The Merry Widow* with Jan Kiepura and Marta Eggerth, interested audiences sufficiently to run 322 performances. The others, which had very short runs, included *The Vagabond King*, 56 performances; *Blossom Time*, 47 performances; *Porgy and Bess*, 24 performances; and *Chauve Souris*, 12 performances.

On October 1, 1943, a musical farce, *Hairpin Harmony*, opened, received brutal reviews, and closed after three performances. One reviewer said that any show that followed would, by comparison, make a better impression. His prediction was correct, for both the critics and the public were eager for a new hit. The very next Broadway production, *One Touch of Venus,* which opened October 7, 1943, benefited from this good timing.

Interest in the production ran high even before the premiere. Advance ticket sales were over $100,000, a startling figure for the 1940s. News stories about the cast and the writers stirred up additional public interest. According to advance reports, the musical, suggested by F. Anstey's story "The Tinted Venus," had been written for Marlene Dietrich. When the role was given to Mary Martin, hopes were still high. Miss Martin had captivated Broadway audiences when she introduced the song "My Heart Belongs to Daddy" in Cole Porter's *Leave It to Me!* She had gone to Hollywood for several pictures, and was now returning to Broadway. Kurt Weill, who wrote the score, had pleased New York audiences with his music for *Lady in the Dark.* Both S. J. Perelman and Ogden Nash, who wrote the book, were prominent, popular authors. Nash had also written the lyrics, and his reputation as a humorous poet made audiences eager to hear them. The cast included John Boles, a handsome Hollywood leading man who had been in retirement for several years but had agreed to return to the stage in *One Touch of Venus* to play Whitelaw Savory, the art dealer. Kenny Baker, the third key member of the cast, was making his Broadway debut but had long been a popular tenor on radio, particularly on the Jack Benny show. Since Agnes de Mille had created the choreography, audiences and critics were hopeful that the dances would be as sprightly and as original as those in *Oklahoma!* Before the opening, rumors began circulating that *One Touch of Venus* was as good as *Oklahoma!* and, perhaps in some ways, might be even better. This resulted, as one critic said, in "an impressive dress-up" first-night audience.

The reviews the following day were contradictory. One critic called the show a hit; another, a disappointment. Some found it clever; others thought it contrived. Most of the critics praised Mary Martin; one dissenter, however, said Miss Martin still did not rate as a singer. Many of the reviews balanced good comments with bad ones. For example, even those critics who did not like

One Touch of Venus admitted that it tried to be different from the ordinary musical, that it was "unhackneyed" and "imaginative"; those who wrote about the production in superlatives often showed reservations, saying that some parts "didn't come off," or that the action lacked lightness and variety.

One Touch of Venus suffered most from unfortunate comparisons with *Oklahoma!* There was some basis for comparison since both productions had de Mille ballets; both integrated the songs with the plot; and both avoided typical musical comedy clichés. The comparisons, however, were often illogical, for the shows were fundamentally different. *Oklahoma!* was rustic, Western, and folksy; it offered a simple romance, a melodramatic villain, a pert heroine, and a virile hero; in many respects, it was family entertainment. *One Touch of Venus,* on the other hand, was urbane, chic, and Manhattanish; it presented pure fantasy, a glamorgoddess heroine, and a likeable but very much bewildered hero; it had no melodramatic villain; it was adult entertainment. The universal qualities inherent in *Oklahoma!* made it a worldwide favorite; the locale and plot of *One Touch of Venus* made it more appealing to New Yorkers than to out-of-towners.

The story of *One Touch of Venus* concerns Whitelaw Savory, an art dealer who brings a priceless, historic statue of Venus to New York. Rodney Hatch, a barber who comes to Savory's museum to shave him, sees the statue, and, to prove to himself that his fiancée's hand is more delicate, slips the wedding ring he has bought for Gloria on the finger of the statue. Thunder rolls and blinding lightning strikes almost immediately. When the air clears, Venus has come to life. The ring, she says, has broken a spell that had turned her to stone, and she now is deeply in love with Rodney, her rescuer. When Rodney tries to evade her, Venus follows him to his rooming house, and is bewildered by his refusal to succumb to her charm as well as by his comment that she should be wearing something other than her flowing, translucent robes. Venus then goes to Radio Center, breaks into a shop window, removes a dress from the window model, and begins changing her clothes. A crowd of people swarm around the shop, but Whitelaw Savory arrives in time to save Venus from being arrested.

Venus then joins Rodney at the bus terminal where he is meeting his shrewish fiancée, Gloria, and her domineering mother; Venus stirs up a quarrel between Gloria and Rodney, and also antagonizes Rodney. She trails him to the barber shop, where Gloria again threatens to be a rival. Venus, however, waves her arms, and Gloria mysteriously disappears. Rodney is accused of murdering Gloria and is sent to the Tombs, but Venus helps him escape and spends a night with him in a hotel room. Rodney begs Venus to bring Gloria back so that he will be free of the murder charge. When Venus does so, the infuriated Gloria staggers out of a closet, regains her composure, makes vindictive accusations about Rodney and Venus, breaks off her engagement, and stalks out of the room. A worshiper of Venus had in the meantime pleaded with her to return to her country, and Venus must now decide whether to go back to her land or stay with Rodney. When she realizes that she could not possibly be happy living with Rodney in a suburb called Ozone Heights, Venus returns to her people by again becoming a statue.

In the final scene, Rodney and Savory both admire the statue. Rodney is disconsolate until a young girl from Ozone Heights, who looks very much like Venus, comes into the museum. Since the girl is also played by Mary Martin, the audience knows Rodney's dream romance will come true.

Credits for the run of 567 performances achieved by *One Touch of Venus* and reasons for its failure to sustain a longer run are equally balanced. Credits include the talented cast in particular Mary Martin, whose acting and singing enhanced the role of the glamour goddess. Miss Martin made the show a personal triumph not only by carrying the burden of the plot but also by being a visual delight. Even the male critics commented on her extensive wardrobe, specially designed by Mainbocher. In almost every scene Miss Martin wore a new, striking outfit that made the production a continuous sequence of exciting fashions for women. She was also completely convincing in the very last scene as the young, unsophisticated girl from Ozone Heights who provides the happy ending. Handsome John Boles was properly suave as Whitelaw Savory; Kenny Baker delighted theater audiences with his singing as much as he had radio listeners. Paula Lawrence as Savory's secretary and Teddy Hart as a taxi driver drifted in and out of the action, but Miss Lawrence's acid gags and Mr. Hart's antics gave the show most of its obvious humor. The featured dancers, Sono Osato, Peter Birch, and Lou Wills, Jr., were all excellent. Miss Osato danced so delightfully in Agnes de Mille's "Ozone Heights" and "Forty Minutes for Lunch," the production's two ballets, that one critic singled her out as the brightest spot in the show. Her success in *One Touch of Venus,* in fact, brought her a leading role the following season in Leonard Bernstein's musical *On the Town.* The critics liked Kurt Weill's music and made specific references to "Speak Low," "The Trouble with Women," and "That's Him," which Mary Martin sang impressively as she leaned over the back of a chair. Miss Martin also sang the number in a television special and once more made the song a delight to hear. Although "That's Him" never became a popular hit, "Speak Low," a beguiling song with a beguine rhythm, has become something of a classic over the years.

People who had tired of hackneyed musicals and wanted to see something different found the show a pleasant surprise, though it may have moved a bit slowly, particularly in the first act. Most certainly the contrived ending in which Rodney meets a modern Venus was a good, popular touch, for audiences would not have been any more content than Venus with Rodney's choice of Gloria. The plot was a variation of the Pygmalion-Galatea story, which had also been the basis for the popular *Adonis* and later, *My Fair Lady.*

The production disappointed critics who compared it with *Oklahoma!* and who thought Perelman and Nash tried too hard to achieve subtle wit by over-emphasizing sophistication at the sacrifice of plain humor. Perhaps, also, the ballets, as one critic suggested, were too long. The dialogue, though sometimes clever, often failed to get the proper audience response. The lyrics did not always have the same verve that Nash's poems have in print. When Nash's lines are read, the reader does not miss even a syllable, but in *One Touch of Venus* the Nash wit, as one critic said, "didn't always come off," because the audience missed an important word or phrase.

Some critics found the lyrics reminiscent of W. S. Gilbert in his popular operettas, but even in Gilbert's fast patter choruses, if the audience missed a word or two, the general tone of the comedy was sufficient to make the songs enjoyable. Perhaps the combination of Weill's music and Nash's lyrics requires that the listeners be as familiar with the songs as are Gilbert and Sullivan audiences.

A comparison of the run of *One Touch of Venus* with the run of *Oklahoma!* fails to indicate the popularity of the Nash-Perelman-Weill production. On the other hand, a comparison of the 567-performance record for *One Touch of Venus* with the list of revivals or failures which preceded and followed it proves that the show was the biggest success of the latter part of 1943, even outrunning *Carmen Jones* which opened in December of that year.

In the four-month period from the premiere of *Carmen Jones* in December 1943, to April 1944, thirty productions, not including a series of Gilbert and Sullivan revivals, opened. Only two of these were musicals—both produced in January 1944—and only one, *Mexican Hayride*, was successful.

The public and the critics were eager for a new musical hit, and when *Follow the Girls* opened in April 1944, it became the success of the season. Unlike *One Touch of Venus* or *Oklahoma!*, *Follow the Girls* made no effort to emphasize story line; the plot, in fact, was almost negligible. In his *Best Plays of 1943–1944*, Burns Mantle wrote a very brief summary and concluded with the opinion that by the second act "everybody had forgotten the plot and nobody cared." The story concerns Bubbles La Marr, a strip-teaser in burlesque, who gives up her stage career to spend all her time in the "Spotlight," a canteen for servicemen. Goofy Gale, who is very much in love with her, has been rejected by the military services and cannot get into the "Spotlight" to see Bubbles. In desperation, he steals a uniform from a British sailor, comes to the canteen, and then discovers that a Navy officer is also interested in Bubbles. A ballet dancer who works at the canteen with Bubbles is in love with another Navy officer. The plot limps along, tangling up these love affairs, but it is shunted aside at every opportunity to make way for specialty numbers. The dancer Anna Viskinova, for example, does an adagio number at the canteen presumably to entertain the boys, but she really hopes a theatrical booking agent will spot her act and get her a contract.

How an agent could get into the canteen if he were not a service-man is unimportant, for no one seemed to care whether the plot made sense or not. Most of the first act consisted of a series of specialties, songs, and comedy sketches. The second act more closely resembled raucous, slapstick burlesque routines.

The plot was so bad, in fact, that the cast seemed to be spoofing the whole nonsensical idea, and the humor carried over to the audience. By the final curtain, all entanglements were solved and the audience left the theater remembering Gertrude Neisen, the star; Jackie Gleason, the principal comedian; the beautiful girls, and the comedy routines, but forgetting what the story was all about.

After the new standards set by *Oklahoma!* the critics might well have bludgeoned *Follow the Girls* for its flimsy plot and patchwork of specialties. Instead, they apparently left the theater as delighted with the show as the audience had been. One critic, who admittedly was prepared to suffer through another bad show, had a wonderful time watching *Follow the Girls,* especially after the long list of failures that had preceded it, and wrote an excellent review calling the production "beautiful."

Gertrude Neisen as Bubbles La Marr stopped the show with the bawdy song "I Wanna Get Married," which featured a procession of show girls dressed as bridesmaids. Miss Neisen, however, held the stage alone as she sang encore after encore with each succeeding chorus becoming bawdier and funnier. Almost every critic praised her performance, and even those critics who said they had not been impressed with her work in night clubs, motion pictures, or radio, thought Miss Neisen was wonderful because she played a rough role, sang raffish lyrics, and yet never resorted to vulgarity to get laughs. By the time *Follow the Girls* was ready to go on the road, most of the original cast had left, but Gertrude Neisen still made the production thoroughly enjoyable with her superb performance.

Among the comedians in the cast, Jackie Gleason as Goofy Gale, the military rejectee, won the best notices. One critic thought Gleason was as funny as Bobby Clark; Lewis Nichols in the New York *Times* predicted that Gleason would become a star. Critics also liked the comedy antics of Tim Herbert and Buster

West, the singing of Frank Parker, well-known radio tenor, and the dancing of Irina Baranova.

The blending of nightclub material, burlesque routines, and bawdy songs made *Follow the Girls* excellent entertainment. In less expert hands, such a *potpourri* of material might have resulted in a hopeless jumble, but almost everyone connected with the production had had experience with different branches of popular entertainment. Harry Delmar, who staged the show, had been one of the founders of the USO and was also general manager for USO shows. In many ways he patterned *Follow the Girls* after USO units which linked a group of acts that had sufficient variety to give the show pace and to eliminate any dull moments that would make audiences restless. Guy Bolton, co-author of the book, had written hit musicals including the very popular long-running *Sally*. His co-author, Eddie Davis, a former taxi driver, provided excellent copy for theater columnists. According to program notes, Davis was driving Eddie Cantor home one night after Cantor had finished a radio broadcast, and Davis was funnier than the Cantor program had been. At Cantor's suggestion, Davis became a writer not only for him but also for Al Jolson, Jimmy Durante, and other stars. Fred Thompson, who wrote additional dialogue and assisted in directing, had worked on more than fifty musical comedies before *Follow the Girls*. Catherine Littlefield, the choreographer, had been a dancer as well as a choreographer. *Follow the Girls* marked the first Broadway hit for the writing team of Dan Shapiro, Milton Pascal, and Phil Charig, but Charig had written the music for several of Jack Buchanan's musicals in London; many stars had used Shapiro's special lyrics in nightclub routines; and Pascal, who was a protégé of Larry Hart, had been a lyric writer for Columbia Varsity shows. Howard Bay, who designed the sets, had also designed *One Touch of Venus* and *Carmen Jones*.

One of Bay's sets included a scene in the Spotlight Canteen for servicemen. The throngs of visitors who crowded the New York area were more than curious about the famous Stage Door Canteen where admission was limited to uniformed men and women in the Armed Services. The theatergoers who saw *Follow the Girls* felt that the Spotlight Canteen gave them an authentic portrait of the canteens; servicemen who saw the show enjoyed making comparisons between the real and the theatrical canteen.

Follow the Girls had two additional interesting sidelights. First, most of the beautiful showgirls were blonde. Second, although the heroine was an ex-burlesque queen, she did not do a striptease. *Follow the Girls* defied tradition by opening at the New Century Theater, which had the reputation of being a jinxed house. The New Century, however, was located uptown and as soon as a theater near the Broadway area became available, the producer moved *Follow the Girls* to the Forty-fourth Street Theater, where it completed its run of 882 performances.

Historians of the American musical theater have had little to say about *Follow the Girls*. One important reference book omits any comment on the show; several others dismiss it as popular wartime entertainment. But all musical comedy histories discuss in rather full detail the "Yip" Harburg–Harold Arlen musical *Bloomer Girl*, which opened in October 1944. Harburg selected a play written by Lilith and Dan James dealing with the rebellion of women during the Civil War period against wearing voluminous hoopskirts. Harburg was satisfied with the general theme, but he knew that in order to compete with *Oklahoma!* a musical would need a very strong plot as well as integrated songs and dances. He asked Sig Herzig and Fred Saidy, who worked on the libretto, to emphasize the themes of women's rights and Negro rights because these could be linked to the fight for freedom in World War II. Since *Oklahoma!* had been a colorful story of the West, it was hoped that the Northern and Southern settings of *Bloomer Girl* would make it equally appealing. Harburg then selected Harold Arlen, who had worked with him on the motion picture *The Wizard of Oz,* to write the score.

A strong plot and emphasis on interesting local customs were not the only influences exerted by *Oklahoma!* The program listings of cast and production staff for the Harburg-Arlen musical read like a list of credits for *Oklahoma!:* the same choreographer, Agnes de Mille; the same musical arranger, Robert Russell Bennett; the same costume designer, Miles White; and the same set designer, Lemuel Ayers. Celeste Holm, in her first starring role as the heroine Evelina, and Joan McCracken, who played an impish maid, Daisy, had both been in the original cast of *Oklahoma!*

Before *Bloomer Girl* opened in October 1944, advance publicity suggested that it was another *Oklahoma!*, and the similarities
in staff and cast easily bolstered that idea. The critics were prepared for another musical that would break away from conventional patterns. Though several reviewers were disappointed,
calling the book labored, the ballets tedious, and the first act
unusually dull, critics who liked the show outnumbered the dissenters. These critics praised the book, the excellent score, the
singers, the dancers, and the beauty and opulence of the production.

The book of *Bloomer Girl* was not comparable to that of
Oklahoma!; yet it was far superior to most of the conventional
musicals with flimsy story lines that had preceded it in the previous seasons.

The plot concerns Evelina, sixth daughter of Horatio Applegate, a manufacturer of ladies' hoopskirts in Cicero Falls, New
York. When her father says she must marry a hoopskirt salesman,
as her five sisters had done before her, Evelina rebels. To prove
her independence, she joins her Aunt Dolly Bloomer's crusade to
have women wear pantalettes, a step which Aunt Dolly believes is
the first women must take in order to get the right to vote. Evelina
scandalizes her father by appearing in pantalettes, but he is even
more appalled by the thought that Evelina's rebellion may ruin his
business. The financial threat is not the Applegates' only concern,
for Evelina is also assisting her Aunt Dolly, an abolitionist, in the
underground movement aiding runaway slaves. Aunt Dolly is
arrested and taken to jail, but, with help from Evelina, remains as
big a problem as she had been when free. Further complications
set in when Jeff Calhoun comes North to find his runaway slave,
Pompey. He meets Evelina and they fall in love, but Jeff discovers
that Pompey is the slave Aunt Dolly has been shielding. At the
end of the first act, political differences threaten to block the love
affair.

The second act begins with the repercussions of Aunt Dolly's
attempt to shield Pompey, and then moves on to the Civil War
which is depicted mainly through a ballet, scenes from *Uncle
Tom's Cabin*—including a slave auction, a short version of Eliza
crossing the ice, and a scene with Joan McCracken playing Topsy
—and the secessionists firing on Fort Sumter. At the end of the

play, Jeff frees Pompey and marries Evelina to provide the inevitable happy ending.

Bloomer Girl proved to be such a box-office hit that shortly after its opening columnists reported that tickets were being sold as much as a year in advance. The show appealed to audiences for many reasons. The excellent cast included, in addition to Celeste Holm and Joan McCracken, Margaret Douglass as Aunt Dolly; Matt Briggs as the hoopskirt magnate, Horatio Applegate; David Brooks as Jeff Calhoun; Dooley Wilson and Richard Huey as the slaves Pompey and Alexander; and James Mitchell, who drew attention as one of the principal de Mille dancers. The role of Evelina proved to be a starring one not only for Celeste Holm but also for Nanette Fabray, who replaced her during the long run.

Bloomer Girl was also a visual treat, for it offered many scenes—particularly the first-act finale, a ballet waltz production—in which the cast was beautifully costumed. During one of the most elaborate scenes, the girls, dressed in billowy, magnificent gowns with voluminous hoopskirts, suddenly stepped out of the skirts to reveal that they were all wearing pantalettes. In the last act, humor was again introduced in the costuming, for when the men returned from war, they were dressed as Zouaves, wearing bright bloomers very similar to those worn by the girls.

Harold Arlen's score and "Yip" Harburg's lyrics were superior. "Evelina," sung by David Brooks, became one of the most popular songs of the 1940s. "Right as the Rain," another love song, is rated by many musicians as one of the best songs in the entire score. Dooley Wilson's "I Got a Song," which he sang in the jail scene, proved to be a show-stopper. "Sunday in Cicero Falls," staged as a beautiful spectacle, had a quality similar to Irving Berlin's "Easter Parade" number in *As Thousands Cheer*. "The Farmer's Daughter" featured an old-fashioned barbershop quartet. And "The Eagle and Me" was a moving song of the Negro's yearning for freedom.

Agnes de Mille's choreography, too, made a strong contribution to the show's success, particularly her Civil War ballet depicting the longing and heartache of the women who waited for their men to return. Miss de Mille, however, also staged a delightful waltz and several lighter numbers in which Joan McCracken proved to be an impish comedienne.

To all these factors relating to the show's success may be added its treatment of more serious issues. The authors handled the issue of women's rights with humor. The issue of civil rights, on the other hand, was presented in a straightforward manner, neither overplaying nor understressing Alexander and Pompey, the slaves. The authors effectively presented the issue by making all the characters attractive. There were no melodramatic villains to pursue victims relentlessly or to be used as scapegoats by militant crusaders. As a result, the musical was neither rabid propaganda nor preaching.

Bloomer Girl easily met the competition of *Oklahoma!* and *Follow the Girls* in the first year of its run. During the second year, in spite of new hit musicals, *Bloomer Girl* continued to draw excellent business and spanned the season, closing with a total of 654 performances. But despite its great success, it has had few revivals because of prohibitive production costs. An amateur director who wanted to present *Bloomer Girl,* for example, discovered that the costume bill alone would be almost double the amount he had allotted for any one show.

Almost four months after the première of *Bloomer Girl,* Michael Todd brought *Up in Central Park* to Broadway on January 27, 1945. Almost everyone connected with the show had been associated with earlier long-running hits. Sigmund Romberg, the composer, had dominated the field of operettas in the 1920s; Herbert and Dorothy Fields, who wrote the book, had written *Panama Hattie;* Miss Fields had written lyrics for the highly successful *Blackbirds of 1928;* Howard Bay, who designed the elaborate sets, had also designed *One Touch of Venus. Up in Central Park* was the second long-running production for Michael Todd (his first being the revue *Star and Garter*) but it was by no means the only other successful venture in his career. In the 1930s, he had produced *The Hot Mikado,* a modernized version of Gilbert and Sullivan's *Mikado,* starring Bill Robinson. The story and lyrics remained virtually the same as the original, but the tempo and rhythm of the music was changed, particularly for the scenes in which Bill Robinson, as the Mikado, performed his famous tap routines in gold-colored shoes. When the New York World's Fair opened, Todd surprised a great many showmen by moving the production from Broadway, where it was still doing profitable business, to the Fair Grounds, where he presented it at lower prices but to much larger audiences.

Todd reportedly got the inspiration for *Up in Central Park* when he first saw the Boston Commons. He suggested the idea of a musical dealing with the development of Central Park to Herbert and Dorothy Fields. In doing research on the history of Central Park, the Fieldses soon discovered that the years 1870 to 1880, which they had selected as the time for the story, provided ample material for the plot, because during 1871 and 1872 *The New York Times* led a crusade against William Marcy Tweed, who had fleeced New York taxpayers out of large sums of money. Tweed, for example, had charged the city over $3.8 million just for carpeting City Hall. To their delight, the writers found that Tweed was definitely connected with a huge swindle involving the development of Central Park.

The site of the present-day park was a large, ugly dump when Tweed and his gang took over. It must be admitted that they did landscape the area, put in paved roads, build the Mall, a museum, a skating rink, a bridle path, and a zoo—but they charged the city exorbitant prices for each item. The bill for park benches alone was over $800,000.

George Jones, owner and publisher of *The New York Times* at that time, printed articles by editor Lewis Jennings exposing Boss Tweed. Jones was joined in his crusade by Thomas Nast, one of the first political cartoonists, who drew a series of caricatures that were printed in *Harper's Weekly* magazine. Tweed and his assistants were reported to have offered huge bribes as well as dire threats to stop the *Times* and *Harper's Weekly* from continuing the series, but these were ignored. Tweed was arrested, convicted, and sent to Blackwell's Island on charges of larceny. In his review of *Up in Central Park* for the New York *World-Telegram,* Burton Rascoe included the information that Tweed had escaped from prison and fled to Spain but had later returned to New York where he was thrown into Ludlow Street Jail and died of exposure.

In shaping their plot from this extensive research, Herbert and Dorothy Fields retained the story of Boss Tweed and his gang and even quoted directly from a Jennings editorial. They changed the name of the *Times* reporter to John Matthews, however, and made him a composite of several men. They also added a love interest with their creation of the fictitious Rosie Moore, daughter of one of Boss Tweed's ward heelers, as the heroine.

John and Rosie fall in love, but, to complicate matters, the writers have Rosie become dazzled by the luxury she enjoys as the daughter of a Tweed henchman. When one of Tweed's cohorts promises to help her become a famous singer in New York, Rosie not only believes him but marries him to show her gratitude. After the Tweed Ring is exposed, however, she realizes her mistake. Her unhappiness increases when her husband, who has run off with a former mistress, is killed. Rosie leaves New York to study music. On her return, one year later, she meets John again at a band concert on the Mall in Central Park. Their reunion provides a happy ending for the final curtain.

Todd, ever the astute showman, gave a party for about 700 people at the Casino in Central Park following the play's opening performance. The reviews were mixed, but all critics agreed that the production was a beautiful series of pageants, and that it was a huge, expensive venture with elaborate and impressive sets and costumes.

In spite of the wealth of research, the book proved to be the prime target for critics, who objected to it as dull, weak, and plodding. Those who liked the book, however, were pleased with its authenticity and dramatization of historical fact. The greatest objections to the book came from those critics who felt that it impeded the procession of magnificent scenes, for Michael Todd evidently had spared no expense in assembling a production which resembled a series of lithographs by Currier and Ives. The scenes included a view of the Park in a snowstorm; the plush red and blue hotel lobby; Central Park as a city dump before Tweed took hold of the project; the bird house; the gardens; the Mall; and the bandstand in the summertime. One production number which began as a series of Currier and Ives tableaux ended with skating in Central Park. In this scene, according to Herbert and Dorothy Fields, Michael Todd used one hundred pounds of very expensive stage snow for each performance. In addition to the opulence and variety of the settings, the costumes by Grace Houston and Ernest Schraps were excellent replicas of those shown in Currier and Ives prints. The dances were directed by Helen Tamiris, who had been a leading dancer before she became a choreographer.

The success of *Up in Central Park* proved to be particularly gratifying for Sigmund Romberg, for it brought him back into the limelight after years of relative neglect once the operetta vogue had subsided. Of the seventy-seven shows with which Romberg had been associated, *Up in Central Park* was not only one of his longest-running successes but also the last that he lived to see produced. Although the score never achieved the popularity of Romberg's earlier works, it did have several excellent numbers including "Close as Pages in a Book," "Carousel in the Park," "When She Walks in the Room," "It Doesn't Cost You Anything to Dream," "April Snow," as well as comedy numbers such as "The Fireman's Bride."

Shortly after the première, tickets were selling at a premium, for audiences were enthralled with the beauty and opulence of the production, the music, and the excellent cast. Noah Beery, Sr., famous motion-picture villain, played Boss Tweed to perfection; Charles Irwin appeared as Timothy Moore, father of Rosie Moore; Maureen Cannon, who stepped into the role of Rosie just before the New York opening, was excellent as the heroine; Betty Bruce, one of Broadway's most scintillating dancers, played Bessie O'Cahane, Rosie's friend; and Wilbur Evans was properly romantic as John Matthews, the *Times* reporter.

Perhaps the book may not have lived up to critics' expectations, but the production pleased audiences and ran for 504 performances.

Carousel, which opened on April 19, 1945, became the season's next long-running hit. The Theatre Guild had long wanted to do a musical based on Ferenc Molnar's *Liliom*. Theresa Helburn, in particular, had thought the fantasy of the story, the carnival setting, and the Hungarian background would all blend into an excellent musical. The Guild had given *Liliom* its first American production in 1921 with Joseph Schildkraut and Eva Le Gallienne. In the 1930s, Miss Le Gallienne revived the play for her Civic Repertory Theater and again appeared in it with Joseph Schildkraut. A new revival on Broadway in 1940 starred Ingrid Bergman and Burgess Meredith. Elia Kazan, who has since become one of Broadway's leading directors, also appeared in the cast. Molnar, however, refused to give the Guild his permission for an adaptation. In the 1940s, when Molnar came to the United States, the Guild directors again approached him, but he again declined, saying that he had even refused to allow Puccini to make an operatic version of his drama. Finally, Miss Helburn and Mr. Langner persuaded Molnar to see *Oklahoma!* After seeing the show, Molnar agreed to a musical adaptation of *Liliom* only if Rodgers and Hammerstein would work on it and only if they would not change the spirit of the play. Rodgers and Hammerstein, however, were undecided, because they were not certain that the foreign locale would lend itself to an adaptation. Rodgers eventually suggested that the musical be given a New England background. Once the change in locale was approved, work on the musical progressed. Liliom became Billy Bigelow; Julie became Julie Jordan; but the basic fantasy element in Molnar's drama, which had been adapted by Benjamin Glazer, was retained.

In working with *Liliom,* Rodgers and Hammerstein encountered problems which they had not had with *Oklahoma!* They did not want to make radical departures from the original plot because *Liliom* was much better known than *Green Grow the Lilacs.*

Molnar's *Liliom* tells the story of a swaggering bully, Liliom, who is a barker at a carousel and charms all the women. In spite of his brashness, he is lonely and, at times, inarticulate. He is attracted to Julie, who is shy and very much in love with him. They have an affair, and when Liliom learns that Julie is pregnant, he attempts to raise money for his unborn child by robbery but is caught. To avoid arrest he kills himself. He is taken into custody by Heavenly policemen whom he tells defiantly that he does not regret his action, and he is sentenced by the Heavenly Court to purgatory. Fifteen years later, he is permitted to return to earth to atone for his sins. He steals a star from Heaven to bring to his daughter, but she refuses to accept it and sends him away. In exasperation, Liliom slaps her, but she does not feel any pain. The play ends unhappily with Liliom returning to purgatory.

In adapting the play to a New England setting, Rodgers and Hammerstein kept the original spirit of the drama but changed the characterizations, for they knew they had to make Liliom, now called Billy, a more sympathetic character. They retained the first scene very much as Molnar had written it but reworked the plot without destroying the original motivations.

In *Carousel,* for example, instead of having Julie become Billy's mistress, Rodgers and Hammerstein have the lovers marry. The owner of the carousel, a vindictive woman who is also very much in love with Billy and infuriated by his marriage, fires him. Unhappy at being away from the carousel, Billy rages at Julie until he learns that he is to become a father. Although he feels proud, he still cannot express himself and is unable to tell Julie how he feels. When he is alone, however, he sings the very emotional "Soliloquy," in which he speculates about his forthcoming role as a father. To get money for the child, he agrees to help Jigger, a disreputable sailor, in a robbery which leads to a murder. To avoid being captured, Billy kills himself. He is sent to purgatory for fifteen years, at the end of which time he meets the starkeeper, who tells him he cannot enter Heaven until he redeems his soul. To do so, he will be given the chance to return to earth for one day to perform one good deed. The starkeeper then shows Billy his fifteen-year-old daughter, and Billy is distressed to discover that she is an unhappy child. He steals a star from Heaven for her, but when he returns to earth and offers her his gift, she refuses to accept it. Just as in *Liliom,* the exasperated Billy slaps her. She feels no pain, however, for his love has made the slap feel like a kiss. In the final scene, Billy appears at his daughter's graduation exercises and sings, "You'll Never Walk Alone." Although the girl does not hear him, she somehow gains confidence, and Billy returns to Heaven, having done his good deed.

Perhaps the most essential difference between Molnar's play and *Carousel* was in the ending, for Molnar's unhappy final scene would never have contented most audiences in the musical theater. By retaining Molnar's basic idea, but by giving Billy a more beneficial influence on his daughter, Rodgers and Hammerstein provided a bittersweet ending that made Billy more sympathetic and the whole production more sentimental. They also redefined the characterization of Billy to show that he did love Julie, and that he was sullen, inarticulate, and often brutal only because he was afraid he would betray himself and tell her he loved her.

To insure the success of *Carousel,* the Guild used practically the same staff that had worked on *Oklahoma!:* Rouben Mamoulian as director, Agnes de Mille as choreographer, Miles White as costume director, and, of course, Rodgers and Hammerstein. Settings were by Jo Mielziner.

Lawrence Langner has written in *The Magic Curtain* that Molnar was very much pleased with the progress of the show. At one of the final rehearsals, he sat in the rear of the theater and wept at many of the scenes. Langner adds that since most of the staff who attended that rehearsal had also been crying, the Guild directors began to worry, for the show represented an investment of $180,000 and they were doubtful if people would pay to see a sad musical. Dress rehearsal did not alleviate their worries, for the show did not run smoothly.

The out-of-town opening for *Carousel* paralleled that of *Oklahoma!* Both musicals opened in New Haven, both had fairly smooth first acts, and both had second-act trouble. Scenes in *Carousel* were changed or added, and musical sequences and ballets were revised or placed in new positions. One story has it that the New Haven opening included one scene in the home of God, with Mr. and Mrs. God in a typical New England living room; if there was such a scene, it was quickly eliminated. A ballet that included a sequence showing the birth of Julie's baby also underwent revisions. Molnar and Mamoulian are both reputed to have suggested changes in the story line so that by the time the show moved to Boston the second act was much stronger.

When *Carousel* opened in New York, it played at the Majestic Theater directly across the street from the St. James Theater which housed *Oklahoma!* As one commentator said, "Rodgers and Hammerstein have become their own worst competitors." Opening night proved to be a trying time for Richard Rodgers, who had injured his back and was forced to watch the performance from behind the curtains, propped up in a stretcher. But the ecstatic reviews the following day must have cheered him immeasurably, for the critics were almost unanimous in their praise. Rodgers and Hammerstein were not surprised that many critics compared *Carousel* with *Oklahoma!* The comparisons, however, were, for the most part, favorable. Louis Kronenberger did predict that *Carousel* would not have so long a run, but he thought *Carousel* made a greater contribution to the American musical theater. Several reviewers objected to the ballets, decried the lack of humor, or thought the production was too long, but almost all were effusive in their praise of the musical score and the acting. They also liked the fact that the original story had not been changed drastically.

A few Broadway showmen were surprised that the Guild had called the show *Carousel;* they quipped that the title would probably hurt box-office sales because it would be mispronounced *CaROWsel.* When the musical prospered, one of the showmen who had criticized the title said, "Now I'm wondering if they would have been just as successful if they had called it *Merry-Go-Round.*"

In keeping with the practice the Guild had followed for *Oklahoma!* the directors selected a cast of comparatively unknown players for *Carousel.* Jean Darling, who played Carrie Pipperidge, Julie's friend, and had been one of the original "Our Gang Comedy Kids" in silent films, received the greatest amount of advance publicity. After the New York opening, however, critics and audiences became equally interested in other performers. Murvyn Vye, who played the villain Jigger, had also appeared as Jud in *Oklahoma!* and was spotted by Hollywood talent scouts. Jan Clayton, who played Julie, made her Broadway debut in *Carousel,* but when Rodgers and Hammerstein decided to revive *Show Boat* they asked Miss Clayton to leave their own hit musical and appear in the revival. The big star of *Carousel,* however, proved to be John Raitt, who was reported to have been a champion athlete at the University of Southern California. According to the program notes, Raitt's physique, appearance, and stage presence won him the role without an audition. In *The Magic Curtain,* Lawrence Langner contradicts this story, for he says that Mrs. Langner's niece had told her about Raitt. When she met him, Mrs. Langner was impressed by his appearance. A few months later, the Guild needed a replacement for Curly in *Oklahoma!* and Mrs. Langner suggested that Raitt be given an audition. As soon as Raitt began to sing, the Guild directors knew they had their replacement. Moreover, Rodgers was sufficiently impressed to tell Langner that

Raitt was the man to play the lead in *Carousel*. Casting him as Billy was an excellent choice, for Raitt had the voice to sing the score properly, the physique to look the part of tough Billy Bigelow, and the smile and charm to please the women in the audience.

To many theatergoers, the best thing about *Carousel* is the score. In revising the show, Rodgers and Hammerstein included a reprise of "If I Loved You" in the second act and discovered that sheet-music sales for the number increased and made it a hit song. After the Broadway opening, several critics named "June Is Bustin' Out All Over" as the hit song.

The score for *Carousel* is probably as well known as that for *Oklahoma!* Some musicologists, in fact, find the opening number, "The Carousel Waltz," superior to any selection in *Oklahoma!* At least one of the hit songs in *Carousel* came from *Oklahoma!* "This Was a Real Nice Hayride" was dropped from *Oklahoma!*, then changed to "This Was a Real Nice Clambake" for *Carousel*. Billy's famous "Soliloquy," reputed to be the first number Rodgers and Hammerstein wrote for the show, has been a favorite selection for John Raitt and Gordon MacRae on television programs. Because "Soliloquy" is a dramatic number, the lyrics are often discussed more than the music. Several recordings of the number without lyrics, however, have revealed the beauty of Rodgers' melodies. The score for *Carousel* also includes "You're a Queer One, Julie Jordan," which leads into the lovely "When I Marry Mr. Snow"; "Blow High, Blow Low," which becomes the background for a spirited hornpipe; "What's the Use of Wonderin'"; "When the Children Are Asleep"; "The Highest Judge of All"; and the final number sung by Billy, "You'll Never Walk Alone," which is even more popular today than it was during the run of the show.

Rodgers and Hammerstein integrated songs with plot even more smoothly in *Carousel* than they had in *Oklahoma!*, the dialogue at times being spoken over a musical background which gradually led into a song.

Carousel has proved to be a durable vehicle. Gordon MacRae played Billy Bigelow in the motion-picture version, and Shirley Jones, who had played Laurey in the motion-picture version of *Oklahoma!* co-starred as Julie. MacRae gave a creditable performance; the dance sequences and New England settings were colorful; but the cameras were unflattering to Miss Jones throughout most of the picture.

Carousel played in London in 1950, where it ran 566 performances with Iva Withers as Julie and Stephen Douglass as Billy. The London critics, however, were not too kind to the production; they objected to its sentimentality and lack of humor. Perhaps the London reception may be explained by the fact that the original play had been banned in Britain on the grounds that it was blasphemous. *Carousel*, nevertheless, was presented with great success at the World's Fair in Brussels in the late 1950s.

Its universality is also evident in the successful revivals in summer theaters all over the United States, as well as at the New York City Center. In 1949, the production featuring Stephen Douglass and Iva Withers ran for several weeks at the City Center and then moved to the Majestic Theater for a total of 49 performances. Again, in 1954, the City Center revival ran for a month with Jo Sullivan as Julie, Barbara Cook as Carrie, and Chris Robinson as Billy. The timelessness of *Carousel* was illustrated even more by the 1965 revival at the New York State Theater in Lincoln Center, which brought ecstatic reviews from critics who called it a masterpiece. John Raitt again played Billy Bigelow and gave a more mature, commanding performance than he had in the original production. Critics who had not seen him when he first appeared as Billy Bigelow doubted that he could have sung the "Soliloquy" as well in 1945 as he did in the revival twenty years later. Richard Rodgers, president and producing director of the Music Theater at Lincoln Center, made certain the revival was produced with the same meticulous care that had characterized the original production. The 1965 *Carousel*, therefore, proved to be a beautiful show that gave older and younger theatergoers alike the opportunity to enjoy what many critics have hailed as the best of the Rodgers and Hammerstein shows.

The original run of 890 performances for *Carousel* is low when compared with the record-breaking run of *Oklahoma! Carousel* opened after *Oklahoma!* had been well established and closed almost a year before *Oklahoma!* completed its run. Perhaps *Carousel*'s shorter run may be partially explained by the fact that even more than *Oklahoma!*, in which a villain had been killed on stage, *Carousel* defied convention in having its hero commit suicide, a much more radical departure from musical comedy conventions. *Oklahoma!* closed on a typically gay, romantic scene, but *Carousel* ended on an emotional, sentimental, and bittersweet note that was definitely not typical of popular musical comedies. The superb staging, music, and acting, however, made the unhappy romance palatable and helped prepare audiences for such later musicals as *The King and I* and *Fanny*, which ended with death scenes. In the twenty-year period since its first presentation, *Carousel* has achieved recognition as one of the classic productions in the history of American musicals.

VII

The Late 1940s

BY THE END of the theatrical season in June 1943, the hit musicals competing at the box office were *Oklahoma!, Bloomer Girl, Up in Central Park, Follow the Girls,* and *Carousel.* Producers realized that any new show, in order to be successful, would have to follow the same pattern or else offer a spectacularly different approach. In October 1945, the revival of *The Red Mill* joined the imposing list of hits, presenting still another obstacle to the course of any new musical.

In October and November of 1945, four new musicals opened. The first, *Polonaise,* with music based on melodies by Chopin, ran for 113 performances. The second, *The Girl from Nantucket,* was an outright failure that closed after 12 performances. *Are You With It?,* the third, was much more successful because it opened the same night as a major dramatic production (*The Rugged Path,* by Robert E. Sherwood and starring Spencer Tracy) which drew all the top critics. The second-string critics who covered the musical, delighted to have the chance to write up a new production, gave it better than average reviews and helped the show achieve a run of 267 performances. The fourth, *The Day Before Spring,* written by Alan Jay Lerner and Frederick Loewe, had a modest run of 165 performances.

The period from January to April 1946 brought a revival of *Show Boat;* one long-running revue, *Call Me Mister;* two failures —*Nellie Bly* (12 performances), and *The Duchess Misbehaves* (5 performances); and four shows which had longer runs: *Lute Song,* with Mary Martin and Yul Brynner (142 performances), *St. Louis Woman* (113 performances), *The Would-Be Gentleman* (77 per-

formances), and *Three to Make Ready*, a revue (327 performances). By May of 1946, *Bloomer Girl* and *Up in Central Park*
had closed; *Follow the Girls* was scheduled to close; and the critics
and the public were ready for a new hit. *Annie Get Your Gun*,
which premiered May 16, 1946, starring Ethel Merman, exceeded
all their expectations and became the only new long-running
musical of the season as well as Irving Berlin's most successful
show. Rodgers and Hammerstein produced *Annie Get Your Gun*
and wisely made no attempt to imitate *Oklahoma!* or *Carousel*.
The result was old-fashioned entertainment at its best.

The story itself was strictly a formula plot that developed a
romance between hillbilly sharpshooter Annie Oakley and Frank
Butler, crack rifle shot in Buffalo Bill's Wild West Show. When
Annie outshoots Frank in an exhibition match and Buffalo Bill
invites her to join the show, she gladly does so to be near Frank.
Annie and Frank fall in love, but Buffalo Bill and his manager
inveigle Annie into doing a trick act—shooting out candles while
riding on a motorcycle—by telling her that the stunt will please
Frank. Instead of being happy, however, Frank is infuriated be-
cause Annie's spectacular act outshines his and makes her a star.
Rather than share the spotlight with Annie, he joins the rival
Pawnee Bill's Far East Show. Chief Sitting Bull, who has been
delighted with Annie's performance, adopts her into his Sioux
Tribe and even breaks one of his rules—not to invest in show
business—by putting money into Buffalo Bill's show. Annie and
the troupe then make a spectacular European tour during which
Annie is decorated by most of the reigning monarchs. Although
the show has gained a good deal of prestige, the troupe returns
home almost penniless. Annie, knowing that Buffalo Bill and
Pawnee Bill must combine their enterprises if either is to survive
and hoping the merger will reunite her with Frank, agrees to sell
her medals to raise funds. But in a very short time, she and Frank
quarrel again and challenge each other to a shooting match.
Finally, Chief Sitting Bull makes Annie realize that if she wins the
match, she will lose Frank. So Annie loses, announces to the world
that Frank is the better shot, and turns her medals over to Frank,
who says he will use them to raise money for the shows. When
Annie says it was a good thing for Frank that he said that or she

would have shot him, the audience knows that Annie will always have the upper hand.

There is no attempt to disguise the old formula story based on two popular situations in American theater: the love story that is blocked by obstacles but finally ends happily, and the Horatio Alger theme of rags-to-riches as it moves Annie up the scale from an awkward hillbilly to the grand, strutting, elegant performer in show business.

Most of the critics wrote rave reviews, but a minority referred to the musical as old-fashioned.

Annie Get Your Gun capitalized on both old and new techniques in the musical theater. In the manner of the older musicals, it minimized the book to emphasize the songs and dances, and any time the plot threatened to slow up the fun, Berlin had a new song ready. Instead of using a cast of unknowns as they had done in *Oklahoma!* and *Carousel,* Rodgers and Hammerstein had the show written especially for Ethel Merman. The plot told an old-fashioned love story with no political messages, no subtleties, no innuendoes, and no real surprises. Helen Tamiris, the choreographer, included several standard chorus and tap routines, but at the same time, the show also incorporated some of the newer innovations in the musical theater, for the dancing also reflected the influence of the ballet, particularly in the Sioux Indian scene. The songs were integrated with the plot and several helped to characterize Annie: "Doin' What Comes Natur'lly," for example, established Annie's hillbilly background.

Opinions differ as to whether Irving Berlin or Ethel Merman was more responsible for the long run achieved by *Annie Get Your Gun.* Certainly, the importance of Merman to the show cannot be minimized. In other musicals, producers would close productions for several weeks during the summer months to give the star a vacation; but when Rodgers and Hammerstein decided to keep *Annie Get Your Gun* running with Merman away for six weeks, receipts fell sharply. When Merman returned to the cast, the show again drew capacity houses, for theatergoers were coming to see Merman's interpretation of Annie. The critics, in fact, reviewed Merman more favorably than they had ever done before. *Variety* said Merman was at the peak of her career; Ward Morehouse liked

Merman better than the score; George Jean Nathan minimized the music and plot but in *Theater Book of 1946–1947* cited both Ethel Merman and Ray Middleton in his list of excellent performances for the season; and Lewis Nichols referred to Merman as "Heaven's gift to musical comedy." More than one critic commented on the fact that up until *Annie Get Your Gun,* Merman had been primarily a singer; then she had become a stage personality; but in this show she proved she had become an actress, and, even more important, a comedienne.

Annie Get Your Gun gave Merman more opportunity to display her many talents than any previous show in which she had appeared. Berlin had given her several excellent comedy songs which she endowed with her own individual style, particularly "I'm an Indian, Too," a number that reminded a great many old-timers of Fannie Brice's comedy routine, "I'm an Indian Squaw." Although Merman did not need to resort to Fannie Brice's Yiddish accent to make the number amusing, Merman made her Indian routine every bit as funny as Miss Brice's. More important, however, Berlin also gave Merman the chance to sing a decidedly new type of song for her—romantic love ballads, which she performed with her usual expert showmanship. In fact, Merman said that by giving her romantic numbers "Berlin made a lady out of me."

Annie Get Your Gun has one of Berlin's best scores. During the run of the show, at least three of the songs were among the top ten tunes played on radio—a record reputed to have been unequalled by any other production of that period. And yet several opening night critics were not at all enthusiastic. One called the songs "undistinguished"; another said Berlin's tunes were "below par"; still another felt the score was "not notable". Those who did like the music, however, accurately predicted that it would become one of Broadway's most popular scores. Howard Barnes called it "excellent"; Vernon Rice said it was impossible to pick a hit tune because "all the tunes are hits"; Louis Kronenberger praised Berlin's lyrics. The tremendous success of *Annie Get Your Gun* was undoubtedly a great source of satisfaction to Berlin, who had always believed that a song or show was good if the public liked it. When someone told Berlin that *Annie Get Your Gun* was old-fashioned, Berlin said, "Yes, an old-fashioned smash."

The hit songs in the show followed one another in rapid succession: "Doin' What Comes Natur'lly"; "Moonshine Lullaby"; "You Can't Get a Man With a Gun"; "I'm an Indian, Too"; the love ballads "I Got Lost in His Arms" and "They Say That Falling in Love Is Wonderful"; and the rhythmic "I Got the Sun in the Morning." Merman made every number she sang a showstopper, and the Merman-Middleton duet "Anything You Can Do I Can Do Better" also proved to be a high spot. Middleton had three excellent numbers on his own, "The Girl That I Marry," "My Defenses Are Down," and "I'm a Bad, Bad Man." "Who Do You Love, I Hope" served as a charming background for a dance routine by the secondary leads. Oddly enough, Berlin showed the greatest concern about the song "There's No Business Like Show Business"—today considered the unofficial anthem of show business—because he felt the producers were not particularly pleased with it. Berlin, in fact, was not sure that he wanted to write the show. Jerome Kern had originally been scheduled to do the score but when he died, Rodgers and Hammerstein asked Berlin to take over the assignment. Although Berlin was reluctant, he did write several numbers at Hammerstein's request and then insisted upon auditioning the songs. Rodgers and Hammerstein, of course, were enthusiastic, and Berlin was persuaded to complete the score.

Kern's death was not the only misfortune that occurred before the show finally reached Broadway. Audiences and critics usually regard certain practices during the try-outs as ominous signs. For example, they usually interpret a Saturday night opening as an indication of the producers' fear that the critics will not like the show, because a Saturday night premiere means that the reviews will not reach the public for at least twenty-four hours. Similarly, a postponed opening date could indicate that a show still needs revising and tightening. When the producers delayed the New York opening of *Annie Get Your Gun* for three weeks, explaining that the delay was caused by a structural defect in the stage equipment, Broadway showmen were skeptical. All doubts were dispelled, however, on opening night, and *Annie Get Your Gun* became the biggest musical hit since *Oklahoma!*

The show had a number of features that attracted audiences. The book by Herbert and Dorothy Fields not only capitalized on traditional dramatic situations but also dealt with the Wild West, always a popular locale in the American theater. Unlike *Oklahoma!*, *Annie Get Your Gun* concentrated on the Wild West show and the glamour of show business. The huge sets designed by Jo Mielziner were especially effective. Joshua Logan's direction kept the show moving at a crisp pace, with only an occasional letdown in scenes when Merman or Middleton were not on stage; but every time the action even started to lag, Merman was back in the spotlight belting out a new number. The colorful costumes designed by Lucinda Ballard ranged from hillbilly outfits to the very chic gowns worn by society debutantes in the second act. And the dance routines staged by Helen Tamiris had variety and vigor.

Critics liked the supporting cast, particularly Harry Bellaver as Sitting Bull, who got one of the biggest laughs in the show when he said dejectedly that he couldn't raise crops on his land because it had too much oil. Reviewers also singled out William O'Neal for his imposing appearance as Buffalo Bill, Marty May as the show manager, and Betty Anne Nyman and Kenny Bowers, who played the young lovers.

Although *Annie Get Your Gun* has been and still is called a Merman show, it also helped the careers of two other actresses. When Rodgers and Hammerstein were casting the road company, they wisely selected Mary Martin to fill the Merman role. According to reports, Miss Martin was eager to play Annie, hoping it would bring her the lead in a new Rodgers and Hammerstein vehicle. She gave a superb performance, not quite the same as Merman's but very definitely one that pleased critics and audiences. The television production also starred Mary Martin, and, as a result of her success in *Annie Get Your Gun,* she later played the lead in two Rodgers and Hammerstein musicals, *South Pacific* and *The Sound of Music.* The London company of *Annie Get Your Gun* featured Dolores Gray and Bill Johnson in a production that ran for 1,304 performances, or about six months less than *Oklahoma!* One or two of the London critics were unenthusiastic about the show, but most were effusive in praising Dolores Gray, who received one of the greatest ovations ever given an American actress in London. *Annie Get Your Gun* also played successfully in Berlin; and in Paris, as *Annie du Far-West,* with Lily Fayol, it ran for more than a year.

The motion-picture version, on the other hand, was less successful than the stage production, partially because of casting problems. When Metro-Goldwyn-Mayer bought the screen rights and announced the picture as a starring vehicle for Judy Garland, hopes ran high, for the story and songs seemed ideally suited to her talents. During the filming, however, it became necessary for studio officials to replace Miss Garland with Betty Hutton, who gave a creditable performance although the picture failed to equal the sparkling stage musical.

The revival of *Annie Get Your Gun,* produced in 1966 at Lincoln Center, turned out to be not only as good, but, in many ways, even better than the original. Broadway showmen were somewhat surprised when Ethel Merman agreed to play for a limited run in the revival, for Merman had turned down the leads in *Hello, Dolly!* and *Mame,* both of which would have been excellent vehicles for her, simply because she did not want to get involved with long runs. When Irving Berlin asked her if she would do the revival of *Annie,* however, Merman consented. One of her reasons, she explained, was that a new generation of theater-goers would be seeing the show. In the revival, Merman demonstrated that she was still the star who could stop the show singing Berlin's tunes.

In the 1966 production, the songs and dances performed by the young lovers were cut. As a replacement, Berlin wrote one new number that topped anything else in the show. Berlin had had luck in *Call Me Madam* with Merman and Russel Nype singing a counterpoint song, and he used this same technique in the new number, "Old-Fashioned Wedding." As sung by Bruce Yarnell, the new Frank Butler, the first chorus told of Butler's wishes for a small old-fashioned ceremony; Merman followed with a chorus in countermelody outlining her own plans for a sumptuous wedding; then Yarnell and Merman repeated their choruses, singing together but paying absolutely no attention to each other. The first contrapuntal chorus came as a pleasant surprise; as the leads repeated the chorus and Merman became more demanding, even beating her fists on Yarnell's chest to get him to listen, the song became a sensation. Audiences insisted on encore after encore, content merely to hear the number in one reprise after another.

Richard Rodgers, who produced the revival, followed the same plan he had used for other Lincoln Center revivals by making certain that the production was as carefully cast and as richly costumed as the original show had been. He chose the handsome Bruce Yarnell to play Frank Butler. Harry Bellaver, the original Chief Sitting Bull, again made his part a memorable one; and Benay Venuta, who, incidentally, had once played the Merman role in a touring company of *Anything Goes,* was an excellent choice for Butler's assistant, Dolly Tate. The dances by choreographer Danny Daniels were as effective as Helen Tamiris' original routines. The hits of the show, however, were still Berlin's score and Merman's performance.

When *The New York Times* asked the president of Columbia Records, Goddard Lieberson, who headed a committee to gather material on musical comedies for the Yale Library, to name the ten musical shows he thought were most worth preserving, Mr. Lieberson included the early long-running hits *Show Boat* and *Oklahoma!* He also chose *Annie Get Your Gun* because he thought it had a superb score and because it had all the advantages of old-fashioned musical comedy with none of the disadvantages. The 1966 revival confirmed the wisdom of Mr. Lieberson's choice, for, after twenty years, the musical remains excellent entertainment.

The original run of *Annie Get Your Gun,* which began in 1946 and ended in February 1949 with a phenomenal record of 1,147 performances, made it the second longest-running musical in the history of the New York theater, a record that was not broken until *South Pacific* surpassed it in 1952. In many ways, *Annie Get Your Gun* served critics as the same sort of standard of excellence in judging musical productions that followed it as *Oklahoma!* had done. For example, Cole Porter's *Around the World,* based on Jules Verne's *Around the World in Eighty Days,* opened May 31, 1946, shortly after the première of *Annie Get Your Gun,* but could not survive the inevitable comparisons made by critics and audiences.

The new season beginning in September 1946, gave *Annie Get Your Gun* little or no competition, for it included two unsuccessful operettas and four new musical productions which also failed. Even the musical adaptation of *Street Scene,* which the critics praised and which Mr. Lieberson also named as one of the ten musicals most worth preserving, failed to win popular approval and closed after 148 performances. The entire season threatened to be a bleak one until January 1947, when *Finian's Rainbow* opened and surprised a great many show people by becoming a hit. There was ample cause for skepticism. Pure fantasy had not been overly popular in the musical theater, and *Finian's Rainbow* was definitely fantasy, dealing with a leprechaun, a pot of gold, and three magic wishes. In presenting the problems of Negroes in the South and exposing the bigotry of Southern politicians, the production, according to some showmen, could have aroused great resentment. And, with the possible exception of Ella Logan, the cast had no star names to add box-office drawing power.

The story, a somewhat radical departure from standard musical comedy plots, resulted from the same planning that had gone into E. Y. Harburg's *Bloomer Girl*. Harburg, who wrote *Finian's Rainbow*, started with two basic ideas, neither of which he had considered developing into a musical. One play was to have dealt with a bigoted Southern senator who was somehow changed into a Negro and thus made subject to the discriminatory laws he had helped to pass. The second play would have developed the story of a leprechaun who had three magic wishes. Just as he had used two separate ideas in *Bloomer Girl*, Harburg again saw the possibility of combining two distinct themes in one production. The link between the two, he realized, could be achieved by having the leprechaun use one of his wishes to change the senator into a Negro. Harburg then decided the material would be better suited to musical comedy than to drama and began to work on this combination of plots as co-author with Fred Saidy, who had written *Bloomer Girl*. He then asked Burton Lane to write the music, which Harburg thought should resemble the type of score Gershwin had composed for *Porgy and Bess*. Lane wrote a simpler but very excellent score with delightful melodies that have remained popular since their first introduction to Broadway audiences.

The musical that emerged told the story of Finian, an Irishman from Glocca Morra, who came to the mythical state of Missitucky to bury a crock of gold he had stolen from a leprechaun in Ireland.

Finian knew that the United States government buried gold in the ground at Fort Knox; presuming that it did so in order to make the money grow, he decided that if he buried his money in the ground near Fort Knox, it too would grow. As the play opens, Finian and his daughter Sharon arrive in Rainbow Valley in the Southern state of Missitucky. Finian buys land from the share-croppers and buries his gold. Sharon falls in love with Woody Mahoney, leader of the sharecroppers, whose sister Susan is a deaf mute. Og, the leprechaun, then arrives in Rainbow Valley in search of Finian and the stolen pot of gold and discovers, to his surprise, that he is turning into a mortal and falling in love with Susan. Rumor spreads that the soil in Rainbow Valley is filled with gold, and the sharecroppers begin spending money freely. Complications arise when Senator Billboard Rawkins, a Southern politician who hates Negroes, tries to rob Finian and the share-croppers of their land. At this point, the three magic wishes are brought into the story. The first wish turns the senator into a Negro evangelist and humanizes him; Og uses the second wish to give Susan the power to speak; the third wish helps the share-croppers, desperate when they hear that the rumor of gold on the land is false, to retain their land. They learn, just in time, that the soil is rich and will be excellent for raising tobacco. Og is trans-formed into a mortal and finds happiness with Susan; Sharon and Woody are united; and Finian and the sharecroppers anticipate the wealth they will get from their tobacco crop.

Overemphasis upon political satire and the problems of big-otry and racial prejudice could easily have made the musical into a propaganda play; the dialogue abounded with barbs about anti-Negro legislation, sharecropping, and sudden wealth. Harburg, however, avoided pitfalls that would have jeopardized the popular appeal of the production. To counterbalance the political satire, Harburg stressed the idea that money was not the most important factor in obtaining happiness. The element of fantasy and the Irish humor also counterbalance the political theme. There might still have been antagonism toward the theme and the book if Burton Lane had not provided an excellent score supplemented by Harburg's equally excellent lyrics. The song hit of the show, "How Are Things in Glocca Morra?", sung by Sharon, had an

Irish flavor, as did "Look to the Rainbow." Two rollicking numbers sung by Og—"Something Sort of Grandish" and "When I'm Not Near the Girl I Love," which had one of the most lilting melodies in the entire score—emphasized the fantasy of the leprechaun. "If This Isn't Love," sung by Woody, helped characterize both Woody and Susan; as the song progressed, Susan danced the words which she wished she could speak, and Woody sang the lyrics. Choral numbers with clever lyrics included four excellent satires, "The Begat," "Necessity," "When the Idle Poor Become the Idle Rich," and "That Great Come-and-Get-It-Day."

The critics raved. George Jean Nathan not only called *Finian's Rainbow* the best new musical of the season but also said it was one of the most original and witty musical comedies in quite some time. Albert Sharpe, as Finian, pleased the critics, and Nathan cited him in his list of "especially interesting performances." David Wayne as Og, the leprechaun, Anita Alvarez as Susan, and Donald Richards as Woody also received good reviews. Most of the critics thought Ella Logan was a delightful Sharon, but one or two objected to her singing Irish lyrics with a Scotch burr.

The critics also applauded the production staff. In his annual honor roll, George Jean Nathan selected Eleanor Goldsmith's costumes as the best of the season. Audiences enjoyed Michael Kidd's choreography, which featured several energetic dance routines that must have left the dancers completely exhausted.

The show abounded in humor ranging from earthy lyrics and pure slapstick to witty lines and sharp satirical episodes such as the one in which the senator taught his Negro servant how to serve a mint julep properly, demonstrating that he must not walk normally but rather shuffle his feet the way Negro actors do in Hollywood films.

Shortly after *Finian's Rainbow* became established as a Broadway hit, the producers faced a new problem. Ella Logan, so the columnists reported, was insisting upon star billing. The producers felt that all the major characters were of equal importance and would not elevate her to stardom. Miss Logan left the show, but the producers discovered that as excellent as the original cast had been, *Finian's Rainbow* prospered just as well when replacements, not only for Miss Logan but also for other performers, joined the cast. The show ran for an impressive 725 performances.

The blend of fantasy and political satire made an effective combination in *Finian's Rainbow,* but *Brigadoon,* the second musical hit of the season, which opened March 13, 1947, relied purely on fantasy. Although it had a shorter run than *Finian's Rainbow, Brigadoon* received far greater acclaim from the critics. The Drama Critics Circle named it the best musical of the year, the first musical to receive such recognition. In his *Best Plays of 1946–1947* Burns Mantle selected *Brigadoon* as one of the ten best plays of the season, a distinction that he had previously given to only two other musical comedies: *Of Thee I Sing* and *Oklahoma!*

Most of the critics were intrigued by the story of a town in Scotland that comes to life only one day in each century; several critics even wondered if Alan Jay Lerner, who wrote the book, had made use of some old Scottish legend. Lerner replied that he had always been an admirer of Sir James Barrie and that he had always wanted to write a musical with a Scottish background, but that he had not based the story on a real legend.

Trouble arose, however, when George Jean Nathan accused Lerner of "barefaced plagiarism," maintaining that the plot was based on a German story, *Germelshausen,* by Wilhelm Friedrick Gerstacker. Nathan pointed out the similarities in plot and listed possible sources where Lerner could have learned of the original tale. Lerner said the similarities were "unconscious coincidence," but Nathan's accusation brought further corroboration from people who had read *Germelshausen.* Today, on many college campuses, German professors who teach *Germelshausen* blandly refer to it as *Brigadoon.*

Gerstacker's story concerned a German town that comes to life for only one day in a century. A young man accidently discovers the town on the one day that it is visible. There he meets a young girl with whom he falls in love. The young man discovers the odd time element by reading birth-date inscriptions on gravestones; when he realizes that in chronological time the girl would be more than two hundred years old, he demands an explanation and is told the story of the miracle that regulates the life of the village and its inhabitants. Although the hero knows that he loves the girl, he leaves the town. When he returns later, he finds that he has lost her forever.

Brigadoon definitely follows the same story line with only minor differences, such as the change in scene from Germany to Scotland, but with several important additions. The young man in *Brigadoon,* Tommy Albright, stumbles onto the town with his friend Jeff Douglass. There he meets Fiona MacLaren and is soon entranced with her, but he discovers her date of birth in the family Bible and cannot fathom the mystery. Fiona takes Tommy to the old school teacher Mr. Lundie, who tells him the story of the minister who had wanted to keep Brigadoon safe from the evil world and had brought about the miracle that would let the town come to life for only one day in every hundred years. In that way, it could never be alive long enough to be contaminated by the outside world. Tommy also learns that a stranger may come to live in Brigadoon, but that no one who lives there may leave the town or the magic spell will be broken and the town will vanish forever. Fiona's sister Jean is to be married to Charlie Dalrymple that same day, and the wedding leads to further complications because Harry Beaton is also in love with Jean. After the ceremony, Harry, in desperation, says he will ruin Brigadoon by running away. The villagers set out in pursuit; during the chase, Jeff trips Harry, who then falls against a rock and is killed. The villagers carry his body back into the town square. As the time draws close when Brigadoon is to vanish once more, Tommy is torn between his love for Fiona, which would keep him in Brigadoon, and his desire to return home. Jeff's inadvertent killing of Harry makes Tommy even more doubtful whether he would be content to remain in the mysterious village. He returns to New York with Jeff.

At this point, the ending of *Brigadoon* diverges completely from the final sequence in *Germelshausen.* Realizing that he loves Fiona and should have stayed with her, Tommy decides that he must return to the site where the village is hidden, even though he has no hope of ever seeing Fiona again. Jeff accompanies him on the trip. When they arrive at the misty spot, Tommy is disconsolate, knowing that somewhere in the mist the girl he loves will be sleeping for one hundred years. Suddenly the mist begins to clear, a very sleepy Mr. Lundie stumbles onto the bridge that leads to

Brigadoon, tells Tommy that his great love for Fiona has wakened him, and leads Tommy slowly back into the gathering mist as the curtains close.

The romantic appeal of the story unquestionably pleased audiences, but the lyrics and music, which established Alan Jay Lerner and Frederick Loewe as one of the top writing teams on Broadway, added greatly to *Brigadoon's* popular appeal. Love ballads such as "Almost like Being in Love" and "Heather on the Hill" became instant favorites. Many people were also enchanted by "I'll Go Home with Bonnie Jean" and "Come to Me, Bend to Me."

Agnes de Mille's choreography further stimulated audience interest. Critics who had begun to weary of ballet and who had said they wished producers would return to old-fashioned dance routines made no such complaint about *Brigadoon*. Miss de Mille not only integrated the dance routines into the plot but also made them masterpieces of showmanship. The Highland flings and vigorous ensemble numbers in the town square had color, rhythm, and grace. Miss de Mille's ballets, in fact, dominated the last act. James Mitchell, who played Harry Beaton, was particularly impressive as he performed an intricate, exciting sword dance just after the wedding ceremony. The chase in pursuit of Harry was staged as a dance routine; in the following scene, Harry's body was brought back into the square and Maggie Anderson, played by Lidija Franklin, performed a somber funeral dance.

Although George Jean Nathan named *Finian's Rainbow* as the best musical of the year, and although he objected to the uncredited source of *Brigadoon,* he was nonetheless delighted with the Lerner and Loewe musical and selected Robert Lewis, the director, as the best musical stage director of the season. He also named Agnes de Mille as the best choreographer. Critics approved the effective costumes designed by David Ffolkes and the settings created by Oliver Smith. Smith's use of mist, which obscured the village during its time of disappearance and then evaporated as the town came to life, became particularly effective in the final scene when the mist cleared only long enough for Mr. Lundie to lead Tommy back into the romantic, sleeping town.

The excellent cast included David Brooks, who made a convincing Tommy Albright; Marion Bell, a newcomer to Broadway, impressed audiences with her sympathetic portrayal of Fiona; Pamela Britton, better known today for her work in television, provided the right touch of comedy as Meg Brockie. Although her two songs, "Love of My Life" and "My Mother's Wedding Day," have never become popular favorites, Miss Britton sang them with a flair that made the most of the comic element but was not out of keeping with the mood of the show. Miss Britton's performance, in fact, kept *Brigadoon* from becoming maudlin or overly sentimental. To some theatergoers, Lee Sullivan as Charlie Dalrymple had one of the best roles in the show. The *Wall Street Journal* review referred specifically to Sullivan's delightful voice which was especially pleasing in the haunting "Come to Me, Bend to Me." In his list of especially interesting performances for the season, George Jean Nathan included George Kean, who played Jeff, and Marion Bell.

Surprisingly enough, *Brigadoon,* which appeared to be an expensive show, is reported to have cost only $167,000, a figure somewhat lower than the cost of *Carousel,* and much lower than the production costs of failures in that same season, which represented average investments of more than $200,000.

Also surprising was the fact that the sets were eliminated from at least one production without detracting from the appeal of the story, the lyrics, and the music. At the University of Pittsburgh, *Brigadoon,* directed by Michael J. McHale, had a very successful run on campus. Mr. McHale and his troupe were invited, under the auspices of the United States Military Air Transport Service, to take the show to the Azores, Iceland, Bermuda, and McGuire Air Force Base in New Jersey. Since lack of space made it impossible to take sets, the production was presented without scenery. Mr. McHale reported that everywhere the show was given, it met with the same enthusiastic audience response. Families of servicemen, who were overseas with the troops, flocked to see *Brigadoon* and loved it. Air Force Commanders heartily approved of the show, for it was, as one officer said, "a family show." And the absence of scenery in no way hampered the entertainment value of the production.

In comparison with other hit musical comedies, the original run of 581 performances for *Brigadoon* may seem short, but time has proved its durability. Each new revival in New York has brought further praise from the critics. *Brigadoon* has been made into a motion picture, has been performed in summer theaters, and has been presented in high schools and colleges from coast to coast. Each new revival comes as a pleasant surprise to audiences who are delighted to find that the score contains songs they have always known and liked.

The 1966 television production of *Brigadoon* with Robert Goulet, Sally Ann Howes, and Peter Falk drew excellent notices, but old timers who remembered the 1947 stage version were somewhat disappointed. They still approved of Harry Beaton's dance, capably performed by Edward Villella, and the use of color which capitalized on the Scotch plaids and made the presentation a beautiful pageant; but they disapproved of changes in the opening and closing scenes. Perhaps the revisions were made in order to win wider appeal with television audiences, but the changes spoiled the effectiveness of the fantasy. Instead of having the town rise out of the mist, Tommy saw Fiona in broad daylight before he entered the town; and, in the final scene, instead of having the mist begin to clear and the sleepy Mr. Lundie slowly lead Tommy back across the bridge, the television version ended with the lovers rushing into an embrace, as though Tommy's love for Fiona could wake up the entire town at any time. Fantasy and romantic mystery were sacrificed to a typical motion-picture ending that was contrary to the mood of the story. The final judgment on *Brigadoon* is perhaps best epitomized by the New York Drama Critics' Circle citation naming it the best musical of 1947, which reads, "To *Brigadoon,* by Alan Jay Lerner and Frederick Loewe . . . because its taste, discretion and thoughtful beauty mark a high note in any season; and because it finds the lyric theater at its best."

Such effusive praise could scarcely be applied to *High Button Shoes* which opened the following season on October 9, 1947, and represented the only long-running musical comedy produced that year. The critics never have called, nor probably ever will call, *High Button Shoes* a major contribution to the American musical theater; but audiences remember it as one of the most entertaining productions of the 1940s. Anyone who saw the 1966 television version of the show would have good reason to wonder about the success of the original production, for although the television presentation used the same plot, it lacked the cast, the dancing, and the tempo that had made *High Button Shoes* a resounding hit in 1947.

When *High Button Shoes* opened on Broadway, *Oklahoma!*, *Annie Get Your Gun*, *Brigadoon*, *Finian's Rainbow*, and *Call Me Mister* were the popular long-running shows. The critics were all waiting for the new Rodgers and Hammerstein show *Allegro*, scheduled to open the following night. They were not enthusiastic about *High Button Shoes*; but did enjoy the Mack Sennett bathing-beauty ballet, the zany antics of Phil Silvers, and the enchanting performance of Nanette Fabray. Lukewarm reviews, however, did not discourage audiences. The nostalgic charm and old-fashioned slapstick humor recalled for older theatergoers the easygoing life of the early 1910s, the sentimental love stories, dumb football stars who win spectacular games, confidence men who outsmart innocent victims, and the golden age of silent-screen comedy.

The story was based on Stephen Longstreet's autobiographical novel *Some Like Them Handsome*, which dealt with life in New Brunswick, New Jersey, near Rutgers University, in 1913. The plot featured Harrison Floy, a confidence man, and his assistant Mr. Pontdue, who come back to their hometown, New Brunswick, hoping to promote any type of scheme that will earn them a fast dollar. Papa and Mama Longstreet become interested in Mr. Floy; Papa thinks Floy can help him sell some swampland, and Mama thinks he would be a good match for her unmarried sister Fran, who is in love with the star football player at Rutgers.

At a big community picnic, Mr. Floy begins selling the land, but in the midst of the excitement, one of the purchasers reports that the land is all swamp and everyone rushes off to investigate. Fran is holding the cash from the sale, and, in order to get the money, Floy makes a whirlwind proposal and rushes her off to Atlantic City, not knowing that Stevie Longstreet, the son, has overheard him. The Longstreets also rush to Atlantic City and, with the aid of a most ludicrous set of policemen, begin searching for Floy. What follows in the next scene is a deliberate parody of the old Mack Sennett two-reel comedies with the bathing beauties, Keystone Cops, and the mad cops-and-robbers chase. Floy finally gets the money bag and is ready to run off with it, only to be held up by Mr. Pontdue, who absconds with the loot.

By the time Floy has caught up with Pontdue, most of the money is gone. Floy returns to New Brunswick and finds that Fran and her football hero are reunited. With the money he has left, Floy bets on Princeton to defeat Rutgers in the big football game; but when he learns that Rutgers is winning, he tries to persuade the Rutgers team to lose the game by singing "Nobody Ever Died for Dear Old Rutgers." Nevertheless, the Rutgers team wins; and Floy, undaunted, starts to promote a new swindle. Before he can get it under way, the police arrive, and Floy escapes to another town, leaving the Longstreets, Fran, and her football hero happy.

The plot in itself would not have drawn people to the theater for the long run of more than two years, but the pleasant music, the ingratiating actors, and the excellent dancing provided a wonderful evening of entertainment that made it the comedy success of the season. George Abbott's direction gave it the same frenzied pace as the long-running farces he had directed in the 1930s, when he had four hit shows running simultaneously. Phil Silvers was superb as the brash, rowdy, conniving Harrison Floy, ably assisted by Joey Faye as Mr. Pontdue. Silvers, a veteran of burlesque, was particularly hilarious when he delivered a fast-moving pitch to get people to buy land—almost as if he were selling boxes of candy in the old burlesque houses—as well as in his ridiculous speech to Mrs. Longstreet's bird-watching society and his fight with a football player. Nanette Fabray as Mama Long-street played the role with a charm that made all her numbers sparkle. The music by Jule Styne and lyrics by Sammy Cahn included two songs, "Papa, Won't You Dance with Me" and "I Still Get Jealous Over You," both sung by Nanette Fabray and Jack McCauley, that were high spots in the show. Probably the most important contributions to the success of the production were the dances by Jerome Robbins, particularly the Keystone Kops ballet.

Once the show became established as a hit, Monty Proser and Joseph Kipnis, the producers, were beset with legal troubles. Mary Hunter brought suit against them, claiming that the producers had substituted George Abbott as director after she had been hired. A three-man arbitration panel awarded her $1,500 plus ¾ of 1 per cent of the weekly gross since the show began, but voted against giving her any sum for personal damages. The decision of the panel was overruled and a restitution of some sort made to Miss Hunter.

A second lawsuit filed against the producers brought into question the use of uncredited material. Mack Sennett, creator of the Keystone comedies, filed a suit for $250,000 against the producers, claiming that they had used his name and that of the Keystone Kops without his permission. Certainly anyone who saw the production immediately recognized the classic Sennett characters—the bathing beauties, the Keystone Kops, the tame gorilla, the long-haired vampire, the black-moustached villain, and the little country girl with long curls. The producers tried to have the case dismissed, but a California judge, according to a news item in *The New York Times,* refused to comply with this request. The outcome is not recorded, but it is known that Sennett was awarded a settlement out of court; and, although the ballet was kept in the show, references to Sennett seemed to be curtailed. Audiences, nevertheless, had no trouble identifying the source of the dance since Robbins succeeded in transplanting the exaggerated actions of a typical Sennett motion picture to the stage by having his dancers do the absurd leaps, stumbles, and acrobatic feats that had crowded the screen comedies. The characters in the Robbins ballet moved in and out of bathing-beach dressing rooms, and constantly got in one another's way. The routine was staged with such precision that the final result was a masterpiece of timing that kept the audience howling. If anything, the stage ballet seemed even more effective than the mad romps on the screen. In print there is nothing funny in the description of a sequence in which a man enters a beach dressing room holding the hand of a bathing beauty who is following him on tiptoe. A moment or two later, he comes out of another dressing room, still doing the same ridiculous tiptoeing step and still thinking he is holding the girl's hand, but this time a huge gorilla is holding his hand and tiptoeing with him.

When the man enters a third door and comes out the fourth, the gorilla has again been replaced by the girl. On the stage, this bit of nonsense was hilarious.

Critics wrote superlatives about the ballet, calling it "one of the comic glories of the age." Robbins' choreography, however, included several other delightful routines such as a tango that burlesqued the sultry dances typical of the Rudolph Valentino motion pictures. To many theatergoers, the "Papa, Won't You Dance with Me" number seemed almost as delightful as the Sennett ballet.

The producers astutely selected a road company that would be as excellent as the New York cast. The Chicago critics were delighted with Eddie Foy, Jr., who had captivated theatergoers in that city when he appeared in *The Red Mill*. Audrey Meadows and Jack Whiting as Mr. and Mrs. Longstreet were ingratiating and charming. One critic who saw both the road company and the New York cast said he found it difficult to make comparisons. Phil Silvers' performance, he felt, was brash and raucous; Eddie Foy Jr.'s, was smooth and slick. "Nanette Fabray," he said, "gave Mama Longstreet a mischievous twinkle, but Audrey Meadows gave her a glittering smile. The casts were different, but I liked them both."

With all their fond memories of the show, old-timers looked forward to the Garry Moore 1966 television version, but the production did not live up to expectations. The famous Mack Sennett bathing beauty ballet was eliminated; Jack Cassidy as Harrison Floy never had a chance to complete any of the ridiculous Phil Silvers routines, for the script writers moved him in and out of the action too rapidly; Garry Moore, who acted as Papa Longstreet and also as a sort of *Our Town* stage director-moderator to bridge gaps in the plot, did not speed up the pace. On the credit side, both Maureen O'Hara and Carol Lawrence, photographed beautifully in color. In the finale, Miss Lawrence satirized the fast dance steps of the period, but the show might have been better had she done the "Papa, Won't You Dance with Me" routine with Cassidy, for their sparkling personalities and musical comedy background might have made the number tingle as it did in the original production.

In 1947, *High Button Shoes* entertained older theatergoers by giving them an opportunity to reminisce about the early 1910s, and younger ones by introducing them to the pre-flapper era and the wonderful world of old-fashioned slapstick. While *High Button Shoes* flourished on Broadway, musicals with more serious themes and with better reviews opened and closed, but *High Button Shoes* kept playing to appreciative audiences for almost two years with a total of 727 performances.

High Button Shoes was the only musical to pass the 500 performance mark in the 1947–1948 season. When none of the five new musicals of the next season reached hit status, prospects for long runs looked bleak until *Where's Charley* opened October 11, 1948, and became a resounding hit. The reviews of the show itself were negative, but the critics liked Ray Bolger.

Most of them had liked *Charley's Aunt,* the old farce upon which the musical was based, and most of them had hoped the combination of Bolger and *Charley's Aunt* would result in a superior show. That it proved to be merely good entertainment came as a letdown. Many critics wrote that Bolger was, as always, in fine form; others thought he was not given sufficient material to do justice to his talents; and still others found that only he made a mediocre show enjoyable.

Public interest in *Where's Charley* ran high even before its opening. The advance sale was reported to have been well over $250,000, which was sufficient to keep the show on Broadway long enough for word-of-mouth advertising to bolster ticket sales. (A famous producer in the 1920s estimated that it took six weeks for a production to overcome bad reviews.) Quite often in the 1940s, when reviews were bad and pre-sold theater parties were over, a show closed immediately, but the advance sale for *Where's Charley* was high enough to insure a normal run. The fact that the public liked Bolger, that one song, "My Darling, My Darling," became a popular number on the hit parade, and that the show was good family entertainment enabled *Where's Charley* to overcome lukewarm reviews.

Many theatergoers were familiar with the original *Charley's Aunt* by Brandon Thomas, first produced in New York in 1893; it had been revived many times on Broadway, had been filmed several times, and had been produced by amateur groups all over the United States. Jack Benny had had a fling in the title role in a motion-picture version; John Mills starred in two London revivals in 1930 and 1953; in 1940 José Ferrer romped through the leading role on Broadway and in 1953 again played the role in a revival at the New York City Center.

The setting for *Charley's Aunt* is Oxford, England. Two young men, Jack Chesney and Charles Wykeham, needing a chaperone in order to have a rendezvous with their lady friends, persuade Lord Fancourt Babberley, another classmate, to pose as Charley's aunt, Donna Lucia, from Brazil. This leads to complications, for an Oxford attorney, who knows that the real Donna Lucia is a wealthy woman, pursues the disguised Lord Babberley at every opportune moment. Lord Babberley is in love with Amy Spettigew, and the plot becomes even more involved as he dashes out of his costume to make love to Amy, and then hastily back into feminine garb when the bogus Donna Lucia is needed as a chaperone. Charley's aunt, the real Donna Lucia d'Alvadorez, arrives, but instead of being the aged spinster-type Babberley is playing, she is a most attractive woman. As soon as she realizes what is going on, Donna Lucia joins in the fun and is very much amused when Babberley keeps saying he is Charley's aunt from Brazil "where the nuts come from." Finally, Babberley is able to drop his disguise and propose to Amy.

The producing team of Cy Feuer and Ernest Martin negotiated for the rights to adapt *Charley's Aunt* as a musical with Ray Bolger as star. They called in George Abbott to write the book and direct the production; Frank Loesser was signed to write the music and lyrics. In making the adaptation, Abbott combined the roles of Lord Babberley and Charles Wykeham so that Charles Wykeham would pose as his own aunt.

Some of the critics felt that *Charley's Aunt,* despite its creaky plot, was more amusing than *Where's Charley;* and their reviews reflected their disappointment. The popular appeal of *Where's Charley,* therefore, surprised some New York show people. But although the production was anything but sophisticated entertainment, older theatergoers enjoyed the satire on Victorian manners, the stilted etiquette of the period, the formal tea parties, the fluttering heroines with fans, and the necessity for chaperones.

Part of the success of both *Charley's Aunt* and *Where's Charley* derived from the device of female impersonation. An actor with feminine gestures and features playing a woman is not always amusing; in fact, if the actor himself seems too feminine, his performance can be offensive. The impersonation in *Where's Charley*, however, was highly diverting, for Bolger, wearing a long black dress, lace gloves, and a gray wig with curls, looked like a caricature of Whistler's mother. Even when he walked with mincing steps or coyly fluttered an eyelid, there was no suggestion of the effeminate female impersonator in his performance, for Bolger was obviously spoofing the whole idea of the masquerade. The scene in a ladies' dressing room, for instance, could have been in bad taste, but Bolger kept it from being offensive without sacrificing any of its genuine humor. As the girls are preening and admiring themselves in front of a mirror, Bolger imitates their actions; looking at his own reflection, he breaks into a fit of laughter that soon has the audience roaring with him in delight. All of Bolger's scenes were played in this same spirit and made the show the kind of entertainment to which parents could and did take their children. Moreover, the young folk loved Bolger as much in *Where's Charley* as they had in *The Wizard of Oz*.

Perhaps the best example of how Bolger ingratiated himself with audiences both young and old is illustrated in the story concerning the song "Once in Love with Amy." On opening night, Bolger clowned, tapped, and mugged his way through the song that became not only the highlight of the show but also a number that is always associated with him. The "Once in Love with Amy" routine gave him the chance to be a sparkling comedian and to do a superb dance routine. It is said that after the show had been running for a while, Bolger noticed at one performance that a little girl sitting down front was singing "Once in Love with Amy" when he did. The delighted Bolger encouraged her to sing along with him, and then asked the audience to join in. This added just the right touch to the show. Whether the story is true or not, Bolger did make audience participation part of the number, and "Once in Love with Amy" revived the old-fashioned, bouncing-ball, sing-along technique. Bolger would rattle off a line, then wait for the audience to sing it, and immediately cue in the next line. The more involved he became with the words, the funnier the whole routine became. And, instead of detracting from Bolger's performance, the audience participation gave him even greater opportunities to mug, to clown, and to make everyone in the theater happy.

Feuer and Martin, being astute showmen, surrounded Bolger with an excellent supporting cast. Byron Palmer, the handsome romantic lead, sang "My Darling, My Darling," and triumphed over the saccharine lyrics. The lovely Doretta Morrow, who was later to have leading roles in *Kismet* and *The King and I,* played Kitty Verdun, Palmer's romantic interest; and Allyn Ann McLerie was an excellent Amy. Miss McLerie, in fact, was so impressive that the producers of Irving Berlin's new musical, *Miss Liberty,* chose her to play the French girl who posed for the Statue of Liberty. In order to get Miss McLerie, they held up their production until her contract with *Where's Charley* had expired.

Where's Charley also established Frank Loesser as a leading lyricist and composer. In addition to the show-stopping "Once in Love with Amy," the score also included "My Darling, My Darling," which became a popular number on the hit parade. The song received an additional unexpected boost from Beatrice Lillie in a rival production, *Inside U.S.A.,* which opened later on Broadway. As part of her routine in one sketch, Miss Lillie had to sing a few phrases of a song. Everyone presumed that she would choose something from *Inside U.S.A.,* but instead she bustled about the stage crooning "My Darling, My Darling." "Make a Miracle," sung by Bolger and Miss McLerie, was one of the first numbers in a Broadway show to demonstrate Loesser's technique of using one vocalist to begin a chorus and then have the second vocalist cut into the song before the chorus had ended, starting on a new set of lyrics. For example, as Bolger sang, he kept trying to gain Amy's attention; Amy's lyrics, however, showed that her mind was elsewhere, and the humor of the song increased with each new chorus and each new interruption of one singer by the other. "The New Ashmoleon Marching Society and Student Conservatory Band," with its complicated title and lyrics and its vigorous marching tempo, also attracted attention. The entire score has not been recorded as an original-cast, long-playing album, but Bolger did record "Once in Love with Amy" and "Make a Miracle" as a single record.

Where's Charley was not a great musical. Many theatergoers would not even call it a good musical, but Ray Bolger drew audiences to the theater for 792 performances. When over-exhaustion forced Bolger to leave the cast, the manager knew that without him, *Where's Charley* could not continue, and, rather than attempt to find a replacement, closed the production.

Bolger's importance to the success of *Where's Charley* became apparent again in 1966, when a Broadway revival without him in the leading role received poor notices; a touring company, also lacking Bolger, failed as a box-office draw and closed.

During the first two months of its run in 1948, *Where's Charley* competed with such long-running hits as *Annie Get Your Gun* and *High Button Shoes*. As the theatrical season continued, Bolger further demonstrated his drawing power by competing successfully with two of the most popular musicals in the history of the New York theater: *Kiss Me, Kate*, which opened in December 1948, and *South Pacific*, which opened in April 1949.

Even before *Kiss Me, Kate* reached New York, reports from out of town indicated that this musical, with songs by Cole Porter and book by Bella and Samuel Spewack, would be a hit. During a four-week tryout in Philadelphia, it did excellent business. The New York opening, according to Burns Mantle, became one of the major social events of the year. The critics wrote rave reviews, some praising Porter's score as his best in years, others as the best of his entire career. The co-stars Alfred Drake and Patricia Morison also received accolades. The critics said that Drake's performance made him "about the most valuable man" in the field of musical comedy; "one of the authentic stars of the American theater"; "handsome, alive, and an ideal woman-tamer." Miss Morison was described as "an agile and humorous actress"; "a delight"; and "a capital comedienne."

The opening night triumph must have been deeply gratifying for Cole Porter, who had never fully recovered from a riding accident in 1937 and was still suffering from bone injuries that were to cause him continual pain for the rest of his life. Furthermore, his last few shows had not been successful and the producers had found potential backers skeptical of investing in a Porter musical. The cast also made some backers a bit hesitant, for although Alfred Drake had been excellent in *Oklahoma!*, most of the shows in which he had appeared after the Rodgers and Hammerstein musical had been failures. Patricia Morison, his co-star, had not been in a Broadway show for ten years, and her work in Hollywood films had not capitalized on her versatility.

Immediately after the newspaper reviews appeared, the demand for tickets became overwhelming. Mail orders poured in, and long lines formed at the box office. Reports began circulating that tickets for *Kiss Me, Kate* were being sold under the counter for fantastic prices, often as high as $100 per ticket. These rumors stirred up the possibility of an investigation of illegal ticket sales, but instead of discouraging theatergoers, this further whetted their desire to see the show.

In writing the book for *Kiss Me, Kate,* Bella and Samuel Spewack juxtaposed the basic plot of Shakespeare's *The Taming of the Shrew* with the trials of a temperamental stage director and his estranged wife, a headstrong star, who are appearing in a revival of the Shakespearean comedy. As the plot of *The Taming of the Shrew* unfolds in on-stage scenes of the revival, the off-stage scenes develop in a parallel manner the turbulent course of the romance between director and star. In this way, *Kiss Me, Kate* followed the pattern of Shakespeare's comedy, which also used the device of a play within a play.

Program notes revealed that during rehearsals the working title had been "Shrew," until the producers discovered that Cole Porter had written the words "Kiss Me, Kate" on some sheet music as possible lyrics for a finale. Taken directly from the Shakespearean text, the phrase provided an excellent title for the production.

The contrast between the modern plot and the Shakespearean story was effected not only through costuming and diction but, even more important, through Porter's score, which contained more than the usual number of hit songs, and was more smoothly integrated into the plot than his previous scores had been. In the modern scenes, Porter used his own style of lyrics, which included the dropping of famous café-society names, sophisticated and often bawdy lines, forced rhymes, and repetitive words. In the Shakespearean scenes, however, he often used words, phrases, and lines taken directly from *The Taming of the Shrew*. These variations are perhaps best illustrated by interlacing the vocal numbers with the synopsis to show Porter's technique in using the score to emphasize contrast. As the curtain rises, a troupe of actors headed by producer-actor Fred Graham and his former wife Lilli Vanessi, sings "Another Openin', Another Show," telling of their preparations for a revival in Baltimore of *The Taming of the Shrew*.

Graham is currently interested in Lois Lane, a singer in the company, but Lois is infatuated with Bill Calhoun, a dancer. When Bill tells Lois that he has lost money in a dice game and has signed Graham's name to an I.O.U. for $10,000, Lois sings "Why Can't You Behave?", a slow, blues number with a pleasant melody to which Porter has set lyrics which repeat the phrase several times in each chorus.

The scene shifts to Lilli's dressing room, where she and Fred reminisce about the shows in which they have appeared together and then sing "Wunderbar," from an old-fashioned operetta they had both liked. Porter intended the song to be a satire on Viennese waltzes, for his lyrics began with a reference to looking down on the Jungfrau, a ridiculous line considering that the Jungfrau is one of the highest mountains in the Alps. But the song appealed to audiences, and today is played for its lilting melody, the satirical lyrics usually being disregarded. By the time Fred and Lilli have finished "Wunderbar," the audience knows they are still in love with each other. Meanwhile, a bouquet of flowers that Fred had sent to Lois is delivered to Lilli by mistake. When she is alone, she sings the ballad, "So in Love." Its minor key and beguine rhythm, first popularized by Porter in "Begin the Beguine," catapulted the song into the hit category. Today, most audiences are familiar with the music, if not with the lyrics.

The next scene represents the first number in the Shakespearean revival, with Fred as Petruchio, Lilli as Kate, Lois as Bianca, and Bill as Lucentio, singing "We Open in Venice." The lyrics are repetitious, changing only to use a comic line each time the name of a different Italian city is mentioned. The action then develops the plot of *The Taming of the Shrew,* with Bianca telling Lucentio why she cannot marry until her older sister Kate gets a husband, and then singing the rhythmic "Tom, Dick, or Harry." Very shortly, Petruchio comes on stage and explains to Lucentio that he wants to marry a rich girl. He develops this idea further in the song "I've Come to Wive It Wealthily in Padua," which is the first time in the score that Porter takes the title and several lines of the lyrics directly from Shakespeare's text. It is to Porter's credit that most audiences cannot tell and do not care to know which lines are original and which are not. Lucentio tells Petruchio that Kate would be eligible, but does not minimize her shrewish temper. Petruchio meets Kate and agrees to marry her, much to the delight of Bianca and her father, who willingly promises Petruchio that Kate will have a handsome dowry. The embittered Kate, left alone on stage, sings "I Hate Men." Later, Petruchio, admitting that Kate is not the type of wife he had hoped to marry, sings "Were Thine That Special Face," which again uses several lines from Shakespeare, although in the original text they were spoken by Bianca.

The scene changes to the adjoining dressing rooms of Lilli and Fred. When Lilli discovers that the bouquet had been meant for Lois, she is infuriated and decides to walk out on the show in the middle of the performance. In Fred's dressing room, however, two gangsters have come to collect the $10,000 I.O.U. signed by Bill. After a bit of fast thinking, Fred tells the hoodlums that he can pay his debt only if Lilli stays in the show, and, as the first act closes, Lilli is raging because the gunmen prevent her leaving the theater.

The second act opens in an alley behind the theater. The song "Too Darn Hot" comments on the weather in Baltimore, but the fast rhythm soon becomes the background for a spirited dance routine that is at complete variance with the inertia expressed in the lyrics. In the next scene, *The Taming of the Shrew* is in progress on stage; Petruchio, now married to Kate, sings about his life as a bachelor in "Where Is the Life That Late I Led," another line from Shakespeare's text. The following scene is set backstage. Bill is scolding Lois for flirting with another man. She begins a reprise of "Why Can't You Behave?", then suddenly swings into

"Always True to You in My Fashion." Several sources have credited Porter's lyrics to Ernest Dowson, a statement which is partially true, for Porter's title does paraphrase Dowson's line "I have been faithful to thee, Cynara! in my fashion." Porter immediately follows this number with "Bianca," sung and danced by Bill. Although the lyrics are not Porter at his best, the song serves its purpose as background music for Bill's solo dance.

After breaking the news that their former boss is no longer top man, the gangsters tear up the now-worthless I.O.U. Lilli makes good her threat and walks out of the show, with Fred unable to stop her. In a number performed in front of the curtain, the two gangsters sing a typically sophisticated Porter number, "Brush Up Your Shakespeare," which begins innocently enough but becomes bawdier with each succeeding chorus. This is perhaps the one song in the show that reverts to the old-fashioned musical comedy technique of using a specialty number that has no direct connection with the plot. The finale brings the Shakespearean troupe back on stage. Fred, certain that Lilli will not return, knows that he must improvise a quick, makeshift ending. Quite suddenly, however, Lilli does appear in costume and sings, "I Am Ashamed That Women Are So Simple," a song that uses Shakespeare's text not only for the title but also for the lyrics. The words "Kiss Me, Kate," also from the text, are used in the finale, which reunites Lilli and Fred.

When Goddard Lieberson selected *Kiss Me, Kate* as one of the ten American musicals most worth preserving, he cited its excellent combination of Shakespeare, sex, and music that stimulated the players to give scintillating performances. Alfred Drake swaggering across the stage as Fred, sang magnificently and acted the role of Petruchio to perfection; Patricia Morison as Lilli was not only beautiful and an excellent actress but also demonstrated that she was a fine singer whose talents had been wasted in a series of grade B Hollywood pictures. Harold Lang, better known as a dancer until *Kiss Me, Kate,* proved that he could also act and sing. Lisa Kirk, who had won excellent notices in *Allegro* by singing "The Gentleman Is a Dope," played Lois and Bianca equally well and stopped the show with "Always True to You in My Fashion." The success of *Kiss Me, Kate,* however, did not depend upon the excellent performances of the original leads, for cast replacements did not dim the lustre of the show. Keith Andes and Anne Jeffreys took over the leading roles in the New York cast during the lengthy run. As a replacement for Andes in the road company, the producers brought in Robert Wright.

Among the further attributes that gave *Kiss Me, Kate* its popular appeal were the choreography by Hanya Holm, ranging from vigorous tap routines by specialty dancers Fred Davis and Eddie Sledge, to nimble solos by Harold Lang and colorful ensemble numbers by the attractive chorus line; the settings and costumes by Lemuel Ayers, co-producer of the show, reflected elegance and good taste.

The motion-picture version of *Kiss Me, Kate* was released during a period of experimentation in which audiences had to hold special red and green glasses for the length of the entire picture to get the new three-dimensional effect. Metro-Goldwyn-Mayer, which had filmed the picture with Howard Keel, Katharine Grayson, and Ann Miller, wisely reissued it in regular technicolor, two-dimensional form that did not distract audiences with scenes such as those in the three-dimensional version, in which actors threw colored bouncing balls and ribbons at the audience.

Kiss Me, Kate was popular abroad, especially in Germany; it was the first American musical comedy presented in Poland; and it enjoyed a phenomenal success in Vienna. Oddly enough, the number which worried the Viennese director most was "Wunderbar," for he did not know if the Viennese would accept it as a satire or would dub it a poor imitation of a Viennese waltz. The reaction in Vienna differed greatly from that in the United States; while the number kept gaining in popularity here as the lyrics were de-emphasized, in Vienna, so the report went, theatergoers appreciated the satirical lyrics and enjoyed the song as a comedy number.

That *Kiss Me, Kate* pleased the public is apparent in its long run. With the heavy demand for tickets, New Yorkers were not surprised when *Kiss Me, Kate* ran into a second season, and then a third, and finally achieved a total run of 1,077 performances, making it the third musical comedy to pass the 1,000 mark. That

Kiss Me, Kate pleased the critics is evident in the fact that it was a very close contender for the Critics' Circle Award as the best musical of the year. Although the prize was awarded to *South Pacific,* several critics expressed their disappointment in the final choice, stating their preference for *Kiss Me, Kate.* Perhaps the best way to epitomize the appeal *Kiss Me, Kate* had for both critics and audiences is to quote the Viennese critic who wrote, "Kiss Me, Kate—again and again and again."

1. Henry E. Dixey was the dashing singing-dancing star of *Adonis* (1884), the first musical to run five hundred or more consecutive performances in New York City

2. Olga Cook and Bertram Peacock starred as Mitzi and Franz Schubert in *Blossom Time* (1921), a fictionalized biography of the composer

3. The original cast of *Oklahoma!* (1943) included (left to right) Lee Dixon as Will Parker, Celeste Holm as Ado Annie, Alfred Drake as Curly, Joan Roberts as Laurey, Joseph Buloff (kneeling) as Ali Hakim, and Betty Garde as Aunt Eller

4. Ethel Merman starred in *Annie Get Your Gun* (1946), her longest-running role. Irving Berlin wrote the score and gave Miss Merman not only comedy and rhythm numbers but a love ballad as well, the first one she introduced on Broadway

5. David Wayne played Og the leprechaun and Ella Logan was the bewitching Sharon who sang "How Are Things in Glocca Morra?" in *Finian's Rainbow* (1947)

6. Mary Martin as Nellie Forbush and Myron McCormick as Luther Billis sang "Honey Bun" in *South Pacific* (1949). McCormick stopped the show by flexing his stomach muscles to make the tattooed ship pitch and roll

VIII

South Pacific

MANY DRAMA critics refer to Rodgers and Hammerstein as the most important creators of musical comedy in the 1940s and credit *Oklahoma!* with setting new standards in the musical theater. Others consider *Carousel* a far superior work even though it had a shorter run; still others call *South Pacific* a major musical, but do not rate it as high as the first two. Records prove, however, that *South Pacific,* in number of prizes, awards, and citations received, exceeded most musical productions in the history of the New York theater and surpassed all of its competitors in the same season. Its distinction as the Pulitzer Prize drama for the 1949–50 season made it the second musical comedy to receive the award.

Previous Pulitzer Prize awards in drama had often stirred up controversy among critics, particularly in 1924 when the award slighted George Kelly's *The Show-Off,* and again in 1935, when Lillian Hellman's *The Children's Hour* was by-passed. There might have been arguments against giving the 1949–50 prize to *South Pacific* on the grounds that it had been produced in the 1948–49 season. The Pulitzer Committee justified its award by explaining that according to the Pulitzer calendar, the musical was produced late enough in the season to be considered eligible for the 1949–50 award. In actual fact, the award of the prize to *South Pacific* received commendation from several newspapers, specifically the New York *Herald Tribune,* which said that the choice of *South Pacific* "will receive confirming cheers from coast to coast."

The Critics Circle named *South Pacific* the best musical production of the year—but not by too great a majority of votes, for *Kiss Me, Kate* ran a very close second. *South Pacific* also won an amazing number of seven Antoinette Perry (Tony) awards and nine Donaldson awards.

Undoubtedly the prize awards at the end of the first season helped *South Pacific* to attain a long run, but even before these were announced, the show had run for almost a year to an unprecedented demand for tickets. Even before the Broadway opening, reports from out of town stimulated interest in the show. Unlike *Oklahoma!* and *Carousel,* which had undergone revisions during the tryouts, *South Pacific* was judged superb even at the first performance, and the show was considered ready for New York at its out-of-town premiere. Ecstatic reviews from New Haven and Boston indicated that Rodgers and Hammerstein had a hit. In Boston, where the top price was $5.40, all tickets were sold in advance. Speculators who had been charging $20 a pair soon raised their price to $50 and even higher, if reports are true. The advance sale in New York became phenomenal. One source reported that advance orders totaled $300,000; others estimate the amount at $500,000. Even more extraordinary was the fact that approximately nine months after the show had opened, the demand for tickets, according to *Variety,* had increased rather than decreased, with the advance sale in January 1950 having risen to more than $700,000.

If audiences had been disappointed, if the advance publicity had promised too much and the show had not lived up to expectations, ticket sales at the box office would have dropped. But *South Pacific* lived up to its reputation. The critics' reviews were almost unanimously raves, with opinion divided only on the question of which feature added most to the entertainment: the romantic story, the excellent book, the good score, or the superb cast. All reviews rated the show as one of Broadway's best in years.

News items, press releases, choice tidbits in newspaper columns, and even lyrics from other songs helped stir up interest in the tight ticket situation. A revival of an old Rodgers and Hart song, "Manhattan," now included two lines referring to the fact that *South Pacific* was terrific and that the singers hoped in some future day to get to see the show. Attempting to stimulate interest in a contest, one commercial firm offered as first prize two choice orchestra seats for *South Pacific,* worth at least $100 apiece in the under-the-counter market.

The rave notices given Mary Martin and Ezio Pinza certainly stimulated ticket sales, but the production proved, almost from the start, that audiences came to see the show and not the star performers. During the first few months of the run, when Pinza missed several performances, disappointed patrons turned their tickets back to the box office for refunds; but these seats were resold immediately, and theatergoers who saw Pinza's replacement, Dickinson Eastham, gave the show favorable word-of-mouth advertising. The same reaction occurred when Mary Martin began missing performances, for tickets turned in were resold immediately to people crowding the lobby in hopes of cancellations. As the show continued with one cast replacement after another, the producers became well aware that audiences wanted to see *South Pacific* regardless of who played the leads.

Oddly enough, *South Pacific* had been used as the title for a drama by Howard Rigsby and Dorothy Heyward produced in 1943. There has been no confusion between the drama and the musical, for the Rigsby-Heyward play ran for only five performances. It might be curious to speculate, however, what could have happened if some producer had decided to revive the drama during the height of the Rodgers and Hammerstein musical success.

South Pacific was based on James Michener's 1947 Pulitzer Prize-winning *Tales of the South Pacific,* a collection of stories based on his Navy experiences on the islands of the New Hebrides and New Guinea. In an article written for the souvenir theater program and entitled "It Could Have Happened," Michener explained that while none of the incidents in his book were true, none of the characters had been based on real people, and none of the islands existed exactly as he had described them, yet in essence the book *was* true, for everything he wrote could have happened. The fictional characters resembled the nurses, officers, seabees, and islanders whom he had met; and the events were typical of those he had heard of or had witnessed on the islands.

Kenneth MacKenna, head of the story department at Metro-Goldwyn-Mayer, first recommended Michener's book as a possible motion picture. When studio officials decided against using it, MacKenna suggested it to Joshua Logan as a stage play. Logan took the idea to producer Leland Hayward, who thought the material would make an excellent musical. Hayward, in turn, approached Rodgers and Hammerstein, who agreed that the book would make a good musical play, and after preliminary negotiations, Rodgers, Hammerstein, Logan, and Hayward joined together as co-producers, Logan agreeing to direct the production as well as to work on the book with Oscar Hammerstein II. Originally, Hammerstein had been scheduled to write the libretto, but the producers realized that Logan's experiences in the Navy would be of invaluable help in writing the play.

The producers agreed on the selection of two stories from Michener's book: "Our Heroine," which dealt with a Navy nurse who fell in love with a French planter; and "Fo' Dolla," the story of an unhappy romance between a Marine lieutenant and a seventeen-year-old Tonkinese girl. "Fo' Dolla" also included a very colorful character, Bloody Mary, mother of the girl. By adding characters which had appeared in other stories, Hammerstein and Logan coordinated the isolated incidents into a singularly uncomplicated, compelling drama with a major plot and minor plot running simultaneously. The stories blended into one episode in the second act when the two heroes set out together on a dangerous mission.

The major plot dealt with the romance between Ensign Nellie Forbush, a nurse from Little Rock, Arkansas, and the middle-aged, dashing, French planter Emile de Becque. Nellie learns that de Becque had lived with a Polynesian woman, now dead, and that the two small Polynesian children whom she had met on his plantation were de Becque's; although greatly attracted to him, she feels that now she could not be happy with him. The minor plot concerns handsome Lieutenant Cable, Bloody Mary, and her daughter Liat. Bloody Mary, deciding that Cable would be the right man for Liat, takes him to meet her. Their romance is passionate and idyllic. A major transition between the two love stories develops at this point, for, just as Nellie objected to de Becque's having lived with a Polynesian, Cable also knows that a marriage to Liat would be impossible because he could not overcome his family's objections to the racial difference.

The stories are further linked in a new development of the plot. Although de Becque is not in the military service, his vast knowledge of the islands makes him an invaluable aid to the United States forces. When Cable is to be sent on a dangerous mission, de Becque, fully aware of the risks involved and of Nellie's reasons for trying to break up their romance, agrees to go with him. While they are away, Nellie grows fond of de Becque's children and also realizes that she is deeply in love with him. de Becque's safe return leads to the happy ending audiences had expected. Cable, however, is killed.

One or two commentators felt that the endings were a bit contrived—that de Becque had been kept alive to provide the audience with a happy ending, and Cable killed in order to end a romance that would eventually have resulted in unhappiness. Allowing de Becque to return, however, was not an illogical development, for earlier episodes in the play had emphasized de Becque's knowledge of the terrain and his ability to maneuver himself safely through enemy-infested territory. One or two drama commentators also compared the love story of Cable and Liat to the story of *Madame Butterfly*, but apart from their unhappy endings, the two plots differed greatly. In John Luther Long's drama, Madame Butterfly commits suicide; in *South Pacific*, Lieutenant Cable is accidentally killed. Pinkerton was not in love with Cio-Cio-San, the heroine in *Madame Butterfly*. That Liat meant more than a transient romance to Cable, however, becomes clear in the song "Carefully Taught," which Cable sings to de Becque. Hammerstein's lyrics emphasize the difference in race, and the prejudices that would keep the young lovers apart.

Equally as important to the musical's phenomenal success as the romantic love interest was the Rodgers and Hammerstein score. The songs not only helped to develop the plot and the characterizations but also were extremely appealing in themselves.

Of the two leading roles, de Becque's had fewer vocal numbers, but each song established the strong personality of the planter. "Some Enchanted Evening," one of the first songs to become a hit, explained why the worldly de Becque would fall in love with the much younger, small town girl, Nellie Forbush. "This Nearly Was Mine" revealed de Becque's knowledge that his romance with Nellie had ended. De Becque also sang a reprise of Nellie's "I'm Gonna Wash That Man Right Outa My Hair," as well as a duet with Nellie in which each told the audience why their romance should not be a success.

Nellie, on the other hand, had at least four excellent solos. In "Cockeyed Optimist," she revealed her happy-go-lucky nature. "I'm in Love with a Wonderful Guy," accentuated Nellie's bubbling good humor as she repeated "I'm in Love" over and over again at the end of the chorus. "I'm Gonna Wash That Man Right Outa My Hair" had a special gimmick that intrigued audiences and provided wonderful copy for columnists and publicity releases, for Nellie sang the number while washing her hair on stage. Women began speculating as to the number of times Mary Martin actually washed her hair, what the effect this constant washing had on her scalp, and what type of shampoo she used. Everything Miss Martin did or said about the song became excellent newspaper copy. For example, Miss Martin had her hair cropped very short so that the washing and drying on stage could be done more quickly. For street wear, she wrapped her short hair in glamorous turbans; both the haircut and the turbans were continuously discussed in women's pages, fashion columns, and magazine articles. *The New York Herald Tribune,* in reporting Miss Martin's departure from the show, ran as its headline "Mary Martin Takes Last Stage Shampoo," and then continued with the story that Miss Martin had rinsed her hair 900 times while playing Nellie. During the London run of *South Pacific,* Miss Martin, in a note which appeared in the program for *Gentlemen Prefer Blondes,* said she had washed her hair 1,886 times since the show opened.

Myron McCormick, who played Luther Billis, was originally slated to sing Nellie's fourth song, "Honey Bun," but the producers decided it would be an ideal comedy number for Miss Martin in an oversized sailor's uniform and McCormick as Honey Bun, in grass skirt, mop wig, and a brassiere made of two large coconuts. The switch worked out beautifully. The song became part of an amateur show presented for the men, and the ridiculous costumes gave the number a touch of homemade theatricality typical of the soldier shows rigged up by Special Service Officers for the troops. The song also received a notable assist from McCormick, who had a ship at full sail painted on his stomach. In one chorus, he wiggled his muscles to make the ship appear to be sailing on the waves, a trick which Joshua Logan said he had seen McCormick perform when they had been at college together.

In addition to the four solos and a duet with de Becque, Nellie also sang a reprise of "Some Enchanted Evening." Rodgers' score, however, did not limit the hit songs to the principal characters. Quite often, so rumor goes, stars have insisted that potential hit numbers sung by other performers must be deleted or cut down. No such situation existed in *South Pacific*. On the contrary, Bloody Mary had two excellent songs in "Bali Ha'i," the beautiful description of an enchanted island, and "Happy Talk," sung to the accompaniment of Liat's graceful hand gestures, which mimed the words.

Audiences reacted quite differently to Cable's two songs. They enjoyed "Younger Than Springtime," Cable's love song to Liat— so much so that it became one of the numbers played most frequently on radio programs. Cable's second number, "Carefully Taught," however, aroused opposition from persons objecting to its "propaganda." Two Georgia legislators, in fact, were sufficiently annoyed to express their distaste for the song publicly. In a newspaper interview, Hammerstein said quite frankly that the lyrics were a protest against racial prejudice as well as a statement of Cable's conflict between his prejudices and his love for Liat.

As a group, the sailors, seabees, and marines also had two show-stopping songs. The first, "Bloody Mary," could perhaps be called a mock serenade to the almost witchlike Tonkinese woman who sold them shrunken heads and grass skirts as souvenirs. The clowning of the singers and Bloody Mary's unusual appearance made the number a delightful comic interlude. In the second chorus number, "There Is Nothing Like a Dame," led by Luther Billis, the music was mere background for Hammerstein's lyrics. In several sections of the song, there is no set rhythm pattern at all. The lyrics were earthy but not vulgar, amusing but not offensive. Probably the best way to judge the lyrics used in the stage version is to compare them with the bowdlerized lyrics used in the motion picture. What had been a highly amusing song in the theater became merely an innocuous ditty in the film.

Although most critics praised the score, a few did not think the songs had sufficient popular appeal. One newspaper critic, however, who felt that the music did not represent Rodgers at his best nevertheless admitted that it fit the play so well that audiences did not miss hearing a series of hit tunes. Rodgers wisely made no attempt to write the type of music usually considered to be typical of the South Sea Islands. The public expressed its approval of the entire score by making the original cast album a best seller. A news item in *The New York Times* reported that the gross sale of records within one year exceeded $4 million, or about $1.5 million more than most shows of that season grossed in ticket sales for the same period of time. The number of long-playing albums sold totalled more than a million. Sheet music sales also reached astronomical figures; the estimate of the total number of copies sold was in excess of two million.

At least two songs were dropped before the production reached New York. "Loneliness of Evening," written for Pinza, was replaced by a reprise of "Some Enchanted Evening." A song for Cable and Nellie, "My Girl Back Home," although dropped from the stage version was sung in the film by Mitzi Gaynor and John Kerr. A third song, "Getting to Know You," was also reputed to have been written for the show and then dropped. Oddly enough, during the out-of-town tryouts for their next show, *The King and I,* Rodgers and Hammerstein added a song called "Getting to Know You" for Gertrude Lawrence.

In establishing the reason for public interest in *South Pacific,* there is no denying the following facts: after Pinza and Martin had left the show, *South Pacific* still played to capacity houses; it broke records on its road tour with other performers in the leading roles; and it fared well in revivals with completely different casts. To discount the importance of Ezio Pinza and Mary Martin in establishing the initial success of the show, however, would be ridiculous, for they represented not only ideal casting but also healthy box-office insurance. The show was a particular triumph for Pinza, a leading basso with the Metropolitan Opera Company, who had been famous for such roles as Don Giovanni, Boris Godunov, and Mephistopheles. Part of his popularity could also be traced to the fact that Pinza, in addition to being a fine basso, was also an excellent actor. Moreover, he had always enchanted women. When Rodgers and Hammerstein learned that Pinza planned to leave the Metropolitan Opera Company and that he wanted to appear in a Broadway musical, they lost no time in offering him the lead, for the role of Emile de Becque gave Pinza the opportunity to capitalize on his singing, acting, and romantic charm.

Fresh from her successful tour in *Annie Get Your Gun,* Mary Martin returned to Broadway, where she had always been a favorite with theater critics, and received ecstatic reviews. She charmed audiences with her clowning, and her acting and singing made each of her numbers a show stopper; moreover, Pinza and Martin surprised those skeptics who doubted whether they could work well together—since he represented opera and she represented musical comedy—by making their duets as well as their romantic scenes highlights of the show.

The original cast also included Juanita Hall, who gave a brilliant performance as Bloody Mary; William Tabbert, excellent as Lieutenant Cable; and Betta St. John, an appealing Liat. Myron McCormick, who gave a splendid performance as Luther Billis, almost made the role a lifetime career, for by the time *South Pacific* had reached its 1,000th performance, Mr. McCormick was the only member of the original cast left in the show. At the final performance, McCormick, still playing Luther Billis, led the cast and audience in singing "Auld Lang Syne."

By the time the production had run two years, critics were saying that even without Ezio Pinza and Mary Martin, *South Pacific* continued to cast its romantic spell on audiences because Rodgers and Hammerstein kept bringing in excellent replacements. Martha Wright, who was an excellent Nellie Forbush, probably sang the role more times on Broadway than any other actress. Along with Ray Middleton and George Britton, Pinza's replacements included Roger Rico, leading basso of the Paris Grand Opera. The public-relations experts, always hunting for items that could keep the show in the news columns, had a field day with Mr. Rico; the story soon circulated that he could not speak a single word of English, that he had learned the dialogue and lyrics by rote, and that he did not understand any of the words. Theatergoers who saw Mr. Rico judged the story to be simply another good publicity stunt, for he certainly spoke and sang with the proper inflections.

Perhaps the most curious bit of casting concerned a replacement for Bloody Mary, the bewigged, black-toothed Tonkinese woman who spoke profanely but sang divinely. In the 1920s, French glamour on Broadway was epitomized by Irene Bordoni. Theatergoers who remembered her chic appearance in those days were startled to find her playing the definitely unglamorous Bloody Mary in the 1950s.

The excellence of the successive cast replacements caused some commentators to speculate on whether *South Pacific* might have prospered just as well without Ezio Pinza and Mary Martin in the original cast. Such assumptions after-the-fact would be difficult to prove; it is perhaps more important to acknowledge the glow and charm with which Miss Martin and Mr. Pinza endowed their roles and gave *South Pacific* its original, strong impact on theater audiences, and to recognize the play's inherent power as a drama with music, which enabled it to continue to please audiences after the original stars had left the show.

South Pacific was not a musical comedy in the traditional sense. At least two startling innovations distinguished it from most of its predecessors. In the first place the show lacked the conventional line of chorus girls; the dancing was kept to a minimum because *South Pacific* had been constructed as a drama with music rather than as a musical comedy. There was, in fact, no choreographer for the production. At the opening of Act II, Archie Savage, who had been one of the leading dancers in the Katharine Dunham group, did a soft shoe dance, and in the comedy number, "Honey Bun," the nurses did a few simple steps which Mary Martin, who had taught dancing in Texas, arranged.

In the second place, the show achieved the fluidity of a motion picture by having no blackouts and by blending one scene into another. The action was continuous, and set changes were made while the cast was on stage or in front of the curtain. Its fluidity was further enhanced through the smooth integration of songs and plot, so that the action led directly into song cues, and the songs, in turn, led into further plot development.

When *South Pacific* opened in 1949, enough time had elapsed after World War II to make the wartime locale subordinate to the romantic love stories. After the production had been running for two years, however, Mary Martin, in an article in *The New York Times*, said the trouble in Korea had given the show "new meaning" and that the story of Lieutenant Cable and his death aroused a greater emotional reponse from families who had boys overseas in the war.

The New York run of *South Pacific* broke financial as well as attendance records. In May 1949, shortly after the Broadway opening, *Variety* reported that *South Pacific* had already paid off 30 per cent of its original investment of $225,000 and that the producers were already planning to make an additional payment of 20 per cent within the next two weeks. In many respects the touring company of *South Pacific* equalled the financial success of the New York production, for it established new gross receipt records in major cities. *South Pacific* earned a greater profit in twenty-six weeks on the road than the New York company had earned in eighty weeks. In Chicago, the production grossed over $1,179,000 in twenty-three weeks. In Cleveland, more than $500,000 had to be returned to people whose mail orders could not be filled.

Internationally, *South Pacific* also set new records, *Time* reporting it as the greatest hit in Spanish theatrical history. The reaction of the London critics, however, surprised a great many American theater men, for the reviews in several cases were definitely unkind—one reviewer, in fact, referred to the show as "South Soporific." The majority of the critics indicated that the production had failed to measure up to the extensive advance publicity. Several of the critics did like the show, however, and most of them were enthusiastic about Mary Martin.

The motion picture starring Mitzi Gaynor and Rossano Brazzi received curious mixed reviews, with emphasis on the excellent sound and beautiful photography. Some critics objected to the dubbed-in voices for several of the principal actors, although most reviewers did not find fault with the fact that Georgio Tozzi's voice was used for Brazzi's songs. Many theatergoers, as well as critics, were more puzzled by the voice dubbing for Juanita Hall, who played her original role of Bloody Mary. What made the dubbing even more curious was the fact that at the time the picture was released, Miss Hall was appearing in a new Rodgers and Hammerstein musical—*Flower Drum Song*—and demonstrating that she could handle her songs effectively without a voice double.

The romantic love stories and excellent score have not lost lustre in more recent revivals of *South Pacific* in New York. Amateur companies and summer stock productions have also drawn large, appreciative audiences, for *South Pacific* still has the same popular appeal which enabled it to earn one of the highest gross receipts in the history of the New York theater—more than $9 million. When *South Pacific* closed in 1954 after 1,925 performances, it became at that time the fifth longest-running production and the second longest-running musical comedy in the history of the New York theater.

The Mid-Century
Musicals

LITTLE ROCK sent two heroines to the New York stage in 1949: Nellie Forbush, the optimistic nurse in *South Pacific,* and Lorelei Lee, the gold-digging "Little Girl from Little Rock" in *Gentlemen Prefer Blondes.* To attempt any other comparison between the two girls would be pointless, for Nellie symbolized sweetness and charm, while Lorelei epitomized the calculating, man-hunting flapper of the 1920s.

The New York première of *Gentlemen Prefer Blondes* on December 8, 1949, not only marked the last of the big, gaudy musicals of the 1940s, but, even more important, it also marked the climax of a saga that had begun in the 1920s, when Anita Loos sent the manuscript of "Gentlemen Prefer Blondes" to *Smart Set Magazine,* edited by George Jean Nathan and H. L. Mencken. Both men enjoyed reading it but rejected it for publication because they thought the story too frivolous. Miss Loos then sent her manuscript to *Cosmopolitan.* Although Ray Long, the editor, bought it, he decided later not to publish the story because he felt it was too trivial for his magazine. Some time later, Henry Sell, editor of *Harper's Bazaar,* found Miss Loos's story while looking through the pile of unused manuscripts Long had bought. He decided to run it as a serial. "Gentlemen Prefer Blondes" became an instant sensation, was reprinted in at least a dozen languages, and prompted Miss Loos to write a sequel, "But They Marry Brunettes."

Edgar Selwyn persuaded Miss Loos to write a straight dramatic play based on her story, but after she signed the contract she discovered to her dismay that Florenz Ziegfeld, Jr. wanted to produce a musical version starring the very popular Marilyn Miller. Although Miss Loos admitted that she would have liked a Ziegfeld production because he would have given the show the type of glamour and glitter it needed, she lived up to the terms of her contract with Selwyn. In collaboration with her husband, John Emerson, she wrote a comic play which starred brunette June Walker, wearing a blond wig to play Lorelei; Edna Hibbard; and Frank Morgan, whose performance as Henry Spofford brought him a Hollywood contract. The show was successful both in New York and on the road, where at least three companies toured simultaneously.

Paramount Pictures bought the film rights. The studio officials, deciding to cast an unknown actress in the role of Lorelei, selected Ruth Taylor, a wide-eyed blonde who, Miss Loos said, played Lorelei off screen as well, for she later married a wealthy broker and retired from films. As Lorelei's wise-cracking companion Dorothy, the studio selected Alice White, a popular screen comedienne in the 1920s.

In an article written for the souvenir program of the 1949 production, Miss Loos said that John C. Wilson had repeatedly asked her to adapt her story as a stage musical comedy, but that she had been too busy writing motion-picture scripts. When she finally decided to write the adaptation, Wilson was busy directing *Kiss Me, Kate*. Nevertheless, Miss Loos went to work on the book and co-authored the adaptation with Joseph Fields. Jule Styne, who had written the music for *High Button Shoes*, and Leo Robin, well-known Hollywood lyricist whose songs included "Louise," "Thanks for the Memory," and "Love in Bloom," were signed to write the score. With *Kiss Me, Kate* successfully launched, Wilson now agreed to direct the production. Herman Levin and Oliver Smith, the producers, signed Agnes de Mille as choreographer and Miles White as costume designer, with Smith to act as set designer. In writing the adaptation, Miss Loos and Mr. Fields kept the spirit of the original book and the atmosphere of the 1920s but gave the story a somewhat different treatment.

The first scene opens aboard the *Île de France*. Lorelei Lee and her friend Dorothy Shaw are sailing to Paris. Dorothy, bemoaning the prohibition laws, is anxious to get to Paris, but Lorelei is not too happy about leaving her fiancé (in the 1920s, the term was "sugar daddy"), Mr. Esmond, a button manufacturer. During the voyage, Lorelei decides that her romance is over and she must find a new love. Explaining how she feels, she sings "I'm Just a Little Girl from Little Rock," a number that tells the story of her life.

Although Dorothy says she could fall in love with a poor man just as easily as with a rich man, Lorelei arranges a match between Dorothy and Henry Spofford, a wealthy bachelor from Philadelphia. Before the boat docks, Dorothy and Henry are very much in love. In the meanwhile Lorelei, whose philosophy is that "Diamonds Are a Girl's Best Friend," sees a diamond tiara belonging to Lady Beekman, a fellow passenger, and knows she must have it. Being a clever manipulator, she decides to wheedle Sir Francis Beekman into lending her $5,000 with which to buy his wife's tiara, and she entices him by singing "It's Delightful Down in Chile." At the end of the number, she has both the money and the tiara.

In Paris, Lorelei finds a new sugar daddy, Mr. Josephus Gage, who manufactures zippers. Meanwhile, Lady Beekman has learned how Lorelei got the tiara, and she hires French attorneys to retrieve it. To add to the complications, Mr. Esmond, Lorelei's fiancé, arrives and finds her with Mr. Gage. Lorelei makes a nightclub debut, is a huge success, and maneuvers Mr. Esmond into forgiving her. She also arranges to pay back the money to Sir Francis. At the final curtain, Dorothy and Henry are to be married; and the elder Mr. Esmond, who had previously objected to the marriage of his son and Lorelei, now realizes that Lorelei is a very shrewd girl, rather than the dumb blonde he had thought, and gives his son his consent to marry her.

The plot was certainly farfetched, but the book was not the primary reason for the musical's phenomenal success. The dances, the music, the sumptuous sets, the costumes, the cast, and, above all, Carol Channing as Lorelei, made the production a fast-moving extravaganza with an emphasis on entertainment. Disregarding integrated score or songs that developed the action, *Gentlemen*

Prefer Blondes followed the pattern of the old-fashioned musicals which shunted plot aside to make way for elaborate production numbers. Even before the show reached New York, reports circulated that it would be a hit. During the two and a half weeks it played in Philadelphia, the show received enthusiastic reviews and played to delighted audiences. In New York the advance sale, according to Robert Coleman in the New York *Daily Mirror,* exceeded $600,000, which he said was the highest figure he could find in his records for any production.

Some time during the rehearsal period and the New York opening, the show must have been altered to build up the role of Lorelei, for in both the original story and in the stage version, Miss Loos had given the characterizations of Dorothy and Lorelei equal importance and had, in fact, relegated many of the best wise-cracking lines to Dorothy. By the time the musical version reached New York, however, Carol Channing—who, along with Yvonne Adair, had appeared previously in only one major Broadway production, *Lend an Ear*—dominated the show. Rumors of backstage friction kept spreading; one or two critics said Miss Adair's talents were being wasted on inferior material. On the other hand, Robert Garland in the New York *Journal-American* felt that Miss Channing deserved to be starred. Before the end of the run, Miss Adair had left the cast, and Miss Channing received star billing.

Any attempt to analyze the popularity of the show must begin with Miss Channing, for she received the most effusive reviews of any actress in the decade. Brooks Atkinson called her performance "the most fabulous comic creation of this dreary period in history"; John Chapman said she was "the funniest female to hit the boards since Fannie Brice and Beatrice Lillie"; William Hawkins referred to her as "one of the most extraordinary people in the entertainment world today." Nor were the reviews exaggerated, for Miss Channing triumphed over what could have been a case of obvious miscasting and made a superb caricature of Miss Loos's original wide-eyed, seemingly helpless heroine whom all the men wanted to protect. In the first place, Miss Channing in no way resembled Miss Loos's diminutive blonde, being instead a tall, well-built girl who looked as though she could deliver an uppercut to any man who got out of line. In fact, she was, as Ward Morehouse said, "about as helpless as a boa constrictor." But Miss Channing, capitalizing on her height, played Lorelei to the hilt. Just to see her trip awkwardly across the stage with mincing steps, as though her high heels were something to which she had not yet become accustomed, made her characterization uproarious by its very incongruity. Her two big songs, "I'm Just a Little Girl from Little Rock" and "Diamonds Are a Girl's Best Friend" topped anything else in the show. In "Diamonds Are a Girl's Best Friend," Miss Channing emphasized the lyrics by manipulating her voice, which ranged from almost a low bass to a high squeak; the number, of course, stopped the show.

Miss Adair, an expert comedienne in her own right, did the best she could with the role of Dorothy, but her songs lacked the zip of Lorelei's two big numbers, for they were either rhythmic ditties leading into a big production number or else conventional love ballads, neither of which had the flair of Channing's songs. Jack McCauley played the sugar daddy, Mr. Esmond, excellently, although except for the opening number, "Bye, Bye, Baby," which he sang with Miss Channing, the role gave him little opportunity to sparkle. Eric Brotherson as Dorothy's fiancé, Henry, had as his best number a duet with Miss Adair, "Just a Kiss Apart." Among the other cast members, Alice Pearce received the best notices as Mrs. Spofford, Henry's mother, a teetering lush constantly in search of a drink.

Agnes de Mille's choreography, which reflected the energetic spirit of the 1920s, also received excellent reviews. The vigorous dance routines surprised a great many critics who had expected Miss de Mille to use the type of ballet integral to the plot that she had devised for *Oklahoma!*, *Carousel*, and *Brigadoon*. Miss de Mille, despite doing extensive research into the vaudeville acts of the 1920s, made no attempt to integrate the dances into the plot, but instead devised amusing numbers reflecting the glitter and speed of the chorus routines used in 1920s musical comedies. Anita Alvarez, the principal dancer, stopped the show, particularly when she did a modern version of Gilda Gray's famous shimmy dance. Carol Channing also did a hilarious samba in the number "It's Delightful Down in Chile," and did a combination Charleston-jig routine in another production number.

Miles White created costumes in keeping with the fashions of the 1920s—they were sometimes beautiful, sometimes ridiculous, but at all times eye-filling. Probably the most striking costumes were those Mr. White designed for the final production number in which he used buttons of all sizes, ranging from small buttons used as mere ornaments to oversized buttons that practically constituted the entire costume. Oliver White, co-producer of the show, added to the opulence with colorful sets which included scenes on shipboard, on Parisian streets, in a Parisian café, at the Ritz Hotel in Paris, and in the Central Park Casino in New York.

Opinion on the merits of the score was divided. Some critics praised the melodies and orchestrations, which sought to reflect the rhythms of the 1920s; others felt the songs were undistinguished. "I'm Just a Little Girl from Little Rock," although a high spot in the show, is seldom heard today; but orchestras still play "Bye, Bye, Baby," and "Diamonds Are a Girl's Best Friend" has become synonymous with Carol Channing and is almost as well known today as it was during the run of the show.

Audience reaction to the show also differed, depending, perhaps, on the age of the theatergoer. Those who disliked the show, particularly the younger audiences, probably accepted *Gentlemen Prefer Blondes* as a true picture of the era and failed to appreciate the element of satire. Those older theatergoers who remembered the 1920s and recognized the fact that Miss Loos and Mr. Fields, instead of trying to give a documentary portrait of the era, were satirizing it, found the show extremely diverting. They saw that even the characterization of Lorelei became a satire on the wide-eyed, innocent-looking heroine Miss Loos had originally created. The outward pose of stupidity and helplessness, embellished with Miss Channing's affected mannerisms, awkward walk, marvelous voice, and physical magnetism in eye-filling costumes, made her Lorelei one of the most amusing caricatures in the history of the American musical comedy theater.

Revivals of *Gentlemen Prefer Blondes* have aroused mixed reactions, depending upon the actress playing Lorelei. From the reviews it would appear that no one had succeeded in approximating Channing's performance. Though Marilyn Monroe, who later made the film version, looked and acted like Miss Loos's original Lorelei, the part has always belonged to Carol Channing, who became a star overnight playing Lorelei Lee and who deserves the credit for the show's long run of 740 performances.

Demonstrating the kind of box-office magnetism that enabled a musical comedy to become a long-running hit was a new experience for Carol Channing—but not for Ethel Merman, who opened the following season in Irving Berlin's *Call Me Madam*. With two long-running hits to her credit, Merman gave another sparkling performance and made *Call Me Madam* her third show to run more than 500 performances.

In 1949, both *South Pacific* and *Gentlemen Prefer Blondes* had established new maximums for advance sales, but *Call Me Madam*, which opened October 12, 1950, with a top admission price of $7.20, broke all records for pre-sold tickets with a total sale of approximately $1 million. In the New York *Daily Mirror*, Robert Coleman said that offers to buy first-night tickets were as high as $400 a pair with no one willing to sell seats even at that price, for publicity about *Call Me Madam* made the opening the most glittering premiere of the season. Autograph hunters jammed the streets to watch the celebrities entering the theater. Among the many notables in that first-night audience, General Dwight Eisenhower drew particular attention because the score featured the song "They Like Ike."

Preliminary out-of-town reports had indicated that *Call Me Madam* would be a hit. Although the Boston reviews were good, the authors felt that the political satire needed to be changed, for the Korean War had made some of the lines too controversial. Irving Berlin also eliminated one song and added another. The biggest song hit of the show, "You're Just in Love," originally sung in Act I, was moved back to the second act. According to Elliot Norton's Boston report in *The Best Plays of 1950–1951*, the dancers performed one new routine in street clothes, for the costumes and set for the number were not finished until after the show had left Boston.

Excellent tryout reports, however, were not the principal reasons for the huge advance sale. More important were the news angles of the plot, which dealt with a socialite, famous for her big Washington parties, who was sent as ambassador to the mythical kingdom of Lichtenburg. Although the authors and producers denied that they had based their story on any real Washington figure, the public knew that Mrs. Perle Mesta, whom Truman had sent to Luxembourg as ambassador, had also been known as one of Washington's famous hostesses. The fact that Miss Merman was also a friend of Mrs. Mesta provided excellent copy for the newspaper stories that further whetted public interest. The combination of the Washington satire, the references to Mrs. Mesta, the Irving Berlin score, and Ethel Merman's drawing power resulted in the unprecedented demand for tickets.

Howard Lindsay and Russel Crouse, co-authors of the book, had wanted to write a show for Merman and decided on the idea of an American ambassador sent to a European court. When the writers suggested the story to Merman, she was not too enthusiastic about doing another musical, for she wanted a dramatic role. Lindsay and Crouse convinced her that they could write a musical comedy with a good dramatic part, and Merman agreed to do the show with a few song numbers. The Irving Berlin songs, however, soon expanded from a few to an entire score.

The basic plot was not a new idea. In 1904 Glen MacDonough had written *It Happened in Nordland,* an operetta with music by Victor Herbert, that dealt with the adventures of a lady ambassador sent to a mythical country called Nordland. There were no other similarities, however, between the two musical productions.

Lindsay and Crouse inserted a program note stating "The play is laid in two mythical countries. The one is Lichtenburg; the other is the United States of America." Merman played Mrs. Sally Adams, famed Washington hostess, whom President Truman has appointed as Ambassador to Lichtenburg. One source credited the appointment to President Eisenhower, a surprising anachronism, for, in 1950, Eisenhower had not even committed himself as being willing to run for office. When Mrs. Adams arrives in Lichtenburg, she becomes attracted to the Prime Minister Cosmo Constantin, played by Paul Lukas, and tries to ingratiate herself by asking Washington to lend his country the staggering sum of $100 million. Mrs. Adams' disregard for protocol and her use of American slang shock the people of Lichtenburg, and Truman recalls her to Washington. In the final scene, however, she triumphs, not only by winning the affection of the Prime Minister but also by proving that she has been successful as a good-will ambassador.

A subplot deals with Mrs. Adams' assistant, Kenneth Gibson, a rather pompous Harvard graduate who knows all the facts and statistics Mrs. Adams does not have in readiness, but who mellows when he falls in love with the Princess Maria, a romance which also ends happily.

Although the plot may have been based on Mrs. Mesta's appointment, the authors wisely did not make the character of Mrs. Sally Adams resemble Mrs. Mesta, nor did Miss Merman make any attempt to give the impression that she was playing Mrs. Mesta. Her Sally Adams was, rather, a composite of many of the roles Merman had played in earlier musicals—the brash, sometimes slangy, extrovert, tripped up by protocol but winning over the opposition just as Merman always won over audiences. As a result, the show was a lampoon that offended no one. To most critics, Merman's telephone conversations with Truman, whose voice was never heard, were extremely funny, starting with Merman's ebullient, "Hello, Harry," to her questions about Margaret's concerts and Bess's bridge games. One or two critics objected to these phone conversations, but most audiences thought them hilarious, and saw nothing offensive in the episodes. At the final curtain, an actor impersonating President Truman took a bow with Miss Merman and received a tremendous round of applause.

The Berlin score gave Merman several good songs including "The Hostess with the Mostes' on the Ball"; two rhythm numbers, "Washington Square Dance" and "Something to Dance About"; a comedy number, "Can You Use Any Money Today?" which Merman sang to Paul Lukas; and a romantic ballad, "Marrying for Love." The hit song of the show, however, was "You're Just in Love," which Miss Merman sang with Russel Nype. Merman and Nype sang different choruses with countermelodies individually; then they sang two choruses as a duet. The interplay intrigued audiences. The routine included several encores during which Miss Merman began gesturing more and more effusively and achieving marvelous audience response. To keep the action moving, Paul Lukas would come on stage and then wait until the unsatisfied audience had heard one more encore. After the show had been running for several months, the story began circulating that at one performance Lukas began imitating Merman's gestures while he waited in the background for the end of the encore.

When the laughs came in the wrong places, Merman turned around, demanded to know what Lukas was doing, and then made him take part in another reprise. Whether the story is entirely true or not, people who saw *Call Me Madam* after the supposed incident had occurred were delighted to find that Lukas had been included in the final encore and that his suave manner, along with Russel Nype's counterpoint singing and Merman's expert timing, added zest to the song.

The score also included Berlin's political propaganda song "They Like Ike," which received a tremendous ovation on the opening night with Eisenhower in the audience and later became the Eisenhower campaign song.

Instead of the usual "original cast" record, complications and contract difficulties resulted in two long-playing albums of the score. RCA Victor was scheduled to make the original cast album, but Ethel Merman was under contract to Decca records. Neither company seemed willing to make compromises, and both companies recorded the show. Decca made a long-playing record with Ethel Merman doing her own numbers and Dick Haymes singing Russel Nype's songs; the RCA album featured Nype and other members of the original cast with Dinah Shore doing the Merman songs.

Leland Hayward, the producer, had selected an excellent supporting cast. Paul Lukas, as the Prime Minister, gave his role the proper charm, dignity, and poise. Russel Nype did not have the type of role that won instant audience sympathy, but as his love affair with the Princess progressed, he became far more likeable, and in his duet with Merman he earned, as one critic said, "second honors" in the show. Critics also praised the performances of Galina Talva as the Princess and Alan Hewitt as a politician.

The cast, the colorful sets and costumes by Raoul Pène du Bois, George Abbott's expert direction, and Jerome Robbins' exciting choreography made *Call Me Madam* a beautiful, fast-moving show; Merman's wardrobe, specially designed by Mainbocher, also brought ecstatic audience response, providing the women with a constant parade of beautiful outfits. But it was her performance, above all else, that kept it running for 640 performances. George Jean Nathan called Merman "Miss Atlas of 1950" because he said the burden of the show rested on her shoulders. Further proof of Merman's importance to the show became evident when the motion-picture rights were sold. Movie producers had bought Merman's earlier stage successes for other actresses: *Panama Hattie* was filmed with Ann Sothern; *Annie Get Your Gun* with Betty Hutton; *DuBarry Was a Lady* with Lucille Ball; but Merman herself was signed to make the film version of *Call Me Madam*.

Call Me Madam might have had a longer run if the competition from other hit musicals had not been so strong. *South Pacific*, which had opened the previous season, was constantly increasing its advance ticket sales. Furthermore, two new shows which opened during the same season as *Call Me Madam* were spectacularly different enough to divert attention from almost all other attractions except *South Pacific*. The first, *Guys and Dolls*, which opened in November 1950, a few weeks after the première of *Call Me Madam*, became the new darling of the critics. And in March 1951, Rodgers and Hammerstein again became their own competitors with the opening of *The King and I*.

Guys and Dolls, more than any other musical produced in the early 1950s, epitomized the new stature of the American musical comedy as a form of dramatic art. Drama critics and historians, in discussing the development of American musical comedy, offered as proof the increased literary merits of the librettos as well as the public's willingness to support musicals with serious themes. The transition from the fairy tale plots of *Sally* and *Irene* to the serious books of *Oklahoma!*, *Brigadoon*, and *South Pacific* had been a gradual rather than a revolutionary one. *Guys and Dolls*, in a sense, recapitulated the history of the American musical theater, for it not only embodied all the assets of the earlier hit musicals but also included the innovations in plot and music integration characteristic of the better productions of the 1930s and 1940s. Conservative critics called *Guys and Dolls* an excellent show; more effusive critics hailed it as the greatest musical ever presented on the Broadway stage. Even in the 1960s, many historians of the drama ranked *Guys and Dolls* and *My Fair Lady* as the two most distinguished American musical dramas.

In selecting plays for his anthology, *From the American Drama*, published in 1956, Eric Bentley included *Guys and Dolls* because he felt that musical comedy had become "the liveliest part of the American theater" and *Guys and Dolls* was possibly the best of all American musical comedies. Bentley also said most musical comedies would not make good reading, but that *Guys and Dolls* was an exception. He was not alone in this opinion, for John Chapman, in *The Best Plays of 1950–1951,* chose *Guys and Dolls* as one of the ten best plays of the season because "of its originality and its avoidance of the usual musical comedy pattern." Chapman thought the book had the same construction as a well-written play, although he did say he wished the reader could also hear the Loesser music. Goddard Lieberson selected *Guys and Dolls* as one of ten musicals most worth preserving because it represented a perfect blending of plot, music, and lyrics. Moreover, *Guys and Dolls* won not only the Critics' Circle Award but also the Donaldson Award, the Antoinette Perry Award, the Outer Circle Critics' award, The Aegis Theater Club Award, and The Show of the Month Award as the best musical produced in the 1950–51 season.

Before the show opened, rumors circulated that *Guys and Dolls* would be a hit because it was based on *The Idyll of Sarah Brown* by Damon Runyan, long a favorite of those who enjoyed stories about the Broadway scene. Originally a newspaperman, Runyan began writing fiction about the assorted characters on Broadway; and although he limited himself to one small section of Manhattan, he fascinated readers all over the United States. Several of his stories had been made into very successful motion pictures—*Little Miss Marker* had been a perfect vehicle for Hollywood's new child star, Shirley Temple; *Lady for a Day* had been an excellent film for May Robson—but none of his stories had yet been adapted for the stage.

When *Guys and Dolls* opened in New York, popular opinion had it that the adaptation of Runyon's story had created no serious problems for the writers, or for Cy Feuer and Ernest Martin, the producers. Those who knew the careful planning Feuer and Martin had given the production, quickly corrected this impression. The producers had actually been painstaking in checking the script. Jo Swerling, a Hollywood scenarist who had also written the book for a Marx Brothers musical, wrote the first libretto, but it did not completely satisfy Feuer and Martin. Because of stipulations in the contract, they retained Swerling's name on the final program as co-author. At least ten different authors then tried to doctor or rewrite the script, but none of their versions seemed to have the approach Feuer and Martin wanted. Finally the producers asked Abe Burrows, a radio scriptwriter, to work on the show, and his libretto apparently gave the Runyan material the right touch. Meanwhile, Feuer and Martin had signed Frank Loesser, who wrote the score for their first production, *Where's Charley*, to do the songs. The producers added still another possible collaborator to their staff when they signed George S. Kaufman as director. The souvenir program, in fact, referred to Kaufman's reputation as an unofficial play doctor for other Broadway productions. Although there have been no statements made to the effect that Kaufman actually did any doctoring on *Guys and Dolls*, nor did Kaufman receive any credit as a writer, his previous experience as a director and collaborator led a great many people to believe that he had probably added touches to the dialogue or suggested some of the surprise gags which were reminiscent of curtain lines in Kaufman's own hit comedies. The musical stage was familiar to Kaufman, who had collaborated on the Pulitzer Prize musical *Of Thee I Sing* and the Rodgers and Hart political satire *I'd Rather Be Right*, as well as the Marx Brothers musical romp *Animal Crackers*.

When *Guys and Dolls* opened in Philadelphia, it was a sell-out from the very start, even though it offered no star names that would attract box-office sales. Some critics felt the show was ready for Broadway, but the producers preferred to keep it out of New York for additional work. The decision to keep a show on the road in order to polish or rewrite often adds extra costs that make out-of-town tryouts lose money. *Guys and Dolls*, however, did not. After three weeks at one theater in Philadelphia, it was moved to another for three additional weeks. During the entire six weeks, while playing to capacity houses, it underwent constant polishing and strengthening. When *Guys and Dolls* opened in New York on November 12, 1950, it had achieved the tight coordination that made its première performance one of the most memorable in the history of the musical theater. The dull spots, if there ever had been any, had disappeared; every song, dance, and line of dialogue served to develop the characterization or the plot. From the very opening scene, which presented in ballet a cross section of typical Broadway characters, to the surprise conclusion that ended with a witty gag, the action moved swiftly; the songs and dances helped accelerate the tempo, and the excellent cast made the Runyanese dialogue sparkle.

The writers had based the libretto somewhat loosely on *The Idyll of Sarah Brown* but had added typical characters from other Runyan stories, such as Harry the Horse, Angie the Ox, and Nicely Nicely Johnson, so-called because when asked how he felt or how things were going, he would say, "Nicely. Nicely." In addition to these characters, the musical also included gamblers, Salvation Army workers, and nightclub chorus girls.

The plot deals with two love affairs. Nathan Detroit, a gambler, and Miss Adelaide, a nightclub singer and dancer, have been engaged for fourteen years, but every time Adelaide tries to get Nathan to set the wedding date, he keeps postponing it because he is involved in a series of floating crap games. He has no trouble organizing the games, but he constantly has to search for a new place—such as the back of a schoolhouse, a garage, or a room behind a bar—because Lieutenant Brannigan keeps trying to break up the gambling racket. The second love story concerns Sky Masterson, a much bigger gambler than Nathan, and Miss Sarah Brown, one of the workers at the "Save a Soul Mission."

In order to promote a new crap game, Nathan, who is desperately trying to raise $1,000 to pay for a place to hold the game, finally maneuvers Sky Masterson into betting that he can get a date with any girl Nathan selects. When Nathan picks Sarah Brown, Masterson knows the odds are against him. Nevertheless, to win the bet, he goes to the Mission, finds that it is in danger of being closed, and offers to bring Sarah a whole flock of penitent sinners if she will go to dinner with him. Sarah finally agrees, although she doesn't understand why Masterson wants to go to Havana for dinner. In Havana, Masterson tricks the unsuspecting Sarah into drinking a native concoction made with Bacardi; thinking it is a flavored milk drink, Sarah keeps reordering, gets high, and even becomes entangled in a brawl when another girl tries to dance with Masterson, who finally drags the belligerent Sarah outside. By the time they return to New York, Sarah and Sky have fallen in love; but when they get to the Mission at about 4:00 A.M., Sarah discovers that Nathan's floating crap game had been held there while she was away and that Masterson had taken her to Havana only to win a bet.

At the end of the first act, the love affair of Sky and Sarah, and the marriage of Adelaide and Nathan seem doomed.

In Act II, the floating crap game is again in full swing, this time in an underground sewer. At the height of the game, Masterson arrives and inveigles every man present to make a fantastic bet. If Masterson loses, he will pay each man $1,000; but if he wins, every loser will have to attend the prayer meeting at the Mission House. Of course, he wins.

In the next scene, set in the street near the Mission, the grumbling losers are moaning about having to go to the prayer meeting. Adelaide meets Nathan and asks him where he is going. When he tells her he has to attend a meeting at the Mission, Adelaide becomes infuriated, saying that that is the worst lie he has ever told her.

At the prayer meeting the gamblers, under pressure, begin giving testimony and reveal that Masterson has lost his bet about being able to date any girl Nathan picked. Sarah rushes out to find Sky but meets Adelaide instead. She assures Adelaide that Nathan actually has attended the prayer meeting. The two unhappy girls then decide that they will have to try a new plan of attack if they want to marry the men—the idea being to get the men to the altar first and start the reformation afterward.

The final scene brings both love stories to a happy conclusion. Masterson not only marries Sarah but also joins the Mission Workers, and Nathan and Adelaide are on their way to the Mission where their wedding ceremony will be performed.

The tightly constructed plot moved so logically and quickly from scene to scene that some drama commentators said the book could be an excellent farce in itself. Whether this would be true or not is rather difficult to judge, for *Guys and Dolls* achieved its pace not only through the dialogue and plot but also from its well-integrated songs and dances. Frank Loesser's songs ranged in type from Tin Pan Alley pop to the "Fugue for Tinhorns," which was constructed as a three-part fugue, and "The Oldest Established," a song about crap games, which had the slow effect of a chorale; while "Take Back Your Mink" and "A Bushel and a Peck," both sung by Adelaide, satirized sleazy nightclub music, with Adelaide and the chorus girls almost shrieking the lyrics in high, shrill voices. Of the two, "A Bushel and a Peck" became one of the show's first hit songs.

"Adelaide's Lament," her best song, in which she complained about her habitual colds, had been written twice. In the first version of the libretto the writers had made Adelaide a stripteaser who caught cold from wearing scanty costumes. When the writers transformed her into a nightclub singer—so that audiences would be more sympathetic to her plight—Loesser rewrote the lyrics to make Adelaide's colds psychosomatic, caused by Nathan's habit of postponing the wedding. The song was definitely one of the wittiest numbers in the entire score. Each verse began with Adelaide's reading the medical symptoms for colds from a textbook and then, in each chorus, rephrasing the technical terms in her own picturesque language. This song illustrates very well Loesser's ability to develop both characterization and plot through ingenious lyrics.

The emphasis in "Take Back Your Mink," essentially a comedy number, was on the droll lyrics in which the chorus girls and Adelaide expressed their disapproval of men's dishonorable intentions in giving them expensive gifts. Their antics as they took off their mink stoles, their pearls, and their dresses certainly attracted more attention than the musical background.

In spite of the sexual innuendoes, and the fact that Nathan and Adelaide had been having an affair for fourteen years, women liked the show because the overtones were almost all romantic. Adelaide and Sarah wanted the conventionality of marriage; Nathan and Sky treated the girls with tenderness; and situations which might have been handled with vulgarity were saved by the characters' honest desire to find happiness and respectability. The dialogue reflected these desires, for the gamblers and dolls never lapsed into vulgarity or crudity, and, in fact, used very stilted, self-conscious language. Most of the time they sounded like second-rate forensic league contestants trying to impress the judges, as in the song "Marry the Man Today," when Adelaide makes a grammatical error and Sarah corrects her.

"Marry the Man Today"—in which Sarah and Adelaide agreed it was better to marry the men first and reform them later—was not the typical Loesser counterpoint song in which one vocalist cut into the lyrics of another. Although the girls sang individual lines separately, they harmonized on the last few bars. On the other hand, the contrapuntal "Sue Me" was even more complicated than Loesser's "Make a Miracle" in *Where's Charley*. In rather quick tempo Adelaide begins berating Nathan, bemoaning all the grief and heartache he has caused her; when she stops to catch her breath or to choke back a tear, Nathan picks up the song in a very different tempo and tries to appease her. In the midst of his protestations, Adelaide again cuts in, changes the tempo, and continues her tirade. Loesser deliberately sacrificed the instant popularity that the use of more conventional techniques might have brought to create a style that demanded perfect coordination and split-second timing from both orchestra and vocalists.

At least two other songs from the score had little trouble making the hit parade. The first, "If I Were a Bell," was a rollicking, rhythmic number which climaxed the Havana episode and was well integrated into the plot. Sarah, still high from too many Bacardi punches, sings about falling in love by making a series of comparisons that reveal how she feels about Sky. More than one vocalist, anxious to have a hit record, was delighted to use "If I Were a Bell" because of its infectious rhythm and clever lyrics. "I'll Know," a duet sung by Sky and Sarah in which she describes the type of man with whom she would fall in love, was not quite so popular as "If I Were a Bell," but it could still be called a hit tune.

"More I Cannot Wish You" did not become a popular hit, perhaps because, as one musician explained it, in a show with so many song hits, something had to get lost in the shuffle. "Sit Down, You're Rockin' the Boat," the big production number which Nicely Nicely sings at the prayer meeting, begins in a bouncy revivalistic rhythm that built up to a feverish climax with everyone on stage, including the Mission Officers, joining in the chorus.

Other numbers in the show included Sky's "My Time of Day," a description of Broadway in the early hours of the morning, and "Luck Be a Lady," a vigorous number sung by Sky during the crap game. Frank Loesser wrote several new songs for the motion-picture version of *Guys and Dolls* including "Your Eyes Are the Eyes of a Woman in Love," but the original stage songs still provided the high spots of the film.

As had Loesser's score, Michael Kidd's choreography also integrated the dancing with the plot as well as with the characterizations. In the nightclub scenes, he had the shrieking girls perform simple routines satirizing typical floor shows, but Kidd made far greater use of dancing to illustrate the plot in at least two other exciting sequences. The first, the opening scene, presented a cross section of Broadway with policemen, chorus girls in slacks, prostitutes, gamblers, sightseers, and sidewalk photographers milling around while sidewalk vendors rushed in, opened a baby buggy that quickly converted into a sales table, plied their wares until they spotted a policeman, quickly hid their merchandise in the buggy, pulled down the hood, and walked slowly past him. Before the end of the number, a sightseer chased a pickpocket who had stolen his watch, the pickpocket searched for the girls who had stolen it from him, and the policeman trailed the street vendors. Throughout this frenzy of activity, three gamblers read their racing forms. As the activity slowly died down, they began singing "Fugue for Tinhorns," in which each tried to pick his favorite horse, and the song got the plot under way. Kidd set his second spectacular routine in the sewer during the crap game, with the players performing what John Chapman called "A Crapshooter's Ballet" which set the mood for the climactic game.

Jo Mielziner's excellent sets and Alvin Colt's costumes, which ranged from the flashy suits worn by the gamblers to the sparse but decorative costumes worn by the nightclub chorines, added color to a technically perfect production.

Instead of selecting familiar Broadway musical comedy players for the key roles, the producers astutely cast experienced actors, who gave excellent performances. Robert Alda, who played Sky Masterson, had appeared in burlesque, vaudeville, nightclubs, and films, and had sung on radio, but *Guys and Dolls* marked his

Broadway debut. Alda, who slightly resembled Cary Grant, convincingly portrayed Sky Masterson as a reckless gambler, a romantic lover, and a semi-reformed mission worker. Vivian Blaine came from Hollywood, where she had starred in musical films, to make her Broadway debut as Adelaide. In a role that might easily have been overplayed, Miss Blaine managed to sound as if she had spoken Runyanese all her life. Those theatergoers who were familiar with Miss Blaine's appearances in motion pictures knew, of course, that she was not using her natural voice. When Sam Goldwyn decided to film *Guys and Dolls* and cast Marlon Brando, Frank Sinatra, and Jean Simmons as Sky, Nathan, and Sarah, he wisely signed Miss Blaine to repeat her role of Adelaide. Isabel Bigley, who played Sarah, was the third newcomer to Broadway. Although she had been Laurey in the London production of *Oklahoma!*, her only previous New York appearance had been in a television show; but the critics heartily endorsed her performance, and several singled out her handling of "If I Were a Bell" as one of the highlights in the show. Sam Levene, who played Nathan Detroit, was by no means a newcomer to Broadway, having regaled audiences in comedies and farces including the long-running *Three Men on a Horse. Guys and Dolls*, however, was his first role in a musical production.

At least two other members of the cast deserve more than a casual reference. Rotund, jolly Stubby Kaye, who stopped the show with "Sit Down You're Rockin' the Boat," started in show business by winning a Major Bowes amateur contest and then played vaudeville houses and resort hotels. His ebullient singing and handling of dialogue made Nicely Nicely Johnson a delightful character. Younger theatergoers may not have remembered Pat Rooney, Sr., who played the Mission Head, but old-timers recalled him as a star attraction in vaudeville. *Guys and Dolls* was his first Broadway show since 1926, and he endowed his brief role with charm and humor.

Most of the reviews were raves. John Chapman's major regret was that the performance lasted only one night, for he would have liked it to run on and on. One or two reviewers did have minor objections to the somewhat jocular treatment given the religious workers and their Mission. People who were familiar with the

Runyan stories, however, thought that *Guys and Dolls* presented the Mission workers as real people and not as idealized religious zealots.

Audiences, for the most part, heartily agreed with the critics, endorsing the show for its attributes of old-fashioned musical comedy—entertainment, girls, gags, comedians, and dance routines —and because everything fit so smoothly into a pattern. Yet so deftly was this accomplished that individual songs and routines stood out as show stoppers without detracting from the continuous action.

A second reason for the show's success might well have been its pace, for the authors moved quickly from one scene to the next without too much explanatory dialogue, and yet the audience knew what had happened or would happen. For example, after Sarah and Adelaide had sung "Marry the Man Today," the audience was not too startled to discover in the next scene that Sarah and Sky had been married and that Adelaide and Nathan were getting ready for a similar ceremony. How the girls accomplished this was unimportant; they had their objectives in the song, and it seemed only natural that they would accomplish them.

Before the end of the run, the principals had all left the cast, but the expert direction, the brilliant score, and the exciting dance routines remained the same. Excellent cast replacements enabled the show to run for 1,200 performances and become one of the few Broadway musicals to pass the 1,000 performance mark. During this long run, *Guys and Dolls* is said to have grossed more than $12 million.

Although *Guys and Dolls* won the Critics' Circle Award as best musical of the year by a majority vote, it had a serious contender in the Rodgers and Hammerstein spectacle *The King and I*. Some members of the Circle, in fact, suggested that awards be given to both productions, but the Circle overruled this idea.

The King and I opened on March 29, 1951, at the St. James Theater, exactly eight years after the première of *Oklahoma!* at the same playhouse. Some critics called it an American opera, for although it was a drama with music, it had the spectacle and pageantry of grand opera.

It was Gertrude Lawrence who first realized that the story of

Anna Leonowens's experiences in Siam in the 1860s would be an excellent stage vehicle for her. She suggested the idea of making it into a musical to her attorneys, who then contacted Rodgers and Hammerstein.

Richard Aldrich, in the biography *Gertrude Lawrence as Mrs. A,* said that his wife had been impressed by Anna Leonowens's book *The English Governess at the Siamese Court* as well as by the motion picture *Anna and the King of Siam* which had starred Rex Harrison and Irene Dunne. Most drama historians refer to Margaret Landon's novel *Anna and the King of Siam* as the source for *The King and I.* Both books, however, tell the same story. Anna Leonowens had written her book in the 1860s; Margaret Landon, who had been very much interested in Mrs. Leonowens's career, wrote *Anna and the King of Siam* in 1939 but is said to have based most of her story on the original autobiographical account. The motion picture and the Rodgers and Hammerstein stage adaptation are both said to have followed Margaret Landon's story, but they were also influenced either directly or indirectly by Mrs. Leonowens's autobiography.

It is easy to understand why Gertrude Lawrence wanted to play the capable, independent, and spirited teacher who matched wits with a domineering monarch, for the role of Anna proved to be perfectly suited to Miss Lawrence's many talents. Moreover, the story itself had strong dramatic possibilities. The widowed Anna Leonowens came to Siam with her two children to teach English to the King's children at the same time that Abraham Lincoln was opposing slave-holding in the United States. King Mongkut of Siam, a barbaric yet charming man, was confused by the influence of Western culture and Western government permeating his kingdom. He soon discovered that Mrs. Leonowens's strong will matched his own, that he could not dominate her as he did the other women in his kingdom, and that she had a vast knowledge of the outside world which fascinated him. Within a short time, Mrs. Leonowens was teaching the King about Lincoln's democratic principles and even suggesting how they could be practiced in Siam.

Rodgers and Hammerstein kept the basic story almost intact in their adaptation, except that they had Anna come to Siam with only one child, her son. The musical begins with Anna's arrival in Siam. Fully expecting the King to meet the terms of their agreement and permit her to live in a house of her own, she soon learns that the King not only makes promises but also breaks them, for he insists that she live in the palace with his wives and children. Anna tries in every way possible to make the King reconsider, even to teaching his sixty-seven children to memorize mottoes and sing songs about the sweetness of home life. Although the King refuses to change his mind, he realizes that he cannot browbeat Anna, and that she will not cater to his whims. At the same time, Anna discovers that in spite of his stubbornness and cruelty, the King has the intellectual curiosity of a child and can also be most gracious and charming. A mutual intellectual admiration (but not a romantic interest) develops between the two.

When the King learns that an English diplomat is about to arrive at the Court, he asks Anna to do what she can to convince the English visitor that the Siamese are not the barbarians the outside world thinks them to be. Anna agrees and makes staggering requests for completely new outfits for the ladies of the Court and for elaborate new settings for the banquet table. The King commands that all comply with Anna's requests. By the time the visitor arrives, Anna has dressed all the women of the Court in magnificent hoopskirt gowns, has instructed the King in various subjects he can discuss to show his knowledge of the Western world, has promised to cue the conversation to these topics, and has also agreed to act as unofficial hostess. Anna's careful planning makes the evening a triumph for the King. Nevertheless, he is puzzled by the way Anna dances with the English visitor. In one of the play's most delightful scenes, the King asks Anna to explain that type of dancing. Anna sings the charming "Shall We Dance?" and the interested King begins his dancing lesson rather awkwardly but soon leads Anna in a lively routine that combines the grace of a waltz step with the vigor of a polka.

A subplot gives the drama its primary, and tragic, love interest. Tuptim, who was brought to the palace against her will to be one of the King's wives, and Lun Tha, one of the King's servants, are in love. They try to run away, are caught, and put to death. Anna had previously considered leaving Siam because the King would not give her a house of her own; now the King's merciless treatment of Tuptim convinces he that she must go.

When she learns that the King is dying, she changes her mind.

Anna finally gets her house, and when the King dies, she decides to remain in Siam to help her former student, the young Crown Prince who has now become the new King.

At the out-of-town opening in New Haven, *The King and I* ran overtime. Rodgers and Hammerstein knew they would have to make extensive revisions before the show reached New York, not only because commuters would be unable to catch trains at a late hour but also because union regulations specified that overtime must be paid for shows which ran past 11:30. In Boston, the authors made extensive cuts to tighten the script, but they also added three new songs. The first, "Western People Funny," added a bit of humor to the second act. The women of the Court, dressed in their new outfits in preparation for the English visitor, ridicule their costumes. At the end of the number, the King objects to the beautiful gowns, pointing out that as the ladies bow in Oriental fashion, the backs of the hoopskirts go straight up and reveal that the ladies are not wearing the proper underclothing.

A second number, "I Have Dreamed," sung by Tuptim and Lun Tha, helps to develop the romantic subplot. Rodgers and Hammerstein wanted another song that would add a light touch to the somber drama, and Gertrude Lawrence asked for a song she could do with the children. The result was "Getting to Know You." Rodgers had first written the melody for a song in *South Pacific* which had been cut from the show. With Hammerstein's new lyrics, this song which Miss Lawrence teaches to her pupils became a show-stopper.

Some New York critics said that any comparison of *The King and I* with earlier Rodgers and Hammerstein hits would be unfair; others did just that, and found *The King and I* more spectacular, more glamorous, and more opulent than any previous musical written by the team. Most audiences readily agreed with these critics, for in sheer beauty *The King and I* surpassed most Broadway productions since the days of Ziegfeld. According to the Rodgers and Hammerstein fact book, there were six carloads of sets and costumes. Irene Sharaff designed elegant costumes of

shimmering silks and satins in brilliant colors, worn with accessories of sparkling Oriental jewelry. Jo Mielziner's elaborate sets
beautifully and tastefully depicted the luxuriousness of the palace.
Gertrude Lawrence looked more glamorous than she had in years,
especially in the billowing white hoopskirted gown she wore
during the "Shall We Dance?" sequence.

John Van Druten, author of the long-running *The Voice of
the Turtle,* directed *The King and I* and further enhanced the
beauty of the production by his staging of the pageantry. The
most impressive and charming episode was the scene in which the
King introduces his children to Anna. To the musical background
of "March of the Royal Siamese Children," the King presents the
children in a pantomime ceremony in which his paternal pride is
revealed only through gestures or smiles. The procession reaches
its climax with the entrance of the Crown Prince and ends with
the entrance of the smallest child.

Jerome Robbins' choreography also added to the visual appeal, for Robbins endowed many of his routines with wit and
grace. The principal ballet, "The Small House of Uncle Thomas,"
depicted the story of *Uncle Tom's Cabin* as the Siamese children
understood it and included little touches of humor which reflected Anna's influence. For example, Anna had had difficulty at
first in convincing the children that such a thing as snow existed.
During the ballet, the Siamese create snowflakes, but not the small,
twinkling kind; their flakes, although shaped like those drawn in
typical children's books, are large and ornate, with several
mounted on poles to resemble Siamese banners.

Several critics who came back to see the show for a second time
found that the score was even better than they had thought on
opening night. No longer distracted by the pageantry, they became more aware of how effective the songs were in providing
deeper insight into the characterizations. One critic, who had said
in his opening night review that he loved the show but did not
think the score was among Rodgers' best, also admitted that he
would not be surprised if he would soon be hearing the tunes
played repeatedly. His prediction was correct.

Perhaps the most remarkable feature of the songs was the
manner in which Rodgers and Hammerstein overcame the many

obstacles that could have spoiled their musical charm. Hammerstein, for example, could not write any love songs for the leading characters, and yet he included love lyrics in Anna's "Hello, Young Lovers," and made certain that Tuptim and Lun Tha had at least two love songs. Rodgers made no attempt to imitate Far Eastern music or even to use Far Eastern instrumentation. The occasional sound of a cymbal or a woodblock helped to create an Oriental effect and became more effective because such sounds were not used continuously.

The score also helped to advance the plot. For example, when Anna and her son arrive in Siam and are somewhat terrified by the grim natives, she sings "I Whistle a Happy Tune" to help them both overcome their fright. Anna's songs also included "Hello, Young Lovers," in which her reminiscences about her own happy marriage explain why she understands the plight of Tuptim and Lun Tha; "Shall We Dance?"; "Getting to Know You"; and "Shall I Tell You What I Think of You," a soliloquy which reveals what Anna really thinks about the King. For his solo number, "Puzzlement," the King half sings and half speaks the lyrics explaining his problems as a monarch. He also joins Anna in the chorus of "Shall We Dance?" Tuptim and Lun Tha sing together the poignant love ballads "We Kiss in a Shadow" and "I Have Dreamed," while "My Lord and Master," sung by Tuptim alone, expresses her disdain for the King, his harem, and his treatment of his wives. Lady Thiang, the King's head wife, persuades Anna not to leave Siam in the number, "Something Wonderful," in which she recognizes the King's faults but also extols his many virtues.

The cast itself made as great an impression on the audience as the beauty of the score and the production. Gertrude Lawrence played Anna to perfection. She was both glamorous and versatile. *The King and I,* the last production in which she appeared, was a fitting climax to her brilliant career. As Anna, she wore magnificent costumes with ease, sang more effectively than other vocalists who probably hit truer notes but who lacked her ability to emphasize the lyrics, played dramatic scenes with force, and fairly twinkled in the comedy sequences when she matched wits with the King, especially in the episode in which the King insisted that her head must be lower than his. As he crouched down, she kept bending lower and lower until she was lying flat on the floor. In the dramatic scenes, Miss Lawrence bristled with righteous anger as she defied the King in front of his Court or defended Tuptim. Anna was certainly one of Miss Lawrence's best characterizations, but it was also her last, for she died of cancer in September 1952.

Yul Brynner's performance as the King surprised many theatergoers, for his previous Broadway appearance opposite Mary Martin in *Lute Song* had not revealed the tremendous power he could exert on stage. In *The King and I,* however, he brilliantly portrayed the semibarbaric, headstrong, merciless, and yet charming monarch. He walked, talked, and spoke like a king, conveying equally well the man's fierceness and tenderness. He made the King's moments of ruthlessness, as in his condemnation of Tuptim, believable; he made his moments of bewilderment understandable; and by assuming a fierce scowl that melted into a smile when his youngest child appeared, he showed the King's capacity for affection.

Mr. Brynner had been a former circus acrobat and was an excellent pantomimist. After his performance in *Lute Song,* he had directed television plays. Miss Lawrence is said to have discovered him at a television studio and suggested to the producers that he might be ideal as the King. Brynner auditioned for Rodgers and Hammerstein by singing gypsy songs to his own guitar accompaniment; he won the role, astounded critics with his performance, and became a star overnight. But the fact that Mr. Brynner received more glowing reviews than Miss Lawrence does not discredit her performance, for the King was a more colorful character than the governess.

The original cast also included the lovely Doretta Morrow, who gave an excellent performance as the unfortunate Tuptim; Dorothy Sarnoff as Lady Thiang, who made the song "Something Wonderful" live up to its title; and Larry Douglass, who was properly romantic as Lun Tha.

When Miss Lawrence, fatally ill, was taken to the hospital, she requested that Constance Carpenter take over the role of Anna. During the long run, Celeste Holm also played Anna for six weeks, and Alfred Drake played the King during Brynner's summer vacation. In London, *The King and I* featured Valerie Hobson and Herbert Lom. The story appealed greatly to English audiences, and most of the critics wrote very favorable reviews. A motion-picture version starred Deborah Kerr and Yul Brynner, Miss Kerr's songs being dubbed in.

By 1955 *The King and I,* despite its huge production cost of $360,000, had earned well over $1 million in profits. The road company, headed by Patricia Morison as Anna, and Leonard Graves—who had played the interpreter in the New York cast—as the King, contributed greatly to this financial success. Miss Morison, who had delighted critics in *Kiss Me, Kate,* again revealed that she was an excellent actress and vocalist and intrigued audiences during the "Soliloquy" scene when she took down her beautiful, long hair and brushed it as she sang.

Reviews written by newspaper critics and by drama historians often differed in discussing the merits of the show. One critic said the production had not introduced any innovations in the musical theater; another hailed it for breaking away from conventional musical comedy patterns. Both critics were right. *The King and I* was unconventional in presenting two leading characters who did not have one love scene, or even one kiss. Yet the musical did follow tradition by including the much more romantic but secondary love story of Tuptim and Lun Tha.

Other critics said the King's death scene set a new precedent in the musical theater by having one of the star performers die on stage, and argued that although Jud had been killed in *Oklahoma!,* he had been the villain. (Rodgers and Hammerstein, however, did have Billy commit suicide in *Carousel.*) Perhaps the greatest departure from the conventional musical comedy pattern was the cast, which consisted mainly of Orientals, with only four characters being English or American. Even *South Pacific,* with its foreign setting, had used a cast in which the Americans outnumbered the natives. When *The King and I* closed after 1,246 performances, it became the thirteenth longest-running production and the third longest-running musical comedy in the history of the New York theater.

In 1952, while both *South Pacific* and *The King and I* were playing to capacity houses, Richard Rodgers again became his own competitor with the revival of *Pal Joey*, a musical which he had written with Lorenz Hart. The original *Pal Joey*, presented in 1940, had run for 374 performances. In spite of an excellent cast and score, the musical had been unpopular among certain audiences and critics because it dealt with unpleasant characters in an unpleasant plot. Based on stories by John O'Hara that had appeared in *The New Yorker*, the plot concerned a tawdry romance between a worthless heel and his wealthy mistress.

O'Hara had suggested to Rodgers that the stories could be adapted for the musical stage, and Rodgers and Hart agreed to write the songs if O'Hara would do the book. The stage version made no attempt to bowdlerize the characters or situations in the life of Joey Evans, an ambitious, immoral hoofer. Joey gives up the girl he might have loved, Linda English, for a wealthy mistress, Vera Simpson, who is willing to pay for his affections. At first Joey is faithful to Vera while she buys him expensive clothes, moves him into a plush apartment, and even gives him his own nightclub. After a while, Joey grows tired of Vera and begins looking for new women to conquer, but the astute Vera, aware of Joey's duplicity, gets rid of him before he can leave her. Linda has also decided that she wants nothing more to do with Joey. Blackmailers further complicate his troubles, and, at the final curtain, he is alone and pennilesss.

The combination of sex, blackmail, frank lyrics, and an unromantic plot made for "adult theater," as some critics called it, praising the production because it differed radically from standard musical comedy fare. *Pal Joey*, however, was too far ahead of its time. Audiences were not yet ready to accept an unpleasant story that contained not a hint of romance, and in which the only wholesome character, Linda, was also the least colorful. Many people who saw the show were embarrassed, and several critics agreed with Brooks Atkinson that the production, the cast, and the music could not redeem the story, for, as Atkinson asked, "Can you draw sweet water from a foul well?"

No one questioned the competence of the talented cast. Rodgers chose Gene Kelly, whose one major role on Broadway had been that of the hoofer in William Saroyan's drama *The Time of Your Life*, to play Joey. Kelly's superb dancing was equalled by his excellent acting, and his performance as the crass opportunist catapulted him into films and stardom. Vivienne Segal, who had delighted Rodgers and Hart with her performance in their musical *I Married an Angel,* again demonstrated her versatility as both singer and comedienne in her portrayal of the wealthy, amoral Mrs. Simpson. An inferior actress might easily have made the character seem ridiculous and the bawdy lyrics offensive, but Miss Segal endowed the role with glitter and sang the lyrics with a naughty twinkle rather than with a lascivious leer. June Havoc, in her first Broadway appearance, played a hard-boiled singer, Gladys, and her striking appearance and successful performance started her on a career that has since included motion pictures, drama, musical comedies, and television. Van Johnson was another cast member who rose from a minor role to stardom in Hollywood.

The Rodgers and Hart songs also were ahead of their time. Certain numbers were integrated with the plot and helped develop the characterizations, while others were included as part of the nightclub scenes, becoming part of a show within a show. Since the story dealt with shoddy affairs, Rodgers and Hart restricted any semblance of a love song to one number, "I Could Write a Book." Even this could not be interpreted as a true love song, for Joey's fickleness negated any belief audiences might have had in his sincerity. Nevertheless, "I Could Write a Book," became popular on radio as a love ballad. "Bewitched, Bothered, and Bewildered," often rated as one of the best Rodgers and Hart songs, eventually became a classic, but during the run of the show it was kept off the radio because of certain of its lyrics. The score also included "What Is a Man?" sung by Vera, and "Our Little Den of Iniquity," a duet sung by Vera and Joey, whose lyrics were equally frank as those in "Bewitched, Bothered, and Bewildered." The most satirical number, "Zip," was also one of the most original. Melba, a newspaper reporter, is discussing show business personalities she has interviewed; "Zip" illustrates her interview with a stripteaser whose intellectual approach to her art was very similar to that of Gypsy Rose Lee in the references to literary, political, and philosophical ideas that had accompanied her removal of her clothing. The speed of the number, its clever lyrics, and rhythmic melody made the song an unusual show stopper.

Audience objections to *Pal Joey* can perhaps best be explained by contrasting the Rodgers-Hart-O'Hara musical with *Guys and Dolls*. While Burrows, Kaufman, and Loesser either glossed over or avoided any unsavory implications of various characters and situations, stressing the elements of humor and romance, *Pal Joey* dealt with its characters completely realistically, not attempting to disguise the fact that Joe was a worthless heel or that Vera paid her paramours. The Rodgers and Hart score, in keeping with this realistic treatment, included frank songs about illicit love, sexual desire, and man's fickleness.

Pal Joey ran for 270 performances in its first season and for an additional 104 performances the next, but it was not a popular success. The revival of *Pal Joey* opened January 3, 1952, in a season which the critics had called "the worst ever" and emerged as its first hit. Unlike many revivals, which often show signs of age, of outmoded techniques, or of outdated books, *Pal Joey* appeared new and bright. Jule Styne and Leonard Key, who produced the revival with Anthony B. Farrell, mounted the show with expensive sets and costumes, and the combination of good production, excellent choreography by Bob Alton, and expert casting helped make the show a sellout. The songs had become popular during the twelve-year interval between the original production and the revival, and such numbers as "Bewitched, Bothered, and Bewildered" and "I Could Write a Book" were sufficiently well known to help draw people into the theater. Even before the revival, Columbia records had made a successful long-playing album of the show featuring Harold Lang and Vivienne Segal.

Rodgers and the producers of the revival had not tampered with the late Lorenz Hart's spicy lyrics. The innuendoes and frank lyrics that had shocked audiences and critics in the 1940s now seemed more acceptable and more palatable.

John O'Hara and Richard Rodgers must have reveled in the reviews of the revival because *Pal Joey* was now hailed almost unanimously as a "classic." The musical theater had changed since 1940. Audiences and critics had become accustomed to seeing productions with stories as unsavory as that of *Pal Joey* and were more able to appreciate the Rodgers-Hart-O'Hara craftsmanship.

Reviewers who had hailed the original production were

pleased with the success of the revival because it justified their opinions; those critics who had disliked the story were now willing to accept it as something superior to the musicals and dramas that had handled similar plots with less wit and with less realism. Brooks Atkinson changed his mind and said that the revival of *Pal Joey* "renews confidence in the professionalism of the theater." The Critics' Circle named *Pal Joey* as the best musical of the year, in spite of the fact that by so doing they violated their own constitution, which specified that prizes should be given only to new productions.

Vivienne Segal once again gave a polished performance as Vera. One critic insisted that Miss Segal looked exactly as young as she had twelve years before; another critic said her performance was even better now than it had been in the original production; still others said she dominated the show, for she intrigued the audience with her every line, gesture, and song. Harold Lang, who played Joey, was excellent in the dance sequences and more than satisfactory in the dialogue and songs. According to several critics, though, his youthful appearance was a disadvantage, for he looked too nice to be a rotter and almost gave the impression that he was a youngster being led astray by the older, more experienced Vera. That he survived the inevitable comparison with Gene Kelly and won the approval of audiences and of most critics is further indication of his skill. Helen Gallagher in June Havoc's former role also received excellent notices. Elaine Stritch as Melba made "Zip" an even greater show-stopper than it had been before.

Goddard Lieberson nominated *Pal Joey* as one of the ten best musicals worth preserving because it marked a change from conventional musicals, and because it had a brilliant score. Although this statement is true, it does not include one important fact. *Pal Joey* required expert performers who could make the story and the lyrics entertaining. The original production benefited from expert casting, but when it toured with several major cast replacements, many audiences were disappointed with the show. In the 1950s when the revival went on tour, inferior performances by supporting players who had not been in the New York cast displeased a great many theatergoers. The motion picture starring Frank Sinatra as Joey, Rita Hayworth as Vera, and Kim Novak as Linda also disappointed audiences. Sinatra's performance was excellent, but Kim Novak was not the ingenue of the original story, and Rita Hayworth, who should have been excellent as Vera, suffered from extremely poor photography.

Even by 1954 *Pal Joey* was still not acceptable to some audiences. The London production with Harold Lang and Carol Bruce received generally good notices, with most of the critics stressing the "adult" story. But an AP release in the *Herald Tribune* for April 4, 1954, said that though three of the lines had been deleted by the Lord Chamberlain, "it was still pretty dirty by British standards."

In New York, however, the revival had the longest run of any Rodgers and Hart show, with a total of 542 performances, or 168 performances more than the original run. *Pal Joey* not only became the second musical revival to run more than 500 performances, but also, by outrunning the revival of *The Red Mill,* established and still holds the record as the longest-running revival in the history of the New York musical theater.

The Early 1950s

WHEN THE theatrical season of 1952–53 opened, *South Pacific, Guys and Dolls, The King and I,* and *Pal Joey* were playing to full houses. Critics had hoped the high standards set by these hits would bring further exceptional productions, but *Wish You Were Here,* the first new show of the season, came as a letdown. Instead of advancing or even keeping pace with recent innovations in the musical theater, it fell back on standard routines and formulas. The majority of the critics wrote unfavorable reviews of everything about the show except its elaborate sets, which included a much publicized $15,000 swimming pool. Most productions receiving such adverse reviews would have closed within a short time, but through astute management and manipulation, *Wish You Were Here* became the musical miracle of the season.

Before the opening, hopes had run high, for the plot was one that New Yorkers had liked when they first encountered it in *Having Wonderful Time,* a comedy by Arthur Kober. The story concerned New Yorkers on a two weeks' summer vacation in the Catskill Mountains. The love interest involved a vacationing young secretary and a young law student who waited on tables during the day and served as a dance partner at night to earn tuition money. The romance flared and flickered, but at the final curtain, there was every hope that the young couple would be able to work out their problems.

Many New Yorkers were familiar with these summer camps. In fact Harold Rome, the composer and librettist of *Wish You Were Here,* had served on the entertainment staff at Green Mansions, an adult summer camp in upstate New York. Arthur Kober's comedy had dealt with Jewish characters and had been successful with John Garfield and Katharine Locke playing the young lovers. R-K-O then filmed it with Ginger Rogers and Douglas Fairbanks, Jr., and disguised or eliminated any trace of Semitic background in the characterizations. Both play and film developed the theme of vacation-time romance, with girls looking for husbands and men looking for new conquests. The standard greeting on postcards sent from these resorts usually consisted of two phrases: "Having wonderful time," and "Wish you were here." Since the play and motion picture had used the first phrase, *Having Wonderful Time,* the second, *Wish You Were Here,* became a natural title for the musical.

Kober had agreed to work on a musical adaptation of his comedy with Rome as composer and lyricist. Rome's previous experience had been with musical revues, including the highly successful *Call Me Mister.* This production was his first book musical comedy. Joshua Logan, who produced the show with Leland Hayward, agreed to serve as co-author, director, and choreographer. Jo Mielziner constructed a series of elaborate settings that depicted all sections of the camp including the picnic grounds, complete with a glowing barbecue pit; a social hall; the woods surrounding the camp; the interior of the cabins; and a basketball court. In addition, he created a realistic rainstorm and a fire that burned down part of the camp. The highlight of the set, however, was the specially designed swimming pool constructed with lights and mirrors that made the interior of the pool visible to the entire audience.

Because of problems involved in assembling and shipping the pool, the producers could not schedule out-of-town tryouts. Instead, they made plans for three weeks of previews in New York, a system that has become almost standard procedure in the 1960s. On opening night, June 25, 1952, New York had one of its record-breaking heat waves, but the theater was filled to capacity. Some critics were disappointed; although they acknowledged the excellence of the sets and costumes, the show's technical perfection, and the ability of the dancers, they objected to the elimination of all the subtlety that had characterized the original play. Whereas the characters in Kober's comedy had been sympathetic, in the musical they were, at best, interesting but lacking in gentleness.

The musical version dealt with Teddy Stern, a secretary who comes to Camp Karefree and falls in love with Chick Miller, a law student. Teddy's romance with Chick, however, faces several obstacles. Not only is she already engaged to Herman Fabricant, but during her vacation at camp finds herself almost compromised by Pinky Harris, a situation saved only by Chick's intervention. At the final curtain, Teddy has broken her engagement to Herman and the audience knows she will marry Chick. Critics objected to this version of the plot; in the original show, Chick had wanted a romance without benefit of marriage; but Logan and Kober made Chick unwilling to marry Teddy because he could not support her. Oddly enough, instead of creating audience sympathy, Chick's honorable intentions made the characterization and the story less realistic and less credible. The secondary plot dealt with Teddy's friend Fay Fromkin, a young woman given to many malapropisms and to numerous romances with men such as "Itchy," the camp social director, and "Muscles," the camp athlete.

Critics were divided on the merits of the cast, although most of them had kind words for Sheila Bond, the soubrette who played Fay, and for Jack Cassidy, who played Chick. Paul Valentine's performance as Pinky Harris, the woman-chasing libertine, brought mixed reactions. Those critics who remembered him as a dancer, when he had appeared as Val Valentinoff, objected to the fact that he was given little or no opportunity to dance or to do any of the sensational leaps he had performed in earlier shows. Patricia Marand appeared as Teddy; Johnny Perkins as "Muscles"; Harry Clark as Herman Fabricant; and Sidney Armus as "Itchy." The cast also included in minor roles Larry Blyden and Florence Henderson, both of whom later became leading players on Broadway.

Logan, who had faith in *Wish You Were Here,* decided to salvage the show despite the reviews. News stories informed the public that Kober, Logan, and Rome were revamping the production. They rewrote the book, discarded several songs, added new ones, and had Jerome Robbins restage the dances. Walter Winchell, one of the most powerful columnists of the time, went into action and plugged the show just as he had done for other musicals which he had catapulted into hits. Eddie Fisher's recording of the title song also helped the show. Meanwhile, word-of-mouth advertising and aroused curiosity among theatergoers began paying off at the box office. Within a few weeks, *Wish You Were Here* was a hit and Logan—in a gracious and shrewd gesture—thanked the critics publicly for their helpful comments.

Wish You Were Here is one of the few productions that began poorly and ended as a triumph, emerging as the financial hit that ran for two seasons with a total of 598 performances. Howard Taubman, wondering about the turn of events, asked, "Was it the swimming pool that dragged them in?" Other commentators looked to the mechanical ingenuity of the sets and the rowdy humor to explain the box-office success. Almost all historians of the theater, however, agreed that the show had benefited from excellent publicity.

By contrast, no one had any difficulty explaining the popular success of *Wonderful Town,* which opened February 25, 1953. The critics called it the best show since *Guys and Dolls.* They liked Rosalind Russell, the star, who more than equalled her fabulous success in Hollywood; and they praised Leonard Bernstein's exceptional score, Betty Comden and Adolph Green's excellent lyrics, and Joseph Fields and Jerome Chodorov's adaptation of their long-running stage success *My Sister Eileen.*

The smooth-running production did not reveal any of the problems involved in its pre-Broadway stage. Five weeks before the show was scheduled to go into rehearsal, trouble arose when the producer had to replace both the composer and the lyricist, who decided not to work on the production. The musical had to go into rehearsal by December 15, 1952, or the option with Rosalind Russell would expire. George Abbott, the director, asked Leonard Bernstein to write one or two numbers; Bernstein offered to write a complete new score. Betty Comden and Adolph Green, who had agreed to write the lyrics if Bernstein worked on the score, were rumored to have been skeptical about the show. Bernstein, however, was enthusiastic, for he felt the story set in Greenwich Village in the torrid thirties provided ample opportunity for diversified music. Bernstein not only wrote fourteen songs for the show but also created various musical interludes to help integrate the action.

Wonderful Town added another triumph to the successful

dramatic career of *My Sister Eileen,* Ruth McKenney's story of her experiences with her sister in New York's Greenwich Village. Joseph Fields and Jerome Chodorov had adapted the story, which ran as a comedy hit for 865 performances. The original cast included Shirley Booth as Ruth and Jo Ann Sayers as Eileen. Within a short time, several road companies were touring the country to highly profitable business. The story next appeared as a motion picture with Rosalind Russell playing Ruth, and her excellent performance made her a logical choice for the starring role in the musical adaptation.

In *Wonderful Town,* Fields and Chodorov retained the basic plot, which dealt with two girls from Columbus, Ohio, who come to New York to seek careers, rent a basement apartment in Greenwich Village, and run into a series of difficulties, mostly with men. Ruth wants to be a writer and Eileen wants to be an actress, but they have difficulty finding jobs. To add to their troubles, a strange man invades their apartment, and after another tenant in the building—an ex-football star—throws him out, they learn that their rooms had formerly been occupied by Violet, a lady of easy virtue. A newspaper reporter interested in Eileen sends Ruth on a faked assignment to get her out of the way, and she meets a group of young Brazilian Naval Officers who follow her home. In the ensuing mêlée Eileen is arrested, charms the policemen, and almost turns the prison into a private apartment with the officers acting as her personal servants.

Eileen's charm also complicates the slight love story. Ruth has fallen in love with Robert Baker, a magazine editor, but when he meets Eileen, he becomes enchanted with her. Realizing that she is breaking up Ruth's romance, Eileen maneuvers things so that Baker becomes aware of the fact that he really loves Ruth.

The original comedy sacrificed a romantic ending for a gag finish. The girls plan to move because the constant drilling for a new subway that would run directly under their apartment rocks the walls at periodic intervals. The landlord has just assured them that the drilling has stopped and the girls agree to stay on when the apartment walls shake from an explosion and the conniving landlord blandly announces that "now they are blasting." The comedy ends on the faint hint that Ruth might marry Baker. In the musical adaptation, Fields and Chodorov changed the ending completely. Ruth gets an offer to work on a newspaper; and as a result of the newspaper publicity about her arrest, Eileen lands a singing job in the Village Vortex, a nightclub. The final curtain comes down on a love scene between Baker and Ruth.

The critics were as pleased with the musical adaptation as they had been with the original comedy, and the Critics' Circle named *Wonderful Town* as the best musical of the season. Burns Mantle had chosen *My Sister Eileen* as one of the ten best plays for his 1940–41 anthology, and Louis Kronenberger, who succeeded John Chapman as editor of *The Best Plays* series, included *Wonderful Town* as one of his ten selections for the 1952–53 season.

The score, which delighted the critics, included numbers that satirized Irish ballads, swing tunes, and old home-town songs. Leonard Bernstein recreated the music of the 1930s in several numbers, but he also added undertones of new musical developments so that each musical routine became a novelty that intrigued audiences. In "One Hundred Easy Ways to Lose a Man," instead of following a standard musical pattern, Bernstein stopped the music after the third line, and Comden and Green filled the pause with gag lines that were perfectly tailored to Rosalind Russell's lightning, staccato delivery. The melody then resumed for the last line of the chorus. "Conversation Piece," said to be Bernstein's favorite number, involved five people trying to make casual conversation. One character spoke a line of dialogue that was followed by a dismal lull. Then all five characters joined in a chorus about nice people making nice talk. Then another character feebly attempted small talk that ended in another lull and another chorus. The entire number built to a climax in which the newspaper reporter began telling what might have developed into a bawdy story, but just as he was about to go too far, the other four began singing the chorus *fortissimo,* and the song, which could have offended a prudish audience if the reporter had spoken one more word, ended on a rollicking, riotous chorus.

In several of the numbers, Bernstein, Comden, and Green satirized old-time songs. "Ohio," intended as a parody on ballads about home towns, and sung by Ruth and Eileen when they reminisced about Columbus, started as a straight number, and then lapsed into patter routines that ended abruptly when the drilling rocked the apartment walls and the two bewildered girls fairly shrieked the lines about wishing they had never left Ohio. The lilting melody, however, could not be submerged by the amusing lyrics, and the song became popular in nightclubs and on radio as a straight ballad. When Eileen got a job that required her to wear a flashing electric sign advertising the Village Vortex and to sing something that would send customers into the club, she started chanting the lyrics to "Swing!" The number gradually developed into an amazing conglomeration of parodies on popular swing tunes of the 1930s with phrases reminiscent of lyrics from "Old Man Mose Is Dead," "A Tisket a Tasket," and "Flat Foot Floogie."

Almost every critic mentioned the number "Conga!" because it led into one of the most vigorous dances seen on the Broadway stage in years. In an attempt to interview the young Brazilian Officers, Rosalind Russell begins singing questions in a Conga rhythm, and the officers join in the chorus doing the Conga. As the number progresses, Miss Russell first vainly and then frantically sings the lyrics while the men dance ever more strenuously. Very soon they are tossing her about and throwing her into the air.

Other parodies included "Pass that Football," which satirized football heroes, college songs, and hero worship; and "My Darlin' Eileen," a delightful take-off on Irish ballads. Bernstein wrote several straight numbers including "Quiet Girl," sung by Baker; "A Little Bit in Love"; and "It's Love," often called the best straight song in the show, first sung by Eileen and later by Baker. In addition to interweaving melodies from the score into the music for several of the dance routines, Bernstein also injected a modern touch in "Wrong Note Rag" by using quarter tones in the harmony. Instead of sounding discordant, the harmony became most intriguing and emphasized the point of the title by making the wrong note sound right.

The speedy pace of George Abbott's direction, the imaginative choreography devised by Donald Saddler, and the colorful costumes and sets by Raoul Pène du Bois were as excellent as the cast, the book, and the score. The critics gave *Wonderful Town* the greatest reception for a musical since *Guys and Dolls* and all hailed Rosalind Russell as the star. They did not exaggerate her singing ability but admitted they enjoyed her throaty numbers, her dancing, and her antics as a comedienne, including one short satirization of a famous Hollywood rival. Miss Russell very definitely was the drawing power at the box office, for she gave an animated, brilliant performance as Ruth. Her Mainbocher costumes were stunning and her vitality kept the show moving. Other motion-picture stars who had attempted Broadway plays and musicals had often failed, but Miss Russell, who was neither a singer nor a dancer, won unqualified bravos. *Wonderful Town,* however, was not her first experience on the musical stage. When she appeared in the 1930 edition of *Garrick Gaieties* both in New York and on the road, critics called her one of the most interesting new personalities on Broadway. Miss Russell had then gone to Hollywood where she became a top-ranking star.

Although Miss Russell dominated the show, she received admirable support from Edith Adams, better known today as Edie Adams, who impressed audiences with her dancing and acting as the helpless Eileen. George Gaynes, a former opera singer who appeared as Robert Baker, added the proper touch of romance in his songs and comedy in his scenes with Miss Russell. Jordan Bentley as the ex-football star, Dort Clark as the woman-chasing newspaper reporter, and Dody Goodman as Violet, the easy-living former tenant, also pleased the critics.

Wonderful Town began with an advance sale of about $400,-000 but soon catapulted into the sell-out list of shows and stayed there until Miss Russell left the show at the end of her contract. As her replacement, the producers brought in Carol Channing. She played the role straight and gave an excellent performance, but the Channing exuberance—her trademark since *Gentlemen Prefer Blondes*—was toned down. She handled the songs, which had definitely been written for Miss Russell, in a more than capable manner with perfect timing, particularly in the "Swing" number. She hurled the gags in the dialogue effectively, but with less zip than Miss Russell. The news releases stressed the fact that this was a new Carol Channing; the reviewers who covered the show for a second time admired her performance; but the show no longer drew so well at the box office. Miss Channing toured in *Wonderful Town,* but the show was not the major success it had been in New

York. *Wonderful Town* did have a long run of 559 performances on Broadway, but showmen wondered just how long the production might have run if Miss Russell had stayed in the cast.

A recent summer revival with a well-known comedienne playing Ruth proved to be a financial disaster, for *Wonderful Town,* despite the excellence of its score and the humor of its dialogue, needs a Rosalind Russell or a Carol Channing to make it click. The successful television special starred Rosalind Russell who, once again, dominated the two-hour spectacular and made it an excellent production.

Columbia Pictures, which had produced the motion picture based on Fields and Chodorov's original comedy, became involved in contractual difficulties over the question of rights to the script for *Wonderful Town* and the price of obtaining the Comden-Green-Bernstein score, and finally decided to go ahead with a different musical version of its own. Judy Holliday, who had been scheduled to play the lead, dropped out of the picture, and Columbia finally produced the film with Betty Garrett as Ruth, Janet Leigh as Eileen, and Jack Lemmon as a publishing executive. The result was an average film which could not compare with the vigor, the pace, or the smooth integration of plot and music that had made *Wonderful Town* the great success it was.

Can-Can, which opened May 7, 1953, paralleled *Wonderful Town* in one respect, for both shows catapulted featured players to stardom. *Wonderful Town* started the successful career of Edie Adams, whose versatility on Broadway, in films, and in nightclubs has become so well known that an astute producer, who recently saw Miss Adams wearing a dark wig on a television commercial, wondered how successful she might be today playing Ruth in a revival of *Wonderful Town. Can-Can* similarly started Gwen Verdon, a featured player, on her way. But while the fresh young talent displayed by Miss Adams in no way offset or detracted from the dynamic Miss Russell, in *Can-Can,* Gwen Verdon overshadowed Lilo, the leading lady, and won unqualified rave reviews. On opening night, she literally stopped the show with her apache number; the audience kept applauding until Miss Verdon, who had already gone back to her dressing room and removed her costume, was sent back on stage, frantically holding her costume in front of her. Columnists soon hinted that Miss Verdon's role had been cut, at Lilo's insistence, or she would have run away with the show.

Publicized feuds are bad for backstage morale, but they are frequently good for the box office. The rumors that Miss Verdon's role had been scissored aroused audience interest and helped, in part, to offset the mixed reviews for the show. With a book by Abe Burrows, score by Cole Porter, and sets by Jo Mielziner, the critics expected a superb production. Many of the reviewers were disappointed in the book and score, but they were all unanimous about the merits of Mielziner's sets, which recreated the era of Toulouse-Lautrec in the Paris of 1893; Michael Kidd's choreography; and Gwen Verdon, who became, as Louis Kronenberger called her, "the musical comedy sensation of the season."

Most reviewers objected to the Burrows book because it offered no new story or unusual plot development. Instead, it dealt with La Mome Pistache, the proprietress of a Montmartre café, who hires laundresses to dance the can-can in the evening at her establishment. A stern, upright, but young and handsome judge is sent to the café to make an investigation of the disgraceful dancing. From the moment he meets the heroine and she sings a sexy song to him, the audience knows he will succumb to her charms. The slight suspense, if there is any at all, comes not from waiting to see how the play will end but to see how long it will take the judge to become part of the Montmartre night life and to fall in love with La Mome. In typical musical comedy style, the judge, instead of prosecuting La Mome, defends her at the trial and clears her and the café of all charges. The secondary plot is also traditional in unfolding a far more humorous story—that of Claudine, a model, who is in love with an eccentric Bulgarian sculptor, but who finds herself equally involved with a suave art critic.

Audiences did not object to the familiar plot because the performers overshadowed it. Peter Cookson, by endowing his role of the judge with charm, good looks, and a pleasant voice, became a new matinee idol and agreeably surprised many of the critics who were accustomed to seeing him only in serious dramatic roles. Most audiences recognized Hans Conried from his numerous appearances in motion pictures and on television. As the ridiculous sculptor, he dominated the comic scenes and regaled audiences with his agonies as he read the bad reviews of his works. He had audiences roaring at his plight when he unwittingly found himself involved in a duel with a cool opponent, and he belted out some of Porter's sauciest lyrics in an amusing rather than offensive manner. Theatergoers had known Eric Rhodes from seeing him on television, in motion pictures, and in stage productions. His coolness and suavity as the critic made an admirable contrast to Conried's frantic movements, especially in the duel scene.

Lilo, as La Mome Pistache, pleased most of the critics, who commented on her resemblance to Betty Hutton; others compared her voice to that of Ethel Merman or Edith Piaf. Although she had top billing, she did not get top reviews, at least one critic objecting to her performance because he thought she mugged too much. Lilo, however, carried the majority of Porter's songs, and her powerful voice did them full justice.

The real sensation of the show was Gwen Verdon, probably the least-known player among the principals when the show opened. Her previous appearances on Broadway had been limited to brief roles in *Magdalena* and *Alive and Kicking*, which had short runs. She had been Jack Cole's dancing partner for five years, had played in nightclubs, and had been in several musical chorus ensembles in motion pictures. In Danny Kaye's picture, *On the Riviera*, Miss Verdon stood out from the chorus every time the camera caught her at close range. In *Can-Can* she won unanimous raves from critics and audiences as she romped through the role of Claudine. Her sparkling personality, her exuberance as a comedienne, and, above all, her superb dancing, made her the top performer in the cast. Playing Eve in a humorous ballet set in the Garden of Eden, she enchanted the audience from the moment she took a bite of the apple and discovered sex. The dance, which could have been offensive if done by a less capable performer, provided a striking showcase for Miss Verdon's versatility. By the time she appeared in her next routine, the apache dance, the audience anticipated something spectacular; but Miss Verdon exceeded all their expectations as she danced with abandon, kicking chairs and sending men spinning with a flick of her ankle. In one sequence, she did a slow motion routine that was even more startling than her whirlwind dancing. It was this apache number that stopped the show opening night when the audience refused to allow the performance to continue until Miss Verdon returned for an extra bow. Miss Verdon, of course, excelled in the finale as she led the dancers in the frenzied can-can.

Cole Porter's music, especially when used as background for Michael Kidd's breathless choreography, was excellent. Even when the music is played without the lyrics, its durability and lilting quality become readily apparent. Some critics, however, who objected to the score were annoyed by certain of the lyrics, which, they felt, were often repetitive and did not measure up to the melodies. This was especially true of Lilo's songs, which repeated words and phrases as often as five and six times in succession. Peter Cookson, on the other hand, had better lyrics, especially in "It's All Right with Me." "Come Along with Me," sung by Conreid and Rhodes, had its share of Porter's spicier rhymes as did the opening chorus, "Maidens Typical of France."

Settings and costumes have not always saved faulty shows, for sometimes excessive ornateness has detracted from simplicity of plot. In *Can-Can*, however, the settings and costumes not only added to the visual enjoyment but also formed a perfect background for the action and the superb dancing. The creation of stunning sets was no novelty for Jo Mielziner, who had designed more than 200 shows before *Can-Can*. He lived up to his reputation for excellence in this production with effective sets which included a Moulin Rouge café that looked as if it might have come out of a Toulouse-Lautrec painting, a garret with typical skylight windows, and a dazzling scene on a rooftop overlooking Paris. Even the map of Paris used as a curtain intrigued audiences. Motley's costumes in the apache and can-can numbers were colorful, and were exceptionally eye-catching in the Garden of Eden ballet, with actors dressed as inchworms, flamingoes, sea horses, leopards, kangaroos, and caterpillars.

Can-Can, the third hit for the producing team of Feuer and Martin, ran far longer than most of its competitors, for it did not close until it had achieved a record of 892 performances. The rowdy comedy, the excellent production, and the sensational dancing that made Gwen Verdon a star all helped to triumph over mixed reviews.

Kismet, which opened December 3, 1953, might have had more difficulty than *Can-Can* in overcoming lukewarm notices if it had not had the good fortune to open while the New York newspapers were on strike. The reviews were not printed until several weeks after the show had been playing to capacity business, and columnists quipped that the show had become a hit before the critics could print their reactions to it. One critic implied that if *Kismet* had opened while papers were being printed, it might not have lasted very long. Not only did it survive, but it also drew long lines to the box office because the astute management capitalized on the strike by advertising through other media. Before the opening, "Stranger in Paradise" had been played at least once a night on most radio stations, often followed by the comment that it was the big song hit from the new show, *Kismet.* By sheer persistence, the producers brought both the show and the music to public notice and stirred up buying fever for tickets before the newspaper strike was settled.

Old-time theatergoers were familiar with the story, for they had first seen it as *Kismet,* a drama by Edward Knoblock, which had its New York première in December 1911, with Otis Skinner as the star. The play became one of his greatest successes. He revived it at periodic intervals, and, in 1930, appeared in a film version. The story was refilmed in 1942 with Ronald Colman and Marlene Dietrich co-starring as the Wazir's wife; anticipating the gilt-painted girl in the motion picture *Goldfinger,* Miss Dietrich's much-publicized legs were painted gold and the resulting publicity emphasized that the glamorous Dietrich's gilded beauty could be seen in technicolor.

The stage musical version, adapted by Charles Lederer and Luther Davis with music and lyrics by George Forrest and Robert Wright, opened in Los Angeles and then came to Broadway. Wright and Forrest, who had adapted Grieg's melodies for *Song of Norway,* turned to the music of Alexander Borodin for *Kismet.* The original drama had told the story of Hajj, a beggar. In adapting the play to the musical stage, Lederer and Davis changed the characterization of Hajj from a beggar to an impoverished poet but kept the basic Arabian Nights type of plot more or less intact.

The entire action takes place in a span of twenty-four hours, during which time Hajj becomes involved in a series of adventures in which he suddenly comes upon wealth; triumphs over a wicked Wazir, who abducts his daughter and places her in his harem; avenges his daughter by drowning the Wazir; and finds a new love in Lalume, the Wazir's widow, whom he takes with him to a place of refuge outside the city. At the beginning of the play his daughter, Marsinah, falls in love with the Caliph, who is disguised as a gardener. After Hajj has rescued her from the harem, she marries the Caliph. With Hajj transformed from beggar to poet, Davis and Lederer were able to build up the role of a rival poet, Omar Khayyam, and insert one sequence in which Hajj and Omar compete with rhymes.

Several theater men predicted that *Kismet* would make Borodin's music as popular as *Song of Norway* had made Grieg's. Wright and Forrest took their melodies from Borodin's first and second symphonies, *Polovetsian Dances,* from *Prince Igor, Suite,* Quartet in D Major, *In the Steppes of Central Asia, Nocturne,* and *Serenade.* The three numbers taken from the *Polovetsian Dances,* —"Stranger in Paradise," "Not Since Nineveh," and "He's in Love"—were largely responsible for a revival of interest in Borodin's work. Quite a few record companies either brought out new recordings or reissued old versions of the "Polovetsian Dances." Wright and Forrest changed some of the tempos to conform with dance rhythms devised by Jack Cole. The basic, somber melodies still remained more or less intact in the ballads, but in the dance sequences the music became a combination of Russian strains and Oriental effects and rhythms.

Critics objected to the story and the score on the grounds that they were cumbersome and lacked variety. The talented cast, on the other hand, forced even the dissenters to qualify their negative reviews. Critics praised Alfred Drake's performance as Hajj, and several repeated almost verbatim what they had said about Drake's talents in *Kiss Me, Kate.* He sang magnificently, with perfect enunciation. In a tricky number, "Gesticulate," he accentuated the lyrics and title through his gestures; he was equally effective in a serious ballad, "The Olive Tree," and in one of the few humorous numbers, "Rhymes Have I," in which he sang banal rhymes with a twinkle that offset the absurdity of the lyrics. In the dialogue, he glossed over lines that could have been ridiculous. Drake's experience as an actor enabled him to make Hajj a romantic, sly but likeable rogue and to make an incredible tale seem plausible. He dominated the show as he swaggered through the humorous, dramatic, and melodramatic scenes. Doretta Morrow as Hajj's daughter, Marsinah, looked and sang even more beautifully than she had in *The King and I*. She was properly romantic as the girl who charmed the Caliph, appropriately harassed as the unwilling bride of the Wazir, and delightful as the respectful daughter in her scenes with Drake. Joan Diener as Lalume, voluptuous wife of the Wazir, was probably the most controversial member of the cast. Audiences either loved or hated her, but they could not remain unmoved by her appearance or her performance. Instead of playing the role straight, as Marlene Dietrich had done in the motion picture, Miss Diener gave Lalume a touch of humor. One critic nominated her as a worthy successor to Mae West. Miss Diener, however, was not burlesquing any screen siren or stage star. She sang lustily, handled several bawdy lines skillfully, and radiated physical charm. Miss Diener's ability to belt out a tune did much to set the pace for the elaborate "Not Since Nineveh" number. Richard Kiley as the Caliph and Philip Coolidge as Omar also pleased the critics.

Jack Cole's choreography won approval from most reviewers, although one or two referred to the dances as being "pseudo-Oriental," or "touches of Minsky." Many of the dances did emphasize sex; the routines of the three barbaric princesses, however, were exotic, intriguing, and performed with grace and artistry. In the tradition of shows presented for "the tired businessman," the chorus girls' costumes were abbreviated, often disguising a minimum of material with a maximum of jewelry. *Kismet* was reputed to have cost $400,000 to produce, and the lavish sets, properties, and costumes explain this high figure.

The objections of the critics did not disturb the audiences. The show had beautiful girls, glittering spectacle, turbulent dances, and a superb cast. The Arabian Nights aura glossed over scenes which might otherwise have seemed dull, and the music provided pleasant entertainment. Even Louis Kronenberger, who had little to say that was complimentary about *Kismet*, selected "Stranger in Paradise" as one of the three hit tunes of the season in his volume *Best Plays of 1953–1954*. The importance of the Broadway cast became apparent when a road show production several seasons later with an inferior cast failed to duplicate the Broadway success. The motion picture of *Kismet*, despite an excellent cast that included Howard Keel as Hajj, Anne Blyth as Marsinah, Vic Damone as the Caliph, and Dolores Gray as La-lume, did not measure up to the stage version. The element of the spectacular, to which critics had objected in the stage presentation, was even more obtrusive on the screen.

Perhaps *Kismet* might have failed to become a great hit if the newspaper critics had had an opportunity to criticize it, but the original box office impetus it received during the newspaper strike enabled it to settle down for a lengthy run of 583 performances.

On the other hand, the critics loved *Pajama Game*, which opened on May 13, 1954. It was one of the few shows to run for more than 1,000 performances. Enthusiastic reviews, good music, excellent publicity, a superb cast, and a novel story kept the show in the standing-room-only class for at least two seasons.

Even before *Pajama Game* opened on Broadway, it was a great hit on the road. In New Haven, during Holy Week—one of the traditionally bad weeks for show business—it drew capacity houses. Tickets during the Boston tryout were at a premium, with brokers charging and getting as much as $60 a ticket. When *Pajama Game* opened, the critics wrote unanimous rave reviews, with many of them calling it the best show of the season.

Pajama Game marked a Broadway first for the producing team of Frederick Brisson, Robert E. Griffith, and Harold S. Prince. Although they were not veteran Broadway producers, they had all worked in the theater or in the entertainment field. Brisson was a film producer, Griffith had been George Abbott's stage manager and assistant, and Prince had worked on Abbott's television shows.

Two veterans of show business—George Abbott and Jerome Robbins—co-directed the production and also collaborated on the adaptation with Richard Bissell, author of the novel, *7½ Cents*, upon which *Pajama Game* was based. Bissell had had no difficulty in making his story credible, for he had drawn on his own experiences working in the pajama factory owned by his family in Dubuque, Iowa.

As the musical begins, a time-study man named Hines steps to the footlights and announces that the audience is about to see a problem play. Hines's statement fools no one, for his mugging leer starts the audience laughing, and he keeps them laughing as he sings about the speed-up plant at the Sleep-Tite Pajama Factory. Sid, the new superintendent, gets into an argument with a union worker and meets a grievance committee headed by Babe. Very soon Babe and Sid are in love. The greatest obstacle to their romance, however, is the fact that he represents management and she represents labor. The workers want a seven-and-a-half-cent raise, and when their demands are turned down, they stage a slowdown. This plan fails, and Babe wrecks one of the machines. The romance runs into further trouble as Sid is forced to suspend Babe from her job. Knowing that Gladys, the president's secretary, has the key to the private ledgers, Sid takes her to a dive called Hernando's Hideaway, gets her drunk, and borrows the key. As soon as he examines the ledgers, Sid presents the president with the true statement of the company's profits and forces him to give the workers their raise. Sid and Babe are reunited, and the final scene shows the entire cast celebrating at Hernando's Hideaway. Running parallel with the main romance is the love story of Gladys and Hines, who is insanely jealous of her. At the finale, the entire cast models Sleep-Tite pajamas with amusing results. Gladys and Hines wear prisoner-striped suits, with Gladys chained to Hines, and Sid and Babe model the economy style, with Sid wearing only the bottoms and Babe only the tops.

The idea of setting a musical comedy in a factory and developing a story that concerns a feud between labor and management seemed unusual to a great many theatergoers. *Pins and Needles* had dealt with labor problems, but it was primarily a revue emphasizing social consciousness. *Pajama Game,* on the other hand, offered no message. The rights of union members and of management were secondary to the zany antics of the characters, the lively dances, the songs, and the standard romance that overcame all obstacles.

The show might well have alienated some members of the audience had the action been slower. For example, one incredible situation among many concerned the president's secret ledgers, in which were recorded hidden profits. How he concealed the information from the directors was never made clear, and before the audience had the opportunity to wonder about this implausible twist, the action moved swiftly into other channels.

Jerry Ross and Richard Adler, who collaborated on music and lyrics, amazed Broadway with their score. They had written Tin Pan Alley songs, had worked on several radio and motion-picture shows, had written special material for stars, and had a few of their songs included in *John Murray Anderson's Almanac*. *Pajama Game*, however, was their first complete Broadway score. Frank Loesser had been asked to write it, but he suggested Adler and Ross, and his recommendation proved to be excellent. For the most part, the songs grew out of the plot and helped establish mood or characterization.

For example, when Sid wanted to tell the audience that he was not happy with his new job in a new town, he sang one of the few straight ballads, "A New Town Is a Blue Town." The score had variety and made use of unusual effects. In "Hey, There," for instance, Adler and Ross used the device of having John Raitt sing the first chorus into a dictaphone. For the second chorus, Raitt listened to the playback, and then joined in with the recording. In Carol Haney's "Steam Heat" Adler and Ross added a hissing effect to the lyrics. "There Once Was a Man," sung by Janis Paige and John Raitt, had a hillbilly flavor. Even the standard love songs had variety. Janis Paige's "I'm Not at All in Love" supposedly aired her feelings of disdain for Sid, but when she shouted that she had not fallen in love, the chorus of girls' voices in the background mocked her protestation. In the duet "Small Talk," in which Sid tried to make love to Babe, she persisted in chattering patter choruses in a losing effort to divert him before finally succumbing in a love scene at the end of the number. "Hernando's Hideaway" satirized tangos, and yet its intriguing melody and rhythm helped it become a popular tango number. On stage it was the basis for a dance routine in a dark nightclub, with actors striking matches for lighting effects. Most composers would be content to have one clever comedy number, but Adler and Ross gave *Pajama Game* more than audiences had expected. In addition to "Hernando's Hideaway" and "Steam Heat," Carol Haney romped through "Her Is" with Stanley Prager, even throwing in a modified striptease. Eddie Foy, Jr. sang the ridiculous "Think of the Time I Save," in which he outlined all his time-saving devices. His top number, however, was "I'll Never Be Jealous Again," which he sang and danced with Reta Shaw. Lively rhythm songs included "Racing with the Clock," which Foy sang to speed up the factory workers; "Once a Year Day," the jubilant song of the factory workers on their annual picnic; and "7½ Cents," in which the workers planned all the ways they could spend their new raise.

Most of the critics were delighted with the score and even Louis Kronenberger, who did not find the libretto exceptional, picked "Hey, There" as one of the three top tunes of the season in his *Best Plays of 1953–1954.*

Original cast albums have often helped publicize shows, particularly if the music and lyrics have audience appeal. Individual records made by popular singers have also helped push show tunes into the list of hit songs. "Hey, There," intrigued listeners on the original cast album, but in 1954 cast albums were not played on radio so frequently as they are in the 1960s. Johnny Ray also recorded the song, but his version did not become popular. Then Rosemary Clooney recorded it; and although the song had been written for a man, Miss Clooney's recording developed into another of her hits and helped both the song and the show.

Jerome Robbins had an established reputation as both dancer and choreographer, the bathing-beauty ballet in *High Button Shoes* marking one of the high spots in his career. With George Abbott he staged *Pajama Game* but delegated the choreography to Bob Fosse, who had been an accomplished dancer on Broadway, in Hollywood, and on the nightclub circuit. For his first venture into Broadway choreography, Fosse devised whirlwind routines that highlighted the action and helped maintain the fast pace set by Abbott and Robbins. Most of the dances were on the frenzied side, particularly "Hernando's Hideway." In "Steam Heat," Fosse devised a show-stopper for Miss Haney, Peter Gennaro, and Buzz Miller; for "Once a Year Day," he put the chorus through a vigorous routine; "The Jealousy Ballet," in which Eddie Foy, Jr.

visualizes what life might be like if he were married to Carol Haney, gathered momentum as Foy dashed on and off stage playing a multitude of parts; "7½ Cents" featured the dancers and singers in front of the curtain going through a series of acrobatics. To a great many people, the real hit was Foy's dance with Reta Shaw in "I'll Never Be Jealous Again." After Miss Shaw has twitted Foy about his jealousy, the two enchant the audience with a soft shoe dance. The number was all the more remarkable because Miss Shaw, an ample woman, danced with ease and grace.

The producers wisely selected a talented cast that could keep up the pace set by Abbott and Robbins and make the antics good entertainment rather than ridiculous slapstick. John Raitt as Sid had his best role since *Carousel*, and handled his comedy scenes, love songs, and romantic sequences with facility. Janis Paige, well known to audiences for her appearances in motion pictures, made her Broadway musical comedy debut in *Pajama Game* and astonished critics by her ability to keep pace with Raitt in the vocal numbers. Eddie Foy, Jr. as the time-study man regaled audiences whether he was doing a soft shoe dance with Reta Shaw, cavorting in a slapstick ballet with Carol Haney, or singing the nonsensical "Think of the Time I Save." The production also capitalized on his ability to do comedy scenes. He had audiences roaring as he modeled defective pajamas that kept falling down or performed an adroitly staged knife-throwing act that had audiences gasping and laughing at the same time. The knife-throwing act looked authentic to anyone sitting beyond the first few rows. As Foy held a knife, he went through a series of weird actions, and then seemed to hurl it at a girl leaning against a board. Actually, he only pretended to throw the knife. As the motion of his arm directed the audience's eyes to the girl, another knife was projected from behind her while Foy concealed the knife he was supposed to have thrown. Carol Haney, a cross between a pixie and a glamor girl, emerged as the surprise hit of the show. Miss Haney had been a dance teacher, a dancing partner for Jack Cole, and an assistant to Gene Kelly. In Hollywood she had done a short dance with Bob Fosse in the motion picture *Kiss Me, Kate,* and it was Fosse who had brought her to Broadway to play Gladys. In "Steam Heat" she wore a tight-fitting black suit and derby, and although she performed the same steps as her partners, her mournful expressions and wide-eyed stares were the highlights of the routine. She more than held her own in the "Jealousy Ballet" with Eddie Foy, Jr., and practically stole "Her Is" away from Stanley Prager who sang the lyrics while Miss Haney mugged, faked a strip-tease, and uttered an occasional low, throaty line or two. The cast also included Reta Shaw in her best Broadway role as a company stenographer; she delighted audiences with her good humor, graceful dancing, and ability to handle comedy lines. Stanley Prager as the union leader and Thelma Pellish as an oversized union member also added to the gaiety.

The story of the understudy who steps into the star's role and becomes a great success has always been a favorite in motion pictures, but on Broadway it has seldom come true. In *Pajama Game*, however, the Cinderella story did come true when a motion picture producer went to the show with the express purpose of seeing Carol Haney. On that particular night, Miss Haney was out of the cast and Shirley MacLaine, her understudy, played the role of Gladys. Intrigued with Miss MacLaine's performance, the producer offered her a contract, and she soon became a Hollywood star.

Pajama Game had no dull spots, for its frenzied pace coupled with its mad antics dispelled any possibility of a lag in interest. What few quiet moments there were offered just enough contrast to give the audience an opportunity to relax before the cast romped into another breathless routine. The effective sets and costumes by Lemuel Ayers also made the show a visual treat.

In understating the sexual element, *Pajama Game* resembled *Guys and Dolls*. The entire show seemed like an innocent lark, even though one scene ended with the heroine taking off her dress and the lovers going into an embrace as the lights blacked out, and despite the fact that the "Jealousy Ballet" portrayed Hines' suspicion of Gladys' infidelity.

When *Pajama Game* was made into a motion picture, Doris Day inherited the role of Babe, but John Raitt, Eddie Foy, Jr., and Carol Haney recreated the roles they had played on Broadway.

Pajama Game closed the 1953–54 theatrical season after a run of 1,063 performances. For almost six months, the new season brought no musical hit until *Fanny* opened on November 6, 1954. David Merrick, the producer of the show, called in Joshua Logan to write the script, and Logan asked Harold Rome, who had worked with him on *Wish You Were Here,* to write the score.

Fanny was not Merrick's first Broadway show, but it is often called his first important production. According to the program notes, three years before *Fanny* reached Broadway, Merrick began working on the idea of combining three plays by Marcel Pagnol—*Marius, Fanny,* and *César*—into a musical production. Merrick went directly to Pagnol, asked for permission to use the plays, and then, while waiting for Pagnol to make a decision, discussed the possibility of a stage version with Joshua Logan. When Pagnol finally agreed to sign a contract, Merrick and Logan began intensive work on the production. Another source, however, says that Merrick had worked first with other writers and composers and, only after becoming dissatisfied with their scripts and scores, asked Logan to work on the adaptation. Logan, who agreed to co-author the script with S. N. Behrman, also directed and co-produced the show.

The work of combining three plays into one musical was a staggering assignment. Behrman, one of America's foremost dramatists, had earned the recognition and respect of critics for his superior comedies of manners, with their particularly excellent dialogue. *Fanny,* however, was his first venture in the musical theater. Although Logan had been an unofficial play doctor as well as an expert producer and director, he realized the difficulty of combining all the material into a unified production—condensing the three stories, yet allowing time for musical numbers and dances.

Behrman and Logan's adaptation tells a story of life on the Marseilles waterfront. Fanny, the daughter of a fishmonger, is in love with Marius, son of César, a local tavern owner. Although Marius loves Fanny, he is possessed by an uncontrollable desire to go to sea. Finally, he does run away, not knowing that Fanny is pregnant. Panisse, a wealthy, middle-aged sailmaker and friend of César, has always loved Fanny. He marries her, willingly accepting Marius's child as his own. Years later Marius returns, discovers that he has a son, and goes to see Fanny. César, finding them together, convinces them that they owe much to Panisse and that they cannot violate the marriage. In the final scene Panisse dies, grateful for his marriage to Fanny but content to know that she will be reunited with Marius.

Critics were divided over the merits of the production, as were most audiences. One reviewer felt that Logan and Behrman, by crowding too much into one show, had made the plot too heavy; another felt that the music intruded on the story and that the story, in turn, clashed with the music; still another thought the lavish production spoiled the simplicity of the story. On the other hand, several critics commended Behrman for his skillful construction of the emotional scenes, his sympathetic treatment of the characters, and his extremely literate dialogue. Still other critics were pleased that Logan and Behrman had placed the emphasis on César and Panisse, the two older men, and that instead of ending with the young lovers reunited, they had closed the show with Panisse's death, giving the production a human, tragic, yet bittersweet finale.

Rome had had problems with the score, for he had to inject numbers that would add a light touch without destroying the basic seriousness of the plot. A few critics thought the score was pleasant but not outstanding; others rated it as one of Rome's best. Certainly it properly carried along the mood of the drama.

All critics, however, praised the exceptional cast. Most certainly Ezio Pinza as César and Walter Slezak as Panisse dominated the stage. Pinza had already enthralled Broadway audiences in *South Pacific*. The role of César was an even better showcase for his diversified talents since it gave him opportunities to display his comic as well as his dramatic ability. He astounded theatergoers with his facility in the comic episodes; and the dramatic climax became plausible through his skillful portrayal of the conflict between his parental desire for Marius' happiness and his realization that Marius could not be allowed to destroy Panisse's marriage.

Rome's songs, though they never reached the popularity of "Some Enchanted Evening," enabled Pinza to display his magnificent voice. In "Why Be Afraid to Dance" he charmed the women in the audience, just as he had done for years at the Metropolitan

Opera, for he not only sang but also danced with the young girls in the chorus line. A few scenes later, when Pinza settled down in a chair and sang, "Welcome Home" to his house and furniture, he won over the male members of the audience. His sincerity and straightforward singing gave certain numbers which might have been melodramatic the impact of honest emotion. "I Like You" a duet sung by Pinza and Bill Tabbert, who played Marius, might have seemed saccharine or overly sentimental, but Pinza and Tabbert conveyed a well-balanced display of mutual admiration, neither overstressing nor underplaying the emotional impact. The role of César, probably the best of Pinza's career, was his last on Broadway; he died May 9, 1957.

Fanny also provided the inimitable Walter Slezak with one of his best roles. Slezak, who was a heavy man, capitalized on his weight, making Panisse a charming, lovable fat man. The characterization, if played by a less gracious actor, could have bordered on the ridiculous; for instance, the episode in which Panisse asks Fanny to marry him and tells her he will be proud to raise her child requires a superb performance to make the scene realistic and to present the character as a grateful old man rather than a ludicrous cuckold. As Slezak played it, the scene aroused great audience sympathy for the older man who wants to marry a much younger woman and have the son he had always wanted. Slezak astounded the critics with his excellence in the serious, emotional scenes as well as in the more humorous episodes.

It is to their credit that Bill Tabbert and Florence Henderson, who played Marius and Fanny, were not overshadowed by the dazzling performances of veterans Pinza and Slezak. Tabbert, who had the difficult role of the young man torn between his love for the sea and his love for Fanny, brought a robust vigor to his characterization. Because Tabbert had appeared with Pinza in *South Pacific,* critics were not surprised that his voice blended well with Pinza's in their duet. He also sang the title number, "Fanny," as well as the haunting "Restless Heart." Florence Henderson, virtually unknown to Broadway, enchanted critics and audiences with her beauty and her sympathetic portrayal of the unhappy Fanny. Her auspicious debut in a major role made good publicity for the news releases, which hailed her as a show business Cinderella. Miss

Henderson sang one of the few light numbers, "Be Kind to Your Parents," as well as the love ballad "I Have to Tell You."

The cast also included Alan Carney as Escartifique, a ferryboat captain who added comic interest in several scenes; the identical twins Tani and Dran Seitz, and Nejla Ates, who appeared briefly as an exotic dancer in the dive where Marius is first tempted to run off to sea.

For a short while, several stories about Nejla Ates, who appeared for only a few minutes in the entire show, began circulating and brought her columns of publicity. Miss Ates, so the first story goes, decided to attract more attention to her brief role which was matched by her sparse costume. She therefore began cutting down on her costume until she wore no more and probably even less than the law required. The police department, notified of her tactics, came back stage at one performance and threatened to stop the show unless Miss Ates wore more than a few well-placed baubles. From then on, Miss Ates wore the costume as it had been designed originally. Whether the story is true or not, it did stir up interest in her performance. The second story concerned the life-size photograph of Miss Ates displayed in front of the theater. It is said that Pinza and Slezak were distressed by the fact that Miss Ates was receiving as much publicity for a performance lasting less than five minutes as they were getting for their starring roles. Although her appearance on stage was as brief as her costume, Miss Ates's belly dance made quite an impression and proved to be a topic of conversation among theatergoers.

Few historians of the drama have credited *Fanny* with making any innovations in the field of musical comedy, and yet the show definitely did not follow the standard formula. Instead of concentrating on the young lovers, the story centered on two middle-aged men. It ended in a death scene. The final curtain, moreover, did not destroy the mood or spoil the realism because Logan and Behrman did not make any concessions to popular romance by ending with young lovers in an embrace.

Because *Fanny* had depended so greatly upon the excellent performances of its original cast, the vitality of the production decreased as these performers gradually dropped out, but the show had a long run of 888 performances. It is also reported to have been successful in Europe, particularly in Munich, where it was only the second American musical comedy to be staged in Germany after the war.

Probably the most vigorous objections raised by critics were to the elaborateness of the production. The critics acknowledged that Helen Tamiris' dances—including an undersea ballet and a circus ballet—were excellent; that Jo Mielziner had created beautiful sets; and that Alvin Colt had designed striking costumes; but they felt that *Fanny* would have been better entertainment if it had been a play with incidental music. The motion-picture adaptation, starring Maurice Chevalier, Charles Boyer, Leslie Caron, and Horst Buchholz, followed this suggestion. The producers eliminated the music and dancing and used the original melodies only as background music. The picture was a visual delight, but those who had seen the stage musical missed Pinza's magnetic voice, his youthful, vigorous dancing, and Slezak's amiable portrayal of Panisse and pleasant singing of "It's Never Too Late to Love."

The unconventional ending in *Fanny* was far different from and far less surprising than the unconventional ending in *Damn Yankees*, the last hit play of the 1954–55 season, in which Gwen Verdon, the scintillating star of the show, ends as a horrible old hag, much to the disappointment of most men in the audience who had hoped she would have a better fate. On the other hand, if ever a show followed a success formula, it was *Damn Yankees*. The producers—Frederick Brisson, Robert Griffith, and Harold Prince—followed the pattern of their earlier hit, *Pajama Game*, by again adapting a popular book for the stage, in this case Douglass Wallop's *The Year the Yankees Lost the Pennant*. They chose almost the same production staff that had worked on *Pajama Game*: George Abbott to direct and collaborate on the adaptation with the novelist; Bob Fosse to do the choreography; and Jerry Ross and Richard Adler to write the score.

The story of *Damn Yankees* deals with Joe Boyd, a plumpish, middle-aged, staunch fan of his home baseball team, the Washington Senators. After watching his team lose a game, Joe says he would sell his soul if the Senators could win the pennant and stop the "damn Yankees." Almost immediately the Devil appears, posing as affable Mr. Applegate, and promises to rejuvenate Boyd and make him a sensational ballplayer in return for his soul. Boyd is ready to make the deal, but, being a shrewd real estate agent, he insists upon an escape clause that will permit him to return to his wife, if he wishes to do so, before the expiration date. Confident that he can make Joe forget his wife, the Devil agrees. Within seconds, Boyd is changed into young, handsome Joe Hardy; and as soon as he joins the Senators, the team begins having a winning streak that puts it in second place in the American League. The Devil, however, has an evil scheme of his own, for he really wants the Yankees to win. His aim is to work the Senators into a pennant fever and then suddenly, at the last moment, make them lose. Meanwhile, Joe, although happy with his baseball success, misses his wife, whom Applegate made him leave suddenly without a word of goodbye. To be near her, Joe rents a room in his former home; his wife, of course, does not recognize the youthful ballplayer as her husband. Joe becomes disillusioned when he discovers Applegate's treachery, and since he is still within the limits of his escape clause date asks to be returned to his former self. The Devil then brings in Lola—whom he has transformed from an ugly woman into a beautiful, sexy siren—to entice Joe to remain with the team and to make him forget about his wife. Applegate's plan fails, however, because Joe remains faithful to his wife and Lola, who has fallen in love with Joe, helps him outsmart the Devil. The Washington Senators win the pennant; Joe returns to his wife; and poor Lola is turned back into an old hag.

The story was, as far as can be determined, the first musical comedy version of the Faust legend. *Damn Yankees* also foiled a traditional show business jinx by making a hit of a baseball story. Previously, superstitious showmen had avoided stories dealing with that sport, because most plays about baseball, with the exception of *Elmer, The Great,* had been failures. (Just for the record, *Damn Yankees* crippled this jinx but did not break it, for the next two comedies about baseball presented on Broadway were failures.) *Damn Yankees* might also have been unsuccessful if the producers had emphasized the sports angle. Instead of concentrating on baseball, however, they capitalized on two popular themes: regained youth, as symbolized by *Faust,* and sex. Most certainly *Faust* has been one of the most popular stories in world literature.

From the time of Christopher Marlowe's *Dr. Faustus* to the present day, authors of dramas, poems, motion-picture scenarios, novels, and short fiction have written variations on the theme of man's willingness to sell his soul to regain his youth. *Damn Yankees* made it a little easier for Joe by providing him with an escape clause that gave him his youth for a time, and yet permitted him to avoid keeping his part of the bargain. But it was the second theme—sex, as personified by Lola and played by Gwen Verdon—that made the great difference between an amusing musical comedy and a phenomenal success. Miss Verdon was more successful in enthralling the men in the audience than in seducing Joe. She danced, sang, twinkled, and stole every scene. Even when she danced with an ensemble and performed the same steps as the chorus line, she remained the center of attraction. She played Lola with a sense of humor, spoofed the very things she was doing to entice Joe, and completely captivated the men and amused the women. During the tryout period, Miss Verdon did not appear on stage until the first act was well under way to sing "Whatever Lola Wants," a routine in which she did a voluptuous striptease that dazzled the audience but failed to impress Joe. The producers realized that every time Miss Verdon appeared the whole show picked up momentum. Before *Damn Yankees* reached New York, therefore, she was given an earlier entrance and a new opening number, "A Little Brains, a Little Talent," in which she proved her ability to handle a clever lyric and to emphasize sex with an underplayed gesture. The lyrics of "Who's Got the Pain," a mock mambo that Miss Verdon danced and sang with Eddie Phillips, were meant to be nonsensical, but they were delightful as Miss Verdon sang them while she and Phillips were performing an amusing yet intricate dance routine. In the second act, Miss Verdon again stopped the show with "Two Lost Souls" which she sang with Stephen Douglass, who played Joe Hardy.

In *Can-Can* Miss Verdon had charmed critics primarily with her dancing, but in *Damn Yankees* she astounded them with her versatility. She had a definite flair for comedy, both in song and dance, and was so intriguing that several critics, speaking also for the men in the audience, asked how Joe could wish he were back with his middle-aged wife, and, even more important, be faithful to her, with the glamorous Verdon tempting him. Although most men wanted Joe to succumb to Lola, the fact that he did not made the story more appealing to women, who delighted in knowing that an obvious but glamorous hussy could not conquer all men. Yet even the women did not resent Miss Verdon, for her ability to make fun of what she was doing converted Lola into a likeable character.

When Joe asked Lola why she had sold her soul to the Devil, she told him she had been the "ugliest girl in Providence, Rhode Island." Therefore, just as Joe symbolized man's desire for youth, Lola symbolized woman's desire for rejuvenation and beauty. She was, in fact, a feminine version of Faust. During most of the play women did not forget that the glamorous, seductive Lola represented an ugly old woman who had become young and beautiful. The major disappointment for women was that Lola, unlike Joe, had no escape clause and ended as a gruesome hag.

Audiences assumed that Miss Verdon's red hair symbolized her association with the Devil, but they had no doubts at all about the symbolism surrounding Ray Walston as Mr. Applegate. Nattily attired in a well-tailored business suit, his trouser legs were nevertheless just short enough to reveal socks of bright red, a shade usually worn by the Devil; his dressing gown was trimmed in the same color. As an added touch, Walston lighted a cigarette without using a match, but he did the trick only once. Walston made one obvious reference to his cloven hoof, but for most of the show, he played the Devil as if he were a brisk business representative of a Madison Avenue firm. He sang "Those Were the Good Old Days" in the style of a veteran song-and-dance man reminiscing about the good old days at the Palace and ended the number without giving any encores, although the audience clamored for more.

Stephen Douglass, as the young Joe Hardy, looked like a ballplayer and did his best to make an impossible role come alive. The major weakness with the characterization of Joe was still the fact that Miss Verdon was more alluring than any other woman on stage, and Joe's ability to withstand her tremendous onslaught never really rang true. Douglass, nevertheless, cut a romantic figure as the young Joe Hardy and was at his best in the "Two Lost Souls" number with Miss Verdon. The cast also included

Robert Schafer as the older Joe and Nathaniel Frey, whose voice, stocky build, and ability to deliver ridiculous lines with a straight face made him stand out in the comparatively small role of Smokey.

Louis Kronenberger picked as one of the top show tunes of the season "Whatever Lola Wants," a number that also became a popular hit. Another song, "Heart," equalled it and today has even excelled it in popularity.

In *Damn Yankees,* Bob Fosse outdid the dance routines he had created for *Pajama Game,* especially in one number, "Shoeless Joe," in which the dancers, dressed as ballplayers, went through an intricate dance routine representing part of a baseball game. The ensemble dances led by Gwen Verdon, of course, were as exciting as those she had performed in *Can-Can.*

Perhaps *Damn Yankees* did fall a bit flat in some places, particularly when Miss Verdon was off stage. Perhaps it did have what the critics called "second act trouble" because Lola's failure to tempt Joe resulted in some rather unbelievable situations. To make certain that the action never lagged for long, however, George Abbott had the actors going through some sort of frenzied motion at all times. As a result, someone on stage was always moving, regardless of whether the characters were singing, talking, or dancing.

Whatever its shortcomings may have been, *Damn Yankees* enjoyed a long, sensational Broadway run. By the time Miss Verdon left the cast, the show had become well established. Capable replacements helped *Damn Yankees* to continue playing to excellent, but not capacity, houses for a total of 1,019 performances.

My Fair Lady

STORIES ABOUT *My Fair Lady,* which broke all attendance records for musical productions in New York with a total of 2,717 consecutive performances, are almost as fantastic as the phenomenal success of the show itself. Before *My Fair Lady* reached New York, out-of-town reports had built up enthusiasm to such a fever pitch that showmen doubted any production could live up to it. Yet *My Fair Lady* exceeded even the highest expectations.

Oddly enough, some superstitious skeptics questioned the possible success of *My Fair Lady* because they felt it had been jinxed by another musical, *Plain and Fancy,* which had opened at the Mark Hellinger Theater. Although *Plain and Fancy* did excellent business, it was forced out of the Hellinger to make way for a much-heralded musical production that opened and failed. In the meantime, *Plain and Fancy* moved to the Winter Garden Theater; but, once again, it was forced out to make way for a new musical, which also failed. *Plain and Fancy* then moved back to the Hellinger, where it continued to do profitable business. When superstitious showmen heard that it was being forced to move for a third time because *My Fair Lady* was booked to open there, they were skeptical; since jinxes usually come in threes, history would probably repeat itself and *My Fair Lady* would fail.

George Bernard Shaw's *Pygmalion,* from which *My Fair Lady* was adapted, had had a long history of successful productions in New York. Mrs. Patrick Campbell had first starred in it. The Theatre Guild later presented it with Lynn Fontanne, who was superb as both Eliza the grand lady and Eliza the guttersnipe. Then, in the 1940s, Gertrude Lawrence appeared in another very successful revival with Raymond Massey and, later, with Dennis King. Gabriel Pascal, who produced the highly successful film version with Wendy Hiller and Leslie Howard, added a touch or two to give the story a more romantic ending but did not completely change the final scene of Shaw's unromantic romance.

Shaw's *Pygmalion* was a variation of the Pygmalion and Galatea legend of the sculptor who fell in love with the statue he had created, and told the story of a phonetics expert who taught a grubby little flower girl, Eliza Doolittle, to be a lady. Shaw, however, did not follow the legend completely because he refused to allow a romance to develop after the professor had changed Eliza. If Shaw had added a romantic ending, *Pygmalion* would have been another version of *Cinderella*. In the foreword to one edition of the play, Shaw said Eliza would probably marry Freddy —an impoverished society lad who had fallen in love with her—and open a flower shop.

Pre-production problems certainly did not do much to raise hopes that *My Fair Lady* would one day turn out to be a record-breaking success. Gabriel Pascal, who had filmed *Pygmalion* and who had the distinction of being the only producer ever to obtain Shaw's consent to use one of his plays for a motion picture, had long wanted to do a musical version of Pygmalion. Although Shaw had indicated that he was pleased with Pascal's film, he flatly refused to allow him to make a musical adaptation, for Shaw had been displeased with *The Chocolate Soldier,* an operetta version of his comedy *Arms and the Man.* Pascal, nevertheless, kept trying to get Shaw's consent, but Shaw refused to change his mind. When Shaw died, Pascal, hopeful that he could now get permission from the Shaw estate, ran into further difficulties; he could not induce writers to work on the proposed musical version. He is said to have asked such eminent lyricists and composers as Arthur Schwartz and Howard Dietz, E. Y. Harburg and Fred Saidy, Cole Porter, and Noel Coward, all of whom, according to reports, refused to consider the idea. Rodgers and Hammerstein also declined Pascal's offer, for Hammerstein felt that *Pygmalion* was not a love story. Shaw's statement that Eliza would probably marry Freddy, not the professor, indicated that he did not want his comedy to have a typical romantic plot, and most writers realized that they could not tamper too much with the ending, even in a musical version.

Pascal finally persuaded Alan Jay Lerner and Frederick Loewe to write an adaptation, but they were dissatisfied with their first attempts. Lerner and Loewe then broke up as a team and each worked with other writers on other productions. When Gabriel Pascal died, Lerner and Loewe decided to attempt again a musical version of *Pygmalion*. According to Lerner, their problems were solved when they realized that instead of changing the play, all they had to do was "just add what happened offstage." When they talked over the possibility of a production with producer Herman Levin, he made arrangements to obtain the rights from the Shaw estate.

Casting the show presented many problems. Most sources agree that Rex Harrison was the ideal choice for Professor Higgins and that he was signed first. The role of Eliza, however, was a different matter. Shaw had described Eliza as a girl between 19 and 20; but few actresses that age could have handled the role, for it required someone who could be a "grubby little cabbage" in the first few scenes and very much the grand lady in the final scenes. Actresses who excelled as the untidy flower girl often failed to capture her regal quality in the final act, and those who were superior in playing the regal lady were often unconvincing in the opening scenes. In comparing Julie Andrews, who originated the role of Eliza in *My Fair Lady*, and Audrey Hepburn, who played in the motion picture, most critics agreed that Miss Hepburn was superior in the last half of the musical, particularly at the Embassy Ball, but that Miss Andrews was superior as the cockney flower girl. Theatergoers who remembered Gertrude Lawrence's vivid characterization in the stage revival of *Pygmalion* agreed that Miss Lawrence had been completely superb, for she played both the cockney Eliza and the regal Eliza to perfection.

The producers of *My Fair Lady* were searching for a young actress who could meet Shaw's specifications; but other sources indicate that the producers wanted a star with box-office appeal. Several drama historians have stated that Mary Martin had expressed an interest in the show; others stated that the producers approached her about playing Eliza; but all sources agreed that they hoped, however, that Mary Martin would consider the part, for although she was older than the girl Shaw had described, she was definitely a box-office star, particularly after her long run in

South Pacific. If reports are accurate, Miss Martin turned down the role because she did not like the score. Several columnists printed items about other prominent actresses, including Judy Holliday, who also were not interested in the part. The producers auditioned over fifty girls, both in New York and in London, before they decided to give the role to Julie Andrews, a comparative unknown whose only Broadway role had been the ingenue in a British import, *The Boy Friend.* Even after Miss Andrews was signed, skeptics wondered if she could handle the role; but once the show opened, there were no doubts about her ability, for she captivated the public and the critics alike with her sprightly performance.

The musical version of *Pygmalion* went into production with the title *My Lady Liza* before it was changed to *My Fair Lady,* which, incidentally, was not a new title. In 1925, George Gershwin had written the music and Ira Gershwin and B. G. deSylva the lyrics for a production that opened out of town with the title *My Fair Lady.* The score even included a song "My Fair Lady." By the time the show opened in New York, however, the title had become *Tell Me More.*

My Fair Lady opened in New Haven in February 1956, then moved to Philadelphia, and one month later opened at the Mark Hellinger Theater in New York on March 15, 1956. Reports from out of town indicated that the production had run long and that two songs were dropped, one of which, "Say a Prayer," later appeared in the motion picture *Gigi.* A ballet called "Decorating Liza" was also cut. By the time the show reached New York, the script was right, the rough spots were ironed out, and the elaborate production with revolving stages worked with superb finesse. The critics were unanimously ecstatic. Even the reserved Brooks Atkinson hailed it as "one of the best musicals of the century." The critics raved not only about the cast, the lyrics, and the music, but also about the fact that Lerner and Loewe had kept the Shavian wit and story almost intact and had not mutilated the plot to add a typical romantic ending. If the critics had any complaint, it was simply that the show, if anything, had too much in it, and that audiences could not assimilate everything. Certainly this criticism was borne out by the number of people who went back to see *My Fair Lady* a second or third time.

Louis Kronenberger, who usually preferred not to include musical comedies among the ten best plays for the volumes he edited because he felt the reader missed the importance of the score, reversed his decision and selected *My Fair Lady* as one of the ten best plays in his 1955–56 selection. The Critics' Circle, as had been expected, named it as the best musical of the season. It also received more than one third of the Tony Awards.

My Fair Lady reflected old-style elegance, for although it represented an investment of over $400,000, a figure that has become common in the 1960s, it looked far more opulent than a great many shows which had cost as much, if not more, to produce. For sheer beauty, *My Fair Lady* excelled most of the shows which had been presented on Broadway since the 1920s, and some critics insisted that it outshone even the glittering extravaganzas of that era.

If there had been any doubt about the success of the show before its opening, the rave reviews and the stampeding lines at the box office soon indicated that *My Fair Lady* would be a financial record-breaker. Scalpers' prices for under-the-counter tickets soared. It is impossible to state accurately just how much brokers charged for these tickets, for figures are sometimes exaggerated and sometimes hushed to prevent investigations, but $100 a ticket would not be an unreasonable estimate. Even in the second and third years of the run, some brokers were charging $12.50 for matinee tickets. During the second year of the run, one man told his ticket agent that he wanted two seats for that evening's performance, that he did not care if the seats were not together, and that he would not quibble over the price. He listened as the broker called one number after another and finally said, "I've called every ticket blood bank in New York and I can't even get you standing room for tonight."

The phenomenal success of *My Fair Lady* has been attributed to many causes, but among the most important factors were Lerner's lyrics, which, as in "I've Grown Accustomed to Her Face," allowed audiences to hope for an eventual happy reunion of Liza and Higgins. Lerner also did more than merely show what happened offstage in *Pygmalion*. In Shaw's play, Eliza tried out her new diction and fascinated Freddy at a tea party in the home of Professor Higgins' mother. Lerner changed the scene to a box at the races; and, although the basic dialogue remained almost the same, the new setting and stunning costumes transformed the quiet tea party into an elaborate production sequence. Lerner, however, did add the scene at the Embassy Ball. The stately procession, the swirling dancers, and the extravagant beauty of the costumes and setting made a brilliant spectacle for an episode that had only been described in Shaw's play. A summary of the musical numbers reveals how cleverly the writers inserted and integrated songs to augment the original plot.

The first scene opens in Covent Garden, where Professor Higgins, a student of speech patterns, is taking notes on the various dialects he hears about him and surprising people by revealing that he can tell what part of England they have lived in from their conversation. To explain what he is doing, Higgins sings, "Why Can't the English," in which he complains about the various dialects in which the English speak. Higgins is interested for a brief moment in the gutteral sounds uttered by Eliza, a flower girl; when she demands to know what he has written about her, he repeats the words she has mumbled with exactly the same intonation. Higgins then meets Colonel Pickering, another linguist, and boasts to Pickering that he could teach even Eliza to speak and act like a lady. When they leave, Eliza tries to imagine what the new life the professor has described might be like in the song "Wouldn't It Be Loverly?"

In the next scene, Eliza comes to the professor's house to take lessons. At first, the professor is not interested in teaching her, although he still boasts that he could transform Eliza—whom he says is so "deliciously low"—and pass her off as nobility; but finally he accepts Pickering's challenge to effect the transformation. Once the lessons begin, the professor becomes exasperated with Eliza's slow progress. His annoyance prompts him to sing "I'm an Ordinary Man," in which he enumerates the irritating habits of women to explain why he will never allow one in his life. Liza, on the other hand, is just as distraught with the professor's constant badgering. To show how much she hates him, she sings "Just You Wait," and states that when she becomes a lady she will show him no mercy, regardless of how much trouble he is in.

As part of her elocution drill, Higgins has Eliza repeat "The rain in Spain stays mainly in the plain" and "In Hartford, Hereford, and Hampshire, hurricanes hardly happen"—lines, incidentally, taken directly from Shaw's play. At the moment when the professor and the audience are beginning to doubt whether Eliza will ever get them right, she suddenly pronounces the words correctly. The startled professor asks her to repeat the lines, and this time she begins to sing them. The disjointed sentences blend into a unified musical number that ends with Eliza, Professor Higgins, and Colonel Pickering all dancing in jubilation.

"The Rain in Spain" was definitely a show-stopper—and also became a popular orchestral number—but Lerner and Loewe performed the almost impossible task of following it with a song that became even more popular. After Eliza has danced with Higgins and Colonel Pickering, the housekeeper tries to get her to go to sleep; but Eliza, still excited from her success, sings, "I Could Have Danced All Night," a song that became an instant hit.

When the professor thinks Eliza is ready to make an appearance in public, he takes her to his mother's box at the Ascot Race Track. To set the mood, the chorus sings "The Ascot Gavotte," a lampoon of British reticence, with the singers showing no emotional reaction as they watch the races. This amusing number, exquisitely costumed and staged, serves as background for Eliza's debut into society. Unlike the other spectators who stand as frozenfaced as they did in the opening song, she cannot control her emotions as she watches the race, and at the climax shouts a cockney vulgarity that shocks everyone on stage as the lights black out.

Young Freddy Eynsford-Hill, one of Mrs. Higgins' guests, has become enchanted with Eliza. In the next scene—set in front of the professor's home—Freddy comes to call, but Eliza, humiliated, refuses to see him. In the ballad, "On the Street Where You Live," he sings about his feelings for her. Rumor has it that one or two critics suggested cutting the number because it did little for the action, but the producer decided to leave it in, and the song became one of the most popular hits from the score. It also provided the necessary lapse of time for Eliza and Higgins to change into costumes for the grand ball.

The professor and Colonel Pickering escort an exquisitely

gowned and jeweled Eliza, and, to the strains of one of Loewe's most delightful waltzes, "The Embassy Waltz," the first act climaxes in a resplendent ballroom scene with couples whirling across the floor in a setting as elaborate as any presented in the old-fashioned operettas.

As the second act opens, Higgins and Pickering are elated. Eliza has been a triumphant sensation and has fooled even a language expert who had hoped to expose her. In their joy, Higgins and Pickering sing, "You Did It," praising each other but completely ignoring Eliza. Finally, giving vent to her rage, Eliza gives back the jewels, demands to know what clothing she may keep, and completely exasperates and bewilders Higgins, who calls her ungrateful. Eliza storms out of the house, meets Freddy again, and sings "Show Me," insisting that he make love to her. The poor fellow, however, has no opportunity even to approach the raging Eliza who storms up and down the stage as she sings.

The next morning, when the professor finds that Eliza has gone, he asks Colonel Pickering why women can't be more reasonable and act like men. He half sings, half talks, "Hymn to Him," detailing the superior male virtues. Finally Higgins locates Eliza at his mother's home. She insists that she is now quite independent and can get along very well "Without You." Returning home, Higgins soliloquizes "I've Grown Accustomed to Her Face," the nearest thing to a love song in the show; he muses about how he has grown used to Eliza; the rhythm of the song changes, and he insists that he would not care what happened to her; yet he always returns somewhat wistfully to "I've Grown Accustomed to Her Face." This song gave the Shavian romance the touch it needed to make audiences realize that the stubborn professor had become fond of Eliza. In the brief final scene, Eliza comes back to the house and finds Higgins listening to a recording he has made of her voice. Eliza turns off the record and continues speaking the lines. The professor looks up, smiles in relief at the audience, but slouches down in the chair and pulls his hat over his eyes so that Eliza cannot see his expression of joy.

Not all of the music was so well integrated into the plot, for Lerner and Loewe did insert two English music hall numbers for Stanley Holloway, who played Alfred P. Doolittle, Eliza's father.

The songs, although delightful, did not advance the main plot but did give the show a definite change of pace and helped to characterize Doolittle. Eliza's father played a more important part in Shaw's *Pygmalion*. In the musical adaptation, his role may have been just as long, but Lerner and Loewe substituted two songs for some of his philosophical speeches; the change gave the musical variety and provided an opportunity for two rousing dance ensembles. The first, "With a Little Bit of Luck," introduces Doolittle to the audience and explains his philosophy of easy living. The song, which he sings with some of his cronies outside a pub, starts simply enough but develops into a full-scale production number. When Doolittle hears that Eliza is living with the professor, he comes to the house with blackmail on his mind. The professor, who at first is ready to throw him out, soon becomes so intrigued by Doolittle's lyrical way of speaking and by his philosophy that he recommends him as a lecturer. The last act finds Doolittle a successful lecturer, bogged down by "middle-class morality," and feeling that he should marry the woman with whom he has been living. He celebrates his last night of freedom with "Get Me to the Church on Time," a song which also develops into a lively production number. To some Shavian admirers, the lyrics for both songs may not seem as pungent as Doolittle's speeches in *Pygmalion*, but to musical comedy devotees, they are far more effective as songs than they would have been as dialogue.

Not everyone was enchanted with the score of *My Fair Lady*, although it should be noted that the dissenters were in the distinct minority. *Variety* carried a story that the composer Rudolf Friml attended a performance of *My Fair Lady* in London but walked out, saying that the score was not of the type he would call music. Other musicians who agreed with Friml were dismayed by the patter-style of Rex Harrison, although they admitted that he did it superbly. There can be no denying the fact that some of Higgins's numbers could scarcely be called songs; but Rex Harrison, Edward Mulhare, Michael Allinson, and all the men who later played Higgins, were selected for their acting ability rather than their ability to sing. The popularity of the score is particularly evident in the sale of original cast albums. Columbia Records, which had provided all the backing for the show, not only earned a fortune on its original investment but also gleaned a fabulous sum from the recording, which outsold every other original cast album issued up to that time. When the show opened in London, Columbia rerecorded it in stereo.

The production, as well as the spirited choreography devised by Hanya Holm, enhanced the score. Expert lighting by Feder blended beautifully with Cecil Beaton's costumes and Oliver Smith's intriguing stage settings, which reflected the England of 1912 with elegance. Beaton achieved striking color combinations, particularly in the Ascot Race scene. The girls of the chorus all wore outfits of black and white. By way of contrast, Miss Andrews appeared in a pink gown and hat, and Cathleen Nesbitt as Mrs. Higgins wore gray. The glittering, jeweled costumes for the Embassy Ball made the scene one of lavish beauty. Beaton and Smith achieved the same opulence even in the Covent Garden scenes, for the opening episode contrasted the grubby flower workers with the elegant society folk who waited outside the theater trying to get taxis; in the "Get Me to the Church on Time" sequence some of the outfits represented the Cockney music hall styles, with several of the dancers resplendent in button costumes.

Moss Hart, expert dramatist and director for many Broadway hits, undertook the job of directing, and not only whipped the show into its perfect form for the Broadway opening but also maintained the original perfection of timing and pace with each change in cast.

The importance of the original cast in establishing *My Fair Lady* as a resounding hit cannot be minimized. In Shaw's *Pygmalion,* Eliza had the starring role, but in *My Fair Lady,* Higgins, particularly as played by Rex Harrison, dominated the action. Higgins' vocal artificialities, his tantrums, his smug confidence, his aloofness towards Eliza, and his snobbish contempt for her, should have made him a despicable character, and yet Harrison made the professor warm, alive, and strangely sympathetic. Harrison's dramatic finesse and perfect enunciation helped him triumph over the singing requirement and enabled him to dominate the stage in the dramatic sequences. Stanley Holloway, an English music hall favorite, delighted audiences with his portrayal of Alfred Doolittle; he excelled in the musical numbers, and cleverly portrayed the man in the dramatic scenes, getting the maximum audience reaction with his handling of Doolittle's philosophical speeches about middle-class manners and morality.

Julie Andrews, a comparative novice in the theater, might easily have been overshadowed by Harrison's ebullience and Holloway's bubbling humor, but she had beauty, a clear voice, and the youthful qualities Shaw had specified for Elisa. By the time the show reached Broadway, Miss Andrews played the role with assurance and was overshadowed by no one.

Most of the critics praised Robert Coote, who was properly stuffy and yet charming as Colonel Pickering; several singled out Cathleen Nesbitt, who played Higgins' mother with wit and elegance, combining warmth toward Eliza with amusement at her son's inability to cope with the girl he had transformed. In his role of Freddy, John Michael King, son of Broadway star Dennis King, made "On the Street Where You Live" one of the score's big hits.

The excellent cast helped the fabulous ticket sales, but box office returns did not diminish when Rex Harrison became the first member of the original cast to leave the show. While *My Fair Lady* continued to do standing-room-only business in New York, Miss Andrews, Mr. Holloway, Mr. Coote, and Mr. Harrison were playing their original roles in the London production. Before the show had completed its run on Broadway, Sally Ann Howes, Pamela Charles, Lola Fisher, Rosemary Rainier, and Margot Moser were some of the actresses who had played Eliza; Edward Mulhare, Michael Allinson, and Tom Helmore were among Rex Harrison's replacements; veteran actor Melville Cooper had a turn in the show as Colonel Pickering, as did veteran motion-picture actor Reginald Denny.

Road companies of *My Fair Lady* also flourished. Brian Aherne and Anne Rogers played the leads in the national touring company and were later replaced by Michael Evans and Diane Todd. Ronald Drake, Carolyn Dixon, and Gaylea Byrne also played in touring companies. Ray Milland played several very successful engagements as Professor Higgins in summer theaters. (Omission of names of principals who played leading roles is not an oversight, for members of the national company were rather frequently replaced by new players while the stars of the touring company took over the roles in New York.)

During the first year or so of the run, when having tickets for the show was a status symbol, audiences may have consisted mostly of out-of-town buyers on expense accounts, or theater parties that had pre-booked the show; but after the show had run for several years and tickets became more available, the show drew a different type of audience—it seemed to become family entertainment. Parents found that children enjoyed the show and that it was singularly free from crudity and nudity.

My Fair Lady broke records not only for number of consecutive performances and gross receipts in New York, but also, possibly, for number of performances given all over the world. Within a few years the show became internationally known, with companies in Australia, Sweden, and Mexico. Four years after the show had opened on Broadway, it was running simultaneously in London, Oslo, Stockholm, Melbourne, Copenhagen, and Helsinki. It was also presented in Amsterdam, Moscow, and Israel.

The motion picture also set a financial precedent, with Warner Brothers paying the record-breaking sum of $5 million for the screen rights. The producers signed Rex Harrison to repeat his stage role, but instead of signing Julie Andrews, they selected Audrey Hepburn, whose name, they felt, meant more at the box office. Failure to sign a stage actress to repeat her original role had been standard practice in Hollywood for years, because film producers preferred to use an established screen star who would attract motion picture audiences all over the country rather than a stage actress who would be unknown outside of the New York area. After the newspaper columnists had stopped discussing the unfairness of the casting, the incident might have died down had Miss Andrews not gone to Hollywood to appear in Walt Disney's film *Mary Poppins,* which turned out to be a great box-office hit. For her performance in that film, Miss Andrews was nominated for an Oscar; Miss Hepburn, on the other hand, did not receive a nomination for playing Eliza because she had not sung the songs. Columnists immediately pointed out the unfairness of excluding Miss Hepburn, because Deborah Kerr had been nominated for her performance in *The King and I* and she had also used a voice double for the songs. The rivalry between Miss Andrews and Miss Hepburn culminated on the night of the Academy Awards. Miss Hepburn presented an Oscar to Rex Harrison for his performance as Professor Higgins. That same night Miss Andrews received an Oscar for playing Mary Poppins. Harrison, the suave diplomat, helped smooth over the situation by thanking both Elizas who had helped him win the award.

Although *My Fair Lady* lacks the distinction of winning a Pulitzer Prize for drama, most judges who would not have voted for it as they did for *Of Thee I Sing* or *South Pacific* would agree with theater critics who have said that *My Fair Lady* represents literary distinction in the American musical theater if only because it remained faithful to the drama by Shaw.

With a total of 2,717 performances, *My Fair Lady* became the longest-running musical comedy and the third longest-running dramatic presentation in the history of the New York theater, exceeded only by *Tobacco Road* and *Life with Father*. It should be noted that *My Fair Lady* did operate in its final year on a two-tickets-for-the-price-of-one policy. Even so, many showmen wondered why the producers closed the show, since it was still playing to profitable houses.

With rising production costs, higher admission prices, and constant cast changes in most hit musicals, it is extremely difficult to predict whether any current musicals, such as *Hello, Dolly!* or *Fiddler on the Roof* will exceed the record established by *My Fair Lady*. The arrival of newer hit musicals, changing economic conditions, or even changes in public taste might influence the length of runs for productions which could be possible contenders for the longevity record and still keep *My Fair Lady* in its top position as the longest-running musical comedy in the history of Broadway.

The Late 1950s

ANY CONVENTIONAL musical production that followed *My
Fair Lady* would have suffered by comparison, but, fortunately,
The Most Happy Fella, which opened in May 1956, only a few
weeks after the première of the Lerner and Loewe record-breaking
hit, differed not only from most musical productions of the 1950s
but also from most musical hits of the past twenty years. Instead of
following standard patterns in dialogue and songs, Frank Loesser,
who wrote book, score, and lyrics, virtually developed the whole
plot through musical numbers that ranged from Broadway and
Tin Pan Alley jukebox tunes to arias, duets, and quartets that
were closer to grand opera.

Loesser based his musical on Sidney Howard's Pulitzer Prize
play *They Knew What They Wanted,* which the Theatre Guild
had produced in 1924 with Richard Bennett, Pauline Lord, and
Glenn Anders in the leading roles. According to Loesser, Samuel
Taylor had originally suggested that he write a musical adaptation
of Howard's drama. At first Loesser had not been convinced that
the suggestion was a good one, but he became more interested
when he realized that despite its serious plot, the play had ample
touches of humor.

Howard's drama dealt with Tony, a middle-aged winegrower
from Napa Valley, California, who writes a letter proposing marriage to Amy, a waitress he had seen in a San Francisco restaurant;
instead of enclosing his own picture, however, he sends a photograph of Joe, his young and handsome hired hand. Amy accepts
the proposal and arrives in Napa Valley. Recognizing Joe from his
photograph, she cannot understand why he acts so aloof. Meanwhile, Tony, en route to meet Amy at the station, has become

involved in an automobile accident and has broken both his legs. Only after he has been brought home does Amy realize that she has been duped and that she is to marry the elderly Tony. Having no job and no money to return to San Francisco, Amy decides to go through with the wedding ceremony that had been scheduled for that day. Later that night, Amy comes out of the house to be alone and breaks into tears. Joe finds her and tries to calm her by giving her a consoling kiss which soon develops into a passionate embrace. The audience later learns that Joe and Amy have slept together.

After her one liaison with Joe, Amy ignores him and devotes herself to taking care of Tony. When she finds that she is pregnant with Joe's child, she feels that she must leave. Tony, however, forgives Amy, asks her to stay, saying that he would be happy to have the world think the child is his.

Howard had based his play on the story of Paolo and Francesca, which dealt with an older man whose wife and friend had betrayed him and who kills them both in revenge. In Howard's adaptation, however, all three characters remain alive.

Loesser kept Howard's story basically intact except for several changes which updated the script. He eliminated one absurd scene in which Joe and the priest find out that Amy is pregnant before she does. In a recent revival of the drama, audiences had laughed during this entire absurd sequence. Loesser, however, has Amy (or Rosabella, as she is called in the musical) collapse while dancing with the workers on the wine ranch. When the doctor examines her, he tells her that she is pregnant. The revival of Howard's drama had also revealed that many of his references to Joe's affiliation with the I.W.W. were dated. In his musical adaptation, Loesser cut all irrelevant and dated political discussions. Howard had also used the priest to act as a Greek chorus expressing doubt about the marriage, and, at times, offering comfort to both Tony and Rosabella. Loesser eliminated the role of the priest and gave some of his speeches to the benign doctor; he used Maria, Tony's sister, to express skepticism and objections to the marriage. Furthermore, by emphasizing the music, Loesser built up the emotional impact of the story and created greater sympathy for both Tony and Rosabella.

The Most Happy Fella became Loesser's third straight long-running success, following *Where's Charley* and *Guys and Dolls*. Along with Cole Porter, Irving Berlin, and Harold Rome, Loesser had established a reputation for writing both music and lyrics, but for *The Most Happy Fella,* he added a third accomplishment by writing the dramatic adaptation. The task was a difficult one that required almost four years, for Loesser used little dialogue but instead developed the story through more than thirty musical numbers, in a score that is said to have been almost as long as that of *Porgy and Bess.* Because of the numerous musical selections, the program did not list individual songs or performers. Loesser called his work a "musical," although it was operatic in conception and included arias, trios, and quartets, as well as songs that were typical musical comedy production numbers. All the songs, despite their variety, not only evolved from the dramatic situations but also helped develop the characterizations. The typical show tunes which became the hits of the production included "Standing on the Corner," sung by a male quartet of girl-watchers; "Big D," a song extolling the virtues of Dallas and setting the background for a full-scale ensemble routine; and "Happy to Make Your Acquaintance," which revealed that Rosabella was growing fond of her husband. Two show-stoppers, "Abbondanza" and "Benvenuta," sung by a trio of Italian workers on the ranch, cleverly satirized Italian operatic trios. The ballads included Rosabella's haunting "Somebody, Somewhere," and Tony's love song, "My Heart Is So Full of You." Many critics rated "How Beautiful the Days," sung by Tony, Rosabella, Joe, and Maria, as the best ballad in the score. Joe also had two show-stoppers in "Joey, Joey," which revealed his restlessness, and "Don't Cry," which he sang in an effort to comfort Rosabella.

Casting the production involved the problem of finding singers who could handle the difficult score and yet who also could be convincing actors. Loesser is said to have even made a trip to Italy in his search for the proper singer to play Tony. Fortunately, he solved the problem by signing Robert Weede, a former member of the Metropolitan Opera Company, who made his Broadway debut playing Tony. Loesser also selected another operatic singer, Mona Paulee, who had won the Metropolitan auditions of the air in 1941, to play Maria, Tony's sister. He signed Jo Sullivan, who had appeared as Polly Peachum in the off-Broadway production of *The Three Penny Opera* and had won recognition for her performance as Julie in a City Center revival of *Carousel,* to play Rosabella; and Art Lund, former vocalist with Benny Goodman's band, to play Joe. Susan Johnson and Shorty Long completed the cast of principal characters.

When *The Most Happy Fella* opened in New York on May 3, 1956, it lived up to the favorable reports from the out-of-town tryouts and began a long, successful run. The fact that it was different in emphasizing music rather than dialogue, and that it told a familiar but poignant December–June love story acted in its favor and helped to eliminate any possible comparisons with *My Fair Lady.* On the credit side, the show also had Loesser's excellent score, Howard's appealing story, Jo Mielziner's colorful sets, Motley's picturesque costumes, and Dania Krupska's sprightly choreography. On the debit side, however, Broadway theatergoers who had expected another Loesser score comparable to *Guys and Dolls* were, if not disappointed, at least very much surprised. People who enjoyed the more serious songs were not particularly impressed by the lighter ones; those who enjoyed the typical Broadway tunes were somewhat bored by the operatic arias.

Several music critics were disturbed by the score because they felt that the combination of popular tunes and operatic arias did not blend. Those critics who preferred the serious numbers regretted Loesser's inclusion of Tin Pan Alley tunes; other critics who preferred the more popular songs thought the operatic interludes were often too powerful, too loud, too overwhelming. Even the recording of the show puzzled record fans, for Columbia issued two different original cast albums. The first contained the complete score of the show in three long-playing records; the second album, consisting of only one record, featured highlights from the production.

The drama critics were also divided in their opinions. Those who thought the show failed as entertainment still acknowledged that it had an excellent score and that it deserved credit for avoiding hackneyed situations and routines. A few critics regretted the fact that *The Most Happy Fella* had lost the simplicity of Howard's drama. Loesser's adaptation, they thought, lessened the emotional impact of the plot by too much emphasis on music. A majority of the critics, however, praised it for its attempt to break away from traditional musical comedy patterns, even though the result may have been, as Louis Kronenberger called it, "a misstep forward."

Most reviewers and audiences were enthusiastic about the cast and were especially impressed by Robert Weede's vivid portrayal of Tony; because of the great demands of the role, Weede sang only at the evening performances. Jo Sullivan made an appealing Rosabella, but Miss Sullivan was perhaps too beautiful for the role. In Howard's drama, Amy was an older waitress, glad to settle down in Napa Valley, but the attractive Miss Sullivan definitely did not appear to be the sort of plain, love-starved girl who would have accepted a proposal from an unknown "lonely hearts" admirer. Yet Miss Sullivan sang and acted the role with such sincerity that she aroused great sympathy for her predicament, making audiences overlook the implausibility of the idea that anyone so young and pretty would have accepted Tony's marriage proposal.

Tall, blond, handsome and athletic, Art Lund appeared to be ideally cast as the virile, restless Joe. Moreover, Mr. Lund had been a popular singer, a featured vocalist with Benny Goodman, and had made several hit records as a solo artist. In *The Most Happy Fella,* he gave an impressive performance, particularly in his song "Joey, Joey."

Susan Johnson, who played Amy's friend, and Shorty Long, who played one of the ranch workers, also proved to be showstoppers, for both singers gave the production a change of pace with their enthusiastic singing. Their duets included "Big D," and "I Made a Fist." The hit song of the show, nevertheless, was "Standing on the Corner," a number still sung frequently. In spite of their excellence, many of the serious numbers from the show are seldom heard today, perhaps because they are too difficult for many singers, and perhaps because they lose their significance out of context.

In spite of mixed notices, *The Most Happy Fella* did win recognition from the reviewers, for in May 1957, it received the Critics' Circle Award as the best musical for the 1956–57 season.

Perhaps *The Most Happy Fella* drew audiences because it dared to be different. Perhaps the entire show may not have appealed to everyone in the audience, but parts of it were certain to please almost everyone, for it catered to many different musical tastes. The show ran for a total of 676 performances, a short run in comparison with other hit musicals which opened at the same time, but very definitely a long run in the history of Broadway musical productions.

Frank Loesser's many problems in adapting *They Knew What They Wanted* were probably exceeded by those which complicated the preparations for the musical version of *Li'l Abner*. Before the show opened on November 15, 1956, several writers, lyricists, and librettists had tried unsuccessfully to whip a working script into shape using Al Capp's well-known characters. Their inability to do so in no way reflected on their talents, for the problem of basing a dramatic production upon established characters has always been a difficult one and with comic-strip characters, it becomes even more so. Audiences unfamiliar with the cartoons knew little or nothing about the characters or the situations in which they were usually involved. The adaptors, therefore, had to devise a basic plot that would be a composite of the typical daily involvements and yet not a mere repetition of what had already appeared in the newspapers. Once a story line has been established, the problem of casting begins, for, unlike the adaptation of a book or story in which the reader creates his own image of the character, the dramatization of a comic strip requires that the actors resemble the cartoonist's creations. The closer the resemblance, the more authentic the characterization becomes.

Buster Brown and *Bringing up Father*—better known as *Jiggs and Maggie*—were two fairly successful stage farces that had been produced in the early part of the century and were based on comic strips, but no dramatic or musical play based on cartoon characters had run for more than 500 performances. Al Capp's widely read, syndicated comic strip, however, seemed to be a good prospect for a musical show. *Li'l Abner* first appeared in the New York *Daily Mirror* in 1935, and during the following twenty-year period, the cartoon drew an ever-increasing number of readers. For years, Capp's creations had satirized politics, public figures, and public corruption. One week in the late 1940s, when Capp began ridiculing a well-known senator, one out-of-town newspaper in a large college city eliminated the comic strip. Thousands of readers complained, and, on the various college campuses in the city, enterprising students sold pirated reprints of that week's cartoons. Within a very short time, the newspaper again began using the feature, offering no explanation for having discontinued it. Capp had also become a favorite author on school campuses for his creation of the Sadie Hawkins Day Race in which all the unmarried women of Dogpatch, the home of Li'l Abner, chased all the eligible males. Any girl who caught a man before he reached the finish line dragged him to Marryin' Sam who ultimately performed a group marriage ceremony. On some campuses, the Sadie Hawkins Day Race, without the inevitable marriage prize, became a yearly event. Capp also intrigued readers with his creation of a loveable little animal called the Shmoo, which soon developed into a national best seller in the toy market.

The wide variety of Capp's characterizations seemed to have sufficient popular interest to attract many different types of audiences. The fighting Scraggs appealed to those people who liked hillbilly stories about feuds and fights; Mammy Yokum, the small, tyrannical matriarch, fascinated youngsters and adventure seekers, for she was superwoman, batwoman, and Tugboat Annie all rolled into one; Daisy Mae appealed to young men, who could not understand Abner's indifference to her; and Li'l Abner, the big, stupid, but handsome all-American boy who preferred bachelorhood to Daisy Mae, appealed to young and old alike.

But the several composers, librettists, and lyricists who worked at various times on the preliminary drafts remained stymied by the problem of adaptation. Alan Jay Lerner, for example, after his first attempt at writing the musical version of *Pygmalion,* had worked first with Burton Lane and later with Arthur Schwartz on *Li'l Abner,* but neither version seemed satisfactory to everyone concerned.

Finally a libretto by Norman Panama and Melvin Frank, with lyrics and music by Johnny Mercer and Gene de Paul, and choreography and direction by Michael Kidd, succeeded in capturing the spirit of Capp's comic strip. Although most of the action took place in and around Dogpatch, the writers included several scenes in Washington, D.C. In addition to Pappy, Mammy, and Li'l Abner Yokum, Daisy Mae and her relatives, and the fighting Scraggs, the writers also included Evil-Eye Fleagle, the man who could cast a spell by giving a single whammy, to say nothing of the even more effective double whammy; General Bullmoose, the tycoon who wanted to get possession of all the money in the world; Senator Jack S. Phogbound, whose political strategy was as ridiculous as his name; a brief appearance of Moonbeam McSwine, the beautiful, shapely girl who, unfortunately, spent too much time around farm animals and too little time trying to rid herself of barnyard odors; Appassionata Von Climax, a magnificently proportioned siren; and Stupefyin' Jones, an even more shapely siren, whose figure stunned men into immobility.

When *Li'l Abner* opened on Broadway, *My Fair Lady* was still the number-one show among musicals. Perhaps Al Capp's characters were no match for Liza Doolittle and Professor Higgins, but they gave serious competition to the other current hit musicals, for the excellent cast brought the citizens of Dogpatch to life. Peter Palmer, who made his Broadway debut as Li'l Abner, had been an all-state football tackle at Missouri and had the proper physique for the role. Moreover, he bore an unusual resemblance to Capp's muscular hero. Edith Adams, who had already impressed Broadway audiences with her portrayal of Eileen in *Wonderful Town,* made a charming, delectable Daisy Mae. Stubby Kaye, ideally cast as Marryin' Sam, again captivated audiences as he had done in *Guys and Dolls.* Diminutive Charlotte Rae endowed the role of Mammy Yokum with the proper zest; Howard St. John, a veteran Broadway actor, superbly played the avaricious General Bullmoose; and Joe E. Marks as Pappy Yokum was properly submissive to Mammy's dictatorship. The minor characters were equally well cast, particularly Tina Louise as Appassionata Von Climax and Julie Newmar as Stupefyin' Jones, two anatomical delights who wore costumes that accentuated their attractiveness. Bern Hoffman as the villainous Earthquake McGoon, Al Nesor as Evil-Eye Fleagle, and Carmen Alvarez in her brief appearance as Moonbeam McSwine also properly resembled Capp's drawings.

The reviews were not all favorable, for several critics who were not devotees of Capp's cartoons said quite definitely that the show meant little to anyone unfamiliar with the comic strip. Others pointed out that the musical had to include explanations for those theatergoers who did not know the citizens of Dogpatch, and, in keeping with the formula for comic strips, the show was forced to include repetitive incidents and ideas. As a result, the plot sprawled out in many directions.

These criticisms were certainly valid, for the book was a jumble of complications and involved situations. The basic plot dealt with Daisy Mae's efforts to get Li'l Abner to marry her, but the authors incorporated Capp's political barbs by having the U.S. Government designate Dogpatch as a suitable place for testing atomic bombs because it was thought to be the most useless place in the United States. A second theme involved Mammy Yokum's concoction of Yokumberry Tonic, which she fed to Li'l Abner to make him strong and healthy. The subplots became interlinked when Li'l Abner took the tonic to Washington to donate it to the government, although General Bullmoose was willing to pay $1 million for the formula. The scientists discover that the tonic does work miracles in building up physiques but that it also, unfortunately, makes men lose interest in women. On Sadie Hawkins Day, Appassionata Von Climax, by means of General Bullmoose's clever strategy and with the able assistance of Evil-Eye Fleagle and Stupefyin' Jones, traps Li'l Abner, who is then bound by Dogpatch tradition to marry her. Broken-hearted Daisy Mae is ready to marry one of the fighting Scraggs, but all complications are solved before the final curtain. When the town inhabitants try to move the statue of Jubilation T. Cornpone into the center of Dogpatch, they discover that it bears a tablet signed by Abraham Lincoln, a fact which makes Dogpatch a national shrine and saves it from being bombed. General Bullmoose is arrested; Li'l Abner is released from having to marry Appassionata; and Mammy Yokum and Marryin' Sam break up the wedding of Daisy Mae and Earthquake McGoon, clearing the way for Li'l Abner to make Daisy Mae his bride.

Most of the critics liked the sprightly score much better than the plot. Johnny Mercer and Gene de Paul had written several delightful numbers such as Li'l Abner's "If I Had My Druthers";

"I'm Past My Prime," an intriguing duet sung by Daisy Mae and
Marryin' Sam; and "Namely You," the love duet sung by Li'l
Abner and Daisy Mae. Stubby Kaye had one rousing number,
"Jubilation T. Cornpone," that set the stage for a vigorous en-
semble routine. General Bullmoose's "Progress Is the Root of All
Evil" and "The Country's in the Very Best of Hands," sung by
Sam and Li'l Abner, both satirized government and politics.
Opinions on these last two numbers were divided, for one or two
reviewers thought the lyrics in bad taste. Most critics, however,
cited Mercer's lyrics for their excellence in adapting the spirit of
Capp's method of lampooning politics and big business.

On the other hand, there was no disagreement about Michael
Kidd's choreography and direction; the critics were unanimous in
praising his contributions to the evening's entertainment. Perhaps
the show did falter in one or two sequences, but once Kidd's
dancers went into action, the pace picked up. In the very opening
scene, Kidd presented the live animals found in Capp's cartoons.
He also devised dance routines that topped anything else in the
show. One sequence begins as a formal ball in Washington. When
the citizens of Dogpatch crash the party, the dancing becomes
more and more accelerated as the ensemble romps through a
frenzied routine in which the Dogpatch characters rout the Washington socialites and practically wreck the ballroom. The high
spot of the show, however, was definitely Kidd's interpretation of
the Sadie Hawkins Day Race. Brooks Atkinson, in his review of
Li'l Abner, pointed out that ballet proved to be the best form for
depicting comic-strip characters because it put them in motion.
The ballet Michael Kidd devised for his rousing first act finale did
exactly that. He put his characters through a series of racing,
jumping, and leaping steps that built to a feverish pitch and
downright warfare between the predatory girls and the unwilling
males. The action sizzled as the girls chased the men across stage, as
Stupefyin' Jones appeared at odd intervals to stop the men dead in
their tracks, and as the victorious women dragged their unwilling
victims to the finish line where Marryin' Sam waited to perform
the marriage ceremony.

Most audiences, particularly those who knew the Al Capp
characters, thoroughly enjoyed the show; many theatergoers who

knew little or nothing about Dogpatch found Michael Kidd's exciting choreography sufficiently fascinating to make the musical comedy delightful entertainment. *Li'l Abner* may have been un-even, but the bouncy music, the excellent cast, and the energetic dancing overbalanced the ridiculous book and helped *Li'l Abner* develop into a long-running hit that played for two seasons and closed with a total of 693 performances.

Two weeks after the premiere of *Li'l Abner,* Judy Holliday came to Broadway in the second musical hit of the season, *Bells Are Ringing,* with book and lyrics by Betty Comden and Adolph Green, and music by Jule Styne. Although the story seemed to have an unusual twist, concerning a telephone operator who worked for an answering service and fell in love with a client, several drama historians pointed out its similarity to *The Five O'Clock Girl,* a musical comedy produced in 1927 that dealt with a girl who started a romantic entanglement by calling a man every day at five o'clock. Comden and Green, however, who had worked with Miss Holliday in a nightclub act, tailored *Bells Are Ringing* to fit her special talents and created a plot almost completely different from *The Five O'Clock Girl.* Ella Peterson, played by Miss Holliday, works for a telephone answering service called Susanswerphone. Although Ella has been warned to keep her calls impersonal, she cannot help becoming involved with the people who use the service. She falls in love with the voice of one client, a playwright-playboy named Jeff Moss. When she discovers that if he does not begin writing his next play, his option with a producer will expire, she decides to become a little Miss Fix-it. Posing as a girl named Melisande, she invades his apartment, surprises him by her supposed intuition into his activities, takes him for a subway ride to show him how friendly people can be, and inspires him to begin writing the play. When he is well on the way to completing the script, Jeff takes Ella to a party where the theatrical social set make her feel out of place. Deciding that she and Jeff live in different worlds and that it would be better if she never sees him again, Ella leaves the party without letting Jeff know where to reach her. In the meantime, she has helped one of her telephone clients, a young actor, to get a part in a play by convincing him that he should stop trying to imitate Marlon Brando and that he should discard his leather jacket outfit for a more dignified business suit. She also has helped another client, Dr. Kitzell, a dentist-song writer, to have his songs accepted for a new show. Jeff finally discovers Ella's true identity, tracks her down to Susanswerphone—followed by all the subscribers she has helped—and the curtain falls on the inevitable reunion between the two lovers.

A subplot concerning a romance between Sue, the owner of Susanswerphone, and Sandor, a bookie, added a few amusing complications. Under the guise of selling recordings via telephone, Sandor in reality is operating a bookie establishment, using the names of composers, numbers of symphonies, and opus numbers as codes for racetracks, horses, and race numbers. Ella, unaware of the booking code, changes one telephone order because she is certain the symphony number was incorrect. The result might have been disastrous if the police had not cracked down, ready to arrest everyone connected with Susanswerphone, and finally decided that Sandor was the real culprit.

The critics almost unanimously belittled the frothy book, although several overlooked the triteness of the story because it gave Miss Holliday ample opportunity to clown, to sing, and to ingratiate herself with the audience. One reviewer said the show was not good enough for Miss Holliday but admitted that she was wonderful. Most of the critics felt, as Brooks Atkinson did, that Miss Holliday "carried on her talented shoulders one of the most antiquated plots." Another critic, in fact, was so impressed by Miss Holliday's sensational performance that he referred to *Bells Are Ringing* as having the "best original book in recent memory."

Comden and Green also helped disguise the time-worn Cinderella story with witty dialogue, clever lyrics, and a variety of characters that included socialites, theatrical personalities, policemen, bookies, gunmen, and subway riders. At times the action paralleled the zany antics in *Wonderful Town* for which Comden and Green had written the lyrics; they incorporated scenes where people danced and sang in subways, a nightclub scene that presented a riotously funny floor show using the dentist's fantastically bad songs to good advantage, and a party where guests dropped names indiscriminately. Comden and Green also included two characters that amused insiders in show business, particularly the characterization of the actor, Blake Barton, which satirized the Marlon Brando cult.

Judy Holliday was most certainly responsible for making the show a tremendous hit, for throughout the proceedings she dominated the action each time she appeared. Oddly enough, in spite of her sensational success in *Born Yesterday*, Miss Holliday had never received star billing on Broadway prior to *Bells Are Ringing*; but this musical, which brought her back from Hollywood, definitely established her as a star. Miss Holliday used her remarkable vocal range to great advantage as she impersonated different people on the answering service, changing her personality and tone of voice for almost every call that came through. When she spoke to Jeff and posed as Mom, she used an old woman's tremulous voice; she squeaked to represent one of Jeff's scatterbrained girl friends; she lapsed into French when taking messages for an exclusive restaurant. In one scene, garbed in a black leather jacket, she did a hilarious imitation of Brando's odd diction. Having a girl put on lipstick before answering a telephone call would, in most plays, be a timeworn gag, not particularly amusing, but when Miss Holliday did it before talking to Jeff, the episode was hilarious.

Jule Styne's infectious music and Comden and Green's clever lyrics provided lilting songs that audiences could remember. Although the patter numbers written for Miss Holliday were not so effective out of context, at least two songs from the show soon became popular favorites. "The Party's Over" and "Just in Time," an intriguing melody based for the most part on only two notes, became hits and are still played quite frequently. Miss Holliday shone particularly in handling such specialty songs as "Is It a Crime?" a satiric plea for happiness in which the music would break while Miss Holliday added a spoken punch line, even including a corny gag explaining what might have happened if Romeo and Juliet had used a telephone answering service. She sang "I'm Going Back" in the Jolson "Mammy" tradition, satirized the Cha-Cha vogue in "Mu-Cha-Cha," and punched home patter lines in "Drop That Name."

The Theatre Guild gave the show a sumptuous production with beautiful sets and costumes by Raoul Pène du Bois. The staging by Jerome Robbins and choreography by Robbins and Bob Fosse also fitted into the sprightly mood of the production. The dancing may have lacked the frenzied pace of Michael Kidd's routines in *Li'l Abner,* but it had far more variety, with numbers that burlesqued waltzes and cha-chas, and one delightful romp that began in a subway and ended on a street corner.

Miss Holliday's co-star, Sydney Chaplin, gave an excellent performance as Jeff Moss and made the playboy-author a likeable character. Jean Stapleton as Sue, Eddie Lawrence as Sandor, Frank Aletter as Blake Barton, and Bernie West as Dr. Kitzell, all gave superb performances. Peter Gennaro as Carl proved to be an effective dancing partner for Miss Holliday in "Mu-Cha-Cha," one of the highlights in the show.

The credit for the long-running success of *Bells Are Ringing,* nonetheless, belonged to Judy Holliday, whose performance kept the show on Broadway for a total of 924 performances. During a two-week summer period when Miss Holliday and Mr. Chaplin were on vacation, Larry Parks and Betty Garrett played the leads, and although they gave excellent performances, box-office receipts dropped sharply, for theatergoers wanted to see Judy Holliday. When the motion-picture version was made, the producers signed Dean Martin to play Jeff, but they wisely chose Miss Holliday to repeat her stage role; once again, she triumphed over the obvious plot and made the picture as delightful as the stage version.

Quite a few theatergoers who enjoyed the old-fashioned, sentimental, Cinderella-type story of such musicals as *Bells Are Ringing* were appalled by the completely different plot of *West Side Story,* the first musical hit of the 1957–58 season. Instead of the happy, carefree people whom Comden and Green had created, Arthur Laurents, who wrote the book for *West Side Story,* filled his stage with juvenile delinquents—angry, belligerent Puerto Ricans, and surly Americans—as he unfolded a story that most commentators defined as a modern version of *Romeo and Juliet.* The musical stirred up much controversy, for, despite its impressive score and brilliant choreography, which delighted a great many people, the plot and some of the lyrics annoyed and infuriated others who felt that at least one song reflected poor taste and that the production as a whole portrayed a seamy side of American life inappropriate for a musical show.

Arthur Laurents had written the book based on an idea by Jerome Robbins. Leonard Bernstein, who had written serious music as well as the score for *Wonderful Town,* had a much greater opportunity in *West Side Story* to incorporate not only numbers that were ballads in the popular style but also remarkable ballet music for the many routines devised by choreographer Jerome Robbins and his assistant, Peter Gennaro. Television writer Stephen Sondheim made his Broadway debut as the lyricist.

Bernstein, Robbins, and Laurents originally had planned to do a special type of musical, presumably to be called *East Side Story* and dealing with a Romeo and Juliet situation in which a Jewish girl and a Catholic boy living on New York's East Side face strong opposition to their romance. Such a plot would have been little more than a variation on Anne Nichols's long-running comedy *Abie's Irish Rose,* which also concerned the marriage problems of a Jewish boy and Catholic girl, and also, as George Jean Nathan had pointed out, stemmed directly from *Romeo and Juliet.* The Bernstein-Robbins-Laurents plan to do a musical involving religious conflicts, however, was abandoned for several years. When the writers decided to resume work on the project, they changed the locale to the West Side and made the newly arrived Puerto Ricans and the native-born Americans the opposing forces. The show was delayed because Bernstein had to finish the score for *Candide,* but once that musical was launched, the men began whipping *West Side Story* into shape.

West Side Story opened in New York in September 1957. The action revolves around a feud between an American gang, the Jets, led by Riff, and a Puerto Rican gang, the Sharks, headed by Bernardo. The Jets plan to challenge the Sharks to a rumble during a dance at the gym, and Riff persuades his friend Tony, who has more or less drifted away from the gang, to help him. At the dance, however, Tony meets Maria, Bernardo's sister, who has come from Puerto Rico to marry Bernardo's friend Chino. Maria and Tony fall in love at first sight, although they know their romance will meet opposition. The rival gangs make plans for the rumble, but Tony persuades them to stage a fair fight, without weapons, between the two best fighters—Bernardo and Riff. The next day, Tony sees Maria again and the two lovers become certain that they want to marry. By the time the gangs meet for the rumble, Bernardo has become furious because of the relationship between Tony and Maria. Within seconds, he and Riff are fighting. Suddenly, Bernardo pulls a knife and kills Riff. The infuriated Tony grabs the weapon and, in retaliation, kills Bernardo. Both gangs rush into battle at fever pitch until they hear a police whistle; they run off, leaving behind the bodies of Riff and Bernardo.

Tony comes to Maria's room via the fire escape, and the lovers are together until Anita, Bernardo's fiancée, knocks at the door; Tony leaves hurriedly. Anita tells Maria she must not have anything more to do with the man who has killed her brother; but Maria finally persuades Anita to find Tony and warn him that the Sharks plan to kill him. The Jets, however, treat Anita brutally when she comes looking for Tony. Infuriated, she tells them that Chino has killed Maria. Tony hears this false report, leaves his hiding place and begins aimlessly wandering in the streets. Suddenly he meets Maria, who has been looking for him to warn him. Within a few moments, Chino appears, shoots Tony, and kills him. Both gangs assemble, stunned by the killing, and declare a truce. As they carry Tony's body off stage, the final curtain falls.

The ending does not hold up too well under strict analysis, for, as one critic pointed out, the gangs should have been just as stunned by the deaths of Riff and Bernardo. Furthermore, the Sharks had already planned to get revenge for Bernardo's death by killing Tony. Nevertheless, during the performance, any idea that the final sequence might be implausible was overshadowed by the grimness of the scene, the expert staging of the episode, and the Bernstein music.

In many ways, *West Side Story* was far more revolutionary than *The Most Happy Fella,* for, unlike Loesser's musical play, it had no compromise happy ending, and, with the exception of two songs, no humor. The first song, "America," sung by Anita and the Shark girls, dealt with the differences between life in Puerto Rico and in America. The second number, "Gee, Officer Krupke!" sung by the Jets, amused some people but annoyed others, who thought it showed bad taste in mocking the police force and in using lyrics they felt unsuitable for the theater.

Critical opinion was not unanimously favorable. Some reviewers hailed *West Side Story* for being different from the standard run of musicals, for its tight script, and for its sensational dancing, but said that despite its merits, they did not enjoy the show. At least two critics considered the unsavory plot unsuitable for musical theater. They also objected to what they felt was a distortion of the Romeo and Juliet story in making it deal with race conflicts, gang warfare, and violence. In their opinion, the distortion involved not only the changed ending, in which Maria survives Tony, but the fact that scenes in *West Side Story* meant to parallel Shakespeare were either overly sentimental or out of keeping with the harshness of the text. For example, two scenes on the fire escape were somewhat similar to Shakespeare's famous balcony scene. In the second sequence, when Tony stood on the fire escape and said good-bye to Maria, the audience knew that he was being hunted by the rival gang and that it was essential that he get away as quickly as possible. Yet the realistic mood of the drama was pushed aside while the lovers sang a ballad. The duet, in fact, not only stopped the action but was also a return to the unrealistic scenes in the old operettas of the 1910s and 1920s when all action or any semblance of reality was shunted aside while the tenor and soprano held the spotlight during an elongated musical farewell.

Perhaps Brooks Atkinson's opening statement in his review best summarized the attitude of some critics and theatergoers: "Although the material is horrifying, the workmanship is admirable." The excellent "workmanship" of which Atkinson spoke included Oliver Smith's impressive sets, Irene Sharaff's costumes, and Jean Rosenthal's lighting—all of which helped to accentuate the stark mood of the drama.

Opinions differed on the merits of Leonard Bernstein's score, but even those who were not impressed with the ballads admitted that the ballet music helped heighten the tension and that its occasional harshness was essential to the choreography. Most certainly Bernstein's score did not fall into the typical old-fashioned musical comedy pattern. His ballads were melodious, but, at the same time, expressed the restless spirit of youth. It is doubtful, however, if even the most optimistic devotees of the score could have predicted its ultimate popularity. The young people, who thought *West Side Story* magnificent, loved the songs and helped make the very numbers that some critics thought sentimental into popular favorites. These included "Maria," sung by Tony after he had met her at the gym; "I Feel Pretty," sung by Maria and the girls; "Tonight," the love duet; and the haunting "Somewhere," in which the lovers expressed the hope that they would find a place where they could be free from opposition and prejudice.

Young people also dominated the excellent cast, which was comprised, for the most part, of comparative unknowns to Broadway audiences. At least two of the leads, however, were soon catapulted into featured billing in other productions. Chita Rivera, who played Anita, had been a dancer in *Guys and Dolls* and in *Can-Can;* she had then appeared in *Mr. Wonderful,* where her talents were completely wasted. During the last half of the show, in fact, Miss Rivera did little more than sit on stage as part of a nightclub audience. In *West Side Story,* though, she revealed her skill as a superb dancer and singer. She proved she could handle the humorous "America," as well as the serious "A Boy Like That," in which she denounces Tony. Carol Lawrence, who played Maria, had first appeared on Broadway in Leonard Sillman's *New Faces of 1952;* in *West Side Story* she emerged as star material, giving a vivid portrayal of the tragic Maria. Miss Lawrence's beauty, as well as her singing and dancing, impressed both audiences and critics. Larry Kert, a former stunt man in Hollywood, had the physical agility as well as the singing voice to make his portrayal of Tony a vibrant characterization. Mickey Calin, who played Riff, won plaudits for his vigorous performance as the leader of the Jets. The entire cast, in fact, intrigued audiences, for it was composed of dancers and singers whose lightning speed and catlike movements made the fighting ballets periods of breathless excitement.

Even those theatergoers and critics who were not enthusiastic about *West Side Story* were impressed by Jerome Robbins' whirlwind choreography, for Robbins, who had also directed the show, made the dances the high spots of the evening. Today, the finger-snapping, crouching, lurching, and leaping dancers of *West Side Story* have become familiar figures on the stage, but in 1957 these dances were excitingly new in the theater. The dance movements not only epitomized perfectly the tensions, the brutality, bravado, and venomous hatred of the gang warriors but also had sufficient variety in themselves to hold audiences spellbound. The few quiet interludes between dances were, by way of contrast, not a letdown in suspense but more an opportunity for the spectator to relax before becoming engrossed in watching another vigorous ballet. Some spectators even felt that Robbins had developed the plot more skillfully through the dancing than through the singing and spoken passages.

After it closed in New York on June 27, 1959, with a total of 732 performances, *West Side Story* was sent on a cross-country tour and then brought back to Broadway on April 27, 1960, this time to uniformly ecstatic notices. Those critics who had liked it the first time repeated their enthusiasm, and those who had been skeptical now hailed it as a masterpiece. The public responded by keeping the second run in New York for an additional 249 performances.

Plans to send *West Side Story* to the World's Fair in Brussels and also to Russia were cancelled when, according to rumors, certain governmental departments frowned on the project. Although many people felt the production should be shown abroad, the opposition believed the decision to cancel the overseas project was sound, for the story of gang warfare, knifing, and feuding between West Side gangs would have presented a negative picture of America to foreign audiences. *West Side Story* was produced in London, where it had considerable success, and, as late as 1967, some English theatergoers still referred to it as a representative picture of New York life. Undoubtedly, headlines dealing with rioting in American cities increased their belief that all of the United States was riddled with gang warfare.

In 1957, the gang warfare and rioting which dominated the show may have seemed far-fetched to New York theater audiences still unwilling to admit that such conditions were reality rather than fancy. Ten years later, however, even the skeptics realized that *West Side Story* could almost be called a documentary portrayal. The public's attitude toward the score has also changed as the music has become more familiar to listeners through constant repetition on radio and television. Singers have used many of the numbers for encores; such songs as "Maria," "Tonight," and "Somewhere" have become classics. Many people now rate the score for *West Side Story* as Bernstein's best and most distinguished contribution to the Broadway theater.

The two hit musicals that followed *West Side Story* differed radically from that somber, pulsating story of warfare in the streets of New York. *Jamaica,* starring Lena Horne, reverted to the musical comedies of the 1910s and 1920s that disguised a creaky plot with stunning scenery, vivid costumes, lilting music, and a beautiful, fascinating star. *The Music Man,* which established Robert Preston on Broadway, introduced Meredith Willson's songs to the Broadway theater in a production with an old-fashioned, homespun plot that was heralded as one of the best family-type shows presented in Manhattan for several decades.

Jamaica opened October 31, 1957, to surprisingly good reviews, for the critics might well have belittled the production for its rambling, almost juvenile book. The plot deals with a seamstress, Savannah, who wants to leave Pigeon Island, off Kingston, Jamaica, to go to New York. Although she and Koli, a handsome but poor fisherman, are in love, Savannah refuses to marry him unless he takes her to New York. When Joe Nashua comes to Pigeon Island from Harlem because he has heard reports of a lucrative but shark-infested pearl bed, he almost persuades Savannah to go back to New York with him. The virile Koli not only dives successfully to obtain the pearls for Nashua but also becomes a hero when he saves Savannah's little brother Quico during a hurricane. Savannah is then content to settle down with Koli in wedded bliss. A subplot concerned two Islanders, Ginger and Cicero, who has always wanted to know how it would feel to rule the Island and has an opportunity to do so for a brief spell after the hurricane. Their on-again off-again romance added a few amusing touches.

E. Y. Harburg and Harold Arlen had originally planned to write a musical about an Island fisherman for Harry Belafonte, but, according to reports, David Merrick wanted the production to deal primarily with the character of Savannah. He shrewdly starred glamorous Lena Horne, whose beauty and magnetic personality gave the production a suave charm. The final production, tailored to fit Miss Horne's talents, had a book by E. Y. Harburg and Fred Saidy, lyrics by Harburg, and music by Arlen, whose melodies admirably fit the mood of the story. Miss Horne entranced audiences as she paraded across stage in a variety of multicolored outfits—some fishtailed, some skintight, but all designed to accentuate her physical attractiveness; and she handled the score as though she believed Arlen's songs were the best she had ever sung. Ricardo Montalban as Koli added the proper romantic touch. With vivid costumes designed by Miles White, beautiful Island sets by Oliver Smith, exotic choreography by Jack Cole, and smooth staging by Robert Lewis, the production moved swiftly from song to song. The slight story served primarily as a thread to hold together a constant change of scene, songs, and dances, and every time the plot threatened to bog down the entertainment, Miss Horne or Mr. Montalban or Josephine Premice or Adelaide Hall picked up a musical cue and charmed the listeners with Arlen's music and Harburg's clever lyrics. The critics were also willing to ignore the plot because, they said, the show had style. According to the program notes, Miss Horne had previously appeared on Broadway in the chorus of *Blackbirds of 1939*, but *Jamaica* marked her first appearance in a starring role, following a successful career in motion pictures and nightclubs. This show was not her first chance to return to New York as a star, for she had previously turned down an offer to play the leading role in another Arlen musical, *St. Louis Woman*. The writers gave her little opportunity for dramatic action in *Jamaica,* but producer David Merrick turned it into a stunning showcase for her talents. Even though the plot never allowed Savannah to get to New York, the production included a dream sequence set in New York's famous Persian Room which permitted Miss Horne to wear a striking gown and sing a sultry ballad, "Take It Slow, Joe." Miss Horne, in fact, was on stage almost constantly and sang most of the numbers, which ranged from ballads to comedy tunes including "Push the Button," which satirized American automation; "Napoleon," which satirized products capitalizing on the names of famous people; "Cocoanut Sweet," a charming lullaby first sung by

Adelaide Hall and Miss Horne and later reprised by Miss Horne; and the rhythmic "Ain't It the Truth," which Miss Horne sang with Josephine Premice. Arlen and Harburg included two comedy numbers for Miss Premice, the excellent comedienne who played Ginger. The first, "Yankee Dollar," showed the attitude of the Islanders toward tourists; the second, "Leave the Atom Alone," handled the serious topic of the atom bomb with deft humor.

Darkly handsome Ricardo Montalban was one of the few non-Negroes in the cast. No reference was made to the fact that *Jamaica* used an integrated cast, nor did audiences even consider the story as one dealing with miscegenation, for the plot simply developed a typical island romance. Montalban not only gave a fine performance as the fisherman but also demonstrated that he could sing and dance as well as, if not better than, a great many actors who played musical comedy leads.

The supporting cast included Adelaide Hall, who had been in the long-running revue *Blackbirds of 1928,* as Grandma Obeah; Josephine Premice as Ginger; Ossie Davis as Cicero; and Erik Rhodes as the governor of the Island. But the show belonged to Lena Horne, and her presence was largely responsible for the show's successful run of 555 performances.

Most certainly, the average musical show with so little plot and so much emphasis upon music, might have folded in a week, but by capitalizing on successful musical comedy techniques of the past—a glamorous star and locale, a handsome leading man, a raucous comedienne, elaborate sets and costumes, a fast moving chorus, and an extensive score—*Jamaica* proved that an old-fashioned musical whose sole purpose was to entertain could be successful when it had a scintillating Lena Horne, a romantic Ricardo Montalban, clever music and lyrics by Arlen and Harburg, and a striking production by David Merrick.

Jamaica satisfied the wishes of theatergoers who wanted to see a relaxing, amusing musical with no serious messages or deep dramatic complications and a production which presented audiences with a continuous kaleidoscopic view of island costumes, native dancing, and rhythmic music. The title and locale of the production were excellent box office lure for tourists en route to the island or for would-be tourists who had never visited Jamaica.

Some drama historians in discussing the history of the American musical stage have omitted any reference to *Jamaica* or have dismissed it with a casual reference along with other productions which they felt did little or nothing to advance the musical comedy theater, but the David Merrick production on Broadway was excellent entertainment, and, thanks to Lena Horne, enjoyed a highly successful run.

Meredith Willson's *The Music Man* opened December 19, 1957, about two months after the première of *Jamaica,* to superlative reviews. The Critics' Circle, in fact, named it the best musical of the season, giving it preference over *West Side Story.*

The plot and atmosphere were old-fashioned, but the production, the music, and the tempo were decidedly modern. Meredith Willson is said to have based the story on events that had happened in Mason City, Iowa, when he was a child. He changed the name of the town to River City and developed a folksy yarn about a fast-talking, somewhat unethical salesman, Harold Hill, who breezes into River City to sell musical instruments and band uniforms. Although Hill cannot read a note of music, he convinces all the townspeople with the exception of the young librarian that he can teach their children to play. With the glibness of a revival preacher, he stirs the placid people into a frenzy, induces them to place large orders, and plans to leave town before his duplicity can be uncovered. Marian Paroo, the librarian and music teacher, presumably annoyed by Hill's advances, is ready to expose him as a fraud until the first-act finale, when she sees what a change he has made in her little brother Winthrop, a shy lad who had seldom spoken because he lisped so badly. As the Wells Fargo wagon bringing the new uniforms approaches and everyone begins singing jubilantly, Winthrop, unable to control his excitement, breaks into song, completely ignoring his speech defect. The grateful Marian changes her mind and tears up the printed information that would have revealed Hill as a liar. By the end of the play, Hill has fallen in love with Marian and realizes that he cannot leave town, even though he may be exposed as a fraud; and Marian, in a very corny but wonderfully sentimental scene, tells the people that Hill's presence has made River City a happier town. The children, resplendent in their new uniforms and brandishing shiny new instruments, rush to Hill's defense and begin playing. Delighted to hear their children making musical sounds, the townspeople are content to have Hill stay with them. What made the final scene so touching was that Willson kept it humorously truthful. In a fairy-tale ending, the children would have come on stage and played a rousing march; but Willson wisely adhered to reality, and when the youngsters played, the music was terrible. Horns squeaked off pitch, and the children butchered the selection. In realistic fashion, however, the townspeople were thrilled to see their children so radiantly happy, and no one on stage or in the audience cared whether the music was in tune or not.

The critics wrote uniformly ecstatic reviews. Some compared the show to the musicals created by George M. Cohan, but *The Music Man* far exceeded Cohan's shows in deftness of pace, in humor, and in song hits. Even the drama historians, who called it old-fashioned, admitted that it gave audiences a wonderful time. The opening night ovation provided definite proof that everyone loved the show, for at the finale the audience broke into applause, keeping rhythm with the stirring music; and *Variety* said, "Nothing like it has ever been seen on Broadway."

Perhaps *The Music Man* was corny, but it was palatable corn. The show had humor without wisecracks and sentiment without exaggerated emotional scenes. Meredith Willson, who wrote libretto, score, and lyrics, incorporated every imaginable trick that might have audience appeal, even to staging a Fourth-of-July picnic. His music reflected the homespun atmosphere, for he sprinkled the score with rhythmic marches, barbershop quartets, love ballads, and songs that led into dances that predated the Charleston era. Willson also made his production appealing by using wholesome characters and plain old-fashioned sentiment in telling the familiar love story of the con-man who is reformed by his love for the beautiful, honest country girl.

Morton DaCosta, who had directed *Auntie Mame* and given it almost breathless speed, managed to inject the same pace into *The Music Man*. The costumes by Raoul Pène du Bois captured the spirit of the times and were amusing without making the ladies look ridiculous; and Howard Bay's sets presented the Iowa scenes with maximum effectiveness. Willson also received able assistance from choreographer Onna White. The steps she devised were much closer to the two-step, the cakewalk, and the square dance, than to the stylized dancing of the 1930s or the influence of ballet in the 1940s. She began the "Shipoopi" sequence simply enough as a comedy number, but soon developed it into a full-scale combination cakewalk and strutting ensemble routine that enabled Robert Preston and Barbara Cook to dance right along with the young, energetic chorus line. Miss White proved equally adept in handling the children, who simulated musical instruments when Hill sang "Seventy-Six Trombones." Watching a portly lady clad in bloomers and middy blouse pumping away at a player piano in the gym for musical accompaniment, or watching the gawky, ungraceful ladies of the town rehearsing a ridiculous fountain ballet not only made the corny humor easily digestible but also even decidedly welcome.

The fact that it was Frank Loesser, who had written book, lyrics, and music for *The Most Happy Fella,* that encouraged Willson to write *The Music Man,* may perhaps have accounted for Willson's decision to write the complete show. Frank Company, of which Loesser was president, co-produced the show with Kermit Bloomgarden and also published Willson's musical score.

The Music Man marked Willson's Broadway debut, although he was well known to a great many people through his radio programs. Even those listeners who were familiar with his musical novelties and his use of choral-speaking groups were amazed by the musical tricks he incorporated into *The Music Man.* Instead of opening the show with the typical singing ensemble, Willson set the scene in a railroad smoking car filled with traveling salesmen and used only the sounds of the train as accompaniment while the men spoke in rhythm. The dialogue began slowly, but as the train picked up speed, the tempo of the dialogue increased. The men bobbed up and down as though they were riding in a bouncy car, and Willson injected repetitive phrases at periodic intervals to act as a break in the dialogue or, at times, to serve almost as a refrain. The rhythmic dialogue established the fact that Harold Hill, the traveling salesman, had taken on a new racket and was now selling band uniforms. When the expository facts had been established and the train began to slow down, the tempo of the dialogue decreased almost to a standstill. The scene ended with a flourish as Hill stepped quickly off the train. The novelty of the entire routine gave the show a zip and pace that seldom slackened during the entire evening.

Willson also gave Robert Preston, who had never sung or danced before, special songs, half-sung, half-spoken, with an emphasis on rhythm rather than melody. In the song "Pool," Preston acted like a frenzied revivalist as he stirred up the townspeople by telling them of the evils lurking in the town pool hall. At the height of the number, while the chorus chanted "trouble, trouble," Preston lapsed into patter rhythm as he asked the people if they had detected any big-city bad habits in their youngsters. He then led them into a rousing finale with the choral ensemble carrying the musical burden but with Preston very much in evidence.

Preston proved that he could be equally adept in handling a melodic number like "Marian the Librarian," which he half-crooned, half-sang while the young dancers almost made a shambles of the quiet library. In the delightful duet "The Sadder-but-Wiser Girl" with Iggie Wolfington, Preston superbly handled the humorous lyrics as well as teaming with Wolfington in a few simple but effective dance steps. Preston's dancing was actually closer to fast walking.

Willson used a clever trick in "Pickalittle," sung by the ladies of River City. The song began as a gossip session but developed into an intricate number as the ladies, nodding their heads like chickens, repeated the title and chorus while a male quartet sang "Goodnight Ladies" as a countermelody. This quartet, played by a group called The Buffalo Bills, did a great deal to reestablish the vogue for barbershop quartets. Willson had them sing four numbers in the show, all designed to give full range to the four voices, and all beautiful examples of barbershop harmony. One song, "Lida Rose," became an almost instant favorite.

Willson again used counterharmony in the songs "Seventy-Six Trombones" and "Goodnight, My Someone," which used basically the same melody but with a different rhythm. In the second act, he combined the two numbers in an effective duet between Hill and Marian. Hill began with "Seventy-Six Trombones" and Marian with "Goodnight, My Someone," and then suddenly Hill switched to "Goodnight, My Someone," and Marian responded with a line from "Seventy-Six Trombones."

Another tricky number, listed in the program as "Piano Lesson," began quietly with Marian's pupil Amaryllis playing a simple scale. Marian and her mother, who had been arguing about Mr. Hill, started singing to the piano accompaniment. Very soon, the orchestra blended in for a full accompaniment. The lyrics set to the scale were especially amusing, and the expert trouping and singing of comedienne Pert Kelton, who played Mrs. Paroo, made the audience wish that Willson had given her more songs.

The big musical hit of the show, "Seventy-Six Trombones," another fast talking and singing number which began with Preston recalling the great name bands, developed into a rousing ensemble number that made the audience feel that it could almost hear all seventy-six trombones. The charm of the number lay in the illusion Willson created which was far more effective than reality, for a television singer who decided to use the number staged it with at least seventy-six trombones both on the screen and in the musical background. Instead of heightening the effectiveness of the song, the overproduction weakened it.

The success of *The Music Man* does not indicate the trouble that beset Willson before the musical finally came to Broadway. Willson is said to have written many drafts of the show before he contacted Kermit Bloomgarden who agreed to produce *The Music Man*. The men who had originally planned to produce the show were not satisfied with the script, and Willson brought in Franklin Lacey to help him with the libretto. Willson also had difficulty in casting the leading role. He had hoped Danny Kaye would play Harold Hill, but Kaye thought the part was not right for him. Dan Dailey and Gene Kelly also were uninterested in the role. On one of Willson's television programs, Phil Harris admitted that he had been offered the part and had turned it down because he thought it was too corny. Harris also admitted that he had foolishly turned down the opportunity to play the lead in the very prosperous road company. Finally, Robert Preston, who had appeared in a series of motion pictures, many of them B grade, was signed for the part and definitely emerged as a top-ranking star.

What Preston lacked in singing and dancing ability he more than made up in energy as he moved quickly on stage, chanting like a revivalist in one song, making sentimental lyrics sound convincing in another, simulating the playing of musical instruments in another. Above all, his glibness and good humor charmed the audience and critics as well as the citizens of River City. Willson wisely delegated the melodious numbers to lovely Barbara Cook, who sang beautifully and gave a thoroughly delightful performance as Marian Paroo. Miss Cook put the right amount of fire in her indignation when she learned Hill was a fraud; she had the necessary ingredients to charm a rival salesman out of exposing Hill; she had the dramatic ability to make her defense of Hill in the final scene convincing; and she had the looks and personality to make audiences believe she could attract and reform a city slicker like Hill.

The cast also included seasoned troupers who glittered in lesser roles. David Burns as Mayor Shinn managed to milk every line for a solid laugh; Iggie Wolfington made a jovial companion for Hill; and Eddie Hodges won audience sympathy as little Winthrop, who emerged from his shyness to sputter out one chorus of "Wells Fargo Wagon" and a rhythmic number, "Gary, Indiana." Al Shea, Wayne Ward, Vern Reed, and Bill Spangenberg, who made up the barbershop quartet, and Helen Raymond as the domineering mayor's wife, also delighted audiences. A special nod, however, must go to Pert Kelton, a veteran trouper of the stage and in television, who played Mrs. Paroo and sparkled every moment she was on stage.

Before *The Music Man* ended its long run of 1,375 performances, Hal March and Bert Parks both played Preston's role of Harold Hill on Broadway, and Forrest Tucker bounced through the lead in the very competent road company. The motion-picture version also starred Robert Preston, with Shirley Jones playing Marian.

The Music Man seemed to have something in it to please almost everyone. Old-timers who had lived in small towns enjoyed the nostalgia of seeing their childhood memories dramatized; city folk who had never known people like those of River City could still enjoy Willson's good-natured lampooning of the ladies who were small-town counterparts of Helen Hokinson's delightful cartoon women; the younger generation could enjoy the rebellious young man who wanted to court the mayor's daughter; and the entire family could enjoy the magic spell cast by the likeable rogue, Harold Hill.

The nostalgic, homespun sentiment that pervaded *The Music Man* and sent audiences home chuckling and humming rhythmic tunes also permeated, but to a lesser degree, *Flower Drum Song*, which opened on December 1, 1958. The two shows differed radically in time and locale, for Rodgers and Hammerstein developed in *Flower Drum Song* a story contrasting Eastern and Western cultures in modern San Francisco; but the principal theme was basically as old-fashioned and sentimental as that of *The Music Man*.

Flower Drum Song came to Broadway in a season that offered several plays dealing with Oriental characters. *The World of Suzie Wong* preceded it, and *Rashomon* and *A Majority of One* followed it. Joseph Fields and Oscar Hammerstein II based *Flower Drum Song* on a book by Chin Y. Lee that concerned the differences between Old World and New World Chinese customs in San Francisco's Chinatown. Hammerstein himself referred to the story as a sort of Chinese "Life with Father," because it dealt with two Oriental fathers and their problems in controlling their families. Public interest in the production before the opening resulted in a huge advance sale of more than $1.5 million, an amount sufficient to keep the show running for several months even if the criticisms were unfavorable.

If *Flower Drum Song* had been written by a different team, it might have fared better with the critics. Although it told an amusing story, offered an excellent cast dressed in striking costumes, had a series of beautiful sets, and included pleasant songs and dances, Rodgers and Hammerstein were again their own worst competitors, for several critics, instead of judging *Flower Drum Song* on its own merits, compared it with *The King and I* for Oriental atmosphere or with *South Pacific* for musical score. One critic said he thought the show lacked charm because the atmosphere was pseudo-Chinese; and Kenneth Tynan, in his review, punned upon the title of *The World of Suzie Wong* by referring to *Flower Drum Song* as "a world of woozy song." On the other hand, some critics accepted the musical favorably as a colorful, entertaining, sentimental production with an obvious story that made no pretense of being profound.

Flower Drum Song may have lacked the force of other Rodgers and Hammerstein shows, but it had its own quaint charm; and if it was not so distinguished a work as *Carousel* or *South Pacific,* it was still far superior to several other Rodgers and Hammerstein shows, notably *Pipe Dream,* for it created a warm glow as it unfolded an uncomplicated tale about nice people, with no out-and-out villains. Perhaps, as some critics said, it pictured Chinatown as an Oriental version of Broadway in its nightclub scenes, but it made the actual nightclub scene more attractive than that found in San Francisco's Grant Avenue section.

Most audiences, especially those who wanted musicals without messages, without propaganda, and without serious dramatic scenes, liked the story of Dr. Li, who brings his daughter Mei Li to San Francisco to marry Sammy Fong, a nightclub owner, whose parents had arranged for the wedding according to Chinese custom. Sammy, however, is infatuated with Linda Low, a stripteaser in his nightclub, and tries to avoid marrying the quiet, lovely little Mei Li. Complications set in when Mei Li and her father arrive at the home of Wang Chi Yang, and Mei Li falls in love with his son Wang Ta. The two fathers are content to have Wang Ta marry Mei Li since Sammy did not object to getting out of his marriage contract. But further complications arise when Wang Ta thinks he has fallen in love with Linda Low and wants to marry her. Wang Chi Yang, angered by the rebellion of his son, informs him that a Chinese father always selects the bride. Sammy Fong, anxious to break up the romance, invites Wang Chi Yang and his family to sit at a ringside table without telling Linda that they will be watching the show.

The nightclub scene begins with a brash master of ceremonies, whom Linda had introduced to the Yang family as her brother, and whose efforts to tell corny jokes fall flat when he sees the shocked visitors at the ringside table. He is only slightly more successful as he sings "Gliding Through My Memoree," which tells about his sweethearts in different countries, with the chorus line appearing in revealing costumes to represent the girls he remembers. The ensemble then sings "Grant Avenue," and Linda comes on stage to do her striptease, disregarding the frenzied signals of the master of ceremonies warning her that the Yang family is watching the show. As the routine increases in tempo, and just as Linda has ripped off part of her bodice, she suddenly finds herself facing Wang Chi Yang, who leaves the club followed by his family. Sammy is overjoyed at the results of his scheme, and the infuriated Linda dumps an ice bucket on him.

Wang Ta now realizes that he has made a mistake, and that Mei Li would have been a much more suitable bride. Dr. Li and his daughter, however, have already gone to the Three Family Association, where Dr. Li and Sammy Fong's parents agree that Sammy will have to follow Old World Chinese tradition by obeying the marriage contract and marrying Mei Li. At the last moment, Mei Li discovers a way of breaking the contract, which leaves her free to marry Wang Ta. Sammy is then reunited with Linda.

No one in the audience took the romance between Wang and Linda too seriously, but the audience enjoyed just sitting back and watching to see how the complications would work out to the obvious conclusion.

A synopsis of the plot does not reveal the warm sentiment and quiet humor that came through in Hammerstein's lyrics. For example, Wang Chi Yang and his sister Madame Liang sang "The Other Generation," in which they bemoaned the difficulty of communicating with the younger generation and expressed their disapproval of the way children acted. Later, Yang's younger son, Wang San, and a group of children reprised "The Other Generation," this time with different lyrics, as they expressed their disapproval of the older generation and bemoaned the difficulty of establishing communication with them. The two generations combined when Madame Liang and her nephew Wang San did "Chop Suey," a clever satire in which they compared life in America to the famous American-Chinese dish. Rodgers and Hammerstein also satirized typical nightclub specialty songs in "Gliding Through My Memoree" and "Fan Tan Fannie." Many people called "Don't Marry Me" the most amusing song routine in the show. As the song began, the Americanized Sammy explained to the tradition-bound Mei Li why they should not marry, but the number ended with both singers doing a typically American strut as they waved hats and trucked down stage. The incongruity of seeing the gentle Chinese girl dressed in an Oriental costume doing an imitation of a Jimmy Durante strut made the entire routine thoroughly delightful. The bouncy rhythmic numbers included "Grant Avenue," which extolled the wonders of China-town's main street and led into a fast-stepping ensemble routine; and "I Enjoy Being a Girl." "Sunday," one of the most tuneful numbers in the score had a simple, effective melody reminiscent at times of Rodgers' "The Blue Room." Audiences also enjoyed "A Hundred Million Miracles," which Mei Li sang with an occasional beat on the flower drum, and the ballads "Like a God," "You Are Beautiful," and "Love, Look Away." During one change of scene, Arabella Hong, who played a seamstress in love with Wang Ta, stepped in front of the curtain to reprise "Love, Look Away," a beautiful number that made the audience sympathize with the girl whose love for Wang Ta would never lead to marriage. Miss Hong had one of the best voices in the show and might well have complicated the plot if Rodgers and Hammerstein had not wisely relegated her to the background after her solo number.

As in all Rodgers and Hammerstein shows, good taste was evident in the direction, the sets, the casting, and the costumes. Oliver Smith created stunning sets; Irene Sharaff designed striking costumes, not so opulent as those in *The King and I* but just right for the half-Oriental, half-American style of *Flower Drum Song;* Gene Kelly's direction kept the leisurely plot moving at a proper tempo; and Carol Haney devised American choreography rather than traditional Chinese steps for the ensembles, although she did include a sprightly Oriental ballet. The American touches were proper, since the story dealt in large part with the younger generation's desire to live as the Americans did.

The excellent cast helped immeasurably to make *Flower Drum Song* enjoyable and entertaining. Miyoshu Umeki, who came to Broadway to play Mei Li after her great success in the motion picture *Sayonara,* entranced the reviewers. She had charm rather than beauty; she made a wistful picture-book bride; and her gentleness and quiet manner of singing provided an appropriate contrast to Pat Suzuki, who played the brassy nightclub stripteaser superbly and who belted out numbers in typically American style. Miss Suzuki stopped the show with "I Enjoy Being a Girl." Keye Luke, whom many people remembered as the Number One Son in Warner Oland's series of *Charlie Chan* motion pictures, made a fine tradition-bound Wang Chi Yang. Ed Kenney gave a convincing performance as the older son, Wang Ta, who realized that his infatuation for Linda was not so great as his love for Mei Li; Patrick Adiarte was amusing as the Americanized younger son. Juanita Hall, who had been an excellent Bloody Mary in both the stage and film versions of *South Pacific,* appeared as Madame Liang, sister of Wang Chi Yang, a role that she played with both dignity and humor. Larry Blyden, with obviously made-up slanted eyes, gave a remarkably suave performance as Sammy, the slick nightclub boss caught between his involvement with Linda and the insistence of his family that he marry Mei Li. Sammy could have been a thoroughly despicable heel, but Blyden's humorous portrayal aroused audience sympathy for him, especially when he was breaking up the romance between Linda and Wang Ta. Mr. Blyden was brought into the show during the out-of-town tryouts, and his deft characterization at the New York première proved that Rodgers and Hammerstein had made a wise decision in casting him as Sammy.

Most people who saw *Flower Drum Song* did not consider it a major work of Rodgers and Hammerstein, for it lacked the dramatic conflict of *The King and I* or *South Pacific;* neither did it have the sweep of *Oklahoma!* It did, however, exude sentimental glow and was, as John Chapman said, "a sweet, gentle story, sweetly and gently treated." As such, it had sufficient popular appeal to run for two seasons and a total of 600 performances.

"Charming" or "gentle" would definitely be inappropriate words to use in describing *Gypsy,* the next big musical to follow *Flower Drum Song* in the spring of 1959. Based on the autobiography by Gypsy Rose Lee, it unfolded the story of a domineering, headstrong stage-mother, superbly played by Ethel Merman, who devoted her life to furthering the careers of daughters Gypsy Rose Lee and June Havoc.

Gypsy, as one critic suggested, could have been just another version of the Cinderella story, this time the tale of the less talented sister, Gypsy, who rose to become the greatest star in burlesque. Miss Lee's autobiography had presented an account of the trials she endured before she entered burlesque and her ultimate triumph as queen of the Minsky shows; but Arthur Laurents, who wrote the libretto, made Gypsy the secondary character and emphasized the role of Mamma to give Merman one of the best vehicles of her career.

Part of *Gypsy*'s appeal stemmed from the fact that it was purported to be authentic, and that it presented the story of the early childhood of two well-known Broadway figures. The producers played down the show-business angle and instead emphasized the role of Mamma. They showed the more sleazy side of burlesque without resorting to the sort of obvious crudity and nudity which eventually killed it in New York in the 1930s. Gypsy Rose Lee herself had found that when she did shows on Broadway, she could get away with a striptease only because she mocked her own act. Instead of offending or shocking women, as other stripteasers had done, she amused them. Perhaps the story of the little lady who went to see the *Ziegfeld Follies* and sat in the front row with her son illustrates the point. When he asked her if she objected to Miss Lee's act, she refused to answer, and when he asked if she enjoyed the show, she said, "I always liked Fannie Brice." As soon as she came home, however, she lost no time in finding her daughter. Her son tiptoed to the closed door to eavesdrop and was amused when he heard her say, "You just have to see this Gypsy Rose Lee. She's wonderful." The writers incorporated this sort of humorous appeal into one raucous number that stopped the show. In it, three burlesque stripteasers try to show Gypsy Rose Lee that to be a success, "You Gotta Have a Gimmick." As each girl does her own bump or grind, she reveals her own special method of holding audiences: one girl blows a trumpet; a second does ballet steps that end in a raucous bump accentuated by her specially constructed costume; and the third presses buttons that light up small bulbs placed at strategic points on her abbreviated costume. Instead of being offensive it was a highlight of the show, for it kidded burlesque just as Miss Lee herself had done.

The story of *Gypsy* was relatively simple. Mamma is determined to make her daughters great vaudeville stars. Since Baby June appears to be the more talented and beautiful of the two girls, Mamma centers the vaudeville act around her and makes her older sister Louise dress in boy's clothing and appear in the chorus line. Mamma battles stage directors, theater managers, and hotel owners as she drags her group from one tank town to another, always hoping to make the big time. When Baby June runs off and marries one of the boys in the show, Mamma builds a new act around Louise; but with vaudeville dying, she finds bookings more and more difficult to obtain. Finally she discovers that the girls have been booked into a burlesque house, and although she was opposed to the idea at first, she relents and permits Louise—now called Gypsy Rose—to do a striptease. Eventually, Gypsy Rose also rebels at her mother's domineering, and Mamma finds that in concentrating on careers for her children, she has lost her own chance to be a success. In a rousing finale, "Rose's Turn," Merman performs one of the most difficult routines of her career, proving that anything her daughters can do, she can do better. She performs part of June's act and part of Louise's, as well as some bumps and grinds, as she showed that now it was her turn to shine. While she performs, the signboard in back which had flashed "Gypsy Rose Lee" in electric lights suddenly flashes only "Rose." In the middle of the number, Mamma breaks down, starts to cry, but snaps out of her despair and finishes to a rousing conclusion. The curtain could have come down on this final song, but Laurents shrewdly added a very brief scene to reunite Miss Lee and Mamma Rose.

The plot also included a romance between Rose and Herbie, a candy salesman, who becomes Mamma's lover as well as manager for the act. Mamma has already been married three times and Herbie is more than willing to be the fourth husband, but Mamma keeps putting off the wedding ceremony in order to devote herself to her daughters' careers. Herbie finally walks out on Mamma, just as Baby June had done. The role of Herbie might have been somewhat ridiculous, but Jack Klugman gave an excellent performance and made Herbie the kind of man whom neither daughter resented, even though they both knew about his affiliation with their mother.

Although the basic story was autobiographical, it was not particularly new, for several other authors had written about domineering stage mothers. Gypsy Rose Lee herself was pleased with the production. Merman made Mamma Rose, despite her faults, an understandable if not always admirable character.

David Merrick and Leland Hayward, who co-produced the show, made no attempt to overglamorize the settings, but the onstage dressing rooms were, as one former burlesque performer said in a private interview, far more tolerable than the ones she was accustomed to. The cheap hotels where Mamma housed her brood and from which she stole blankets that Louise later made into wool coats looked much cleaner than the rundown hotels where travelling vaudeville players were often forced to stay. Jo Mielziner's sets gave the production an air of authenticity without overemphasizing the sleaziness of the locale. Raoul Pène du Bois designed costumes that ranged from the ridiculous burlesque outfits to several striking gowns worn in the final sequence. Sandra Church, who played Gypsy Rose Lee, began her striptease in a long-skirted, tight-fitting gray gown, which she did not remove. She stepped off stage and within seconds reappeared wearing a bright red dress cut along the same lines, which she again did not completely doff as she exited. A few seconds later she returned to the stage in a bright blue outfit. Whether she was whisked out of one dress into another, or whether, as one electrician suggested, the gown reflected different colors by a change in lighting was unimportant, but Miss Church's split-second changes added a slick, intriguing touch to the routine.

During the out-of-town tryouts, New Yorkers heard rumors that certain sections of the musical were undergoing revision, with new scenes being added and old scenes being scrapped. If the reports are true that the producers decided to eliminate a burlesque routine, the decision was sound, for nothing on stage could have topped the hilarious scene in the dressing room with the three stripteasers. And if ensemble routines were cut to build up the striking Merman finale, the decision was again sound, for Merman's concluding solo would have made anything that followed anticlimactic.

Gypsy opened in New York in May 1959. The burden of the

musical interludes fell to Merman. Jerome Robbins, who directed both the show and the choreography, kept the dancing to a minimum except for the vaudeville act performed by the youngsters, which turned out to be virtually the same act each time except for costume changes.

All the critics wrote in glowing superlatives about Ethel Merman, and most of them wrote good, if not enthusiastic, reviews of the production, but opinions on the book were divided.

One critic objected to the fact that *Gypsy* really had two heroines—Mamma and Gypsy Rose Lee—and that one of them had to be shunted aside. There is no denying the truth of his statement, but the show would not have been so powerful if the production had overemphasized the spectacular rise of Miss Lee. The ultimate defeat of Mamma had more dramatic depth than the glamour story of the girl who became a star, a story which, although true, had been done in many variations before.

In spite of its merits, *Gypsy* needed Ethel Merman to make it click. Shortly after the show had opened, Miss Merman became ill and had to drop out of the cast temporarily. For several weeks, box-office receipts dropped, but when Merman returned to the show and again strutted across stage, business bounced back to capacity.

Ethel Merman had proved her versatility with each new show. Critics knew that she could sing, but she soon convinced them that she was also a deft comedienne. In *Annie Get Your Gun* she demonstrated her ability to sing serious ballads, but in *Gypsy* she had the greatest role of her career, for she proved that she was also a dramatic actress. The Merman flair for wearing high fashion was not included in the script; neither was she given the bouncing, rhythmic songs that led into dance ensembles. Instead, her songs developed the characterization and reflected the seriousness of the show. Her comedy number, "Mr. Gladstone, I Love You," was handled with typical Merman proficiency, but it was a new Merman who performed the moving finale "Rose's Turn," or the ballad "Small World," or the love duet "You'll Never Get Away from Me."

Many critics felt that Jule Styne's score for *Gypsy* was the best he had ever written, and with Ethel Merman doing the songs *Gypsy* had more than a few numbers that became popular hits.

Stephen Sondheim, lyricist for *West Side Story,* wrote even better lyrics for *Gypsy.*

During rehearsals, rumor had it that Merman and Styne did not see eye to eye on some of the numbers, but if there had been any differences of opinion no signs were evident when the show opened, for Merman handled the score superbly. The songs in the first act were virtually all Merman's. In "Some People," she expressed her desire to get out and do things; "Everything's Coming Up Roses," was the expression of her unfailing optimism in the face of defeat. "I Had a Dream," reprised periodically, became almost a theme song to express Mamma's new ideas about revising Baby June's act. Styne and Sondheim used the song "May We Entertain You" in two different forms to excellent advantage, first as the musical background for Baby June's act, and later, in a much slower tempo, as "Let Me Entertain You" for the accompaniment to Gypsy Rose Lee's striptease.

Several actresses who played Mamma in out-of-town productions of *Gypsy* were far less successful than Merman; they often lacked her warmth, drive, and personality, as well as her ability to hold an audience. Miss Merman made no effort to tone down Mamma's driving ambition or her ruthless tactics on behalf of her children, but Merman made Mamma's forcefulness and domination understandable, and her vibrant personality even engendered audience sympathy. In "Rose's Turn," when she demonstrated that she was more talented than anyone else in the family, she made audiences almost forget her ruthlessness and the unhappiness she had caused. Instead, the audience found itself feeling sorry for this woman whose daughters had left her. Sandra Church was properly appealing as young Gypsy Rose Lee, but if, as some critics suggested, she was kept in the background, the fault may have been in the libretto, which required her to be placid so that the contrast between her and Mamma would be more marked. Miss Lee had a type of animation that Miss Church was not permitted to reveal. Even the striptease routine in *Gypsy* lacked the flair which Miss Lee injected into her act. When *Gypsy* first opened and Miss Lee appeared as a mystery guest on *What's My Line?,* she regaled John Daly and the audience as she silently peeled off her gloves as though she were doing a striptease act before answering questions posed by the blindfolded panel. Whether or not Sandra Church could have captured this spirit is not the point; the script simply did not permit her to do so.

The motion-picture version featured Rosalind Russell as Mamma Rose and Natalie Wood as Gypsy, and although both actresses gave excellent performances, the magnetism that Merman had generated on stage was missing.

After seeing *Gypsy* on Broadway and watching Merman stop the show in the final number, a veteran Broadway theatergoer said, "It's too bad they didn't do this show ten years ago. Merman would have made a wonderful Gypsy Rose Lee." True as the statement may be, Merman was an even more wonderful Mamma Rose; and she kept *Gypsy* on Broadway for a total of 720 performances.

The biographical authenticity of *Gypsy* was not equalled by *The Sound of Music*—the first long-running hit of the next season —which was based on the factual account of the escape of the famous singing Trapp family from Austria during the Nazi regime. The production, for which Rodgers and Hammerstein did the score, was based on Maria Augusta Trapp's *The Trapp Family Singers;* but Howard Lindsay and Russel Crouse, who wrote the libretto, emphasized sentiment, played down the harshness of the Nazi invasion, and created a musical that seemed far more fictional than *Gypsy*.

The true story of the Trapp Family Singers was fairly well known and seemed to have infinite possibilities for dramatization. A motion picture based on the family had been made in Germany, and Vincent J. Donehue was interested in doing an American motion-picture version. When Paramount Pictures decided not to make the film, Donehue then got in touch with Mary Martin, who was very eager to appear in the show. Her husband, Richard Halliday, planned to co-produce *The Sound of Music* with Leland Hayward, and obtained permission from all the members of the Trapp family to portray them on stage. Howard Lindsay and Russel Crouse, co-authors of New York's longest-running hit, *Life with Father,* as well as *State of the Union* and the Irving Berlin musical *Call Me Madam,* were signed to write the book. Richard Rodgers and Oscar Hammerstein II agreed not only to write the score but also to co-produce the show if they could create entirely new music and not have to depend on songs from the Trapp family's repertoire. With Vincent J. Donehue to direct the production, Oliver Smith to create the sets, Lucinda Ballard, the costumes, and Jean Rosenthal, the lighting, work began on the show as soon as Rodgers and Hammerstein had finished *Flower Drum Song,* the musical on which they had been working when negotiations for *The Sound of Music* were begun.

Lindsay and Crouse began the musical with a scene in Austria's Nonnberg Abbey in 1938. The nuns are distressed that a new postulant, Maria, is not in the abbey as she should be, and are discussing whether or not she should be permitted to become a member of their order. Maria, who had gone to the mountains, finds upon her return late that evening that the Mother Abbess thinks that she is unready to lead a cloistered life. Instead, she has decided to send Maria to the estate of Captain Von Trapp, where she will act as a governess for the Trapp children, whose mother has died. Captain Von Trapp rules his family with the same type of discipline he had enforced in the Austrian Navy. During his absence Maria teaches the children to sing and becomes the confidante of Liesl, the oldest child, aged sixteen, who is in love with Rolf Gruber, aged seventeen. By the time Captain Von Trapp returns home with his new fiancée Elsa Schraeder and his friend Max Detweiler, the children have fallen in love with Maria. The Captain is stunned to see that Maria has taken material he had selected for curtains and made it into new outfits for the children, but he is even more astounded when he hears the children sing.

During a party that Von Trapp gives for Elsa, several guests discuss the ominous rise of the Nazi regime in Austria. Fears and arguments are temporarily forgotten, though, when Maria has the children sing "So Long, Farewell," in which they bid the guests goodnight and withdraw one at a time. Maria, who has danced with the Captain, knows that she has fallen in love with him and, frightened, runs back to the abbey. The understanding Mother Abbess advises her to go back to the Trapp home, saying that Maria must not be afraid to accept true love.

Captain Von Trapp, discovering that both Max and Elsa are willing to go along with the Nazi party, breaks off his engagement

with Elsa, but is not too distressed, for he readily admits that he
has grown fond of Maria—a fact the audience had known from
the moment he first danced with her. Two weeks later Maria
and the Captain are married in the abbey, with the children
making up the bridal procession and the nuns in the background
watching the radiant Maria walk down the aisle. By the time
Maria and the Captain return from their honeymoon, the Nazis
have invaded Austria. Maria tries to comfort Liesl when it turns
out that Rolf has joined the party, but Maria is soon faced with a
greater problem—the Nazis are determined to force Captain Von
Trapp into their service. Stalling for time and hoping to find a
way of escape, Maria jumps at Max's suggestion that the Trapp
family sing at a local music festival. At the end of the concert,
knowing that a Nazi escort is waiting for the Captain, the Trapps
sing "So Long, Farewell," exit one at a time, and flee to the abbey
for safety. The Nazis organize a search party and come to the
abbey where Rolf discovers the Trapps but, seeing Liesl, realizes
that he cannot betray her and calls out that he sees no one. At the
final curtain the Trapp family begins its flight to freedom over the
mountain roads.

The producers selected an unusual cast. Mary Martin, of
course, had already become established as a Rodgers and Hammerstein star in *South Pacific,* but she had also won new admirers
for her appearance with Helen Hayes in *The Skin of Our Teeth.*
She enchanted both audiences and critics with her performance as
Maria. She handled the songs superbly, was delightful in the
scenes with the children, and sparkled in both the humorous and
serious scenes. Theodore Bikel, who played Captain Von Trapp,
was not a newcomer to Broadway either, having appeared in
several plays and motion pictures. He was probably even better
known for his recordings of folk songs. He, too, impressed audiences with his performance of the stern father who softened under
the persuasive charm of Maria. Patricia Neway, who played the
Mother Abbess, had won recognition for her appearances in Gian
Carlo Menotti's operas as well as for her performances with the
New York City Opera. Her dignity, her remarkable warmth,
and her rich voice made her a marvelous Mother Abbess. Kurt
Kasznar, who played Max, had appeared in a great many motion

pictures, television programs, and stage plays. His expert sense of timing, as well as his mobile face, enabled him to make Max, the man who was willing to cooperate with the Nazi party, a convincing character who did not arouse audience antipathy. Elsa Schraeder, the lady who almost married Captain Von Trapp, was played by the striking brunette Marion Marlowe, who had been on the Arthur Godfrey show for several years. *The Sound of Music* was her first Broadway show, but her performance was that of a veteran.

Brian Davies as Rolf Gruber, the young man in love with Liesl, and Lauri Peters as the oldest child in the Trapp family, made a delightful team. In addition to Miss Peters, the children in the original cast included William Snowden, Kathy Dunn, Joseph Stewart, Marilyn Rogers, Mary Susan Locke, and Evanna Lien. Replacements in these roles were to be expected, for the musical ran on and on and the children kept outgrowing their parts.

Interest in the show before the Broadway opening ran high. Advance sales, according to some sources, were well over $2 million; others placed the figure in excess of $3 million. Reports from the out-of-town tryouts were extremely favorable, and New York audiences anticipated seeing a sensational show when *The Sound of Music* opened on November 16, 1959.

The critics were divided in their opinions. Those who liked the show found it the most mature work of Rodgers and Hammerstein. Those who were less impressed thought it corny, conventional, and overly sentimental. One critic blamed Lindsay and Crouse for making the book too saccharine; another objected to director Vincent J. Donehue's placement of so much emphasis on the children; still another felt that the play ended too abruptly without showing the audience how the Trapps escaped to safety. The inevitable comparisons with other Rodgers and Hammerstein shows were made, to the definite disadvantage of *The Sound of Music*. Most audiences, though, found the sentiment wholesome, the songs delightful, and the children adorable. In fact, the public seemed to disregard all the unfavorable comments by making *The Sound of Music* a hit show for which tickets were almost unobtainable.

Even the critics who disliked the show agreed, for the most

part, in praising Mary Martin's scintillating performance and the excellence of the score. Instead of opening with a conventional overture, the show began with the nuns at the abbey singing "Preludium" *a capella* and then launching into "Maria," a far different song from the type audiences had expected the cloistered sisters to sing. The tune was sprightly, and the lyrics revealed that the nuns thought the new postulant was a delightful girl but that she was a problem and that they did not know how to handle her. The scene then shifted to the outdoors where Maria sang "The Sound of Music." These two scenes set the pace and tone of the entire play. (Rodgers and Hammerstein made certain that the public would be aware of this unusual opening by refusing to allow latecomers to be seated during the first two scenes; news soon spread that stragglers did not have the usual five or ten minute leeway after announced curtain time because there was no orchestral overture.)

Mary Martin's songs with the children appealed to most audiences. The favorite was unquestionably "Do Re Mi," in which she taught the children to sing by making each child represent a note in the scale. As the song progressed, she added lyrics, changed the order of the notes, and constructed a melody from the scale they had sung in the first chorus. "The Lonely Goatherd," which Miss Martin sang with the children, sparkled particularly when Miss Martin yodeled. "These Are a Few of My Favorite Things" began as a simple listing of the pleasures Maria enjoyed, but the number became deeply moving as a duet between Miss Martin and Patricia Neway, whose rich voice complemented Miss Martin's. The lyrics for this song are considered by many writers to be among Hammerstein's most poetic, for he used precise, concrete imagery that made each recollection a vivid memory.

Miss Martin made her opening number, "The Sound of Music," a lovely bit of sentiment. Her duet with Mr. Bikel, "An Ordinary Couple," had excellent lyrics and music, which enabled both singers to express their affection for each other without resorting to hackneyed phrases. Miss Neway sang "Climb Ev'ry Mountain" superbly, as she tried to convince Maria that she must not be afraid to grasp the good things in life. The reprise of this number, sung by the ensemble as the Trapps begin their trek to freedom, made a stirring finale. "You Are Sixteen," a delightful number about teen-age love, was first sung by Liesl and Rolf, but acquired depth and sentiment when Mary Martin reprised it in the second act to console Liesl over her disappointment in Rolf. Miss Marlowe teamed with Kurt Kasznar in the novelty "How Can Love Survive?" in which Kasznar questions whether Elsa Schraeder and Captain Von Trapp can be happy together even though they will not have to suffer from poverty; Miss Marlowe joined him in developing the idea. In "No Way to Stop It," Miss Marlowe and Mr. Kasznar tried to persuade the Captain that he should cooperate with the Nazi party, accept the transitions that were taking place in the world, and conform to them; but Von Trapp remained unconvinced. People who felt that *The Sound of Music* glossed over unpleasantness too smoothly would have preferred a non-musical passage in which the three characters would have argued about the Nazi invasion. Such a scene, however, would have been out of keeping with the emphasis Lindsay, Crouse, Rodgers, and Hammerstein had placed on the emotional involvements of the Trapp family. Resorting to a form of euphemistic song to make a serious topic more acceptable for popular taste may have been less dramatic, but it still made its point effectively. In many ways the song paralleled "Carefully Taught" in *South Pacific,* for "No Way to Stop It" handled the same type of serious subject matter, but with a more sprightly rhythm and tuneful melody.

Everything about *The Sound of Music* reflected good taste and elegance. Oliver Smith's settings were not only colorful but also, at times, almost breathtaking in their loveliness, especially in the mountain scenes, which actually conveyed the impression of height, and the living room of the Trapp home with its palatial center staircase. Jean Rosenthal's lighting was particularly effective in making the abbey colorful. Lucinda Ballard's costumes were impressive, particularly the robes of the Mother Abbess and the costumes of the children. Miss Martin's clothes, designed by Mainbocher, were, for most of the show, eye-catching, except for the plain, unbecoming dress she wore when she first appeared at the Trapp home. One of the children said the dress was ugly, and Miss Martin, with a twinkle, replied that it had belonged to a new postulant at the abbey.

Excellent cast replacements helped the show achieve its long run. Martha Wright took over for Mary Martin and was later replaced by Jeannie Carson, who was followed by Nancy Dussault. When *The Sound of Music* closed with a total of 1,443 performances, making it the third longest-running Rodgers and Hammerstein musical and the fourth longest-running musical in the history of the New York theater, many of the songs were still popular. The motion-picture version helped to keep them popular, for the film, starring Julie Andrews and Christopher Plummer, was perhaps even more popular than the stage play. In one city, which ordinarily thought a six-month run for a picture sensational, *The Sound of Music* ran for well over a year and would have continued running if a conflict in bookings had not arisen.

The Sound of Music became Rodgers and Hammerstein's final collaboration, for during the run of the show Hammerstein died. The night after his death the show did go on, but reporters hounded the grief-stricken performers, and people who saw that performance said that Miss Martin appeared in the first scene with tear-streaked makeup. Nevertheless, she gave her usual magnificent performance, even though people who sat in the front rows were certain they saw her break into tears when the final curtain came down.

Rodgers and Hammerstein wrote more long-running musical hits than any other duo, and Hammerstein himself was associated in one capacity or another with more long-running musical hits than any other writer or lyricist.

The Sound of Music was not the greatest musical Rodgers and Hammerstein wrote together, but it epitomized those qualities that had marked all their work: excellent taste and unashamed sentiment. They had always emphasized characters who had the courage to face life: Julie, who overcame the handicap of Billy Bigelow's mistreatment in *Carousel;* Curly, in *Oklahoma!,* who had the courage to defy Jud; Nellie Forbush of *South Pacific,* who learned the meaning of courage when she realized that Emile might be killed; Anna Leonowens of *The King and I,* who had the courage to stand up for her rights against the half-barbaric monarch; and the Trapps, who had the courage to attempt an escape from the Nazis. The final scene did not need to dramatize their trek over the mountains and their eventual safe arrival in a neutral country. Audiences that remembered *The Sound of Music* was based on biographical material knew that the Trapp family had escaped, and audiences unfamiliar with the history of the family felt instinctively that the Trapps would reach their destination.

Oscar Hammerstein II has often been called one of the finest poets in the musical theater. He had written "The Last Time I Saw Paris" not as a song but as a poem, and Jerome Kern had been sufficiently inspired to set it to music. Hammerstein's lyrics in *The Sound of Music* were on a par with the best he had written, and if they were too sentimental and perhaps a bit too sugary for some critics, they still made *The Sound of Music* a warm-hearted climax to an illustrious career.

Following in the pattern of *Gypsy* and *The Sound of Music*, *Fiorello!* became the third successive long-running musical hit based on biographical material. It was also the third musical comedy to win the Pulitzer Prize for drama.

When *Fiorello!* opened in New York on November 24, 1959, it arrived with little advance fanfare. The fact that it was booked into the Broadhurst Theater raised some skepticism, for certain showmen had always insisted that potential hit musicals opened in more desirable theaters. The Broadhurst, on 44th Street, although ideally located, had a comparatively small seating capacity that made it less suitable for musicals because of the limited gross. When *Fiorello!* was announced for the Broadhurst, therefore, some insiders assumed that the show had limited appeal. But once it opened to ecstatic reviews, and word got out that the production had excellent songs and dances and that Tom Bosley was sensational in the leading role, long lines formed at the box office.

The use of a political figure as a leading character was not an innovation on Broadway. The Rodgers and Hart musical *I'd Rather Be Right* featured George M. Cohan as Franklin Delano Roosevelt; the George S. Kaufman-Morrie Ryskind satire *Of Thee I Sing* had dealt with politicians, albeit fictitious ones. *Fiorello!* however, was presented as a true account of La Guardia's life—a life sufficiently colorful and exciting as to require no exaggerated episodes that might detract from its authenticity.

The critics almost unanimously wrote glowing reviews. They felt that even though the show may have been uneven, the high spots certainly made up for any weaker scenes. By the end of the season, *Fiorello!* had won three major awards: the Pulitzer Prize for drama, the Critics' Circle award for the best musical of the season, and the Tony Award. Louis Kronenberger in *The Best Plays of 1959–1960,* again overcame his reluctance to select musicals by including *Fiorello!*

The prologue began with Mayor La Guardia reading the comic strips to children over the radio during a newspaper strike. Then followed a flashback to 1914, when he was practicing law in Greenwich Village. La Guardia becomes involved in settling a strike, the first in which women picketed, because the leader, Thea, had been arrested on a trumped-up charge of soliciting. La Guardia meets Thea, falls in love with her, and fights her case. Then, under the sponsorship of Ben Marino, he runs against Tammany Hall for congressman in the Fourteenth District. In the one musical sequence involving La Guardia, the fighting candidate starts his campaign on a street corner, singing "The Name's La Guardia." Very soon, through the ingenious shifting of a few props, the scene becomes an Italian neighborhood, where first Thea speaks to the people and then La Guardia takes over, singing "The Name's La Guardia" in Italian. The scene then shifts to a Jewish neighborhood where Morris, La Guardia's assistant, speaks to the group. When La Guardia takes over and is asked why he never mentions his Jewish background, he says that he doesn't feel that being only half Jewish is "enough to brag about," and then sings a Yiddish version of his campaign song. The scene culminates in a spirited street dance.

La Guardia wins the election, goes to congress, refuses to take Marino's advice and vote against the draft, and reveals that he has enlisted in the service. At a farewell party given by Marino, La Guardia asks Thea to marry him. She does not accept his proposal but admits that she had spoken to a priest about the possibility of such a marriage. La Guardia tells her that he can understand why a Catholic girl would hesitate to marry someone who was half Jewish, half Italian, and now an Episcopalian, but he also tells her that they will be married when he comes back from the war.

The next scene shows some old motion-picture newsreel shots of the real La Guardia leaving Washington, shooting down his first German plane, and being hailed as a hero in Trieste. At the finale of Act I, the stage La Guardia comes down a gangplank and presents Thea with a key to Trieste, her native city.

As Act II opens, Thea and La Guardia are married, and he has decided to run for the position of mayor against Jimmy Walker. He quarrels with Ben Marino, refuses again to take his advice, and loses his support. La Guardia then suffers two major setbacks: he loses the election, and Thea, who has been ill, dies. For three years he remains out of politics, until Judge Seabury offers to nominate him as his candidate for mayor. Marie, La Guardia's faithful secretary, who had always been in love with him, persuades Marino to back Fiorello. The play ends with La Guardia planning to marry Marie, and Ben and his politicians preparing to help him win the election.

Audiences did not need to have his ultimate triumph and winning campaign dramatized. His decision to run again was a fitting conclusion, for most people remembered how ably he had governed the city of New York. Moreover, some audiences were as enthusiastic over the victory of the stage Fiorello as they had been over that of the real Fiorello; at some performances, when news of his election to congress came through, there were bursts of spontaneous applause.

There were no stars in the cast of capable performers, but Tom Bosley, in his Broadway debut, made the role of La Guardia a major triumph. Bosley not only resembled La Guardia but also managed to imitate his excitable, quick movements and even, to a degree, his voice. *Fiorello!* avoided the pitfalls that often caused musicals to falter when a fine dramatic actor is assigned to a leading role. Instead of forcing Bosley to half-sing his songs or do overly simplified dance routines, the writers concentrated his appearances in the dramatic scenes—with the exception of the campaign song routine—and delegated the typical musical comedy assignments to other performers. As a result, Bosley gave an almost straight dramatic performance, portraying La Guardia's virtues—his warmheartedness, his fight for the underdog, and his battle against political corruption—as well as his compelling drive, his temperamental outbursts, and his occasionally dictatorial methods. Bosley delighted both audiences and critics.

Howard da Silva, remembered as a "bad guy" in the movies and as Jud in *Oklahoma!*, gave a superb performance as Ben Marino, the political boss. Da Silva, in fact, made three of his satirical numbers the musical highlights of the show. Ellen Hanley made a charming Thea; Patricia Wilson as Marie, the patient secretary who became the second Mrs. La Guardia, won the audience's sympathy; and Pat Stanley was enchanting as Dora, the girl in the picket line who defied the huge policeman on the beat, played by Mark Dawson, and finally married him. Dawson gave an amusing performance as this thick-headed policeman who rose from the Police Department to the Sewer Department and then on to Garbage, with proportionate increases in income that finally enabled him and Dora to live in a penthouse. Nathaniel Frey's mobile face, which often made him look like a sad hound dog, and his mournful voice helped him to give an excellent performance as Morris, La Guardia's faithful assistant. Eileen Rodgers, who appeared briefly in the second act as singing star, Mitzi Travers, made the most of her song, "Gentleman Jimmy," ably recalling the singing style of the period.

La Guardia's life story made excellent theatrical entertainment because he had been such a colorful figure. The book written by George Abbott and Jerome Weidman presented him as a sturdy fighter without making him a faultless hero. Abbott and Weidman also vividly recreated the corrupt period from 1917 to 1933, exposing the politicians of Tammany Hall and lampooning various political campaigns.

George Abbott directed the show with his usual acute sense of timing, balancing the few quiet moments with more frenzied scenes involving La Guardia. Much of the action concerned political intrigue in the backrooms where strategy was planned, but Abbott made certain that no scene ever bogged down. He often varied the pace by contrasting the action. For example, La Guardia's excitability and quick movements were balanced by Morris' resigned placidity in the office and by Thea's quiet understanding in the home.

The score for the show was excellent; lyricist Sheldon Harnick and composer Jerry Bock were acclaimed by critics as the best young writers of the season, with some people suggesting that

Harnick should have received a special prize for his lyrics. Three of the songs, all handled superbly by da Silva and his henchmen, were excellent political satires. "The Bum Won" was an amusing ditty, but "Politics and Poker" and "The Little Tin Box" lampooned politicians and politics so deftly that many people were not aware of the fact that both numbers also had delightful melodies. Many critics rated "The Little Tin Box," which dealt with the investigations conducted by Judge Samuel Seabury, as the best song in the show. Its lyrics satirized the outlandish explanations politicans gave when they were accused of spending public funds for their own use. In addition to the satirical numbers, Bock and Harnick wrote several ballads: "When Did I Fall in Love?" sung by Thea; "The Very Next Man," Marie's outburst as she waited for La Guardia to realize that she loved him; and "On the Side of the Angels," sung by La Guardia's office staff. The most popular ballad, "Till Tomorrow," led into a beautiful hesitation waltz danced by the ensemble at Marino's farewell party for Fiorello. The excellence of Harnick's lyrics was readily apparent, but orchestral arrangements of the songs revealed the tunefulness of Bock's score, particularly in such songs as "On the Side of the Angels," "Politics and Poker," and even "The Little Tin Box."

The routines devised by choreographer Peter Gennaro added immeasurably to the entertainment. As La Guardia toured through the New York neighborhoods during the election campaign, Gennaro created show-stopping routines that reached a climax in the Jewish neighborhood when the chorus line broke into a spirited number that resembled a hora. Gennaro also satirized the high-kicking chorus lines and toe-tapping routines of the 1920s in "Gentleman Jimmy," the number performed in honor of Mayor Jimmy Walker. Pat Stanley's amusing novelty song, "I Love a Cop," also had a romping dance devised by Gennaro.

Costumes by William and Jean Eckart faithfully depicted the long skirts and huge hats worn by the women of the day, but the outfits were amusing rather than ludicrous. The Eckarts also devised rotating sets that eliminated delays and helped speed up the action.

Many New Yorkers called *Fiorello!* a fitting tribute to La

Guardia, since it portrayed him as a warmhearted fighter whom most people liked and many people loved. Because it told a straightforward, but pleasantly sentimental, story of a beloved public figure, the show appealed to audiences and ran through two seasons with a total of 795 performances.

7. In Rodgers and Hammerstein's *The King and I* (1951) Yul Brynner was the irascible King and Gertrude Lawrence, in her last role on Broadway, played Anna

8. Judy Holliday and Sydney Chaplin were Ella and Jeff in *Bells Are Ringing* (1956), the musical about an answering service operator who falls in love with a client

10. One of the dance highlights in *West Side Story* (1957) was a gang fight, in ballet form, between the American Jets and the Puerto Rican Sharks

9. Julie Andrews and Rex Harrison played the original leads in Broadway's longest-running musical, *My Fair Lady* (1956). In this opening scene outside London's Covent Garden, Liza Doolittle demands to know what Professor Higgins has written about her

11. *Jamaica* (1957), a tropical romance story, starred Lena Horne as Savannah the seamstress and Ricardo Montalban as Koli the pearl fisherman

12. *La Plume de Ma Tante* (1958) featured monks leaping several feet into the air during a bell-ringing dance. The show was one of the last successful revues on Broadway

13. Ethel Merman reached dramatic heights in *Gypsy* (1959). Here Sandra Church as Gypsy and Miss Merman as Mama Rose meet Maria Karnilova as Tessie, a burlesque ballerina

XIII

The Early 1960s

THE FIRST long-running musical comedy produced in 1960, *Bye, Bye, Birdie,* opened April 14 with little advance ballyhoo and became an unexpected hit. The critics were more than pleasantly surprised, and most of them wrote enthusiastic reviews. One critic stressed the fact that most of the people connected with the show were comparatively unknown. Edward Padula, the producer, had been a stage manager; composer Charles Strouse had been a rehearsal pianist; librettist Michael Stewart had written for television; and lyricist Lee Adams had worked for *Time.* Strouse, Adams, and Stewart, however, had worked together on material used in revues and nightclubs. Gower Champion, the director and choreographer, was better known to the public as a dancer who had delighted motion-picture and television fans when he and his wife, Marge Champion, whirled through their fast-stepping routines.

The timely story dealt with the shrieking adulation felt by teen-agers toward a popular singer, named Conrad Birdie, who very much resembled Elvis Presley. As the play opens, Albert Peterson, a teacher-turned-songwriter who also manages Conrad Birdie, is facing a crisis, for Conrad is to be inducted into the United States Army. To capitalize on the situation, Albert's secretary, Rose Grant, suggests that he write a ballad about a farewell kiss. Conrad could sing it during his final television appearance on the Ed Sullivan show, then kiss a young girl goodbye, and the resulting publicity would make the number a big hit. From the many members of Conrad Birdie fan clubs all over the United States, Rose selects Kim MacAfee, who lives in Sweet Apple, Ohio, to be the lucky girl. Very soon, Albert, Rose, and Conrad invade the MacAfee home in preparation for the telecast. Conrad's arrival upsets the town, for when he sings in the public square, twanging his guitar and swinging his hips, youngsters shriek and the mayor's wife swoons in delight. A group of teen-agers who have decided to give Conrad an all-night serenade perch under his window and chant chorus after chorus of "We Love You, Conrad," until the frantic Mr. MacAfee is ready to strangle them.

Kim's boy friend, Hugo Peabody, does not approve of Conrad, nor does he approve of Kim's getting kissed during the program, even if it does make her, as she insists it will, the most envied girl in America. On the night of the telecast, everyone is panic-stricken, for the show is running behind schedule and Conrad's time allotment must be shortened. The cameras finally focus on Conrad, with the MacAfee family in the background; the act ends in a shambles, for Mr. MacAfee, overwhelmed by appearing on the Sullivan show, begins mugging outrageously and ruins Conrad's song. Moreover, before Conrad can kiss Kim, the jealous Hugo suddenly steps on stage and flattens Conrad with a punch.

All ends well, however, for Conrad is shipped off to the Army, and Albert and Rose, in a quiet finale that is a decidedly pleasant change of pace from the feverish frenzy that has preceded it, plan to marry and go to a small town where Albert will resume his teaching career.

Michael Stewart did not limit the scope of the book to the activities of the younger generation and the story of Conrad, for he developed even more fully the love story of Albert and Rose. Instead of handling it as pure romance, however, he made it into farce by the addition of Albert's domineering mother, Mae Peterson, who either ignores Rose or else insults her. To make certain that Albert will continue to support her and not take Rose's advice to go back into teaching, Mrs. Peterson does everything possible to break up the affair. She protests her solicitude for Albert's welfare at one moment, hurls slow-pitched, acid barbs at Rose the next, and interlaces everything with moaned enumerations of the great sacrifices she has made for her son. The audience, as well as Rose, could gladly have choked her, except for the fact that she was too amusing to be annihilated. Stewart also built up the role of Mr. MacAfee, the frenzied father who protests against having his meals ruined, his home invaded by show people, and his family's kowtowing to Conrad's slightest whim, but eventually succumbs to all the excitement.

Many of the critics who liked *Bye, Bye, Birdie* were particularly impressed with its excellent cast. The role of Rose gave Chita Rivera even greater opportunity than she had had in *West Side Story* to demonstrate her adeptness as a comedienne, as a singer, and as a dancer. She was delightful as a vengeful Rose, ready to murder Albert; she was persuasive as an older girl disappointed in love when she sang "What Did I Ever See in Him?" with Kim; and she was sensational in a dance routine called "Shriner's Ballet." The role of Albert catapulted Dick Van Dyke into a brilliant career in television and in motion pictures, for he revealed that he was one of the most versatile young men in the musical comedy theater. He danced nimbly, sang well, and his double-takes were hilarious. He fluttered nervously in the scenes with his mother, mugged delightfully in the comedy bits, and enchanted audiences with his fresh, wholesome personality. Susan Watson as Kim was sweet and appealing, even when dressed in an outlandish shapeless sweater. Paul Lynde and Marijane Maricle as Mr. and Mrs. MacAfee made the song "Kids" an amusing commentary on the younger generation, and Miss Maricle's portrayal of the somewhat bewildered Mrs. MacAfee provided an admirable contrast for Mr. Lynde's lunacy. Dick Gautier, ideally cast as the hip-swinging, undulating Conrad, handled the dialogue as skillfully as he did the songs. Kay Medford, as Mrs. Peterson, the vitriolic mother, almost ran away with the show, for she squeezed a laugh out of every line. She regaled audiences, regardless of whether she was shuffling on stage in space shoes and dripping in full-length mink, or trying to sing a nasal accompaniment for her new discovery as a replacement for Conrad—a dancer who performed a split and then couldn't get up.

Gower Champion's famed exuberance as a performer carried over into *Bye, Bye, Birdie,* the first Broadway show he directed. He kept the action moving quickly through scenes that might otherwise have been awkward or exaggerated, emphasized the humor, and seldom allowed the pace to slacken, even in the musical interludes. Champion, who also devised and directed the choreography, incorporated touches that heightened the fun by satirizing the nonsensical habits of young people; particularly effective was a telephone sequence with teen-agers perched in odd positions on an elevated set, all making calls, and all slouching, kneeling, crouching, or simply lying stretched out on the floor. The conversations blended into a musical number that was fresh and imaginative.

For the ensembles, Champion had the youngsters move with rhythmic verve in routines that captured the exuberant spirit of the young. He also created two ballets for Chita Rivera. In the first, Miss Rivera, assisted by Dick Van Dyke, dreams of various methods of killing him and then puts each plan into action. The second ballet starts placidly as she crashes a Shriners' party and heads for the speaker's table but soon develops into a frenzied Mack Sennett chase with dancing on the table, under the table, and around the table until the meeting ends in bedlam.

If, as some critics felt, the score by Strouse and Adams was not particularly inspired, it still had numbers that were far better than the rock 'n' roll songs blaring on television and radio. Conrad Birdie's solos, "Honestly Sincere" and "One Last Kiss," were clever lampoons of the rock 'n' roll style, although they lost some of their special flavor when taken out of context. A third Birdie number, "A Lot of Livin' to Do," which had better rhythm and melody than the first two, became a popular hit and is still played frequently. Probably the best number in the score, "Put on a Happy Face," sung by Dick Van Dyke to charm two little girls who were sulking, has developed into a standard. One sad-faced little girl, played by Sharon Lerit, was an admirable foil for Van Dyke, whose singing, lithe dancing, and amusing attempts to get her to smile, made the song a standout.

The costumes designed by Miles White were colorful and effective, and his outfits for Conrad Birdie were hilarious exaggerations of garish bad taste, particularly a skintight, gold combination of jacket and trousers that sent the girls and women of Sweet Apple into ecstasies. Picturesque sets designed by Robert Randolph also helped the show by reflecting the wholesome, small-town atmosphere of Sweet Apple.

The appeal of *Bye, Bye, Birdie* was not limited to Broadway;

the show became a popular amateur production in a great many schools across the country because it gave students an opportunity to be uninhibited in their acting. One community theater in a mid-Eastern town scheduled a local production of *Bye, Bye, Birdie* for five weeks, but the demand for tickets was so heavy that the management extended the run for the balance of the season.

The motion-picture version was not so amusing as the stage production, although Dick Van Dyke repeated his excellent performance as Albert Peterson and Janet Leigh made an intriguing Rose Grant. The screen adaptation included changes that destroyed much of the original humor. The stage play, for example, spoofed the real problems that occur when untaped shows do not run on schedule, but the screen version introduced a slapstick change that taxed credibility by forcing ballet dancers to perform routines at an impossible speed. Moreover, Kim, as played by Ann-Margaret, was not quite the same wide-eyed girl portrayed by Susan Watson, and the characterization of Mrs. Peterson, as played by Maureen Stapleton, was altered, even to the point of marrying her off in the final reel.

In the last decade or so, the changing attitude of adults towards hysterical teen-agers has somewhat dimmed the amusing qualities of *Bye, Bye, Birdie*. In reviewing a recent summer revival of the show, one critic said that *Bye, Bye, Birdie* was not a production for adults who had seen it before. In 1960 and 1961, however, *Bye, Bye, Birdie* was an entertaining satire. It was not a great show, but it was a pleasant diversion that merited its run of 607 performances.

None of the four long-running musicals produced in the 1960–61 season was the surprise success that *Bye, Bye, Birdie* had been. Broadway showmen had predicted that three of them would be hits. *Camelot,* written by Alan Jay Lerner and Frederick Loewe, opened while their greatest success, *My Fair Lady,* was still running; Meredith Willson's *The Unsinkable Molly Brown* also opened while his first big hit, *The Music Man,* was still on Broadway; and *Carnival* was based on a very popular motion picture, *Lili.*

The fourth production, *Irma La Douce,* which opened September 29, 1960, and became the first musical hit of the season, had been a great success in Paris, where it opened in 1956. Two years later, it was presented in London where it also pleased large audiences, and then was brought to New York. The story was not particularly well constructed or startlingly new, but David Merrick's Broadway production of the London version, with the same director—Peter Brook—and the same three English players—Elizabeth Seal, Keith Michell, and Clive Revill—was a saucy novelty and pleased most of the critics.

The plot concerned Irma, a prostitute who is in love with Nestor, a poor law student, and is supporting him while he continues his schooling. Nestor becomes jealous of Irma's other clients, and, disguising himself with a false beard and derby hat, poses as a prospective protector, Monsieur Oscar, who becomes Irma's only client and for each visit pays her ten thousand francs, which she gives to Nestor. And so it goes—the same ten thousand francs changing hands as Nestor changes roles. In order to raise the initial sum, Nestor is forced to take on a variety of jobs. Between rushing from one type of work to another, jumping in and out of disguises, and pretending to be two different men with Irma, he grows wearier and wearier. Irma soon finds herself entranced by Oscar; Nestor, growing jealous of himself in the role of Irma's protector, decides to kill the imposter Oscar. He is arrested for the "murder" and sent to Devil's Island, but he manages to escape, clear himself of the murder charge, and return to Irma in time for the birth of their child on Christmas Eve.

In adapting the play for English and American audiences from the original French book and lyrics by Alexandre Breffort, the writers—Julian More, David Heneker, and Monty Norman—made certain situations, dialogue, and lyrics which could have been much more ribald seem almost harmless. By using French words—such as *milieu* for underworld, *grisbi* for money, *poule* for tart, and *mec* for procurer—they were able euphemistically to disguise references that could have offended some audiences and annoyed others. *Irma La Douce* made audiences overlook the more tawdry angles of the plot by blending sin with sentiment, by glossing over immorality with disarming innocence—and by diverting audiences with charming music, whirlwind dancing, superb sets, and a brilliant cast.

"The story of the bad girl with the heart of gold has been done many times," Miss Seal said in an interview, "but not like this." Her statement could not apply to the story itself, for the plot offered few new twists; but she was right about the production's being unusual, because Broadway audiences, accustomed to seeing musicals with many girls on stage, were surprised to find that she was the only girl to leaven an otherwise all-male cast. Miss Seal, making her first appearance in New York as Irma, dazzled audiences and critics with her sprightly performance. After watching her in action, more than one reviewer said that any idea of augmenting the cast with other women seemed absurd. She was pert, vivacious, and adorable. She sang the French numbers beautifully, as though she had been a Left-Bank chanteuse all her life, and she danced magnificently, high-kicking, whirling, and swirling through one intricate routine after another. Moreover, she was a capable actress who somehow managed to make Irma an alluring combination of French *poule* and helpless child.

Keith Michell, who played Nestor/Oscar, gave an exhausting performance in his dual role, changing costumes and donning and doffing his false beard with split-second speed. He was equally impressive in singing the ballad "Our Language of Love" with Miss Seal and in handling the comedy number "Wreck of a Mec." Both Mr. Michell and Clive Revill, who also played many parts, had been members of the Old Vic Company in England. The versatile Mr. Revill gave a deft comic performance as narrator, travel guide, proprietor of the bar where the underworld characters assembled, interpreter, and judge.

Peter Brook's direction and Onna White's choreography gave *Irma La Douce* a faster pace than a George Abbott farce. Rolf Gerard's excellent sets glided quickly on and off the stage, and Joe Davis' lighting further enhanced the production, at times turning the show into a kaleidoscopic spectacle of light and speed.

If the entire production had not been so diverting, and if audiences had had time to consider the book seriously, *Irma La Douce* might have fallen flat, but every time the plot threatened to get out of hand, the orchestra played Marguerite Monnot's very listenable music and one of the characters began to sing. Many people, in fact, considered the score to be the show's principal asset, the melodious songs charmingly orchestrated for accordion, xylophone, and trombone by Andre Popp to sound as if they were being played in a French music hall. Some of the lilting tunes included "Valse Milieu," an enchanting number similar to the title song; the rhythmic "Dis-Donc," sung by Miss Seal and leading into one of her dance routines; "There Is Only One Paris for That," with its toe-tapping tempo; and "Our Language of Love," sung by Irma and Nestor, which was a typical French ballad with an appealing melody.

Irma La Douce could definitely not be classified as "family entertainment," for many people found the story of the *poule* and her *mec* objectionable. In spite of its raffishness, however, *Irma La Douce* pleased many theatergoers and ran through one season and into the next with a total of 524 performances.

A few weeks after the première of *Irma La Douce,* another unconventional heroine invaded Broadway in Meredith Willson's *The Unsinkable Molly Brown,* which opened on November 3, 1960. Unlike Irma, whose easy virtue offended some audiences, Molly Brown was rough and raucous—but respectable.

Even before the premiere, audiences and critics were anticipating another sensational musical treat in *The Unsinkable Molly Brown,* and showmen were predicting that it would be a hit because Meredith Willson had written the score. The book by Richard Morris was based on the true story of an Irish girl, Molly Tobin, who was one of the few survivors of the shipwrecked *Titanic*. Morris' biographical account begins with a description of Molly's rough and tumble life in Hannibal, Missouri. Although she is illiterate, Molly is determined to get an education and to make a better life for herself. She goes to Colorado, works in a saloon, and meets Leadville Johnny Brown. They fall in love, marry, and become fabulously wealthy when Johnny strikes a rich mine. Molly's driving ambition, however, is to be a lady. Her adoring husband, who would get her anything she wanted, buys her a magnificent home in the most fashionable section of Denver, but the socialites of the city snub the uncultured Browns, and when Molly tries to make friends by inviting the social leaders to her home, no one comes. Realizing that she and Johnny lack the proper social graces, Molly persuades him to take her to Europe where they can acquire polish. The Browns' unlimited wealth brings them a host of European friends including members of the nobility, who seem to be enchanted by Molly's frankness and insatiable appetite for knowledge. By the time the Browns decide to return to Denver, Molly has learned to speak several languages, to play the piano, and to paint. The Browns invite a prince and several princesses to come back with them as house guests, and although the socialites in Denver are impressed by the royal visitors, they still refuse to accept Molly as an equal. This latest snub makes her determined to go back to Europe and never return; but Johnny, who wants to settle down and lead a more placid life, is equally determined that he will not leave. Molly goes alone. Although she mingles in prominent social circles and receives a proposal of marriage from a prince, Molly knows that she was wrong in leaving Johnny, that she still loves him, and that she has to go back to him. She sets sail on the ill-fated *Titanic*. When the ship is wrecked and begins to sink, she is one of the fortunate survivors. Her courage in the face of disaster makes her a heroine whom people afterward called "The Unsinkable Molly Brown." At the finale, although she has also become a heroine to the Denver socialites, it is her reunion with Johnny that makes her content at last.

Another element detracting from the plot's Cinderella quality and even adding a somewhat sordid note was the implication that it was their wealth alone that gained for Molly and Johnny entrance into European social circles. Having a prince propose marriage to Molly underlined still further the fact that these aristocrats were "selling" their titles to acquire financial security.

The Unsinkable Molly Brown opened on Broadway to mixed reviews. Some critics hailed the show as a hit; some thought it was spotty and uneven; and one review carried a headline stating that Molly "Fails to Float." Whether or not a theatergoer enjoyed the show depended almost entirely upon his response to Tammy Grimes, who played Molly Brown. She gave an excellent performance as the unkempt tomboy in the early scenes and convincingly portrayed Molly's gradual development into a smartly dressed, but still uninhibited, hoyden as the play progressed. Most of the critics praised her performance and, in their annual poll at the end of the season, acclaimed her as the best feminine performer in a musical comedy, by-passing Elizabeth Seal of *Irma La Douce* and Julie Andrews of *Camelot*. The vote was not unanimous, however, for one critic, who admitted that Miss Grimes was dynamic, said her appeal was limited to a special cult. After the show had been running for several months, it became clear that audience reaction to her performance was divided. Most people thought she was magnificent, but some theatergoers insisted that they could not hear or understand her because she often slurred words, garbled syllables, or threw away lines. On the other hand, opinions were unanimously favorable for the performance of tall, blond, and handsome Harve Presnell, who had the best voice in the company and made the role of Johnny believable.

Oliver Smith's brilliant sets included a saloon in Colorado, the elegant residential section of Denver, the sumptuous rooms in the Browns' mansion, a Parisian salon, and a scene in Monte Carlo. The scene in mid-Atlantic, which attempted too much and achieved too little, was the only setting that failed to impress. Miles White's costumes, particularly for the episodes in Denver and Paris, were elaborate and stunning. Audiences enjoyed Peter Gennaro's choreography, and Dore Schary's direction made the opening scenes vibrant. Schary also kept the play moving as briskly as possible in the second act, but he had to contend with an uneven script, for the early scenes were lusty and well paced, but the dialogue and action slowed down when Molly decided to crash society. Her experiences as a social climber in Denver and her mingling in European social circles were not half so amusing as her brawls and fights in Hannibal, Missouri, and Leadville, Colorado, had been. Furthermore, her decision to leave Johnny and go back to Europe did not create any sympathy for the headstrong heroine.

Instead of capitalizing on the wreck of the *Titanic* and Molly's heroic behavior in the lifeboat, the producers relegated the episode to one short scene, none too convincingly staged, and made it incidental to the rags-to-riches theme. The backdrop showed the *Titanic* going down; Molly stood up in the rowboat and spurred everyone on; but the scene was short, unrealistic, and inconclusive. What could have been a momentous episode became a mere transitory interlude.

Many people who compared the two Willson shows running simultaneously on Broadway felt that *The Unsinkable Molly Brown* lacked the humor and sentiment of *The Music Man*. The comparison was not quite justified, for *The Unsinkable Molly Brown* was a rowdier show with more emphasis on slapstick, especially in the first few scenes. Its contrast of backwoods life in Leadville with the elegance of Denver and Monte Carlo, and the shifting of scenes from America to Europe, gave it greater variety in types of dancing, costumes, and settings. Nevertheless, many audiences preferred the old-fashioned, nostalgic charm of *The Music Man*.

Meredith Willson shared the same experience as Rodgers and Hammerstein in being his own worst competitor, for critics said the music and lyrics for *The Unsinkable Molly Brown,* were too reminiscent of the songs he had created for *The Music Man*. For example, "I Ain't Down Yet" had the same rhythmic march style as "Seventy-Six Trombones." "Belly Up to the Bar, Boys" and "Chick-a-pen" were also rhythmic, but the score included two lovely ballads, "Dolce Far Niente," and "I'll Never Say No," while "Are You Sure" represented the jazz beat of Tin Pan Alley. Orchestral versions of the songs further revealed the excellence of the music, much of which was quite different from that of *The Music Man*.

In addition to its jaunty score, *The Unsinkable Molly Brown* contained several intriguing episodes. For example, in the opening number, Molly fights with her brothers shouting "I Ain't Down Yet," her diction down to earth and her ambition overpowering. At one point she grabs a broom and wields it like a scepter, drapes a tablecloth over her shoulders as a cape, places a pail on her head for a crown, and struts like a queen. Later in the show, Molly holds a prince's cane as a scepter, wears a fur cape draped just as the tablecloth had been, and, instead of a pail, wears a glittering tiara on her head. As she struts on stage just as she had in the first act, the similarity of her walk and the contrast of her costume make this moment a high spot.

Molly was delightful when she poked fun at herself, saying "I'm just a hog for knowledge"; when she fought with brawling customers in the saloon; and when she kicked off her shoes, picked up her skirt, and broke into a wild dance with Johnny in the scene when no one comes to her party.

The major difficulty with *The Unsinkable Molly Brown* was that, unlike *Gypsy* or *Fiorello!* which impressed audiences with their biographical authenticity, Molly Brown's plot seemed contrived. Even incidents that were supposedly based on fact seemed like fiction, for example, the scene in which Johnny asks Molly to guard the money from his first mine strike. The sum is enormous, and Molly, in desperation, tries hiding it first in one place and then in another. She finally decides that the pot-bellied stove would be the safest hiding place because since it is summer, no one would think of lighting a fire. While Molly is out of the room, Johnny comes home from a drinking bout, feels that he is getting a chill, and lights a fire. When Molly discovers that the money has burned, she becomes hysterical. The scene was hilarious but implausible; and it was followed by an equally fantastic episode in which Johnny promises to get Molly another strike, which he does almost immediately, finding a mine much more lucrative than the first. According to the reviewers, these incidents really occurred, but many people thought they were fictional. Later in the play, not knowing what to give Molly as a gift, Johnny sends her the same amount of money that he had burned in the stove—and a match. This scene added a bright touch to the on-again, off-again status of the marriage, but it still did not convince skeptics that the first episode had been true.

The Unsinkable Molly Brown reminded some people very much of Ethel Merman's hit show, *Annie Get Your Gun,* which also dealt with a hillbilly who rose to fame. The basic difference between the characterizations of Annie and Molly, however, partially explains why *Annie Get Your Gun* seemed to have more popular appeal; Annie won audience sympathy almost from the start because her desire for culture and fame was depicted humorously, whereas Molly's ambition and brashness were made to seem much more hard-boiled and calculating.

Miss Grimes and Mr. Presnell dominated the action because the script kept the supporting characters in the background. Edith Meiser, however, did manage to impress audiences with her brief appearance as Denver's social leader, and Mitchell Gregg, as the prince who wanted to marry Molly, sang one of the show's best numbers, "Dolce Far Niente."

The motion-picture version, with Debbie Reynolds and Harve Presnell, benefited a great deal from Miss Reynolds' performance; she pleased audiences and surprised those critics who had maintained before the picture was released that she might have been miscast. Miss Reynolds was not quite the comic-strip character in the opening scenes that Miss Grimes had been, but she was much more effective in the last half as the unhappy Molly who knew she should never have left Johnny.

In spite of its shortcomings, the stage production did entertain audiences. The magnificent staging, the performances of Miss Grimes and Mr. Presnell, and above all, Meredith Willson's songs almost disguised the hackneyed plot and kept *The Unsinkable Molly Brown* floating for 532 performances, a long run by Broadway standards, but a disappointing run for those who had expected *Molly Brown* to be a success of the same magnitude as *The Music Man.*

Meredith Willson was not the only composer who suffered comparisons in the 1960–61 season because two of his shows were running simultaneously on Broadway. Alan Jay Lerner and Frederick Loewe faced even more damaging comparisons when *Camelot* opened December 6, 1960, and the critics and public both found it a decided let-down from their triumphant *My Fair Lady,* which was still drawing capacity houses and moving ever closer to establishing a longevity record for musical comedies. One critic, in fact, said that *Camelot* would be gone before *My Fair Lady* closed. His prediction was almost correct, for *My Fair Lady* ended its run on September 29, 1962, and *Camelot* closed January 3, 1963.

Figures differ on the actual cost of production, which ran over $500,000 before *Camelot* reached New York. Estimates also vary on the advance ticket sales, but most sources agree that the box office was deluged with orders that totaled well over $3 million. The advance sale was so large, in fact, that the press agent was reported to have said, after reading the unfavorable reviews, that *Camelot* could become the first failure to run for two years.

The public's tremendous interest in the show even before it opened stemmed from many causes. The principal reason seemed to be the fact that Lerner and Loewe, who had written *Camelot;* Moss Hart, who directed it; and Julie Andrews, who starred in it, had all been connected with *My Fair Lady.* Miss Andrews had not only won national publicity for her performance as Eliza Doolittle both in New York and London but also had become known to millions of television fans for her performances in *High Tor* and in the Rodgers and Hammerstein special *Cinderella.* Furthermore, Richard Burton, who was to play King Arthur, had appeared on Broadway with Helen Hayes in *Time Remembered,* had established an excellent reputation as a Shakespearean actor with the Old Vic Company, and had built up a following for his performances in motion pictures.

Public interest in *Camelot* remained high even when newspapers reported a series of misfortunes that began when famous Hollywood designer Adrian, who was working on the costumes, died. Tony Duquette took over the assignment and completed the job superbly. Before the show reached New York, Moss Hart, the director, had had a heart attack, and Alan Jay Lerner was suffering from ulcers. When *Camelot* opened in Toronto, it ran more than an hour overlength, and cutting became a necessity. By the time it reached Broadway, the production had been whittled down but still seemed to drag in spots, and the producers eventually cut an additional twenty-five minutes after the New York première.

Lerner and Loewe had based *Camelot* on T. H. White's *The Once and Future King,* which had offered a new version of the Arthurian legends, and included King Arthur's hopes for a peaceful world, the marriage of Arthur and Guenevere, the unhappy love story of Lancelot and Guenevere, the villainy of Modred, the wizardry of Merlin, who lived his life backwards, and the escapades of Sir Pellinore, the dragon-hunter. The story of King Arthur and the Knights of the Round Table had been told many. times before T. H. White's account, and each version, although generally faithful to the main story line, varied the incidents or characterizations slightly. Malory's *Morte d'Arthur* and Tennyson's *Idylls of the King* were standard reading requirements in high schools and colleges for a great many years. T. H. White's book revived contemporary interest in the Arthurian legends.

Lerner found himself confronting an almost impossible task in writing the adaptation. Shaw's *Pygmalion,* by comparison, had been simple to adapt into the musical *My Fair Lady,* for Shaw had provided a clear-cut basic plot that could be augmented with music. *The Once and Future King,* on the other hand, contained a variety of episodes, characters, and incidents that Lerner had to organize and condense into a production that could not run longer than three hours. Furthermore, Lerner could not try a radically new approach which might have raised objections from people who had preconceived notions about the characters, nor could he rely on any one version of the legend, since there were so many variations in the treatment of the main characters.

Instead of trying to retain the somberness of the legend, Lerner and Loewe tried to lighten *Camelot* with songs and sprightly numbers that were, despite their tunefulness, at times incongruous with the action. Lerner and Loewe also tried to follow the pattern of *My Fair Lady* by integrating the songs with the story; but in many scenes the musical numbers merely repeated what the complicated action had already disclosed. Even an attempt to integrate the musical selections into a scene by scene synopsis results in a choppy, disjointed summary.

At the beginning of Act One, Arthur, nervous about his approaching marriage to Guenevere, sings "I Wonder What the King Is Doing Tonight" to express his doubts, and then hides in a tree; Guenevere appears, and she, too, is apprehensive about the marriage. Her first number, "The Simple Joys of Maidenhood," tells of her yearning to enjoy a little more of life before becoming a bride. Arthur and Guenevere meet, and Arthur describes the charms of his kingdom in "Camelot."

To dispose of Merlin early in the plot, the writers use "Follow Me," sung by a spirit-creature who entices Merlin into a magic trap.

Arthur establishes the Round Table, and Lancelot comes from France to become one of the Knights, stating his qualifications in "C'est Moi." The song conveys the impression that Lancelot is smug and priggish. His assurance and egotism do not endear him to the Court or to Guenevere, who sings "Then You May Take Me to the Fair" to three knights who she hopes will defeat Lancelot in the tournaments. This number was cut from the show after the Broadway opening.

Arthur, unable to persuade Guenevere to conceal her dislike

for Lancelot, muses over his problem in a musical soliloquy, "How to Handle a Woman." At the tournament, Lancelot defeats his opponents and delivers what appears to be a fatal blow to Sir Lionel. By means of his intense faith, however, Lancelot brings Sir Lionel back to life and thereby wins the admiration of Guenevere and the knights.

Lancelot realizes that he has fallen in love with Guenevere. Unwilling to betray his friend King Arthur, he decides to leave Camelot. Before doing so, he sings of his love for the Queen in "Before I Gaze on You Again." Two years later, Lancelot returns and Arthur knights him in a very impressive ceremony, not revealing that he knows Lancelot and Guenevere are in love. In one of the show's best numbers, "If Ever I Would Leave You," Lancelot then clearly defines the great love he had for Guenevere.

Arthur's troubles increase when Modred, his illegitimate son, plans to depose him and take over the throne. In "The Seven Deadly Virtues," Modred expresses his contempt for all that Arthur represents. One of the quietest and most delightful scenes in the production follows, in which Arthur and Guenevere are shown trying to keep up the pretense of being happily married by singing "What Do the Simple Folk Do."

As his first step in deposing Arthur, Modred plans to trap him in the forest and keep him there for the night. Although Morgan Le Fay, the sorceress, seems reluctant to help him, Modred finally convinces her by plying her with one of her favorite delicacies, chocolates. Modred has also stirred up the knights, who express their discontent in "Fie on Goodness." During the time that Arthur is trapped in the enchanted forest, Lancelot comes to Guenevere's room, and Guenevere, in the ballad "I Loved You Once in Silence," confesses her love for him. Hoping to trap Guenevere and Lancelot, Modred breaks into Guenevere's chambers and accuses her of treason. Lancelot manages to escape, but Guenevere is arrested, tried, and sentenced to burn at the stake. Although Lancelot succeeds in rescuing Guenevere, his action forces Arthur to wage war against him. In the final scene, which takes place before the battle begins, Arthur meets with Guenevere and Lancelot and forgives them. A young boy then approaches, saying that he wants to join the Round Table. Before sending the child home, Arthur reprises the song "Camelot," instructing the boy to tell future generations the story of that kingdom and what it had represented.

Lerner and Loewe were not always successful in using musical numbers to develop the plot. For example, the necessity to condense lengthy episodes from the book into one short scene in the play resulted in the use of a choral group singing "Guenevere" to relate what had transpired at Guenevere's trial. The oratorio quality of the number negated the dramatic effect that might have resulted if Guenevere had been shown defending herself against her accusers. Such a trial scene, however, would have added more running time to a show that needed cutting rather than expanding. As a result, the musical interlude glossed over the trial far too quickly to make the scene the dramatic highlight it might have been.

The production opened in New York to mixed reviews. Several critics wrote kind reviews about certain parts of the show but expressed disappointment in the production as a whole. Others expressed complete disapproval. The reviewers, however, differed in the reasons for their objections. One critic thought *Camelot* would have been a better show if it had been written in the same light-hearted style as *A Connecticut Yankee,* which Rodgers and Hart had adapted from Mark Twain's humorous story about King Arthur's Court. A second critic also felt that Lerner would have been more successful had he treated the story as a farce; and a third critic objected to the unhappy ending. *A Connecticut Yankee* had been an amusing musical because Mark Twain's story had been amusing, but White's *The Once and Future King* was not a satire; and Lerner, in making the adaptation, could not tamper with the basically serious plot. Even though the ending of *Camelot* was unhappy, Lerner did compromise by not showing the death of Arthur. He also tried to inject as much humor as possible, but unfortunately these lighter scenes overshadowed the rest of the production and made the show uneven.

The critics were divided in their opinions on some of the humorous touches which Lerner used. Several reviewers liked the scene in which Morgan Le Fay agrees to trap Arthur in the forest; others thought her ecstasies over the chocolates ridiculous. Most of the reviewers said Sir Pellinore, the dragon-hunter, had his amusing moments, but the dissenters felt that his funny scenes were thin. The original source material also limited Lerner's opportunities in other ways. For example, the villainous Modred, who added animation to the plot, could not be introduced until the second act.

Although the critics were not in agreement on the merits of the score or the libretto, they were unanimous in their approval of the sets and costumes. Oliver Smith's magnificent settings included parks, terraces, grandstands, jousting fields, forests, battlefields, and a stupendous throne room complete with gold throne. The costumes were equally brilliant, with soft pastels in some scenes, brilliant colors in others, and sparkling gold in the throne-room sequence. No one could minimize the effectiveness of the sets and costumes, but magnificent scenery and glittering gowns could not disguise the ponderousness of the action.

Several members of the excellent cast received rave notices, which helped draw theatergoers to the box office. Richard Burton, ideally cast as King Arthur, surprised audiences with his ease in handling the musical numbers and dance steps. His distinguished acting made for effective portrayals of Arthur as bewildered young man, idealistic king, unhappy husband, and, finally, disillusioned warrior. Robert Goulet triumphed over Lancelot's smugness in the first act, for he was handsome, romantic, and personable. As *Camelot* continued its run on Broadway, and as Mr. Goulet began making appearances on television programs, he soon developed into a popular matinee idol and became one of the biggest drawing attractions in the show. His first number, "C'est Moi," may not have aroused any audience sympathy for Lancelot, but his striking appearance in shining armor and his remarkable voice stirred up audience interest in Mr. Goulet. Later in the show he sang the ballad "If Ever I Would Leave You" superbly. Julie Andrews, who looked even more strikingly beautiful than she had in the Embassy Ball scene from *My Fair Lady,* sang Guenevere's songs magnificently, but the script did not permit her to be the jealous, passionate queen of the legends. Miss Andrews's portrayal made Guenevere a much gentler, more charming, and more sympathetic character. In their scenes together, she and Mr. Burton did a great deal to enliven the action. Almost every critic singled out their opening songs and "What Do the Simple Folk Do" as the bright spots in the show. Roddy McDowell as Modred, Robert Coote as Sir Pellinore, and M'el Dowd as Morgan Le Fay gave excellent performances in small roles that added a sparkling glow to some of the somber, slow-moving scenes.

Before *Camelot* completed its run, the cast had changed. William Squires replaced Richard Burton as King Arthur; when Julie Andrews left the show, Patricia Bredin, followed by Janet Pavek, and motion-picture actress Kathryn Grayson, played Guenevere. Robert Peterson replaced Robert Goulet as Lancelot late in the run.

Camelot might have received better reviews and might have run much longer if Lerner and Loewe had not written *My Fair Lady* first. Unquestionably *Camelot* suffered from the inevitable comparisons.

Camelot had sufficient merit, however, to win several awards in the New York Drama Critics' Annual Poll. Richard Burton was voted the best male performer in a musical; Oliver Smith, the best set designer; Adrian and Tony Duquette, the best costumers; and Alan Jay Lerner, the best lyricist.

These awards, the huge advance sale, and the popularity of such songs as "If Ever I Should Leave You," "Camelot," and "Follow Me," which was played more frequently as an orchestral number, helped the show span a second season on Broadway. Robert Goulet, the last of the three principals to leave the cast, developed into an even stronger box-office name in the second season. *Camelot* definitely became a financial hit that not only lasted longer' than skeptics had predicted but also outran the other three hit musicals produced in the 1960–61 season with a total of 837 performances.

Camelot also became a major road attraction for two seasons. After the Broadway production closed, it was sent on tour with William Squires as Arthur, Katharine Grayson as Guenevere, and Robert Peterson as Lancelot. Later, Louis Hayward and George Wallace played Arthur, and Anne Jeffreys replaced Katharine Grayson as Guenevere before the tour ended. A second company with Biff McGuire as Arthur and Jeannie Carson as Guenevere also began touring in November 1963. The following year, a London production opened with Laurence Harvey as Arthur. Before the season ended, Paul Daneman took over the lead.

In spite of the hit status of *Camelot, The Unsinkable Molly Brown,* and *Irma La Douce,* the 1960–61 season had disappointed many critics. Theatergoers and critics alike were eager for a different type of show. *Carnival,* the fourth musical hit of the season, opened April 13, 1961, and through its imaginative use of puppets, its wistful heroine, and its poignant hero, recreated a magic wonderland of childhood that induced a greater sympathetic and emotional response from audiences than any of its predecessors in the same season. The newspaper critics unanimously approved the production and showered it with praise. The Critics' Circle endorsed *Carnival* by selecting it as the best musical of the season.

Those critics who made references to the motion-picture *Lili* from which *Carnival* had been adapted, limited their comments, for the most part, to factual information about the original material. The Metro-Goldwyn-Mayer film, written by Helen Deutsch and based on a story by Paul Gallico, featured Leslie Caron and Mel Ferrer. Instead of booking *Lili* into one of the larger New York houses, the producers had presented it in the small Trans-Lux Theatre on Lexington Avenue where it proved to be a sleeper, delighting audiences with its wistful charm. When the picture ran on and on, and the title song became a popular hit, many theaters that had already shown the film brought it back for highly successful re-runs.

The stage version, *Carnival,* produced by David Merrick and adapted for the stage by Michael Stewart, featured Anna Maria Alberghetti as Lili, Jerry Orbach as the puppeteer Paul, and James Mitchell, Kaye Ballard, and Pierre Olaf as carnival performers. The story remained faithful to the screen version and dealt with Lili, a wide-eyed waif who takes a job with a carnival owned by a friend of her late father. She falls in love with the magician, Marco the Magnificent, but is equally intrigued by the puppet show, whose marionette walrus and fox talk to the lonely girl and become her friends. Within a short time, Lili's conversations with the puppets, whom she treats as real creatures, become a major audience attraction. The temperamental puppeteer, em-

bittered because of an accident which left him lame, falls in love
with Lili but can only express his affection by remaining hidden
and allowing the puppets to speak for him. When he tries to speak
directly to her, he rages and shouts. Eventually the innocent Lili
learns that Marco has long been involved in a liaison with his assistant, Rosalie. No longer wanting to compete for his affections, Lili
decides to leave the carnival but stops to say good-bye to her
friends the walrus and the fox. When they plead with her to stay,
she suddenly realizes that she loves not them, but the man who has
used them to reveal his love for her.

Even before *Carnival* reached Broadway, rumors spread that
Merrick had another hit, one that benefited from imaginative
staging, excellent direction, a good score, and a fine cast. Gower
Champion, who had delighted critics with his work on *Bye, Bye,
Birdie,* had even greater opportunities in *Carnival* to demonstrate
his skill as a director and choreographer. The plot unashamedly
emphasized sentiment, for *Carnival* was, despite its exotic circus
atmosphere and tawdry gaiety, the simple romance of a winsome
girl and a lame boy who find true happiness together. But by coun-
terbalancing moments of tenderness with moments of humor and
scenes of multiple action, Champion never permitted sentiment to
lapse into sentimentality.

When the audience entered the theater, the curtain was already up, revealing a stage bare except for a backdrop that depicted a countryside scene. As the houselights dimmed, Pierre
Olaf, one of the carnival workers, wandered onto the set and
began playing the show's theme song on a concertina. Very soon
the audience had the same thrill that children experience when
they crowd circus grounds to see a show being assembled, for
Will Steven Armstrong's mobile sets were rapidly transforming
the stage into a magical carnival world. While the roustabouts
were putting up the main tent, booths glided on stage, flags were
raised, and lights turned on. The circus music blared, and carnival
players in gaudy costumes paraded onto the set. In several sequences, Champion had performers or souvenir vendors coming
up the aisles on their way onto the stage so that the audience felt
more and more that it was right in the midst of the carnival.
Champion also included one exciting sequence in which jugglers

tossed flaming torches while actors milled around and roustabouts shifted scenery. Acrobats, dancers, and even a dog act added authenticity to the circus atmosphere. In the final scene, the carnival set was struck in the manner in which it had been raised, and the show closed on a barren stage with a fake countryside in the distance.

Champion made certain that James Mitchell, who played Marco, the magician, actually performed feats of magic, such as pulling a lighted cigarette from Lili's ear. For one of Mitchell's routines, Champion staged the song "Always, Always You" in a very clever manner. Marco placed his assistant, Rosalie, in a basket; and as they sang the duet, he plunged large swords into the basket. Regardless of how the trick was done, it looked authentic and made the number both a novelty and an enigma. Mitchell, moreover, performed the trick so adeptly that audiences forgot he was a dancer and not an experienced sleight-of-hand artist.

Expert performances added to the charm of *Carnival*. Anna Maria Alberghetti made an excellent Lili. She demonstrated that her reputation as a singer was well deserved and also revealed considerable acting ability in her portrayal of the innocent girl who found solace in the puppets. Jerry Orbach in the difficult role of Paul, the crippled puppeteer, expertly handled the dialogue and his manipulation of the puppets' voices. Kaye Ballard, a facile comedienne, played Rosalie; and James Mitchell, whom audiences remembered for his brilliant dancing in such shows as *Brigadoon,* performed one of Champion's most dazzling routines in the number "Sword, Rose, and Cape." Pierre Olaf, the bespectacled, cherubic little man who had appeared in Merrick's production of *La Plume de Ma Tante,* played the puppeteer's friend. In the second act, when the troupe heard rumors of the carnival's being taken to Paris, Mr. Olaf, in one of Gower Champion's best routines, began doing an intricate dance step. The carnival dancing girls picked up the step and kept pace with Mr. Olaf until the dance became an exciting, vigorous, and almost abandoned romp.

To many people the puppets, created and supervised by Tom Tichenor, were the most important characters in the show; their scenes with Lili were wistful, charming and often amusing as they reprimanded her, gave her advice, or sang with her. The puppets, of necessity, had to be large enough to be seen in the balcony but still small enough to be manipulated by hand, and Tichenor made them just the right size to create the kind of magic that enthralled youngsters and amused adults. The element of fantasy was always present, but the puppeteer and Lili also managed to create in their conversations a very strong illusion of reality. The puppeteer's ability to make the animals speak brought a nostalgic response from those people who had wanted to have that same experience when they were children and whose play-acting with toys was never so satisfactory as Lili's delightful interludes with the walrus and the fox.

Instead of using the theme song from the motion picture, "Lili," Bob Merrill, who wrote both music and lyrics, created an entirely new score. The critics singled out for special praise such numbers as "Her Face," sung by Paul; "Mira," sung by Lili; and "Beautiful Candy," sung by Lili and the puppets. The theme song, "Love Makes the World Go Round," became a hit that retained its popularity long after the show had closed.

In addition to naming *Carnival* the best musical of the season, the New York Drama Critics also named Merrill the best composer of the season, and tied the vote for best director between Gower Champion and Franklin Shaffner (*Advise and Consent*). Tony Awards were given to Anna Maria Alberghetti for the best female performer in a musical and to Will Steven Armstrong for the best scene designer.

During the run of *Carnival*, rumors of friction between David Merrick and Miss Alberghetti were mentioned vaguely in several drama columns, and Miss Alberghetti at one point dropped out of the cast. Merrick used a number of actresses as her replacements, including Anita Gilette, Julie Migenes, Wendy Waring, Susan Watson, Mimi Turque, and Carla Alberghetti, sister of Anna Maria. Miss Alberghetti returned to the cast, however, and later played the lead in the touring company. In spite of cast changes, *Carnival* spanned two seasons on Broadway with a run of 719 performances.

None of the musicals produced in the 1960–61 season, however, had the tremendous appeal of *How to Succeed in Business Without Really Trying*, which opened October 14, 1961, and immediately became Broadway's biggest hit in several years. Unanimous rave reviews sent buyers scurrying to the box office for tickets, regardless of how far in advance they might be; ticket agents told prospective customers that no seats would be available for months; and business executives with expense accounts paid exorbitant under-the-counter prices to see a show that lampooned their activities.

Many people, who knew that the musical had been based on a popular book written by Shepherd Mead, wondered why the producers had not shortened the original title. Columnists and critics tried to abbreviate it to "How to Succeed in Business," and then "How to Succeed." One or two even resorted to using only the first letter in each word—HTSIBWRT. The men who set up the marquee managed to devise a sign that included the names of the two featured players as well as the full-length title in the limited space, but when a second musical opened that same season with an even longer title, *A Funny Thing Happened on the Way to the Forum,* one puzzled producer, not affiliated with either production, said, "What ever happened to the good old days when we had shows like *Sally* and *Irene?*"

In *The Best Plays of 1961–1962,* Henry Hewes, the editor, explained that Jack Weinstock and Willie Gilbert had originally adapted Shepherd Mead's book *How to Succeed in Business Without Really Trying* as a straight comedy, and only later agreed to make it into a musical with the collaboration of Abe Burrows, who also became the director. The musical reunited producers Cy Feuer and Ernest Martin, composer-lyricist Frank Loesser, and director Burrows, all of whom had been associated with *Guys and Dolls.* Once again the group created a show that had the satirical wit of *Of Thee I Sing;* the integration of plot and music and the slick production of *Guys and Dolls;* and a tight script with sufficient merit as a play to win the Pulitzer Prize for drama and the Critics' Circle Award as best musical comedy of the season.

The plot satirized one of the most popular dramatic situations in American drama, the famous Horatio Alger "rags-to-riches" story. The musical also made use of the equally popular theme of Cinderella and Prince Charming. Loesser even included one song, "Cinderella, Darling," in which the office girls pleaded with Rosemary, the heroine, to make the fairy tale come true by marrying the hero, J. Pierrepont Finch, whose meteoric rise has made him the Prince Charming of the World Wide Wicket Company. Moreover, the authors aptly fulfilled the promise of the show's title by lampooning big business, executive board meetings, yes-men, nepotism, rigged television quiz shows, office wolves, coffee breaks, and office romance.

The play opens with J. Pierrepont Finch, a window washer, studying Mr. Mead's book while an offstage voice reads the passages aloud to the audience. From time to time throughout the performance, Finch refers to the text, which serves to explain Finch's next strategic move in his phenomenal rise from window washer to Chairman of the Board. He begins working for the World Wide Wicket Company in the mail room alongside Frump, the president's despicable nephew, but through his book he becomes aware that the position has no future. When he is selected to become head mail clerk, Finch magnanimously declares that Frump, rather than he, is the logical man for the job—an underhanded trick that makes Frump ineligible for the junior executive post Finch really wants. From then on, Finch knifes or leaps over each opponent as he advances in the organization. He pretends to work overtime to impress Mr. Biggeley, the president; capitalizes on Biggeley's loyalty to his Alma Mater to get rid of a man who had graduated from a rival college; and sends Hedy LaRue, his voluptuous but incompetent secretary, to deliver a letter to an important executive, a notorious office wolf who, not suspecting that the glamorous Hedy is the personal property of Mr. Biggeley, tries to date her. The lights black out and come on within seconds to reveal Finch seated at the ex-executive's desk. After maneuvering himself into the top position in the planning and development department, Finch, as his first advertising gimmick, persuades Biggeley that the company should sponsor a treasure-hunt program on television featuring Hedy LaRue. To avoid any accusation of rigging, Finch makes certain that no one except Biggeley and himself would know where the treasure had been hidden; but he completely overlooks the fact that Biggeley might tell Hedy. On the very first telecast, when the announcer asks her to swear on a Bible that she does not know where the treasure has been buried, Hedy blurts out the hiding place. Finch's future prospects look bleak until Mr. Womper, Chairman of the Board, and a former window washer, too, begins to investigate the television fiasco and is delighted to discover that Finch began as a window washer. The final scene shows Womper preparing to go on a honeymoon with his new bride, the seductive Hedy, and Finch by-passing even Biggeley to become the new Chairman of the Board.

The satire on rigged television programs was particularly timely, for during the run of *How to Succeed in Business Without Really Trying,* millions of people were still dazed by the startling disclosure that several quiz shows offering fabulous sums of prize money had given information beforehand to contestants. The investigation of this malpractice had also revealed that many programs offering only nominal prizes had also been rigged to make panelists or contestants seem more astute and, therefore, more interesting to audiences. The show's lampoon of these television scandals served a double purpose, for it not only ridiculed the rigging but also provided a temporary—but necessary—setback for Finch's spectacular rise to power.

Abe Burrows' direction and Bob Fosse's staging of the musical scenes both emphasized humor. By using gags and blackouts effectively, Burrows built up each episode to a hilarious climax. In the musical sequences, Fosse often used novel tricks that made these numbers quite different from the standard song and ·dance routines. Sometimes he broke the chorus line into small groups with only two or three performers on stage at a time. In one of the early scenes, he had the actors stand motionless, suddenly become animated for a moment or, two, and then freeze back into position. This way of depicting all workers as puppets was amusing, and the constant change in action and movement also quickened the tempo.

The scenery, lighting, and costumes were all as slick as the script. Robert Randolph's rapidly-changing sets depicted the offices, corridors, and even the executive washroom in the World Wide Wicket Company; Robert Fletcher designed typical Madison Avenue–style business suits, which varied from somber, neutral shades to light pastels. His garish, tight-fitting outfits for Hedy

LaRue made her the focal point of interest on stage and provided an effective contrast to the bright but conservatively-tailored dresses he had created for the attractive secretaries.

Frank Loesser won both a Tony and the Critics' Circle Award as the best lyricist of the year, a distinction he well deserved; but the fact that he did not receive any award for his music does not indicate that his melodies were inferior. The satirical wit of the lyrics simply overshadowed the music, for Loesser carefully tailored each song to advance the plot or the characterization. The duet "Rosemary" served well as the conventional love song found in most musical comedies, but it was not half so impressive as two other satirical ballads. The first, "Love from a Heart of Gold," sung by Biggeley and Hedy, lampooned Rudy Vallee's famous old love songs and also ridiculed the shouting female vocalist, for Hedy began the first chorus in a normal tone and then gradually increased the volume so that by the second chorus she was letting loose with powerful blasts that drowned out the orchestra. The second ballad, "I Believe in You," was written for a scene set in the washroom. Finch, who had come in to shave, sang the lyrics to his own reflection in the mirror while the orchestra imitated the buzz of electric razors, and the other executives, in a counter melody, sang about stopping Finch in his rise to power. In the context of the show the song was Finch's love song to himself. Outside the show (and in the movie version) it has gained lasting popularity as a standard love song.

"Brotherhood of Man" had a bouncy rhythm that helped the number develop into a spirited chorale with almost the fervor of a revivalist chant. "The Company Way" also had an effective rhythm, but Loesser's bright lyrics satirizing yes-men and "company policy" again obscured the excellence of the melody. "A Secretary Is Not a Toy" had the most adult lyrics of any number in the show, but the clever staging and tricky dancing made audiences overlook certain of its innuendoes.

The number "Coffee Break," on the other hand, used an almost unmelodic accompaniment, for the lyrics did not need a particularly tuneful background. As the scene opened, employees rushed to their desks just in time to avoid being late, set up their work material, and then immediately prepared for a coffee break.

After the coffee wagon was wheeled on stage, the startling announcement that the urn was empty led into a musical lament expressing the misery of an office staff unable to eat breakfast on company time.

Loesser's score also included delightful little touches in the orchestral accompaniments, such as the use of kazoos to imitate the sound of electric razors, and—during the romantic ballad "Rosemary," in which Finch first kisses his sweetheart—the inclusion of a romantic strain from a Grieg piano concerto to make the accompaniment sound like background music for a Hollywood love epic.

The original cast, which did much to enhance the appeal of the production, included Robert Morse as Finch; Rudy Vallee as J. B. Biggeley; Charles Nelson Reilly as Frump; Virginia Martin as Hedy LaRue; Bonnie Scott as Rosemary; Claudette Sutherland as Smitty; Ruth Kobart as Miss Jones; and Sammy Smith, who doubled in the roles of Mr. Twimble, head of the mail room, and Mr. Womper, Chairman of the Board.

Both Vallee and Morse, the two featured performers, were popular box office attractions. Morse had become known to Broadway audiences through his appearances in *The Matchmaker, Say, Darling,* and *Take Me Along.* The role of Finch fit his many talents and won him the Tony Award, the *Variety* Poll of Drama Critics award, and the endorsement of Henry Hewes, the *Best Plays* editor, for the best male performance in a musical comedy of that season. Rudy Vallee, one of the leading stars in show business during the 1920s and 1930s, had become famous as the bandleader of the Connecticut Yankees orchestra, had appeared in several Broadway shows and motion pictures, and had been the host and star of "The Fleischman Variety Hour" radio program.

Vallee's performance as J. B. Biggeley surprised a great many people who remembered him only as a popular singing idol. When Vallee cupped his hands as if he were singing through his famous megaphone his fans broke into spontaneous applause. Ladies who had adored him as "The Vagabond Lover" sighed with nostalgic joy when he sang "Love from a Heart of Gold" with Hedy LaRue. The role of Biggeley, however, also capitalized on his talent as a comedian, and parents who took their teen-age children to see the show often found that the younger set's reaction to Vallee was quite different from their own. In the lobby during the intermission at an evening performance, a teen-age girl said to her mother, "Why did you tell me he was a singer? He's a comedian, and I think he's a riot."

By playing the role straight and always maintaining his dignity, Vallee contributed an excellent characterization of the typical big business executive, susceptible to flattery. The contrast between Vallee, who looked dignified even when dressed in old-fashioned golf knickers, and the ebullient Robert Morse highlighted their duet, "Grand Old Ivy," with Vallee singing it straight and Morse purring, cuddling, and squirming around Vallee to ingratiate himself. The duet was an amusing lampoon of college songs and a spoof of "The Maine Stein Song"—Vallee's most durable trademark.

If played by the wrong actor, Finch could have been a despicable, scheming rascal, whose downfall would have pleased audiences. Morse, however, exuded innocence and charm as he trampled his opponents, and his youthful appeal effectively glossed over Finch's conniving aggressiveness. To make Finch even more likeable, the script built up the role of Frump, Biggeley's nephew, who was equally as ruthless and as determined to succeed as Finch, but was presented in contrast as a nasty young man with no talent, succeeding only because he used family influence. Frump's whining, malicious badgering, and petty rages were no match for Finch's dimpled smile, and innocent baby stare. The more hostile the audience became to Frump, the more anxious it was for Finch to succeed; the contrast between the rivals made Finch appear an all-American hero compared to Frump, the all-American heel. Charles Nelson Reilly's excellent performance as the nasty Frump won him not only the *Variety* Poll of Drama Critics award but also the Tony Award as the best supporting male player in a musical production. Henry Hewes in *The Best Plays of 1961–1962* also cited Reilly as having given an outstanding performance.

Virginia Martin, who had first appeared on Broadway in *New Faces of 1956,* in which she did an impersonation of Marilyn Monroe, emerged as a deft comedienne in her characterization of Hedy LaRue. Miss Martin made Hedy a combination of Mae West,

Marilyn Monroe, and practically all the other screen sirens rolled into one. Bonnie Scott as Rosemary, the patient girl who loved Finch, and Ruth Kobart as Mr. Biggeley's formidable secretary, also gave excellent performances.

In addition to the prizes already mentioned, Tony Awards were given to producers·Cy Feuer and Ernest Martin; authors Abe Burrows, Jack Weinstock, and Willie Gilbert; and music director Elliot Lawrence. Burrows also received the Tony Award and won the *Variety* Poll of Drama Critics as the best director of a musical production of that season.

When Robert Morse and Rudy Vallee left the cast, skeptics thought the show might lose its drawing power, but the musical continued in spite of numerous cast replacements. Morse, who left the show after two years was replaced by Darryl Hickman, who was succeeded a year later by Ronnie Welsh; Vallee, who stayed with the production for three years, was followed by Jeff deBenning as Biggeley; Ralph Purdom took over Reilly's role as Frump; Joy Claussen and, later, Maureen Arthur replaced Virginia Martin as Hedy; and Lois Leary, Michele Lee, and Suzanne Menke appeared as Rosemary.

The popularity of *How to Succeed in Business* was not limited to Broadway. Two road companies began profitable tours in 1963, and a third was sent out in 1965 after the production had closed in New York with a phenomenal run of 1,417 performances, making it, at that time, the fifth longest-running musical comedy in the history of the Broadway theater.

In the 1961–62 season, Frank Loesser's accomplishment in writing both words and music for *How to Succeed in Business Without Really Trying* was not unique, for Richard Rodgers also worked in the dual capacity of composer-lyricist that season.

How to Succeed in Business Without Really Trying had emphasized speed and humor, but *No Strings,* the Richard Rodgers-Samuel Taylor musical, highlighted settings, costumes, and melody. After the death of Oscar Hammerstein II, many show people wondered whom Rodgers would select as his lyricist; when Rodgers decided that for the first time he would write his own lyrics, they were even more curious about the outcome.

The show opened to mixed reviews, but most critics felt that

Rodgers had again created delightful melodies and that he had also written good lyrics which, at times, seemed to reflect the influence of his two former associates. The words of "The Sweetest Sounds," for instance, were reminiscent of Oscar Hammerstein's poetic phrasing; lyrics of other songs bore similarities to Lorenz Hart's bold rhyme schemes.

The book by Samuel Taylor dealt with Barbara Woodruff, a Negro high-fashion model in Paris who becomes involved in a love affair with David Jordan, a Pulitzer Prize-winning author. Jordan has lost confidence in himself as a writer and is beginning to fall into the same sort of lazy existence led by his friend Mike Robinson, who is being supported by an Oklahoma heiress named Comfort O'Connell. Barbara gives up her job and goes away with David to a secluded spot, hoping to encourage him to write; they quarrel and he joins Mike and Comfort on one of their trips, fully aware that this aimless drifting will offer him only temporary relief, and that he will not be content until he again turns out a successful novel. Barbara finally convinces David that he might regain confidence if he returns to Maine. Although David wants to marry her and take her back home with him, she refuses, realizing that she would be unhappy in Maine, that she would not be accepted by the New Englanders, and that she would miss the social freedom she had enjoyed in Paris. The book made no direct references to the racial difference between David and Barbara, but the unhappy ending did not come as a surprise, for the love affair had seemed doomed from the start. In Paris, Barbara was treated with respect by her associates, was admired by the world of fashion, and was extremely well paid, whereas David simply drifted from one resort to another using any pretext to avoid getting back to work. Returning to Maine could regenerate David and again establish him as a novelist, but Barbara would lose the independence and prestige she had gained abroad. The second act, particularly, developed the hopelessness of the romance through a series of songs which were melodic and sung superbly by Diahann Carroll, but tied to a static plot.

No Strings, however, attracted attention for its unusual technical production, its excellent cast, its novel use of musicians, its mobile sets, and its striking costumes. One critic commented on the fact that the title of the show also could have described the orchestra, which consisted of a flute, clarinet, trumpet, trombone, oboe, bassoon, and drums, but no stringed instruments. Instead of keeping them in the pit, the director placed the musicians in the wings and had individual players drift in and out of the action as part of the background. For example, in the opening scene, the flutist, seated on stage, played an obbligato as Miss Carroll sang "The Sweetest Sounds." When Richard Kiley began the second chorus, a clarinetist appeared and picked up the strain. This use of individual musicians playing countermelodies onstage while the full orchestra played offstage enabled the vocalists to emphasize the lyrics without being forced to sing over a loud, brassy accompaniment. The director added another refreshing touch by bringing the entire orchestra onstage for one of the final curtain calls.

Visually, the show was a delight both in the sets and in the costuming. Diahann Carroll, as the Parisian model, wore a series of beautiful outfits, including a particularly striking chiffon gown that fascinated women in the audience. Miss Carroll stood on a platform to pose for a photograph while the cameraman strategically placed electric fans nearby to set the material in motion and reveal the multi-layered, multi-colored, chiffon petticoats beneath the full-length skirt. Donald Brooks and Fred Voelpel designed tights for the chorus girls that made them resemble shop-window mannequins; during most of the show the girls struck poses, became part of the background, or served as scene-shifters by turning panels, moving props, and adding scenic accessories with amazing speed.

Instead of designing elaborate sets, David Hayes created unusual effects by means of panels, moveable platforms, and a few props. With the aid of the mannequin-chorus girls, everything seemed to glide quickly into place; and by setting out a few potted plants, a bench, and a paneled backdrop, within seconds Hayes converted a corner of the stage into a meeting place for the lovers. The scenes varied from sections of Paris to Monte Carlo, Deauville, Honfleur, and St. Tropez, but most of the set changes involving the mannequins were limited to the scenes in Paris, especially in the photographer's salon.

The cast, another of the show's principal assets, worked hard to overcome the limitations of the book. Diahann Carroll made the difficult role of Barbara a personal triumph, for she not only impressed audiences with her acting and singing but also with her ability to look as if she well deserved to be the highest-paid fashion model in Paris. Richard Kiley in the thankless role of David made Jordan's shiftlessness as well as his attraction for Barbara understandable. Since most of the action in the second act dealt directly with the unhappy romance, and since Miss Carroll and Kiley sang all but one of the numbers, their handling of the songs and their convincing performances helped to offset the immobility of the plot.

The few lines spoken by Noelle Adam, who played the photographer's assistant, were in French; but the curvaceous Miss Adam, wearing black silk tights and a bulky sweater, needed no dialogue to attract attention. She brightened up the scenes in the studio as she swirled in and out of the plot with the grace of a ballerina. Polly Rowles as Molly Plummer, a fashion-magazine writer noted for her sense of humor, conveyed the idea that she had wit even though the dialogue gave her little chance to prove it. Bernice Massi as Comfort, the wealthy playgirl; Don Chastain as Mike Robinson, her unfaithful lover; and Alvin Epstein as the photographer, also livened up the action in the first act. Mitchell Gregg as Louis de Pourtal, euphemistically called Barbara's tutor in the script, impressed audiences with his song "The Man Who Has Everything."

Richard Rodgers' score included several songs that had popular appeal. "The Sweetest Sounds" became an immediate hit. Diahann Carroll sang magnificently regardless of whether she was punching home a humorous line in "Loads of Love" or emphasizing sentiment in "An Unorthodox Fool." Both Miss Carroll and Richard Kiley effectively handled most of the score, and made one of their five duets, "Maine," a highlight in the second act. "La, La, La," a saucy French number, acquired much of its zest from Noelle Adam, who whirled about the stage and sang the title phrase delightfully.

Since *No Strings* opened on March 15, 1962, almost at the close of the season, the publicity it received from the prize awards shortly after its première helped box-office sales. The *Variety* Poll of Drama Critics, for example, named Diahann Carroll as the best female lead in a musical, David Hays as the best scene designer, Richard Rodgers as the best composer, and tied the vote for best costume designer between Donald Brooks and Fred Voelpel (*No Strings*) and Lucinda Ballard (*The Gay Life*). Joe Layton was runner-up in the *Variety* Poll as best director of a musical. The list of Tony Awards included a special award for Richard Rodgers, and a tied vote between Joe Layton (*No Strings*) and Agnes de Mille (*Kwamina*) as best choreographer.

No Strings amazed superstitious showmen because it became a hit even though it had opened at the 54th Street Theater, reputed to be a jinxed house. Some time later, however, the production was moved to a more centrally located theater on 44th Street. Barbara McNair and Howard Keel, who replaced Diahann Carroll and Richard Kiley, also played the leads in the road company. In spite of the labored story, the slow second act, and the unhappy ending, *No Strings* had sufficient audience appeal to keep the production running for 580 performances.

A Funny Thing Happened on the Way to the Forum, which opened in May 1962, was almost the antithesis of *No Strings.* Instead of elaborate settings and lavish costumes, it broke away from musical comedy tradition by using only one stage set and no change of costumes. *No Strings* had been almost devoid of humor, but *A Funny Thing Happened on the Way to the Forum* had few, if any, serious moments. The action, the dialogue, the dances, and the songs were all farcical, designed to provoke only laughter.

Burt Shevelove and Larry Gelbart had based *A Funny Thing Happened on the Way to the Forum* on comedies by Plautus, who had died in 184 B.C. Despite its modern touches, the musical that resulted proved that raucous and rowdy comedy had not changed much since the days of the Romans.

The idea for the show originated with Burt Shevelove. While still a student at Yale, he had used some of Plautus' works as the basis for a musical and later decided to delve further into the Roman farces as source material for a full-length Broadway musical. Larry Gelbart, who had worked with Shevelove on television, became co-author of the book; and Stephen Sondheim, who had written the lyrics for *West Side Story* and *Gypsy,* was signed to do both music and lyrics. Instead of limiting themselves to one comedy by Plautus, the authors combined many of his works, taking the names of characters from one, an incident from another, a scene from still another, and creating a new plot that, despite its patchwork inheritance, emerged as a unified farce with all complications and subplots ingeniously woven into one major story.

A Funny Thing Happened on the Way to the Forum had a slight plot, but one so involved with various petty schemes that it seemed far more complicated than it actually was. The curtain rose to reveal a street in ancient Rome with three houses on it: the center house owned by Senex; to its left, the house of Lycus, a dealer in courtesans; and to its right, the home of Erronius, who had for twenty years been in search of his son and daughter, who had been stolen from him. The story dealt with Pseudolus, slave to Hero, the son of Senex and Domina. Hero sees the beautiful Philia in Lycus' house and falls in love with her. Pseudolus promises to get Philia for Hero in return for his freedom.

Pretending that he wants to buy a courtesan for himself, Pseudolus has Lycus bring out the girls. Lycus, however, does not exhibit Philia. When Pseudolus sees her at a window and asks specifically for her, Lycus explains that Philia is a virgin whom he has already sold to Captain Miles Gloriosus. The wily Pseudolus then exclaims that Crete, where Lycus had bought Philia, has been suffering from a dreadful plague. Lycus, fearful that she will contaminate the other courtesans, willingly consents to Pseudolus' suggestion that she stay at the house of Senex until the captain arrives. Philia admits that she has fallen in love with Hero, but when Pseudolus offers to help the lovers run away she insists it is her duty to marry the captain who has bought her. Further complications ensue when Senex sees Philia, who mistakes him for Captain Gloriosus. The infatuated Senex, now his son's rival, plans a rendezvous in Erronius' deserted house. Erronius returns unexpectedly, and Pseudolus, at Senex' command, talks him into rushing off on another quest for his missing children. To add to Pseudolus' difficulties, Captain Gloriosus arrives to claim his bride. When she cannot be found and the captain learns that she had been entrusted to Pseudolus, Gloriosus is ready to kill the slave. At this point Pseudolus asks if he might say just one word. The captain consents. "Intermission!" Pseudolus bellows, and the curtain comes down on the first act.

The second act begins exactly where the first act had ended. Pseudolus, after talking himself out of his predicament by promising to find Philia, decides to tell Gloriosus that Philia has died. By threatening to blackmail a fellow slave, Hysterium, if he does not comply, Pseudolus has him dress as a girl and pretend to be the dead Philia. The plan almost succeeds until the captain decides to give Philia a farewell kiss. The frightened Hysterium runs off, and everyone begins rushing in and out of wrong doors in a frenzied comedy chase. Erronius arrives at a strategic moment, notices that Gloriosus and Philia are both wearing a piece of jewelry with the same design, and delightedly identifies the warrior and the girl as his long-lost children. Philia is now able to marry Hero; Gloriosus is content to obtain two courtesans, the Gemini; and Pseudolus gains his freedom.

Just how much of the plot Shevelove and Gelbart borrowed from Plautus was not so important as the fact that they maintained the spirit of the old comedies. *A Funny Thing* would never win any prizes for literary merit or for subtlety, but it proved that lowbrow humor could still be very entertaining if done properly. Most of the critics agreed that the show lived up to its title, for it was funny in the same ways that had made burlesque good theater at the turn of the century. Howard Taubman, who liked the show, pointed out that no one even started to go to the Forum. For that matter, most audiences did not care whether anyone ever arrived there or not. Some theatergoers were offended by the raucous action and raffish humor, and one critic felt that the show strained too hard for laughs. His objection may have been true, but most audiences, including some who were a bit skittish about certain scenes, were won over by the principal comedians, who mugged and hammed with professional slickness, as though they were burlesquing the roles they assumed.

Zero Mostel as Pseudolus, David Burns as Senex, Jack Gilford as Hysterium, and John Carradine as Lycus were zestfully uninhibited. Their seemingly effortless ability to make audiences laugh, however, came from years of theatrical experience that had schooled them in the arts of timing, gesturing, and enunciating. Zero Mostel had been equally adept in handling both serious and humorous roles in nonmusical productions; Jack Gilford had been particularly effective in a semicomic yet basically serious role in *The Diary of Anne Frank;* John Carradine, a noted Shakespearean actor, had also given an impressive performance as the ragpicker in *The Madwoman of Chaillot;* and David Burns had salvaged a number of musical shows with his deft performances.

Regardless of whether *A Funny Thing* lapsed into pure slapstick, ridiculous chases in the Mack Sennett tradition, or burlesque sketches, Zero Mostel dominated every scene, rolling his eyes and posturing like a figure on a Roman vase. Mostel, a large man, pranced about with grace, and the incongruity of seeing one so huge move with such dexterity made his antics a source of amazement. In scenes that were basically vulgar, Mostel's pretences of surprise or shock that such actions should be taking place made them hilarious. For example, when Lycus presented his courtesans and each girl performed a frenzied dance, Mostel would leer at one moment and then look askance at such unseemly gyrations.

David Burns had audiences chortling over Senex' would-be romantic escapades with Philia. Simply by quivering his lips, Burns, a superb comedian, could enrich a gag line in a comedy song. Jack Gilford's agitated histrionics were perfect for the hysterical Hysterium, and John Carradine added to the ribaldry by making Lycus an amusing rather than lecherous dealer in courtesans. When Burns, Mostel, Gilford, and Carradine sang "Everybody Ought to Have a Maid," they stopped the show. Burns started the song, and then, one by one, each man joined him in what appeared to be a series of encores with different lyrics until all four comedians were on stage getting bigger laughs with each new chorus.

Preshy Marker's beauty and her expert trouping made audiences understand why father and son would both be infatuated with her. Brian Davies as Hero added the proper touch of romance, an accomplishment not to be minimized. If played improperly, Hero could have spoiled the whole first act, which began with Zero Mostel cavorting and clowning as he explained to the audience that the show would be "Comedy Tonight"; while he sang the number, the cast joined him in a series of slapstick routines; if Hero, who followed the madcap opening with the ballad "Love I Hear," had sung it badly, the number would have been a decided letdown. Davies not only established the romantic interest with "Love I Hear," but also proved, in the duet "Free" with Zero Mostel, and in "Impossible" with David Burns, that despite his youth, he could keep pace with the veteran performers.

Ruth Kobart, who had formerly sung with the New York Opera Company, and who earlier in the same season had played Miss Jones in *How to Succeed in Business Without Really Trying*, was an excellent Domina, imperious wife of Senex. Raymond Walburn, a veteran motion-picture actor, made the most of his comparatively brief appearances as Erronius. Eddie Phillips, George Reeder, and David Evans, as three proteans, played a multitude of roles ranging from eunuchs to warriors, and their popping in and out of the action, first in one role and then in another, added variety as well as humor.

The direction of George Abbott, a master of farce technique, emphasized speed, never letting the action lapse. Even when the slim plot remained static, it seemed to develop rapidly because Abbott kept the actors in motion, bumping, kicking, chasing one another, or colliding in doorways. The few quiet moments during the love duets gave audiences a chance to relax before the comedians would appear again, whizzing from one ridiculous situation into another.

One episode that might have misfired, but did not, involved Mostel's forcing Gilford to dress up as Philia. To convince Gilford that he looked the part, Mostel sang "Lovely" as though he were actually serenading a beautiful girl. Gilford, in his ridiculous disguise, made theatergoers and even critics who had never enjoyed female impersonators think the whole episode hilarious.

Jack Cole, the choreographer, had little opportunity to do much more than stage individual routines for the courtesans in the first act. His dances may have been, as one critic said, straight out of burlesque, but they were amusing because the names of the courtesans—Vibrata, Tintinabula, Gymnasia, Panacea, and the Geminae—aptly described their routines.

Although the courtesans had little to do in the show apart from their gyrating solos, they intrigued audiences every time they appeared. During the Christmas season, when theaters took up their annual collection for the Actors Benefit Fund, the girls in the show came off the stage in their abbreviated costumes and took charge of the collection in the orchestra section of the theater. Instead of dropping in coins, most men reached into their pockets for paper money, which rapidly lined and padded the baskets.

One man, who normally attended six or seven shows during that week, usually divided up the total amount of money he intended to contribute and dropped a coin or two into the basket for each show, but when he saw *A Funny Thing* he put a dollar bill in the basket. "I think almost every man sitting around me did the same thing," he said. "Besides, I was too busy looking at Gymnasia to realize what I was doing."

Stephen Sondheim wrote clever songs but integrated them so well that they meant little out of context. Even when they were quite melodious, they became so closely linked with the action that the audience remembered the lyrics rather than the tunes. "Everybody Ought to Have a Maid" had a pleasant, lilting melody and rhythm that audiences were apt to overlook because the four comedians who sang it emphasized the lyrics. "Lovely," as sung by Philia and Hero, was a pleasant ballad, but theatergoers remembered it best as the humorous ditty sung by Mostel to reassure Gilford that his disguise as Philia was convincing. "I'm Calm," Gilford's solo, satirized various suggestions for treating hysteria, with Gilford trying to subdue his nerves and almost succeeding until just as he was finishing the number, he heard Senex call and went screaming off stage in a hysterical fit. Regardless of the music's effectiveness, it could not help but become secondary to Gilford's frenzied delivery of the lyrics.

At the end of the first season, *A Funny Thing* brought Tony Awards to Zero Mostel and David Burns as best performers in a musical, to Harold Prince as best producer, to Burt Shevelove and Larry Gelbart as best authors of a musical, and to George Abbott as best director. The success of the Shevelove-Gelbart-Sondheim production inspired an off-Broadway revival of the Rodgers and Hart musical *The Boys from Syracuse*, which stemmed indirectly from Plautus and directly from Shakespeare. The producers of *The Boys from Syracuse* even altered one or two scenes to incorporate the same type of activity that had so amused audiences in *A Funny Thing*.

Careful cast replacements helped keep the show running. Jerry Lester played Pseudolus when Zero Mostel was on vacation, and in February 1964, Dick Shawn took over the role. Before the production closed, both Danny Drayton and Eric Rhodes appeared on Broadway as Lycus, and Frank McHugh took over as Senex. During the latter part of the run, the show operated on a two-for-one ticket policy and finally closed with a total of 964 performances.

A Funny Thing Happened on the Way to the Forum may not have done anything to advance the development of the musical comedy, but it proved that skillful actors can make some of the world's oldest jokes and situations come alive, and that the universal appeal of slapstick, low comedy, and farce have not changed in over two thousand years.

XIV

The Latest Hits of the 1960s

THE 1962–63 theatrical season disappointed a great many musical comedy enthusiasts, for it brought forth no American long-running successes. Even though such productions as *Tovarich* with Vivien Leigh, *Little Me* with Sid Caesar, *She Loves Me* with Barbara Cook, Daniel Massey, and Jack Cassidy, and *Mr. President* with Nanette Fabray, Robert Ryan and an excellent score by Irving Berlin all had fairly good runs, they were listed as failures in *Variety*'s tabulation of the season's "Hits and Flops." On the other hand, the only three musical hits which ran for 500 or more performances were British imports: *Beyond the Fringe,* an intimate revue featuring four English comedians; *Stop the World—I Want to Get Off,* which used pantomime, symbolism, and English music-hall humor to develop its plot; and *Oliver!* an adaptation of Oliver Twist which skirted around and about the Dickens novel.

Some New Yorkers thought the 114-day newspaper strike, which began December 7, 1962, and lasted until March 31, 1963, may have caused the poor attendance at American musicals. The fallow season, however, was reflected more concretely in the attitude of the critics. For the first time in years, none of the musical productions nominated for the Drama Critics' Circle Award had sufficient strength to pull a majority of votes, and the Circle did not name a best musical, although it did give a special citation to *Beyond the Fringe.*

David Merrick, one of Broadway's greatest showmen, whose long-running musical comedies and revues included *Fanny, La Plume de Ma Tante, Jamaica, Gypsy, Irma La Douce,* and *Carnival,* produced two of the successful British imports, *Oliver!* and

Stop the World—I Want to Get Off, again demonstrating that he had the knack of knowing which type of foreign production would appeal to American audiences.

Stop the World—I Want to Get Off, with book, music, and lyrics by Leslie Bricusse and Anthony Newley, came early in the season, opening on October 3, 1962. It was preceded only by a summer revival of *Fiorello!;* a review starring Eddie Fisher; and a British drama, *The Affair.* The critics and the public were ready for a new hit, and the advance publicity indicated that *Stop the World* might be it. Called the best show of the year in England, its big number "What Kind of Fool Am I?" had been named the best song of the year, and the score had also been designated the best of that year. Advance sales were good. Theatergoers, spurred on by the publicity, expected to see a spectacularly different type of musical that would epitomize British wit and style.

The American critics, however, were not uniformly impressed by the production. Several hailed its different approach, but others objected to an overemphasis on sentiment and sporadic humor. The audiences were as divided as the critics.

The plot developed the life story of Littlechap from birth to death, showing that the more he conformed to conventional patterns, the more successful he became. The setting, which remained the same throughout the entire production, represented the interior of a circus tent; the members of the cast, dressed in loose-fitting tights and looking somewhat like circus clowns, were seated on the side benches. As the play begins, Littlechap enters through a tunnel, the symbol of life—for those who entered—and death—for those who exited—and twists himself into the position of a child about to be born. He portrays the newborn infant and then the small child who does not speak but conveys ideas through body movement. Soon he is a young boy working his way up the executive ladder. After marrying the boss's daughter, who is pregnant with his child, he quickly makes progress in the firm until he becomes the top executive. He advances in social prestige, becomes a Member of Parliament, and reaches the exalted position of being knighted "Master of Doubletalk," receiving a medal for his ability to speak a great deal and say nothing. During his phenomenal rise, he has had affairs with a Russian, a German, and an American girl.

When his older daughter, who has followed her mother's example and become pregnant out of wedlock, has to marry, he is still enough aware of his family responsibilities to attend the wedding; but when his next daughter is married, he is too busy to appear at the ceremony. Engrossed in his own affairs, he does not realize that his wife has been critically ill until after she has died. As the play nears its conclusion, he sings "What Kind of Fool Am I?" which depicts the emptiness of his life and his failure to ever fall in love with anyone but himself. Finally Littlechap enacts his own death by exiting into the symbolic tunnel. He reappears, however, assuming the same position that he had taken in the opening scene, to show that the cycle of life will start again—he will once more be born, grow up, and live the same sort of existence.

Much of the progress in the play was demonstrated through the use of symbolic gestures. For example, when Littlechap first approached the boss's office, he had to reach high up for the door-knob, but as he advanced in the firm, the imaginary knob kept getting lower and lower as it became more and more accessible.

The advance publicity, which had heralded *Stop the World* as an original production with a new approach to musical theater, did not misrepresent the facts, even though some commentators remarked upon its resemblance to Marcel Marceau's famous pantomime "The Seven Ages of Man." Anthony Newley was reported to have acknowledged his indebtedness to Marceau. Newley's makeup and costuming gave further proof that he was not attempting to hide Marceau's influence, though Newley wore loose trousers with large suspenders and an undershirt, rather than the exact duplicate of Marceau's outfit, and instead of Marceau's bold whiteface, Newley used a pallid white that more closely resembled the makeup of a circus clown, even to the red-tipped nose.

Newley's version of the seven ages of man has also been compared more recently to the sketches presented by both Red Skelton and Dick Van Dyke on television specials, as well as to the original source for all the pantomimists, Shakespeare's passage in *As You Like It*. The Newley-Bricusse production, however, differed from the others because it presented a more fully developed treatment of the idea.

Henry Hewes, editor of *The Best Plays of 1962–1963,* selected

Stop the World—I Want to Get Off as one of the ten best plays of the season. Although many commentators found the plot basically one-dimensional, Mr. Hewes's condensation effectively demonstrated dramatic values in both the script and the lyrics. These assets were further enhanced in the stage production by the music. When the show first opened, the song "What Kind of Fool Am I?" became an instant hit. In more recent years, two other numbers from the score, "Build a Mountain" and "Once in a Lifetime" have increased in popularity and have been played frequently on radio and television.

Critics were not always in agreement on the humor, which included quips about English, Russians, Germans, and Americans. Periodically Newley would step to the front of the stage, shout "Stop the world!" as though he were symbolically trying to stop the meaningless progress of life, and then tell a joke that had no relevance to the plot and sometimes destroyed the mood that had been created by the preceding action. Perhaps the greatest objection may have been to the manner in which the humor was injected rather than to actual quips themselves, many people objecting to certain jokes primarily because Newley had stepped out of character to tell them.

Because the setting and costumes did not change, *Stop the World* had to rely upon its performers to add variety and sustain interest. The production gave them ample opportunity to offset the basic repetitiousness of the script; it provided a tour de force for Anthony Newley as Littlechap and for Anna Quayle as the four women in his life. Newley, an accomplished pantomimist, was even more effective as a vocalist. He alone was responsible for making three of the songs outstanding hits, and his dramatic singing of "What Kind of Fool Am I?" became the high spot of the show. At the end of the season Newley won the *Saturday Review*'s dramatic poll; received the endorsement of Henry Hewes, the *Best Plays*' editor; and was runner-up in the *Variety* poll of dramatic critics for the best male performer in a musical. The *Variety* poll also named Mr. Newley as best director of a musical.

Anna Quayle, playing four different roles, proved her versatility as a pantomimist as well as a singer. She sang the same number to represent Evie, the English girl; Anya, the Russian; Ilse, the

German; and Ginnie, the American. The idea and melody in each version remained basically the same, but the lyrics differed. In spite of an unfeminine costume resembling a gym suit, with long cotton tights and a gray blouse, the attractive statuesque Miss Quayle held interest, particularly as she switched from one nationality to another with a gesture or a change in dialect. For her performance as the best supporting female player in a musical, Miss Quayle won the *Saturday Review* and *Variety* drama critics' polls and the Tony Award.

In addition to the two leads, who carried the burden of the show, the cast included a talented group of young singers and dancers headed by the attractive twins Jennifer and Susan Baker, who played the daughters of Evie and Littlechap.

In November 1963, after *Stop the World* had run for more than a year, Joel Grey and Joan Eastman took over the leading roles and kept the show on Broadway until February 1, 1964, when it closed after 555 performances.

Sean Kenny, who designed the set for *Stop the World*, had greater opportunity to reveal his ingenuity in *Oliver!*, David Merrick's second British import of the season. The set for the opening scene which included long, dark, and narrow stairways, recalled the starkness of the circus tent and benches in *Stop the World*. For *Oliver!*, however, Kenny had constructed a much more complicated revolving set. The stairs became an effective part of a workhouse, a smoke-filled tavern, and a part of London Bridge. As the stairs revolved on stage, they provided an excellent way of showing Oliver's attempts to escape from the police. A few backdrops gliding into place, and John Wyckham's excellent lighting, worked wonders in transforming a dismal, prisonlike workhouse into a brightly lighted London street. Moreover, the sets changed with amazing rapidity, making complex changes seem relatively simple.

The smoothness of the technical production and the assured performances of the cast were achieved during a long road tour before Merrick brought *Oliver!* into New York, at the time of the newspaper strike. Several other producers had tried to postpone opening dates, hoping the strike would be settled. Rumors had circulated that Merrick was planning to keep *Oliver!* on the road until newspapers again appeared on the stands. Merrick did postpone the opening, but when there seemed to be no immediate settlement of the dispute in sight, he brought the show in on January 6, 1963.

The newspaper strike eliminated the threat of unfavorable reviews but many producers were more concerned that the public would not know which shows were still running and which were opening. When *Oliver!* opened, the reviews were printed in the January 14 issue of *FIRSTNITE*, a publication which the seven New York newspapers allowed to print reviews written by their drama critics. Radio and television programs kept the public informed about openings, and often presented the critics' opinions about new shows. David Merrick gave his own highly favorable review of *Oliver!* on a radio program that discussed opening-night performances.

Lionel Bart, who wrote book, music, and lyrics, had, according to the program notes, "freely adapted" *Oliver!* from Charles Dickens' *Oliver Twist* but had not radically changed the basic plot. In the opening scene, Oliver, an orphan who lives in the workhouse, musters up enough courage to ask the Beadle, Mr. Bumble, for more food. The infuriated Bumble takes Oliver to an undertaker's establishment and sells him to Mr. Sowerberry, who needs a worker. After being treated even more abusively there than he had been at the workhouse, the rebellious Oliver runs away, meets the Artful Dodger, a cheerful youngster about his own age, and goes with him to the hideout of Fagin and the boys whom he trains to be thieves. Fagin proceeds to instruct Oliver in the art of picking pockets, and the next morning Oliver is sent out with the boys. While they are filching, one of their victims discovers that he has been robbed and starts a chase; Oliver, who has merely been a bystander, is arrested because he looks guilty.

The boys rush back to an underworld tavern to find Fagin and his accomplices, Nancy and Bill Sikes, her brutal lover. When the boys tell Fagin that Oliver has been arrested, cleared of the charge, and taken home by Mr. Brownlow, a rich, elderly gentleman, Fagin and Bill Sikes, fearing that Oliver might inform the police of their hideout, tell Nancy to bring him back. At first Nancy objects, but Bill manhandles her until she agrees.

Mr. Brownlow, struck by Oliver's resemblance to his daughter, who had disappeared long ago and whom he now believes to be dead, decides to have Oliver live with him. When Mr. Brownlow has to return a package of books to a shop, Oliver asks if he might do the errand, and Mr. Brownlow consents. Nancy, however, has been waiting for just such an opportunity; when she sees that Oliver is alone, she forces him to go back to Fagin's with her.

Meanwhile an old woman on her deathbed in the workhouse confesses that years before she had stolen a brooch from Oliver's mother when she had died. Bumble and his wife, piecing together the facts, realize that Oliver's mother must have been Mr. Brownlow's long-lost daughter. Armed with evidence, Bumble goes to Mr. Brownlow's home hoping to be paid for returning the brooch. Instead of rewarding Bumble, Brownlow threatens to have him fired for mistreating the inmates of the workhouse, for feeding the boys starvation rations, and for selling the boys as though they were slaves. Before Mr. Brownlow can make plans to find Oliver, Nancy comes to see him, not letting Fagin or Bill know where she has gone. After confessing that she had taken Oliver away and convincing Mr. Brownlow that she regretted what she had done, she promises to bring Oliver to Mr. Brownlow at midnight on London Bridge. Sikes, however, learns of her plans, follows her, and kills her. He then grabs Oliver and starts to take him back, but an angry mob, incensed by Nancy's death, gathers quickly, and Bill, trying to make a getaway, releases the boy. During the ensuing chase, Sikes is killed. Oliver is then reunited with his grandfather. As the play ends, Fagin, who has been forced to abandon both his hideout and the wealth he had accumulated, is unsure of his future. He reprises the musical soliloquy, "Reviewing the Situation," wondering whether he can turn over a new leaf, and, if so, what changes he will have to make in his mode of living. The entire cast, assembled for curtain calls, then reprises two of the livelier numbers to help audiences forget the somberness of the preceding action and leave the theater in a happy mood.

Dickens enthusiasts were displeased with the adaptation of *Oliver Twist* and accused Lionel Bart of treating the novel irreverently. The liberties he took with the story, however, made the difference between a production that became a hit and one that would have aroused antagonism and kept New York audiences away from the theater. Dickens' novel had emphasized the evils of workhouses and the ill-treatment of orphans; but in *Oliver!* Dickens' cries for social reform were minimized. The complaints against *Oliver!* were somewhat similar to those lodged against *The Sound of Music* for minimizing the Nazi invasion and stressing the sentimental love story. But the popular appeal would have been lessened considerably had Bart included all of Dickens' indictments, for very few plays or musical comedies dealing with social reform have ever become hits.

The greatest change, as had been anticipated, came in the depiction of Fagin. The script removed all of the anti-Semitic references and transformed Fagin from a character who would have aroused the protests of religious organizations and anti-defamation leagues into a humorous rascal. In fact Norman Nadel, in his review, said that Fagin had been described "by a Jewish newspaper in California . . . as the kind of lovable old codger you'd invite to a Hadassah tea." Moreover, the Habimah Theater presented a Hebrew edition of *Oliver!* in Israel in 1966.

Reports from critics who had seen the original production of *Oliver!* in London stated that the characterization of Fagin had been softened and toned down for the American version, but the London revival in 1967 appeared to be exactly the same as the Merrick production in New York.

Although Fagin was not pure Dickens, the script did include a number of Dickens' remarkable, one-trait characters: the Falstaffian Mr. Bumble, who oppressed the workhouse inmates; Mrs. Corney, the workhouse matron, who wheedled Mr. Bumble into marriage and only then revealed her shrewish disposition; Mr. Sowerberry, the dour undertaker, and his irascible wife; Charlotte, their slatternly daughter; Noah Claypoole, their bullying apprentice, who infuriated Oliver; the brutal Bill Sikes; Nancy, his unhappy mistress; and the Artful Dodger, Fagin's best-trained disciple.

When *Oliver!* followed the novel and tried to condense important action into one short scene, such as the one in which old Sally confessed that she had stolen a brooch from Oliver's mother, the hastily drawn episode was less interesting than the more fully developed song and dance routines. Bill Sikes, limited to one or

two brief appearances, had little opportunity to convey the menacing brutality that Dickens had given him in the novel. Furthermore, the tragedy of Nancy's death was largely offset by the finale,
with Nancy very much in evidence reprising the sprightlier songs.
On the other hand, when *Oliver!* strayed from the original plot
and Bart eliminated much of the overemphasis Dickens had placed
on sentimentality and coincidence, the production had more popular appeal. The resultant humor prompted Henry Hewes, in *The
Best Plays of 1962–1963*, to ask "whether Oliver was fortunate to
find his wealthy grandparents later on."

Lionel Bart had a reputation in England for writing hit songs
that appealed to young singers and young audiences. The
sprightly tunes in *Oliver!* reflected this type of music, but "As
Long as He Needs Me," "Where Is Love?" and an impressive
street-scene interlude, in which vendors sang beneath Oliver's
window, demonstrated his ability to create more dramatic ballads
as well. Dissenters objected to some of Bart's songs, calling them
music-hall numbers not in keeping with the plot. The score, however, helped make the show a success, for many of the songs had a
rollicking lilt. The characters may not have been particularly
Dickensian in the musical interludes, but they were delightfully
entertaining when they sang, "Consider Yourself at Home," which
provided a touch of melodious high spirits as contrast to the op-
pressive workshop and undertaker scenes that had preceded it,
"Come Back Soon," and "You've Got to Pick a Pocket or Two."
The duet in which Mr. Bumble courted Mrs. Corney and she kept
singing "I Shall Scream," also added a delightful touch of humor.
Georgia Brown throbbed "As Long as He Needs Me" into the hit
ballad of the season, but she was equally adept in the lively "Oom-
Pah-Pah," as well as "I'd Do Anything," which she first sang and
danced with the Artful Dodger and then taught Oliver to perform
with little Bet. *Oliver!* also intrigued American audiences with its
typically English finale, using the entire cast to reprise the hit
songs.

The entire cast won rave notices. Clive Revill, who had received excellent reviews when he appeared in Merrick's production of *Irma La Douce*, impressed critics with his portrayal of
Fagin. His experience with the Old Vic as well as with the Royal

Shakespeare Company helped him in the difficult task of engendering audience understanding for Fagin. His excellent performance made Fagin's songs, "Reviewing the Situation" and "You've Got to Pick a Pocket or Two," diverting rather than offensive. Georgia Brown, who originated the role of Nancy in England, had been known in London as a popular singer. She gave her numbers, particularly "As Long as He Needs Me," a dramatic quality that made them highlights in the show. Bruce Prochnik as Oliver also pleased the critics, but he soon outgrew the part. During the long run on Broadway, several youngsters played the role.

Peter Coe, the director, worked wonders with the young boys, never letting them lapse into mere precociousness. Under his direction, they performed like disciplined actors rather than precocious amateurs. Coe also kept the show moving rapidly. He built the opening scene, which began at a slow pace, to a rousing climax when Oliver asked for "More," and he capitalized on the revolving sets to give the fast action even greater acceleration.

At the end of the first season, Sean Kenny won both the *Saturday Review* and *Variety* polls as well as the Tony Award for the best scene designer. Lionel Bart also received Tony Awards as the best composer and the best lyricist. The show went on a two-for-one ticket basis before it concluded its run. The cast also changed, with Robin Ramsey playing Fagin and Maura K. Wedge, later followed by Judy Bruce, playing Nancy.

The London production of *Oliver!* has erroneously been reported as having achieved the world's record for long-running musical productions. Its 2,618 performances ran far ahead of the 774 achieved by the New York company, but it did not surpass the record of 2,717 performances established in New York by *My Fair Lady*. If musical revues are included in the tabulations, *The Black and White Minstrel Show,* still current in London, now holds the world's record for musical productions with more than 3,500 performances.

Oliver! was the last of the British musical comedies to become a long-running hit, for in the four seasons from 1963 through 1967, the eight musicals that ran for more than 500 performances were all American productions. As of May 1, 1968, six of these shows—*Mame, Man of La Mancha, Fiddler on the Roof, Hello, Dolly!, Cabaret,* and *I Do! I Do!* were still playing on Broadway. The two productions that had completed their runs—*Sweet Charity* and *Funny Girl*—had both become hits because the public wanted to see Gwen Verdon and Barbra Streisand. *Funny Girl,* however, continued to do profitable, but not capacity, business for more than a year after Mimi Hines had replaced Miss Streisand. *Sweet Charity,* on the other hand, relied almost entirely on the drawing power of Miss Verdon; when illness caused her to miss performances, box-office receipts dropped sharply. Shortly after Miss Verdon left the cast, the show closed.

Neil Simon had adapted *Sweet Charity* from the motion picture *The Nights of Cabiria* by Federico Fellini, Tullio Pinelli, and Ennio Flaiano. The show was tailored to Miss Verdon's talents and kept her onstage throughout almost the entire production, giving her very little time to make even a change in costume. The basic plot concerned Charity Hope Valentine, a bubble-headed, sentimental dance-hall hostess, who, according to the subtitle of the show, was "a girl who wanted to be loved." Every one of her romantic entanglements, unfortunately, ended unhappily. In the opening scene, Charity is in the park with a man who takes her money and pushes her into the lake. A crowd gathers, but no one helps her, even though it appears that she is drowning. Charity somehow manages to save herself, and when she returns to the Fandango Ballroom, where she works as a hostess, she vows never again to throw herself at the next man who comes along. Her resolution is short-lived, for Vittorio Vidal, an Italian film star, picks her up after he has quarreled with his latest amour, and takes her to his apartment. His lady love, however, returns penitent, and Charity is forced to hide in the closet for several hours so as not to provoke another lovers' quarrel. Again she returns to the Fandango unloved. Deciding to improve herself, she goes to New York's 92nd Street YMHA to attend a lecture and becomes trapped between floors in an elevator with Oscar Linquist, an accountant who suffers from claustrophobia. Although Charity does her best to calm the frightened Oscar, she is only partially successful; but by the time the power is restored and she is able to get Oscar out of the elevator, Charity is ready once more to fall in love. Oscar takes Charity on a parachute ride in Coney Island, and they again become stuck in mid-air. This time Charity is frightened and Oscar solicitous, easing her fears until they reach the ground safely.

Although Charity has told Oscar that she works in a bank, she decides to confess the truth about herself, even though she knows she may lose him. To her surprise, she discovers not only that Oscar already knows that she works at the Fandango but also that he wants to marry her. Charity is more than willing to give up her job and settle down as Mrs. Linquist, but at the last moment Oscar finds that he cannot overlook her past and will not be able to go through with the wedding. In the final scene, Charity is alone again, still hoping to meet and fall in love with the right man.

Enthusiastic out-of-town reports had stirred up interest in *Sweet Charity,* Philadelphia critics rating it the best pre-Broadway musical of the season. The interest of New York theatergoers was also stimulated by the fact that *Sweet Charity* would be playing at the newly redecorated Palace, once the most important vaudeville house in the United States, but in recent years a motion-picture theater. News stories informed the public that the original glamour of the Palace, including its famous sculptured ceiling, would be restored. When *Sweet Charity* opened, audiences were delighted with the refurbished theater. Some of the critics, in fact, were more enthusiastic about the restoration of the Palace to the legitimate stage than they were about *Sweet Charity,* but most of the reviewers predicted that the show would be a commercial success.

In adapting *The Nights of Cabiria,* Neil Simon had altered the characterization of the heroine from a lady of easy virtue to a dance-hall hostess whose name—Charity Hope Valentine—symbolized her poignant longing for love. Moreover, he glossed over her sordid life with an even greater sheen of innocence than the writers had given the heroine in *Irma La Douce.* Critics who compared *The Nights of Cabiria* with *Sweet Charity* approved of Simon's making Charity a smarter girl than the original heroine had been but disapproved of the unhappy ending. Many theatergoers shared this opinion. Charity may have been amoral, the dance-hall girls may have been obvious hussies, and the story may have bordered on the tawdry, but Gwen Verdon's wistful performance aroused sympathy for the heroine and made her broken romance a distinct disappointment.

Sweet Charity gave Neil Simon three hit shows running simultaneously on Broadway. Critics had anticipated that he would pepper the script with the same type of witty lines he had used in his other two successes, *Barefoot in the Park* and *The Odd Couple*. They were surprised, therefore, to find that the gags were relatively infrequent. He did inject laughs whenever possible, but much of the humor in *Sweet Charity* was ironic rather than comical.

Apart from their disappointment in the book and its development, most critics were pleased with the direction, the performers, and Robert Randolph's striking sets, particularly the elevator in which Charity and Oscar were trapped, and the Coney Island set. The reviewers also praised Irene Sharaff's excellent costumes. One unusual element in the costuming was the fact that throughout most of the action Miss Verdon, the star, wore the same outfit, a short black dress, somewhat like a slip, which started above the knees and was split even higher on the sides.

Opinions about the music by Cy Coleman and lyrics by Dorothy Fields were mixed, but almost everyone rated "If My Friends Could See Me Now," which Gwen Verdon sang during the scene in Vittorio Vidal's apartment, the best number in the show. "I'm a Brass Band" gave Miss Verdon the opportunity to perform an exciting dance routine in the second act. "Big Spender" was sung by the hostesses at the Fandango who lined up at the railing in the dance hall to entice the customers. Helen Gallagher and Thelma Oliver, who led the girls, made the number a show-stopper.

Bob Fosse, Miss Verdon's husband, received a Tony Award as best choreographer for *Sweet Charity*. He devised vivid dances for Miss Verdon and staged impressive routines for the ensemble, particularly "The Rich Man's Frug," which satirized new dance fads as well as the discotheques where this type of rhythmic frenzy had become popular. Fosse, who also directed the show, used to excellent advantage an electric signboard on which titles, reminiscent of silent motion-picture subtitles, flashed periodically as gags or diversions during the seconds needed to make a shift in sets, and as effective transitions.

Most critics praised the cast and singled out Thelma Oliver and Helen Gallagher, as the dance-hall hostesses, and John Mc-Martin as Oscar, for special mention. All of the critics were unanimous in their delight with Miss Verdon's dynamic performance as Charity. She was magnificent in the role. At the end of the season, she won the *Variety* poll as the best actress in a musical production. She charmed audiences when she sang, when she danced, or when she merely twinkled. Her training as a dancer was evident in every gesture and movement, even when she stood still and merely waved an arm. Whether alone in the spotlight or surrounded by an entire group, she dominated the action. She needed only to hold a cane, don a silk hat, cock it at a rakish angle, and then grin, and she had won over the audience before she even took a step.

As long as Miss Verdon appeared in *Sweet Charity*, box-office receipts were high. According to stories printed by columnists, the physical demands of the role were so exhausting that Miss Verdon cut at least one routine from the matinee performances. When illness caused her to miss performances, box-office receipts dropped, despite the excellence of her standby. Since the show depended entirely upon Miss Verdon for its popular appeal, her sporadic absences, which made audiences uncertain whether she would or would not appear, also affected advance ticket sales. Miss Verdon, nevertheless, kept *Sweet Charity* running on Broadway for almost two seasons and continued playing the role after the management had resorted to a two-for-one ticket policy. When she left the cast in the summer of 1967, the show soon closed with a total of 608 performances.

Sweet Charity had opened in Philadelphia on December 6, 1965, and was originally scheduled to open at the Palace on December 28. The New York première was postponed, however, until January 29, 1966. To many Broadway theatergoers, such delays usually indicate book trouble or casting problems, but when *Funny Girl*, which came to Broadway two years earlier, in 1964, postponed its opening date five times while the production played to preview audiences, New Yorkers were certain that rumors about difficulties were not exaggerated.

Funny Girl, originally scheduled to open in New York on February 13, 1964, did not have its première until March 26. During the extended period of previews in New York, the writers, the director, and the producer kept reworking the script, adding and deleting musical numbers. Jerome Robbins, who was brought in to assist director Garson Kanin, became production supervisor, but it is difficult to estimate just what responsibilities each man assumed in getting the show into its final form. When *Funny Girl* finally did open, it became a great hit. The critics, for the most part, felt that the book was weak, but they were delighted with Barbra Streisand. Their praise, plus excellent publicity catapulted her into the limelight and stirred up audience interest in seeing Broadway's newest star.

Funny Girl was based on the life of Fanny Brice, and traced her career from her girlhood on the lower East Side of New York to her appearance in the *Ziegfeld Follies.*

The opening scene, set backstage in the New Amsterdam Theatre, shows Fanny waiting in her dressing room for her husband, Nick Arnstein, who has just finished serving a prison term for embezzlement. Uncertain about the coming reunion Fanny begins to reminisce about her past. The action flashes back to the lower East Side where the young Fanny, gawky and not pretty, is determined to get into show business. Her audition for Kenny, manager of a music hall, is unsuccessful, but when she sings "I'm the Greatest Star" for Eddie Ryan, a vaudeville hoofer, she convinces him that she has talent and Eddie agrees to coach her. Kenny eventually hires Fanny, and she becomes a hit singing "Cornet Man." Nick Arnstein, who has come backstage to pay off a gambling debt to Kenny, meets Fanny. Shortly after that, she receives an offer from Florenz Ziegfeld to appear in the *Follies.* On opening night Arnstein comes backstage to congratulate her. Fanny takes him back to Henry Street to a block party her mother has arranged to celebrate her daughter's success. Although Fanny has already fallen in love, Nick, instead of pursuing the romance, leaves for Kentucky, and they do not meet again until Fanny is in Baltimore on tour with the *Follies.* Nick takes Fanny to dinner in a private dining room at a very elegant restaurant and makes love to her. The next day, Fanny decides to give up her career and follow Nick. The first act closes as she sings "Don't Rain on My

Parade," in which she declares that she will not allow anything to stand in the way of her finding happiness with Nick.

The second act opens with Nick and Fanny married. Fanny soon returns to the stage in a new edition of the *Follies*. During a rehearsal, she hears Nick trying to persuade Ziegfeld to invest in a gambling casino. Although Ziegfeld refuses, Fanny provides the necessary financial backing. On the opening night of the *Follies,* Fanny is upset because Nick has not come to see the show. After the performance, Nick arrives very much dejected and tells Fanny that the casino has failed and he has lost all the money invested. Fanny accepts the news placidly, whereupon Nick objects to her pampering him. Realizing that she has hurt Nick's pride, Fanny plans to make Nick a partner in a talent firm but tries to keep him from knowing that she is financing the venture. When Nick discovers what Fanny has done, he becomes angry. To show his independence, he becomes involved in an illegal bond deal, is arrested for embezzlement, and sentenced to eighteen months in prison.

The final scene, again set in the New Amsterdam Theatre, shows Fanny at her dressing table as Nick enters. Although Fanny and Nick still love each other, he makes her realize that their marriage could never again be a happy one. After Nick leaves, Fanny reprises "Don't Rain on My Parade," this time with a different connotation as she expresses her determination to let nothing stand in the way of her success.

In some respects, *Funny Girl* was more authentic than most stage biographies, but the musical comedy covered only part of Fanny Brice's life story. The script depicted her meteoric rise in the 1910s and 1920s but did not include her later successes in Hollywood and in radio in the 1930s when she created the character of Baby Snooks. Miss Brice soon appeared only in that role, and, with the advent of television, did a weekly series as Snooks. The incongruity of the tall, angular Miss Brice dressed as a child and using a child's voice and gawky gestures in her portrayal of the precocious brat, Baby Snooks, made the program a national favorite.

In the 1930s Miss Brice returned to the stage in another edition of the *Follies* that included one sketch in which she appeared as Snooks. Although Fanny Brice had been hailed as one of the great stage comediennes, she sang serious ballads with equal effectiveness. On her vaudeville tours, she did several of her well-known comedy routines, but in one scene she appeared on a darkened stage, lighted only by a street lamp, leaned against the post, and without resorting to gestures or affected mannerisms sang "My Man" so effectively that many people assumed that she was singing about her own life. Miss Brice, however, according to some insiders, had not selected the number herself. Ziegfeld had discovered "Mon Homme," written by Maurice Yvain with French lyrics by Albert Willemetz and Jacques Charles. The well-known playwright Channing Pollock wrote the English lyrics and gave the number the title "My Man" and Ziegfeld had Miss Brice sing it in the *Follies of 1921*. One source indicated that Miss Brice had also used it in one of Ziegfeld's Midnight Frolic shows. The song not only became an instant hit but also became linked directly with Miss Brice.

After Miss Brice died in 1951, many people felt that her life story would provide excellent material for a theatrical production. Interest in her career had never waned. Isobel Lennart, who wrote the book for *Funny Girl*, had originally planned her script as the basis for a motion picture; Miss Brice's third husband, Billy Rose, had written a story of her life; several authors had attempted biographical dramatizations; and Kaye Ballard had made a successful recording of Miss Brice's most famous songs.

Miss Brice's life story, however, was not an easy one to recreate. Although it embodied, in essence, the popular theme of the ugly duckling who became a Ziegfeld star, it did not end with the conventional "and they lived happily ever after." The writers could not falsify the biography with a trumped-up bittersweet ending after Arnstein returned from prison, for it was well known that Miss Brice's marriage to Mr. Arnstein had ended in divorce. Another difficulty in preparing the script derived from the fact that Nick Arnstein, who was still alive, would have to give his permission to be portrayed on stage. Furthermore, the producer, Ray Stark, was married to Frances Arnstein, daughter of Miss Brice and Mr. Arnstein, and reports indicated that Stark wanted to present Arnstein as favorably as possible. He finally succeeded in doing this, for the characterization, particularly as played by Sydney Chaplin, depicted Arnstein as a suave, dashing, and very handsome gambler.

The liner notes on the original cast album for *Funny Girl* stated that Ray Stark had long wanted to do a musical based on Fannie Brice's life, but as late as 1962 the list of future David Merrick productions had included *My Man,* the story of Miss Brice, with book by Isobel Lennart, music by Jule Styne, and lyrics by Bob Merrill. A great many people had assumed that Merrick would star Barbra Streisand, who had appeared in his production of *I Can Get It for You Wholesale.* The Ray Stark production of *Funny Girl* had the same author, composer, and lyricist as announced for Merrick's *My Man.* Stark is said to have made certain that none of the material written about Miss Brice by other authors whom he had asked to work on possible dramatizations would be included in this script. Nor did he include any of the songs Miss Brice had made famous.

When *Funny Girl* opened in Boston, it had second-act trouble and also ran too long. At least thirty minutes were cut before the production opened in Philadelphia. From the time of the first performance in Boston to the première in New York, at least five songs, "A Helluva Group," "It's Home," "Took a Little Time," "Sleep Now, Baby Bunting," and "Absent-Minded Me," were cut. Judging from the out-of-town reviews, the producers must have cut some of Carol Haney's dance routines, several of the *Follies* ensembles, and changed the opening scene. In rewriting the book, the producers had to work primarily on the second act, for the breakup of Fanny Brice's romance had less appeal than her meteoric rise and love affair with the dashing Arnstein, which had given the first act its excitement. By the time the production had finally opened in New York, the burden of keeping the second act moving had been placed on Miss Streisand.

Newspaper columnists hinted that Stark had had trouble finding anyone who could play Miss Brice until Miss Streisand impressed audiences with her performance as Miss Marmelstein in *I Can Get It for You Wholesale.* Most of the critics praised Miss Streisand's virtuoso performance but felt that the book gave Sydney Chaplin, although he was charming and handsome as Nick, little opportunity to make the characterization come alive. Critics also blamed the book rather than Miss Streisand for the show's failure to evoke the warm stage personality of Fanny Brice. Moreover, enjoyment of the production often depended upon the theatergoer's knowledge of Miss Brice's career. Those people who had seen her in the Ziegfeld shows and heard her sing "My Man," "Rose of Washington Square," "Second Hand Rose," or "I'm an Indian," were none too enthusiastic about *Funny Girl,* from which all these songs identified with Miss Brice had been excluded. Although they admitted that Miss Streisand had great talent and that she carried the burden of the show more than capably, they still felt that she was not playing the fabulous Fanny.

The decision to avoid such numbers as "My Man," however, was sound, for Jule Styne's songs showed Miss Streisand to good advantage and permitted her to develop an individualized characterization rather than a mere imitation of Miss Brice.

On the other hand, younger theatergoers, who had never seen or heard Miss Brice, were enthralled with Miss Streisand's dynamic performance as the ugly duckling who married the handsome gambler. Miss Streisand created for them a new character, the girl who triumphs over lack of beauty and becomes a great star. Moreover, many commentators felt that Miss Brice's original routines would have meant little or nothing to the newer generation of theatergoers.

After *Funny Girl* had become established as a hit, Miss Streisand used several of Miss Brice's songs on her television program, and helped revive interest in "My Man" and "Second Hand Rose." The Styne-Merrill songs for *Funny Girl* did resemble some of Fanny Brice's routines. "Sadie, Sadie" was based on the same idea as "Rose of Washington Square"; "The Music That Makes Me Dance" was, in a sense, a counterpart of "My Man"; and "Rat-Tat-Tat" and "Beautiful" gave Miss Streisand the opportunity to clown through typical Ziegfeld production numbers. But the hit song of the show, "People," was definitely a Streisand rather than a Brice song.

Miss Streisand and the successful *Funny Girl* became synonymous. Audiences crowded the theater to see the new star. A Streisand cult developed that not only catapulted *Funny Girl* into the "standing room only" category but also boomed the sales of Streisand records and developed huge television audiences for her two television "specials." When Johnny Desmond took over the role of Arnstein, critics again reviewed the show and stated that Miss Streisand had developed stature as a comedienne and as an actress, but that she spoke lines so rapidly that audiences could not always catch all of her dialogue.

On the last night in which Miss Streisand would appear in the show, the capacity audience was startled to hear an announcement on the loudspeaker that the role of Fanny Brice would be played—pause, while the audience gasped—by Barbra Streisand. The audience, according to *Variety*, whooped in relief. At the end of the show, Miss Streisand made a curtain speech and then sang "My Man," the one number many theatergoers wished had been included in the score.

There can be no minimizing the tremendous box-office power that Miss Streisand developed during her stay with *Funny Girl*. Originally, the top price for orchestra seats, for example, had been $8.80 with an increase to $9.40 for weekends; but shortly after the opening, the price was raised to $9.60 for all evening performances. Furthermore, the management at the Winter Garden added an extra row of thirty-seven seats in the orchestra.

During most of the period in which Barbra Streisand played the role of Fanny Brice, the theater was filled to capacity despite the questionable authenticity of the book. For example, many showmen doubted that Ziegfeld would ever have selected Miss Brice to sing the production number "Beautiful," or that the real Miss Brice would have clowned during the routine. These same dissenters also felt that the two scenes in the *Follies* lacked the glamour of Ziegfeld's production numbers. Robert Randolph's sets did incorporate the stairways that Ziegfeld liked to use in his revues; but *Funny Girl* did not have a lengthy parade of stunning show girls walking serenely down the stairs in elaborate costumes, often so heavy and ornate that the ladies of the ensemble had to practice as rigorously as if they were training for a dance routine in order to acquire the proper grace. Here again the commentators argued, and rightfully, that many theatergoers who flocked to see *Funny Girl* had never seen a production staged by Ziegfeld and would, therefore, have no basis for comparison. But many of these same commentators found the scene in which Miss Streisand succumbed to the charms of Sydney Chaplin as funny as any of the sketches Miss Brice had performed in Broadway revues.

Although the members of the supporting cast had even less opportunity than Chaplin to develop their characterizations, Kay Medford, with her ability to drawl a fairly amusing line into a howling gag, impressed audiences with her performance as Fanny's mother.

After Miss Streisand left the New York cast of *Funny Girl* she appeared for fourteen weeks in the London production. Most of the English critics wrote favorable reviews, but one or two dissenters, who had objected to the tremendous advance publicity hailing her talents, said that Miss Streisand did not always project clearly, and that they were unable to follow parts of her dialogue and some of the lyrics.

The London papers reported that the New York production of *Funny Girl* was operating at considerably lower grosses since Miss Streisand had left the cast. Gross receipts had indeed fallen. Any actress who followed Barbra Streisand in *Funny Girl* had to overcome the handicap of playing a role that had been tailored for her in both songs and dialogue. A road company, however, which began with Marilyn Michaels in the leading role, played to excellent houses. In New York those theatergoers who saw Miss Streisand's understudy, Lainie Kazan, perform the lead when Streisand suffered from laryngitis, were enthusiastic about her performance.

The real test, however, came when Mimi Hines replaced Miss Streisand in the New York company, for Miss Hines was not a Fanny Brice type of comedienne. Miss Streisand, dark and angular, resembled Miss Brice to some extent, but the blonde and petite Miss Hines had none of the Semitic features that had distinguished Miss Brice. Nevertheless, she gave a very convincing performance. Although her television and nightclub appearances as a comedienne had frequently overshadowed her remarkable talent as a singer, she had ample opportunity in *Funny Girl* to demonstrate both. She handled the serious ballad "People" capably, and was even more effective in the comedy songs, which permitted her to include some of the clowning actions and gestures that she had used to good advantage on television programs. Despite the fact that Miss Hines definitely did not look Jewish, she was excellent as Private Schwartz in the song, "Rat-Tat-Tat." In "You Are Woman," which she sang with Johnny Desmond, she punched home gag-lines with the unerring timing of a nightclub comedienne who knew how to handle audiences.

Miss Hines and her partner-husband, Phil Ford, also worked together as a team in *Funny Girl,* for he took over the role of Eddie Ryan, the vaudeville hoofer who befriended Fanny. Broadway audiences were skeptical about how long the production would run without Barbra Streisand. Miss Hines, however, played Fanny Brice from December 27, 1965 until July 1, 1967, when *Funny Girl* closed with a total of 1,348 performances. During the latter part of the run, the show operated on a two-for-one ticket policy and continued to draw large audiences but lower gross receipts.

The road tour also did profitable business, and during the summer of 1967 both Edie Adams and Carol Lawrence appeared in successful summer stock presentations. The initial success of the show, nevertheless, must be credited to Streisand, who triumphed over a book that most critics rated only average. Her "funny girl" may have only slightly resembled the real Fanny Brice, but her performance was a tour de force that established her as a star and *Funny Girl* as one of Broadway's greatest musical hits.

When *Funny Girl* closed, four musical comedy hits that had passed the 500-performance mark were still running in New York: *Man of La Mancha,* which opened at an off Broadway theater but used Broadway Equity contracts; *Hello, Dolly!,* which broke the longevity record set by *My Fair Lady;* and *Fiddler on the Roof,* which established a new record for musicals. *Mame,* the most recent arrival in the group, opened May 24, 1966.

No one seemed surprised when Robert Fryer and Lawrence Carr, producers of *Auntie Mame* which Jerome Lawrence and Robert E. Lee had adapted from Patrick Dennis' best-selling novel, announced that they would co-produce *Mame,* a musical adaptation of the comedy, with Sylvia and Joseph Harris. *Auntie Mame* had been a long-running hit with Rosalind Russell, who later starred in the very successful film version.

When *Mame* opened in Philadelphia, one critic said he wondered why it had taken ten years for someone to decide to adapt *Auntie Mame* into a musical, for the new show provided delightful entertainment. Reports from Boston, where *Mame* did capacity business during its entire stay, were even more favorable; the critics called it the most popular musical of the season and predicted that it would be a hit in New York.

The plot of *Mame* adhered more or less to the original story of *Auntie Mame* and concerned the adventures of the unconventional Mame Dennis, whose nephew Patrick comes to live with her when his father dies, leaving him in Mame's care. Mame sends Patrick to an avant-garde school against the wishes of the banker who controls Patrick's estate, loses all her money in the stock-market crash of 1929, and marries the wealthy Southern gentleman Beauregard Jackson Picket Burnside. When Burnside dies, Mame returns to New York and discovers that Patrick, now nineteen, has become a young snob and is preparing to marry a rattle-brained society debutante. The clever Mame skillfully maneuvers to break up the engagement, and Patrick eventually marries an interior decorator, Pegeen, of whom his aunt approves. In the final scene Mame is about to take Patrick's young son Peter with her on a trip, thus bringing the plot full circle.

The story held few, if any, surprises, since a great many people had read the book or had seen the stage or screen versions. Audiences, however, were surprised by certain of the incidents in the musical, for in making the adaptation, Lawrence and Lee had changed some events, combined two characters into one, and eliminated others. In the original play, after Mame has lost her money, she gladly takes a walk-on role in a production starring her friend Vera Charles; but the eccentric Mame wears an excessive number of jingling bracelets that ruin the scene; when one bracelet becomes caught in Miss Charles's dress, Mame cannot pry it loose and is forced to remain on center stage for all the curtain calls. In the musical version, Mame still becomes an actress, but this time she appears in a musical within a musical, playing the lady in the Moon. Mame's performance is a fiasco, for she slides off her perch and goes through a series of gyrations that ruin Vera's big number. In both the comedy and the musical, when Mame goes to Beauregard's Southern home to meet his family and is trapped into riding in a fox hunt on a wild horse that might have killed her, she manages to stay in the saddle and even brings the fox back alive. The musical offered no explanation for Mame's success as a horsewoman, but in the comedy it becomes clear that Mame remained on the horse simply because she had become stuck in the saddle and couldn't get loose. The cast of characters in *Auntie Mame* had included an Irish poet hired to help Mame write her memoirs after Beauregard died; and Agnes Gooch, an efficient but spinsterish secretary who fell under Mame's spell and permitted her to dress her in a seductive gown and send her out on a date with the poet. When Agnes returned six months later, she told Mame she had "lived"—perhaps too unwisely, for she was pregnant. The musical eliminated the Irish poet and combined the role of Agnes Gooch with that of the family servant who had originally brought Patrick to Mame's apartment. Agnes, however, still succumbed to Mame's persuasive powers and allowed herself to be togged out by Mame and Vera Charles and sent off in search of adventure. Lawrence and Lee also modified Mame's plans for breaking up Patrick's marriage to the snobbish Gloria Upson. In both the musical and the play, the Upsons inform Mame that they intend to buy a lot in a restricted area of Connecticut where the young couple can build a home. In the comedy Mame infuriates the Upsons when she buys an adjacent lot with the money she expects to earn from her memoirs and announces that she is going to build a home for Jewish refugees. In the musical, Mame buys the lot, but decides to build a home for unwed mothers such as Agnes Gooch. The bite was less vicious, perhaps, but the idea was still strong enough to infuriate the Upsons and break up the marriage.

Oddly enough, in cutting down and condensing scenes to allow time for musical numbers, Lawrence and Lee managed to develop the mutual affection between Mame and Patrick more fully than they had in their comedy. They accomplished this partly by showing Mame taking Patrick to art classes, to a four-alarm fire, and even to a nightclub, which the police raid. Such songs as "Open a New Window" and "My Best Girl" further emphasized the growing affection between young Patrick and his aunt. Even more important, Angela Lansbury's characterization of Mame and Frankie Michaels' of Patrick gave their scenes a sentimental, touching quality that had been glossed over in the comedy.

Before *Mame* went into rehearsal, rumors circulated about potential stars who had either turned down the role or who had hopefully auditioned for it. Ethel Merman, who had been offered the part, said she had refused simply because she did not want to become involved in another long-running production on Broadway. Angela Lansbury, who won the role, gave a scintillating performance that made her Broadway's newest celebrity. *Mame* benefited from Miss Lansbury's extensive experience both in films and on the stage. In spite of her beauty, she had seldom played glamour roles, for she was too versatile an actress to be stereotyped as a clotheshorse. Her film performances had brought her two nominations for Academy Awards. In 1957 she made her Broadway debut in *Hotel Paradiso* and demonstrated that she was an excellent farceur. In the 1960–61 season she handled a difficult dramatic role in *A Taste of Honey* and won the approval of the critics. Miss Lansbury then appeared in a short-lived musical, *Anyone Can Whistle,* and convinced Broadway showmen that she could be a musical star if she had the proper vehicle. *Mame* gave her that opportunity. It utilized all her talents as a comedienne, dramatic actress, singer, and dancer. It also capitalized on her beauty, for Miss Lansbury dazzled the audience by wearing a series of striking outfits designed by Robert Mackintosh.

Miss Lansbury's portrayal of Mame was less bizarre than Patrick Dennis' original characterization and more subdued than Rosalind Russell's. Her charm and deft performance created a more sympathetic Mame and heightened the sentimental quality of her scenes with young Patrick, superbly played by Frankie Michaels as an average, rather than precocious, child. Moreover, his appealing performance made audiences share his affection for Auntie Mame. At the end of the first season three members of the cast won Tony Awards: Angela Lansbury as the best actress in a musical; Frankie Michaels as the best featured actor in a musical; and Beatrice Arthur as the best featured actress in a musical. As Vera Charles, Miss Arthur emphasized every acid line, regaling audiences with her almost deadpan interpretation of Mame's dipsomaniac friend. In many ways Miss Arthur's portrayal was slower-moving, less frenzied, but much wittier than the Vera Charles that Lawrence and Lee had originally created for *Auntie Mame*.

Any actor who played the grown-up Patrick had to overcome the handicap of competing with the far more charming character of young Patrick, aged ten; but tall, handsome Jerry Lanning pleased audiences with his effective performance. The excellent cast also included Jane Connell as Agnes, and Charles Braswell as Beauregard.

At the end of the season, costume designer Robert Mackintosh and lyricist Jerry Herman both won the *Variety* Poll of Drama Critics. Herman had also written the score which many critics hailed for its tuneful melodies. The title song, "Mame," effectively staged as the first-act finale, may not have been so spectacular as Herman's "Hello, Dolly," but it had a rollicking rhythm and melody that easily made it the hit of the show. "If He Walked into My Life," the number in which Miss Lansbury wonders about the possible mistakes she may have made in raising Patrick, also became a resounding hit. Other songs that pleased audiences included "My Best Girl," sung by Frankie Michaels and Angela Lansbury; and "We Need a Little Christmas," a delightful quartet sung by Angela Lansbury, Frankie Michaels, Jane Connell, and Sab Shimono, who played Ito, Mame's butler. "Open a New Window," sung by Miss Lansbury, benefited not only from imaginative staging but also from the mobile sets designed by William and Jean Eckart. As Mame sang the number, she and Patrick walked up a magnificent staircase. When they reached the top landing, the surrounding scenery glided off, and Mame and Patrick, sitting on a large window frame that had been lowered onto the platform, were transported into a new scene. The score also included several comedy numbers. Miss Lansbury and Miss Arthur threw barbs at each other in "Bosom Buddies," and Miss Arthur's throaty voice accentuated the ridiculous lyrics in "The Man in the Moon," a burlesque of the songs used in old-fashioned musical comedy routines. "Gooch's Song," Agnes's lament about the consequences of the emancipated life, provided still another humorous set of lyrics.

Onna White's sprightly choreography, which drew on many

dances of the depression era, highlighted the first-act finale with a cakewalk routine while the ensemble sang "Mame." In the second act she staged a vigorous Charleston, danced by Mame and the young guests at the Upson estate, to the number "That's How Young I Feel."

By the summer of 1967 Stuart Getz had replaced Frankie Michaels as young Patrick, and Anne Francine had become the new Vera Charles. In August 1967, when Miss Lansbury took a well-earned two-week vacation, Celeste Holm, in preparation for the starring role in the road company, played Mame and received glowing reviews. The weekly gross receipts quoted in *Variety* indicated that *Mame* continued to do capacity business during the two weeks Miss Holm played the lead.

Gene Saks, who directed the production, sacrificed none of the comedy of the original plot even though he slowed down the frenzied pace that had dominated many of the scenes in *Auntie Mame*. The tempo he sustained, in fact, made Mame's antics more credible and Patrick's adoration for her more contagious.

Any discussion of *Mame* as a Broadway hit, however, would be incomplete without a specific reference to the author of the novel. As Hobe Morrison pointed out in his *Variety* review, credits for *Mame*'s phenomenal success should include Patrick Dennis, whose material had provided such an excellent basis for the dramatic versions that followed.

Mame introduced no startling innovations in the musical theater, but it did offer excellent entertainment. It may have been, as one or two dissenters suggested, old-fashioned and sentimental, but it had appeal for audiences that wanted to sit back and relax, listen to pleasant tunes, look at a beautiful heroine, and watch an opulent production unfold a familiar story without forcing the listener to probe for hidden meanings.

When Miss Lansbury's contract expired at the end of the second season, *Mame* had surpassed *Auntie Mame's* record of 619 performances. Janis Paige, who replaced Miss Lansbury, helped draw excellent, although not capacity houses, and Miss Paige was in turn replaced by Sheila Smith, Jane Morgan, and finally Ann Miller, who introduced several of her show-stopping tap routines. *Mame* prolonged its run by using two-for-one tickets and closed in January 1970 with a total of 1,508 performances, making it one of Broadway's great musical hits.

Man of La Mancha opened November 22, 1965, approximately six months earlier than *Mame*. The ANTA Washington Square Theater where *Man of La Mancha* played had a seating capacity of approximately 1,115 with a possible total gross of approximately $56,800, while the Winter Garden Theater, which housed *Mame*, had a seating capacity of 1,479 and could gross more than $94,000 a week, with an additional $1,000 for standees. The performance record for *Man of La Mancha*, therefore, although it clearly established the production as a long-running hit, did not reveal the fact that the number of people who saw the show each week was about 3,000 less than the number who saw *Mame*.

Some commentators have questioned whether *Man of La Mancha* should be included in a list of Broadway hits, for the ANTA Washington Square Theater, located on the edge of Greenwich Village, is not in the Broadway sector. Technically, however, *Man of La Mancha* is a Broadway show because all contracts, including those for authors and actors, were in accordance with royalty or salary scales established for Broadway shows rather than the lower scales established for off-Broadway productions.

After *Man of La Mancha* had become a definite hit, rumors circulated that it would move uptown to a larger house; for although it was drawing capacity houses at the ANTA Washington Square Theater, it was earning only marginal profits. The owners of the theater, however, readjusted the contract to a flat rental and eliminated the percentage of the gross over a stipulated sum that it had formerly received. The new terms gave the production an additional profit of about $1,500 a week, and the producers of *Man of La Mancha* decided to remain at the ANTA Theater.

In his introduction to the play, Dale Wasserman, author of *Man of La Mancha,* wrote that he had been in Madrid working on a motion picture when, to his surprise, he read a newspaper item stating that he was in Spain doing research for a dramatic version of Cervantes' *Don Quixote*. The news item was wrong, but Wasserman decided to read the book. When he had finished the two volumes, he decided not to write a stage adaptation of the story—

which had already been used as the basis for ballets, motion pictures, dramas, and operas—because he felt that none of these adaptations had been able to condense the rambling story into a practicable dramatic version. On the other hand Wasserman had become intrigued with the mystery that surrounded Miguel de Cervantes y Saavedra, the author. In his search for information about the man who had written so important a literary classic, Wasserman found several documents which indicated that Cervantes' life had been a series of misfortunes. From the limited biographical material, Wasserman learned about Cervantes' service in the army, his disablement, his five years of slavery in Algiers, his excommunication from the Church, his three terms in prison, his broken marriage, his illegitimate daughter, and finally, his writing of *Don Quixote,* begun when he was already in his fifties, impoverished, ill, and nearly blind.

Wasserman decided to write a play combining the characters of Cervantes and Don Quixote because he felt that the author and the fictional hero were alike in remaining idealists despite adversity. As his theme, Wasserman used a quotation from Miguel Unamuno: "Only he who attempts the absurd is capable of achieving the impossible."

The first dramatic version, *I, Don Quixote,* was presented as a ninety-minute original television drama on November 9, 1959, as part of the *Du Pont Show of the Month* series, with Lee J. Cobb playing the dual role of Cervantes-Quixote. The show won three television awards. Wasserman then planned to convert the television script into a stage play. Albert Marre, who had been extremely successful as a director of both plays and musicals, convinced Wasserman that his novel idea would provide an excellent basic plot for a musical.

As composer, Marre selected Mitch Leigh, who had studied with Paul Hindemith at the Yale School of Music, founded Music Makers, Inc., and won major awards for writing music used in radio and television commercials. Leigh had also written incidental music for several Broadway plays but had never worked on the score for an entire musical production. Although he realized that he would have to create melodies that could be integrated into the plot rather than typical musical comedy tunes that might become popular favorites, Leigh agreed to undertake the difficult task and spent two years working on the score. To fit the mood of the drama, he used a form of flamenco music which, as he admitted, had come considerably later than the era in which Cervantes lived. The score, nevertheless, provided appropriate background for the drama through its rhythm and unusual orchestration, which used two guitars, a string bass, a few woodwinds and brass instruments, and percussion. The success of *Man of La Mancha* brought Leigh two major awards and lucrative offers from advertisers who were now willing to pay higher prices for his television commercials.

Joe Darion, the lyricist, had worked on two versions of Don Marquis' saga of Archy and Mehitabel. The first version, *Archy and Mehitabel,* had been in the form of an opera; Darion later readapted it into a Broadway musical, *Shinbone Alley.* He had also written the lyrics for several popular songs, among them "Ricochet," which had sold an astronomical number of records.

After Wasserman, Leigh, and Darion had completed the libretto and score, they tried out the production in East Haddam, Connecticut, at an old opera house that had been reconverted into a small summer theater. As part of a community project that operated on a nonprofit basis, Albert Selden had taken over the Goodspeed Opera House and had reputedly spent three quarters of a million dollars on renovations. During his first two years as managing director, Selden presented a variety of productions, including revivals of musical comedy hits of the 1920s and 1930s as well as several Gilbert and Sullivan operettas. In the summer of 1965, he planned to produce, in conjunction with director Albert Marre, three new musicals that could later be presented on Broadway. Selden and Marre formed a repertory company that included Richard Kiley, Ray Middleton, Robert Rounseville, Jon Cypher, and Joan Diener, all five of whom appeared in the first production, *Man of La Mancha,* which proved to be the only successful one of the three. Richard Kiley, who played Cervantes, and Joan Diener, who played Aldonza, had worked together in *Kismet,* which Marre had also directed. Before the end of the summer, *Man of La Mancha* was brought back to the Goodspeed Opera House. The late Hal James, who had come to see the play, offered to help finance a New York production and became co-producer with Albert Selden.

The ANTA Washington Square Theater, one of the few theaters available to the producers of *Man of La Mancha* at the beginning of the season, had been built to provide temporary quarters for the Lincoln Center Repertory Company and had several disadvantages. The location, Fourth Street, was far removed from the theatrical center; the limited seating capacity indicated that the show would need to draw capacity houses to be profitable; and the semicircular stage presented problems for Howard Bay, the scene designer. On the other hand, the theater had one definite advantage: audiences could see the stage clearly from all parts of the auditorium because the semicircular rows of seats were even more steeply banked than the balcony seats in typical Broadway theaters. To facilitate entrances and exits, Bay ingeniously contrived a long staircase that could be lowered onto the stage, trap doors that led to a lower dungeon, and a series of passageways below the stage. By slanting the platform at a rather sharp angle, he created problems for Jack Cole, the choreographer, but at the same time he further improved the visibility.

The production opened in New York with the same cast that had performed *Man of La Mancha* at East Haddam. The action, continuous, without any intermission, begins with Cervantes and his servant entering a prison in Seville, where Cervantes is to await trial by the Inquisition for an offense against the Church. The thieves and trollops who surround him try to take away his possessions, including the manuscript of *Don Quixote,* but Cervantes persuades a kangaroo court set up by his fellow prisoners to permit him to offer as his defense a dramatization of his manuscript. During the first musical number, Cervantes puts on makeup, including a moustache, pointed beard, and thick eyebrows, to resemble Don Quixote. His servant becomes Sancho Panza, and the other prisoners assume supporting roles, including several who appear as horses.

At the start of the story of the eccentric knight whose aim is to restore chivalry, Quixote and Sancho Panza come to a roadside inn, which Quixote tells Sancho Panza is a castle. There he meets Aldonza, a servant girl and strumpet. When he insists upon calling her Dulcinea, the ideal lady of quality whom he would worship, the confused and somewhat irate Aldonza cannot understand why Quixote does not see her as she really is.

The scene then changes to Quixote's home, where his niece, Antonia, and his housekeeper are asking the padre for help in dealing with Quixote's madness. As they sing "I'm Only Thinking of Him," the padre realizes that they are less interested in Quixote's welfare than in stopping him from causing further embarrassment. Nevertheless, he agrees to help Dr. Carrasco, Antonia's fiancé, bring Quixote back to his home.

At the inn, Quixote, waiting to be dubbed a knight, sees a barber wearing his shaving basin as a helmet. Quixote usurps it, calling it the magic helmet of Nambrino. Aldonza, still confused by Quixote's chivalry, asks why he behaves so strangely. Quixote explains his actions in the song "Impossible Dream." After he has defended Aldonza against the attacks of the muleteers, the innkeeper knights him in a ceremony called "The Dubbing." Aldonza's experience of chivalry is short-lived, however, for when she is alone with the muleteers, they carry her off and criminally assault her. Disillusioned, Aldonza will have no more of Quixote and his impossible dream.

The doctor and the padre, having failed in their first attempt to bring Quixote back to his home, then return with a new plan. Disguised as the Knight of the Mirrors, the doctor challenges Quixote and forces him to look into the mirror of reality where he sees himself as an old, demented man. The doctor then takes Quixote back, defeated and dying. Aldonza, realizing that his defeat means that he will no longer be the knight who had treated her as a lady of quality, goes to his home. After fighting her way into his room, she begs him to become again that chivalrous knight. Roused by hearing Aldonza repeat the lyrics of "Impossible Dream," Quixote attempts to get out of bed and put on his armor in preparation for another quest, but the effort is too much. He collapses and dies. Quixote's death, however, has changed Aldonza, for she now calls herself Dulcinea, as though she has literally become the ideal woman of Quixote's dreams.

The final scene shows Cervantes back in the dungeon with the prisoners who, inspired by his story, have returned his manuscript.

As the play ends, Cervantes, who seems now to have acquired Quixote's bravery, leaves to face his Inquisitors.

Most of the critics wrote superlative reviews, expressing admiration for the hero Cervantes-Quixote and his romantic story of hope and chivalry. To these critics, *Man of La Mancha* brought a welcome change from the theater of the absurd or dramas that dealt only with the evils or the decadence of humanity. Wasserman's libretto never treated Quixote, in spite of his absurdities, as a clown, but rather engendered audience sympathy for the idealistic, pathetic, and somewhat foolish knight whose mission had been to correct the wrong in the world.

Audiences and critics were also intrigued by the excellent lighting and ingenious staging, which used only a few props, very little moving scenery, and the imagination of the spectators to depict such scenes as Quixote's tilting at the windmills. Equally fascinating were the scene in which Cervantes applied makeup on stage to transform himself into Quixote, and Jack Cole's choreography, particularly the skillful manner in which he circumvented the problems of the slanted stage.

Several critics did object to one or two earthy lines and to what they felt was an overemphasis on sentiment, but even the dissenters agreed that *Man of La Mancha* had merit as a production that broke away from traditional musical comedy patterns and used singers who could really sing. Richard Kiley, who gave a magnificent performance in the dual role of Cervantes-Quixote, had appeared in serious dramas and in musical comedies on Broadway. In *Man of La Mancha,* he had ample opportunity to demonstrate his ability both as a singer and as an actor. Joan Diener, the wife of Albert Marre, the director, gave a superb performance in the exhausting role of Aldonza. Most of the critics also praised Ray Middleton as the innkeeper, Robert Rounseville as the padre, Irving Jacobson as Sancho Panza, and Jon Cypher as Dr. Carrasco.

Many of the critics further endorsed the production for its excellent score and lyrics, and also for the novelty of placing one half of the orchestra on either side of the stage to give the effect of stereophonic sound. Anyone who has not seen the production could, by reading the synopsis and listening to the excellent original cast album, discover how well the songs had been integrated into the text. The dramatic quality of "The Impossible Dream," however, even out of context, has made it a popular hit.

At the end of the first season, *Man of La Mancha* led all other productions in prize awards. It received Tony Awards for the following:

Best musical of the season
Best actor in a musical—Richard Kiley
Best composer and lyricist—Mitch Leigh and Joe Darion
Best scenic designer—Howard Bay
Best director of a musical—Albert Marre

It won the *Variety* Poll of Drama Critics in the following categories:

Best musical of the season
Best actor in a musical—Richard Kiley
Best composer—Mitch Leigh
Best scene designer—Howard Bay

The New York Drama Critics' Circle named it the best musical of the season; Otis L. Guernsey, Jr., editor of *The Best Plays of 1965–1966,* selected it as one of the ten best plays of the year; and the Joseph Maharam Foundation awarded Howard Bay $1,000 for the excellence of his sets.

Despite the glowing reviews it received, *Man of La Mancha* did not become an instant success. For several weeks after it opened, it attracted enthusiastic but definitely not capacity audiences. Some skeptics doubted that the show would run very long, even though it had received an excellent boost on the Ed Sullivan program, where the leading characters performed several scenes from the production. Gradually, however, as word-of-mouth advertising spread, box-office sales and mail orders increased until *Man of La Mancha* became a sell-out hit. The limited seating capacity and the increasing interest of theatergoers made tickets virtually impossible to obtain for months in advance.

By the end of the second season, several of the original cast members, including Richard Kiley and Joan Diener, had gone on tour with the production, but the cast changes seemed to have little or no effect on the demand for tickets. The New York cast replacements in the Cervantes-Quixote role included José Ferrer, John Cullum, and David Atkinson; Miss Diener's role of Aldonza was played by Maura K. Wedge and later by Bernice Massi; and Wilbur Evans took over Ray Middleton's role of the innkeeper.

Reviews of the road company were very favorable. A report from one city indicated that the producers had turned down an offer to present the show in a large theater because they felt that *Man of La Mancha* needed the intimacy of a small house to be effective.

Early in 1967 plans were made to present *Man of La Mancha* in Amsterdam and in Vienna. The show became an even greater financial success when United Artists bought the screen rights for a sum in excess of $2 million. By October 1, 1967, although the management was announcing the availability of tickets for some performances, the production still drew well. In March, 1968, the musical was forced to move from the ANTA Theater and was brought to the Martin Beck Theater on Broadway. Transferring the show uptown to a larger house proved to be profitable, for *Man of La Mancha* played to excellent houses. Early in 1971, it was moved temporarily off Broadway to the Eden Theater and then was brought back to the Mark Hellinger Theater on Broadway where it completed its run of 2,329 performances.

During the 1966–67 theatrical season, *Man of La Mancha* was listed as one of the three most successful touring attractions. The other two, *Fiddler on the Roof* and *Hello, Dolly!*, had already established long runs in New York, and *Fiddler on the Roof* had played to capacity houses from its opening, September 22, 1964 through December 1967.

Fiddler on the Roof certainly did not resemble a typical Broadway musical. Almost every man in the cast wore a beard. The girls were dressed in peasant costumes, authentic but not spectacular. The story was amusing but ended almost tragically, with only the slightest hope that the characters exiled from their homeland would find a more peaceful existence in a foreign land.

Joseph Stein based the musical on a collection of stories about a milkman named Tevye, written by Sholom Aleichem, famed

Yiddish writer. Zero Mostel, who originated the role of Tevye in *Fiddler on the Roof,* had also played the role of Tevye in an off-Broadway production of *The World of Sholom Aleichem.* Joseph Stein, however, did not simply readapt that play or the original stories to a musical form, although he did include some of the important episodes and, of course, certain of the main characters. Instead, he created a fresh story that dealt with the gradual breakdown of traditions, partially illustrated through the marriages of Tevye's daughters. Stein explained that he used very little of the original dialogue because some of it sounded too melodramatic in translation, and some of it, such as Tevye's habit of misquoting the Scriptures, meant little to people who did not know the original passages. He kept to the original idea, however, by inventing misquotations that had the same effect. Sholom Aleichem had created Tevye as a mild man, not always clever; but Stein changed the characterization to give Tevye wit, leadership, and forcefulness. He also added new characters and included specific references to the oppression and violence that had not been emphasized so strongly in the original stories. Stein, nevertheless, retained the spirit of Aleichem's stories and succeeded in paraphrasing the almost untranslatable Yiddish idioms into colloquial English. Many people, in fact, who had read Sholom Aleichem found it difficult to determine where Aleichem's contributions ended and where the ingenious Mr. Stein's new material began.

Stein said that everyone connected with the production of *Fiddler on the Roof* had grown to love Tevye, his family, and his community. The proof of this statement was evident in Stein's skillful handling of the characters and dialogue; in the excellence of the music and lyrics by Jerry Bock and Sheldon Harnick; and in Jerome Robbins' choreography, which ranged from traditional folk dances to vigorous Russian steps that sent dancers leaping and jumping in breathless routines.

The story, as Stein fashioned it, dealt with life in the village of Anatevka and with the traditions of its people. The play opened without an overture to reveal a fiddler seated precariously on a roof, playing his music even though he was in danger of falling off and getting hurt. Tevye enters and explains to the audience that the people in Anatevka are similar to the fiddler: they also live precariously. In the first number, "Tradition," Tevye introduces the townspeople, including his family, the matchmaker Yente, the rabbi, the rabbi's son, the butcher, the bookseller, the beggar, and the Russian constable. Most of the ensuing action develops the story of Tevye, his wife, and his daughters. Yente has arranged a wedding between Tevye's oldest daughter Tzeitel, and Lazar Wolf the butcher, a man old enough to be her father. Tzeitel pleads with Tevye not to force her to go through with the wedding. Although bound by tradition to honor his agreement, Tevye agrees to let Tzeitel marry the man she loves, Motel the tailor. Knowing that he will have trouble persuading his wife Golde to agree to the change in grooms, Tevye pretends to have a dream in which Golde's grandmother appears and sanctions the marriage between Tzeitel and Motel. The second daughter Hodel also defies tradition by telling her father she intends to marry Perchik, a young radical, and asking for Tevye's blessing rather than his permission. Chava, the third daughter, marries a Russian gentile. Although Tzeitel's marriage and Hodel's romance were not what Tevye and Golde had planned for their daughters, they had accepted Motel as a son-in-law and hoped that Hodel would be happily married to Perchik when she joined him in Siberia. Chava, however, has married outside the faith; in keeping with tradition, Tevye cuts her off from the family as though she were dead.

The Czar orders that all Jews must evacuate their homes in Anatevka. The villagers pack their belongings. When Chava returns to bid her parents farewell, Golde wants to embrace her but knows she cannot defy tradition or Tevye, who has deliberately turned his back on his daughter and refused to speak to her. Yet when Tzeitel bids her sister farewell, Tevye prompts her to say, "God be with you." Golde's inability to caress her daughter, and Tevye's refusal to acknowlege the child he loved, had far greater emotional impact through underplaying and the use of almost no dialogue than it might have had if it had been played more theatrically.

In the final moment of the play, Tevye, Golde, and their two youngest daughters set out for America, hoping that Tzeitel and Motel will eventually join them. The unhappy ending was not a surprise to people who knew the stories of Jewish life in Russia and the forced exodus in the early 1900s. Any attempt to change the ending would have been incongruous with the historical facts of emigration during the Czarist regime.

The focus on Tevye and his family gave the play its unity. Although Tevye was literally the head of the family, his wife carried out his wishes only when they agreed with hers. To prevent her from crossing him openly, Tevye had learned to handle Golde with tact, as he did in conjuring up the dream to make her consent to Tzeitel's wedding. When Tevye hears his children talk about love, he is puzzled, and asks Golde if she loves him; after her initial shock, she sings a duet with Tevye in which they decide that after twenty-five years of marriage, they are probably in love, although this discovery will not change their behavior toward each other. The audience sensed their affection more concretely in the wedding scene. In Orthodox Judaism, the men and women do not sit together during religious services, even at a wedding ceremony. Dancing together would have been an even greater defiance of tradition. But after Perchik has begun dancing with Hodel, Tevye decides that he wants to dance with his wife. Golde, knowing that she is shocking some of the people by breaking away from custom nevertheless dances with her husband.

Boris Aronson's striking sets, Patricia Zipprodt's costumes, and Jean Rosenthal's lighting, particularly during the impressive candle-lighting ceremony, all enhanced the production, as did Jerome Robbins' directing and choreography. Robbins' whirlwind routines in the first act dazzled audiences. During the wedding ceremony, for example, four dancers balanced bottles on their heads while performing a series of intricate steps. At the scene in the inn, when Tevye has arranged for Tzeitel's marriage to Lazar, the members of the ensemble start to dance in jubilation. Some young Russians add their vigorous steps, and the tempo increases until the number climaxes in a heap of exhausted dancers.

Jerry Bock and Sheldon Harnick added immeasurably to the show by creating songs that steadily gained in popularity. Several of Tevye's numbers, such as "If I Were a Rich Man," had a decided Chassidic touch, with Tevye embellishing the melody with cantorial flourishes that were musical sounds rather than lyrics.

Bock and Harnick created three numbers that had a decided musical comedy flavor: "Matchmaker, Matchmaker," which became a popular hit; "Miracle of Miracles," sung by Motel when he knew he would marry Tzeitel; and "Now I Have Everything," sung by Perchik to Hodel. Several critics mildly objected to these songs because they seemed to be catering to Broadway taste, but they were not completely incongruous, for they did illustrate the desire of the young people to break with tradition. These songs also pleased theatergoers who might not have liked the show so well if the entire score had represented only traditional music. "Sunrise, Sunset," however, which was more in keeping with the overall mood of the production, became a popular hit.

Several critics also objected to the duet "Do You Love Me?" sung by Golde and Tevye, because they thought the lyrics sounded like gag lines. The song, nonetheless, was authentic in its characterization of such couples as Golde and Tevye, who never met until the day of their wedding but learned to live with each other without ever giving serious thought to romance until their children decided to marry for love. A confused Tevye might well have wondered if he understood his daughters, and a bewildered Golde might well have been perplexed by her husband's sudden display of emotion.

Some theatergoers observed that the dialogue had a great many lines that were typical of the Jewish humor used by popular comedians. This humor often came, not from the character's intention to be witty, but from his attempt to camouflage sentiment.

Several of the most delightful episodes were those in which Tevye spoke directly to God, asking why he could not have been a rich man, or why his horse had to be lame. He even rebuked God for allowing the Russians to stage a demonstration that made a shambles of Tzeitel's wedding party. When Tevye, at one point, stopped his complaining and asked God if he were bothering Him, the audience almost expected to hear the question answered. The scene was humorous but not irreverent.

Commentators and critics have written a great deal about Zero Mostel's magnificent portrayal of Tevye, expressing their delight in his dynamic interpretation of the role when the show first opened, and their dissatisfaction with his ad libbing after the show had been running for a while. If, as some critics intimated, he destroyed the mood, he still gave a brilliant performance that helped establish *Fiddler on the Roof* as one of the great musical comedies in the history of the American theater. Mostel could be riotously funny one moment, and then suddenly heartbreaking in the more emotional scenes, as in his refusal to speak to Chava. Mostel's ability to balance the humor and the sadness, to put across the musical numbers, and to establish exceptional rapport as he spoke directly to the audience, gave the play much of its appeal.

Mostel overshadowed everyone else on stage and dominated the action, but Maria Karnilova almost equalled Mostel in holding the spotlight. Her sharp performance made Tevye's scenes more credible. Miss Karnilova had been a devastatingly comical ballerina in one of Jerome Robbins' dance troupes, and one of the highly amusing striptease dancers in *Gypsy,* but she surprised even her steadfast admirers with her brilliant performance as Golde, who might easily have been portrayed as a scolding nag but through Miss Karnilova's skillful portrayal emerged, despite her sharp tongue, as warm and human.

With far less opportunity to command attention, the other members of the cast—including Beatrice Arthur as Yente; Joanna Merlin, Julia Migenes and Tanya Everett as the three older daughters; Austin Pendleton as Motel; Bert Convy as Perchik; Joe Ponazecki as Fyedka; and Michael Granger as Lazar Wolf—were nevertheless uniformly excellent. The list of credits could be much longer, for every person on stage contributed to the success of the production.

The success of *Fiddler on the Roof* did not depend entirely upon the original cast, for the show continued to do capacity business in New York regardless of who played Tevye. The major difference between Mostel's performance and those of his successors was in the somewhat changed characterization of Tevye. Luther Adler, who replaced Mostel after the show had run for about eleven months, was perhaps less effective in the musical numbers, but more effective in the dramatic scenes. Mostel had emphasized humor as well as compassion; Adler emphasized emotion. Herchel Bernardi, who succeeded Adler, and Harry Goz, who took over the role when Bernardi left the cast, were both definitely amusing and believable. The Israeli performer Topol, who starred in the London production, emphasized sentiment.

In the past, some theatergoers had complained that plays dealing with Jewish life were frequently meaningless to anyone unfamiliar with Orthodox Jewry. There were fewer objections to *Fiddler on the Roof* on this point, for Joseph Stein in the opening scene explained many of the traditional costumes, such as the skullcap and the dangling prayer shawl, and several of the traditional customs. One bit of costuming, however, continued to raise questions. The women always wore headcoverings of shawls or scarves, and even when Golde appeared without a scarf she wore an obvious wig (*sheitle*), which represented a form of headcovering. The general explanation that both men and women always covered their heads clarified this use of all types of headpieces. Harnick's lyrics also were designed to help the non-Jewish theatergoer, for he generally followed a Yiddish term with its English equivolent. *L'Chaim* was followed by *To Life,* for instance, and *Mazeltov* by *Congratulations.*

Stein, nevertheless, did include two names with special connotations that simply could not be translated into English. Fruma-Sarah and Yente were both authentic Jewish names, having a special significance for people who understood Yiddish. The word "Fruma" could have been part of the proper name or it could have been an adjective describing Lazar Wolf's first wife. A literal translation would be "pious" or "deeply religious," but the word meant someone who strictly observed all customs and rituals of Orthodox Jewry. Since neither "pious" nor "deeply religious" would have had quite the same connotation, it was much simpler for Stein to leave the word in Yiddish rather than supply a faulty translation. The word "Yente" would be even more difficult to translate. Yente was a proper name, but it was also a word used to describe a certain type of woman. Twelve women who were asked to define the word gave twelve different definitions including "busybody," "gossip," "fishwife," "loudmouth," "coarse woman," "upstart," "meddler," and "informant." All twelve agreed that any translation would destroy part of the connotation because "Yente" meant a combination of several of those words. An awareness of the meanings and connotations of "Fruma" and "Yente" added a touch of humor to the names, but unfamiliarity with the double meanings did not detract from the enjoyment of the show.

Most of the critics showered the production with superlatives, but some were disappointed because it seemed to have too much "Broadway" in its humor and songs. Several critics thought the script had a little too much self-pity, but this may have resulted from Stein's handling of those episodes concerning the pogroms and the forced evacuation of the Jews.

The printed text included the statement, "You don't have to be Jewish to enjoy *Fiddler on the Roof*," as well as a reference to Sholom Aleichem as the Jewish Mark Twain. Although Aleichem's stories dealt with the struggles of a Russian Jew, they were understandable to people in other countries. Stein's adaptation further emphasized the universality of the original plots. A man from Dublin, for example, after seeing the show in New York, said that the theme of *Fiddler on the Roof* was not merely Russian-Jewish in application, for the story of a poor but hard-working father trying to earn a living for his family, to uphold the traditions of his community, and refusing to sanction a marriage outside of his faith could just as well have taken place in Ireland.

When *Fiddler on the Roof* first opened, some showmen said that the production would appeal primarily to Jewish audiences in New York. But the phenomenal success of *Fiddler on the Roof* in London disproved this. In the summer of 1967, when tickets for most productions were available on the day of the performance, *Fiddler on the Roof* was selling tickets several months in advance. Seventeen of the eighteen London critics voted Topol, who played Tevye, the best performer in a musical, and sixteen critics named *Fiddler on the Roof* the best foreign musical of the season.

At the end of its first season in New York, *Fiddler on the Roof* won most of the awards that were available for a musical production. It received fourteen out of a possible nineteen votes to win the New York Drama Critics' Circle Award as the best musical of the year. It also received Tony Awards for the following:

Best musical
Best actor in a musical—Zero Mostel
Best actress in a supporting role in a musical—Maria Karnilova

Best producer of a musical— Harold Prince
Best author of a musical—Joseph Stein
Best composer and lyricist—Jerry Bock and Sheldon Harnick
Best costumes—Patricia Zipprodt
Best choreographer—Jerome Robbins

Awards in the *Variety* Poll of Drama Critics included:

Best actor in a musical—Zero Mostel
Best score—Jerry Bock
Best lyrics—Sheldon Harnick
Best scene designer—Boris Aronson (tied with Oliver Smith for *Baker Street* and *Luv*)

Fiddler on the Roof became a financial hit in its first season and had made well over a million dollars by the end of the second season. During the third year, profits had risen to 276 per cent of the original investment, and showmen were predicting that the production would probably be the greatest money-maker Harold Prince had produced.

In June 1966, when *Fiddler on the Roof* was finishing its second season, a full-page advertisement in *The New York Times* announced that a national company with Luther Adler was already on tour, a special company with Paul Lipson as Tevye would play the Dallas State Fair, and productions had opened in Finland and Israel. By 1967 *Fiddler on the Roof* was scheduled to play in England, France, Holland, Denmark, Sweden, Germany and Australia. When the production opened in Japan, in 1967, it received additional publicity, for the CBS evening news telecast showed fascinating scenes of the Japanese company in performance.

Fiddler on the Roof opened in New York at the Imperial Theater, where it could gross approximately $88,000 a week. Later it moved to the larger Majestic Theater, where the weekly gross was approximately $100,000. By May 1, 1968, *Fiddler on the Roof* had run for 1,508 performances. New Yorkers had not only seen Zero Mostel, Herschel Bernardi, and Luther Adler play Tevye, but also Paul Lipson and Harry Goz, who took over the role for a month while Bernardi recuperated from an operation. During this period, Harold Prince placed Goz's name above the title, a rarity in show business under such circumstances. Prince is reported to have said that he thought anyone who could play the lead in *Fiddler* deserved star billing. After Bernardi left the cast, Goz took over the starring role.

When box-office receipts began to drop, *Fiddler on the Roof*, acclaimed as "one of the most memorable musical shows in a generation, if not all time," began operating on cut rates. As of May 1, 1972, with Jan Peerce of the Metropolitan Opera Company as Tevye, it established a new record for musicals with 3,171 performances. Approximately a month and a half before closing, Paul Lipson returned to his role as Tevye and was on stage on June 17, 1972, when *Fiddler on the Roof* had its 3,225th performance, breaking the record set by *Life with Father*, and in so doing became the longest-running production in the history of the Broadway theater. It continued until July 2, 1972 when it closed after 3,242 performances. *Fiddler* played to capacity houses longer than *Hello, Dolly!*, which shattered existing box-office records on the road, particularly in cities where Carol Channing played Dolly.

The basic plot for *Hello, Dolly!* has a long history of adaptations. The original version was an English play, *A Day Well Spent*, by John Oxenford, produced in London in 1835. Several years later Johann Nestroy wrote a German adaptation, *Einen Jux Will Er Sich Machen*, produced in Vienna in 1842. Almost one hundred years elapsed before the comedy next appeared in 1938 as *The Merchant of Yonkers* by Thornton Wilder, who had followed Max Reinhardt's suggestion that he write an English adaptation of Nestroy's comedy. The production, starring Jane Cowl, had only a short run in New York. Approximately fifteen years later Wilder did another adaptation of the play, titling it *The Matchmaker*. When it opened in London in the 1954–55 season, it became an instant hit with Ruth Gordon giving a raucous performance as the meddlesome Dolly Levi. On December 5, 1955, co-producers David Merrick and The Theatre Guild brought *The Matchmaker* to Broadway, where it duplicated its London success, running for 486 performances, and was rated as one of the ten best plays of the season. The cast included Ruth Gordon, Loring Smith, Eileen Herlie, Arthur Hill, and Robert

Morse. A film version followed with Shirley Booth as Dolly Levi, and Shirley MacLaine, Anthony Perkins, and Robert Morse in supporting roles. David Merrick then produced *Hello, Dolly!*, the musical adaptation of Wilder's play, which opened January 16, 1964, and became Merrick's longest-running Broadway show!

Michael Stewart, who wrote the musical adaptation, followed the main plot fairly closely but judiciously cut some of the characters. He eliminated most of Wilder's soliloquies, except those spoken by Dolly, and deleted the entire sequence in which Cornelius and Barnaby were disguised as girls to elude an irate Mr. Vandergelder. In spite of the changes, Stewart retained the flavor and spirit of Wilder's comedy. The story still took place in Yonkers and New York City in the 1880s and concerned the widow Dolly Gallagher Levi, who pretends to be a matchmaker for Horace Vandergelder, a wealthy Yonkers merchant. Though she professes to be helping Vandergelder in his courtship of a charming widow, Mrs. Irene Molloy, Dolly has already decided to marry him herself. When Vandergelder comes to New York, where he is to meet Dolly and Mrs. Molloy, his clerks, Cornelius and Barnaby, decide to close shop and go to New York for the day in search of adventure. As they are walking near Mrs. Molloy's hat shop, they suddenly see Vandergelder approaching and take refuge in the shop, not realizing that Vandergelder will be coming into the shop to see Mrs. Molloy. After Vandergelder and Dolly arrive, the scene becomes a series of frantic attempts by Cornelius and Barnaby to hide. Eventually Vandergelder realizes that two men are in the shop, and although he does not discover who they are, he is sufficiently angered to cancel any plans of marrying Mrs. Molloy. Dolly, however, sends him off in fairly good spirits by promising to introduce him to an heiress. She then maneuvers Cornelius and Barnaby into taking Mrs. Molloy and her assistant, Minnie Fay, to dinner at the Harmonia Gardens, where she is planning to meet Mr. Vandergelder.

In Wilder's play, Vandergelder never met the heiress, whom Dolly had called Miss Money. Stewart, however, included her in his version, presenting her as a ridiculous, portly young woman who ordered enormous portions of food. After making a triumphant entrance with the song "Hello, Dolly," Dolly maneuvers to get rid of Miss Money. During the scene in the Harmonia Gardens, Vandergelder loses his wallet, which is turned over by mistake to Cornelius, who is in a private dining room with Mrs. Molloy, Barnaby, and Minnie Fay. While Dolly has dinner with Vandergelder, she strategically keeps telling him that she will not marry him, although he insists that he has no intention of asking her to be his wife. When he discovers that Cornelius is in the Harmonia Gardens with Mrs. Molloy, he fires him. He becomes even more incensed when he finds that Dolly has also arranged for his niece Ermengarde, and her sweetheart Ambrose, of whom he disapproves, to be at the Harmonia Gardens. The scene ends riotously with everyone except Dolly being arrested for creating a disturbance. In the courtroom, Cornelius declares that he is in love with Mrs. Molloy, and she admits that she has fallen in love with him. Dolly shrewdly chooses this moment to tell Vandergelder that she is walking out on him.

In the final scene back in Yonkers, Cornelius and Barnaby come to demand their back wages; Ermengarde asks for her inheritance money; and Cornelius and Mrs. Molloy are planning to marry and open a store across the street from Vandergelder's. At Dolly's suggestion, Vandergelder decides to take Cornelius in as a partner, and, finally coming to his senses, he asks Dolly to marry him.

The cast then assembles in preparation for curtain calls, reprising several songs until Dolly reappears, beautifully gowned in an elaborate white dress and hat befitting a bride, and leads everyone in a rousing finale of "Hello, Dolly."

Anyone who saw the slick New York production, the superb performance by Carol Channing, and the smooth transitions from witty dialogue into show-stopping musical routines would never suspect that the show had run into trouble during its try-out period. On February 19, 1967, *The New York Times* printed an interview with Gower Champion in which he said that *Hello, Dolly!* had been "a disaster in Detroit." According to Champion, Merrick had not been pleased with the production, which then had only four good musical numbers. The writers immediately went to work on revisions. Such numbers as "You're a Damned Exasperating Woman," "Penny in My Pocket," and "No, a Million Times No," were taken out, and almost every part of the show was rewritten. The combined efforts of Champion, Merrick, the writers, and the cast worked wonders; for when *Hello, Dolly!* came to New York, it revealed the precision and pace of American theater at its best, with routines that floated across the stage, spilled out on to a runway that circled the orchestra pit, and brought the performers practically into the audience. To build up Carol Channing's spectacular second act entrance in the Harmonia Gardens, Champion put the dancers through a routine, "The Waiter's Gavotte," that combined slapstick, hijinks, and nimble footwork, with the waiters racing across stage carrying trays loaded with dishes, dueling with enormous skewers of shish kebab, and jostling, bumping, and running into each other. Yet through all the zany antics, the waiters miraculously never dropped a single tray or dish. All this frenzied activity led into one of the most sensational entrances in show business, for, with the announcement that Dolly Levi had arrived at the Gardens, the spotlight focused on the entrance at the top of a center stairway, with the waiters lined up on both sides. Suddenly Channing appeared, resplendent in a red gown set with jewels, and came down the stairs to sing "Hello, Dolly." As the boys took up the second chorus, Channing went through a shuffle routine on the stage, on the runway, and back on stage to make the song one of the biggest show-stoppers in the history of the musical theater. Channing needed only to smile at the audience, wave her arms gracefully, and begin strutting to have the audience break into spontaneous applause. The number could have gone on and on, but Champion wisely started a final encore that deliberately led into a new plot development before the ensemble finished the chorus.

Jerry Herman's score for *Hello, Dolly!* has erroneously been called a one-hit score. Many other songs in the score were quite delightful, but they simply could not compete with the staging, the bounce, and the catchy lyrics of "Hello, Dolly." The number received additional publicity when Carol Channing sang another version, "Hello, Lyndon," at the White House during the Presidential campaign; David Merrick was reputed to have threatened to sue the Republican party for an astronomical figure if anyone tried to change the words to "Hello, Barry." It was Herman who was sued, however. The composer of "Sunflower," a popular tune of the 1940s, claimed that Herman had stolen his melody. Herman paid a settlement in excess of $250,000.

Herman's melodies for "Dancing," "Ribbons Down My Back," "Put on Your Sunday Clothes," "Motherhood," and "So Long, Dearie," were lilting. The main difficulty with the score was not that it lacked merit, but that Channing's throaty delivery of the humorous lyrics attracted more attention than the melodies so that audiences, who had no trouble remembering the clever lines, often could not recall the tunes.

Almost all of the critics were enthusiastic about Gower Champion's direction and choreography. When Channing was on stage, he wisely allowed her to dominate every scene and song; but when she was off stage, he kept the action flowing with colorful dance routines, such as "The Waiter's Gavotte" and "It Takes a Woman," in which he had the male dancers doing nimble tricks, leaping from elevated platforms on to the stage, or popping in and out of doors and trapdoors with amazing speed. Champion's direction profited from the excellence of Oliver Smith's sets, which floated on and off stage and also from his construction of the runway that brought parts of the show right into the audience. Jean Rosenthal's lighting and Freddy Wittop's colorful costuming also made the show a beautiful extravaganza. Wittop's costumes for Dolly, including full-length, magnificent gowns, elaborate hats, and intricate headpieces of feathers, were especially striking.

Above all, the critics and the audiences loved Carol Channing. The glowing reviews she had received for her portrayal of Lorelei Lee in *Gentlemen Prefer Blondes* were surpassed by the extravagant superlatives the critics used to describe her performance as Dolly Levi. The gold-digging Lorelei Lee had been a caricature, but the matchmaking Dolly was a full-blown characterization of a lonely widow determined to wed the wealthy Horace Vandergelder. Never once did Channing give the impression that she was acting Dolly Levi; she *was* Dolly Levi. Channing's ingratiating smile, her wide-eyed stares, and her conversations with her late husband Ephraim fascinated both audiences and critics and made them feel that Vandergelder was a very lucky man to marry her and that, by comparison with Dolly, Irene Molloy, who did not resort to man-baiting tactics to trap a husband, was far less interesting.

Whether singing in her remarkable husky voice, gliding through a dance routine, stepping onto the runway to ask Ephraim to give her a sign that he approved of her marriage, meddling into other people's affairs, or simply outwitting Vandergelder, Carol Channing was magnificent. From the moment she stepped out front and confided that she intended to marry Vandergelder, she established marvelous rapport with the audience.

Theatergoers were stimulated to see the superb Channing performance not only by the ecstatic reviews and word-of-mouth advertising but also by her appearances on various television programs. When Ginger Rogers was ready to take over the role of Dolly in New York, Miss Channing and Miss Rogers appeared as mystery guests on *What's My Line,* where Channing succeeded in publicizing not only Miss Rogers as the new star of the New York cast but also her own appearances in the road company. Perhaps her best television appearance on behalf of the show was as guest star with the chorus boys from *Hello, Dolly!* on *I've Got a Secret*—her secret being that she acted as the cast barber and cut the boys' hair. Whether the story was dreamed up by a press agent or was true was not half so important as the wonderful rapport that Miss Channing seemed to have with the young men, which became another factor stimulating audiences to try to obtain tickets for the show.

Carol Channing's magnetic performance received immeasurable assistance from the excellent supporting cast. David Burns as the baffled Horace Vandergelder, frustrated in the battle of wits with Dolly, made an excellent foil for Channing. Every time he twitched his nose in anger or glared at Channing, who glared right back, he was riotously funny. Eileen Brennan repeated the triumph she had scored in the off-Broadway production of *Little Mary Sunshine,* with her performance as Mrs. Molloy; Charles Nelson Reilly, who had played the whining, nasty Frump in *How to Succeed in Business Without Really Trying,* gave a very convincing performance in the more romantic role of Cornelius; and diminutive Sondra Lee sparkled as the elfin Minnie Fay.

Hello, Dolly! had opened with a top price of $8.80 for Monday through Thursday evenings, and $9.40 for weekend performances. The price was soon raised to $9.60 for all evenings. Receipts were increased even more when the St. James Theater, which had not sold standing room for other productions, adopted a new policy and sold advanced standing-room tickets for *Hello, Dolly!*

At the end of the first season, interest centered on prize awards, for *Hello, Dolly!* was running simultaneously with another great hit, *Funny Girl*. When the awards were announced, *Hello, Dolly!* proved to be the champion, probably establishing a new record for number of prizes. The New York Drama Critics' Circle named it the best musical comedy of the season with a total of thirteen out of a possible eighteen votes. It received the remarkable total of ten Tony Awards:

> Best producer of a musical— David Merrick
> Best author of a musical—Michael Stewart
> Best conductor of a musical—Shepherd Coleman
> Best female lead in a musical—Carol Channing
> Best director of a musical—Gower Champion
> Best scene designer—Oliver Smith
> Best costume designer—Freddy Wittop
> Best choreographer—Gower Champion
> Best lyricist—Jerry Herman
> Best composer—Jerry Herman

Hello, Dolly! also received the highest number of votes in the *Variety* Poll of Drama Critics in the following categories:

> Best female lead—Carol Channing
> Best director of a musical—Gower Champion
> Best scene designer—Oliver Smith
> Best lyricist—Jerry Herman

In August 1965, after *Hello, Dolly!* had run for approximately eighteen months, Carol Channing, whose contract had stipulated that she would go on tour with the show, left the New York cast; David Merrick brought in Ginger Rogers, with whom Miss Channing had played in the motion picture, "The First Traveling Saleslady," as her replacement. Merrick and his staff launched Miss Rogers as the new Dolly Levi with excellent publicity in newspapers and magazines and with frequent appearances on television.

Ginger Rogers' appeal as Dolly Levi differed from Miss Channing's. She was more subdued and more feminine. Moreover, Gower Champion restaged the show to emphasize Miss Rogers' dancing. To a great many people, she represented Hollywood at its best, for she was the motion-picture star who had delighted them in a series of musical films with Fred Astaire. Miss Rogers needed only to break into a simple time step with two of the dancers to have her admirers break into spontaneous applause. The women who remembered seeing her in films gloried in the fact that the popular star was still the epitome of glamour.

Miss Rogers stayed with *Hello, Dolly!* until February 1967, drawing excellent, if not capacity, houses. When she left the New York cast to play the lead in a road company, Martha Raye became the third Dolly Levi for a few months. Betty Grable, who had starred in one of the road companies, replaced Miss Raye, and several critics who reviewed the show rated Miss Grable as second only to Carol Channing. An excellent dancer and one of Hollywood's top musical comedy stars, Miss Grable provided a sparklingly different interpretation of Dolly Levi from that of her predecessors and, in the dance sequences flashed her famous legs.

The phenomenal success of *Hello, Dolly!* in New York was exceeded by at least two of the road companies. While Miss Channing was still playing the lead in New York, David Merrick organized his first touring cast with Mary Martin as Dolly and Loring Smith as Horace Vandergelder, a role he had played in *The Matchmaker*. Miss Martin, who offered still another excellent and individualized characterization of Dolly, broke existing box-office records in Texas and Louisiana before Merrick sent the show to the Orient, where it did phenomenal business. In Tokyo Miss Martin sang a special chorus of "Hello, Tokyo!" and Merrick ran an extremely clever newspaper ad publicizing both the road company and New York production by including the caption that if people could not get tickets to see Carol Channing, they could come to Tokyo and see Miss Martin. When the Russian authorities cancelled performances scheduled for Moscow and Leningrad, Merrick arranged to have the company give performances for the

American troops in Korea, Okinawa, and Vietnam. During the latter engagement, President Johnson sent Miss Martin the message, "You are making your President and all of Texas proud of of you." The Mary Martin company next opened in London where the critics were none too enthusiastic about the show but were delighted with Mary Martin's portrayal of Dolly.

When Carol Channing began her road tour, David Merrick predicted that she would break records, but the final tabulation must have amazed even Merrick himself. Miss Channing, who had played to capacity business for every performance in New York, also played to capacity business for every performance on the road. She broke all records in St. Louis with a gross of more than $176,000 in the first week, and then broke her own record with a gross of approximately $198,000 in the second week. In Oklahoma City, where the entire engagement was completely sold out in advance, she drew the staggering total of $295,025 in ten performances. The Pittsburgh engagement, originally scheduled for two weeks, was extended to four, with an average gross of $158,000 each week, breaking all records for gross receipts for any show in the history of the city.

Sources vary on the total amount of money grossed by the Channing company, but several sources have credited Miss Channing with drawing over $14 million during the 141 weeks she played the role of Dolly in New York and on the road.

While the show was playing in Chicago, Miss Channing left the cast for several months to make a film in Hollywood, and Eve Arden, whose understudy Carol Channing had been in *Let's Face It,* took over the role. Before the end of the Chicago run, Betty Grable replaced Miss Arden.

Hello, Dolly! remained the number one road attraction during the 1966–67 season, with one troupe headed by Carol Channing, a second by Betty Grable, and a third by Dorothy Lamour and Ginger Rogers, who alternated in the role during the Las Vegas engagement. Martha Raye also appeared in a special overseas company that performed for the American troops.

The film rights brought Merrick more than $2.5 million, plus a percentage of the gross. One newspaper columnist stated that when the studio officials announced their intention of starring

Barbra Streisand rather than Carol Channing in the film, they were deluged with letters of protest. A new, sensational Dolly, Pearl Bailey, came to Broadway in 1968 when Merrick starred her and Cab Calloway in an all-Negro version of *Hello, Dolly!* Enthusiastic audiences in Washington during the try-out prompted him to cut the tour and bring the show into New York immediately. Critics wrote rave reviews for Pearl Bailey, Cab Calloway, and the superb supporting cast. Their brilliant performances revitalized the show and put it back into the hit category. When Merrick decided to send the Bailey-Calloway production on the road, where it did sensational business, he starred Phyllis Diller in the original all-white version in New York for several months. In April, 1970, Merrick finally persuaded Ethel Merman, to whom he originally offered the show, to play Dolly for a limited engagement. Two new numbers were added for Merman who received accolades from the critics. Audiences gave her such enthusiastic ovations that she stopped the show with almost every song. Miss Merman stayed with *Hello, Dolly!* until it broke the longevity record set by *My Fair Lady* and closed with a total of 2,844 performances, a record surpassed only by *Fiddler on the Roof.* During its long run, *Hello, Dolly!* was not only one of the greatest commercial successes on Broadway but also was one of the greatest touring box-office attractions in the history of American musicals.

Two later well-staged, innovative musicals, *I Do! I Do!* and *Cabaret,* were both produced in the 1966–67 season. *I Do! I Do!* was based on *The Fourposter,* a two-character play by Jan de Hartog which opened on October 24, 1951, and ran for 632 performances. Both the original play and the musical adaptation dealt with the married life of Michael and Agnes. De Hartog had made deft use of a bedroom setting to give the play an intimacy that would have been spoiled by the intrusion of a third character.

In recent years, several critics have complained that too many musicals have been based on already established works, with the adaptors straining too hard to follow the original plays. Most of the critics, however, agreed that *I Do! I Do!* was not only successful as an adaptation but also as a new kind of musical comedy, breaking all precedents by using only two characters—no chorus line, no singing ensemble, no offstage voices. In doing so, it kept the intimate quality of *The Fourposter* and intrigued audiences with the idea that they were sharing secrets with the couple on stage.

During the tryout period, reports from the road were mixed; Gower Champion, the director, is reported to have said that the show had not gone well in Boston. But apparently all difficulties had been eliminated before the New York première, for when *I Do! I Do!* opened on December 5, 1966, critics were enthusiastic about the ability of Mary Martin and Robert Preston to sustain their vigorous roles for the complete evening's performance. Theatergoers who had seen *The Fourposter* were delighted to find that *I Do! I Do!* had kept not only the spirit but also the plot of the original play almost intact, and that the songs and dances helped to advance the story which dealt with fifty years of a marriage that had begun in the late 1890s and continued through the 1950s.

The Fourposter began with Michael carrying Agnes over the threshold into their bedroom on their wedding night. *I Do! I Do!* began just before the wedding ceremony and then moved to the bedroom. From then on, the bedroom remained the setting except for one or two brief sequences. The first act of *I Do! I Do!* dealt with the early married life of Michael and Agnes and the birth of their children. As the years roll by, Michael becomes a famous author and thinks he has found a new romance; Agnes wins him back. In the second act, with the children grown up and married, Agnes feels that her life with Michael is over and that she has found a new romance with a young poet; Michael's persuasive powers win her back. In the final scene, Agnes and Michael, now an elderly couple, are preparing to move into a smaller house. Michael has always objected to a pillow embroidered with the words "God Is Love," which he had found on the bed on his wedding night. He tells Agnes that she must not leave the pillow for the new young couple that will be moving in. Agnes tries to hide the pillow in the bed; Michael throws back the bed covers, discovers the pillow, decides to let it stay on one side, puts a bottle of champagne for the groom on the other, and then leaves with Agnes.

Mary Martin sang magnificently, Robert Preston acted superbly, and their teamwork made the production delightful. Because their roles were so strenuous, Merrick scheduled only six evening performances a week during the early part of the run. Later, he starred Carol Lawrence and Gordon MacRae in the matinee performances. At the end of the first season, Preston won both the *Variety* Drama Critics Poll and a Tony award.

Gower Champion's imaginative direction never permitted the action or song sequences to lag. In the last scene, for example, Champion installed two dressing tables equipped with mirrors on the runway. Sitting at the tables, the stars applied makeup to add lines and wrinkles to their faces, and aged twenty years in a matter of minutes. Theater audiences had been fascinated with this same bit of stage business in *Man of La Mancha*, but the effect upon the audience was even greater in *I Do! I Do!*, for the change in appearance was more drastic.

The original play had given the players sufficient time to change costumes between scenes, but the musical adaptation, with its uninterrupted action, cleverly used solo numbers to permit each of the actors a moment offstage to change. Michael, however, made several changes on stage, shouting to Agnes as he dressed; the dialogue, the banter, and the action all seemed charmingly realistic in that bedroom setting. The clever costumes and wigs created by Freddy Wittop helped immeasurably in portraying the passage of time. Oliver Smith's ingenious set, with props that moved on and off stage, further helped speed up the action. The orchestral accompaniment came from backstage because Smith was using the runway covering the orchestra pit as part of a hospital hallway that Michael paced as he waited for the birth of his child. During the musical interlude at the end of the intermission, the back curtain was raised to reveal the orchestra, and was lowered when the music led into the second act.

Librettist-lyricist Tom Jones and composer Harvey Schmidt, who had written the highly successful off-Broadway musical, *The Fantasticks*, wrote a well integrated score that not only advanced the plot but also gave both stars ample opportunity to display their versatility. Several critics singled out "Love Isn't Everything" and "Nobody's Perfect," sung by Agnes and Michael together, as well as two of Agnes' solos. In the first, Agnes, angered by Michael's admission that he is infatuated with another woman, reaches down into a trunk, pulls out a ridiculous huge hat, pulls up her nightgown, and sings the torchy "Flaming Agnes," a definite show-stopper. In the second, "Somebody Needs Me," a ballad, she weeps as she sings about love. The number was sentimental but not maudlin.

After Mary Martin and Robert Preston left the show, Carol Lawrence and Gordon MacRae continued in the leads, playing both matinee and evening performances. *Variety* began reporting the number of times the standbys, Stephen Douglass and Drani Seitz, had appeared as Michael and Agnes, but did not explain whether illness or the strenuous demands of the roles had caused MacRae and Lawrence to be out of the show.

After running for several months on two-for-one tickets, *I Do! I Do!* closed with a total of 584 performances. It had been the runner-up in the Critics' Circle vote for the best musical, and might have received greater consideration as a prize play if *Cabaret,* which won most of the major drama awards, had not been produced in the same season. The Critics' Circle named *Cabaret* the best musical for 1966–67. Boris Aronson, the scene designer, won the *Variety* Poll of New York drama critics, a Tony award, and the Brandeis Creative Arts award. Joel Grey won both a Tony and the *Variety* Poll as best actor in a supporting role in a musical. Patricia Zipprodt, costume designer; John Kander, composer; and Fred Ebb, lyricist, also won both Tonys and the *Variety* Poll. Additional Tony awards went to *Cabaret* as the best musical, to Harold Prince as producer as well as director, to Joe Masteroff as librettist, to Peg Murray as a featured, supporting actress in a musical, and to Ronald Field as choreographer. Otis Guernsey, Jr. also selected *Cabaret* as one of the ten best plays for his 1966–67 volume.

Cabaret also followed the successful formula of basing a musical on an established play, in this case John van Druten's adaptation of Christopher Isherwood's stories about a young writer living in Berlin during the pre-Hitler era. Van Druten's *I Am a Camera,* produced in 1951 with Julie Harris in the leading role, ran for 214 performances and won the Drama Critics' Circle Award for the best American play of the season. *Cabaret* far exceeded the run of the play, for it closed with a total of 1,166 performances.

Van Druten's adaptation had dealt with an amoral heroine, Sally Bowles, who moves in with the hero, Isherwood, but maintains only a platonic relationship with him. When she discovers that her affair with an American has resulted in pregnancy, she has an abortion. At the end of the play, Isherwood tries to persuade Sally to leave Germany with him, but she refuses. In writing the musical adaptation, Masteroff modified the characterizations and the plot by having Sally become involved in an affair with the hero, now called Clifford Bradshaw. Masteroff also built up the role of the landlady, Fräulein Schneider, by creating a romance between her and Herr Schultz, a Jewish merchant. Instead of following the play by limiting the action to Cliff's room, Masteroff added a colorful cabaret setting and a scene in Schultz's store. He also added many new characters including a Nazi bully, Ernst, and a master of ceremonies in the cabaret, who introduced the musical turns and epitomized the decadence of the Kit Kat Club.

The musical begins with the master of ceremonies singing "Willkommen" (welcome), and inviting the audience to watch the show. Very soon entertainers, waiters, the stage orchestra, and patrons appear, and the scene develops into a full scale production number. The next scene introduces the hero, Clifford Bradshaw, and a young German, Ernst, who are on a train *en route* to Berlin. When Clifford, who has become aware that Ernst is concealing a package from the custom officials, does not give him away, Ernst becomes affable, learns that Cliff plans to teach English, and agrees to be his first pupil. He also sends Cliff to Fräulein Schneider's to rent a room. Cliff later joins Ernst at the Kit Kat Club, where he meets the club's featured singer, Sally Bowles, an English girl living with a German. Sally soon moves in with Cliff, Fräulein Schneider making little protest although she had berated one of her other tenants, Fräulein Kost, for taking sailors to her room. Fräulein Schneider herself is having an affair with Herr Schultz, which leads to a marriage proposal. During the celebration party, Ernst warns her that marrying a Jew would be unwise. Fräulein Schneider breaks off the engagement and returns the wedding gifts.

Sally tells Cliff that she is pregnant with his child. In order to raise money, Cliff accepts Ernst's offer to go on a well-paying, underground mission to Paris. Sally returns to the Kit Kat Club against Cliff's wishes, and Cliff, who comes to the cabaret for Sally, gets into a fight with Ernst and is manhandled by Ernst's henchmen. Sally finds Cliff in his room, tells him that she has had an abortion and has paid for it by selling her fur coat. Infuriated, Cliff slaps her, but then tries to persuade her to leave Berlin with him. Sally refuses to go. On the train to Paris, Cliff begins writing his memoirs. In the final scene, set in the cabaret, the master of ceremonies brings Sally on to reprise the title song. The cabaret characters leave the stage, and the master of ceremonies, alone in the spotlight, signals goodbye, the lights dim, and the curtain falls.

Cabaret opened on November 12, 1966, at the Broadhurst Theater, with a top price of $12.00. At the end of the first season, in spite of its capacity business, Cabaret was listed in Variety as only a potential hit, for it had not yet recovered its investment cost. By the end of May, 1968, however, Cabaret had become an established hit. Profits for Cabaret increased when producer Harold Prince moved Fiddler on the Roof from the Imperial Theatre to the Majestic and then moved Cabaret into the Imperial, thus making it possible for both shows to have larger weekly gross receipts.

Most of the critics liked the show and the cast headed by Jill Haworth as Sally, Bert Convy as Cliff, Jack Gilford as Schultz, and Lotte Lenya as Fräulein Schneider. The critics praised Lotte Lenya and Jack Gilford, but they were most enthusiastic about Joel Grey as the master of ceremonies and Peg Murray as Fräulein Kost. Word-of-mouth advertising helped stir audience interest in Grey, who was later given equal billing with the other four principals. When Miss Lenya was out of the show, Peg Murray took over the role of Fräulein Schneider.

Cabaret was definitely a show for adults. Several of the songs, particularly those performed by the master of ceremonies, were far more earthy than those seen in most musical comedies. He did one number with a gorilla dressed as a girl, and another in which he sang bawdy lyrics with two chorus girls; in a third, the interlude which opened the second act, he joined the line-up dressed as one of the chorus girls but ended the number by breaking into a goose step; in "The Money Song," he described love for sale, with each of the girls costumed to represent a different form of currency. The gestures, posturing, and costumes in this number were more erotic than in many of the raffish burlesque shows seen on 42nd Street in the 1930s.

Though it shocked some people, *Cabaret* was an interesting show, for the staging was superb. When the audience entered the theater, the curtain was up, revealing a stage bare except for a huge tilted mirror which reflected the audience, in a sense making the theatergoer a part of the show. From this opening to the final scene, Boris Aronson's sets moved deftly on and off stage; during the intermission, the all-girl orchestra of the Kit Kat Club played. The mobility of the sets and the use of stairs on either side of the stage for entre-scene movements gave the show fluidity.

Several critics compared *Cabaret* to plays by Bertold Brecht and the score to tunes written by Kurt Weill (who had been married to Lotte Lenya). According to Miss Lenya, who had lived in Berlin until 1933—when she and Weill escaped to Paris—*Cabaret*'s atmosphere and plot, and many of the routines in the Kit Kat Club, were authentic representations of life in 1930s Berlin. Miss Lenya, who had built up a following by singing Weill's music, drew many of her admirers to *Cabaret*. Most of the songs written by John Kander and Fred Ebb meant little out of context, though, for the title song was the only number which developed into a popular hit. As sung by Sally, "Cabaret" was as harsh as the show, but the version used on radio and television emphasized the lilting melody and accentuated the rhythm. A second number, "Meeskite" (ugliness or odd-looking), a standout as sung by Jack Gilford, also intrigued radio audiences.

Cabaret epitomized the change from the conventional musicals of the 1940s and 1950s to the musicals of the 1960s. It mocked emotion and emphasized decadence and immorality in its depiction of the mood of pre-Nazi Germany. Moreover, it had few if any admirable characters. As an authentic representation of decadent Berlin, however, *Cabaret* skillfully presented a harsh story which intrigued many theatergoers and had, at least, a morbid fascination for others.

The last three long-running successes of the 1960s all differed from other popular musicals of the decade. *Hair,* the "American tribal love-rock musical," broke down barriers of conventionality in dialogue, in action, and in nudity. The leading character in *Promises, Promises* was an amoral non-hero who allowed his superior executives to use his apartment for their assignations. The cast of *1776* included only two women, no chorus line, and emphasized plot and dialogue rather than music.

Hair, the most controversial musical of the decade, opened off-Broadway at the Public Theater October 29, 1967, where it ran 49 performances before moving to the Cheetah, a Greenwich Village club, for 45 additional performances. The production, directed by Gerald Freedman, had no nudity. The plot, although thin, dealt with a young man and his parents who try to bridge the generation gap in voicing their views on the war. The young draftee cannot make up his mind whether to burn his draft card or go to war. He goes to Vietnam and is killed. The antiwar protestations had a strong emotional impact, but the production also delighted theatergoers with its brash humor and rhythmic score.

When Michael Butler decided to produce the show on Broadway, Thomas O'Horgan redirected it. The story line was pared to a minimum and new songs and comments on everything from pollution, sex, and drugs to military service and religion were added. During the preview period, skeptics predicted that audiences would not pay $12 a ticket for a production with dialogue, lyrics, and action that were certain to offend a great many theatergoers; had virtually no story line; and used bedraggled costumes. Advance publicity stating that one scene would include total nudity aroused further skepticism as well as speculation about the possibility of censorship.

Hair opened at the Biltmore Theater April 29, 1968, to definitely mixed reviews. Several critics condemned its irreverence, desecration of the flag, and obscenity by calling the show "vulgar," "offensive," "dirty," or "juvenile backyard fence graffiti." Other critics hailed it with such effusive praise as "fresh," "frank," "the most significant musical of the decade," or "an important contribution to the American stage" because it unshackled the theater and gave it new freedom. Three members of the Critics' Circle—Clive Barnes, Henry Hewes, and Emory Lewis—voted for *Hair* as the best musical of the year. Most critics were in agreement on one point—the excellence of the score. In *Variety*'s poll of eighteen New York drama critics, *Hair* won two awards: Gerome Ragni and James Rado were selected as best lyricists of the season with seven votes; Galt MacDermot was named as best composer with eight votes. MacDermot also received the Drama Desk–Vernon Rice Award for his score.

However, by minimizing plot and concentrating on sensationalism in action and dialogue to shock audiences, the Broadway version lost the poignancy of the off-Broadway production. To emphasize their overstepping of the bounds of propriety, the authors, early in the Broadway run, had actors dressed as policemen running down the aisles to stop the show. This routine was later dropped. Shortly after the opening, Ragni and Rado, who also played the leading roles, began experimenting with new material. Producer Michael Butler, who objected to this practice, not only replaced them with other actors but also barred them from the theater. Within a short time, however, Butler and the authors reached an agreement as to how new material would be presented, and peace was restored. During all this time, the show continued playing to capacity houses.

Audience reaction to *Hair* differed widely. Older theatergoers who disapproved of it expressed their condemnation by walking out during the performance; those who liked it voiced their approval by claiming that *Hair* was a significant expression of the youthful rebellion. Younger theatergoers who thought *Hair* was symbolic and sophisticated because the cast indulged in simulated sexual antics on stage and spoke the language of the gutter were bewildered to learn that older patrons often referred to the actors as young children pretending to be naughty. This viewpoint was not farfetched, for young performers reveal their skill at playacting in the ease with which they demand or prevent audience participation. At one performance, a man, obviously drunk, tried to heckle the actors who walked, ran, or danced up the aisle near him. They completely ignored him, giving no indication that they saw or even heard him, and before the end of the first act, the man left the theater. On the other hand, the youthful exuberance of the actors was at its best in the finale when the cast had no difficulty in cajoling people in the orchestra seats to come on stage and dance with them. The performers in *Hair* danced effortlessly with a rhythmic abandon and animal magnetism that was very evident when contrasted with the less graceful members of the audience who tried doing the same steps.

Many people of college age recommended *Hair* as entertainment for anyone under thirty. A survey of a group of college students who had seen the production revealed that most of them were surprised to discover that several stunts they thought were original were variations of older routines. Many of the students said they had never seen another production in which the actors came out into the audience. A few remembered that *Carnival* had had a parade in the aisles, but most of them had never heard about *Hellzapoppin'* or *Sons o' Fun,* the Olsen and Johnson shows in which stooges came up and down the aisles or chorus girls danced with some of the patrons. They had also not known that another novelty they enjoyed—an actor swinging on a rope out over the heads of the audience in Tarzan fashion—was a variation of a Beatrice Lillie skit in *The Show Is On* in which Miss Lillie sat on a half-moon that moved out over the first few rows of the audience while she dropped garters to the men sitting below. The young people who had seen *Hair* particularly liked such stunts as the barefooted actor, wearing only a loin cloth, walking nimbly on the backs of seats in the front rows, or the devastating satire on the popular singing group The Supremes, in which three girls, who appeared to be wearing tight-fitting sequin gowns, suddenly branched out and revealed that all of them were huddled into one large dress that hung from their shoulders like a tent. The young people who answered the questionnaire said the fact that the routines were not always new did not lessen their approval of *Hair*. They did not object to the vulgarity or obscene language, but neither did they take it too seriously. Almost unanimously they agreed that they enjoyed the music, although they admitted that the lyrics were unintelligible unless they had heard the recording before attending the show. This has also been one of the most frequent complaints made by both theatergoers and critics.

On the credit side, *Hair* had definite pace, moving quickly from one gag or song to another. The performers worked harmoniously as a group and their spirit of comradeship was always apparent. On the debit side, the jokes were not always amusing, and the serious moments were ineffective because scenes that could build to an emotional crisis were cut short to insert a joke or a bit of irrelevant action.

Several members of the New York company subsequently played leading roles in other Broadway productions. To mention but a few: Jill O'Hara, the original Sheila in the off-Broadway version of *Hair*, took a major role in *Promises, Promises;* Gail Dixon, the ingenue in *Coco*, starring Katharine Hepburn, also appeared in the off-Broadway version of *Hair*, Lynn Kellogg, who originated the role of Sheila on Broadway, made frequent appearances on national television programs; and Donny Burks, who appeared as Hud on Broadway, played the title role in an off-Broadway drama, *Billy Noname*.

Any review of *Hair* is apt to be misleading, because the original script underwent many changes and the printed text was not the same as the version playing in New York. Moreover, the road company versions differed from the New York production. In some cities, more than one nude scene is reputed to have been inserted. Early in 1970, producer Michael Butler told a reporter that he had staged *Hair* as a local production in many cities because he preferred to use local actors rather than "second rate" touring companies, and that the script had been revised to include topical references to the cities in which it played. In the same interview, Butler discussed the international recognition *Hair* received—twenty-three companies played in ten countries. By the end of the year, Butler said, he hoped to have as many as thirty-five companies. Variations in the foreign productions were made to fit the individual countries. Not all of the productions included nudity, and in some countries the style of dancing was changed.

In Los Angeles, Butler took over the Earl Carroll Theater, renamed it the Aquarius after the hit song of the show, and launched a local company that caught the public's fancy. In London, Butler held up the production until the office of play censor was abolished in September 1968. When *Hair* opened, it became an immediate hit and the London critics rated the music as the best part of the show. In London, as in New York, the sales of original cast recordings helped increase the popularity of the production.

Hair was not without censorship problems. In Mexico, it was ordered closed after the first performance; in Paris, the Salvation Army Commander voiced a strong protest. There had been complaints in cities across the United States, but the show ran into trouble in Boston where the advance ticket sale was over $600,000. The district attorney who saw the show at a preview tried to stop it from opening but finally agreed to withhold judgment until the seven judges of the Massachusetts Supreme Court had a chance to see *Hair* for themselves. When they did, they ordered *Hair* to be closed unless the actors in the nude scene wore at least a minimal costume, and they ordered the scene desecrating the flag to be eliminated. Since the producer refused to make these changes, the show remained closed, although counter litigations were undertaken. During early 1970, champions of *Hair* were calling for its reopening, but the company was being forced to make refunds on tickets. In late May, however, the Court decision was overruled, and the show reopened.

In spite of these skirmishes with censors, *Hair* was one of the great money-makers in theatrical history. According to *Forbes* Magazine, *Hair* played to approximately 4 million people in the first two years and grossed over $22,300,000. By May 1, 1972, road companies were still flourishing, and in New York, *Hair* was operating on cut rates and had run 1,670 performances.

Critics who doubted that *Hair* would succeed had no such misgivings about David Merrick's production of *Promises, Promises*. They predicted it would be a hit because some of the most successful writers in show business were connected with the musical. The book was based on the Academy Award film *The Apartment* by Billy Wilder and I. A. L. Diamond which starred Jack Lemmon, Shirley MacLaine, Fred MacMurray, and Edie Adams. Neil Simon, whose unbroken record of hits included both comedies and musicals, made the stage adaptation. Composer Burt Bacharach and lyricist Hal David, hailed as one of the foremost teams of songwriters, wrote the score. The director, Robert Moore, had staged the hit off-Broadway drama *The Boys in the*

Band; and David Merrick, the producer, had already presented two successful plays in a fallow season.

When *Promises, Promises* opened December 28, 1968, most of the critics felt that in spite of the advance ballyhoo the show lived up to their expectations. Even those who had reservations about its merits either praised the score, the acting, or Neil Simon's adaptation. Merrick had his third hit of the season, and even at a top price of $15 a ticket on weekends, the show did capacity business of more than $100,000 a week during the first year of the run.

Simon did not change the basic story of Chuck Baxter who finds that he can get promotions and higher salaries by letting his superior executives use his apartment for trysts with their mistresses. Chuck falls in love with Fran Kubelik who works in the same building, not knowing that she is having an affair with J. D. Sheldrake, the top executive. When Sheldrake and Fran have a quarrel in Chuck's apartment and Sheldrake leaves, Fran tries to commit suicide, but Chuck and Dr. Dreyfuss, a neighbor, save her life. Refusing to play the stooge any longer, Chuck gives up his apartment, loses his job but wins Fran.

The basic immorality of the plot as well as the odd love story of an unconventional heroine and a young opportunist who is a willing foil for his lecherous bosses were a far cry from the early Cinderella musicals of the 1920s, the brittle musical comedies of the 1930s, the romantic love plots of *Oklahoma!* and *Brigadoon* of the 1940s, and the sophisticated wit of *My Fair Lady* in the 1950s. In setting, slick production, and pace, *Promises, Promises* was more closely related to *How to Succeed in Business Without Really Trying* of the 1960s.

In his adaptation, Neil Simon not only peppered the script with gags but also used two additional devices which made Chuck, in spite of his involvements with office trysts, a young man who aroused audience sympathy. Simon inserted monologues, a technique used by many dramatists, that enabled Chuck to talk directly to the audience. Thornton Wilder had used the same technique effectively in *Our Town* and *The Matchmaker* when he had a leading character stop the action, step to the footlights, and discuss the situation. *Hello, Dolly!,* the musical adaptation of *The Matchmaker,* also used a modified version of the monologue.

The characters in Wilder's dramas, however, were inherently more likeable than Chuck from the very start. Simon used the monologue to give Chuck the opportunity not only to discuss the action and plot development but also to confide his thoughts, his frustrations, and his despairs. As a result, instead of being merely an unimpressive young man who happens to love the wrong girl, he established a rapport with audiences that grew stronger as the play progressed and made theatergoers sympathetic to his seemingly hopeless love affair. Another technique Simon used was reminiscent of Elmer Rice's *Dream Girl,* in which the heroine kept romanticizing her adventures in a series of daydreams. In *Promises, Promises,* Simon had Chuck indulge in his own brand of dream world. He would see Fran, for example, imagine their conversation as he hoped it would be, suddenly snap out of his reverie, tell the audience that it never happened that way, and then replay the scene to show what actually had been said. These sequences were delightful, for Simon clearly showed the difference between imagination and reality. The combination of daydreaming and monologues made spectators forget the shoddiness of Chuck's amoral willingness to help his bosses in their extramarital affairs. Simon also made the serious or morbid situations, such as the scene following Fran's suicide attempt, light and even amusing by interlacing the dialogue with gag lines.

When *Promises, Promises* first opened, Merrick listed the cast alphabetically, giving none of the performers special mention, but he soon raised Jerry Orbach and Jill O'Hara to featured billing. Orbach, who received unanimously rave reviews, overshadowed most of the performers with his brilliant performance as Chuck and won the Tony Award as the best actor in a musical. In addition to the warmth of his characterization, particularly in the monologues, Orbach sang the complicated, rhythmic songs by Bacharach-David so effortlessly that they sounded as if they were simple, melodic numbers. Jill O'Hara, in the difficult role of Fran, worked uphill throughout the first act but won over the audience when she sang the best number in the score, "I'll Never Fall in Love Again." Marian Mercer, who played a kookie pickup in a bar, also won a Tony as the best supporting actress in a musical. In her few brief moments, Miss Mercer stopped the show, and her costume—a coat made of owl feathers—intrigued the women. A. Larry Haines as Dr. Dreyfuss and Edward Winter as Sheldrake, also received excellent notices.

The Bacharach-David score pleased most of the critics who liked its decided novelty, trick arrangements and rhythms, electronic sounds, modern beat, and clever lyrics. There were a few critics, however, who regretted that the songs seemed to lack melody. The music, nevertheless, provided an excellent background for the action and was effective in the dance sequences choreographed by Michael Bennett, particularly in an exuberant rock routine performed by three office girls at the Christmas party that increased in crescendo until it reached a frenzied climax.

Life Magazine named *Promises, Promises* the best musical of the year, and the London production also received excellent reviews. In New York, the musical drew well for over two years and then resorted to cut-rate tickets before completing a run of 1,281 performances.

1776, the Critics' Circle choice as the best musical of the year, also proved to be the sleeper of the year. The production opened with little fanfare, and its success came as a surprise. Bookers for theater parties and ticket brokers had been skeptical about a musical dramatization of a historical episode. Advance reports that it dealt with debates in the Second Continental Congress leading up to the signing of the Declaration of Independence and that it had no chorus line also caused agencies to avoid buying blocks of tickets. When the show opened to generally excellent reviews, lines began forming at the box office and *1776* developed into a sell-out hit.

1776 was indeed a phenomenon. In contrast to *Hair*, which featured total nudity and hippie outfits, everyone in *1776* was well dressed in proper period costumes. Instead of the rhythmic, electronic musical devices in *Promises, Promises,* it had more melodic accompaniment for its dramatic, literate songs. It had none of the "liberated freedom of speech" used in popular plays emphasizing sex, but it did have adult humor. Ben Franklin indulged in ribaldry, and Thomas Jefferson was portrayed as a warm-blooded young husband, but the characterizations and dialogue did not offend or shock even the staid theatergoers. *1776* also broke with tradition not only with its unusual title but also by having only two women in a cast that featured robust male actors. *Irma La Douce* had succeeded with only one woman, who played the leading role, but the women in *1776* played secondary roles.

Not all of the reviews were favorable. Dissenters who wanted to see girlie-girlie shows, or who preferred entertainment that lampooned patriotism, referred to it as "wooden" or "souvenir-ship patriotism." One reviewer objected to William Daniels' characterization of John Adams and rated the show satisfactory but not great; another said the ending did not reach an emotional climax; still another called it "semidocumentary" because the historical episodes were not quite accurate. More people had signed the Declaration than were represented on stage. Although this decrease in number may have been an economy measure, it definitely did not detract from the spirit of authenticity. Most of the critics, however, wrote ecstatic reviews calling *1776* "exciting," "moving and artistic," "brilliant," and "exhilarating." The number of prizes *1776* received also stimulated audience interest. It won the Critics' Circle Award as the best musical of the year with nine votes; Otis Guernsey, Jr., selected it for his 1968–69 volume as one of the best plays of the year. The Tony Award for the best musical of the season was given to Peter Stone, the librettist; Sherman Edwards, composer and lyricist; and Stuart Ostrow, the producer. Tony Awards were also given to Peter Hunt as best director of a musical and to Ronald Holgate as best supporting actor in a musical. William Daniels, whose performance most critics had rated as one of the best of the year, had also been nominated for a Tony in the category of best featured or supporting performer, but he withdrew his name from the competition. According to reports, Daniels felt that his nomination in that category slighted his professional standing because he was listed as one of the starring actors. The Joseph Maharam Foundation Awards were given to Jo Mielziner for best musical stage design and to Patricia Zipprodt for best costume design. Peter Stone also received the Drama Desk Award for the best musical book.

Sherman Edwards, a history teacher, combined his two interests—music and history—in writing the music and lyrics. He had worked on the show for nearly ten years and then had suggested the idea for *1776* to Peter Stone, who had written librettos for Broadway musicals and scenarios for Hollywood motion pictures. When Stone heard Edwards talk about his plans for a show dealing with the signing of the Declaration of Independence, he realized how much he had learned from Edwards about the historical background.

Writing the libretto was a challenge, for Stone had to build up suspense, even though it was obvious that the document would eventually be signed. By including the arguments of the congressmen, their insistence upon deletions, and the objections of several members to the basic principle of the document, Stone succeeded in arousing interest. The audience never doubted that the Declaration would be passed, but it did not know how Franklin, Adams, and Jefferson could wheedle the objectors into giving them the necessary unanimous vote. Suspense mounted, therefore, as Franklin, Adams, and Jefferson kept maneuvering to win over the delegates, reaching a climax when all colonies except Pennsylvania were ready to sign. Although two of the three delegates were against the Declaration, Adams shrewdly needled James Wilson into siding with Franklin against the lone dissenter, John Dickinson, to give Pennsylvania a majority of assenting votes. The play also revealed that Adams and Jefferson wanted a statement denouncing slavery, but Edward Rutledge of South Carolina insisted on having it deleted and blamed the New England shipowners for importing slaves. This incident was typical of the concessions Adams was forced to make and dramatized the fact that the document which declared America's desire for freedom was a political compromise that was not half as democratic as the original draft had been.

Audiences interested in ribald entertainment or typical chorus girl routines might well be disappointed in the production, but a great many theatergoers have been fascinated by the historical revelations and literate dialogue and have also been aroused by the patriotic appeal of the story. Moreover, Stone and Edwards did not resort to such familiar techniques as flag waving, men in uniform, or even typically patriotic music to achieve their effect. Instead, they presented John Adams as a stubborn politician fighting for independence; Ben Franklin as a shrewd politician who makes Adams realize that compromises must be made; Dickinson of Pennsylvania as a strong supporter of the English government; and Thomas Jefferson as a brilliant writer. The play also clearly showed those members of Congress who were afraid to vote or take a definite stand, those who objected to freedom for slaves, and those who were opposed to the war. *1776* presented these historical figures as men, revealing their strength and their weakness, rather than as legendary heroes. Members of the Congress called John Adams a bore, but he won audience sympathy for his integrity. Thomas Jefferson was portrayed not only as an idealist but also as a lusty young man who would rather be with his wife than attend congressional meetings. No attempt was made to tone down the humor or ribaldry of Ben Franklin to make him represent the whitewashed, legendary figure depicted to school children. Many people had been indignant about a similar characterization in an earlier musical, *Ben Franklin in Paris,* but if there were any such complaints about *1776,* they were apparently less vehement.

The songs were a definite asset to the dramatic action, for they helped establish moods or provided a definite change of pace. Richard Henry Lee, for example, sings a rousing number before going back to Virginia to explain the necessity of the Declaration of Independence. At another point, a young soldier returning from the battles of Lexington and Concord sings a ballad of a dead soldier to his mother that is more poignant, meaningful, and literate than many of the current antiwar ballads. It also emphasizes the fact that American soldiers were suffering from lack of food and clothing. The vigorous "Molasses to Rum" expresses Rutledge's condemnation of the New England shipowners, and the love duets sung by Abigail and John Adams are charming interludes between dramatic congressional debates.

Jo Mielziner's principal set faithfully reproduced the congressional chambers as represented in latter-day photographs, but Mielziner ingeniously constructed the set so that sections could be closed off in order to show other scenes in Philadelphia. He also made effective use of scrim curtains. As the play opened, a curtain showed the top section of the Declaration of Independence; at the finale, when the delegates were ready to sign the document, another scrim curtain was lowered, the lights on stage were dimmed, and the curtain showed the signatures at the bottom of the Declaration.

The cast included twenty-six actors, all of whom had significant parts, but William Daniels as John Adams, Howard da Silva as Benjamin Franklin, and Ken Howard as Thomas Jefferson dominated the action. Virginia Vestoff as Abigail Adams and Betty Buckley as Martha Jefferson added the proper touch of femininity, and Ronald Holgate gave an exuberant, high-spirited performance as Richard Henry Lee.

A road company of *1776* was highly successful as was a London production which opened in 1970. In New York, the musical operated on cut rates in its last year before closing with a run of 1,217 performances. The distinction of *1776* is that its treatment of history is vibrant and energetic. By presenting the characters and the political arguments so vividly that audiences have little difficulty in understanding what took place in Philadelphia, it demonstrates a teaching process that even dissenting critics cannot overlook.

Long-running off-Broadway musicals have not been included in this volume mainly because they have been produced in theaters with small seating capacities. Since the average Broadway musical plays to as many patrons in one performance as an off-Broadway production would draw in an entire week, the off-Broadway show would have to run approximately seven or eight years to equal a one-year run on Broadway in audience attendance. Special mention, however, must be made of one off-Broadway musical, *The Fantasticks*, which opened May 3, 1960, at the Sullivan Street Playhouse. On May 1, 1972, it had run 4,993 performances, a record that press agents have heralded as the longest run in the history of the American theater. Although this run is not comparable in attendance records with long-running Broadway musicals, it is, nevertheless, a major achievement, and the fact that it is in its thirteenth year entitles *The Fantasticks* to a place in any list of long runs on Broadway.

Tom Jones, the librettist and lyricist, and Harvey Schmidt, the composer, based their work on Edmond Rostand's *Les Romantiques*. They wrote a charming, intimate musical about a boy and girl who are in love because they think their parents disapprove of the romance. The fathers, however, are anxious to have the young people get married and try to help the romance without letting the young lovers know of their plans. The romance runs into complications, the boy learns about the difficulty of the outside world, but all ends happily.

The musical, with a small cast of nine, profits from the intimacy of a small playhouse. In London, for example, although several critics thought *The Fantasticks* was pleasant and charming, others felt that it was presented on too large a stage. In New York, director Word Baker, aided by Ed Wittstein's setting, made the production appear to be a delightful masque. The melodic songs profited from the simple accompaniment of piano and harp, and one of the numbers, "Try to Remember," introduced in the first act and reprised at the finale, has developed into a standard hit.

During its ten-year run, the cast has undergone many changes, but it is significant to note that Jerry Orbach originated the role of narrator, a characterization that enabled him to speak directly to the audience just as he does in his current hit *Promises, Promises*. Kenneth Nelson, who originated the role of the boy, had a leading role in the more recent off-Broadway drama *The Boys in the Band* and is scheduled to have a major role in a new Broadway musical. Other performers who appeared in *The Fantasticks* include Bert Convy who played the hero in *Cabaret,* and John Cunningham, who later took over the same role.

Despite the cast changes and slight plot, *The Fantasticks* has continued to charm audiences with its story of young lovers, its whimsy, and its melodic score. It has not only remained popular in New York but also has been produced successfully by amateur groups and resident companies all over the United States.

14. *Hello, Dolly!* (1964) was a highly successful musical adaptation of Thornton Wilder's *The Matchmaker*. When an all-Negro company starring Pearl Bailey and Cab Calloway played Washington in 1967, President and Mrs. Lyndon Johnson appeared on stage to join in singing the title song

15. A symbolic hair-cutting sequence was one of the first-act routines in the controversial rock musical *Hair* (1968). The cast underwent extensive changes as talent scouts offered roles in other productions to youthful members of the company.

16. The young cast in *Grease* (1972), the musical affectionately satirizing the teen-agers growing up in the 1950s, their rock'n' roll music, and their idolatry of James Dean and Sandra Dee. *Grease*, still playing as of May 1, 1977, has surpassed the performance record set by *Hair*. The original cast included Adrienne Barbeau (in striped blouse) who has since become a top-ranking performer in television.

17. In *Cabaret* (1966) Lotte Lenya played Fräulein Schneider the German landlady, who dances here with three sailors to celebrate her engagement.

18. A scene from the revival of *Candide* (1974), the Leonard Bernstein musical based on the work by Voltaire with settings and costumes by Eugene and Franne Lee and staged by Harold Prince.

19. Glynis Johns (center) as Desirée greeting Len Cariou as Frederick Egerman at her mother's chateau, one of the elaborate scenes in the spectacular Stephen Sondheim—Hugh Wheeler musical *A Little Night Music* (1973), based on a film by Ingmar Bergman.

20. In *A Chorus Line* (1975), which won the Pulitzer Prize for Drama as well as the Tony and Critics Circle awards as best musical of the season, the dancers auditioning for a show are holding photos of themselves. Performers in this lineup who won Tony Awards include Donna McKechnie (second from left), Carole (Kelly) Bishop (third from left), and Sammy Williams (second from right).

XV

Miscellaneous
Productions

IN THE entire history of the New York theater, only fourteen musical productions that were not musical comedies or operettas have run for 500 or more performances. These miscellaneous shows range from one-man shows to opulent revues, and most of them reflect prevailing economic conditions. Critics who bemoan the lack of revue-type entertainment overlook the fact that stars who draw well at the box office often demand such enormous salaries or percentages that profits are almost negligible, and that television variety shows often present more elaborate divertissements—which the public can see free of charge. As a result, the number of revues presented on Broadway in the 1960s has been extremely small.

Victor Borge has the unique distinction of being the only solo performer to establish a record of more than 500 performances with his one-man show, *Comedy in Music,* produced in 1953. Moreover, he performed without orchestral or assisting piano accompaniment. Borge did have a dog run on stage when he played "Trees," and a stagehand would occasionally come on for a moment, but apart from that, the program was entirely Borge. He talked a great deal, played a great deal, and kept the audience entertained during the full evening's performance. Many of the routines such as the punctuation lesson, in which he used vocal sounds to represent punctuation marks, were already familiar to the audience. Even when Borge played seriously, he kept the audience laughing. For example, he discussed the tendency of audiences to cough during a performance, and then encouraged everyone to cough while he played Debussy's "Clair de Lune." When someone, undoubtedly a stooge, gave a particularly penetrating bellow, Borge would say, "Oh, that's a good one," and continue playing without missing a note. A run of 500 performances for a solo performer would be phenomenal, but Borge's *Comedy in Music* did not close until it had run for 849 performances.

In recent years, television appearances by stars have often hurt them at the box office, for the public is no longer willing to pay high theater prices to see the same routines that it could watch on television for no cost at all. Perhaps Borge's frequent television appearances curtailed the run of his second version of *Comedy in Music,* produced in 1964, in which he did two-piano work with Leonid Hambro. Although the production was successful, it did not draw the capacity houses Mr. Borge had entertained in the 1950s, and closed with a total of 192 performances.

The first long-running revue, *A Society Circus,* produced in 1905, played at the old Hippodrome Theater which seated about 5,000 people—a capacity approximately 1,200 seats less than Radio City Music Hall. The Hippodrome is reputed to have had an enormous stage that could hold anything from a ballet to a circus, as well as the most elaborate stage equipment in New York. Audiences were intrigued not only by *A Society Circus,* the second production at the new Hippodrome, but also by the theater itself. Program notes indicate that *A Society Circus* included such production numbers as "The Court of the Golden Fountains," which probably had the same appeal that the elaborate "Dancing Waters" number has had in spectacular stage presentations at such theaters as the Radio City Music Hall in recent years. Among the solo performers, *A Society Circus* featured Marceline, a famous French clown.

Most of the spectacular shows at the Hippodrome, which presented two performances daily, had very successful runs, but *A Society Circus* achieved a record of 596.

Seventeen years elapsed between the presentation of *A Society Circus* and *Chauve Souris,* the second long-running revue, produced in 1922. The *Chauve Souris,* or Bat Theater of Moscow, included members of Stanislavski's Art Theater who had fled to

Paris during the Revolution, where they had organized a troupe and presented informal entertainments. Nikita Balieff reorganized the group and presented a show in London, and Morris Gest then brought the company to New York. The production was similar to a vaudeville revue and constantly underwent changes and added new routines during its long run of 520 performances. Among the songs that became popular, the best remembered is "The Parade of the Wooden Soldiers," a precision dance number which ended with the soldiers falling one by one. During the several revised editions, the show also included "The Volga Boatman," "Katinka," and "Dark Eyes."

Theatergoers found that the language barrier posed no difficulty, and they were delighted with the novelty of the production, the music, and the droll comedy of the corpulent Mr. Baileff.

A theater's small seating capacity can help to prolong the run of a show, and this was particularly true for *Chauve Souris*. During the summer months of 1922, the production was moved from a large Broadway theater to the Century Roof, which seated only 500 people. Most of these performances, however, drew capacity houses even during the summer heat.

Several years later, *Blackbirds of 1928* opened on May 9, 1928, with an all-Negro cast featuring Bill "Bojangles" Robinson, Adelaide Hall, Aïda Ward, and Eloise Uggams, mother of Leslie Uggams, who has herself become a popular television singer, and, more recently, a musical comedy performer. *Blackbirds* was the most successful all-Negro musical revue ever staged on Broadway, and much of its success belonged to Bill Robinson, who did not appear until the second half of the show. He sang "Doin' the New Low Down" and tap-danced on the stage, then up and down a small flight of stairs, and, at one point, on top of a piano. His nimble feet, warm personality, and ingratiating smile immediately won over the audience and established him as a Broadway star. Robinson later became one of Hollywood's best-known performers, famous particularly for his dancing in several Shirley Temple pictures.

At least two musical numbers in *Blackbirds*, both sung by Adelaide Hall, have remained popular favorites. The first was the infectious "Dig-a Dig-a Doo," which provided a vigorous tempo for an energetic dance routine. According to a great many news columnists and drama commentators, Dorothy Fields and Jimmy McHugh, who wrote the lyrics and music for *Blackbirds,* were inspired to write the second song hit when they were on upper Fifth Avenue near one of the exclusive jewelry stores and saw a young couple looking in the window. The boy said he'd like to buy the girl something expensive but couldn't give her anything but love. The songwriters immediately had the idea for "I Can't Give You Anything but Love, Baby," one of the best-known show tunes of all times.

In 1928 and 1929, talking motion pictures had not yet curtailed theater attendance, and the booming prosperity of the late twenties was reflected in the box-office success of *Blackbirds of 1928,* which kept audiences entertained for 518 performances.

During the early years of the Depression, no musical revue reached 500 performances. In 1937, however, *Pins and Needles,* a revue quite different from the usual popular Broadway production, opened as an amateur show at the Labor Stage Theater, formerly the Princess Theatre, home of the successful Jerome Kern musicals in the 1920s. Its entire cast was comprised of members of the International Ladies Garment Workers Union. The producers, who had thought of their effort as an intimate revue, were amazed when critics not only treated it as a professional production but lavished praise upon it. When *Pins and Needles* opened, theatergoers just recovering from the Depression were becoming aware of the problems of labor organizations and the rights of the workingman. By presenting these problems humorously rather than as serious propaganda, and by occasionally laughing at both sides of the labor situation, the producers attracted not only members of labor unions and their friends but also the "carriage trade" theatergoers whom the show ridiculed. The production satirized capitalism, politics, foreign affairs—even labor itself—and helped establish Harold Rome as a songwriter, particularly for his number "Sunday in the Park," one of the few sentimental songs in an otherwise humorous show.

A revised version, *Pins and Needles 1939,* opened at the same theater in April 1939, and later moved uptown to the Windsor Theater with a top price of $1.65. During the long run, new sketches or songs were inserted to fit changing world conditions; among such numbers was "The Red Mikado," which lampooned the Stalin-Nazi pact. Other songs, such as one ridiculing English politics, and the opening theme, "Sing Me a Song of Social Significance," were eliminated. Excellent reviews, clever sketches, and enthusiastic performers enticed audiences for more than three years. Perhaps the length of the run should be qualified, for the Labor Stage Theater seated only approximately 300 people, but the run at the Windsor Theater indicates its tremendous popular appeal; *Pins and Needles* did not close until it had achieved a total of 1,108 performances.

Just as *Pins and Needles* reflected the public's growing awareness of the workingman, *Hellzapoppin,* produced in 1938, reflected the aftermath of the Depression years. Prosperity and the war boom were still to come, but the theatergoing public, eager to find something to laugh about, flocked to see the revue Olsen and Johnson had compiled from gags and sketches they had used in vaudeville shows around the country.

The program labeled *Hellzapoppin* "A screamlined revue," and listed a series of numbers in the program as though the revue were going to follow a standard pattern. The skits were clever, the songs amusing; but the hits of the show were the unprogrammed stunts and pranks, some of them outlandishly insulting. Olsen and Johnson, however, made certain that no one would really be offended, for they planted stooges in the audience. One number, for example, featured a raffle in which seat numbers were pulled out of a box and prizes awarded to the lucky stubholders. Although the raffle seemed to be conducted legitimately, it was not, for each prize-winner was carefully selected. The first prize, a beautiful corsage, was usually awarded to a lady down front. The prize became a perfect tribute for any celebrity attending the performance and also provided good copy for theater columnists and press agents. As the raffle continued, however, the prizes became more and more ludicrous until 50 pounds of ice was dumped unceremoniously into a man's lap. Audiences were so busy laughing that most people failed to see that the "victim" was part of the cast, that he had a piece of burlap stretched across his knees in preparation, and that he left with the ice as soon as he received it.

At one point, the lights were dimmed, and a voice came over the loudspeaker warning the audience that the auditorium would be showered with spiders. At once puffed rice or some similar product was thrown at the theater patrons, who roared in delight.

The opening number set the pace—particularly the news shot of Hitler speaking with a Yiddish accent. From then on, performers constantly streamed up and down the aisles or popped up in the boxes. The revue had the speed of a three-ring circus interspersed with just enough songs to permit the audience to rest from its laughter. In addition to Olsen and Johnson, who appeared in numerous skits, the large cast included the popular Radio Rogues, comedians Barto and Mann, and a long list of performers who doubled as singers, stooges, and members of the audience.

In spite of the general pandemonium, the show was geared to split-second timing and complete professionalism. People who had the opportunity to sit near the stooges were often surprised at their seriousness. For example, a young lady would unobtrusively come into a box, politely ask the regular seat-holder to move back a bit, and then wait. Suddenly, on cue, she would scream as a man dressed in a gorilla suit rushed in and dragged her out. Similarly, the stooges in the audience would quietly slip in and out of the aisle seats without distracting attention from the stage activity.

Several critics labeled the show "ordinary," but the public enjoyed the gags, the zany antics, and, above all, the chance to laugh and forget their troubles. A great deal of the tremendous popular success must also be credited to Walter Winchell, who constantly inserted items about the show in his widely read column. A Winchell reference to a celebrity who had seen the revue was just the right touch to send celebrity-watchers not only to the lobby but also to the box office.

When *Hellzapoppin* closed with a total of 1,404 performances, Olsen and Johnson opened a second revue, *Sons o' Fun*, produced in 1941, which followed the same pattern. The cast included such well-known performers as Carmen Miranda, Ella Logan, and Spanish dancers Rosario and Antonio. Frank Libuse, one of the principal comedians, greeted people as they entered the theater; he often acted as an usher and escorted patrons to the wrong seats, which started the confusion even before the curtain went up.

The show resembled *Hellzapoppin* by having the same stooges in the aisles, on the stage, and in the boxes. In addition to the routine comedy sketches, the revue also included burlesques of current Broadway hits. Audience participation was even greater than it had been in *Hellzapoppin*. For one routine, the chorus came into the aisles and danced with members of the audience. Celebrities who attended the show were, of course, immediately chosen as dancing partners. The audience was often hard-pressed to know who was a ticket-holder and who was a paid stooge, but in the uproarious confusion, no one really cared. Certainly the people forced by "usher" Frank Libuse to climb a ladder to get into the upper-tier box seats, and the man in an aisle seat who suddenly found a stork depositing a baby in his lap, and the women who came on stage and then had their skirts blown over their heads must have been stooges—but the constant stream of gags and surprises made the audience feel that it was witnessing a series of impromptu occurrences.

Olsen and Johnson balanced sheer slapstick with more serious numbers, and the production ran for 742 performances, approximately half as long a run as *Hellzapoppin's* but nevertheless an impressive number of performances for a show that so closely resembled its predecessor.

Among the productions that might be classified as revues, *Stars on Ice* and *Hats Off to Ice,* both of which followed *Sons o' Fun* on Broadway, belong in a special category as ice-skating extravaganzas produced at the former Center Theater in Radio City. The Center, built as a companion house to Radio City Music Hall, was originally designed to present stage and film entertainment while the Music Hall was to present concerts and possibly operas. After the management converted the Music Hall into a motion-picture theater, the Center presented a variety of stage spectacles including such operettas as *The Great Waltz,* which allowed full scope for all the stage devices, moveable platforms, and scenic effects available at the Center. When ice-skating revues proved successful, the Center presented annual shows featuring many of the foremost skaters in the world. The shows were staged extravagantly, costumed lavishly, and presented at economy prices. The best seats sold for approximately one half the price charged for orchestra seats at most Broadway musicals. The revues concentrated on lavish spectacles but provided sufficient contrast by presenting fine solo figure skaters as well as hilarious skating comedians. Most of the ice shows ran for a season, but *Stars on Ice,* which opened on June 24, 1942, ran for two years with a total of 830 performances. *Hats Off to Ice* opened June 22, 1944, and ran for 889 performances. Both of these long-running ice shows flourished during the booming war years, and their economy prices, brilliant spectacles, and superb skaters all attracted appreciative audiences.

The World War II years also influenced the run of two opulent revues. Soldiers and civilians crowding into New York joined the regular theatergoers who were seeking escape entertainment, particularly shows with beautiful chorus girls; and at least two revues filled this need. The first, *Star and Garter,* opened June 24, 1942. Michael Todd capitalized on the fact that burlesque houses had been banned in New York by staging the show as if it were a typical Broadway revue but incorporating all the old tricks of burlesque—including double-entendre songs, stripteasers, and slapstick sketches. Todd, an astute showman, disguised the warmed-over burlesque material by mounting the show beautifully. He hired Bobby Clark, always a Broadway favorite, as top comedian; for glamour, he co-starred Gypsy Rose Lee, who had left the burlesque circuit in the 1930s to appear in a *Follies* production. He selected beautiful chorus girls and show girls, whose shapeliness made audiences forget their negligible singing voices; he hired excellent dancers; and he engaged Hassard Short to stage the entire production so lavishly that all theatergoers, and not just seekers of burlesque, would be spellbound.

Clark romped, ogled the girls in the show, and regaled audiences as a judge at a murder trial. When the defendant, Gypsy Rose Lee, sat on the witness chair and crossed her legs, Clark slipped down from his chair and suddenly poked his head out of the curtains at the bottom of the judge's bench to get a better view of Miss Lee's shapely legs. Georgia Sothern and Gypsy Rose Lee both did their striptease routines, and Miss Lee proved to be an expert comedienne as she spoofed her own act. Professor Lamberti, a gum-chewing, bedraggled musician, played the xylophone while a beautiful girl standing behind him did a striptease. The act become progressively more hilarious as the audience kept applauding for encores and the delighted Lamberti, unaware of the girl behind him, kept playing.

The first act finale, an Irving Berlin song, "The Girl on the Police Gazette," was a magnificent array of pinks and blacks. Gypsy Rose Lee, featured as The Girl, had only to walk on stage and the audience broke into applause.

Although several critics said *Star and Garter* was little more than a burlesque show moved from Forty-Second Street to Broadway at much higher prices, the many people who swarmed into New York during the war years looking for just this type of entertainment kept the show running for 609 performances.

The *Ziegfeld Follies,* which opened a year later in April 1943, presented a more conventional type of entertainment than *Star and Garter* and had a longer run than any *Follies* ever produced by Florenz Ziegfeld, Jr., or any edition of the *Follies* produced after his death. The *Ziegfeld Follies of 1943* starred Milton Berle, who dominated the show. In fact Berle seemed to be on stage almost constantly except during the production numbers. His broad, fast comedy included a sketch in which he satirized the 1943 meat shortage by playing a butcher who carefully hid a steak in a safe. In another sketch he did a takeoff on *Hellzapoppin.* At times, he came to the footlights and talked to and with the audience. The cast also included the lovely singer Ilona Massey; Jack Cole, who performed an intriguing Hindu dance in the Oriental style he was later to use in many of the shows he choreographed; and Dean Murphy, who delighted audiences with his impersonations of celebrities in show business and politics. In keeping with the Ziegfeld tradition, the production numbers were beautifully staged and costumed, particularly in one scene in which the costumes shimmered with coffee-colored variations. The combination of beautiful women, Milton Berle, good humor, and the economic prosperity of the New York theater helped the *Ziegfeld Follies of 1943* run for 553 performances.

Call Me Mister, produced in 1946, profited from the prosperity on Broadway which continued after the war. The revue capitalized on the foibles of army life and the experiences of soldiers in readjusting to civilian life. Audiences were intrigued by the fact that almost everyone connected with the production was an ex-serviceman, ex-servicewoman, or an ex-USO entertainer. Harold Rome, who wrote the lyrics and music, had served in the Armed Forces, as had Arnold Auerbach and Arnold B. Horwitt who wrote the sketches. Co-producer Melvyn Douglas was a veteran of the Special Services Division of the Army. According to the program notes, Betty Garrett, the only cast member to receive featured billing, had made numerous appearances in the G. I. Jane shows that played in Army bases and hospitals. The talented cast also included Jules Munshin, an expert comedian; Laurence Winters, an impressive baritone who later became a member of the New York Opera Company; and Maria Karnilova, a superb dancer who later appeared as Tessie in *Gypsy* and more recently as the mother in *Fiddler on the Roof*.

For the most part, the revue depicted the humorous side of military life. Betty Garrett sang "Poor Little Surplus Me," in which she bemoaned the fate of the canteen waitress who had no one left to serve. Miss Garrett, who knew just how to emphasize every clever line in the lyrics, was particularly effective as she sang about the high-ranking officers who returned to menial positions in civilian life while the little private whom she had ignored was now connected with the New York Stock Exchange. *Call Me Mister*, however, was not all satire. At least two numbers, both sung by Laurence Winters, dealt with more significant themes. The first, "The Face on the Dime," was a tribute to the late President Franklin Roosevelt. The second, "The Red Ball Express," was a strong indictment against racial prejudice.

The production also included several numbers that had little or no connection with Army life. "South America, Take It Away," a wonderful spoof on South American dances sung by Betty Garrett, was made to fit the general theme of the revue by having Miss Garrett appear as a USO hostess entertaining the troops. Miss Garrett's devastating performance made the song one of the biggest hits in the show. "Yuletide, Park Avenue" had absolutely no connection with Army life, for in it a Park Avenue family sings its gratitude to the prominent business houses where the family had shopped during the Christmas season. Its clever lyrics included the name of every leading department or specialty store in New York.

The glowing reviews, the youthful zest of the company, the chance to laugh at Army nonsense with just enough serious numbers to provide the right touch of contrast, all helped *Call Me Mister* achieve its tremendous popularity. Its appeal was not limited to servicemen, for all audiences could appreciate the witty sketches, the lilting music, the broad comedy, and the general enthusiasm of the brilliant cast. Nor was the appeal limited to the New York area, for a second company, headed by Jane and Betty Kean, toured successfully on the road.

Call Me Mister, which closed after 734 performances, was the last American long-running revue. Only two revues produced since 1946 have run for more than 500 performances. The first, *La Plume de Ma Tante,* a French import, opened in 1958. The second, *Beyond the Fringe,* a British intimate revue produced in New York in 1962, was an extended series of sketches featuring four talented young men—Alan Bennett, Peter Cook, Jonathan Miller, and Dudley Moore.

Although the critics wrote enthusiastic reviews, *Beyond the Fringe* puzzled some audiences, for enjoyment came in proportion to the audience's ability to understand the satirical references to British and American politics, prominent English political figures, and British eccentricities. The humor ranged from slapstick to irony in sketches that exposed British snobbishness, the evils of the class system, stuffy officials, and political blunders. The revue also lampooned the church; stuffy college professors belaboring obscure points in academic double-talk; and discussions of the fine arts. The finale developed into a riotous satire on Shakespeare, with all four men romping through a variety of Shakespearean antics in which they used exaggerated gestures and spoke an almost incomprehensible language.

The performers were ingratiating, and each seemed to have a special cult of his own. The critics of *Variety* and the *Saturday Review* cited Jonathan Miller as the performer who made the most auspicious Broadway debut of that season. Peter Cook became familiar to television audiences, for he appeared several times on popular programs. Musicians enjoyed the musical satires of Dudley Moore, an accomplished pianist who was particularly funny when he donned a wig to portray Dame Myra Hess. Alan

Bennett, the quietest member of the cast, was impressive in the sequences that provoked thought rather than laughter. In the fall of 1963, the revue underwent revisions, although many of the original numbers were still retained, and the production did not close until May 1964, with a total of 667 performances.

La Plume de Ma Tante, produced in 1958, was the last of the long-running opulent revues. In a season that also produced *Flower Drum Song* and *Gypsy,* the Critics' Circle by-passed the musical comedies and awarded its prize for the best musical entertainment of the year to *La Plume de Ma Tante.* Several critics, in fact, called the production a French edition of *Hellzapoppin,* which it resembled in speed and in precision timing but from which it differed by confining the action to the stage and by emphasizing pantomime. Some of the skits resemble the old two-reel, silent motion-picture comedies in which the action rather than dialogue provoked the laughter.

The production numbers varied from lengthy pantomimes and ballet sequences to short blackouts, such as the scene in which a man climbs the stairs leading to an airplane, finds that the trip has been cancelled, stands at the stairs staring into space, suddenly spins his bow tie as if it were a propeller—and flies off into the air as the lights black out.

Precision was particularly evident in the first-act finale. As the scene opened, four monks began to pull long bell ropes. As they started to interweave the ropes, they broke into a maypole dance and accelerated the tempo until they were jumping into the air and swinging off the ground. At the height of the frenzied dance, the head monk entered, and the four monks reversed their steps, making the leaps shorter and shorter until the ropes were untwined and the monks were again tolling the bells as they had been doing at the start of the scene. The four men danced with such gleeful abandon that they made a very difficult routine appear to be quite simple.

Split-second timing was also evident in a routine danced by a group listed on the program as "The Royal Croquettes." The chorus line did a series of high kicks in perfect time except for Colette Brosset, who invariably kicked the wrong leg in the wrong direction. When the line had crossed the stage, Robert Dhery, who acted as narrator between many of the scenes, brought the group back to correct the error. This time the girls reversed the kick, and again Miss Brosset kicked wrong. Although performing a wrong step in precision dancing is more difficult than keeping in line with the chorus, Miss Brosset kicked so perfectly in split timing that even the wrong steps became part of the precision instead of making the entire routine a jumble of legs.

Unlike American revues, which build up musical numbers, *La Plume de Ma Tante* subordinated music to comedy. Even solo vocal numbers were peppered with farce. In one scene, for example, the curtains opened to reveal a soprano wearing a floor-length evening gown which had a series of ruffled tiers from the waist to the floor. As she sang, she seemed to grow taller each time she reached a high note. What appeared to be an optical illusion soon became a reality as the audience noticed that each time she grew taller, another tier of ruffles in the skirt would emerge as though the skirt were a set of escalator stairs. Before the number had ended, the soprano had reached a towering height, although the bottom of the skirt still clung to the floor.

Probably the most deceptive element in the revue was the impression it gave of being a large, lavish production. Yet the entire cast consisted of fourteen men and women—and one horse. Several scenes bordered on the ribald, but the natural charm of the performers, their innocent yet impish expressions, and their superb timing won over even the more prudish members of the audience. In one scene, the stage set included four beach bathhouses. The men discovered that the door of the third bathhouse would swing open if they slammed the other doors properly. When one of the girls entered the third bathhouse and began taking a shower, the men kept swinging their doors to no avail, and the entire sketch became as ludicrous as an old Mack Sennett comedy. Yet the maneuvering of the doors was as intriguing to the audience as it was frustrating to the men. During a scene in which the horse appeared, one performer kept coming on stage with a brush and pan, looking at the horse, and then walking off stage disgusted. Each time he reappeared, the running gag brought a louder laugh from the audience.

Robert Dhery, who wrote and directed the show, and Colette

Brosset, who directed the choreography, appeared in many of the skits and routines. Pierre Olaf, an elderly, wide-eyed cherub, enchanted audiences as one of the monks and also as a clown in a beautiful production number, "In the Tuileries Gardens." The emphasis upon pantomime, the excellent dancing, the charm of Mr. Dhery and Miss Brosset, and the zest and enthusiasm of the entire cast delighted audiences, who kept *La Plume de Ma Tante* running for 835 performances.

If the secret of producing a successful revue lay in patterning it after a resounding hit, then *La Grosse Valise,* produced in 1965, should have been a long-running production; the show was reported to have the same charm and humor as *La Plume de Ma Tante.* Robert Dhery was again the author; and Colette Brosset again directed the choreography. Perhaps the critics and audiences, who had hoped to see another version of *La Plume de Ma Tante,* expected too much, for reaction to *La Grosse Valise* was decidedly negative. The critics were unimpressed by the trick stage effects and thought the slapstick humorless. The principal actors who had helped to make *La Plume de Ma Tante* diverting were not in this new cast, and *La Grosse Valise* closed after only seven performances.

No revue produced since *La Plume de Ma Tante,* with the exception of *Beyond The Fringe,* has been able to run for even 500 performances. And, with the increasing costs of production, higher salaries, and competition of free television variety shows, it is unlikely that producers will hazard another revue to match the opulence of *Star and Garter,* the *Ziegfeld Follies of 1943,* or *La Plume de Ma Tante.*

These Also Ran

IN THE 1960s and 1970s, several productions which ran more than 500 performances could have been excluded from a list of Broadway's greatest musical hits because they ended their New York runs as failures; according to figures quoted in *Variety,* they had not recovered their production costs. Since a 500-performance record was the basis for selecting hit musicals, eliminating these shows would establish a new standard—financial success—to determine hits and would necessitate the inclusion of musical comedies which had shorter runs but which earned higher profits than several shows which did run for 500 or more performances. Moreover, to many people the length of the run established by the shows listed as failures still indicates popular success. The financial failures, however, demonstrate that rising costs of production have made long runs a necessity, and that a run of 500 performances, considered sensational in the 1920s, is no longer an assurance that a show will break even. Several of these failures resorted to two-for-one tickets after the shows had been running for almost a year, proving only that a cut-rate policy could keep a production running but could not increase profits unless it attracted larger audiences.

Before *Milk and Honey* opened on Broadway in September 1961, commentators predicted that the Israeli setting, the folk dancing, and the score would appeal to the large Jewish population in the New York area. The cast included Robert Weede and Mimi Benzell, who had been members of the Metropolitan Opera Company, and Molly Picon, a favorite of the Yiddish theater, making her first appearance in a Broadway musical.

The libretto by Don Appell dealt with seven American

women touring in Israel. One of the women, Ruth, meets Phil, an American contractor whose daughter is married to an Israeli farmer. Phil and Ruth fall in love, but Ruth learns that Phil is separated from his wife who refuses to divorce him. They become involved in an affair that ends unhappily, with Ruth returning to the United States not very hopeful that Phil will ever get a divorce. A second romance, involving the widowed Clara Weiss, played by Molly Picon, ends happily with the final episode showing the newly married Clara wearing a huge diamond that must have dazzled even the people sitting in the last row of the balcony. Two subplots depicted the pride of the Israeli farmers and the rigorous hardships they endured to make their land productive.

Milk and Honey opened to favorable reviews. The critics lauded the performances of Robert Weede as Phil and Mimi Benzell as Ruth, but they were even more effusive in praising Molly Picon's performance as Clara. The diminutive actress stole the show every moment she was on stage and entranced audiences whether she was doing a buck and wing or a somersault, singing amusing lyrics, or acting as a matchmaker. The settings by Howard Bay, costumes by Miles White, choreography by Donald Saddler, as well as the score by Jerry Herman, which evoked the flavor of Israeli folk music in several numbers, presented what many people considered to be an authentic picture of Israeli life.

In spite of its attributes, however, *Milk and Honey* did not please those people who disapproved of the romance of Phil and Ruth because the lovers were encouraged in their affair and were told that if they remained in Israel, practically no one would object to their living together. Those who disapproved of the plot wanted Israel depicted as a land of milk and honey and not as a haven for common-law liaisons.

During the first few months of the run, *Milk and Honey* drew capacity houses and might have continued to draw well if Molly Picon had not left the cast for several months to make a motion picture in Hollywood. While she was gone, box office receipts dropped. By the time Miss Picon rejoined the show, interest in *Milk and Honey* had already waned. When the production closed in January 1963 with a total of 543 performances, *Variety* reported a loss of $70,000 on the show's original investment.

The final deficit for *What Makes Sammy Run?*, which opened February 27, 1964, more than quadrupled the amount lost by *Milk and Honey*. Budd and Stuart Schulberg adapted the musical from Budd Schulberg's highly successful novel, the story of Sammy Glick, a ruthless heel who rose to the top of the motion-picture industry. The first section of the novel had depicted Sammy's early life on the East Side of New York, but the musical eliminated most of this background material and traced Sammy's rise to power from copyboy on a New York newspaper to chief of a large motion-picture studio. On the way up, Sammy crushes his opponents, steals ideas, betrays friends, and drives one of his benefactors to suicide. He bypasses Kit, an attractive writer who has fallen in love with him, to marry Laurette Harrington, daughter of a prominent banker, only to discover at the final curtain that his wife is even more ruthless and immoral than he.

The critics differed on the merits of the show, but agreed that Steve Lawrence, Robert Alda, Sally Ann Howes, and Bernice Massi gave convincing performances. There was also favorable comment on the costumes by Noel Taylor and the score by Ervin Drake. Steve Lawrence's performance during the first few months of the run definitely headed the list of credits, for Lawrence won the New York Drama Critics' Poll as the best male performer in a musical production during the 1963–1964 season. Lawrence's hit records and his appearances on television and in nightclubs made him the show's strongest box-office attraction.

Paradoxically, the Hollywood story, which had made the novel popular in the 1940s, was dated by the 1960s, for a new generation of theatergoers unfamiliar with former studio intrigues had grown up in the twenty-three-year period since the book first appeared. By 1964, very few, if any, of the veteran motion-picture tycoons were still in control of studios. Even Abe Burrows' direction, and, as most critics suggested, unofficial play doctoring, failed to add sufficient humor to lighten the unpleasant story and make it more acceptable to musical comedy audiences. Moreover, the songs and dance routines provided only temporary diversion and were, at times, inconsistent with the basic story of Sammy Glick's bludgeoning tactics to conquer Hollywood. On the other hand, using an unappealing character as the lead in a musical might have been too radical when the novel first appeared, but Broadway audiences had learned to accept such a character in the successful revival of *Pal Joey*. Several commentators made comparisons between the Rodgers and Hart musical and the adaptation of Schulberg's novel to explain why *Pal Joey* had become a musical classic and why *What Makes Sammy Run?* appeared to be merely a carbon copy. Joey was worthless but not evil. Sammy was vicious, calculating, and clever; and no one, with the exception of Laurette, was able to escape his machinations. Joey, despite his faults, was amiable; Sammy was sinister.

By the time the show had run five months, attendance had dropped. Despite the lukewarm notices, *What Makes Sammy Run?* might have survived if rumors had not begun to circulate about dissension in the show. Budd Schulberg was displeased with the ad-libbing being inserted into the dialogue; the producers threatened to bring legal action against Steve Lawrence unless he reinstated one of the songs he had cut. Lawrence began missing performances, and *Variety* reported threats of suits and counter-suits. By the end of the first year, the producers stated that Lawrence had missed seven out of eight performances in one week and that during a four-month period he had missed a total of twenty-four performances. Box-office receipts continued to drop because theatergoers did not know whether Lawrence would or would not appear in the title role.

Steve Lawrence, however, had sacrificed a great deal to star in the show, for he had turned down lucrative offers that would have paid him more for one night's appearance than he received as a weekly salary in *What Makes Sammy Run?* The producers, on the other hand, did not want to release Lawrence, for without him the show had little drawing power. After 540 performances, *What Makes Sammy Run?* closed with a deficit of more than $285,000 on its original investment.

Golden Boy, starring Sammy Davis, Jr., represented a greater investment than *What Makes Sammy Run?* and earned back a higher percentage of its costs, but still closed with a large deficit. *Golden Boy* was similar to *What Makes Sammy Run?*, for it de-pended upon its star for success. Sammy Davis, Jr., in the demand-ing role of Joe Wellington, had suffered with laryngitis during the arduous road tour and played the opening performance on Broadway wearing a body microphone. During the long run in New York, Davis not only fought off laryngitis but also suffered a muscular injury at one performance, appearing in the last act with a bandaged ankle. When illness forced him to miss several performances or when he took a week's vacation to get a well-earned rest, the box office receipts dropped drastically.

Clifford Odets' drama *Golden Boy*, on which the musical was based, was presented on Broadway in 1937. Its plot deals with an Italian boy, Joe Bonaparte, whose father wants him to become a musician. Joe, however, becomes a boxer because he thinks the ring offers better opportunities for making quick money. When Joe breaks his hand in a fight, the drama reaches its emotional crisis, for Joe realizes he will never be able to resume his musical career. Joe and Lorna, his manager's mistress, fall in love but know that their affair is doomed. In his big fight, Joe knocks out his opponent and then learns that his blow has killed the man. Dazed by this information, Joe and Lorna drive off in his high-powered car and are killed in a crash.

Odets began working on the musical adaptation but died before finishing the script; his former pupil, William Gibson, author of *The Miracle Worker* and *Two for the Seesaw*, took over the assignment. The adaptation changed Joe from an Italian boy to a young black who is determined to fight his way to the top to overcome the racial injustices he has suffered. The musical retained the incident of the crucial injury to Joe's hand, but it was ineffective. Joe Bonaparte had been a musician; Joe Wellington was not. As a result, what had been an emotional crisis in the original play was merely an unfortunate episode in the musical. Joe had broken his hand but had not destroyed a potential career. The ending also was changed. Instead of Lorna and Joe dying together in the car crash, Joe drives off alone and is killed.

Changing the script to develop the racial problem enabled the production to include a musical sequence in Harlem that stopped the show. Joe Wellington returns to his old neighborhood and sings "Don't Forget 127th Street," and everyone in the block joins him in a spirited dance routine. The musical was at its best in scenes such as this which had nothing in common with Odets' original drama.

When *Golden Boy* opened on the road, the producer knew the show was rough, and instead of rushing it into New York, he extended the road tour. After months of revisions and exhausting rehearsals, *Golden Boy* came to Broadway on October 20, 1964. Most of the New York critics agreed that Sammy Davis gave a convincing portrayal of Joe, handled the vocal numbers remarkably well in spite of his laryngitis, and demonstrated a new talent in agile dancing. *Golden Boy* may have failed to score a knockout, as one critic remarked, but Sammy Davis made his role of Joe Wellington a personal triumph. Donald McKayle's choreography, particularly in the big fight scene, the most exciting and most skillfully staged routine in the entire production, helped audiences forget the unmanageable book. With only the percussion instruments as accompaniment, Sammy Davis and dancer Jaime Rogers slugged each other, fell, jumped up, and again traded blows as though they were in a real fight. Rogers executed the difficult steps as though he were a fighter and not a dancer; Davis surprised many people with his skill in matching Rogers' nimble footwork.

For a while, the gross receipts for *Golden Boy* were among the highest on Broadway, but the operating expenses and production costs were too high to be recovered unless the show played to capacity houses for a long period. When producer Hillard Elkins closed *Golden Boy* after 569 performances, he still had a deficit of $120,000 on his original investment of $575,000.

Unlike the three preceding financial failures, *Half a Sixpence* had no star with the box-office appeal of Sammy Davis, Steve Lawrence, or Molly Picon. The musical, which had been adapted from H. G. Wells's novel *Kipps*, was set in turn-of-the-century Folkstone, in the southern part of England. Arthur Kipps, an apprentice in a drapery emporium, gives his sweetheart, Anne, who works as a maid, half a sixpence as a love token. He enrolls in an evening class for workers and falls in love with his teacher, Helen Walsingham, and when he learns that he has come into a large inheritance, Kipps asks Helen to marry him. She agrees, but Kipps, dismayed by her snobbishness and class consciousness, breaks off the engagement and marries Anne. Unable to adjust to being the wife of the wealthy, extravagant Kipps, Anne is miserable. After Helen's brother swindles Kipps out of most of his money, Kipps and Anne open a small shop and find happiness by returning to the modest life to which they had been accustomed.

The adaptation by Beverley Cross followed the original story, but the music and lyrics by David Heneker and the choreography by Onna White dominated the production, turning *Half a Sixpence* into a typical musical comedy in which a slender plot served primarily as background for songs and dances. The show, originally produced in London as an intimate musical, was expanded in the American version, particularly with the addition of dance routines devised by Miss White, such as ballet miming the bustling activity in the drapery shop.

Most of the critics wrote rave reviews, calling *Half a Sixpence* a humorous, tuneful, and visual delight. Loudon Sainthill's sets and costumes faithfully re-created the period atmosphere. David Heneker created songs that were not only well suited to the story but also varied in type. The amazing Tommy Steele, who had pleased London audiences with his performance in the Rodgers and Hammerstein production of *Cinderella* and who had then originated the role of Kipps, handled most of the songs and captivated audiences with his boyish charm, his dancing, strutting, singing, and banjo playing.

When *Half a Sixpence* opened on April 25, 1965, it gave every indication of becoming a hit, but when Steele left the cast before the end of the next season, the show lost some of its verve. By the end of the first year, the cast had undergone many changes, and when the production closed on July 16, 1966, with a total of 512 performances, *Variety* reported that it had lost $100,000 of its original investment of $300,000. In June 1967, however, *Variety* reclassified *Half a Sixpence* as a hit because the touring companies had recovered the loss and had earned a profit.

At least three long-running musicals produced in the 1970s also failed to recover their initial investment. *The Rothschilds*, adapted by Sherman Yellen from the book *The Rothschilds* by Frederic Morton, opened October 19, 1970. The story, which dealt with the history of the famous banking family, begins in the ghetto of Frankfurt where Mayer Rothschild's shop is wrecked during a pogrom. Rothschild builds up his dynasty by sending his five sons to European centers to become banking heads. In the last act, the Rothschilds, now established as influential bankers, are accepted in the courts of Europe.

A few critics tried to compare *The Rothschilds* to *Fiddler on the Roof* because Jerry Bock and Sheldon Harnick had written the scores for both. The only parallel between the two productions, however, was that both musicals dealt with Jews. *Fiddler* had universality in its story of a farmer who struggles to eke out a living, never loses his belief in God, and disowns a daughter when she marries someone of another faith. In Japan, in Ireland, and in England, for example, audiences said the story could have applied to deeply religious members of their working classes. Although *The Rothschilds* presented a realistic portrait of intolerance, it dealt too specifically with one unusual family. Audiences had difficulty finding a common bond that would link them with the Rothschilds who had broken out of the ghetto to become a powerful banking family.

Hal Linden, who played Mayer Rothschild, won the Tony Award for best actor in a musical; Keene Curtis, who played a variety of anti-Rothschild villains from European noblemen to Prince Metternich, also won the Tony Award for best supporting actor in a musical. The critics thought *The Rothschilds* had a good dramatic plot, but that it lacked humor, had no outstanding songs, and very few dance routines. When *The Rothschilds* closed on January 2, 1972, after 507 performances, it had not recovered its production costs. Moreover, a plan to send the musical on tour to help recoup losses was cancelled.

Follies, with book by James Goldman, loomed as a potential hit. Stephen Sondheim, who wrote the songs, was widely acclaimed both as a lyricist and a composer. The large cast was studded with such former stars as Alexis Smith, Gene Nelson, Yvonne de Carlo, and Fifi d'Orsay who had been popular motion-picture players; Dorothy Collins, a leading singer on *The Hit Parade*; Mary McCarty, one of the principals in the Broadway musical *Miss Liberty*; Ethel Shutta, Eddie Cantor's leading lady in *Whoopee*; and Arnold Moss, the distinguished Shakespearean actor.

The setting was the bare stage of a theater that was being razed. A group of middle-aged former show people come to a farewell party, and the story deals primarily with four principal characters—two couples whose marriages are breaking up. A beautiful former actress is married to an unfaithful politician and diplomat. The second actress, who has married a traveling man, is still in love with the politician-diplomat. As the play progresses, the four principals are depicted as they were in the early twenties by four young people. To emphasize the symbolism, the memory characters are costumed in black and white to contrast with the mature characters. The title referred to the foolishness and heartaches of its characters, and these follies are developed in a "Loveland" sequence with lace curtains, valentines, showgirls in lavish costumes, and chorus boys in powdered wigs. Each of the four characters explains his and her problems in a song sequence, and when the party is over, the four principals face grim reality in the empty theater.

Follies opened April 4, 1971, to mixed reviews. Critics who liked the show called Goldman's book "powerful," and commended Sondheim on his excellent music and lyrics. Others said *Follies* was an exciting innovation in the theater. Those who did not like the show thought the book was slow and weak. The numerous prizes awarded to *Follies* should have counteracted the negative reviews. At the end of the 1970–1971 season, *Follies* won the Critics Circle Award as the best musical of the year. Boris Aronson received the Joseph Maharam Foundation Award for best design by an American. Drama Desk Awards were given to Boris Aronson, set designer; Florence Klotz, costume designer; Stephen Sondheim, composer and lyricist; Harold Prince and Michael Bennett, directors; and Michael Bennett, choreographer. In the 1971–1972 season, *Follies* won eight Tony Awards: Alexis Smith, best actress in a musical; Michael Bennett and Harold Prince, directors; Boris Aronson, set designer; Stephen Sondheim, best score; Florence Klotz, costumes; Tharon Muser, best lighting; and Michael Bennett, best choreographer.

One of the major drawbacks was the misleading title. Theatergoers who had expected to see a Ziegfeld extravaganza were disappointed to find they were seeing a serious, dramatic production. The well-known show people who studded the cast also proved to be a disappointment, for most of these performers were limited to cameo appearances and were primarily symbolic figures who enhanced the background. There seemed to be no midpoint of appreciation for *Follies*. People either hated it or loved it, and apparently those who loved it were in the minority, for attendance kept dropping. The musical closed July 1, 1972, with a run of 521 performances and a deficit of more than $640,000.

The first musical version of *Candide*, with book by Lillian Hellman, adapted from the story by Voltaire, and with lyrics by Richard Wilbur, John LaTouche, and Dorothy Parker, opened December 1, 1956, and closed after a short run of 73 performances. The principal asset of the production was Leonard Bernstein's music, which critics said represented some of Bernstein's best work for the Broadway theater. Although the musical failed, the original cast album became a popular recording.

Harold Prince's production of *Candide*, which began a limited run at the Chelsea Theater Center in the Brooklyn Academy of Music on December 19, 1973, was classified as a revival, but, with the exception of Leonard Bernstein's score, it was virtually a new show. The production had a new book by Hugh Wheeler and additional lyrics by Stephen Sondheim. Some of the characterizations were changed, but basically the story remained the same and developed Voltaire's satirical concepts of good and evil. Dr. Pangloss has taught his pupil Candide to believe "all for the best in the best of all possible worlds." Candide and his sweetheart Cunegonde go out into the world and face banishment, rape, the Spanish Inquisition, and betrayal. They come back disillusioned but still hopeful that the world may improve. Some of the critics thought Voltaire's fast-paced story would have been better suited for motion pictures, but the critics generally agreed that Leonard Bernstein had written a glittering score in which he satirized such musical forms as coloratura arias, duets, quartets, and dance rhythms.

Candide closed at the Chelsea Theater Center on January 20, 1974, and on March 10, 1974, it was transferred to the Broadway Theater. To permit more continuous action, Prince reconstructed the entire orchestra section of the theater. He set up ten different acting areas connected by ramps, bridges, platforms, and trap doors. The seating capacity was cut to nine hundred, and the audience sat in the equivalent of bleachers or on stools in clumps of seats or benches in various parts of the orchestra, some of them in almost direct contact with the action. At the end of the 1973–1974 season, *Candide* received the Critics Circle Award as the best musical of that year. Tony Awards were won by Franne and Eugene Lee for best scenic design; Harold Prince for best director of a musical; and a special Tony Award to *Candide* as "an outstanding contribution to the artistic development of the musical theater."

Despite the accolades given *Candide* during its run in Brooklyn and in New York, the production drew mixed reactions from spectators. A great many people objected to the circus atmosphere, the new seating arrangement, and the uncomfortable seats. According to *The New York Times*, the management was refunding as much as $200 a week. *Candide* ran almost two years, but the limited seating capacity cut down on the potential gross, and when *Candide* closed on January 4, 1976, after 740 performances, it still had a deficit of approximately $150,000.

Purlie, with book by Ossie Davis, Philip Rose, and Peter Udell, music by Gary Geld, and lyrics by Peter Udell, was based on the play *Purlie Victorious* by Ossie Davis which was produced in 1961 and was filmed under the title *Gone Are the Days* in 1963. The play, set in southern Georgia, mocked white plantation owners, laughed at the Uncle Toms who worked on plantations, and tried to prove that blacks could outwit and triumph over the whites without violence. Purlie, a self-educated black preacher, tries to free the plantation workers from the domination of overbearing Ol' Cap'n, the owner, to whom they are all in debt. Purlie wants to buy his own church and asks a young girl named Lutiebelle to help him swindle money from Ol' Cap'n. His plan does not work, but with the help of Charlie, Ol' Cap'n's son, he gets his church and marries Lutiebelle. The musical, which followed the original story, was primarily a play with songs rather than a standard musical comedy, for production numbers were limited to the opening and the finale.

Several critics thought the story was somewhat dated, that Purlie was an amusing but cowardly young man, that Ol' Cap'n was a stereotyped Southern gentleman, and that Lutiebelle was an impish but appealing young Topsy. The critics who reacted negatively to this emphasis upon humor said the racial issues involved were no longer funny. With the rise of black militants and activists, neither the story nor Purlie's wheedling and scheming, they felt, depicted the attitudes of the black leaders who had become national figures. Most of the critics, however, wrote favorable reviews. Even the dissenters admitted that the cast was excellent. Cleavon Little's performance as Purlie won him both the Tony Award and the Variety Poll of Drama Critics as the best actor in a musical produced in the 1969–1970 season. Melba Moore also won both the Tony Award and the Variety Poll as the best supporting actress in a musical for her performance as Lutiebelle.

Joyce Brown, the first black woman to conduct the opening of a Broadway show, was a further asset. Miss Brown had previously conducted the orchestra for *Bye, Bye, Birdie* on tour and had also taken over the orchestra for *Golden Boy*. During the run of *Purlie*, theatergoers sitting in the front rows found distinct pleasure in watching Miss Brown, who mouthed the lyrics, swayed to the music, and, in perfect control of the orchestra, made the musical accompaniment secondary to the vocalists without minimizing the importance of the intricate rhythms.

Purlie opened in March 1970 and soon had backing from black religious and social groups. The awards won by Cleavon Little and Melba Moore that same spring also promoted box-office sales. The production had further support from Sylvester Leaks, public relations director of the Stuyvesant Restoration Company, who had worked with other black-oriented entertainments. Instead of trying to organize the white groups that usually booked theater parties, Leaks contacted such groups as the NAACP and arranged to bring busloads of black patrons from other cities to see the musical.

When attendance began to drop, the management used cut-rate tickets. *Purlie*, which represented an investment of $400,000, prolonged its run to 689 performances, but closed with a deficit. Unlike the other three failures in the 1970s, however, *Purlie* was reputed to have recovered its losses on a successful road tour with a cast headed by Robert Guillaume and Patti Jo, and with Joyce Brown as conductor.

The 1970s

THE EXTENSIVE advance publicity for *Oh, Calcutta!* aroused speculation as to whether the nudity, earthy language, and simulated sex sequences would run into difficulties with the censors. *Hair* had already broken down many of the barriers, but *Oh, Calcutta!* was rumored to go to greater extremes, even to full lighting for the nude scenes. The newspapers announced a distinguished list of contributors that included Kenneth Tynan, Samuel Beckett, John Lennon, Bruce Jay Friedman, and Jules Feiffer, among others. Hillard Elkins, in association with Michael White and Gordon Crowe, produced the revue which had been devised by Kenneth Tynan and conceived and directed by Jacques Levy. George Platt later became associated as one of the producers.

Oh, Calcutta! was originally scheduled to open on Broadway, but plans were changed and it was booked into the off-Broadway Eden Theater which seated only 499. Admission prices were the highest in New York, with seats in the first two rows priced at $25; most of the other tickets were $15. Because the New York authorities had already cracked down on *Che!*, another off-Broadway production, for its nudity and simulated sex and had arrested the company and refused to allow the production to continue unless changes were made, the producers of *Oh, Calcutta!* invited city officials to a preview to check on the erotic revue. Very few comments were printed about the reactions of the officials, but the invitation evidently had been a shrewd move, for *Oh, Calcutta!* opened June 17, 1969, apparently without restrictions.

A few critics commended *Oh, Calcutta!* for breaking down taboos and bringing new freedom to the stage, but most of the critics, instead of being shocked or even amused, rated *Oh, Calcutta!*

a bore. Several reviewers said the most offensive scenes were not those in which the actors were nude but were, rather, the sketches in which fully or partly dressed actors indulged in tasteless antics or dialogue that represented conventional burlesque at its worst. The lyrics, which may or may not have been bawdy, were not always distinguishable. One or two critics thought the sketches represented adolescent humor and fell flat, and that the cast, with the exception of the dancers, was often inadequate, particularly in handling the dialogue. Still another complaint was the fact that individual authors were not credited for specific sketches so that critics could not identify just what scenes such men as Beckett or Tynan had written. The choreography, particularly a nude *pas de deux* performed by Margo Sappington and George Welbes, received favorable comments, although dance critics said it was not a novelty, for they had seen nude routines performed by professional ballet companies.

The show profited from the widespread publicity, however, and from its opening through December 1970, it earned a profit of more than $280,000. In February 1971, after 704 performances, it was moved uptown to the Belasco Theater with a new top price of $15. Cut rates went into effect for all but the first few rows of the orchestra and mezzanine. *Oh, Calcutta!* was also produced in several European countries. When the London edition began previewing in September 1970, it aroused more interest than the New York production. Rumors circulated that the London brokers were asking and getting as much as $50 per ticket.

In the United States, a road company which opened in Los Angeles was panned by the critics and closed by city officials who charged that the show was obscene and arrested the entire cast. The producers, nevertheless, decided to gamble on a closed-circuit television production to be shown in theaters across the country. The producers had hoped originally to have over two hundred bookings, but the number dropped to less than fifty. In Louisville, pressure from the FBI was reputed to have cancelled the showing; the closed circuit program was also cancelled in such cities as Ottawa, Peoria, Oklahoma City, Baltimore, and Lexington, Kentucky. In Columbus, Ohio, the film was stopped after the first showing and the theater manager was arrested. Despite these setbacks, the stage version of *Oh, Calcutta!* continued playing to profitable grosses in New York where it ran until August 1972 with a total of 1,314 performances.

The critics were much kinder to *The Me Nobody Knows*, which opened at the off-Broadway Orpheum Theater in May 1970. The revue, a musical study of the underprivileged children of New York, was based on *The Me Nobody Knows*, a collection of writings by children between the ages of seven and eighteen living in the New York ghetto areas and attending public schools in Bedford-Stuyvesant, Harlem, Jamaica, Manhattan, and Youth House in the Bronx. The book had been compiled by Stephen M. Joseph, a teacher who had selected material from his own classes and from those taught by his friends. Herb Schapiro devised the idea of making the book into a musical; lyrics for four songs were poems the children had written; Will Holt provided additional lyrics; and the music composed by Gary William Friedman was primarily a form of rock with emphasis on rhythm rather than melody.

The sketches and songs ranged from thoughts about birds and summer to the dirt, violence, drugs, and prostitution in the ghetto. The first act revealed the curiosity of the children and their ideas about the world in general; the second act showed the grimness of the slums. Sketches included a scene involving a thirteen-year-old boy who takes heroin as a means of escape; a boy who is happy that his baby brother, bitten by rats, is dead, for now he doesn't have to baby-sit, there will be no more doctor bills, and he will have more to eat. Sketches also dealt with the problems of being black and the fear of the night.

The Me Nobody Knows had first been presented as a thirty-minute revue in Trenton, New Jersey. When it opened in New York as a full-length production, it featured a cast of twelve talented young people—eight black and four white. Three had had no professional experience; several came from the ghetto; and the rest were professional actors. The youngest member of the cast, Douglas Grant, aged eleven, had never lived in the slums or in a low-income neighborhood. Beverly Ann Bremers, the only blonde in the group, was over twenty and had appeared in other productions, including *Hair*. Most of the critics were impressed with the cast, the musical staging by Patricia Birch, the direction by Robert H. Livingstone, and the stage setting by Clarke Dunham— a series of ramps that suggested tenement alleys, rooftops, and fire escapes. Scene changes were also effected by photographs of tenements, poolrooms, or open fields projected on the backdrop. A few of the reviewers felt that the production presented a realistic portrait of the seamy side of New York. Critic John Simon said that if legislators saw *The Me Nobody Knows*, they might soon put an end to the ghettos.

By November 15, 1970, the revue had run 208 performances, but a conflict between actors and managers in off-Broadway theaters resulted in a strike which continued for six months and closed seventeen shows including *The Me Nobody Knows*. The producers decided to bring it to the Helen Hayes Theater on Broadway where it opened December 18. The production benefited from the new location, for the theater had a better sound system, better lighting equipment, and a larger stage that gave the actors more freedom of movement. When *The Me Nobody Knows* closed in November 1971, it had run 587 performances including the 208 off-Broadway performances.

In direct contrast to *The Me Nobody Knows* and its depiction of the New York ghettos, *Company*, with book by George Furth and music and lyrics by Stephen Sondheim, dealt with the other side of New York, the residents in the high-rise apartments in the better neighborhoods. Furth had originally written a play about eleven marriages, and the possibility of starring Kim Stanley portraying all the wives was discussed, but the production plans were changed, and Furth's script was adapted into a musical dealing with Bobby, a bachelor in his mid-thirties, and five married couples. The wives all want to believe that Bobby is lonely and try to persuade him to marry; the husbands envy Bobby's freedom but go along with their wives in trying to encourage him to join their ranks. In the opening scene, the five couples give Bobby a birthday party. The episodes that follow develop a series of sketches showing that each couple has its own problems and is forced to make compromises. Bobby becomes a casual observer who realizes the couples he visits are not happy. He therefore decides he wants no part of marriage.

The out-of-town reviews during the tryout tour were not favorable. *Variety*'s Boston critic, for example, said that *Company* would appeal only to homosexuals and misogynists. *Company* also received mixed notices in New York. Critics who disliked it admitted that it was slick and brittle but complained that it dealt with uninteresting people and that the series of vignettes involving the individual couples all followed the same pattern. Those who liked it, however, wrote rave reviews. Almost all the critics, including those who were not partial to the production, wrote in superlatives about Stephen Sondheim's score and brilliant lyrics. Moreover, although Sondheim's songs were integrated into the plot, often serving as comments on the action, they had variety and revealed his talent in creating a versatile score. Critics said it would be difficult to take Sondheim's songs out of context, but, nevertheless, they cited two numbers for their excellence. "Another Hundred People" dealt with some of the inanities and ironies of contemporary urban life. The best song, "The Ladies Who Lunch," ridiculed the dull ladies who go to luncheons, continually drink too much, and fritter their lives away on trifles. The critics also commended George Furth for his original and striking plot.

Most of the characterizations, with the exception of Bobby, were of equal importance, but critics singled out several members of the cast including Dean Jones as Bobby; Susan Browning as a rattle-brained air hostess; Barbara Barrie as a karate expert; and Charles Kimbrough as her husband. The best reviews, however, went to Elaine Stritch who played the cynical, oft-married Joanne. Miss Stritch's adeptness in handling acid barbs and in singing "The Ladies Who Lunch" made her role sufficiently outstanding to earn feature billing not only for her but also for the actresses who followed her. A superb set by Boris Aronson, which appeared to be a steel framework that included an elevator and several stories in the apartment building, also received high praise, as did Harold Prince's direction of the musical. About one month after the Broadway opening, Dean Jones became ill. His standby, Larry Kert, who took over the lead, also pleased the critics.

Company opened April 26, 1970, too late to be a candidate for the 1969–1970 Tony Awards, but it did win the Critics Circle Award as the best musical of that season, getting thirteen votes, or almost double the number of its nearest contender. The Variety Poll of Drama Critics for 1969–1970 selected Stephen Sondheim as best composer and best lyricist, Harold Prince as best director, and Boris Aronson as best set designer. Aronson also received the Joseph Maharam Foundation Award for best stage design by an American, and *Theater World* included Susan Browning in its annual list of promising young performers.

The following season, *Company* received the 1970–1971 Tony Award as the best musical of the year. Other Tony Awards were given to Stephen Sondheim as best lyricist and best composer, Harold Prince as best director, Boris Aronson as best scene designer, Michael Bennett as best choreographer, and George Furth as author of best book for a musical.

By the end of the first year, most of the principals had left the cast, but the producers made theatrical news with shrewd replacements, particularly for the role of Joanne. When Elaine Stritch left the New York cast to head the road company and later the London production, motion-picture star Jane Russell took over the role. The former Hollywood pin-up girl brought *Company* ample publicity, for almost every major New York columnist wrote an article on the glamorous Miss Russell. When Vivian Blaine replaced Miss Russell, *Company* again received good publicity, for many of the columnists said that Miss Blaine, who had made theatrical history with her performance as Adelaide in *Guys and Dolls*, was very much at home as Joanne. During the latter part of its profitable stay in New York, *Company* operated on two-for-one tickets before completing its run of 690 performances.

Company and *Applause*, which also opened in 1970, both instituted higher admission scales by raising the price of matinee tickets from $8 to $9. Unlike *Company*, which had only one set, no chorus line, and virtually no changes of costume, *Applause* was a traditional backstage glamour musical that included such familiar scenes as an opening-night celebration, the Tony Awards ceremony, and the backstage friction between performers; it featured elaborate costumes; and in the full-scale production for the title song "Applause," it parodied current Broadway musicals, including a brief touch of nudity to satirize *Oh, Calcutta!* Instead of the cynical wit that pervaded *Company*, *Applause* emphasized old-fashioned sentiment with the heroine triumphing over the villainess.

Applause was based on the motion picture *All About Eve*, starring Bette Davis with Anne Baxter in the cast. Although many people thought the film concerned Tallulah Bankhead, Mary Orr, who wrote the original story, revealed that the plot was based on an incident involving Elisabeth Bergner and a young actress whom Miss Orr did not identify. The musical adaptation with book by Betty Comden and Adolph Green, music by Charles Strouse, and lyrics by Lee Adams, followed the film version in its story of Margo Channing, a middle-aged actress. Eve Harrington, a ruthless, ambitious young actress, comes to Margo's dressing room and ingratiates herself by flattering Margo, who takes Eve home with her. Within a short time, Eve induces the author and the producer of Margo's current play to hire her as Margo's understudy without consulting Margo. Eve then schemes to have Margo miss a performance so that she can appear in the play and then becomes the star in a drama Margo had wanted to do. Eve also tries but fails to seduce Bill Sampson, a director whom Margo loves. In the motion picture, the final scene showed an apprehensive Eve in her dressing room with an aspiring young actress who is trying to ingratiate herself, just as she had done with Margo. The stage version ends with Margo and Bill reconciling and planning to marry. Instead of the dressing room episode, Eve is denounced in two sequences. In the first, she attempts to seduce Bill. At most performances, audiences broke into applause when he rejected her and walked out. In the second, Eve tells the producer, with whom she has been having an affair, that she is in love with the playwright. The producer slaps her, tells her he knows she still has a husband somewhere, and orders the defeated Eve to pack her clothes, go to his apartment, and, if he is not there, to wait. A few critics thought the marriage plans for Bill and Margo were unrealistic, but audiences approved of the happy ending.

When *Applause* opened in Baltimore, the major problem facing the producers was that Lauren Bacall's performance was so vibrant that in order to make the part believable they had to recast several roles, particularly that of Eve, for she had to be a clever actress who seemed better suited for the roles Margo was too old to play. Penny Fuller, who was brought into the cast during the road tryouts, gave a convincing portrayal as Eve, but Bacall still dominated the production.

By the time *Applause* opened in New York in March 1970, all production problems had been worked out and the musical received glowing reviews. *Applause* was cited for its strong plot as well as for its glittering presentation of life backstage, fast-moving choreography, and impressive sets and costumes. In the supporting cast, critics singled out Len Cariou as Bill Sampson, Penny Fuller as Eve, and Bonnie Franklin as a young actress who sang the title number.

Applause, however, was Lauren Bacall's show. Although she was playing a middle-aged actress, she was anything but a fading star, and was effective not only as a comedienne but also as a dramatic actress in the scenes in which she battled with the producer and the playwright about Eve or tried to convince Bill that she would give up her career to marry him. *Applause* was Lauren Bacall's first musical on Broadway, but she was right at home half-talking, half-singing her numbers or leading the chorus in a spirited dance routine. Moreover, Bacall also made *Applause* a one-woman fashion show by wearing an assortment of outfits that ranged from slinky evening gowns and fluffy negligees to casual sportswear.

Applause, which cost over $725,000 to produce, played to capacity houses and earned back its investment in less than a year. A few weeks after the New York opening, *Applause* won the Tony Award as the best musical of the season. Tony Awards were also given to Ron Field as best director and choreographer and to Lauren Bacall as best actress in a musical. The Outer Circle cited Bonnie Franklin for her outstanding performance, and *Theater World* included Len Cariou and Bonnie Franklin in its annual list of promising new actors.

When Lauren Bacall was ready to leave the New York company for a vacation before starting a long road tour, the producers announced that Rita Hayworth would be the new Margo Channing, but Miss Hayworth withdrew from the assignment and the producers shrewdly signed Anne Baxter to replace Bacall, a fact which the newspaper columnists widely publicized because Miss Baxter had played Eve in the motion picture. In the fall of 1971, Lauren Bacall started the road tour of *Applause* which drew capacity houses across the country. In New York, during the second year, *Applause* continued to operate profitably on cut-rate tickets. On May 1, 1972, Anne Baxter left the cast and Arlene Dahl became the third motion-picture actress to play Margo Channing on Broadway. *Applause* closed May 27, 1972, with a run of 896 performances.

Updating the old story with topical references and new dialogue made *Applause* seem as modern as any of the current attractions on Broadway. On the other hand, the 1971 revival of the 1925 musical *No, No, Nanette* retained much of the dated plot, dialogue, and corny jokes of the 1920s but capitalized on nostalgia, a talented cast, and the excellent score which had made the original production a popular success. It had run 321 performances in the 1925–1926 season, and had surpassed most of its competitors in worldwide recognition. Approximately twenty-five companies toured the United States; seventeen different companies played in foreign countries; and the production earned a profit of more than $2 million.

When the original *No, No, Nanette* opened in Detroit in 1924, it appeared to be a failure. The director was replaced; librettists Frank Mandel and Otto Harbach rewrote the script and discarded several of the songs; lyricist Irving Caesar and composer Vincent Youmans wrote four new numbers including the now classic "Tea for Two" and "I Want to Be Happy"; and H. H. Frazee, the producer, recast several of the leads. *No, No, Nanette* was then booked into Chicago where it became a hit and ran for almost a year. During this time, touring companies began playing both in the United States and abroad, and by the time *No, No, Nanette* reached New York in September 1925, it was an established international success.

The highlights of the musical were the score and the dance routines rather than the book which was based on Frank Mandel's farce *My Lady Friends*, published in 1923. The frothy plot dealt with a wealthy Bible publisher who decides to help three young protégées financially. Complications arise when the girls, who live in different cities, come to visit the publisher at the same time. His attorney tries to get rid of the girls, but the attorney's wife misunderstands the situation. By the final curtain, the girls have been paid off and the publisher and the attorney are reunited with their wives. Nanette, the publisher's niece, and her fiancé, a young lawyer, provide the principal romance.

The 1971 *No, No, Nanette*, if produced improperly, might have been little more than a museum piece, for the revival did not change the ridiculous plot. The excellent original score, however, enhanced by shrewd casting, show-stopping choreography, and elaborate sets and costumes, made the musical one of the highlights of the 1970–1971 season. The numerous prizes awarded the revival indicate only partially the favorable reaction of the critics. Burt Shevelove, for example, won a Drama Desk Award for his adaptation of the creaky book. Instead of permitting the actors to ridicule the 1920s, Shevelove, who also directed the revival, had them playing the story straight, as if it were a new show, and, as a result, the musical became a delightful nostalgic experience. The Drama Desk also made awards to Helen Gallagher for her outstanding performance, to Raoul Pene du Bois for costumes, and to Donald Saddler for choreography. Tony Award winners included Helen Gallagher as best actress in a musical, Patsy Kelly as best supporting actress in a musical, Raoul Pene du Bois as best costume designer, and Donald Saddler as best choreographer. Raoul Pene du Bois also won the Joseph Maharam Foundation Award for his costumes, and the Outer Circle cited the revival as a distinctive achievement in the New York theater.

The costumes designed by Raoul Pene du Bois were reproductions of styles worn in the 1920s, such as heavily beaded gowns, fluffy two-piece bathing suits for the girls, and knitted sweaters, argyle socks, and knickers for the boys. He added a new touch, however, by using colors that varied from soft pastels to modern psychedelic shades of blue. His stage sets also helped make *No, No, Nanette* a visual delight. In the first and third acts, he used old-fashioned wallpaper with patterns similar to those created by Dufy; the brilliant show curtain was patterned after Matisse.

The program listed Busby Berkeley, director of famous Hollywood musicals of the 1930s, as production supervisor, but the song-and-dance routines were staged by Donald Saddler, who had danced with Helen Gallagher in *High Button Shoes*. In addition to Ruby Keeler's two show-stopping routines, "I Want to Be Happy" and "Take a Little One-Step," Saddler's varied choreography included an old-fashioned number during which the chorus girls danced on huge beach balls, a routine that had been popular in such theaters as the Roxy and Radio City Music Hall. In the expertly staged "Tea for Two," sung and danced by the juvenile leads and chorus, the dancers glided on and offstage for chorus after chorus. Helen Gallagher and Bobby Van made "You Can Dance with Any Girl" another show-stopper. The dance critics, in fact, were sufficiently impressed to review *No, No, Nanette* solely for its choreography.

The talented cast, one of the best New Yorkers had seen in years, was also one of the revival's major assets. Susan Watson and Roger Rathburn were excellent as the juvenile leads, but Ruby Keeler, Helen Gallagher, Bobby Van, Patsy Kelly, and Jack Gilford dominated the show and made even the creaky plot amusing.

Many people remembered Ruby Keeler for her starring roles in Hollywood musicals of the 1930s. She had previously appeared on the New York stage in a minor role in *Whoopee*, starring Eddie Cantor, produced in 1928, and had played the lead in Ziegfeld's *Show Girl*, produced in 1929. Shortly after she married Al Jolson, she left *Show Girl* and went to Hollywood where she became a film star. A year after her second husband, John Lowe, an industrial engineer, died, she was persuaded to come out of retirement and return to Broadway as Sue Smith, wife of the Bible publisher, in *No, No, Nanette*. Although she was playing a mature woman, she danced as though she were still the young heroine of the 1930 musicals. Her first number, "I Want to Be Happy," was sung by Nanette and Mr. Smith, just as it had been in the original musical. Miss Keeler then appeared and started tapping, but when the entire chorus came onstage, she accelerated the tempo and led the young dancers in a fast-stepping routine, very similar to the elaborate full-scale dance sequences in her films, and made "I Want to Be Happy" the high spot of the revival.

Patsy Kelly had also appeared on Broadway before becoming a

famous comedienne in Hollywood. Although she had only a minor role as Pauline, the maid, in *No, No, Nanette,* she dominated the stage every time she appeared briefly to shout at the telephone, curse the electric sweeper, or regale the audience with a corny gag. The young theatergoers loved her, for she was a key figure in their newfound interest in the comics and comediennes of the 1920s and 1930s.

Bobby Van, who played the attorney, was one of the most agile dancers to come out of Hollywood, and was effective whether dancing with Miss Gallagher, doing a whirlwind solo, or cavorting in comedy scenes with Jack Gilford. Helen Gallagher, who played the attorney's wife, had appeared in numerous Broadway musicals, but she had her best role in *No, No, Nanette,* for her performance, which won the Tony Award, demonstrated her versatility as a comedienne, singer, and dancer.

When *No, No, Nanette* opened out of town, Hiram Sherman played Jimmy Smith, the Bible publisher, but he left the cast and Frank McHugh took over the role. Jack Gilford then replaced McHugh before the musical reached Broadway and gave a highly amusing performance as the harassed publisher who cannot cope with his three protégées.

No, No, Nanette benefited from wide television coverage, as most of the principals appeared on talk shows to plug the production. Irving Caesar, the seventy-six-year-old lyricist, also gained new recognition for his television appearances, particularly on the David Frost show, singing his own numbers. The revival received further excellent coverage in the 1972 Tony Awards telecast, in which Helen Gallagher and Bobby Van appeared in the "You Can Dance with Any Girl" sequence, and Ruby Keeler did her entire "I Want to Be Happy" routine. As a fitting climax, the entire cast of the Tony program appeared at the finale strumming ukuleles and singing "I Want to Be Happy."

The road company headed by June Allyson in the Ruby Keeler role, Judy Canova as the maid, and Dennis Day as the errant husband drew well in most of its bookings. The out-of-town reviewers, although less ecstatic than the New York critics, liked the cast, the opulent production, and the familiar score. Among the many favorable New York reviews, *Variety* correctly predicted that the revival would outrun the original production, for the 1971 *No, No, Nanette* continued for 861 performances.

Of the five long-running musicals produced in the 1971–1972 season, the rock opera *Jesus Christ Superstar*, based on the last seven days in the life of Jesus of Nazareth, with music by Andrew Lloyd Webber and lyrics by Tom Rice, was the most controversial. It was also the most popular of the five during its first season on Broadway.

Webber and Rice had written a song "Superstar" and then had expanded the idea into a complete score that was recorded. The success of the album prompted the writers to present the songs in concert form, an attraction which became popular internationally. Tom O'Horgan then conceived the idea of presenting the score on Broadway in a rock opera version and apparently changed the original concept, for the character of Jesus was overshadowed by O'Horgan's flamboyant production and his emphasis upon the colorful scenery by Robin Wagner and costumes by Randy Barcelo. O'Horgan resorted to bizarre, sometimes vulgar imagery, such as having priests suspended from a framework of dinosaur bones, or Judas on a trapeze filled with beautiful girls and peacock feathers.

Jesus Christ Superstar opened in New York on October 17, 1971. Two critics endorsed the show; four wrote mixed reviews; and five condemned it in scathing terms such as "cheap," "shoddy," "vulgar," and "a stage catastrophe." Norman Nadel called it "a trashy distortion of the Biblical story." John Simon headlined his review with "closer to rock bottom than to rock opera." In *Best Plays of 1971–1972*, Otis L. Guernsey, Jr. referred to it as "a nightmare version of the passion and crucifixion," and described it as "an evening of raw, often indigestible stage imagery, sometimes in questionable taste, but as unstoppable as a circus." Several critics thought the characters in O'Horgan's production were shadowy figures rather than realistic characterizations. One notable exception was Judas, played by Ben Vereen, a black actor, who received the most favorable comments for his performance and won a *Theater World* Award for outstanding new acting talent. Opinions also varied on the lyrics and music. The negative reviewers called the lyrics "doggerel" and the music "monotonous." Those who liked the songs praised them for their lyrics and rhythmic melodies. Moreover, Andrew Lloyd Webber won the Drama Desk Award as the most promising composer of the season.

Jesus Christ Superstar ran into vigorous opposition from religious leaders of various faiths who strongly protested against the production. Catholics and Baptists, for example, objected to the sexual relationship between Christ and Mary Magdalene. Other clergymen objected to the scene showing Jesus having a tantrum as well as to O'Horgan's exaggerated pretentiousness which they called "camp entertainment," a treatment unsuited for the Biblical story. The American Jewish Committee and Anti-Defamation League branded the show as "anti-Semitic," particularly in portraying the priests as evil, bloodthirsty, and inhuman in their condemnation of Christ.

In spite of the protests and the negative reviews, a great many theatergoers were interested in seeing the production. Some agreed that *Jesus Christ Superstar* may have been lacking in artistry and good taste, but they were impressed by the pageantry and costumes. People who were familiar with the popular concert recording were curious to see how it had been converted into a dramatic stage presentation. As a result, *Jesus Christ Superstar* had a popular, profitable run of 720 performances on Broadway. When it was presented in London with a different director and much simpler staging, it was even more successful and had a longer run than the New York production.

The musical version of Shakespeare's *Two Gentlemen of Verona*, produced December 1, 1971, by Joseph Papp, not only received excellent reviews but also won a great many of the major drama awards. The production with music by Galt MacDermot, his first Broadway score since *Hair*, lyrics by John Guare, and book adapted by Guare and Mel Shapiro had first been produced during the summer of 1971 at the Delacorte Theater in Central Park as part of the Joseph Papp New York Shakespeare Festival of free productions. For this musical adaptation, the Shakespearean setting was changed from Verona to San Juan and from Milan to New York. The success of the summer presentation prompted Papp to open the musical version on Broadway. The production was somewhat enlarged, the cast underwent a few changes, but the new version still dealt with the love stories of Proteus and Julia,

Valentine and Silvia. Proteus is pledged to Julia but tries to double-cross Valentine who is in love with Silvia. After all complications are ironed out, Proteus and Julia and Valentine and Silvia are reunited.

Instead of objecting to the revisions in the text, the use of colloquialisms in the dialogue, and the addition of songs, most of the critics said the changes were not in bad taste nor did they detract from the humor in Shakespeare's comedy. They might not have accepted such distortions of Shakespeare's tragedies, but they thought the revisions were acceptable because *Two Gentlemen of Verona* was not one of Shakespeare's major plays. The critics liked the structured stage setting which allowed actors to perform scenes on different levels and to accelerate the action by eliminating scene changes. They also liked the four leads in the integrated cast played my Raul Julia and Diana Davila as Proteus and Julia, and Clifton Davis and Jonelle Allen as Valentine and Silvia.

Although the critics heartily endorsed *Two Gentlemen of Verona*, public support was negligible at first, possibly because theatergoers were reluctant to pay $12 and $15 a ticket for a musical that had been presented without an admission charge during the summer. Word-of-mouth advertising, however, soon bolstered ticket sales and the show developed into a substantial hit that ran 627 performances.

Two Gentlemen of Verona won further recognition for its excellence by receiving a majority of the prizes and awards for the 1971–1972 season. It received the Critics Circle Award as the best musical of the season, winning with thirteen votes on the first ballot. It also won the Tony Award as best musical. John Guare and Mel Shapiro won the Tony Award for best book of a musical. In its list of outstanding new actors for the season, *Theater World* included Jonelle Allen. Drama Desk Awards were given to Galt MacDermot as outstanding composer; John Guare, outstanding lyricist; Mel Shapiro, one of the season's outstanding directors; Raul Julia and Jonelle Allen, outstanding performances; Jean Erdman, outstanding choreographer; and John Guare and Mel Shapiro, outstanding book writers. *Variety*'s poll of Drama Critics selected Jonelle Allen, best female lead in a musical; Theoni V. Aldredge, best costume designer; Galt MacDermot, best composer; and John Guare, best lyricist. In addition, Joseph Papp was cited by the Variety Poll as best director of the season for all his productions including *Two Gentlemen of Verona*. Papp also received the 1972 award given by the New York State Council on the Arts.

The finale of *Two Gentlemen of Verona* epitomized the humor, the fast-paced action, and the rhythmic music that dominated the entire production, for, in the last scene, simultaneously, on various parts of the stage, a basketball game was in progress, a group of actors were blowing large soap bubbles, and actors perched high on ramps on opposite sides of the stage tossed and caught Frisbees with amazing accuracy.

In the 1960s, mature theatergoers had laughed at the antics and harmless prattle of the adolescents in *Bye, Bye, Birdie,* a musical which satirized the teen-age hysteria over Elvis Presley. *Bye, Bye, Birdie,* however, was juvenile entertainment in comparison with *Grease,* a musical produced in February 1972, which satirized the Elvis Presley-James Dean-Sandra Dee era. *Grease* amused the young people who had grown up in the late 1950s but shocked some of their parents with the direct references to sex, pregnancy, and virginity. A number of women objected to *Grease* because the vulgarities and earthy expressions were spoken by girls as well as by boys. In the 1920s, newspaper editorials and critics would probably have condemned the musical, but in 1972, the earthy language had lost its shock value. A few critics referred to the "foul mouthed young louts," but most of the critics ignored the dialogue and praised *Grease* for its satirical portrait of the 1950s, its lampoon of rock 'n' roll music, and its sprightly choreography.

Grease by Jim Jacobs and Warren Casey, who wrote the book, music, and lyrics, had first opened off-Broadway at the Eden Theater on Second Avenue, but it operated on first-class Broadway contracts and was classified as a Broadway production. In June 1972 it was moved to the Broadway theater sector, first to the Broadhurst Theater and later to the Royale. The title referred to the grease with which the teen-agers slicked down their hair, and the musical, facetiously billed as the *No, No, Nanette* of the thirty-year-olds, dealt with the manners and morals of the high school students who grew up in the 1950s and who idolized the hip-swinging, guitar-playing singing stars and the young Hollywood film rebels. As a symbol of this idolatry, the stage set featured a blow-up of James Dean's portrait surrounded by a group of oversized pictures from high school yearbooks.

Critics singled out Barry Bostwick for his effective performance as a young man who imitates the James Dean mannerisms and strut especially when he is in an embarrassing predicament and uses the posturing as a cover-up. In addition to Bostwick, critics also liked Adrienne Barbeau (who has since become a featured player in the TV program *Maude*), Timothy Meyers, and Carole Demas.

The score received mixed reviews. Some critics called it bright; others referred to it as monotonous. Although none of the songs hit the top of the popularity list, *Grease* developed a strong following not only with people who had grown up in the 1950s but also with older and younger audiences who enjoyed the rhythmic music, the posturing and exaggerated mannerisms of the cast, and the authentic outfits of the 1950s worn in the show.

Within the next two years, two national companies in the United States and three foreign companies began extensive tours. Meanwhile, the Broadway production continued to draw well at the box office. As of March 1, 1977, *Grease* had run more than 2,070 performances, making it the longest running attraction on Broadway at the time, and the sixth longest running musical comedy in the history of the Broadway theater.

Sugar, produced by David Merrick and directed and choreographed by Gower Champion, was reminiscent of the popular musical comedies of the 1920s which critics said were "designed to please the tired businessman." It had no serious theme, moral, or message. Its sole purpose was to amuse audiences. Based on the successful motion picture *Some Like It Hot*, which had starred Marilyn Monroe, Jack Lemmon, and Tony Curtis, *Sugar* emphasized humor, particularly in the episodes in which the two leading men are disguised as women. Robert Morse and Tony Roberts, in the Lemmon and Curtis roles of Joe and Jerry, played two musicians who witness a gangster killing. To avoid being caught by the mobsters, they dress up as women and join an all-girl orchestra. Complications set in when they meet Sugar, the voluptuous vocalist with the orchestra. By the final curtain, Sugar and Jerry are in love.

Robert Morse as Joe squeezed every possible laugh out of his masquerade. Tony Roberts as Jerry was equally diverting in his disguise. Of particular interest, however, was the contrast between the two female impersonations. Roberts was somewhat brittle, a slick character constantly trying to make a play for Sugar without revealing his identity. Morse, on the other hand, was more cuddly. Women in the audience thought he was an adorable little doll whose characterization became hilarious when he began thinking and acting as if he actually were a woman. Stunning Elaine Joyce, who played Sugar, the Marilyn Monroe sex symbol role, was a clever comedienne, a gorgeous beauty ideally cast. The fourth principal character, Cyril Ritchard, was excellent as the older man (the role played by Joe E. Brown in the motion picture) who thinks Robert Morse is a delectable woman, falls in love with him, and proposes marriage.

Before *Sugar* opened in New York, however, it ran into serious problems on the tryout tour and underwent extensive revisions. Rumors circulated that the original book, which had been written by Michael Stewart, would be revised by George Axelrod. Then word spread that Neil Simon might doctor the book, but the final draft, as credited in the program, was written by Peter Stone. Rumors also circulated that Jerry Herman would write new songs to supplement the Jule Styne-Bob Merrill score, but these songs were either not written or not used in the final score, for Herman's name was not listed in the program credits.

When *Sugar* opened on Broadway in April 1972, it was a fast-paced comedy. The dancing was excellent, and the entire production was brilliantly staged. The music was typical of the jazz era of the 1920s, but offered no outstanding hit songs. Several reviewers, in fact, thought *Sugar* was most entertaining in the non-musical sequences. Clive Barnes, for example, did not like the score and thought that the cast was superior to the material. Most of the critics praised Robert Morse and Tony Roberts for their excellent performances. Elaine Joyce also charmed the critics who wisely did not try to compare her with Marilyn Monroe other than to comment that Miss Joyce was cute, well proportioned, and delightful.

Sugar drew large audiences because it was an amusing show, expertly staged, choreographed, and costumed, with expert farceurs in the leading roles. Robert Morse's appearances on several television programs, particularly one in which he showed how he had to be transformed from the man into the woman, complete with women's clothing, makeup, and wig, in a matter of minutes, was an intriguing revelation of what takes place backstage and definitely stimulated box-office sales. At the end of the first season, Robert Morse was included in the Drama Desk Awards for outstanding performances, and Elaine Joyce was included in *Theater World*'s awards for outstanding new acting talent. *Sugar* remained a popular favorite for more than a year and closed with a run of 505 performances.

Before *Don't Bother Me, I Can't Cope*, a musical revue by Micki Grant, opened in New York, it had first been presented in a slightly different version in Washington, D.C., at Ford's Theater, and in small theaters in the New York area. The revue, a collection of songs and dances with musical themes based on ballads, calypso music, Gospel music, and other musical forms, was first called a black theater presentation for blacks, but theatergoers soon discovered that it was black entertainment for both black and white audiences. It handled ghetto themes with finesse and wit. It also included songs that were strongly emotional. The entire revue was an intelligent black protest but was not bitter or militant.

The production opened on Broadway at the Playhouse Theater on April 19, 1972. The reviews ranged from good to excellent with special praise for Vinnette Carroll's direction and for the songs and dances which portrayed a variety of black experiences and were performed on a bare stage.

In some respects, *Don't Bother Me, I Can't Cope* was an adult version of *The Me Nobody Knows*, the former dealing exclusively with black themes, while the latter with ghetto problems of both blacks and whites.

Critics who preferred the second half of the program said that one major flaw in the revue was that Miss Grant did not appear in the first half. Moreover, the songs she wrote sounded better when she sang them. The critics and audiences generally agreed that *Don't Bother Me, I Can't Cope*, instead of being depressing or predominantly militant, offered a variety of moods in an entertaining, enlightening, and refreshing revue. *Don't Bother Me, I Can't Cope*, which had an excellent run of 1,065 performances, did not close until October 17, 1974.

Pippin, the first musical success produced in the 1972–1973 season, was a personal triumph for Bob Fosse who directed and choreographed the production. At the end of the season when Fosse won Tony Awards for both his direction and choreography, he became the first director to win three different major awards in one year. In addition to the Tony Awards for *Pippin*, Fosse received the Emmy Award for the television program *Liza with a Z*, starring Liza Minnelli, and an Oscar for the motion picture *Cabaret*.

The book for *Pippin*, written by Roger Hirson, dealt with Pippin, son of Charlemagne (real name, Pepin), who goes out into the world, has affairs with women, becomes involved in a war and a revolution, and finally settles down to a placid life of marriage. The story resembled somewhat the basic plot of *Candide*, but Bob Fosse converted it into a fast-paced, dancing musical. Fosse did not receive program credit as collaborator on the script, but it is generally known that he wrote much of the show. Fosse, for example, had episodes in Pippin's career performed by a group of clowns, the idea patterned closely on the *commedia dell'arte*, the Italian popular comedy developed from the sixteenth to eighteenth century in which masked entertainers improvised actions on themes or topics associated with a basic plot. To head this group of entertainers, Fosse created the role of the Leading Player, performed by Ben Vereen, who maintained contact with the audience by acting as commentator and master of ceremonies. Vereen's role was reminiscent not only of the minstrel song-and-dance man but also of the master of ceremonies in *Cabaret*. During rehearsals, Fosse, who was delighted with Vereen's performance, kept enlarging his role.

Beginning with the opening number, "Magic to Do," which dealt with the world of illusion, Fosse staged most of the production as a series of sketches, similar to a vaudeville revue with touches of a minstrel show, a magic show, and fast-stepping dance routines. Critics were not impressed with the book, but they approved of the similarity between *Pippin* and *Cabaret* in dancing, costumes, and sets. They wrote in superlatives about Bob Fosse's staging, Tony Walton's sets, and Ben Vereen's dazzling performance. Several critics also mentioned Irene Ryan, known nationally as the grandmother in the TV program *The Beverly Hillbillies*, who played an earthy grandmother. Miss Ryan, who died during the run of the show, was replaced by Dorothy Stickney. Critics also singled out John Rubenstein's performance as Pippin.

At the end of the season, both the Tony Awards and Drama Desk Awards were given to Bob Fosse as best choreographer and director; Ben Vereen, best performer in a musical; and Tony Walton, best scene designer. Jules Fisher also won a Tony Award as best lighting designer, and Patricia Zipprodt received the Drama Desk Award for best costume designer.

Pippin, which opened October 23, 1972, played to excellent houses. As of March 1, 1977, it was still drawing well and had run 1,790 performances.

A Little Night Music, a Harold Prince production with score by Stephen Sondheim, opened February 25, 1973, and received excellent reviews. The title was taken from a Mozart composition, and the book by Hugh Wheeler was based on an Ingmar Bergman motion picture *Smiles of a Summer Night*. The story, set in Sweden at the turn of the century, and as readapted for the stage, dealt with Frederick Egerman, a middle-aged attorney, whose second wife, a teen-ager, is still a virgin after eleven months of marriage. Egerman resumes an affair with his former mistress, Desiree Armfeldt, an actress, whose current lover is Count Malcolm, a dragoon. Egerman, Desiree, Count Malcolm and his wife meet at the country estate of Mme. Armfeldt, Desiree's mother, and by the final curtain, Egerman is relieved to learn that his wife and his eighteen-year-old son have fallen in love and run off. Egerman and Desiree are reunited, and the Count is reconciled to being reunited with his wife.

Most of the critics referred to *A Little Night Music* as elegant, beautiful, or the handsomest show in town. Clive Barnes called it "an adult musical." The majority of the critics praised the performances of Glynis Johns as Desiree, Hermione Gingold as Mme. Armfeldt, Len Cariou as Frederick Egerman, and D. Jamin-Bartlett, a maid, who stopped the show with her number "The Miller's Son." Boris Aronson's well-constructed sets had a mobility that enabled the action to flow from one scene to the next as panels were moved offstage while others were moved on. Critics also agreed on the excellence of Stephen Sondheim's clever rhyme schemes and score, particularly since all the songs were written as waltzes or as waltz variations.

A Little Night Music won a great many of the major prizes, including the Critics Circle and Tony Awards as the best musical of the season. Other Tony Awards were given to Hugh Wheeler for best book of a musical; Stephen Sondheim, best score; Glynis Johns, best actress in a musical; Patricia Elliott (who played the Count's wife), best supporting actress in a musical; and Florence Klotz, best costume designer. The *Theater World*'s list of most promising new performers of the season included Patricia Elliott and D. Jamin-Bartlett. Drama Desk Awards were given to Glynis Johns and Patricia Elliott for outstanding performances; Harold Prince, direction; Hugh Wheeler, book writer; D. Jamin-Bartlett, most promising new performer; and Stephen Sondheim who received more than 80 percent of the votes as best composer and more than 95 percent of the votes as best lyricist. Although Sondheim's songs were integrated into the action, one number, "Send in the Clowns," has become a favorite with many of the top-ranking vocalists in the country because it demonstrates Sondheim's skill in using an enchanting melody to emphasize dramatic lyrics.

A Little Night Music closed after a successful run of 600 performances and then was sent on tour. In April 1975, with Jean Simmons and Hermione Gingold heading the cast, it opened in London where it ran more than 400 performances.

In the 1972–1973 season, Harry Rigby, who had helped to produce the successful revival of *No, No, Nanette*, decided to revive *Irene*, another popular musical comedy of the 1920s. Rigby, with Albert Selden and Jerome Minskoff as co-producers, signed Debbie Reynolds, one of MGM's top musical stars, to play *Irene*, the distinguished Shakespearean actor John Gielgud to direct the production, comedian Billy de Wolfe to play Madame Lucy, a male fashion designer, and Patsy Kelly to play Mrs. O'Dare, Irene's mother.

The heavily publicized pre-Broadway tour of *Irene* was turbulent. Billy de Wolfe dropped out of the show because of illness and George S. Irving took over the role. The opening in Toronto was rough, and the reviews were negative. The audience was incensed at one performance when Debbie Reynolds, who was stricken with laryngitis, appeared on stage but Gielgud read her lines. In Philadelphia, the reviews were also bad. Since the producers realized that the show needed a great deal of work, they kept *Irene* on the road for three months while changes were made. Harry Rigby had adapted the book from the original libretto by Harry Tierney, but Hugh Wheeler and Joseph Stein were both brought in to readapt the book. New songs were added and one interpolated number, "I'm Always Chasing Rainbows," was dropped. Dissatisfaction with the direction and pace of the musical brought further changes when John Gielgud withdrew as director and was replaced by Gower Champion with Peter Gennaro acting as choreographer.

In the original story, Irene O'Dare, who works for an upholsterer, is sent to the home of wealthy Donald Marshall. He hires her and two of her friends to model gowns designed by Mme. Lucy, whom he has set up in business, falls in love with Irene, and marries her. In the revised version, Irene is a piano tuner, a twist in plot that gave Peter Gennaro the chance to insert a whirlwind routine with Debbie Reynolds and the male chorus dancing on top of upright pianos. The new version featured Debbie Reynolds in several spectacular dance routines, presented her as a model wearing beautiful gowns created by Hollywood designer Irene Sharaff, and, in one scene, enabled her to do her devastating imitation of the Gabor sisters by posing as a Hungarian countess. Only five of the songs from the original score were used and eight numbers were interpolated, some of them old-time favorites such as "You Made Me Love You," and "They Go Wild Simply Wild Over Me."

After several postponements, *Irene* opened at the new Minskoff Theater in New York on March 13, 1973, and surprised those critics who thought the bad out-of-town reviews indicated the show might fail. The critics thought the book was still weak but it was not a museum piece. Moreover, they hailed Miss Reynolds for her beauty, her dancing, and her energetic performance. Miss Reynolds won an Outer Circle Award, voted by out-of-town critics for distinction in the New York theater. George S. Irving as Madame Lucy won the Tony Award for best supporting actor in a musical, and *Theater World* included Monte Markham, who played Donald Marshall, in its list of promising new performers. A few critics objected to Patsy Kelly's mugging and gestures, but audiences enjoyed the Kelly characterization, particularly in her scenes with Debbie Reynolds.

Irene became one of Broadway's most popular attractions, and Debbie Reynolds, who received a percentage of the weekly gross and profits, helped build up goodwill for the show by appearing in the lobby after performances to sign autographs and souvenir booklets. Her personal box-office magnetism helped set a new all-time record Broadway gross for a nonholiday week with a total of $143,567.

When Debbie Reynolds was ready to leave the New York cast to start a national road tour, she selected Jane Powell, who also had starred in MGM musicals, as her replacement. Gower Champion declined to direct Miss Powell, but Debbie Reynolds helped coach her for the role. The dance routines were reportedly changed for Miss Powell, and the song "I'm Always Chasing Rainbows" was put back into the show. The critics liked Jane Powell's performance, and *Irene* continued playing to large audiences for 604 performances.

Irene should have been a financial success, for, in addition to breaking records in New York, Miss Reynolds set a new all-time high for a week's gross, $242,867, for eight performances in Chicago. Her total gross for two weeks in Chicago was $479,553, which was also believed to be a new record. Yet, when *Irene* ended its run in New York, *Variety* reported that it had closed with a loss. There were also reports that the financing of *Irene* was under investigation to discover why the production had not shown a profit or why the backers had not received any payment on their investment. It was known that Miss Reynold's percentage had been high, that Gielgud, despite his withdrawal from the production, was still receiving payment, and that the extensive revisions and changes out of town had raised production costs. To the public, however, the response both in New York and on the road indicated that the revival of *Irene* was a popular hit, and the record-breaking grosses indicated that if there were a loss, it was due to ill-advised management of funds and not to the lack of public support or dissatisfaction with the show.

Raisin, a black-oriented musical, was similar to *Don't Bother Me, I Can't Cope* in that it was persuasive rather than militant in depicting the black man's struggle for a decent home in the pre-civil rights period. Robert Nemiroff and Charlotte Zaltzberg, who wrote the book for the musical, based it on the play *A Raisin in the Sun* by Lorraine Hansberry which was produced in 1959. Miss Hansberry's drama starred Sidney Poitier as Walter Lee Younger and dealt with a black family in the Chicago tenements. Lena Younger, Walter's mother, uses her late husband's insurance money to make a down payment on a new home in a white neighborhood. Walter insists that he be allowed to manage the rest of the money, and when Lena turns it over to him, he loses all of it to a swindler. To recover his loss, Walter is ready to accept money from the people who are ready to buy the house because they don't want Lena and her family to move into their neighborhood. When Lena insists that Walter explain to his young son Travis why he is going to accept the money, Walter suddenly matures. He tells the man making the offer that the Youngers do not want their money, that they will move into their new home, and that he, his wife, and his mother will all work to meet payments on the house. Although Poitier had the starring role, the play epitomized Lena's desire to find truth and dignity in her life, and when Poitier left the cast, Claudia MacNeil, who played Lena, was quickly elevated to stardom.

The musical version kept to the original plot, but the role of Lena was emphasized without minimizing the entire family's struggle to get out of the black ghetto. *Raisin* was first presented at the Arena stage in Washington, D.C., and then was remounted and restaged for the Broadway production which opened October 18, 1973. Most of the critics praised Virginia Capers' performance as Lena and said the success of *Raisin* depended largely upon her. At the end of the season, Miss Capers won the Tony Award for best actress in a musical. Running a close second in the reviews was Ralph Carter, the personable young lad who played Travis, Walter's son. Carter has since become one of the leading players in the television program *Good Times*. In spite of the shift in emphasis to Lena, Joe Morton as Walter Lee gave an effective performance, particularly in the difficult scene in which he breaks down and cries onstage. Critics who commented on the episode praised Morton's ability to make the scene effective without making it seem exaggerated or maudlin. In general, most of the reviewers liked the musical adaptation and the cast.

In addition to the Tony Award, *Raisin* received further recognition from *Theater World*, which included Joe Morton, Ralph Carter, and Ernestine Jackson, who played Ruth, Walter's wife, in its list of promising new performers both on- and off-Broadway during the 1973–1974 season. *Raisin* was more successful than its predecessor, *Purlie*, in attracting Broadway audiences to see a production dealing with blacks and their struggle for recognition.

When *Raisin* closed in December 1975, it had run 847 performances. It then began a lengthy, highly profitable road tour. By November 1976 it had grossed over $4 million and had established several new records. On its opening night in Hartford, Connecticut, it set an attendance record of 1,400 for an election night. In Detroit, it set a record gross of $550,000 during its run of eight weeks. In San Francisco, it set a house record at the Orpheum Theater of $147,000. In commenting on the road tour, *Variety* reported that *Raisin* was booked through January 1978.

The Magic Show, which opened May 28, 1974, set a different type of record on Broadway. Magicians and magic shows had always been popular attractions in the theater. For years, such famous illusionists as Thurston and Blackstone toured the United States with their magic revues. Harry Houdini, the famous escape artist, was a headline attraction in vaudeville houses. The illusionists were also successful in nightclubs, but none of them ever played a long-running engagement on the New York stage.

The Magic Show, however, set a precedent. Although it was classified as a musical comedy, it was basically a showcase for a new master of illusion, Doug Henning. The production followed the show-within-a-show formula by combining a musical comedy with a magic act. The story involves a nightclub owner who hires a new magician to replace an old act, and the new performer becomes a sensation with his amazing bag of tricks. Most of the critics either minimized or ignored the story line and musical comedy features but wrote in superlatives about the magician, Doug Henning, who embellished familiar tricks with new illusions that completely baffled audiences. Not only did he saw a woman in half but he also separated the two parts and took them to opposite sides of the stage. He then went one step further by dividing a woman into three parts and then separated the parts. Henning's amazing feats not only attracted people who had seen Thurston and Blackstone but also the public which had been interested in such television shows as *Houdini* and the Bill Bixby series *The Magician*.

When Henning began appearing on television programs and performing his tricks using such subjects as Liza Minnelli as the woman sawed in half, his amazing skill brought more people to the theater. In later television specials in which he demonstrated that he was equally adept at performing several of Harry Houdini's famous escape routines, he had the assistance of such performers as Gene Kelly and Michael Landon, and again he performed seemingly impossible illusions with Joey Heatherton. Each of Henning's television appearances seemed to stimulate interest in the stage production *The Magic Show*.

A road company with Peter DePaula in the Henning role opened a prosperous tour in December 1974, and when Joe Abaldo replaced Doug Henning in the New York company in March 1976, *The Magic Show* continued to draw excellent audiences. On March 1, 1977, it had run 1,116 performances and gave no indication that the show would soon be closing.

Shenandoah, a musical based on the 1965 motion picture *Shenandoah*, written by James Lee Barrett and starring James Stewart, was first produced during the summer of 1974 at the Goodspeed Opera House in East Haddam, Connecticut. The success of the summer booking prompted the producers to bring it to Broadway with the same cast headed by John Cullum, who played Charlie Anderson, a widowed farmer in the Shenandoah Valley during the Civil War. Anderson refuses to let his sons be dragged off to the war until his youngest son is kidnapped by Union troops. His oldest son and his son's wife are killed, and, before the play ends, another son is killed. The ending is sentimental, even tearful, but not maudlin.

During the out-of-town tryouts, *Shenandoah* was not hailed as a great musical, but it was called good family-oriented entertainment with a tender, old-fashioned story, a serious theme, and an emotional appeal. When the musical opened in New York in January 1975, the reviews were mixed. Walter Kerr, who liked the show, thought it was beautiful and moving. Other critics thought its simplicity and wholesomeness were a refreshing contrast to the decadence and immorality in other musical productions. Those critics who were not impressed with *Shenandoah* thought there were not enough dance routines and that too much emphasis was placed upon sentiment. On the other hand, most theatergoers liked the moments of tenderness such as the scenes in which Charlie Anderson talks to his dead wife. It was readily apparent that a number of people in the audience were crying during several of the emotional scenes. Critics and audiences almost unanimously agreed that John Cullum was excellent in the leading role. In a period when actors rather than singers were playing leads in musicals and talking rather than singing the lyrics, it was refreshing to hear Cullum who, with his robust voice, could handle the rhythmic numbers and make the sentimental songs sound convincing rather than maudlin. The supporting cast members, all of whom had been in the original production at the Goodspeed Opera House, gave Cullum excellent support.

Shenandoah drew large if not capacity audiences, and word-of-mouth advertising from contented theatergoers kept it running profitably. At the end of the first season, John Cullum not only won a Tony Award as best actor in a musical but also received one of the Drama Desk Awards for outstanding contribution to the 1974–1975 season. Despite the comments of some critics that the book was old-fashioned, the co-authors, James Lee Barrett, who also wrote the original screenplay, Peter Udell, and Philip Rose won the Tony Award for best book of a musical. Outer Critics Circle Awards were also given to John Cullum and to Chip Ford, who played one of the sons. The combination of sentiment, wholesomeness, and pacifism helped *Shenandoah* draw well even after John Cullum left the cast, and, as of March 1, 1977, it had run over 870 performances.

The Wiz, based on Frank L. Baum's book *The Wonderful Wizard of Oz,* with music and lyrics by Charlie Small and book by William F. Brown, was the most successful all-black musical presented in the 1970s. It was also the one which seemed doomed to failure, for on January 5, 1975, its opening night in New York, a closing notice was posted backstage. The advance ticket sale had been negligible, for the show had run into serious problems on the road. Geoffrey Holder, who had designed the costumes, was brought in as director to replace Gilbert Moses. After Holder assured the entire company that no one was to be fired and that they would rework the production, he began revamping the show with George Faison as choreographer.

The tornado routine, which came in the opening scene, had started with a dancer dressed in black, whirling across the empty stage. A strip of black material, attached to her hair, swirled up into the lofts and, as the dancer spun across the stage, the strip of material grew longer. The chorus moved quickly on stage, catching the ribbon, keeping it moving, and preventing it from becoming entangled until the dancer was in the center of a fast, whirling sea of black. Even though the symbolic tornado effect had made the routine a show stopper, the tornado was dropped during the road trip, but Holder shrewdly reinstated it. He also changed the costume for Stephanie Mills, who played Dorothy. Instead of letting her wear a nondescript outfit, he made her more appealing by having her wear a little girl's white dress. He also made certain that the costumes he had designed did not impede the dance routines. The yellow brick road was represented by four dancers wearing blonde Afro wigs and carrying yellow poles, and as Dorothy and her friends danced down the yellow brick road, they did so between the symbolic dancers. Holder's clever costumes for the Munschkins made them look half their height as they sat on small tables with wide, voluminous skirts covering their legs. The Wiz was costumed to represent a black superdude wearing glittering clothes to a prize fight at Madison Square Garden.

In spite of the revisions, the skeptical producers had posted the closing notice. *The Wiz* had lost a great deal of money on its road tour, and there was little reserve left to attempt a run in New York. The press agents, however, made an all-out effort to build a demand for tickets and immediately began contacting radio and television talent scouts to plug their show on the air. Tickets for *The Wiz* were sold at half price since the cut-rate ticket deal had worked well for other black productions. Moreover, the producers contacted people who might be interested in bringing special groups of people, who ordinarily would not patronize the Broadway theater, to see *The Wiz*. They also managed to get an excellent booking on the *New York AM* show. This frenzied concentration paid off, for at the end of the first week, the Saturday matinee was a sell-out. The producers then sponsored a television commercial to plug the show; this immediately brought results as gross box-office receipts soon spurted to over $100,000 a week.

Audience reaction also helped ticket sales. Theatergoers who had come out of curiosity to see how badly the Judy Garland motion-picture version had been distorted found that *The Wiz* was least interesting when it faithfully followed the film but that it sparkled with excitement when Holder's costumes and directorial touches as well as George Faison's choreography dominated the stage. Critics were pleased that the music was soft rock rather than the brassy, unmelodic hard rock 'n' roll. Instead of trying to compare Stephanie Mills with Judy Garland, audiences soon found that the moment Miss Mills began to sing, she developed a vibrancy of her own, and when she began dancing, she sparkled.

At the end of the season, *The Wiz* won the Tony Award as best musical. Tony Awards were also given to Charlie Small, best music and lyrics; Ted Ross, best supporting actor in a musical; Dee Dee Bridgewater, best supporting actress in a musical; Geoffrey Holder, best director of a musical; Geoffrey Holder, best costume designer; George Faison, best choreographer. Geoffrey Holder, Charlie Small, Ted Ross, and George Faison also won Drama Desk Awards. As of March 1, 1977, *The Wiz* was a well established hit which had run over 867 performances and was still attracting large audiences both in New York and on a national road tour.

Chicago, a musical with book by Fred Ebb and Bob Fosse, was based on a play by Maurine Watkins, produced in 1926, dealing with the gangster era in Chicago. Roxie Hart, the principal character, murders her lover, but a conniving lawyer builds up sympathy for her and wins her an acquittal. Bob Fosse, who not only co-authored but also directed and choreographed the musical version, used devices and gimmicks he had incorporated in some of his other productions. In *Pippin* he had expanded a simple plot into a dancing extravaganza, and in *Chicago* he expanded Miss Watkins' play into a jazz-age spectacular with emphasis on dancing and songs epitomized by such numbers as "Razzle Dazzle" and "All That Jazz." He also used the *commedia dell'arte* technique just as he had in *Pippin*. In depicting the corruptness of society, the gangsters, molls, and murderesses in the 1920s, he re-created the decadence of *Cabaret*. Even the costumes by Patricia Zipprodt were reminiscent of those used in *Cabaret* with the girls wearing black stockings, red garters, and garish, abbreviated costumes.

The set, created by Tony Walton, was constructed of shiny panels, and the band was perched onstage on top of a large center cylinder. The band vocalists singing at the microphones and the band playing under a glittering globe of twirling mirrors were reminiscent of the ballrooms in the 1920s.

In the musical version, Roxie is striving for a career in show business if she is acquitted. The musical included a second murderess, Velma, played by Chita Rivera, who has been in show business and who keeps fighting to get more attention than Roxie. At the finale, both Roxie and Velma appear onstage as a team. Critics pointed out that neither the story nor the characters are likable. The tone of the plot development is satirical; Roxie and Velma are unsympathetic, vulgar, heartless murderesses; and Billy Flynn, their conniving attorney, is willing to do anything for a fast dollar.

Chicago was billed as "a vaudeville," for Fosse included vaudeville sketches, songs, and dance routines held together by the slight plot. This format permitted Chita Rivera and Gwen Verdon, both superb dancers, to do show-stopping production numbers such as Miss Rivera's "All That Jazz." Gwen Verdon, who pretends she is pregnant to win sympathy from the newspaper reporters, sings "Me and My Baby" assisted by six male dancers wearing baby bonnets and sucking their thumbs. In the courtroom scene, Miss Verdon sits on Jerry Orbach's knee acting like a dummy while Orbach, the ventriloquist, does all the talking. Orbach also has several vaudeville routines. In one he does an imitation of a suspendered, bespectacled Clarence Darrow. In another Orbach does a semi-striptease to the song "All I Care About," backed by chorus girls waving feathered fans. At periodic intervals, the dancers strutted, glided, or shuffled onstage in an assortment of bizarre, revealing costumes.

On August 8, 1975, Liza Minnelli took over Gwen Verdon's role for five weeks while Miss Verdon underwent surgery for a throat ailment. Miss Minnelli, who had worked with Bob Fosse on her television special *Liza with a Z* and the motion-picture version of *Cabaret*, insisted that she did not want billing for the role outside the theater or in the Playbill program. The dances were reportedly modified for her, and her five-week engagement was a complete sell-out. The producer did not want the show reviewed again, but Clive Barnes argued that Miss Minnelli's appearance was news. He covered the show as did other critics who made little or no comparison between Gwen Verdon and Liza Minnelli other than to comment that Miss Verdon was primarily a dancer; Miss Minnelli, a singer.

Despite the sleazy plot and unsavory characters, *Chicago*, which *Variety*'s reporter in Boston said was reminiscent of shows for the "tired businessman," became a hit in New York. On March 1, 1977, it had run 699 performances.

The idea for *A Chorus Line*, the most widely acclaimed musical of the 1970s, was conceived by Michael Bennett, the director and choreographer of the production. Bennett first met with twenty-four dancers for two long taping sessions in which they discussed their backgrounds, their problems, and their frustrations. Bennett then turned the tapes over to Nicholas Dante, one of the dancers involved in the sessions, who then collaborated with James Kirkwood in writing a play based partially on the taped material. Some time later, Marvin Hamlisch and Edward Kleban were brought in to write the music and lyrics.

A Chorus Line established precedents in plot, development, and staging. The setting is deceptively simple, for the action takes place on a bare stage with large mirrors as backdrops, allowing both the audiences and the dancers to see themselves. Twenty-eight young chorus dancers are auditioning for a director who will hire only eight of them. As the musical progresses, he cuts the number down to nineteen and finally to eight.

The final script expanded the original taped interviews. In order to learn more about the applicants, several of whom might be given a few lines of dialogue in the production, the director asks the dancers to tell him about their background and problems. One dancer talks about an alcoholic father, another about a domineering mother, still others about sexual experiences, religious beliefs, or training for the ballet. The story goes beyond character revelation, for it also presents such problems as the tragedy of a dancer who breaks his leg and can no longer perform. Although most of the dancers have their individual moments, the story of Cassie, played by Donna McKechnie, is the most prominent. Cassie, who has one of the best routines in the production, "The Music and the Mirror," had been a successful dancer. She also has had an affair with Zach, the director, who now opposes her returning to the chorus. When the number of applicants is narrowed down, however, Cassie is included in the final eight.

A Chorus Line, produced by Joseph Papp for the New York Shakespeare Festival Public Theatre, opened off-Broadway on April 15, 1975, at the Newman Theatre. Shortly after the opening, *A Chorus Line* won the Critics Circle Award as the best musical of the season. The Joseph Maharam Foundation award for distinguished stage design by an American was given to Robin Wagner. The critics wrote in superlatives, not only for the story, the score, and the choreography but also for the talented cast and the general production. Edward Kleban was cited for his lyrics, which helped to develop the characterizations. Marvin Hamlisch's music was praised for its rhythmic quality, its unobtrusiveness in not detracting from the plot, and its melodic excellence in such numbers as "What I Did for Love," which has become the hit song of the score. Although the story deals with dancers and their problems, its appeal was not limited to people familiar with the New York theater, for it signified the struggle of all young people searching for success, often hampered by obstacles that they cannot overcome. Some of the critics singled out a few of the performers such as Donna McKechnie, Sammy Williams as the dancer who breaks a leg, and Priscilla Lopez who sings "What I Did for Love," but the critics generally agreed that the performers, just like the dancers in *A Chorus Line*, blended together to create a unified impression of excellence.

On July 25, 1975, *A Chorus Line* was moved to the Shubert Theater on Broadway where it became the most successful musical of the season. The demand for tickets was so great that, for the first time in years, rumors began circulating about under-the-counter scalping and hot ticket sales. At the end of the season, it won nine Tony Awards including one for best musical. The other Tony Awards were given to James Kirkwood and Nicholas Dante for best book of a musical; Marvin Hamlisch and Edward Kleban, best score; Donna McKechnie, best actress in a musical; Sammy Williams, best featured actor in a musical; Carole Bishop, best featured actress in a musical; Michael Bennett, best director of a musical; Tharon Musser, best lighting; and Michael Bennett and Bob Avion, best choreography. Drama Desk Awards were given to James Kirkwood, Nicholas Dante, Marvin Hamlisch, Carole Bishop, and Donna McKechnie. Obie Awards were won by Marvin Hamlisch, Edward Kleban, Sammy Williams, and Priscilla Lopez. A special Obie was also awarded to Michael Bennett, James Kirkwood, and Nicholas Dante for book and direction. In addition, *A Chorus Line* won the Pulitzer Prize for best drama in the 1975–1976 season, the first musical to win that distinction since 1961–1962 when *How to Succeed in Business Without Really Trying* received the Pulitzer Prize.

As of March 1, 1977, *A Chorus Line* was playing to capacity houses in New York where it had run over 640 performances. Two road companies were also playing to standing-room only, and a London company was enjoying a successful run.

It is impossible to predict the future of the American musical theater, for higher ticket prices and the competition of free television entertainment have affected theater attendance. The importance of box-office stars in establishing musical hits, however, cannot be minimized. Ethel Merman has been responsible for the success of more musical comedies than most of her contemporaries. Only two productions in which she appeared ran fewer than 200 performances. *Panama Hattie, Call Me Madam, Annie Get Your Gun,* and *Gypsy* all ran 500 or more performances. Even more important, Miss Merman remained with these hit shows in New York until they completed their long runs. As a general rule, however, when a production has run 1,000 or more performances, the original stars have already left the cast. A show that runs three or more years, therefore, must be sustained by the strength of the production rather than by its cast.

The top price of $17.50 and $20 a ticket for some musicals has made the public more selective. There are such long-running exceptions as *Grease,* which has already been playing for more than five years. *A Chorus Line* is the most successful musical of the decade, but it would be purely speculative to estimate how long either of these productions will run.

People of moderate means have become conditioned to the feeling that Broadway musicals, with their escalating prices, are catering to executives with unlimited expense accounts or to out-of-towners who are willing to order tickets directly from the box office months in advance and not quibble about less desirable seat locations or changes in cast.

A perplexing situation has developed, therefore, for most musical comedies must run longer in the 1970s than was necessary in earlier decades to be financial successes. The number of musicals that will run 500 or more performances in the 1970s may include a larger number of financial failures if production costs and ticket prices keep rising and theater attendance does not improve.

Bibliography

Newspaper articles (particularly *The New York Times* drama and magazine sections); magazine articles, particularly in *Theatre Arts,* and *Stage;* printed texts.

Best Plays series from 1894 to 1967, edited by G. P. Sherwood and John A. Chapman (1884–1899), Burns Mantle, G. P. Sherwood (1894–1899), Burns Mantle (1919–1920 to 1946–1947), John A. Chapman (1947–1948 to 1951–1952), Louis Kronenberger (1952–1953 to 1959–1960), Henry Hewes (1960–1961 to 1962–1963), Otis L. Guernsey, Jr. (1963–1964 to 1975–1976). New York: Dodd Mead.

Blum, Daniel C., editor *Theatre World* (1944–1945 to 1965–1966). New York: Crown.

Chapman, John A. *Theatre* (annual volumes from 1953). New York: Random House.

Nathan, George J. *The Theatre Book of the Year* (from 1942–1943 to 1949–1950). New York: Knopf.

New York Critics Reviews. N. Y. Critics Reviews Inc. (from 1940 to 1967).

Variety (from 1925).

The following books have also provided source material:

Atkinson, Brooks, *Broadway Scrapbook.* New York: Theatre Arts, 1947.

Baral, Robert, *Revue.* New York: Fleet, 1962.

Blum, Daniel C., *Pictorial History of the American Theatre 1860–1960.* Philadelphia: Chilton, 1960.

Churchill, Allen, *The Great White Way.* New York: Dutton, 1962.

Ewen, David, *American Musical Theater.* New York: Henry Holt and Co., 1958.

Engel, Lehman, *The American Musical Theater.* New York: CBS Legacy, 1967.

Gaver, Jack, *Curtain Calls*. New York: Dodd, Mead, 1949.

———, *Season In, Season Out*. New York: Hawthorn, 1966.

Green, Abel, and Laurie, Joe., Jr., *Show Biz*. New York: Holt, 1951.

Green, Stanley, *Encyclopedia of the Musical Theatre*, New York: Dodd Mead, 1976.

———, *The World of Musical Comedy*, New York: Ziff-Davis, 1960.

Hoyt, Charles H., *Five Plays*, edited by Douglas L. Hunt. New Jersey: Princeton University Press, 1941.

Katkov, Norman, *The Fabulous Fanny*. New York: Knopf, 1953.

Langner, Lawrence, *The Magic Curtain*. New York: Dutton, 1951.

———, *The Play's the Thing*. New York: Putnam, 1960.

Lee, Gypsy Rose, *Gypsy*. New York: Dell, 1959.

Lewine, Richard, and Simon, Alfred, *Encyclopedia of Theatre Music*. New York: Random House, 1961.

Mattfeld, Julius, *Variety Music Cavalcade 1620–1961*. New York: Prentice-Hall, 1962.

McSpadden, J. Walker, *Operas and Musical Comedies*. New York: Crowell, 1946.

Morehouse, Ward, *Matinee Tomorrow*. New York: Whittlesey House, 1949.

Nathan, George J., *Encyclopaedia of the Theater*. New York: Knopf, 1940.

———, *The Entertainment of a Nation*. New York: Knopf, 1940.

———, *The Morning After the First Night*. New York: Knopf, 1938.

———, *The Theatre of the Moment*. New York: Knopf, 1950.

Rodgers and Hammerstein Fact Book (published by Rodgers and Hammerstein) 1955.

Sobel, Bernard, *The Theatre Handbook and Digest of Plays*. New York: Crown, 1946.

Taubman, Howard, *The Making of the American Theatre*. New York: Coward-McCann, 1965.

Webster's Biographical Dictionary. New York: G. C. Merriam, 1943.

Zolotow, Maurice, *No People Like Show People*. New York: Random House, 1951.

Appendix
The Long-Running Musicals

As of May 1, 1972, the following musical productions had run for 500 or more performances. (*Abbreviations:* PP = Pulitzer Prize drama. CC = Critics' Circle selection as best musical of the season. * = Still running March 1, 1977.)

3,242 PERFORMANCES   *Fiddler on the Roof* (CC)

Book by Joseph Stein; music by Jerry Bock; lyrics by Sheldon Harnick; based on stories by Sholom Aleichem.

Produced by Harold Prince at the Imperial Theatre, September 22, 1964. Directed and choreographed by Jerome Robbins; settings by Boris Aronson; costumes by Patricia Zipprodt; lighting by Jean Rosenthal.

ORIGINAL CAST INCLUDED: Zero Mostel, Maria Karnilova, Joanna Merlin, Julia Migenes, Tanya Everett, Marilyn Rogers, Linda Ross, Beatrice Arthur, Austin Pendleton, Bert Convy, Michael Granger, Joe Ponazecki.

PRINCIPAL SONGS: "Tradition," "Matchmaker, Matchmaker," "If I Were a Rich Man," "Sabbath Prayer," "To Life," "Miracle of Miracles," "The Tailor, Motel Kamzoil," "Sunrise, Sunset," "Now I Have Everything," "Do You Love Me?," "I Just Heard," "Far from the Home I Love," "Anatevka."

2,844 PERFORMANCES   *Hello, Dolly!* (CC)

Book by Michael Stewart; music and lyrics by Jerry Herman; based on *The Matchmaker,* by Thornton Wilder.

Produced by David Merrick at the St. James Theatre, January 16, 1964. Directed and choreographed by Gower Champion; assistant director, Lucia Victor; special assistant, Marge Champion; scenery by Oliver Smith; costumes by Freddy Wittop; lighting by Jean Rosenthal.

ORIGINAL CAST INCLUDED: Carol Channing, David Burns, Eileen Brennan, Charles Nelson Reilly, Sondra Lee, Jerry Dodge, Alice Playten, Igors Gavon.

PRINCIPAL SONGS: "I Put My Hand In," "It Takes a Woman," "Put on Your Sunday Clothes," "Ribbons Down My Back," "Motherhood," "Dancing," "Before the Parade Passes By," "Elegance," "Hello, Dolly," "It Only Takes a Moment," "So Long Dearie."

2,717 PERFORMANCES *My Fair Lady* (CC)

Book and lyrics by Alan Jay Lerner; music by Frederick Loewe; based on *Pygmalion,* by George Bernard Shaw.

Produced by Herman Levin at the Mark Hellinger Theatre, March 15, 1956. Production staged by Moss Hart; choreography by Hanya Holm; settings by Oliver Smith; costumes by Cecil Beaton; lighting by Feder.

ORIGINAL CAST INCLUDED: Rex Harrison, Julie Andrews, Stanley Holloway, Robert Coote, Cathleen Nesbitt, John Michael King, Viola Roache.

PRINCIPAL SONGS: "Why Can't the English?," "Wouldn't It Be Loverly?," "With a Little Bit of Luck," "I'm an Ordinary Man," "Just You Wait," "The Rain in Spain," "I Could Have Danced All Night," "On the Street Where You Live," "Get Me to the Church on Time," "A Hymn to Him," "Show Me," "Without You," "I've Grown Accustomed to Her Face."

2,329 PERFORMANCES
Man of La Mancha (CC)

Book by Dale Wasserman; music by Mitch Leigh; lyrics by Joe Darion; suggested by the life and works of Miguel de Cervantes y Saavedra.

Produced by Albert W. Selden and Hal James at ANTA Washington Square Theatre, November 22, 1965. Directed by Albert Marre; choreography by Jack Cole; scenery and lighting by Howard Bay; costumes by Howard Bay and Patton Campbell.

ORIGINAL CAST INCLUDED: Richard Kiley, Irving Jacobson, Joan

Diener, Ray Middleton, Robert Rounseville, Jon Cypher, Mimi Turque, Eleanor Knapp.

PRINCIPAL SONGS: "Man of La Mancha," "It's All the Same," "Dulcinea," "I'm Only Thinking of Him," "I Really Like Him," "What Does He Want of Me?," "Little Bird, Little Bird," "Barber's Song," "Golden Helmet," "To Each His Dulcinea," "The Quest (The Impossible Dream)," "Knight of the Woeful Countenance," "Aldonza," "The Knight of the Mirrors," "A Little Gossip," "The Psalm."

2,248 PERFORMANCES   *Oklahoma!* (†)

Book and lyrics by Oscar Hammerstein II; music by Richard Rodgers; based on *Green Grow the Lilacs,* by Lynn Riggs.

Produced by the Theatre Guild at the St. James Theatre, March 31, 1943. Direction by Rouben Mamoulian; choreography by Agnes de Mille; settings by Lemuel Ayers; costumes by Miles White.

ORIGINAL CAST INCLUDED: Alfred Drake, Joan Roberts, Celeste Holm, Betty Garde, Joan McCracken, Bambi Linn, Howard da Silva, Joseph Buloff.

PRINCIPAL SONGS: "Oh, What a Beautiful Mornin'," "I Cain't Say No." "Kansas City," "Oklahoma," "People Will Say We're in Love," "The Surrey with the Fringe on Top," "Out of My Dreams," "Pore Jud Is Daid," "All er Nothin'," "The Farmer and the Cowman," "Many a New Day."

2,070 PERFORMANCES*   *Grease*

Book, music, and lyrics by Jim Jacobs and Warren Casey.

Produced by Kenneth Waissman and Maxine Fox in association with Anthony D'Amato at the Eden Theater, February 14, 1972. Directed by Tom Moore; musical numbers and dances staged by Patricia Birch; scenery by Douglas W. Schmidt; costumes by Carrie F. Robbins; lighting by Karl Eigsti.

ORIGINAL CAST INCLUDED: Barry Bostwick, Carole Demas, Adrienne Barbeau, Dorothy Leon, Ilene Kristen, Tom Harris, Garn Stephens, Katie Hanley, James Canning, Walter Bobbie, Timothy Meyers, Jim Borrelli, Marya Small, Don Billett, Alan Paul, Kathi Moss.

PRINCIPAL SONGS: "Alma Mater," "Summer Nights," "Those Magic

† Also listed as 2,212 performances.

Changes," "Freddy, My Love," "Greased Lightnin'," "Mooning," "Look at Me, I'm Sandra Dee," "We Go Together," "Shakin' at the High School Hop," "It's Raining on Prom Night," "Born to Hand-Jive," "Beauty School Dropout," "Alone at a Drive-in Movie," "Rock 'n' Roll Party Queen," "All Choked Up."

1,925 PERFORMANCES
South Pacific (PP) (CC) (†)

Music by Richard Rodgers; lyrics by Oscar Hammerstein II; book by Oscar Hammerstein II and Joshua Logan; based on *Tales of the South Pacific,* by James A. Michener.

Produced by Richard Rodgers and Oscar Hammerstein II in association with Leland Hayward and Joshua Logan at the Majestic Theatre, April 7, 1949. Production staged by Joshua Logan; sets by Jo Mielziner; costumes by Motley.

ORIGINAL CAST INCLUDED: Mary Martin, Ezio Pinza, William Tabbert, Juanita Hall, Betta St. John, Myron McCormick, Martin Wolfson.

PRINCIPAL SONGS: "Dites-Moi," "A Cockeyed Optimist," "Some Enchanted Evening," "Bloody Mary," "There Is Nothin' Like a Dame," "Bali Ha'i," "I'm Gonna Wash That Man Right Outa My Hair," "I'm in Love with a Wonderful Guy," "Younger than Springtime," "Happy Talk," "Honey Bun," "Carefully Taught," "This Nearly Was Mine."

1,790 PERFORMANCES* Pippin

Book by Roger O. Hirson; music and lyrics by Stephen Schwartz.

Produced by Stuart Ostrow at the Imperial Theater, October 23, 1972. Directed and choreographed by Bob Fosse; scenery by Tony Walton; costumes by Patricia Zipprodt; lighting by Jules Fisher.

ORIGINAL CAST INCLUDED: Ben Vereen, John Rubenstein, Eric Berry, Leland Palmer, Irene Ryan, Christopher Chadman, John Mineo, Roger Hamilton, Richard Korthaze, Paul Solen, Gene Foote, Jill Clayburgh, Shane Nickerson.

PRINCIPAL SONGS: "Magic to Do," "Corner of the Sky," "Welcome

† Also listed as 1,694 performances.

Home," "War Is a Science," "Glory," "Simple Joys," "No Time at All," "With You," "Spread a Little Sunshine," "Morning Glow," "On the Right Track," "Kind of Woman," "Extraordinary," "Love Song."

1,750 PERFORMANCES   *Hair*

Book and lyrics by Gerome Ragni and James Rado; music by Galt MacDermot.

Produced by Michael Butler at the Biltmore Theater, April 29, 1968. Directed by Tom O'Horgan; dance director, Julie Arenal; musical director, Galt MacDermot; scenery by Robin Wagner; costumes by Nancy Potts; lighting by Jules Fisher; sound by Robert Kiernan.

ORIGINAL CAST INCLUDED: James Rado, Gerome Ragni, Lynn Kellogg, Lamont Washington, Melba Moore, Ronald Dyson, Steve Curry, Sally Eaton, Shelley Plimpton, Diane Keaton, Lorri Davis, Suzannah Norstrand, Leata Galloway, Steve Gamet, Paul Jabara, Natalie Mosco, Emmaretta Marks, Robert I. Rubinsky, Jonathan Kramer.

PRINCIPAL SONGS: "Aquarius," "Donna," "Hashish," "Sodomy," "Colored Spade," "Manchester," "Ain't Got No," "I Believe in Love," "Air," "Initials," "I Got Life," "Going Down," "Hair," "My Conviction," "Easy to Be Hard," "Hung," "Don't Put It Down," "Frank Mills," "Hare Krishna," "Where Do I Go?," "Electric Blues," "Black Boys," "White Boys," "Walking in Space," "Abie Baby," "Prisoners in Niggertown," "What a Piece of Work Is Man," "Good Morning Starshine," "The Bed," "The Flesh Failures."

1,508 PERFORMANCES   *Mame*

Book by Jerome Lawrence and Robert E. Lee; music and lyrics by Jerry Herman; based on *Auntie Mame,* by Patrick Dennis, and dramatic adaptation by Jerome Lawrence and Robert E. Lee.

Produced by Robert Fryer, Lawrence Carr, Sylvia Harris and Joseph Harris at the Winter Garden Theatre, May 24, 1966. Directed by Gene Saks; dances and musical numbers staged by Onna White; scenery by William and Jean Eckart; costumes by Robert Mackintosh; lighting by Tharon Musser.

ORIGINAL CAST INCLUDED: Angela Lansbury, Beatrice Arthur, Frankie Michaels, Jane Connell, Sab Shimono, Charles Braswell, Jerry Lanning, Diana Walker, Johanna Douglas, John C. Becher, Diane Coupe, Michael Maitland.

PRINCIPAL SONGS: "St. Bridget," "It's Today," "Open a New Window," "The Man in the Moon," "My Best Girl," "We Need a Little Christmas," "Mame," "Bosom Buddies," "Gooch's Song," "That How Young I Feel," "If He Walked into My Life."

1,443 PERFORMANCES *The Sound of Music*

Book by Howard Lindsay and Russel Crouse; lyrics by Oscar Hammerstein II; music by Richard Rodgers; suggested by *The Trapp Family Singers,* by Maria Augusta Trapp.

Produced by Leland Hayward, Richard Halliday, Richard Rodgers, and Oscar Hammerstein II at the Lunt-Fontanne Theatre, November 16, 1959. Staged by Vincent J. Donehue; settings by Oliver Smith; musical numbers staged by Joe Layton; costumes by Lucinda Ballard; Mary Martin's clothes by Mainbocher; lighting by Jean Rosenthal.

ORIGINAL CAST INCLUDED: Mary Martin, Theodore Bikel, Patricia Neway, Marion Marlowe, Kurt Kasznar, Brian Davies, Muriel O'Malley, Lauri Peters.

PRINCIPAL SONGS: "The Sound of Music," "Maria," "My Favorite Things," "Do Re Mi," "You Are Sixteen," "The Lonely Goatherd," "How Can Love Survive?," "So Long, Farewell," "Climb Every Mountain," "No Way to Stop It," "Ordinary Couple," "Edelweiss."

1,417 PERFORMANCES
How to Succeed in Business Without Really Trying (PP) (CC)

Book by Abe Burrows, Jack Weinstock, and Willie Gilbert; music and lyrics by Frank Loesser; based on *How to Succeed in Business Without Really Trying,* by Shepherd Mead.

Produced by Cy Feuer and Ernest Martin, in association with Frank Productions, Inc., at the Forty-Sixth St. Theatre, October 14, 1961. Staged by Abe Burrows; musical staging by Bob Fosse;

settings and lighting by Robert Randolph; costumes by Robert Fletcher; choreography by Hugh Lambert.

ORIGINAL CAST INCLUDED: Robert Morse, Rudy Vallee, Charles Nelson Reilly, Virginia Martin, Bonnie Scott, Claudette Sutherland, Ruth Kobart, Sammy Smith.

PRINCIPAL SONGS: "How To," "Happy to Keep His Dinner Warm," "Coffee Break," "The Company Way," "A Secretary Is Not a Toy," "Been a Long Day," "Grand Old Ivy," "Paris Original," "Rosemary," "Cinderella, Darling," "Love from a Heart of Gold," "I Believe in You," "The Yo Ho Ho," "Brotherhood of Man."

1,404 PERFORMANCES   *Hellzapoppin*

Assembled by Ole Olsen and Chic Johnson; music by Sammy Fain; lyrics by Charles Tobias; additional words and music by Annette Mills, Teddy Hall, Don George, Paul Mann, Stephen Weiss, Sam Lewis.

Produced by Olsen and Johnson at the Forty-Sixth St. Theatre, September 22, 1938. Staged by Edward Duryea Dowling.

ORIGINAL CAST INCLUDED: Ole Olsen, Chic Johnson, Dewey Barto and George Mann, Shirley Wayne, Ray Kinney and the Aloha Maids, The Radio Rogues, The Charioteers, Bettymae and Beverly Crane, Hal Sherman, Walter Nilsson, Berg and Moore, Reed, Dean and Reed, Whitey's Steppers.

PRINCIPAL SONGS: "Blow a Balloon Up to the Moon," "Fuddle-Dee-Duddle," "It's Time to Say 'Aloha'," "When McGregor Sings Off Key," "Boomps-a-Daisy" (music and words by Annette Mills), "We Won't Let It Happen Here" (music by Teddy Hall, words by Don George), "When You Look in Your Looking Glass" (words by Sam Lewis, music by Paul Mann and Stephen Weiss).

1,375 PERFORMANCES *The Music Man* (CC)

Book, music, and lyrics by Meredith Willson; story by Meredith Willson and Franklin Lacey.

Produced by Kermit Bloomgarden with Herbert Greene (in association with Frank Productions, Inc.) at the Majestic Theatre, December 19, 1957. Staged by Morton Da Costa; settings and lighting by Howard Bay; choreography by Onna White; costumes by Raoul Pene du Bois.

ORIGINAL CAST INCLUDED: Robert Preston, Barbara Cook, David Burns, Iggie Wolfington, Pert Kelton, Eddie Hodges, Helen Raymond, Dusty Worrall, Danny Carroll, "The Buffalo Bills" (Al Shea, Wayne Ward, Vern Reed, Bill Spangenberg).

PRINCIPAL SONGS: "Rock Island," "Iowa Stubborn," "Trouble," "Piano Lesson," "Goodnight, My Someone," "Seventy-Six Trombones," "Sincere," "The Sadder-but-Wiser-Girl," "Pickalittle," "Marian the Librarian," "My White Knight," "Wells Fargo Wagon," "It's You," "Shipoopi," "Lida Rose," "Will I Ever Tell You," "Gary, Indiana," "Till There Was You."

1,348 PERFORMANCES   *Funny Girl*

Book by Isobel Lennart; music by Jule Styne; lyrics by Bob Merrill. Produced by Ray Stark, in association with Seven Arts Productions, at the Winter Garden Theatre, March 26, 1964. Directed by Garson Kanin; production supervised by Jerome Robbins; musical numbers staged by Carol Haney; scenery and lighting by Robert Randolph; costumes by Irene Sharaff.

ORIGINAL CAST INCLUDED: Barbra Streisand, Sydney Chaplin, Kay Medford, Danny Meehan, Jean Stapleton, Buzz Miller, Roger De Koven.

PRINCIPAL SONGS: "If a Girl Isn't Pretty," "I'm the Greatest Star," "Cornet Man," "Who Taught Her Everything?," "His Love Makes Me Beautiful," "I Want to Be Seen with You Tonight," "Henry Street," "People," "You Are Woman," "Don't Rain on My Parade," "Sadie, Sadie," "Find Yourself a Man," "Rat-Tat-Tat-Tat," "Who Are You Now?," "The Music That Makes Me Dance."

1,314 PERFORMANCES   *Oh, Calcutta!*

Devised by Kenneth Tynan; contributions by Samuel Beckett, Jules Feiffer, Dan Greenburg, John Lennon, Jacques Levy, Leonard Melfi, David Newman and Robert Benton, Sam Shepard, Clovis Trouille, Kenneth Tynan and Sherman Yellen; music and lyrics by The Open Window.

Produced by Hillard Elkins in association with Michael White and Gordon Crowe at the Eden Theater, June 17, 1969. Directed by Jacques Levy; choreography by Margo Sappington; scenery by James Tilton; costumes by Fred Voelpel; lighting by David Segal; projected media designed by Gardner Compton and Emile Ardolino; still photography by Michael Childers; audio design by Robert Liftin.

ORIGINAL CAST INCLUDED: Raina Barrett, Mark Dempsey, Katie Drew-Wilkinson, Boni Enten, Bill Macy, Alan Rachins, Leon Russom, Margo Sappington, Nancy Tribush, George Welbes. The Open Window: Robert Dennis, Peter Schickele, Stanley Walden.

PROGRAM: "Taking off the Robe," "Dick and Jane," "Suite for Five Letters," "Will Answer All Sincere Replies," "Paintings of Clovis Trouille," "Jack and Jill," "Delicious Indignities," "Was It Good for You, Too?," "Much Too Soon," "One on One," "Rock Garden," "Who: Whom," "Four in Hand," "Coming Together, Going Together."

1,281 PERFORMANCES *Promises, Promises*

Book by Neil Simon; music by Burt Bacharach; lyrics by Hal David; based on motion picture *The Apartment,* by Billy Wilder and I. A. L. Diamond.

Produced by David Merrick at the Sam S. Shubert Theater, December 1, 1968. Directed by Robert Moore; musical numbers staged by Michael Bennett; musical direction and dance arrangements by Harold Wheeler; scenery by Robin Wagner; costumes by Donald Brooks; lighting by Martin Aronstein.

ORIGINAL CAST INCLUDED: Jerry Orbach, Jill O'Hara, Marian Mercer, A. Larry Haines, Edward Winter, Ken Howard, Paul Reed, Norman Shelly, Vince O'Brien, Dick O'Neill, Donna McKechnie, Margo Sappington, Baayork Lee.

PRINCIPAL SONGS: "Half as Big as Life," "Upstairs," "You'll Think of Someone," "Our Little Secret," "She Likes Basketball," "Knowing When to Leave," "Where Can You Take a Girl?," "Wanting Things," "Turkey Lurkey Time," "A Fact Can Be a Beautiful Thing," "Whoever You Are," "A Young Pretty Girl Like You," "I'll Never Fall in Love Again," "Promises, Promises."

1,246 PERFORMANCES *The King and I*

Music by Richard Rodgers; book and lyrics by Oscar Hammerstein II; based on *Anna and the King of Siam,* by Margaret Landon.

Produced by Richard Rodgers and Oscar Hammerstein II at the St. James Theatre, March 29, 1951. Staged by John van Druten; choreography by Jerome Robbins; sets by Jo Mielziner; costumes by Irene Sharaff.

ORIGINAL CAST INCLUDED: Gertrude Lawrence, Yul Brynner, Doretta Morrow, Dorothy Sarnoff, Larry Douglas, Leonard Graves, Sandy Kennedy, John Juliano.

PRINCIPAL SONGS: "I Whistle a Happy Tune," "My Lord and Master," "Hello, Young Lovers!," "The Royal Siamese Children," "A Puzzlement," "Getting to Know You," "We Kiss in a Shadow," "Shall I Tell You What I Think of You?," "Something Wonderful," "Western People Funny," "I Have Dreamed," "Shall We Dance?"

1,217 PERFORMANCES *1776* (cc)

Book by Peter Stone; music and lyrics by Sherman Edwards; based on an idea by Sherman Edwards.

Produced by Stuart Ostrow at the Forty-Sixth St. Theatre, March 16, 1969. Directed by Peter Hunt; musical numbers staged by Onna White; musical direction and dance music arrangements by Peter Howard; scenery and lighting by Jo Mielziner; costumes by Patricia Zipprodt.

ORIGINAL CAST INCLUDED: William Daniels, Howard da Silva, Ken Howard, Ronald Holgate, Virginia Vestoff, Betty Buckley, Scott Jarvis, David Ford, Paul Hecht, David Vosburgh, Dal Richards, Roy Poole, Ronald Kross, Henry Le Clair, Edmund Lyndeck, Emory Bass, Robert Gaus, Bruce MacKay, Duane Bodin, Philip Polito, Charles Rule, Clifford David, Jonathan Moore, Ralston Hill, William Duell, B. J. Slater.

PRINCIPAL SONGS: "Sit Down, John," "Piddle, Twiddle and Resolve," "Till Then," "The Lees of Old Virginia," "But, Mr. Adams," "Yours, Yours, Yours," "He Plays the Violin," "Cool, Cool, Considerate Men," "Momma Look Sharp," "The Egg," "Molasses to Rum," "Is Anybody There?"

1,200 PERFORMANCES   *Guys and Dolls* (CC)

Music and lyrics by Frank Loesser; book by Jo Swerling and Abe Burrows; based on "The Idyll of Miss Sarah Brown," short story by Damon Runyan.

Produced by Cy Feuer and Ernest Martin at the Forty-Sixth St. Theatre, November 24, 1950. Staged by George S. Kaufman; dances and musical numbers staged by Michael Kidd; sets by Jo Mielziner; costumes by Alvin Colt.

ORIGINAL CAST INCLUDED: Robert Alda, Vivian Blaine, Sam Levene, Isabel Bigley, Pat Rooney, Sr., Stubby Kaye, B. S. Pully.

PRINCIPAL SONGS: "Fugue for Tinhorns," "Follow the Fold," "The Oldest Established," "I'll Know," "A Bushel and a Peck," "Adelaide's Lament," "Guys and Dolls," "Havana," "If I Were a Bell," "My Time of Day," "I've Never Been in Love Before," "Take Back Your Mink," "More I Cannot Wish You," "Luck Be a Lady," "Sue Me," "Sit Down, You're Rockin' the Boat," "Marry the Man Today."

1,166 PERFORMANCES   *Cabaret* (CC)

Book by Joe Masteroff; music by John Kander; lyrics by Fred Ebb; based on *I Am a Camera,* by John van Druten, and stories by Christopher Isherwood.

Produced by Harold Prince in association with Ruth Mitchell at the Broadhurst Theatre, November 20, 1966. Directed by Harold Prince; dances and cabaret numbers by Ronald Field; scenery by Boris Aronson; costumes by Patricia Zipprodt; lighting by Jean Rosenthal.

ORIGINAL CAST INCLUDED: Jill Haworth, Jack Gilford, Bert Convy, Lotte Lenya, Peg Murray, Joel Grey, Edward Winter, John Herbert, Mara Landi.

PRINCIPAL SONGS: "Willkommen," "So What?," "Don't Tell Mama," "Telephone Song," "Perfectly Marvelous," "Two Ladies," "It Couldn't Please Me More," "Tomorrow Belongs to Me," "Why Should I Wake Up?," "The Money Song," "Married," "Meeskite," "If You Could See Her," "What Would You Do?," "Cabaret."

1,147 PERFORMANCES *Annie Get Your Gun*

Book by Herbert and Dorothy Fields; music and lyrics by Irving Berlin.

Produced by Richard Rodgers and Oscar Hammerstein II at the Imperial Theatre, May 16, 1946. Staged by Joshua Logan; dances by Helen Tamiris; settings and lighting by Jo Mielziner; costumes by Lucinda Ballard.

ORIGINAL CAST INCLUDED: Ethel Merman, Ray Middleton, Marty May, Lea Penman, Betty Anne Nyman, Kenny Bowers, William O'Neal, Harry Bellaver.

PRINCIPAL SONGS: "Doin' What Comes Natur'lly, "Anything You Can Do," "The Girl That I Marry," "I Got Lost in His Arms," "I Got the Sun in the Morning," "I'm an Indian, Too," "Who Do You Love, I Hope," "You Can't Get a Man with a Gun," "They Say It's Wonderful," My Defenses Are Down," "There's No Business Like Show Business," "Moonshine Lullaby," "I'm a Bad, Bad Man."

1,116 PERFORMANCES* *The Magic Show*

Book by Bob Randall, music and lyrics by Stephen Schwartz, magic by Doug Henning.

Produced by Edgar Lansbury, Joseph Beruh and Ivan Reitman at the Cort Theater, May 28, 1974. Directed and choreographed by Grover Dale; scenery by David Chapman; costumes by Randy Barcelo; lighting by Richard Nelson.

ORIGINAL CAST INCLUDED: Doug Henning, Robert Lupone, David Ogden Stiers, Annie McGreevey, Cheryl Barnes, Dale Soules, Ronald Stafford, Lloyd Sannes, Anita Morris, Sam Schacht.

PRINCIPAL SONGS: "Up to His Old Tricks," "Solid Silver Platform Shoes," "Lion Tamer," "Style," "Charmin's Lament," "Two's Company," "The Goldfarb Variations," "A Bit of Villainy," "West End Avenue," "Sweet, Sweet, Sweet," "Before Your Very Eyes."

1,108 PERFORMANCES *Pins and Needles*

Music and lyrics by Harold Rome; sketches by Arthur Arent, Marc Blitzstein, Emanuel Eisenberg, Charles Friedman, and David Gregory.

Produced by the International Ladies' Garment Workers' Union at the Labor Stage Theatre, November 27, 1937. Staged by Charles Friedman; choreography by Benjamin Zemach; dances directed by Gluck Sandor.

ORIGINAL CAST INCLUDED: All non-professional actors, members of the International Ladies' Garment Workers' Union.

PRINCIPAL SONGS: "Chain Store Daisy," "Doing the Reactionary," "Nobody Makes a Pass at Me," "One Big Union for Two," "Sing Me a Song with Social Significance," "Sunday in the Park," "What Good Is Love?"

1,070 PERFORMANCES   *Kiss Me, Kate*

Music and lyrics by Cole Porter; book by Bella and Samuel Spewack; based on Shakespeare's *The Taming of the Shrew*.

Produced by Saint Subber and Lemuel Ayers at the New Century Theatre, December 30, 1948. Staged by John C. Wilson; settings and costumes by Lemuel Ayers; dances by Hanya Holm.

ORIGINAL CAST INCLUDED: Alfred Drake, Patricia Morison, Lisa Kirk, Harold Lang, Harry Clark, Jack Diamond.

PRINCIPAL SONGS: "Another Op'nin', Another Show," "Why Can't You Behave?," "Wunderbar," "So in Love Am I," "We Open in Venice," "Tom, Dick or Harry," "I've Come to Wive It Wealthily in Padua," "I Hate Men," "Were Thine That Special Face," "Kiss Me, Kate," "Too Darn Hot," "Where Is the Life That Late I Led?," "Always True to You (In My Fashion)," "Bianca," "Brush Up Your Shakespeare," "I Am Ashamed That Women Are So Simple."

1,065 PERFORMANCES
                 Don't Bother Me, I Can't Cope

Musical revue by Micki Grant.

Produced by Edward Padula and Arch Lustberg in Vinnette Carroll's Urban Arts Corps production at the Playhouse Theater, April 19, 1972. Conceived and directed by Vinnette Carroll; choreography by George Faison; scenery by Richard A. Miller, supervised by Neil Peter Jampolis; costumes by Edna Watson, supervised by Sara Brook; lighting by B. J. Sammler, supervised by

Ken Billington. Produced in association with Ford's Theater Society, Washington, D.C.

ORIGINAL CAST INCLUDED: Alex Bradford, Hope Clarke, Micki Grant, Bobby Hill, Arnold Wilkerson.

PRINCIPAL SONGS: "I Gotta Keep Movin'," "Lookin' Over from Your Side," "Don't Bother Me, I Can't Cope," "When I Feel Like Moving," "Help," "Fighting for Pharaoh," "Good Vibrations," "Love Power," "You Think I Got Rhythm?" "They Keep Coming," "My Name Is Man," "Questions," "It Takes a Whole Lot of Human Feeling," "Time Brings About a Change," "So Little Time," "Thank Heaven for You," "So Long, Sammy," "All I need."

1,063 PERFORMANCES   *Pajama Game*

Book by George Abbott and Richard Bissell; music and lyrics by Richard Adler and Jerry Ross; based on *7½ Cents*, by Richard Bissell.

Produced by Frederick Brisson, Robert E. Griffith, and Harold S. Prince at the St. James Theatre, May 13, 1954. Staged by George Abbott and Jerome Robbins; scenery and costumes by Lemuel Ayers; choreography by Bob Fosse.

ORIGINAL CAST INCLUDED: John Raitt, Janis Paige, Eddie Foy, Jr., Carol Haney, Stanley Prager, Reta Shaw, Ralph Dunn.

PRINCIPAL SONGS: "The Pajama Game," "Racing with the Clock," "A New Town Is a Blue Town," "I'm Not at All in Love," "I'll Never Be Jealous Again," "Hey There," "Her Is," "Once a Year Day," "Small Talk," "There Once Was a Man," "Steam Heat," "Think of the Time I Save," "Hernando's Hideaway," "7½ Cents."

1,019 PERFORMANCES   *Damn Yankees*

Book by George Abbott and Douglass Wallop; music and lyrics by Richard Adler and Jerry Ross; based on *The Year the Yankees Lost the Pennant,* by Douglass Wallop.

Produced by Frederick Brisson, Robert E. Griffith, and Harold S. Prince, in association with Albert B. Taylor, at the Forty-Sixth St. Theatre, May 5, 1955. Staged by George Abbott; dances and musical numbers staged by Bob Fosse; scenery and costumes designed by William and Jean Eckart.

ORIGINAL CAST INCLUDED: Gwen Verdon, Stephen Douglass, Ray Walston, Shannon Bolin, Robert Shafer, Nathaniel Frey, Rae Allen, Jean Stapleton.

PRINCIPAL SONGS: "Goodbye, Old Girl," "Six Months Out of Every Year," "Heart," "Shoeless Joe from Hannibal, Mo.," "A Man Doesn't Know," "A Little Brains—a Little Talent," "Whatever Lola Wants," "Who's Got the Pain?," "Near to You," "Those Were the Good Old Days," "Two Lost Souls."

964 PERFORMANCES

A Funny Thing Happened on the Way to the Forum

Book by Burt Shevelove and Larry Gelbart; music and lyrics by Stephen Sondheim; based on the plays of Plautus.

Produced by Harold Prince at the Alvin Theatre, May 1, 1962. Staged by George Abbott; choreography and musical staging by Jack Cole; settings and costumes by Tony Walton; lighting by Jean Rosenthal.

ORIGINAL CAST INCLUDED: Zero Mostel, David Burns, Jack Gilford, John Carradine, Raymond Walburn, Brian Davies, Preshy Marker, Ruth Kobart, Ronald Holgate.

PRINCIPAL SONGS: "Comedy Tonight," "Love, I Hear," "Free," "Lovely," "Pretty Little Picture," "Everybody Ought to Have a Maid," "I'm Calm," "Impossible," "Bring Me My Bride," "That Dirty Old Man," "That'll Show Him."

924 PERFORMANCES   *Bells Are Ringing*

Book and lyrics by Betty Comden and Adolph Green; music by Jule Styne.

Produced by The Theatre Guild at the Sam S. Shubert Theatre, November 29, 1956. Staged by Jerome Robbins; dances and musical numbers staged by Jerome Robbins and Bob Fosse; sets and costumes designed by Raoul Pene du Bois; lighting by Peggy Clark.

ORIGINAL CAST INCLUDED: Judy Holliday, Sydney Chaplin, Jean Stapleton, Bernie West, Frank Aletter, Eddie Lawrence, Dort Clark.

PRINCIPAL SONGS: "It's a Perfect Relationship," "On My Own," "You've Got to Do It," "It's a Simple Little System," "Is It a

Crime?," "Hello, Hello There," "I Met a Girl," "Long Before I Knew You," "Mu-Cha-Cha," "Just in Time," "Drop That Name," "The Party's Over," "Salzburg," "The Midas Touch," "I'm Goin' Back."

896 PERFORMANCES *Applause*

Book by Betty Comden and Adolph Green; music by Charles Strouse; lyrics by Lee Adams; based on film *All About Eve* and original story by Mary Orr.

Produced by Joseph Kipness and Lawrence Kasha in association with Nederlander Productions and George M. Steinbrenner III at the Palace Theater, March 30, 1970. Directed and choreographed by Ron Field; scenery by Robert Randolph; costumes by Ray Aghayan; lighting by Tharon Musser.

ORIGINAL CAST INCLUDED: Lauren Bacall, Len Cariou, Penny Fuller, Lee Roy Reams, Brandon Maggart, Robert Mandan, Bonnie Franklin, Ann Williams.

PRINCIPAL SONGS: "Backstage Babble," "Think How It's Gonna Be," "But Alive," "The Best Night of My Life," "Who's That Girl?," "Applause," "Hurry Back," "Fasten Your Seat Belts," "Welcome to the Theater," "Inner Thoughts," "Good Friends," "She's No Longer a Gypsy," "One of a Kind," "One Hallowe'en," "Something Greater."

892 PERFORMANCES *Can-Can*

Music and lyrics by Cole Porter; book by Abe Burrows.

Produced by Cy Feuer and Ernest H. Martin at the Shubert Theatre, May 7, 1953. Staged by Abe Burrows; dances and musical numbers staged by Michael Kidd; settings and lighting by Jo Mielziner; costumes by Motley.

ORIGINAL CAST INCLUDED: Lilo, Peter Cookson, Hans Conried, Erik Rhodes, Gwen Verdon.

PRINCIPAL SONGS: "Maidens Typical of France," "Never Give Anything Away," "C'est Magnifique," "Come Along with Me," "Live and Let Live," "I Am in Love," "If You Loved Me Truly," "Montmartre," "Allez-Vous-En," "Never, Never Be an Artist," "It's

All Right with Me," "Every Man Is a Stupid Man," "I Love Paris,"
"Can-Can."

890 PERFORMANCES *Carousel* (CC)

Music by Richard Rodgers; book and lyrics by Oscar Hammerstein
II; based on play adapted by Benjamin F. Glazer from Ferenc
Molnar's *Liliom*.

Produced by The Theatre Guild at the Majestic Theatre, April 19,
1945. Staged by Rouben Mamoulian; supervised by Lawrence
Langner and Theresa Helburn; choreography by Agnes de Mille;
settings by Jo Mielziner; costumes by Miles White.

ORIGINAL CAST INCLUDED: John Raitt, Jan Clayton, Jean Darling,
Christine Johnson, Eric Mattson, Murvyn Vye, Jean Casto, Jay
Velie, Ralph Linn, Bambi Linn.

PRINCIPAL SONGS: "The Carousel Waltz," "If I Loved You," "June
Is Bustin' Out All Over," "Mister Snow," "This Was a Real Nice
Clambake," "Soliloquy," "You're a Queer One, Julie Jordan,"
"Blow High, Blow Low," "What's the Use of Wond'rin',"
"There's Nothing So Bad for a Woman," "When the Children Are
Asleep," "You'll Never Walk Alone."

889 PERFORMANCES *Hats Off to Ice*

Lyrics and music by James Littlefield and John Fortis.

Produced by Sonja Henie and Arthur M. Wirtz at the Center
Theatre, June 22, 1944. Staged by William H. Burke and Catherine Littlefield; skating directed by May Judels; choreography by
Catherine and Dorothie Littlefield; settings by Bruno Maine;
costumes by Grace Houston.

PRINCIPAL SKATERS: Freddie Trenkler, Carol Lynne, the Brandt
Sisters, Geoffe Stevens, Lucille Page, Rudy Richards, Claire Wil-
kins, Bob Ballard, Peggy Wright, Paul Castle, Jean Sturgeon.

PRINCIPAL SONGS: "Hats Off to Ice," "Love Will Always Be the
Same," "Isle of the Midnight Rainbow," "Headin' West," "With
Every Star," "Here's Luck."

888 PERFORMANCES *Fanny*

Book by S. N. Behrman and Joshua Logan; music and lyrics by Harold Rome; based on trilogy (*Marius, Fanny,* and *César*) by Marcel Pagnol.

Produced by David Merrick and Joshua Logan at the Majestic Theatre, November 4, 1954. Staged by Joshua Logan; scenery and lighting by Jo Mielziner; costumes by Alvin Colt; dances by Helen Tamiris.

ORIGINAL CAST INCLUDED: Ezio Pinza, Walter Slezak, William Tabbert, Florence Henderson, Gerald Price, Alan Carney, Nejla Ates.

PRINCIPAL SONGS: "Never Too Late for Love," "Octopus Song," "Restless Heart," "Why Be Afraid to Dance?," "Welcome Home," "I Like You," "I Have to Tell You," "Fanny," "Panisse and Son," "To My Wife," "Love Is a Very Light Thing," "Be Kind to Your Parents," "Other Hands, Other Hearts."

882 PERFORMANCES *Follow the Girls*

Book by Guy Bolton and Eddie Davis; dialogue by Fred Thompson; lyrics and music by Dan Shapiro, Milton Pascal, and Phil Charig.

Produced by Dave Wolper in association with Albert Borde at the Century Theatre, April 8, 1944. Staged by Harry Delmar; dances and ensembles by Catherine Littlefield; settings and lighting by Howard Bay; costumes by Lou Eisele.

ORIGINAL CAST INCLUDED: Gertrude Niesen, Jackie Gleason, Irina Baronova, Bill Tabbert, Frank Parker, Val Valentinoff, Tim Herbert, Buster West.

PRINCIPAL SONGS: "I Wanna Get Married," "Follow the Girls," "Twelve O'Clock and All Is Well," "You're Perf," "Where Are You?" "I'm Gonna Hang My Hat."

873 PERFORMANCES *Camelot*

Book and lyrics by Alan Jay Lerner; music by Frederick Loewe; based on *The Once and Future King,* by T. H. White.

Produced by Alan Jay Lerner, Frederick Loewe, and Moss Hart at the Majestic Theatre, December 3, 1960. Staged by Moss Hart; settings by Oliver Smith; choreography and musical numbers staged by Hanya Holm; costumes by Adrian and Tony Duquette; lighting by Feder.

ORIGINAL CAST INCLUDED: Richard Burton, Julie Andrews, Robert Goulet, Robert Coote, Roddy McDowall, John Cullum, Bruce Yarnell, Michael Kermoyan, M'el Dowd.

PRINCIPAL SONGS: "I Wonder What the King Is Doing Tonight?," "The Simple Joys of Maidenhood," "Camelot," "Follow Me," "C'est Moi," "The Lusty Month of May," "Then You May Take Me to the Fair," "How to Handle a Woman," "Before I Gaze at You Again," "If Ever I Would Leave You," "The Seven Deadly Virtues," "What Do the Simple Folk Do?," "Fie on Goodness," "I Loved You Once in Silence," "Guenevere."

870 PERFORMANCES*   *Shenandoah*

Book by James Lee Barrett, Peter Udell, and Philip Rose; music by Gary Geld; lyrics by Peter Udell. Based on the original screen play by James Lee Barrett.

Produced by Philip Rose, Gloria and Louis K. Sher at the Alvin Theatre, January 7, 1975. Directed by Philip Rose; choreography by Robert Tucker; scenery by C. Murawski; costumes by Pearl Somner, Winn Morton; lighting by Thomas Skelton.

ORIGINAL CAST INCLUDED: John Cullum, Ted Agress, Joel Higgins, Jordan Suffin, David Russell, Penelope Milford, Robert Rosen, Joseph Shapiro, Donna Theodore, Chip Ford, Charles Welch, Gordon Halliday, Marshall Thomas, Gary Harger, Gene Masoner, Ed Preble, Graig Lucas, Casper Roos.

PRINCIPAL SONGS: "Raise the Flag of Dixie," "I've Heard It All Before," "Pass the Cross to Me," "Why Am I Like Me?" "Next to Lovin' (I Like Fightin')," "Over the Hill," "The Pickers Are Comin'," "Meditation," "We Make a Beautiful Pair," "Violets and Silverbells," "It's a Boy," "Freedom," "Papa's Gonna Make It Alright," "The Only Home I Know."

867 PERFORMANCES*   *The Wiz*

Music and lyrics by Charlie Small; book by William F. Brown, based on L. Frank Baum's *The Wonderful Wizard of Oz*.

Produced by Ken Harper at the Majestic Theatre, January 5, 1975. Directed by Geoffrey Holder; choreography and musical numbers staged by George Faison; scenery by Tom H. John; costumes by Geoffrey Holder; lighting by Tharon Musser.

ORIGINAL CAST INCLUDED: Stephanie Mills, Hinton Battle, Tiger Haynes, Ted Ross, Andre De Shields, Dee Dee Bridgewater, Mabel King, Clarice Taylor, Tasha Thomas, Ralph Wilcox, Evelyn Thomas, Danny Beard, Carl Weaver, Andy Torres.

PRINCIPAL SONGS: "The Feeling We Once Had," "He's the Wizard," "Soon as I Get Home," "I Was Born on the Day Before Yesterday," "Ease on Down the Road," "Slide Some Oil on Me," "Mean Ole Lion," "Be a Lion," "So You Want to Meet the Wizard," "To Be Able to Feel," "No Bad News," "Everybody Rejoice," "Who Do You Think You Are?" "Believe in Yourself," "Y'all Got It!," "A Rested Body Is a Rested Mind," "Home."

861 PERFORMANCES

No, No, Nanette (revival)

Book by Otto Harbach and Frank Mandel; music by Vincent Youmans; lyrics by Irving Caesar and Otto Harbach. (Based on the farce *My Lady Friends,* by Frank Mandel.)

Produced by Pyxidium Ltd. at the Forty-Sixth Street Theater, January 19, 1971. Production supervised by Busby Berkeley; adapted and directed by Burt Shevelove; dances and musical numbers staged by Donald Saddler; designed by Raoul Pene du Bois; lighting by Jules Fisher.

REVIVAL CAST INCLUDED: Ruby Keeler, Patsy Kelly, Helen Gallagher, Jack Gilford, Bobby Van, Roger Rathburn, Susan Watson, K. C. Townsend, Loni Zoe Ackerman, Pat Lysinger.

PRINCIPAL SONGS: "Too Many Rings Around Rosie," "I've Confessed to the Breeze," "Call of the Sea," "I Want to Be Happy," "No, No, Nanette," "Peach on the Beach," "Tea for Two," "You Can Dance with Any Girl," "Telephone Girlie," "Where-Has-My-Hubby-Gone-Blues," "Waiting for You," "Take a Little One-Step."

860 PERFORMANCES   *Song of Norway*

Music and lyrics by Robert Wright and George Forrest; music adapted from works by Edvard Grieg; book by Milton Lazarus; based on play by Homer Curran.

Produced by Edwin Lester at the Imperial Theatre, August 21, 1944. Staged by Charles K. Freeman; choreography by George Balanchine; production designed by Lemuel Ayers; settings by Carl Kent; costumes by Robert Davison.

ORIGINAL CAST INCLUDED: Lawrence Brooks, Irra Petina, Helena Bliss, Sig Arno, Robert Shafer, Walter Kingsford; also members of The Ballet Russe de Monte Carlo including Alexandra Danilova, Frederic Franklin, Nathalie Krassovska, Leon Daniellan, Maria Tallchief, Ruthanna Boris, Mary Ellen Moylan, Nicholas Magallances.

PRINCIPAL SONGS: "At Christmastime," "Freddy and His Fiddle," "I Love You," "Now," "Strange Music," "Three Loves," "Midsummer's Eve," "The Legend," "To Spring," "Hill of Dreams," "Nordraak's Farewell."

849 PERFORMANCES   *Comedy in Music*

Victor Borge's One-Man Show; produced by Harry D. Squires at the John Golden Theatre, October 2, 1953.

847 PERFORMANCES   *Raisin*

Book by Robert Nemiroff and Charlotte Zaltzberg, music by Judd Woldin, lyrics by Robert Brittan; based on *A Raisin in the Sun* by Lorraine Hansberry.

Produced by Robert Nemiroff at the Forty-sixth Street Theatre, October 18, 1973. Directed and choreographed by Donald McKayle; scenery by Robert U. Taylor; costumes by Bernard Johnson; lighting by William Mintzer.

ORIGINAL CAST INCLUDED: Virginia Capers, Joe Morton, Al Perryman, Loretta Abbott, Ernestine Jackson, Ralph Carter, Helen Martin, Deborah Allen, Elaine Beener, Ted Ross, Walter P. Brown, Robert Jackson, Chief Bey, Herb Downer, Marenda Perry, Richard Sanders.

PRINCIPAL SONGS: "Man Say," "Whose Little Angry Man," "Runnin' to Meet the Man," "A Whole Lotta Sunlight," "Booze," "Alaiyo," "African Dance," "Sweet Time," "You Done Right," "He Came Down This Morning," "It's a Deal," "Sidewalk Tree," "Not Anymore," "Measure the Valleys."

835 PERFORMANCES
La Plume de Ma Tante (CC)

Written, devised, and directed by Robert Dhery; music and arrangements by Gerald Calvi; English lyrics by Ross Parker.

A Jack Hylton production, presented in the United States by David Merrick and Joseph Kipness at the Royale Theatre, November 11, 1958. Staged by Alec Shanks; choreography by Colette Brosset; curtain designed by Vertès; scenery supervised and lighting by Charles Elson; sets and costumes by Erté, Vertès, Dignimont, Lilla de Nobile, Alec Shanks, Jacques Esterel, and Henri Pennec.

ORIGINAL CAST INCLUDED: Robert Dhery, Colette Brosset, Pierre Olaf, Jacques Legras, Roger Caccia, Jean Lefèvre, Ross Parker, Nicole Parent, Pamela Austin, Michael Kent, Henri Pennec, Michel Modo, Yvonne Constant, Genevieve Coulombel.

PRINCIPAL SONGS: "Song of the Swing," "Frères Jacques," "Le Bal Chez Madame de Mortemouille," "Ballet Classique," "Precision," "Femmes Fatales," "In the Tuileries Gardens," "Ballet Moderne," "Le Finale de Paris."

830 PERFORMANCES   Stars on Ice

Music by Paul McGrane and Paul Van Loan; lyrics by Al Stillman.

Produced by Sonja Henie and Arthur M. Wirtz at the Center Theatre, June 24, 1942. Staged by William H. Burke; choreography by Catherine Littlefield; costumes by Lucinda Ballard; lighting effects by Eugene Braun.

PRINCIPAL SKATERS: Carol Lynne, Skippy Baxter, Twinkle Watts, Brandt Sisters, Paul Castle, Three Rookies, Freddie Trenkler, The 4 Bruises.

PRINCIPAL SONGS: "Big, Broad Smile," "You're Awfully Smart," "The Cavalier Cat," "Juke Box Saturday Night," "Like a Leaf Falling in the Breeze," "Gin Rummy, I Love You."

796 PERFORMANCES *Fiorello!* (PP) (CC)

Book by Jerome Weidman and George Abbott; music by Jerry Bock; lyrics by Sheldon Harnick.

Produced by Robert E. Griffith and Harold S. Prince at the Broadhurst Theatre, November 23, 1959. Staged by George Abbott; choreography by Peter Gennaro; scenery and lighting by William and Jean Eckart; costumes by William and Jean Eckart.

ORIGINAL CAST INCLUDED: Tom Bosley, Patricia Wilson, Howard da Silva, Ellen Hanley, Pat Stanley, Mark Dawson, Eileen Rodgers, Nathaniel Frey, Bob Holiday.

PRINCIPAL SONGS: "On the Side of the Angels," "Politics and Poker," "Unfair," "Marie's Law," "The Name's La Guardia," "The Bum Won," "I Love a Cop," "Till Tomorrow," "Home Again," "When Did I Fall in Love?," "Gentleman Jimmy," "Little Tin Box," "The Very Next Man."

792 PERFORMANCES *Where's Charley?*

Book by George Abbott; words and music by Frank Loesser; based on *Charley's Aunt,* by Brandon Thomas.

Produced by Cy Feuer and Ernest H. Martin in association with Gwen Rickard at the St. James Theatre, October 11, 1948. Staged by George Abbott; sets and costumes by David Ffolkes; dances by George Balanchine, assisted by Fred Danielli.

ORIGINAL CAST INCLUDED: Ray Bolger, Allyn Ann McLerie, Byron Palmer, Doretta Morrow, Horace Cooper, Jane Lawrence, Paul England.

PRINCIPAL SONGS: "The Years Before Us," "Better Get Out of Here," "The New Ashmolean Marching Society and Students' Conservatory Band," "My Darling, My Darling," "Make a Miracle," "Serenades with Asides," "Lovelier Than Ever," "The Woman in His Room," "Pernambuco," "Where's Charley?," "Once in Love with Amy," "The Gossips," "At the Red Rose Cotillion."

774 PERFORMANCES *Oliver!*

Book, music, and lyrics by Lionel Bart; adapted from *Oliver Twist,* by Charles Dickens.

Produced by David Merrick and Donald Albery at the Imperial Theatre, January 6, 1963. Staged by Peter Coe; designed by Sean Kenny; lighting by John Wyckham.

ORIGINAL CAST INCLUDED: Clive Revill, Georgia Brown, Bruce Prochnik, David Jones, Willoughby Goodard, Hope Jackman, Barry Humphries, Alice Playten, Danny Sewell.

PRINCIPAL SONGS: "Food, Glorious Food," "Oliver!," "I Shall Scream," "Boy for Sale," "That's Your Funeral," "Where Is Love?," "Consider Yourself," "You've Got to Pick a Pocket or Two," "It's a Fine Life," "I'd Do Anything," "Be Back Soon," "Oom-Pah-Pah," "My Name," "As Long As He Needs Me," "Who Will Buy?," "Reviewing the Situation."

742 PERFORMANCES *Sons o' Fun*

Material by Ole Olsen, Chic Johnson, and Hal Block; music by Sammy Fain; lyrics by Jack Yellen; additional lyrics by Irving Kahal and songs by Will Irwin.

Produced by the Shuberts at the Winter Garden Theatre, December 1, 1941. Staged by Edward Dowling; dances and ensembles by Robert Alton; costumes and settings by Raoul Pene du Bois.

ORIGINAL CAST INCLUDED: Olsen and Johnson, Carmen Miranda, Ella Logan, Frank Libuse, Blackburn Twins, Rosario and Antonio.

PRINCIPAL SONGS: "Happy in Love," "Why?," "Cross Your Fingers," "Let's Say Goodnight with a Dance," "Oh, Auntie," "The Joke's on Us," "It's a New Kind of Thing," "Thank You, South America," "Thank You, North America," "It's a Mighty Fine Country We Have Here."

740 PERFORMANCES
Gentlemen Prefer Blondes

Book by Joseph Fields and Anita Loos; music by Jule Styne; lyrics by Leo Robin; based on *Gentlemen Prefer Blondes*, by Anita Loos.

Produced by Herman Levin and Oliver Smith at the Ziegfeld Theatre, December 8, 1949. Staged by John C. Wilson; sets by Oliver Smith; costumes by Miles White.

ORIGINAL CAST INCLUDED: Carol Channing, Yvonne Adair, Jack

McCauley, Alice Pearce, Eric Brotherson, Anita Alvarez, Peter Birch, Reta Shaw, Rex Evans.

PRINCIPAL SONGS: "It's High Time," "Bye, Bye, Baby," "A Little Girl from Little Rock," "I Love What I'm Doing," "Just a Kiss Apart," "It's Delightful Down in Chile," "Sunshine," "I'm A'Tingle, I'm A'Glow," "House on Rittenhouse Square," "You Say You Care," "Mamie Is Mimi," "Diamonds Are a Girl's Best Friend," "Gentlemen Prefer Blondes," "Homesick Blues," "Keeping Cool with Coolidge," "Button Up with Esmond."

740 PERFORMANCES

Candide (revival) (CC)

Music by Leonard Bernstein; lyrics by Richard Wilbur; additional lyrics by Stephen Sondheim and John Latouche. New book by Hugh Wheeler, adapted from story by Voltaire.

Produced by the Chelsea Theatre Center of Brooklyn in conjunction with Harold Prince and Ruth Mitchell at the Broadway Theatre, March 10, 1974, (First presented on December 11, 1973, at the Chelsea Theatre Center of Brooklyn at the Brooklyn Academy of Music for 48 performances.) Directed by Harold Prince; choreography by Patricia Birch; design by Eugene and Franne Lee; lighting by Tharon Musser.

ORIGINAL CAST INCLUDED: Lewis J. Stadlen, Mark Baker, Maureen Brennan, Jim Corti, David Horwitz, Deborah St. Darr, Mary-Pat Green, Joe Palmieri, Sam Freed, Robert Henderson, Peter Vogt, Gail Boggs, Lynne Gannaway, Carolann Page, Carlos Gorbea, Kelly Walters, Chip Garnett, Jeff Keller, Becky McSpadden, Kathryn Ritter, Renee Semes, June Gable, Rhoda Nutler.

PRINCIPAL SONGS: "Life Is Happiness Indeed," "The Best of All Possible Worlds," "Oh Happy We," "It Must Be So," "O Miserere," "Glitter and Be Gay," "Auto Da Fe," "This World," "You Were Dead, You Know," "I Am Easily Assimilated," "My Love," "Alleluia," "Sheep's Song," "Bon Voyage," "Make Our Garden Grow."

734 PERFORMANCES   *Call Me Mister*

Music and lyrics by Harold Rome; sketches by Arnold Auerbach and Arnold B. Horwitt.

Produced by Melvyn Douglas and Herman Levin at the National Theatre, April 18, 1946. Staged by Robert H. Gordon; dances directed by John Wray; settings by Lester Polokov; costumes by Grace Houston.

ORIGINAL CAST INCLUDED: Jules Munshin, Betty Garrett, Maria Karnilova, Bill Callahan, Lawrence Winters, George Hall, Harry Clark, Alan Manson, Danny Scholl, Chandler Cowles, George Irving, Glenn Turnbull, Paula Bane, Betty Lou Holland, Ruth Feist, Kate Friedlich, Virginia Davis, Evelyn Shaw, Betty Gilpatrick, Joan Bartels, Marjorie Oldroyd.

PRINCIPAL SONGS: "Going Home Train," "Welcome Home," "Surplus Blues," "The Red Ball Express," "Military Life," "Call Me Mister," "Yuletide, Park Avenue," "The Face on the Dime," "South America, Take It Away," "When We Meet Again," "Along with Me."

732 PERFORMANCES *West Side Story*

Book by Arthur Laurents; music by Leonard Bernstein; lyrics by Stephen Sondheim; based on idea by Jerome Robbins.

Produced by Robert E. Griffith and Harold S. Prince (by arrangement with Roger L. Stevens) at the Winter Garden Theatre, September 26, 1957. Staged and choreographed by Jerome Robbins; co-choreographer, Peter Gennaro; scenic production by Oliver Smith; costumes by Irene Sharaff; lighting by Jean Rosenthal.

ORIGINAL CAST INCLUDED: Mickey Calin, Larry Kert, Ken Le Roy, Carol Lawrence, Chita Rivera, Lee Becker, David Winters, Tony Mordente.

PRINCIPAL SONGS: "Jet Song," "Something's Coming," "The Dance at the Gym," "Maria," "Tonight," "America," "Cool," "One Hand, One Heart," "I Feel Pretty," "Somewhere," "Gee, Officer Krupke," "A Boy Like That," "I Have a Love."

727 PERFORMANCES *High Button Shoes*

Book by Stephen Longstreet; music and lyrics by Jule Styne and Sammy Cahn; based on novel by Stephen Longstreet.

Produced by Monte Proser and Joseph Kipness at the Century

Theatre, October 9, 1947. Staged by George Abbott; choreography and staging of dance numbers by Jerome Robbins; settings by Oliver Smith; lighting by Peggy Clark; costumes by Miles White.

ORIGINAL CAST INCLUDED: Phil Silvers, Joey Faye, Jack McCauley, Johnny Stewart, Nanette Fabray, Helen Gallagher, Mark Dawson, Nathaniel Frey, Lois Lee, Paul Godkin.

PRINCIPAL SONGS: "He Tried to Make a Dollar," "Can't You Just See Yourself in Love with Me?," "There's Nothing Like a Model T," "Next to Texas, I Love You," "Security," "Bird Watcher's Song," "Get Away for a Day in the Country," "Papa, Won't You Dance with Me?," "On a Sunday by the Sea," "You're My Girl," "I Still Get Jealous," "Nobody Ever Died for Dear Old Rutgers."

725 PERFORMANCES   *Finian's Rainbow*

Book by E. Y. Harburg and Fred Saidy; music by Burton Lane.

Produced by Lee Sabinson and William R. Katzell at the Forty-Sixth St. Theatre, January 10, 1947. Staged by Bretaigne Windust; choreography by Michael Kidd; settings and lighting by Jo Mielziner; costumes by Eleanor Goldsmith.

ORIGINAL CAST INCLUDED: Ella Logan, David Wayne, Albert Sharpe, Donald Richards, Eddie Bruce, Anita Alvarez, Robert Pitkin, Tom McElhany.

PRINCIPAL SONGS: "This Time of Year," "How Are Things in Glocca Morra?," "If This Isn't Love," "Look to the Rainbow," "Old Devil Moon," "Something Sort of Grandish," "Necessity," "When the Idle Poor Become the Idle Rich," "The Begat," "When I'm Not Near the Girl I Love," "That Great Come and Get It Day."

720 PERFORMANCES   *Jesus Christ Superstar*

Music by Andrew Lloyd Webber; lyrics by Tom Rice; based on the last seven days in the life of Jesus of Nazareth; conceived for the stage by Tom O'Horgan.

Produced by Robert Stigwood in association with MCA, Inc., by arrangement with David Land at the Mark Hellinger Theatre, October 12, 1971. Directed by Tom O'Horgan; scenery by Robin Wagner; costumes by Randy Barcelo; lighting by Jules Fisher.

ORIGINAL CAST INCLUDED: Ben Vereen, Jeff Fenholt, Yvonne Elliman, Alan Braunstein, Michael Meadows, Bob Bingham, Phil Jethro, Steven Bell, Dennis Buckley, Barry Dennen, Michael Jason, Linda Rios, Peter Schlosser, Paul Ainsley.

PRINCIPAL SONGS: "Heaven on Their Minds," "What's the Buzz," "Strange Thing Mystifying," "Everything's Alright," "This Jesus Must Die," "Hosanna," "Simon Zealotes," "Poor Jerusalem," "Pilate's Dream," "The Temple," "I Don't Know How to Love Him," "Damned for All Time," "The Last Supper," "Gethsemane," "The Arrest," "Peter's Denial," "Pilate and Christ," "King Herod's Song," "Could We Start Again, Please," "Judas' Death," "Trial Before Pilate," "Superstar," "The Crucifixion," "John 19:41."

719 PERFORMANCES *Carnival* (CC)

Book by Michael Stewart; music and lyrics by Bob Merrill; based on material by Helen Deutsch.

Produced by David Merrick at the Imperial Theatre, April 13, 1961. Staged and choreographed by Gower Champion; settings and lighting by Will Steven Armstrong; costumes by Freddy Wittop; assistant choreographer, Gene Bayliss; puppets created and supervised by Tom Tichenor; designer and supervisor of magic and illusion, Roy Beonson.

ORIGINAL CAST INCLUDED: Anna Maria Alberghetti, Jerry Orbach, James Mitchell, Kaye Ballard, Pierre Olaf, Henry Lascoe.

PRINCIPAL SONGS: "Direct from Vienna," "A Very Nice Man," "Fairyland," "I've Got to Find a Reason," "Mira," "Sword, Rose and Cape," "Humming," "Yes, My Heart," "Everybody Likes You," "Magic, Magic," "Tanz Mit Mir," "Theme from 'Carnival',", "Yum Ticky," "The Rich," "Beautiful Candy," "Her Face," "Grand Imperial Cirque de Paris," "I Hate Him," "Always Always You," "She's My Love."

702 PERFORMANCES   *Gypsy*

Book by Arthur Laurents; music by Jule Styne; lyrics by Stephen Sondheim; suggested by *Gypsy*, the memoirs of Gypsy Rose Lee.

Produced by David Merrick and Leland Hayward at the Broadway Theatre, May 21, 1959. Staged and choreographed by Jerome Robbins; settings and lighting by Jo Mielziner; costumes by Raoul Pene du Bois.

ORIGINAL CAST INCLUDED: Ethel Merman, Sandra Church, Jack Klugman, Maria Karnilova, Faith Dane, Chotzi Foley, Lane Bradbury, Paul Wallace, Karen Moore, Jacqueline Mayro, Mort Marshall.

PRINCIPAL SONGS: "Let Me Entertain You," "Some People," "Small World," "Mr. Goldstone, I Love You," "Little Lamb," "You'll Never Get Away from Me," "If Momma Was Married," "All I Need Is the Girl," "Everything's Coming Up Roses," "Madame Rose's Toreadorables," "Together, Wherever We Go," "You Gotta Have a Gimmick," "Rose's Turn."

699 PERFORMANCES*   *Chicago*

Book by Fred Ebb and Bob Fosse; music by John Kander; lyrics by Fred Ebb. Based on the play by Maurine Watkins.

Produced by Robert Fryer and James Cresson in association with Martin Richards, Joseph Harris, and Ira Bernstein at the Forty-sixth Street Theatre, June 3, 1975. Directed and choreographed by Bob Fosse; scenery by Tony Walton; costumes by Patricia Zipprodt; lighting by Jules Fisher.

ORIGINAL CAST INCLUDED: Gwen Verdon, Chita Rivera, Jerry Orbach, Barney Martin, Mary McCarty, Gary Gendell, Richard Korthaze, Cheryl Clark, Michon Peacock, Candy Brown, Graciela Daniele, Pamela Sousa, Michael Vita, M. O'Haughey, Charlene Ryan, Paul Solen, Gene Foote, Ron Schwinn, Ross Miles.

PRINCIPAL SONGS: "All That Jazz," "Funny Honey," "Cell Block Tango," "When You're Good to Mama," "Tap Dance," "All I Care About," "A Little Bit of Good," "We Both Reached for the Gun," "Roxie," "I Can't Do It Alone," "Chicago After Midnight," "My Own Best Friend," "I Know a Girl," "Me and My Baby," "Mister

Cellophane," "When Velma Takes the Stand," "Razzle Dazzle," "Class," "Nowadays," "R.S.V.P. Keep It Hot."

693 PERFORMANCES   *Li'l Abner*

Book by Norman Panama and Melvin Frank; lyrics by Johnny Mercer; music by Gene de Paul; based on characters created by Al Capp.

Produced by Norman Panama, Melvin Frank, and Michael Kidd at the St. James Theatre, November 15, 1956. Staged by Michael Kidd; choreography by Michael Kidd; scenery and lighting by William and Jean Eckart; costumes designed by Alvin Colt.

ORIGINAL CAST INCLUDED: Peter Palmer, Edith Adams, Stubby Kaye, Joe E. Marks, Charlotte Rae, Bern Hoffman, Julie Newmar, Howard St. John, Tina Louise, Al Nesor, Ted Thurston.

PRINCIPAL SONGS: "A Typical Day," "If I Had My Druthers," "Jubilation T. Cornpone," "Rag Offen the Bush," "Namely You," "Unnecessary Town," "What's Good for General Bullmoose," "The Country's in the Very Best of Hands," "Oh, Happy Day," "I'm Past My Prime," "Love in a Home," "Progress Is the Root of All Evil," "Put 'Em Back," "The Matrimonial Stomp."

690 PERFORMANCES   *Company* (CC)

Book by George Furth; music and lyrics by Stephen Sondheim.

Produced by Harold Prince in association with Ruth Mitchell at the Alvin Theater, April 26, 1970. Directed by Harold Prince; scenery and projections by Boris Aronson; costumes by D. D. Ryan; lighting by Robert Ornbo.

ORIGINAL CAST INCLUDED: Dean Jones, Barbara Barrie, George Coe, John Cunningham, Charles Kimbrough, Merle Louise, Teri Ralston, Beth Howland, Steve Elmore, Elaine Stritch, Pamela Myers, Charles Braswell, Susan Browning, Donna McKechnie.

PRINCIPAL SONGS: "Company," "The Little Things You Do Together," "Sorry-Grateful," "You Could Drive a Person Crazy," "Have I Got a Girl for You," "Someone Is Waiting," "Another Hundred People," "Getting Married Today," "Side by Side by Side," "What Would We Do Without You?," "Poor Baby," "Tick Tock," "Barcelona," "The Ladies Who Lunch," "Being Alive."

689 PERFORMANCES   *Purlie*

Book by Ossie Davis, Philip Rose, and Peter Udell; music by Gary Geld; lyrics by Peter Udell; based on *Purlie Victorious,* by Ossie Davis.

Produced by Philip Rose at the Broadway Theater, March 15, 1970. Directed by Philip Rose; choreography by Louis Johnson; scenery by Ben Edwards; costumes by Ann Roth; lighting by Thomas Skelton.

ORIGINAL CAST INCLUDED: Cleavon Little, Melba Moore, Linda Hopkins, Novella Nelson, Sherman Hemsley, C. David Colson, Helen Martin, John Heffernan.

PRINCIPAL SONGS: "Walk Him Up the Stairs," "New Fangled Preacher Man," "Skinnin' a Cat," "Purlie," "The Harder They Fall," "Charlie's Songs," "Big Fish, Little Fish," "I Got Love," "Great White Father," "Down Home," "First Thing Monday Mornin'," "He Can Do It," "The World Is Comin' to a Start."

676 PERFORMANCES
            The Most Happy Fella (CC)

Book, music, and lyrics by Frank Loesser; based on *They Knew What They Wanted,* by Sidney Howard.

Produced by Kermit Bloomgarden and Lynn Loesser at the Imperial Theatre, May 3, 1956. Staged by Joseph Anthony; choreography by Dania Krupska; scenery and lighting by Jo Mielziner; costumes by Motley.

ORIGINAL CAST INCLUDED: Robert Weede, Jo Sullivan, Susan Johnson, Art Lund, Mona Paulee, Shorty Long, Arthur Rubin, Rico Froehlich, John Henson, Keith Kaldenberg.

PRINCIPAL SONGS: "Ooh, My Feet," "The Most Happy Fella," "Joey, Joey, Joey," "Abbondanza," "Don't Cry," "Big 'D,' " "Warm All Over," "My Heart Is So Full of You," "Song of a Summer Night," "Somebody, Somewhere," "Standing on the Corner," "Rosabella," "Happy to Make Your Acquaintance," "How Beautiful the Days," "I Like Everybody," "I Made a Fist," "Mama, Mama," "Sposalizio."

670 PERFORMANCES *Irene*

Book by James Montgomery; music by Harry Tierney; lyrics by Joe McCarthy.

Produced by Joseph McCarthy at the Vanderbilt Theatre, November 18, 1919. Scenery by Robert Law Studios; second act designed by Clifford Plumber; women's costumes by Lucille, Ltd.; men's outfits by Fashion Park.

ORIGINAL CAST INCLUDED: Edith Day, Walter Regan, Bobbie Watson, Eva Puck, Dorothy Walters, Gladys Miller.

PRINCIPAL SONGS: "Alice Blue Gown," "Irene," "Castle of My Dreams," "Hobbies," "The Talk of the Town," "To Be Worthy of You," "We're Getting Away with It," "To Love You," "The Last Part of Any Party," "There's Something in the Air," "Sky Rocket."

667 PERFORMANCES
Beyond the Fringe (CC special citation)

Production written by the performers.

Produced by Alexander H. Cohen, by arrangement with William Donaldson and Donald Albery, at the John Golden Theatre, October 27, 1962. Staged by Alexander H. Cohen; original London production directed by Eleanor Fazan; scenery by John Wyckham; lighting by Ralph Alswang.

CAST: Alan Bennett, Peter Cook, Jonathan Miller, Dudley Moore.

657 PERFORMANCES *A Trip to Chinatown*

Book by Charles H. Hoyt; music by Percy Gaunt; also interpolated numbers by a variety of authors unknown.

Produced by Charles H. Hoyt at Hoyt's Madison Square Theatre, November 9, 1891.

ORIGINAL CAST reported to have included J. Aldrich Libby and Loie Fuller. Program for 1891 lists the following: Harry Conor, George A. Beane, Lloyd Wilson, Lillian Barr, Blanche Arkwright, Arthur Pacie, Harry Gilfoil, Geraldine McCann, Maggie Daly, Lucy Daly, Allie Archmere, Anna Boyd.

PRINCIPAL SONGS: "The Bowery," "Reuben and Cynthia," "The Widow," "Push Dem Clouds Away," "The Chaperone," "Out for a Racket," and "After the Ball" (by Charles K. Harris).

654 PERFORMANCES *Bloomer Girl*

Book by Sig Herzig and Fred Saidy; music by Harold Arlen; lyrics by E. Y. Harburg; adapted from a play by Lilith and Dan James.

Produced by John C. Wilson in association with Nat Goldstone at the Shubert Theatre, October 5, 1944. Staged by E. Y. Harburg; book directed by William Schorr; choreography by Agnes de Mille; settings and lighting by Lemuel Ayers; costumes by Miles White.

ORIGINAL CAST INCLUDED: Celeste Holm, David Brooks, Joan Mc-Cracken, Mabel Taliaferro, Matt Briggs, John Call, Margaret Douglass, Doolie Wilson, Richard Huey.

PRINCIPAL SONGS: "When the Boys Come Home," "The Eagle and Me," "Right as the Rain," "Sunday in Cicero Falls," "Evelina," "It Was Good Enough for Grandma," "The Rakish Young Man with the Whiskers," "I Got a Song," "T'morra, T'morra."

644 PERFORMANCES *Call Me Madam*

Book by Howard Lindsay and Russel Crouse; music and lyrics by Irving Berlin.

Produced by Leland Hayward at the Imperial Theatre, October 12, 1950. Staged by George Abbott; dances and musical numbers staged by Jerome Robbins; scenery and costumes by Raoul Pene du Bois; Miss Merman's dresses by Mainbocher.

ORIGINAL CAST INCLUDED: Ethel Merman, Paul Lukas, Russell Nype, Pat Harrington, Galina Talva.

PRINCIPAL SONGS: "The Hostess with the Mostes' on the Ball," "Washington Square Dance," "Lichtenburg," "Can You Use Any Money Today?," "Marrying for Love," "The Ocarina," "It's a Lovely Day Today," "The Best Thing for You Would Be Me," "Something to Dance About," "Once Upon a Time Today," "They Like Ike," "You're Just in Love."

640 PERFORMANCES*
A Chorus Line (PP) (CC)

Conceived by Michael Bennett; book by James Kirkwood and Nicholas Dante; music by Marvin Hamlisch; lyrics by Edward Kleban.

Produced by New York Shakespeare Festival Public Theater, Joseph Papp, director, at Public Theater, April 15, 1975. Closed after 101 performances and moved to Sam S. Shubert Theater on Broadway, July 25, 1975. Directed and choreographed by Michael Bennett; co-choreographer, Bob Avian; scenery by Robin Wagner; costumes by Theoni V. Aldredge; lighting by Tharon Musser.

ORIGINAL CAST INCLUDED: Scott Allen, Renee Baughman, Carole Bishop, Pamela Blair, Wayne Cilento, Chuck Cissel, Clive Clerk, Kay Cole, Ronald Dennis, Donna Drake, Brandt Edwards, Patricia Garland, Carolyn Kirsch, Ron Kuhlman, Nancy Lane, Baayork Lee, Priscilla Lopez, Robert LuPone, Cameron Mason, Donna McKechnie, Don Percassi, Michael Serrecchia, Michel Stuart, Thomas J. Walsh, Sammy Williams, Crissy Wilzak.

PRINCIPAL SONGS: "I Hope I Get It," "Joanne," "And," "At the Ballet," "Sing!" "Hello Twelve, Hello Thirteen, Hello Love," "Nothing," "Dance: Ten, Looks: Three," "The Music and the Mirror," "One," "The Tap Combination," "What I Did for Love."

627 PERFORMANCES
Two Gentlemen of Verona (CC)

Music by Galt MacDermot; lyrics by John Guare; based on the play by William Shakespeare, adapted by John Guare and Mel Shapiro.

Produced by the New York Shakespeare Festival, Joseph Papp, producer, at the St. James Theater, December 1, 1971. Directed by Mel Shapiro; choreography by Jean Erdman; scenery by Ming Cho Lee; costumes by Theoni V. Aldredge; lighting by Lawrence Metzler.

ORIGINAL CAST INCLUDED: Raul Julia, Clifton Davis, Diana Davila, Jonelle Allen, Frank O'Brien, Jose Perez, Alix Elias, John Bottoms, Frederic Warriner, Norman Matlock, Alvin Lum, Georgyn Geetlein, Sheila Gibbs.

PRINCIPAL SONGS: "Summer, Summer," "I Love My Father," "That's a Very Interesting Question," "I'd Like to Be a Rose," "Thou, Julia, Thou Hast Metamorphosed Me," "Symphony," "I Am Not Interested in Love," "Love, Is That You?," "Thou, Proteus, Thou Hast Metamorphosed Me," "What Does a Lover Pack?," "Pearls," "Two Gentlemen of Verona," "Follow the Rainbow," "Where's

North?" "Bring All the Boys Back Home," "Love's Revenge," "To Whom It May Concern," "Night Letter," "Calla Lily Lady," "Land of Betrayal," "Thurio's Samba," "Hot Lover," "What a Nice Idea," "Who Is Sylvia," "Love Me," "Eglamour," "Kidnapped," "Mansion," "What's a Nice Girl Like Her," "Dragon Fight," "Don't Have the Baby," "Milkmaid," "Love Has Driven Me Sane."

609 PERFORMANCES   *Star and Garter*

Sketches, music and lyrics by various writers and composers including Irving Berlin, Al Dubin, Will Irwin, Harold Rome, Lester Lee, Irving Gordon, Alan Roberts, Harold Arlen, Frank McCue, Doris Tauber, Dorival Caymmi, Jerry Seelen, Jerome Brainin, John Mercer, Sis Willner, Al Stillman.

Produced by Michael Todd at the Music Box Theatre, June 24, 1942. Staged by Hassard Short; dances directed by Al White, Jr.; sets by Harry Horner; costumes by Irene Sharaff.

ORIGINAL CAST INCLUDED: Bobby Clark, Gypsy Rose Lee, Georgia Sothern, Professor Lamberti, Pat Harrington, Carrie Finnell.

PRINCIPAL SONGS: "The Girl on the Police Gazette," "Brazilian Nuts," "Bunny, Bunny, Bunny," "I Don't Get It," "Star and Garter Girls," "Clap Your Hands," "For a Quarter," "Blues in the Night," "Robert the Roue."

608 PERFORMANCES   *The Student Prince*

Book and lyrics by Dorothy Donnelly; music by Sigmund Romberg; based on Richard Mansfield's adaptation of *Old Heidelberg,* by Wilhelm Meyer-Forster.

Produced by the Shuberts at the Jolson Theatre, December 2, 1924. Staged by J. C. Huffman; settings by Watson Barratt; dances by Max Scheck; costumes by Wedley of Paris, Vanity Fair Company; scenery by United Scenic Studios.

ORIGINAL CAST INCLUDED: Howard Marsh, Ilse Marvenga, George Hassell, Greek Evans, Fuller Mellish.

PRINCIPAL SONGS: "Golden Days," "Drinking Song," "Deep in My Heart, Dear," "Serenade," "Just We Two," "Student Marching Song," "Come, Boys, Let's Be Gay Boys," "Student Life."

608 PERFORMANCES *Sweet Charity*

Book by Neil Simon; music by Cy Coleman; lyrics by Dorothy Fields; based on motion picture *Nights of Cabiria,* by Federico Fellini, Tullio Pinelli, and Ennio Flaiano.

Produced by Robert Fryer, Lawrence Carr, Sylvia Harris, and Joseph Harris at the Palace Theatre, January 29, 1966. Directed, conceived, and choreographed by Bob Fosse; scenery and lighting by Robert Randolph; costumes by Irene Sharaff.

ORIGINAL CAST INCLUDED: Gwen Verdon, John McMartin, Helen Gallagher, Thelma Oliver, James Luisi, Ruth Buzzi, Arnold Soboloff, Harold Pierson, Eddie Gasper.

PRINCIPAL SONGS: "You Should See Yourself," "Big Spender," "Charity's Soliloquy," "Rich Man's Frug," "If My Friends Could See Me Now," "Too Many Tomorrows," "There's Gotta Be Something Better Than This," "I'm the Bravest Individual," "Rhythm of Life," "Baby Dream Your Dream," "Sweet Charity," "Where Am I Going?," "I'm a Brass Band," "I Love to Cry at Weddings."

607 PERFORMANCES *Bye, Bye, Birdie*

Book by Michael Stewart; music by Charles Strouse; lyrics by Lee Adams.

Produced by Edward Padula at the Martin Beck Theatre, April 14, 1960. Staged and choreographed by Gower Champion; scenery by Robert Randolph; costumes by Miles White; lighting by Peggy Clark.

ORIGINAL CAST INCLUDED: Dick Van Dyke, Chita Rivera, Susan Watson, Paul Lynde, Kay Medford, Dick Gautier, Marijane Maricle, Michael J. Pollard, Johnny Borden.

PRINCIPAL SONGS: "An English Teacher," "The Telephone Hour," "How Lovely to Be a Woman," "We Love You, Conrad," "Put on a Happy Face," "Normal American Boy," "One Boy," "Honestly Sincere," "Hymn for a Sunday Evening," "One Last Kiss," "What Did I Ever See in Him?," "A Lot of Lovin' to Do," "Kids," "Baby, Talk to Me," "Spanish Rose," "Rosie."

604 PERFORMANCES   *Irene* (revival)

Book by Hugh Wheeler and Joseph Stein, from an adaptation by Harry Rigby, based on the original play by James Montgomery; music by Harry Tierney; lyrics by Joseph McCarthy; additional lyrics and music by Charles Gaynor and Otis Clements.

Produced by Harry Rigby, Albert W. Selden, and Jerome Minskoff at the Minskoff Theater, March 13, 1973. Directed by Gower Champion; musical numbers staged by Peter Gennaro; scenery and costumes by Raoul Pene du Bois; Miss Reynolds' costumes by Irene Sharaff; lighting by David F. Segal.

ORIGINAL CAST INCLUDED: Debbie Reynolds, Monte Markham, Patsy Kelly, Ruth Warrick, Janie Sell, Carmen Alvarez, George S. Irving, Bruce Lea, Bob Freschi, Ted Pugh, Kate O'Brady.

PRINCIPAL SONGS: (from original score of *Irene*) "The Family Tree," "Alice Blue Gown," "The Last Part of Every Party," "We're Getting Away with It," "Irene." (Songs added for revival) : "The World Must Be Bigger Than an Avenue" (music, Wally Harper; lyrics, Jack Lloyd) ; "They Go Wild Simply Wild Over Me" (lyrics, Joseph McCarthy; music, Fred Fisher) ; "An Irish Girl" (lyrics, Otis Clements; music, Charles Gaynor) ; "Stepping on Butterflies (by Wally Harper) ; "Mother Angel Darling" (by Charles Gaynor) ; "The Riviera Rage" (by Wally Harper) ; "The Great Lover Tango" (music, Otis Clements; lyrics, Charles Gaynor) ; "You Made Me Love You" (music, James Monaco; lyrics, Joseph McCarthy) .

603 PERFORMANCES   *Adonis*

Book and lyrics by William F. Gill and Henry E. Dixey; music by Edward E. Rice.

Produced by William F. Gill at the Bijou Opera House, September 4, 1884.

ORIGINAL CAST INCLUDED: Henry E. Dixey, Amelia Summerville, George Howard, Lillie Grubb.

PRINCIPAL SONGS: "The Invocation," "We Are the Duchess' Daughters," "I'm a Merry Little Mountain Maid," "The Susceptible Statuette," "Most Romantic Meeting," "He Would Away," "The Blushing Bride," "It's English, You Know" (words by H. S. Hewitt) .

600 PERFORMANCES *Flower Drum Song*

Book by Oscar Hammerstein II and Joseph Fields; lyrics by Oscar Hammerstein II; music by Richard Rodgers; based on *Flower Drum Song*, by C. Y. Lee.

Produced by Rodgers and Hammerstein, in association with Joseph Fields, at the St. James Theatre, December 1, 1958. Staged by Gene Kelly; scenic production by Oliver Smith; choreography by Carol Haney; costumes by Irene Sharaff; lighting by Peggy Clark.

ORIGINAL CAST INCLUDED: Miyoshi Umeki, Pat Suzuki, Larry Blyden, Keye Luke, Juanita Hall, Ed Kennedy, Arabella Hong, Jack Soo, Patrick Adiarte, Anita Ellis, Conrad Yama.

PRINCIPAL SONGS: "You Are Beautiful," "A Hundred Million Miracles," "I Enjoy Being a Girl," "I Am Going to Like It Here," "Like a God," "Chop Suey," "Don't Marry Me," "Grant Avenue," "Love, Look Away," "Fan Tan Fannie," "Gliding Through My Memoree," "The Other Generation," "Sunday."

600 PERFORMANCES

A Little Night Music (CC)

Book by Hugh Wheeler; music and lyrics by Stephen Sondheim; suggested by Ingmar Bergman's film *Smiles of a Summer Night*.

Produced by Harold Prince in association with Ruth Mitchell at the Shubert Theater, February 25, 1973. Directed by Harold Prince; choreography by Patricia Birch; scenery by Boris Aronson; costumes by Florence Klotz; lighting by Tharon Musser.

ORIGINAL CAST INCLUDED: Glynis Johns, Len Cariou, Hermione Gingold, Benjamin Rayson, Teri Ralston, Barbara Lang, Gene Varrone, Beth Fowler, Judy Kahan, George Lee Andrews, Mark Lambert, Victoria Mallory, D. Jamin-Bartlett, Despo, Will Sharpe Marshall, Laurence Guittard, Patricia Elliott, Sherry Mathis.

PRINCIPAL SONGS: "Night Music," "Now," "Later," "Soon," "The Glamorous Life," "Remember?" "You Must Meet My Wife," "Liaisons," "In Praise of Women," "Every Day a Little Death," "A Weekend in the Country," "The Sun Won't Set," "It Would Have Been Wonderful," "Perpetual Anticipation," "Send in the Clowns," "The Miller's Son."

598 PERFORMANCES   *Wish You Were Here*

Book by Arthur Kober and Joshua Logan; music and lyrics by Harold Rome; based on *Having Wonderful Time*, by Arthur Kober.

Produced by Leland Hayward and Joshua Logan at the Imperial Theatre, June 25, 1952. Staged and choreographed by Joshua Logan; settings and lighting by Jo Mielziner; costumes by Robert Mackintosh.

ORIGINAL CAST INCLUDED: Sheila Bond, Jack Cassidy, Patricia Marand, Sidney Armus, Paul Valentine, John Perkins, Sammy Smith, Harry Clark, Larry Blyden, Florence Henderson, Phyllis Newman.

PRINCIPAL SONGS: "Camp Karefree," "Goodbye Love," "Social Director," "Shopping Around," "Bright College Days," "Mix and Mingle," "Could Be," "Tripping the Light Fantastic," "Where Did the Night Go?," "Certain Individuals," "They Won't Know Me," "Summer Afternoon," "Don Jose," "Everybody Love Everybody," "Wish You Were Here," "Relax," "Flattery."

596 PERFORMANCES   *A Society Circus*

Book by Sydney Rosenfeld; lyrics by Sydney Rosenfeld and Manuel Klein; music by Manuel Klein and Gustav Luders.

Produced by Thompson and Dundy at the New York Hippodrome, December 13, 1905. Staged by Edward P. Temple and Frederic Thompson; settings by Arthur Voegtlin; costumes by Alfredo Edfel and Archie Gunn.

ORIGINAL CAST INCLUDED: Marceline, Francis J. Boyle, Leila Romer, Olive North, The Four Marnos, The Flying Dunbars, Claire Heliot and her twelve lions, Edwin A. Clark, James Cherry, Harry F. Siegfried, Thomas J. Daly, Rose La Harte, Rita Dean, Stella Martine, H. E. Cluett, Felix Haney, Frank Silvers Oakley, Barlow's Elephants, Miss Marquis and Ponies, Ralph Johnstone, Mlle. Leris, Marguerite and Hanley.

PRODUCTION NUMBERS INCLUDED: "Song of the Flowers," "Court of the Golden Fountains," "Motoring in Mid-Air."

592 PERFORMANCES *Blossom Time*

Book and lyrics by Dorothy Donnelly; adapted from German operetta *Das Dreimädlerhaus*, by A. M. Willner and H. Reichert; music adapted by Sigmund Romberg from works by Franz Schubert and H. Berte.

Produced by the Shuberts at the Ambassador Theatre, September 29, 1921. Staged by J. C. Hoffman; scenes by Watson Barratt; dances arranged by F. M. Gillespie; costumes and hats by Mode Studios; scenery by United Scenic Studios.

ORIGINAL CAST INCLUDED: Bertram Peacock, Olga Cook, Howard Marsh, William Danforth, Roy Cropper.

PRINCIPAL SONGS: "Song of Love," "Tell Me Daisy," "Only One Love Ever Fills the Heart," "My Springtime Thou Art," "Three Little Maids," "Serenade," "There Is an Old Vienna," "Ave Maria."

587 PERFORMANCES *The Me Nobody Knows*

Book by Stephen M. Joseph; music by Gary William Friedman; lyrics by Will Holt; original idea by Herb Schapiro; edited from the book *The Me Nobody Knows*, by Stephen M. Joseph.

Produced by Jeff Britton in association with Sagittarius Productions, Inc. at the Orpheum Theater, May 18, 1970. Directed by Robert H. Livingstone; musical numbers staged by Patricia Birch; scenery and lighting by Clarke Dunham; costumes by Patricia Quinn Stuart.

ORIGINAL CAST INCLUDED: Northern J. Calloway, Beverly Ann Bremers, Irene Cara, Gerri Dean, Jose Fernandez, Douglas Grant, Melanie Henderson, Kevin Lindsay, Paul Mace, Laura Michaels, Carl Thoma, Hattie Winston.

PRINCIPAL SONGS: "Dream Babies," "Light Sings," "This World," "Numbers," "What Happens to Life," "Take Hold the Crutch," "Flying Milk and Runaway Plates," "I Love What the Girls Have," "How I Feel," "If I Had a Million Dollars," "Fugue for Four Girls," "Rejoice," "Sounds," "The Tree," "Robert, Alvin, Wendell and Jo Jo," "Jail-Life Walk," "Something Beautiful," "Black," "The Horse," "Let Me Come In," "War Babies."

584 PERFORMANCES   *I Do! I Do!*

Book and lyrics by Tom Jones; music by Harvey Schmidt; based on *The Fourposter*, by Jan de Hartog.

Produced by David Merrick at the Forty-Sixth Street Theatre, December 5, 1966. Directed by Gower Champion; scenery by Oliver Smith; costumes by Freddy Wittop; lighting by Jean Rosenthal.

ORIGINAL CAST: Mary Martin, Robert Preston.

PRINCIPAL SONGS: "All the Dearly Beloved," "Together Forever," "I Do! I Do!," "Good Night," "I Love My Wife," "Something Has Happened," "My Cup Runneth Over," "Love Isn't Everything," "Nobody's Perfect," "A Well Known Fact," "Flaming Agnes," "The Honeymoon Is Over," "Where Are the Snows?," "When the Kids Get Married," "The Father of the Bride," "What Is a Woman?," "Somebody Needs Me," "Roll Up the Ribbons," "This House."

583 PERFORMANCES   *Kismet*

Book by Charles Lederer and Luther Davis; music based on works of Aleksandr Borodin; musical adaptation and lyrics by Robert Wright and George Forrest; based on *Kismet*, by Edward Knoblock.

Produced by Charles Lederer at the Ziegfeld Theatre, December 3, 1953. Staged by Albert Marre; dances and musical numbers staged by Jack Cole; settings and costumes by Lemuel Ayers; lighting by Peggy Clark.

ORIGINAL CAST INCLUDED: Alfred Drake, Doretta Morrow, Joan Diener, Richard Kiley, Henry Calvin, Florence Lessing, Lucy Andonian, Beatrice Kraft, Patricia Dunn, Bonnie Evans, Reiko Sato, Philip Coolidge.

PRINCIPAL SONGS: "Sands of Time," "Rhymes Have I," "Fate," "Bazaar of the Caravans," "Not Since Nineveh," "Baubles, Bangles, and Beads," "Stranger in Paradise," "He's in Love!," "Gesticulate," "Night of My Nights," "Was I Wazir?," "Rahadlakum," "And This Is My Beloved," "The Olive Tree," "Presentation of Princesses."

581 PERFORMANCES *Brigadoon* (CC)

Book and lyrics by Alan Jay Lerner; music by Frederick Loewe.

Produced by Cheryl Crawford at the Ziegfeld Theatre, March 13, 1947. Staged by Robert Lewis; choreography by Agnes de Mille; settings by Oliver Smith; costumes by David Ffolkes; lighting by Peggy Clark.

ORIGINAL CAST INCLUDED: David Brooks, Marion Bell, George Keane, James Mitchell, Pamela Britton, Lee Sullivan, Virginia Bosler, Lidija Franklin, William Hansen.

PRINCIPAL SONGS: "Once in the Highlands," "Brigadoon," "Down on MacConnachy Square," "Waitin' for My Dearie," "I'll Go Home with Bonnie Jean," "The Heather on the Hill," "Come to Me, Bend to Me," "Almost Like Being in Love," "There But for You, Go I," "My Mother's Wedding Day," "Jeannie's Packin' Up," "From This Day On."

580 PERFORMANCES *No Strings*

Book by Samuel Taylor; music and lyrics by Richard Rodgers.

Produced by Richard Rodgers, in association with Samuel Taylor, at the Fifty-Fourth Street Theatre, March 15, 1962. Staged and choreographed by Joe Layton; settings and lighting by David Hays; costumes by Fred Voelpel and Donald Brooks.

ORIGINAL CAST INCLUDED: Diahann Carroll, Richard Kiley, Noelle Adam, Alvin Epstein, Polly Rowles, Don Chastain, Mitchell Gregg, Bernice Massi.

PRINCIPAL SONGS: "The Sweetest Sounds," "How Sad," "Loads of Love," "The Man Who Has Everything," "Be My Host," "La La La," "You Don't Tell Me," "Love Makes the World Go," "Nobody Told Me," "Look No Further," "Maine," "An Orthodox Fool," "Eager Beaver," "No Strings."

572 PERFORMANCES *Show Boat*

Book and lyrics by Oscar Hammerstein II; music by Jerome Kern; adapted from *Show Boat,* by Edna Ferber.

Produced by Florenz Ziegfeld at the Ziegfeld Theatre, December

27, 1927. Dances and ensembles arranged by Sammy Lee; settings by Joseph Urban; costumes by John Harkrider; staged by Florenz Ziegfeld, Sammy Lee, Zeke Cohan.

ORIGINAL CAST INCLUDED: Charles Winninger, Howard Marsh, Norma Terris, Helen Morgan, Edna May Oliver, Jules Bledsoe, Aunt Jemima, Eva Puck, Sammy White, Charles Ellis.

PRINCIPAL SONGS: "Make Believe," "Ol' Man River," "Can't Help Lovin' Dat Man," "Life Upon the Wicked Stage," "You Are Love," "Why Do I Love You?," "I Might Fall Back on You," "Till Good Luck Comes My Way," "In Dahomey," "Hay, Feller," "Bill" (lyrics by P. G. Wodehouse).

570 PERFORMANCES *Sally*

Book by Guy Bolton; lyrics by Clifford Grey; music by Jerome Kern and Victor Herbert (ballet music).

Produced by Florenz Ziegfeld, at the New Amsterdam Theatre, December 21, 1920. Staged by Edward Royce; settings by Joseph Urban; costumes by Mme. Nookerov, Pascaud, Alice O'Neill, Lucille, Ltd., Lady Duff Gordon.

ORIGINAL CAST INCLUDED: Marilyn Miller, Leon Errol, Walter Catlett, Irving Fisher, Mary Hay, Stanley Ridges, Dolores, Catherine Littlefield.

PRINCIPAL SONGS: "Wild Rose," "The Lorelei," "Sally," "Look for the Silver Lining" (lyrics by B. G. deSylva), "Whip-poor-will" (lyrics by B. G. deSylva), "The Church 'round the Corner" (lyrics by P. G. Wodehouse), "Butterfly Ballet."

568 PERFORMANCES *Golden Boy*

Book by Clifford Odets and William Gibson; music by Charles Strouse; lyrics by Lee Adams; based on *Golden Boy*, by Clifford Odets.

Produced by Hillard Elkins at the Majestic Theatre, October 20, 1964; directed by Arthur Penn; choreography by Donald McKayle; settings, costumes, and projections by Tony Walton; lighting by Tharon Musser; projections devised by Richard Pilbrow; assistant choreographer, Jaime Rogers.

ORIGINAL CAST INCLUDED: Sammy Davis, Paula Wayne, Billy Daniels, Kenneth Tobey, Johnny Brown, Jaime Rogers, Roy Glenn, Lola Falana, Ted Beniades, Lester Wilson.

PRINCIPAL SONGS: "Workout," "Night Song," "Everything's Great," "Gimme Some," "Stick Around," "Don't Forget 127th Street," "Lorna's Here," "The Road Tour," "This Is the Life," "Golden Boy," "While the City Sleeps," "Colorful," "I Want to Be with You," "Can't You See It?," "No More," "The Fight."

567 PERFORMANCES *One Touch of Venus*

Book by S. J. Perelman and Ogden Nash; lyrics by Ogden Nash; music by Kurt Weill; suggested by F. Anstey's *The Tinted Venus.*

Produced by Cheryl Crawford in association with John Wildberg at the Imperial Theatre, October 7, 1943. Staged by Elia Kazan; choreography by Agnes de Mille; settings by Howard Bay; costumes designed by Paul du Pont, Kermit Love and Mainbocher.

ORIGINAL CAST INCLUDED: Mary Martin, John Boles, Kenny Baker, Paula Lawrence, Teddy Hart, Harry Clark, Helen Raymond, Ruth Bond, Sono Osato, Lou Wills, Jr., Allyn Ann McLerie.

PRINCIPAL SONGS: "One Touch of Venus," "How Much I Love You," "I'm a Stranger Here Myself," "Speak Low," "West Wind," "Foolish Heart," "The Trouble with Women," "That's Him," "Wooden Wedding," "Very, Very, Very.",

559 PERFORMANCES *Wonderful Town* (CC)

Book by Joseph Fields and Jerome Chodorov; music by Leonard Bernstein; lyrics by Betty Comden and Adolph Green; based on *My Sister Eileen,* by Joseph Fields and Jerome Chodorov, and stories by Ruth McKenney.

Produced by Robert Fryer at the Winter Garden Theatre, February 25, 1955; staged by George Abbott; dances and musical numbers arranged by Donald Saddler; sets and costumes by Raoul Pene du Bois; lighting by Peggy Clark; Miss Russell's clothes designed by Mainbocher.

ORIGINAL CAST INCLUDED: Rosalind Russell, Edith Adams, George Gaynes, Henry Lascoe, Jordan Bentley, Dody Goodman, Chris Alexander, Dort Clark, Michele Burke.

PRINCIPAL SONGS: "Christopher Street," "Ohio," "Conquering New York," "One Hundred Easy Ways," "What a Waste," "Never Felt This Way Before," "Pass the Football," "Conversation Piece," "A Quiet Girl," "Conga!," "My Darlin' Eileen," "Swing!," "It's Love," "Wrong Note Rag."

557 PERFORMANCES · Rose Marie

Book and lyrics by Otto Harbach and Oscar Hammerstein II; music by Rudolf Friml; also numbers by Herbert Stothart.

Produced by Arthur Hammerstein at the Imperial Theatre on September 2, 1924. Staged by Paul Dickey; costumes by Charles LeMaire.

ORIGINAL CAST INCLUDED: Dennis King, Mary Ellis, William Kent, Arthur Deagon, Edward Ciannelli, Dorothy Mackaye, Pearl Regay.

PRINCIPAL SONGS: "Rose Marie," "The Mounties," "Indian Love Call," "Totem Tom-Tom," "The Door of My Dreams," "Pretty Things," "Why Shouldn't We?," "Lak Jeem," "Minuet of the Minute."

555 PERFORMANCES · Jamaica

Book by E. Y. Harburg and Fred Saidy; music by Harold Arlen; lyrics by E. Y. Harburg.

Produced by David Merrick at the Imperial Theatre, October 31, 1957. Staged by Robert Lewis; production designed by Oliver Smith; choreography by Jack Cole; costumes by Miles White; lighting by Jean Rosenthal.

ORIGINAL CAST INCLUDED: Lena Horne, Ricardo Montalban, Adelaide Hall, Josephine Premice, Ossie Davis, Erik Rhodes, Augustine Rios, Joe Adams.

PRINCIPAL SONGS: "Savannah," "Savannah's Weddin' Day," "Pretty to Walk With," "Push the Button," "Incompatibility," "Little Biscuit," "Pity the Sunset," "Yankee Dollar," "What Good Does It Do?," "Monkey in the Mango Tree," "Take It Slow, Joe," "Ain't It the Truth," "Leave the Atom Alone," "Cocoanut Sweet," "For Every Fish," "I Don't Think I'll End It All Today," "Napoleon."

555 PERFORMANCES

Stop the World—I Want to Get Off

Book, music, and lyrics by Leslie Bricusse and Anthony Newley.

Produced by David Merrick, in association with Bernard Delfont, at the Sam S. Shubert Theatre, October 3, 1962. Staged by Anthony Newley; scenery and lighting by Sean Kenny; John Broome's choreography restaged by Virginia Mason.

ORIGINAL CAST INCLUDED: Anthony Newley, Anna Quayle, Jennifer Baker, Susan Baker.

PRINCIPAL SONGS: "The A. B. C. Song," "I Want to Be Rich," "Typically English," "Lumbered," "Welcome to Sludgepool," "Gonna Build a Mountain," "Glorious Russian," "Meilinki Meilchick," "Family Fugue," "Typische Deutsche," "Nag! Nag! Nag!," "All-American," "Once in a Lifetime," "Mumbo Jumbo," "Welcome to Sunvale," "Someone Nice Like You," "What Kind of Fool Am I?"

553 PERFORMANCES *Florodora*

Lyrics by Owen Hall; music by Leslie Stuart; book revised by Frank Pixley.

Produced by Dunne, Ryley, and Fisher at the Casino Theatre, November 10, 1900. Staged by Lewis Hopper.

ORIGINAL CAST INCLUDED: Fannie Johnston, Edna Wallace Hopper, R. E. Graham, Sydney Deane, May Edouin, Willie Edouin, Cyril Scott. The original sextette: Margaret Walker, Marjorie Relyea, Daisy Greene, Vaughn Texsmith, Marie L. Wilson, Agnes Wayburn.

PRINCIPAL SONGS: "The Credit's Due to Me," "The Silver Star of Love," "Somebody," "Come and See Our Island," "I Want to Marry a Man," "The Shade of the Palm," "The Millionaire," "Tell Me, Pretty Maiden," "I've an Inkling," "The Fellow Who Might," "The Queen of the Philippine Islands," "I Want to Be a Military Man," "The Island of Love."

553 PERFORMANCES *Ziegfeld Follies of 1943*

Music by Ray Henderson; words by Jack Yellen; sketches by Lester

Lee, Jerry Seelen, Bud Pearson, Les White, Charles Sherman, Joseph Erens, Harry Young, Lester Lawrence, Baldwin Bergensen, Ray Golden, Sid Kuller, William K. Wells; also material by Buddy Burston, Dan White, Harold Rome.

Produced by the Shuberts at the Winter Garden Theatre, April 1, 1943. Staged by John Murray Anderson; dialogue staged by Arthur Pierson; sets by Watson Barratt; costumes by Miles White; dances by Robert Alton and Jack Cole.

ORIGINAL CAST INCLUDED: Milton Berle, Ilona Massey, Dean Murphy, Jack Cole, Nadine Gae, Arthur Treacher, Sue Ryan, Tommy Wonder, Christine Ayers, the Rhythmaires, Jack McCauley, Imogene Carpenter, Jaye Martin, Bill and Cora Baird, Arthur Maxwell, Ben Yost's Vi-Kings, Charles Senna.

PRINCIPAL SONGS: "Come Up and Have a Cup of Coffee," "Hold That Smile," "Thirty-Five Summers Ago," "Hindu Serenade," "The Wedding of the Solid Sender," "Love Songs Are Made at Night," "Micromania" (by Harold Rome).

551 PERFORMANCES   *Good News*

Book by Laurence Schwab and B. G. deSylva; lyrics by B. G. deSylva and Lew Brown; music by Ray Henderson.

Produced by Laurence Schwab and Frank Mandel at the Forty-Sixth Street Theatre, September 6, 1927. Staged by Edgar MacGregor; sets by Donald Oenslager; frocks by Kiviette; gowns by Milgrim; men's clothes by Stratford.

ORIGINAL CAST INCLUDED: John Price Jones, Mary Lawlor, Zelma O'Neal, Inez Courtney, Gus Shy, Shirley Vernon, George Olsen and his Band.

PRINCIPAL SONGS: "Varsity Drag," "Good News," "The Best Things in Life Are Free," "Lucky in Love," "The Girls of Pi Beta Phi," "He's a Ladies' Man," "Just Imagine."

547 PERFORMANCES   *Let's Face It*

Book by Herbert and Dorothy Fields; music and lyrics by Cole Porter; based on *The Cradle Snatchers*, by Russell Medcraft and Norma Mitchell.

Produced by Vinton Freedley at the Imperial Theatre, October 29, 1941. Staged by Edgar MacGregor; dances and ensembles staged by Charles Walters; settings by Harry Horner; costumes by John Harkrider.

ORIGINAL CAST INCLUDED: Danny Kaye, Eve Arden, Mary Jane Walsh, Edith Meiser, Benny Baker, Jack Williams, Vivian Vance, Nanette Fabray.

PRINCIPAL SONGS: "Let's Face It," "Farming," "Ev'rything I Love," "Ace in the Hole," "You Irritate Me So," "A Little Rumba Numba," "I Hate You, Darling," "Let's Not Talk About Love," "Rub Your Lamp," "Melody in Four F" (by Sylvia Fine and Max Liebman), "A Modern Fairy Tale" (by Sylvia Fine and Max Liebman).

543 PERFORMANCES   *Milk and Honey*

Book by Don Appell; music and lyrics by Jerry Herman.

Produced by Gerard Oestreicher at the Martin Beck Theatre, October 10, 1961. Staged by Albert Marre; choreography by Donald Saddler; settings and lighting by Howard Bay; costumes by Miles White.

ORIGINAL CAST INCLUDED: Robert Weede, Mimi Benzell, Molly Picon, Tommy Rall, Juki Arkin, Lanna Sanders, Ellen Madison, Thelma Pelish.

PRINCIPAL SONGS: "Shepherd's Song," "Shalom," "Independence Day Hora," "Milk and Honey," "There's No Reason in the World," "Chin Up, Ladies," "That Was Yesterday," "Let's Not Waste a Moment," "Like a Young Man," "I Will Follow You," "Hymn to Hymie," "As Simple as That."

540 PERFORMANCES   *Pal Joey* (revival)

Book by John O'Hara; music by Richard Rodgers; lyrics by Lorenz Hart.

Revived by Jule Styne and Leonard Key, in association with Anthony B. Farrell, at the Broadhurst Theatre, January 3, 1952. Production supervised by Robert Alton; book directed by David Alexander; dances by Robert Alton; sets by Oliver Smith; costumes by Miles White.

REVIVAL CAST INCLUDED: Harold Lang, Vivienne Segal, Helen Wood, Helen Gallagher, Elaine Stritch, Lionel Stander, Pat Northrop.

PRINCIPAL SONGS: "You Mustn't Kick It Around," "I Could Write a Book," "Chicago," "That Terrific Rainbow," "What Is a Man?," "Happy Hunting Horn," "Bewitched, Bothered and Bewildered," "Pal Joey," "The Flower Garden of My Heart," "Zip," "Plant You Now, Dig You Later," "In Our Little Den," "Do It the Hard Way," "Take Him."

540 PERFORMANCES

What Makes Sammy Run?

Book by Budd and Stuart Schulberg; music and lyrics by Ervin Drake; based on *What Makes Sammy Run?* by Budd Schulberg.

Produced by Joseph Cates at the Fifty-Fourth Street Theatre, February 27, 1964. Directed by Abe Burrows; musical staging by Matt Mattox; scenery and lighting by Herbert Senn and Helen Pond; costumes by Noel Taylor.

ORIGINAL CAST INCLUDED: Steve Lawrence, Robert Alda, Sally Ann Howes, Bernice Massi, Arny Freeman, Walter Klavun.

PRINCIPAL SONGS: "A New Pair of Shoes," "You Help Me," "A Tender Spot," "Lites-Camera-Platitude," "My Hometown," "Monsoon," "I See Something," "Maybe Some Other Time," "You Can Trust Me," "A Room Without Windows," "Kiss Me No Kisses," "I Feel Humble," "Something to Live For," "Paint a Rainbow," "You're No Good," "The Friendliest Thing," "Wedding of the Year," "Some Days Everything Goes Wrong."

533 PERFORMANCES

The Unsinkable Molly Brown

Music and lyrics by Meredith Willson; book by Richard Morris.

Produced by The Theatre Guild and Dore Schary at the Winter Garden Theatre, November 3, 1960. Staged by Dore Schary; choreography by Peter Gennaro; settings by Oliver Smith; costumes by Miles White; lighting by Peggy Clark.

ORIGINAL CAST INCLUDED: Tammy Grimes, Harve Presnell, Cameron Prud'homme, Mitchell Gregg, Edith Meiser, Joseph Sirola, Christopher Hewett, Wanda Saxon.

PRINCIPAL SONGS: "I Ain't Down Yet," "Belly Up to the Bar, Boys," "I've A'ready Started In," "I'll Never Say No," "My Own Brass Bed," "The Denver Police," "Beautiful People of Denver," "Are You Sure?," "Happy Birthday, Mrs. J. J. Brown," "Bon Jour," "If I Knew," "Chick-a-pen," "Keep-a-Hoppin'," "Leadville Johnny Brown," "Up Where the People Are," "Dolce Far Niente," "Colorado, My Home."

531 PERFORMANCES   *The Red Mill* (revival)

Book and lyrics by Henry Blossom; music by Victor Herbert; additional lyrics by Forman Brown.

Revived by Paula Stone and Hunt Stromberg, Jr. at the Ziegfeld Theatre, October 16, 1945. Staged by Billie Gilbert; technical supervision by Adrian Awan; choreography by Aida Broadbent; settings by Arthur Lonergan; costumes by Walter Israel and Emile Santiago.

ORIGINAL CAST INCLUDED: Michael O'Shea, Eddie Foy, Jr., Dorothy Stone, Ann Andre, Charles Collins, Odette Myrtil, Edward Dew, P. J. Kelly, Hal Price, George Meador.

PRINCIPAL SONGS: "The Isle of Our Dreams," "When You're Pretty and the World Is Fair," "Everyday Is Ladies' Day with Me," "The Streets of New York," "Because You're You," "Moonbeams," "Mignonette," "Whistle It," "A Widow Has Ways."

526 PERFORMANCES   *Irma La Douce*

Original book and lyrics by Alexandre Breffort; music by Marguerite Monnot; English book and lyrics by Julian More, David Heneker, and Monty Norman.

Produced by David Merrick, in association with Donald Albery and H. M. Tennent, Ltd., and by arrangement with Henry Hall, at the Plymouth Theatre, September 29, 1960. Staged by Peter Brook; choreography by Onna White; settings and costumes by Rolf Gerard; lighting by Joe Davis.

ORIGINAL CAST INCLUDED: Elizabeth Seal, Keith Michell, Clive Revill, Zack Matalon, Stuart Damon, George S. Irving, Fred Gwynne, Aric Lavie, Osborne Smith.

PRINCIPAL SONGS: "Valse Milieu," "Sons of France," "The Bridge of Caulaincourt," "Our Language of Love," "She's Got the Lot," "Dis-Donc," "Le Grisbi Is le Root of le Evil in Man," "Wreck of a Mec," "That's a Crime," "From a Prison Cell," "Irma-la-Douce," "There Is Only One Paris for That," "The Freedom of the Seas," "But," "Christmas Child."

521 PERFORMANCES   *Rosalinda*

Adapted from Max Reinhardt version of *Die Fledermaus* by Gottfried Reinhardt and John Meehan, Jr.; music by Johann Strauss; additional lyrics by Paul Kerby.

Produced by New Opera Company at the Forty-Fourth Street Theatre, October 28, 1942. Sets by Oliver Smith; costumes by Ladislas Czettel.

ORIGINAL CAST INCLUDED: Everett West, Ralph Herbert, Dorothy Sarnoff, Virginia MacWatters, Leonard Stocker, Gene Barry, Paul Best, Oscar Karlweis.

521 PERFORMANCES   *Follies* (CC)

Book by James Goldman; music and lyrics by Stephen Sondheim.

Produced by Harold Prince in association with Ruth Mitchell at the Winter Garden Theater, April 4, 1971. Directed by Harold Prince and Michael Bennett; choreography by Michael Bennett; scenery by Boris Aronson; costumes by Florence Klotz; lighting by Tharon Musser.

ORIGINAL CAST INCLUDED: Alexis Smith, John McMartin, Gene Nelson, Dorothy Collins, Yvonne De Carlo, Dick Latessa, Marti Rolph, Ethel Barrymore Colt, Fred Kelly, John J. Martin, Justine Johnston, John Grigas, Sheila Smith, Peter Walker, Michael Bartlett, Helen Blount, Sonja Levkova, Mary Jane Houdina, Marcie Stringer, Charles Welsh, Victor Griffin, Jayne Turner, Michael Misita, Graciela Daniele, Fifi D'Orsay, Mary McCarty, Ethel Shutta, Virginia Sandifur, Kurt Peterson, Harvey Evans, Arnold Moss, Ralph Nelson, Victoria Mallory.

PRINCIPAL SONGS: "Beautiful Girls," "Don't Look at Me," "Waiting for the Girls Upstairs," "Rain on the Roof," "Ah, Paris!" "Broadway Baby," "The Road You Didn't Take," "Bolero d'Amour," "In

Buddy's Eyes," "Who's That Woman," "I'm Still Here," "Too Many Mornings," "The Right Girl," "One More Kiss," "Could I Leave You," "Loveland," "You're Gonna Love Tomorrow," "Love Will See Us Through," "The God-Why-Don't-You-Love-Me Blues," "Losing My Mind," "The Story of Lucy and Jessie," "Live, Laugh, Love."

520 PERFORMANCES   Chauve Souris

Entire production devised by M. Nikita Balieff; music by Gretchaninoff, Aliabieff, Liadoff, Glinka, Archangelsky, Levine, Betove, and others.

Produced by F. Ray Comstock and Morris Gest at the Forty-Ninth Street Theatre, February 4, 1922. Sets by Sergei Soudeikine and Nicolas Remisoff; costumes by Granier of Paris; intermission curtain by Ralph Barton.

ORIGINAL CAST INCLUDED: M. Nikita Baileff, Messrs. Dalmatoff, Gorodetsky, Salama, Doubinsky, Boreo, Davidoff, Jourist, Kotchetovsky, Marivesky, Stoianovsky, Zotoff, Malakoff, Wawitch; Mesdames Deykarhanova, Dianina, Fechner, Birse, Ershova, Karabanova, Vassilkova, Lomakina, Komisarjevskaia.

PRINCIPAL SONGS: "The Parade of the Wooden Soldiers" (Leon Jessel, composer), "Katinka."

518 PERFORMANCES   Blackbirds of 1928

Lyrics by Dorothy Fields; music by Jimmy McHugh.

Produced by Lew Leslie at the Liberty Theatre, May 9, 1928. Staged by Lew Leslie; costumes by Kiviette.

ORIGINAL CAST INCLUDED: Bill Robinson, Adelaide Hall, Aida Ward, Tim Moore, Ruth Johnson, Marjorie Hubbard, Eloise Uggams, Billie Cortez, Crawford Jackson, Blue McAllister, Lloyd Mitchell, George Cooper, Mantan Moreland, Harry Lucas, Willard McLean, Elizabeth Welch, Mamie Savoy, Baby Banks, Philip Patterson, Earl Tucker, the Plantation Orchestra.

PRINCIPAL SONGS: "I Can't Give You Anything But Love, Baby," "I Must Have That Man," "Dig-a Dig-a Doo," "Bandanna Babies,"

"Doin' the New Low Down," "Dixie," "Here Comes My Blackbird," "Magnolia's Wedding Day," "Porgy," "Shuffle Your Feet and Roll Along."

517 PERFORMANCES *Sunny*

Book and lyrics by Otto Harbach and Oscar Hammerstein II; music by Jerome Kern.

Produced by Charles Dillingham at the New Amsterdam Theatre, September 22, 1925. Staged by Hassard Short; dances arranged by Julian Mitchell and Dave Bennett; settings and costumes by James Reynolds; special dances arranged by Alexis Kosloff, John Tiller, Fred Astaire.

ORIGINAL CAST INCLUDED: Marilyn Miller, Jack Donahue, Mary Hay, Clifton Webb, Joseph Cawthorn, Paul Frawley, Cliff "Ukulele Ike" Edwards, Pert Kelton, George Olsen and his Orchestra.

PRINCIPAL SONGS: "Who?," "Sunny," "Two Little Bluebirds," "D'Ye Love Me?," "When We Get Our Divorce," "Sunshine."

512 PERFORMANCES *Half a Sixpence*

Book by Beverley Cross; music and lyrics by David Heneker; based on *Kipps,* by H. G. Wells.

Produced by Allen-Hodgdon, Stevens Productions and Harold Fielding at the Broadhurst Theatre, April 25, 1965. Directed by Gene Saks; dances and musical numbers staged by Onna White; scenery and costumes by Loudon Sainthill; lighting by Jules Fisher.

ORIGINAL CAST INCLUDED: Tommy Steele, Polly James, Carrie Nye, Ann Shoemaker, John Cleese, Eleanore Treiber, Will Mackenzie, Norman Allen, Grover Dale, Trescott Ripley, James Grout, Mercer McLeod.

PRINCIPAL SONGS: "All in the Cause of Economy," "Half a Sixpence," "Money to Burn," "A Proper Gentleman," "She's Too Far Above Me," "If the Rain's Got to Fall," "The Old Military Canal," "Long Ago," "Flash, Bang, Wallop," "I Know What I Am," "The Party's on the House."

511 PERFORMANCES   *The Vagabond King*

Book and lyrics by Brian Hooker and W. H. Post; music by Rudolf Friml; based on *If I Were King*, by Justin Huntley McCarthy.

Produced by Russell Janney at the Casino Theatre, September 21, 1925. Staged by Max Figman; costumes by James Reynolds; sets by James Reynolds; musical numbers by Julian Alfred.

ORIGINAL CAST INCLUDED: Dennis King, Carolyn Thomas, Max Figman.

PRINCIPAL SONGS: "Song of the Vagabonds," "Some Day," "Only a Rose," "Huguette Waltz," "Love Me Tonight," "Nocturne," "Love for Sale."

509 PERFORMANCES   *The New Moon*

Book and lyrics by Oscar Hammerstein II, Frank Mandel, and Laurence Schwab; music by Sigmund Romberg.

Produced by Schwab and Mandel at the Imperial Theatre, September 19, 1928. Musical numbers staged by Bobby Connelly; costumes by Charles LeMaire; stage settings by Donald Oenslager.

ORIGINAL CAST INCLUDED: Robert Halliday, Evelyn Herbert, William O'Neal, Esther Howard, David Barnes, Max Figman, Gus Shy.

PRINCIPAL SONGS: "Lover, Come Back to Me," "Softly, As in a Morning Sunrise," "One Kiss," "Wanting You," "Stouthearted Men," "The Girl on the Prow," "Marianne," "Try Her Out at Dances."

507 PERFORMANCES   *The Rothschilds*

Book by Sherman Yellen; music by Jerry Bock; lyrics by Sheldon Harnick; based on *The Rothschilds* by Frederic Morton.

Produced by Lester Osterman in the Hillard Elkins production at the Lunt-Fontanne Theater, October 19, 1970. Directed and choreographed by Michael Kidd; scenery and costumes by John Bury; lighting by Richard Pilbrow.

ORIGINAL CAST INCLUDED: Hal Linden, Keene Curtis, Michael Maitland, Robby Benson, Lee Franklin, Mitchell Spera, Timothy Jerome, David Garfield, Chris Sarandon, Paul Hecht, Allan Gruet, Leila Martin, Nina Dova, Peggy Cooper, Jill Clayburgh, Roger Hamilton, Kim Michels, Thomas Trelfa, Kenneth Bridges, Jon Peck, Paul Tracey, Leo Leyden, Elliott Savage, Carl Nicholas, Howard Honig, Christopher Chadman.

PRINCIPAL SONGS: "Pleasure and Privilege," "One Room," "He Tossed a Coin," "Sons," "Everything," "Rothschild and Sons," "Allons," "Give England Strength," "This Amazing London Town," "They Say," "I'm in Love! I'm in Love!" "In My Own Lifetime," "Have You Ever Seen a Prettier Little Congress?" "Stability," "Bonds."

505 PERFORMANCES   *Sugar*

Book by Peter Stone; music by Jule Styne; lyrics by Bob Merrill; based on the screenplay *Some Like It Hot* by Billy Wilder and I. A. L. Diamond (based on a story by Robert Thoeren).

Produced by David Merrick at the Majestic Theater, April 9, 1972. Directed and choreographed by Gower Champion; scenery by Robin Wagner; costumes by Alvin Colt; lighting by Martin Aronstein; associate choreographer, Bert Michaels.

ORIGINAL CAST INCLUDED: Tony Roberts, Robert Morse, Elaine Joyce, Cyril Ritchard, Sheila Smith, Steve Condos, Alan Kass, Harriet Conrad, Linda Gandell, Nicole Barth, Leslie Latham, Marylou Sirinek, Terry Cullen, Kathleen Witmer, Pam Blair, Eileen Casey, Debra Lyman, Sally Neal, Mary Zahn, Gerard Brentte, Dick Bonelle, Igors Gavon, Ken Ayers, George Blackwell, Andy Dew.

PRINCIPAL SONGS: "Windy City Marmalade," "Penniless Bums," "Tear the Town Apart," "The Beauty That Drives Men Mad," "We Could Be Close," "Sun on My Face," "November Song," "Sugar," "Hey, Why Not!" "Beautiful Through and Through," "What Do You Give to a Man Who's Had Everything?" "Magic Nights," "It's Always Love," "When You Meet a Man in Chicago."

504 PERFORMANCES   *Shuffle Along*

Book and lyrics by Eubie Blake and Noble Sissle.

Produced by Nikko Producing Company at the Sixty-Third Street Music Hall, May 23, 1921. Staged by Walter Brooks.

ORIGINAL CAST INCLUDED: Noble Sissle, Florence Mills, F. E. Miller, Aubrey Lyles.

PRINCIPAL SONGS: "I'm Just Wild About Harry," "Bandana Days," "Love Will Find a Way."

504 PERFORMANCES   *Up in Central Park*

Book and lyrics by Herbert and Dorothy Fields; music by Sigmund Romberg.

Produced by Michael Todd at the Century Theatre, January 27, 1945. Staged by John Kennedy; dances by Helen Tamiris; settings and lighting by Howard Bay; costumes by Grace Houston and Ernest Schraps.

ORIGINAL CAST INCLUDED: Wilbur Evans, Maureen Cannon, Noah Beery, Sr., Betty Bruce, Daniel Nagrin, Charles Irwin, Maurice Burke.

PRINCIPAL SONGS: "Close as Pages in a Book," "Carousel in the Park," "It Doesn't Cost You Anything to Dream," "April Snow," "The Big Back Yard," "When You Walk in the Room," "The Fireman's Bride."

503 PERFORMANCES   *Carmen Jones*

Adaptation and lyrics by Oscar Hammerstein II, based on Meilhac and Halévy's adaptation of "Carmen," by Prosper Mérimée; music by Georges Bizet.

Produced by Billy Rose at the Broadway Theatre, December 2, 1943. Staged by Hassard Short; libretto directed by Charles Friedman; choreography by Eugene Loring; settings by Howard Bay; costumes by Raoul Pène du Bois.

ORIGINAL CAST INCLUDED: Muriel Smith and Muriel Rahn (alternating as Carmen), Luther Saxon and Napoleon Reed (alternating as Joe), Carlotta Franzell and Elton J. Warren (alternating as Cindy Lou), Glenn Bryant, June Hawkins, Cosy Cole.

PRINCIPAL SONGS: "Dat's Love," "Dere's a Cafe on de Corner," "Beat Out Dat Rhythm on a Drum," "Stan' Up and Fight," "Dis Flower," "My Joe," "Our Man."

501 PERFORMANCES *Panama Hattie*

Book by Herbert Fields and B. G. deSylva; music and lyrics by Cole Porter.

Produced by B. G. deSylva at the Forty-Sixth Street Theatre, October 30, 1940. Staged by Edgar MacGregor; dances by Robert Alton; costumes and settings by Raoul Pène du Bois.

ORIGINAL CAST INCLUDED: Ethel Merman, James Dunn, Betty Hutton, Arthur Treacher, Rags Ragland, Joan Carroll, Pat Harrington, Frank Hyers, Phyllis Brooks, Nadine Gay, June Allyson, Betsy Blair, Lucille Bremer, Doris Dowling.

PRINCIPAL SONGS: "My Mother Would Love You," "I've Still Got My Health," "Fresh as a Daisy," "Make It Another Old-Fashioned, Please," "Let's Be Buddies," "Visit Panama," "Who Would Have Dreamed?," "All I've Got to Get Now Is My Man."

LONGEST RUN (OFF BROADWAY)

7,059 PERFORMANCES* *The Fantasticks*

Book and lyrics by Tom Jones; music by Harvey Schmidt; suggested by the play *Les Romantiques,* by Edmund Rostand.

Produced by Lore Noto at the Sullivan Street Playhouse, May 3, 1960. Staged by Word Baker; production designed by Ed Wittstein; musical direction and arrangements by Julian Stein.

Original cast included Jerry Orbach, Rita Gardner, Kenneth Nelson, William Larsen, Hugh Thomas, Thomas Bruce, George Curley, Richard Stauffer, Jay Hampton.

PRINCIPAL SONGS: "Try to Remember," "Much More," "Metaphor," "Never Say No," "It Depends on What You Pay," "Soon It's Gonna Rain," "Happy Ending," "This Plum Is Too Ripe," "I Can See It," "Plant a Radish," "Round and Round," "They Were You."

Index of Titles

The following abbreviations are used in the Index of Titles.

Index of Names